I0754606

AMERICANISMS;

THE ENGLISH OF THE NEW WORLD.

By

M. SCHELE DE VERE, LL.D.,

PROFESSOR OF MODERN LANGUAGES IN THE UNIVERSITY OF VIRGINIA,
AUTHOR OF "STUDIES IN ENGLISH," ETC.

NEW YORK:
CHARLES SCRIBNER & COMPANY.
1872.

JOSEPH J. LITTLE,
Stereotyper, Electrotyper, and Printer,
108 to 114 Wooster St., N. Y.

PREFACE.

Mr. Marcy, when Secretary of State, issued a circular to the diplomatic and consular agents of the United States in foreign countries, requiring them to make all communications to his department in the American Language. The order excited much comment abroad and at home, and the American Language, thus for the first time introduced into official documents, was everywhere gravely discussed. Did the Americans really have an idiom of their own? or did the order refer to the Choctaw or Cherokee, the Sioux or Comanche tongue? A few years later the same term reappeared in a diplomatic circular of gravest import. The late Emperor Alexander of Russia, smarting under the defeat he had suffered in the Crimea at the combined hands of the French and the English, decreed that certain documents should be translated from the Russian into the American tongue. The Czar was, as R. W. Emerson would say, wiser than he knew, and unconsciously uttered a half-truth.

But a half-truth only, for as yet there is no American Language. We are far too practical a people, not to appreciate fully all the admirable qualities of the speech of our fathers, and are really far too busy with the task allotted us by Providence of creating a New World, to find time for studying grammar and making words. It is only now and then, when the old tools cannot do the new work required of them, that we cast them aside and invent a better one; or perhaps in the rich virgin soil of the great West an old root sends up new suckers, full of vigor and new meaning, but still bearing the image of the parent stock in all their features. As English itself is omnivorous, and this great continent has opened its doors wide to many millions of men of other races, we have, besides, freely admitted the useful foreign word with the foreign immigrant and granted to both full citizenship after a short trial.

Hence we still speak English, but we talk American. The native of the New World may, in dress and appearance, in culture and refinement, pass unnoticed in European society, but no sooner does he open his lips, than his intonation, choice of words, and structure of sentence, betray his foreign birth. The difference is, in reality, very slight, but it is characteristic, and as there is no better key to the habits and temper of a people, than the study of its watchwords and nicknames, its likes and dislikes of terms and phrases, we have endeavored to collect enough of these peculiarities to furnish an idea of *the way we talk.*

The whole literature of Americanisms is so far limited to three works, the Vocabulary of the late John Pickering, the Dictionary of John Russell Bartlett, and the Glossary of supposed Americanisms by Alfred L. Elwyn. Mr. Bartlett's admirable and exhausting work has naturally supplied many words and a few illustrations (marked *B.*) even to this compilation, nor would it have appeared desirable to attempt a new collection, if the time between its publication and the present, had not been unusually productive in changes and great events. In the interval many millions of immigrants have been added to our population, and new Territories and new States to our Union; a civil war of gigantic proportions has shaken the political edifice to its foundations and altered every feature of the aspect of society, and the mind of the whole nation has received a new impulse. Language, always a faithful mirror of the life of a people, has been proportionately enriched and modified. The war alone has added a large number of new words to our idiom; every branch of industry, every new way of thinking, every change in politics, is fully represented by a new word or a peculiar phrase. Many of these will, no doubt, pass away again, while others will become parts of our speech; but in either case it seemed to be desirable to record them before they are set aside once more, or, if preserved, before their origin is forgotten.

The author has been most kindly and courteously aided by friends and strangers. He owes especial thanks to the Hon. John Hammond Trumbull, of Hartford, Connecticut, for a master's guidance in Indian matters; to Professor S. S. Haldeman, of Chickis, Pennsylvania, for like aid in scientific terms, and to Mr. Hugh Blair Grigsby, of Edge Hill, Charlotte County, Virginia, for valuable hints as to old English terms preserved in the South. The names mentioned in the chapter on Natural History are taken from the various publications of the Smithsonian Institution, courteously supplied by its distinguished officers.

On the other hand, it must be stated that the task of collecting so-called Americanisms is necessarily one of overwhelming difficulty. The license of the press, the independent freedom of daily speech, the very small number of strictly American works, and the utter indifference of the people to the minutiæ of speech, are so many obstacles. A collection like the present must, therefore, be unavoidably imperfect and incomplete, and the author will feel himself amply rewarded, if his good intentions shall awaken a deeper interest in so important a feature of our national life, and lead to more satisfactory results hereafter.

University of Virginia,
August, 1871.

CONTENTS.

I.

The Indian.

THE INDIAN.

"Lo, the poor Indian!"
Pope.

PROVIDENCE seems to have ordained that by an act of poetical justice many races that have been conquered and even exterminated by foreign invaders, should nevertheless survive in the names of the great landmarks of their native land. Thus the ancient Briton still speaks to us in the mountains and rivers of England, and the Indian in the geography and natural history of the United States. The prairie and the backwoods, once the home of the Red man, are full of his memory, and objects abound there, known to us by names which are indigenous and peculiar among so much that is of foreign origin or common to many countries. The North American savages play no unimportant part in our literature; they have their war-whoops and yells, their paint and their feathers, in prose as well as in poetry, in Hiawatha and in Cooper's novels. These names and these things—though, perhaps, not legitimately included in a very strict definition of the term Americanisms—are almost the only really old things which we have, the only relics left to remind us that human beings roamed over our hills and floated on our waters before the Pilgrims landed at Plymouth and brave Captain Smith sailed in his frail boat up the Potomac.

It is much to be regretted, that the proportion of these really ancient names is not larger, especially in our geography; for we could well have submitted to it, that the unfortunate race, after becoming the victims of Anglo-Saxon enterprise, should have taken their conquerors captive and imposed upon them their own favorite words. Their names are so musical and full of meaning, and ours so harsh and commonplace, that we should have been the gainers by the exchange. There is music even in the roughest of Indian names; and some like *Susquehanna*, *Iowa*, *Hochelaga*, *Minnehaha*, *Dahlonega*, and *Taloolah*, are smooth and melodious almost to perfection. They were at one time much more numerous in the land, although, as J. K. Paulding already wrote: "the first settlers of an Indian country not only took away from the copper-colored villains their lands and rivers, but gave them new names, like the gypsies, who first steal children, and then, to disguise the theft, christen them anew." (Letters from the South, II. p. 17.) After the successful struggle for independence, an evil taste for modernizing set in, and, as a British writer says complacently, "æsthetic loyalists in the mother country must have felt avenged for their defeat in the substitution of names like Adamstown and Gainesville for such melodious syllables as heretofore graced the village." Even *Pawcatuck* (the river which divides Connecticut and Rhode Island), and *Wut-a-qut-o*, properly *Wicataquoc*, are less grating upon the civilized ear than Ovid and Palmyra, to say nothing of Sodom and Babylon, which the old Puritans inflicted, they alone knew why, upon some places in their new dominion. There is a slight compensation for this injury to be found in the fact that this double nomenclature at times proves the history of certain localities. Thus we find that in Pennsylvania the older counties bear English names, since the English colonists used their own names by preference in those parts of the State with which they came in contact. Northampton, Lancaster, York, Somerset, and Chester (for Cheshire), counties in the eastern and southern part of that State, show clearly that they were the first to be colonized and named. Lehigh and Delaware, Susquehannah and Alleghany, Juniata and Erie, on the contrary, prove by their Indian names the change in public opinion produced by the War of Independence. Later still came the Germans, and not by conquest but by superior industry and great thrift, became the owners of large tracts of land on which they built their towns of Womelsdorf, Mannheim, and Hannover. Even the religious body of Moravians, large numbers of whom settled in this State and built here their missions and their convents, left their mark behind them in *Bethlehem* and *Litiz* (perhaps from *laetitia?*), in *Shiloh* and *Canaan*, *Salem* and *Ephrata*.

In another instance, that of Virginia, the history of the State may be read in bright letters in its local names. The first settlers, headed by that paragon of romantic adventurers, John Smith,

> "Of name
> Most homely, yet unmatched in fame
> By those of Arthur's Table Round;"

when they found themselves amid the fairest scenes of nature in her prime, with coast, river, and woodland expanding around in all her magnificence of novelty and extent, remembered that they were still patriots, and their loyalty prevailed over their poetical taste. Hence they replaced the stately and sonorous name of *Powhatan* (Father of Waters) by that of the reigning monarch, and their first permanent settlement was "Old *Jamestown*, on the river *James*." This inauspicious opening was followed up through all the succeeding years, while Spenser dedicated his wondrous allegory to "The most high, mighty, and magnificent Empresse, renowned for pietie, virtue, and all gracious government, Elizabeth, by the grace of God Queen of England, France, and *Virginia*"—while the colony faithfully adhered to the Stuarts and was honored with the title of the *Old Dominion*—and while she remained an ill-treated colonial dependence. There are no less than sixteen princes and princesses inscribed on her broad lands in as many counties, called after these royal personages, beginning with *Henrico*, the first of the eight original shires. By their side stand names of historic note, still sounding grand in their ancient renown: York and Lancaster, Warwick and Northumberland, all redolent of Shakespeare and Rapin. Then come the governors, each one commemorated by a county, and Patrick Henry honored by two. "Happily most of the rivers have been allowed to retain their original appellation, and the majestic *Potomac*, the *Opecquon*, the *Rappahannock*, the fourfold *Ma-Ta-Po-Ni*, its banks famous as our bloodiest battle-ground on this Continent, the *Pamunkey* and the *Appomattox*, immortal as the closing scene of a woful struggle, and the *Roanoke*, all rejoice in the beauty and dignity of their aboriginal names, hereafter to afford full scope to the acumen of the historian and the philologist." (Hugh Blair Grigsby.)

For it is not only the euphony but also the historical interest and the moral weight of these Indian names, which should have made them sacred to our forefathers. It is the duty of the brave man to honor the enemy whom he has conquered, and rarely has such a conquest called forth greater virtues and more heroic courage than the long and fearful struggle between the Red man and the Saxon. What sad memories are not associated in the minds of all Americans with the *dark and bloody ground*, as the present State of Kentucky, and part of upper Ohio, were called for many a generation! First, the ill-fated locality was shunned by the Indians with superstitious dread, because their ancient traditions spoke of a frightful carnage which had taken place centuries before the arrival of the Europeans, on the beautiful banks of the river. Then immigrants settled here and there in the blood-stained region, had suddenly been assailed and overwhelmed by the treacherous Indians, and once more the locality became the scene of a long, relentless struggle between two hostile races. But not only here—everywhere in the great West—the sonorous names of rivers and mountains are full of bright memories of matchless heroism and resistless perseverance, and these beautiful words ought to be treasured up and held as precious as an inheritance of gold. The giant Himalaya would lose half its dread majesty, if it were rechristened Wellington, and Chimborazo would be reduced from its grandeur under the name of Pizarro. How much more, however, was lost when *Horicon* was dubbed by flattering loyalists Lake George, when the silvery *Winooski* received the odorous and incongruous name of *Onion River*, and the hills, of which the poet sings:

> "Then did the crimson streams that flowed,
> Seem like the waters of the brook
> That brightly shine, that loudly dash
> Far down the cliffs of *Agiochook*,"
>
> *Lovewell's Flight.*

began to bear the common name of *White Mountains!*

It is true, that occasionally efforts have been made to secure the Indian nomenclature of well-known points, and even to imitate the process in forming new names. Mr. Schoolcraft, himself a master of the Ojibway dialect of the Algonquin, acted both systematically and judiciously in this matter, when his position as Commissioner of Indian Affairs enabled him to assume authority. He tells us in one of his admirable and most interesting reports, that whenever a place in the Northwest was to be named, its exact situation, and the particular tribe of aborigines that inhabited the neighborhood, were first carefully ascertained. Then the most striking features of the landscape and local peculiarities were considered, and some expression describing them was chosen and translated into the dialect of the original occupants. Thus the name of the lake which forms the source of the Mississippi, was successfully formed. Mr. Schoolcraft had established the fact that all the fanciful derivations of the name of the river were far more poetical than true, and that *Misi-sepe,* as it was originally written, meant simply Vast River, just the title which such a magnificent river ought to have. The *Misi,* he taught us, was the same in *Missouri,* in *Mich*ili Mackinac—which Father Hennepin actually wrote *Miss*ili Mackinac—and in *Mich*igan. How much more imposing and suggestive this Indian name than the *Rivière Colbert* of Hennepin's Louisiana, the *Rivière Saint Louis* of La Salle, and the *Hidden River* of the Spanish discoverers! To this noble term, a worthy companion was to be found in naming its first fountain. Mr. Schoolcraft had discovered the latter himself when ascending the river with his party, but too modest to give it, after the example of other discoverers, his own name, he took the Algonquin word *totosh,* a woman's breast, and adding to it the usual local termination of Indian words, he fused the parts into the beautiful and appropriate word *Itasca,* typifying the support and sustenance which the lake affords to the great river at its very birth. How different was this systematic and suggestive method of the enthusiastic philologist and philanthropic explorer, to the popular way of bestowing names! States are created by Congress, and encumbered with the name of the martyr president; new counties are formed within the older States, and have to bear the name of the lucky member of the local legislature who proposed the measure, and towns built up by the energy and enterprise of successful men become known as Titusville, or Bungtown. The absurdity of such nomenclature was once unconsciously exhibited, when a great poet, unfortunately not yet known to the world at large, incorporated in perfectly good faith, the following local names in his National Poem:

" Hard Scrabble, Fair Play, Nip and Tuck, and Patch,
With Catholic, Whig and Democrat to match,

Blue River, Strawberry and Hoof-Noggle steep,
And Trespass, and Slake Bag, Clay Hole deep,
Bee Town, Hard Times, and Old Rattlesnake,
Black Leg, Shingle Ridge, Babel and Stake,
Satan's Light House, Pin Hook and Dry Bone,
And Swindler's Ridge, with hazels overgrown,
Buzzard's Roost Injunction, and The Two Brothers,
Snake Hollow Diggings, Black Jack, Horse and others,
And Lower Coon, Stump Grove, and Red Dog bleak,
Menomenee, Rattail Ridge, may measure out this sonnet,
With Bull Branch, Upper Coon,—pour no curses on it!"

Black Hawk by Elbert H. Smith. p. 191.

Even such atrocities are, however, occasionally surpassed by willful absurdities, as when a beautiful sheet of water in the State of Vermont was wantonly deprived of its fair and legitimate Indian name, to be called *Llama* water (written now Lama water) in honor of General Wool!

The Indian names, on the other hand, which were anew given by discoverers and persons in authority, were generally taken from the dialects of the Algonquin languages, which Mr. Schoolcraft first proposed to call by the generic name of *Algic*, and which were spoken by all the tribes of New England, the Middle States, Virginia, and part of North Carolina; a few only from the *Ojibway* (Chippewa) family, and other Western tribes. Thus, *Niagara* and *Saratoga* are Iroquois, like their kindred, full and sonorous even in their sadly corrupted form of the present day; *Alabama* and *Tuscaloosa*, *Talladega* and *Pensacola*, not less musical, have been traced to a kindred form spoken by the *Muscogees* (Creeks) and *Seminoles*, while *Wenona* and *Minnehaha*, immortalized by Longfellow's poem, belong to the great family of *Dahcotah* Indians. If such names have not more frequently retained their hold on the places they once designated and the memory of early settlers, there is some excuse for the latter found in the extreme length of most Indian words. This difficulty was already complained of by the great Eliot during his pious labors in writing his noble work, the Indian Bible; and he adduces words like—"Nummatchekodtantamoonganunnonash" (thirty-two letters) meaning "our lusts;" "Noowomantammoonkanunonnaso," meaning "our loves;" and "Kummogkodonattootummooetiteaonganunnonash" (forty-three letters), meaning "our question." (Magnalia, Bk. III., p. 193.) In the Book of Common Prayer, translated into the language of the Six Nations, there are also many long words, such as—"Tsinihoianerenseratokentitser-oten." (Daniel, ix. 9.) No wonder, therefore, that so many of these words, especially those belonging to the Dahcotah branch, which is rough and full of nasal sounds, have either been entirely lost or at least transformed till they can no longer be recognized.

In some instances it is a special matter of regret that the Indian names of places and States no longer suggest their original meaning. This was occasionally simple enough, as in Connecticut—originally written *Quonaughticot*—which meant in the Mohegan dialect "long river;" and in Massachusetts—in the Natic dialect *Masasuset*—signifying "the place of great hills," with reference to the Blue Hills, eleven miles to the southwest of Boston, the highest point of land in the eastern part of that State. Of cities thus designated, *Milwaukie*, recalls its original name, meaning "rich lands," and *Sing Sing*, the Algonquin word *Asingsing*, "a place of stones," with all the greater force as it is now, "the residence of gentlemen," in Artemus Ward's language, "who spend their days in poundin' stun." Other names, however, have more or less picturesqueness in their meaning, and are not so easily improved by recent changes. Thus *Chicago* represents in its French pronunciation very fairly the actual sounds heard by the first French explorers, when the Potawatomies, who dwelt there, called it *Shecaugo*, "playful waters." (?) *Dahlonega* is the softened form of the *Talauneca* of the Cherokees, which meant "yellow metal," for the Indians were well aware of the gold found in the neighborhood, which made the city in later years the seat of a government mint, because of its happy position in the very centre of the gold-mine district of Northern Georgia. Lake *Erie* is almost the only remainder now of the once powerful tribe of Eries, who lived where the State of Ohio now is; the latter name, as given to the river, owes its origin to the Iroquois, who called it the *Oheo*, "beautiful water," by the same instinctive admiration which prompted the French to name it, La Belle Rivière. It had a lucky escape from Father Marquette's baptism, who christened it Ouaboukigon—a name which subsequently shrunk into *Ouabache*, and has finally as *Wabash* been given to the last tributary of the Ohio. It is curious that a kind of stigma seems to adhere to the name, for even now the good people of Indiana and the West generally, are fond of saying of a man who has been cheated, that "he has been *Wabashed*." At one time, when the "dark and bloody ground" of Kentucky and Ohio became famous among the whites, the Indians also felt inclined to call their beautiful river rather the Blood River, so fearful had been the scenes of carnage and cruelty enacted on its fair banks. One of the youngest states, Idaho, well deserves its poetical name, *I-da-hoe*, the "gem of the mountains," and the name of the river *Monongahela* flows as smoothly from the lips with its liquid notes as the far-famed rye whisky distilled on its banks, which is known all over the Union by the same term, in contradistinction from Scotch and Irish rivals. On the other hand, the much-discussed name of the greatest waterfall on our continent has been stripped of all the poetical meanings given it by writers whose imagination exceeded their knowledge. *Neagara*, the original word, taken from the Seneca-Iroquois dialect, has no connection with cataracts, but means prosaically, "across the neck," alluding to the course of the river across the neck or strip of land that lies between Lakes Erie and Ontario. A similar idea underlies the word *Mitchikan* in the Ottawa dialect, which was originally given to Mackinac, and meant "fences," as if the island were lying fence-like before the Upper Lake. At least so says the Rev. Mr. Pierz, a missionary among the Ottawas; but Allouez, his French predecessor, calls it, a few years before, *Machihiganing;* the present word *Michigan* is evidently an improvement upon both the former names.

The word *Esquimaux*, though not denoting any tribe inhabiting the United States, is still so frequently regarded as belonging to our speech that it may not be amiss to correct the common error, by which it is considered a French term, probably only because of its French-looking termination. A learned linguist of France went so far in his patriotic zeal to reclaim it as his own, that he insisted upon its being a contraction of *ceux qui miaulent!* The word obtained its French appearance from the Canadian voyageurs, who introduced it, after having in vain tried to imitate in any better way the sounds by which the *Innuits*, as they call themselves, were designated by the Kenisteno Indians in their language. This was *Ashkimai* or "eaters of raw meat," which practice appeared to them strange enough to give its name to the whole race, and hence the present name of *Esquimaux*.

Since the acquisition of Alaska, for which a new term, *Walrussia*, was proposed, but deservedly failed to obtain currency, a few words have become familiar to the American ear, which belong to the Indians of that district. This is the *Chinook Jargon*, a conventional language like the Lingua Franca of the Mediterranean, and the Pigeon-English of India, which dates back to the fur-droguers of the last century. Those mariners, whose enterprise before 1800 explored the northwest coast of America, picked up at their general rendezvous, Nootka Sound, various native words useful in barter, and thence transplanted them, with additions from the English, to the shores of Oregon. When the great Astor's expedition arrived at the mouth of the Columbia, the Jargon received its principal impulse; many more words of English were brought in, and for the first time the French, or rather the Canadian and Missouri patois of the French, was introduced. The principal seat of the company being at Astoria, not only a large addition of Chinook words was made, but a considerable number was taken from the *Chihalis*, who immediately bordered that tribe on the north. The language continued to receive additions, and assumed a more distinct and settled meaning under the Northwest and Hudson's Bay Companies, who succeeded Astor's party, as well as the American settlers in Oregon. Its advantage was soon perceived by the Indians, and the Jargon became to some extent a means of communication between natives of different speech and between them and the whites. It was even used between Americans and Canadians. First in vogue upon the Columbia and Willamette, it spread to Puget Sound, and with the extension of trade found its way far up the coast and the rivers, so that there are now few tribes between the 42d and 57th parallels of latitude, in which there are not found interpreters through its medium. Notwithstanding its apparent poverty of words and the absence of grammatical forms, it possesses much flexibility and power of expression, and really serves almost every purpose of ordinary intercourse.

Mr. George Gibbs, who has furnished the Smithsonian Institution with an admirable Dictionary of the "Chinook Jargon," estimates the total number of words at about five hundred, of which about one hundred and sixty are French and English, eighteen of unknown derivation, and all the others belonging to the Chinook and kindred dialects. Both elements have been slightly modified in the Jargon: the Indian gutturals are softened or dropped, and the *f* and *r* of the English and French, unpronounceable to the Indians, are modified into *p* and *l*. Grammatical forms are reduced to their simplest expression, and variations in mood and tense only conveyed by adverbs or by the context.

The conversational language of the Indians has, of course, left no traces in our English, mainly because of the great diversity of dialects, which has deprived even such masterly works as Eliot's Indian Bible, of all but historic interest. Among the rare exceptions is the word *netop*, used by the New England Indians in the sense of "my friend," which Mr. Pickering tells us was in his day still used, colloquially, in some towns in the interior of "Massachusetts, to signify a friend or (to use a cant word) a crony." It is doubtful, however, whether it is now-a-days used in any intercourse, even with Indians, as the Narragansett word would hardly be intelligible to other tribes. The term *pokeloken*, an Indian term, signifying, "marsh," has apparently more vitality in it, for it is still very largely used by lumbermen in Maine, and by their brethren in the Northwest, mostly their kinsmen and always their pupils, when they speak of marshy ground extending inland from a lake or a stream. "I had unawares pushed the canoe into a *pokeloken* and was aground, remembering too late the half-breed's admonitions, who has specially warned me against these mysterious *pokelokens*." (Hon. C. A. Murray's *Letters*, No. 27.) In North Carolina and further South, similar swamps are called *pocasans*. They are lands filled with water during winter and the spring months, and overgrown with cypress and juniper trees, with a heavy undergrowth of reeds. "After passing this swamp or *pocasan*, on the east side of the Chowan, you come to sandy lands covered with large pines, a country famous for tar-making." (*Southern Magaz.*, Aug. 1871, p. 195.) The lumbermen employ also the Indian term *wangan*, "a boat," very generally for a peculiar kind of boat, in which they carry their tools and provisions. "Among the dangers (of lumbering in Maine), where life and property are hazarded, is that of *running the wangan*, a phrase well understood on the river." (*The Americans at Home*, III. p. 257 *B*.)

Another Indian term surviving at least as a provincialism, is the *tarboggin* of the extreme North and of Canada, the *tarbogin* of the Far West, known as *travée* to the French voyageurs. This is a kind of light wagon, often drawn by dogs, on which Indian squaws are in the habit of bringing home their loads of cotton-wood, etc., consisting simply of a couple of tent-poles with two cross-bars to support the freight. The Canadians have improved them, mainly for the purpose of using them as sleds in sliding on the snow from great heights, in which case they are often made to carry a double load, the owner finding it no easy task to steer the frail vehicle rightly, and to keep his fair charge from slipping from his hold. A term which has only lately found its way into our English, through the increasing number of hunters who make up parties in search of elk, moose, etc., is *whiggiggin*, as it is written from the sound merely. The Indian word is the Abenaki, *awikhigan*, meaning "a letter, book, or anything written," and is in Maine and Canada, as well as in the Northwest, now generally used to designate the written permit which has to be obtained from the local authorities—often an Indian chief—before non-residents are allowed to hunt there. It is in these same districts, also, that a trap set by hunters, is sometimes called by its Indian name *Killhag*. "The first furs were brought into town yesterday, and already a number of *Killhags* have been put up everywhere." (*Bradford Times*, 1864.) If we add, finally, the term *mocuck*, which designates in the Abenaki dialect a large, peculiarly-shaped cake of sugar, we shall have mentioned all the more familiar terms of this class. "Covered by a blanket, and pillowed by a *mocuck* of sugar, each Indian was asleep upon his rush-mat." (C. Lanman, *Summer in the Wilderness*.)

It is well known that the very word *Indian*, as given to the race found here by the first settlers, rests upon a mistake, as if the natives also must needs be involved in the evil fortune, which gave to the whole continent, at the expense of the discoverer, the name of a man who had no title to such an honor. For whatever merit recent investigations may have secured to the bold and persevering navigator, Amerigo Vespucci, his claims are as nothing by the side of those of Columbus, and yet already in 1507, in the *Cosmographiæ Synopsis*, the name of *America* is entered as current among men.

In like manner the poor *Redskin* also, as the early colonists called him on account of his color, has ever since been known to the world by the name of distant *Ind*, which Columbus thought he had reached, when he discovered Hispaniola. Nor has he been allowed to retain even that name long, for already Charles Cotton rhymes the verb "cringes" with "Indies," and thus proves to us that even in his day the poor Indian had to submit to being called *Injun*, which is now his common name with common people, producing an odd and detestable resemblance in sound between the Indian, the engine, and the onion of New England. Along the frontier line he was perhaps as frequently called a *Copperhead*, an ancient term of contempt, of which W. Irving makes frequent use in his quaint History of New York. "These were the men," he says, "who vegetated in the mud along the shores of Pavonia, being of the race of genuine *copperheads*;" and elsewhere: "The Yankees sneeringly spoke of the round-crowned burghers of the Manhattoes as the *Copperheads*." In the year 1861, a Mr. Burtt, then Quartermaster in the United States Army, is said to have first applied the term to a class of so-called Anti-War Democrats, Northern sympathizers with the Southern rebellion, though it is not unlikely that in his patriotic zeal he may have rather compared them to the venomous and noisome serpent, which is also known under the name of *Copperhead* (Trigonocephalus contortrix). Can the Indian be blamed if he really, as is generally supposed, retorted by fixing upon the first invader on his soil the equivocal name of *Yankee?* The best authorities on the subject now agree upon the derivation of this term from the imperfect effort made by the Northern Indians to pronounce the word "English." The Rev. Mr. Heckewelder, than whom few men have been more thoroughly at home in Indian speech and Indian character, distinctly states, that they pronounced it *Yengees*, and knew how to distinguish them "by their dress and personal appearance, and that they were considered as less cruel than the Virginians or Long-knives." (*Hist. Acc. of the Indian Nations*, p. 132.) In like manner Judge Durfee refers to them in his remarkable poem, "What Cheer; or, Roger Williams in Banishment," thus:

"Ha! *Yengee*," said the Sachem, "wouldst thou go
To soothe the hungry panther scenting blood?"
(Canto III. 32.)

Nor is it less curious to notice how early the term began to be used in a disparaging sense by political or personal antagonists of the bold pioneers and bigoted puritans. The Dutch on the banks of the Hudson probably first of all applied it contemptuously to their formidable rivals on the Connecticut, and subsequently the regular troops took it up, if we may credit the Rev. Mr. Gordon, as quoted by T. Westcott of Philadelphia, when he says: "They (the British troops) were roughly handled by the *Yankees*, a term of reproach when applied by the regulars." (*Notes and Queries*, 1852, p. 57.) Subsequently the daily-increasing animosity between the North and the South made the term *Yankee* in Southern minds an incarnation of all that was uncongenial and distasteful, and hence during the war *the Yanks* became the universal designation of Federal soldiers in the Confederacy, even as they were called *Rebs*—not Rebels—by Northern men. With a strange confusion of ideas the poor Confederate soldier, who succumbed morally to the privations and sufferings of Northern prisons and penitentiaries, and in his dire need took the oath and enlisted in the United States Army, was contemptuously called a *galvanized Yankee*—probably by an indistinct association with the worthless galvanized imitations of gold and silver, now so popular with the masses.

The same fatality which made the words America, Yankee, and Indian genuine misnomers, seems to have followed even the national songs of the American people. *Yankee Doodle*, at least, and the well known tune which bears this name, are anything but American. Where their birthplace really was, is, however, quite a mystery yet. New discoveries are constantly made: Kossuth was reported to have recognized it as one of the national airs of his own Magyar race, and a learned diplomat of the United States discovered it among the Basque, in one of their ancient Sword-Dances. This much only is certain, that the wicked wits of the court of Charles II. whistled the tune in the ears of the Nell Gwynnes of that time, and it is found jingling in a song on a famous lady of easy virtue in those days:

"Lucy Locket lost her pocket,
Kitty Fisher found it;
Nothing in it, nothing on it,
But the binding round it."

Those indefatigable students, the Duyckincks, track it still farther back to the old songs of the land of their ancestors, Holland, and claim that Dutch laborers used to sing:

"*Yanker* didel, *doodel* down,
Didel, dudel, lenter;
Yanker viver, voover vown,
Botermilk and Tanter,"—

which certainly has a suspicious look of originality about it, and might well shake our faith in the assertion that one Dr. Shackburg of the British Army composed the famous song. Its adoption as a national air dates from the day on which a country fifer happened to play it as a quick-march at the head of a small detachment of gallant countrymen going to the fight at Bunker Hill.

The true *Yankee* of our day is the son of New England, the descendant and worthy representative of the Pilgrim fathers, the heir to all their noble qualities, homely virtues, and violent prejudices. The type does not find its fullest expression in the accomplished Bostonian, though he live at the "Hub of the World," and be firmly persuaded that modern culture radiates from his native town to all parts of the earth; but rather in the thrifty farmer and hardy mechanic, who can do anything from running a plough to ruling a State, from selling wooden nutmegs to winning a seat in the Senate, and now and then in a master-mind like Emerson's or Lowell's. Very different is he, indeed, from the gay, generous *Southron*, as the Southerners are apt to be called, whom, at an early period of our history the Indians distinguished by the name of *Long-knives*. The origin of the term is said to have been this: "In the year 1764, a Colonel Gibson of Fort Pitt came accidentally upon a party of Mingoes, encamped on Cross Creek, a tributary of the Ohio. Little Eagle, a distinguished chief, commanded the party, and upon discovering the whites, gave a fearful whoop and at the same time discharged his gun at the Colonel. The ball passed through Gibson's coat without injuring him. With the quickness of a tiger he sprang upon his foe, and with one sweep of his sword, severed the head of Little Eagle from his body. Two other Indians were killed by the whites, but the others escaped and reported that the white captain had cut off the head of their chief with his long knife. This was the origin of the celebrated and fearfully significant term *Long-knives*. It was applied throughout the war to Virginians, and even to this day has not been forgotten by some of the Western tribes." (W. De Hass, *History of Indian Wars*, p. 216.) Even the mutual aversion of the white against the red man has by no means become quite extinct, and it must not be forgotten that this feeling was, on the part of the former, all the stronger and deeper as the poor Indians were—thanks to early preachers—for a long time looked upon as worshippers and agents of Satan. Hence the term *Indian hating*, is still of frequent use in the Far West, and represents a passion, which is even now a mingled ferocity and fanaticism, inconceivable to quiet Christians and perhaps to any other men but border adventurers.

Of the many words designated as *Indian*, we omit here all names of plants and animals, which will be mentioned elsewhere, and allude only to those which are characteristic of the language or the habits of the American. Thus he has learned from the cautious savage to traverse woods and march to distant points of attack in a single line, so that every man steps in the footsteps of the man before him, and baffles any guess at the number that may have passed. This is called walking *Indian file*, and applied to any occasion where people walk one behind the other. *Indian Forts* are inclosures, found in large numbers in New York and Pennsylvania, and less frequently in New England, Canada, and Virginia, occupying high bluff points or headlands, scarped on two or more sides and naturally easy of defence. When found on lower ground, they are generally raised on some dry knoll or little hill in the midst of a swamp, or where a bend in the river lends security to the position, but they stand invariably near an unfailing supply of water. The embankments are seldom over four feet high, pierced by one or more gateways, and surrounded by a ditch of some depth. It has been questioned, however, whether these fortifications belong to the present race of Indians or the Aztecs that preceded them in the country.

In the State of New York and in Canada there are, besides, many places found, where the Indians buried their dead, and these are known as *bonepits*. The bones are usually deposited in long trenches or pits, forming very extensive works and accumulations.

The ceremony of thus interring the bones of the departed was called by the Indians the "second burying," and took place among some tribes, like those visited by Charlevoix, every eight years, but among the Iroquois and the Hurons every ten years. Early settlers occasionally quote these burials as the *festival of the dead.* (H. R. Schoolcraft.)

These *Indian Forts* are, moreover, carefully to be distinguished from the *Indian Mounds* which are found in nearly every State of the Union, but in all probability have but rarely any connection with the Aborigines. The habit of the people of ascribing any unusual form of the surface ground to the agency of the former owners of the land, has, no doubt, led to the designation of these mounds as Indian. In many cases they are, of course, burial-places of the Red man, and when opened, are found to contain bones, tomahawks, and other rude tools and weapons. Such abound especially in the Middle and Southern States, and, within the memory of men now living, the Indians of the Far West have come to visit once more the graves of their forefathers in the Atlantic States, startling the quiet dwellers there by their sudden and uncouth appearance, and vanishing again like a dream, after having deposited some simple memorial on one of these mounds. In other parts of the country every rounded knoll is so called, and thus in California, especially in times of flood, "cattle and sheep are gathered on *Indian Mounds,* waiting the fate of their companions, whose carcasses drift by or swing in eddies with the wrecks of barns and outhouses." (F. B. Harte, *The Luck of Roaring Camp,* p. 221.) But here also they are strangely mixed up with the Indians, and thus the same author speaks of the end of one of his most graphically described heroes: "He was buried in the *Indian Mound,* the single spot of strange, perennial greenness, which the poor aborigines had raised above the dusty plain." (p. 234.)

The State of Florida has a peculiar kind of mounds, which are familiarly known as *Chunk* Yards or *Chunkee* Yards, consisting of oblong yards adjoining high mounds and "rotundas," built by the Seminoles. In the centre stands a mysterious obelisk, and at each of the more remote corners a post or strong stake, to which their captives were bound previous to being tortured and burnt. The able historian of Florida, Mr. Bartram, says: "The pyramidal hills or artificial mounts, and highways or avenues, leading from them to artificial ponds or lakes, vast tetragon terraces, *chunk-yards*, and obelisks or pillars of wood, are the only monuments of labor, ingenuity, and magnificence that I have seen, worthy of notice." Later researches have led to the discovery that *Chunkee* was the Indian name of a game played with a flat, round stone and a pole about eight feet long; the former was rolled forward and the pole thrown at the same time, by two players, and he whose pole came nearest to the stone won the game.

As the Indians have been led by their white friends to consider a present in the light of an exchange only, being always expected to give much land for little value, this has given rise to the term *Indian Giver*, meaning a child, or a man, who desires the return of his gift. Among the articles which unfortunately still constitute the staple of all such presents, spirits of some kind, or *fire-water*, as the English-speaking Indians often call it, holds, of course, a prominent rank. It is a sad index to the nature of the vast majority of such transactions between white and red men, that the term *Indian Liquor* is universally known to mean adulterated whiskey. Nor is water the only element of adulteration: tobacco, red pepper, and other condiments are apt to be added in large quantities by dishonest dealers and agents.

Wild orchards of ungrafted apple and peach trees are frequently called *Indian orchards*, under an erroneous impression that they were planted by the red men; but, except in the more prosperous *Indian Reservations* or *Reserves*, tracts of land secured to them by the government, and in regions where they have long been permanently settled, as in the Territory of the Choctaws, the poor Indian is not apt to plant trees; besides, he is fully aware that ungrafted peach-trees are apt to be hardier and more productive than the finer varieties.

Of all the subjects connected with the original race in American life none holds probably a more prominent place in the mind of the masses than the *Indian Summer*, a short but surpassingly beautiful season in the latter part of autumn. A similar *spell* of fine weather, as it is called by another Americanism, is noticed, in other countries also, and frequently compared to the halcyon period of the Greeks, so that Shakespeare could pointedly say:

"Expect Saint Martin's summer, halcyon days,"—(*Henry VI., Part* 1, *B.*)

in allusion to what he elsewhere calls:

> "Farewell thou latter spring,
> Farewell all hallown summer."—(*Henry IV.*)

In England the season derived its name of Saint Martin's or Martin Mass Summer, from the fact that it commonly begins there about November 11, St. Martin's day; on the Continent it is called Summer Close and "l'été de St. Martin," with an ungallant double meaning, which allows the term to be applied to ladies of advancing years. It may be that there is an association of the same idea, though less delicately expressed, in the German "Alte Weiber Sommer," while in Chili it is called St. John's Summer. In the United States, this season, when "twinkle in the smoky light the waters of the rill," generally begins in November, though the period varies within a month. It is characterized by fair but not brilliant weather; the air is smoky and hazy, perfectly still and moist; and the sun shines dimly, but softly and sweetly, through an atmosphere that some call copper-colored and others golden, in accordance with their power of poetical perception. The name of *Indian Summer* is differently explained. The Rev. James Freeman derives it from the fact that the Indians are particularly fond of it, regarding it as a special gift of their favorite god, the god of the Southwest, who sends the soft southwest winds, and to whom they go after death. Daniel Webster said that the early settlers gave that name to the season because they ascribed its peculiar features, the heat and the haze, to the burning of the prairies by the Indians at that time. Mr. Kercheval, however, gives a more plausible explanation: "It sometimes happened, that after the apparent onset of winter, the weather became warm; the smoky time commenced, and lasted for a considerable number of days. This was the *Indian Summer*, because it afforded the Indians—who during the severe winter never made any incursions into the settlements—another opportunity of visiting them with their destructive warfare. The melting of the snow saddened every countenance, and the genial warmth of the sun chilled every heart with horror. The apprehension of another visit from the Indians and of being driven back to the detested fort, was painful in the highest degree." (*Hist. of the Valley of Virginia*, p. 190.)

Many Indian terms have become so incorporated into American speech, and have, at times, struck their roots so deep into public institutions, as to have become almost true Americanisms. Such are *wigwam* and *wampum*. The former is the Anglicized form of a phrase in the Natic dialect of the Algonquin family; here *wĕkouomŭt* meant "in his or her house," and the curtailed word *wĕkouam* was the true ancestor of the modern *wigwam* in the sense of an Indian's hut or cabin. The original hut, generally made of skins and affording but scanty shelter in protracted bad weather, stands in strange contrast with the imposing building in New York, in which the *wigwam, i. e.*, the headquarters of a Democratic organization of great power and influence are now established. This political body derives its name of *Tammany*, and that of *Tammany Hall*, from an ancient chief of the *Narragansett* Indians, called Miantonomu, who had his seat on *Tammany*, a hill north of Newport, where he and Canonicus sold, in 1638, Aquiduct or the Isle of Peace, now the State of Rhode Island, for twenty-three broadcloth coats and thirteen hoes, "as also two torkepes." Political adversaries will have it that this mode of "selling" has not yet gone out of practice at the place that now bears the name.

Ordinarily such sales were made, and if not made, confirmed in *wampum*, the current coin of the Indians. This consisted of strings of shells, which were frequently united into a broad belt, worn as an ornament or a girdle. *Wampum*, an Algonquin word, meant originally nothing more than "white" and served to designate only inferior shells, which were white, and, according to the accounts of colonial chroniclers, were held equal to silver, while the *peac*, or "black"—whence *wampumpeage*—were compared to gold. *Sewan* was in Algonquin the name of shell-money generically and *Roanoke* in Virginia, for which now *wampum* is used. The white money was made from the shells of *Pyrula caniculata*, a large pear-shaped univalve, sometimes called "periwinkle." The part used was the *columella* or pillar, the whorls being broken off; they were not eatable, like the English periwinkle, and attained considerable size. The more costly beads came from the largest shells of the *Quahaug* or *Cohog*, a welk, known in the Middle and Southern States as the Round Clam, and belonging to the genus *Venus mercenaria*, which is so called on account of their being used as currency. The inner surface of these shells is beautifully polished, the centre of the valves pure white, and part of the outside mantle of a rich violet. This border the Narragansett Indians made into the blue shell-money, which they call *Suckanhock*, by breaking it into small pieces and rubbing them with stones till they were cylindrical and could be drilled lengthwise. It seems almost incredible that the Indians should have done this, and done it so very neatly, without metallic tools, and yet Roger Williams says, expressly: "before ever they had awle-blades from Europe they made shift to bore this, their shell-money, with stones." (*Key to the Indian Languages*, p. 150.) Of the use of *sewan* a writer on the "New Netherlands in 1679," says, quoting from a journal of that year: "We sat down before the fire. There had been thrown upon it, to be roasted, a pailful of Gowanus oysters, which are the best in the country. They are large and full, some of them not less than a foot long. We had for supper a haunch of venison, which he had bought of the Indians for three guilders and a half of *seewant*, that is, fifteen stuivers of Dutch money, and which weighed thirty pounds." (*Putnam's Magazine*, April, 1858.)

Like the precious metal, these shells served at the same time for ornaments and for money, and being strung were worn in bracelets and necklaces. The Indians have always been exceedingly fond of personal ornaments, and the great chief who now-a-days delights the crowds in Washington by stalking down the avenue in all his bravery and finery, had his prototype in the warrior described thus a hundred years ago: "One of them was a Delaware chief; he wore the badges of his office, the *wampum* belt, three half-moons, and a silver plate on his breast; bands of silver on both arms, and his ears cut round and ornamented with silver; the hair on the top of his head was done up with silver wire." (*The Johnson Boys' Account of their Escape in* 1788.) When made up into belts or bands, four inches wide and three to five feet long, they were exchanged in ratification of treaties, and given and received as title-deeds. The two colors were at times wrought together in patterns, and by a methodical arrangement made to aid the memory. As the female revolutionists of Paris registered, according to Dickens's account, the doomed aristocrats in their knitting, so the Indians wove the story of the past and the promise of the future into wampum belts. Father Marquette tells us, moreover, that words addressed to the Indians, when not accompanied by a wampum belt, were considered not important, and that the missionary, who first announced the gospel in a village, always spoke by the "belt of the prayer," which he held in his hands, and which remained to witness his words when the sound had died away. A similar use is made on the Pacific Coast of another variety of shells, called *Haiqua* (Dentalium), which the natives use mainly for ornaments, but in certain localities also employ after the manner of *wampum*. "The men did not think their gala-equipments complete, unless they had a jewel of *haiqua*, or wampum, dangling at the nose." (W. Irving's *Astoria*, II. p. 87.)

Another Indian term still prominent in the organization of great political bodies in America is the name of the presiding officer of the before-mentioned fraction of the Democratic party, their *Sachem*. This term seems to have been peculiar to Northern Indians, since Captain John Smith calls the head of the Virginia Indians *King*, and then continues: "His (Powhatan's) inferior kings, whom they call Werowances, are tyed to rule by custom; the commander they call *Caucorouse*, which is captain" (*Hist of Va.*, I. p. 143), while Beverley says, "a *cockarouse* is one that has the honor to be of the king or queen's council, with relation to the affairs of government." (*Hist. of the Valley of Va.*, III. 117.) The word, which has a suspicious English sound about it, became, perhaps on that account, a favorite in the South, and was long used to designate a person of consequence among the Red men, although already the Swedish-Indian Dictionary of 1696 calls the chief *Saccheeman*. This term *Sachem* and the equally familiar *Sagamore*, often considered distinct terms, are in reality one and the same; so far from meaning two different things, they are simply variations of the original *Sakemo*, the name for a chief in all the New England dialects. Captain John Smith explained the meaning thus: "For their government: every *Sachem* is not a king, but their great *Sachems* have divers *Sachems* under their protection, paying them tribute, and dare make no warres without his knowledge, but every *Sachem* cares for the widowes, orphans, the aged, and maimed." (*Hist. of Va.*, II. p. 238.) The modern poet, for his part, describes his appearance in these words:

"He looks like a *Sachem*, in red blanket wrapt,
Who 'mid some council of the sad-garbed whites,
Erect and stern, in his own memory wrapt,
With distant eye broods over other sights."
(J. R. Lowell, *An Indian Summer Reverie.*)

The rule of the Sachem has long since passed away; a *Sachemdom*, such as the older writers spoke of, when describing the territorial extent of a Sachem's power, cannot be said to exist in our day, yet the word still survives and is in constant use. This is even more strikingly the case with the Indian's wife, his *squaw*, a word originating in the Algonquin language, and appearing in the New England dialects as *squah* or *esquah*, while in Ojibway it is more simply *quah* or *equah*, a form which has led to a comparison with the old English cven (queen), a woman. Her child is strangely disguised under the name of *pappoose*, which even so great a scholar as Mr. Schoolcraft fancied to be of Indian origin, because *papoïs* resembled a root meaning "to laugh." Now, as Indian children alone ever laugh, such an exhibition of glee and mirth being regarded as undignified by older people, the designation appeared to be very appropriate. As such it was used by W. Irving: "Marching fearlessly forward, our valiant heroes carried the village of Communipaw by storm, notwithstanding that it was vigorously defended by some half a score of squaws and *pappooses*" (*Hist. of New York*, p. 321); and J. G. C. Brainard sings of one:

"Here his young squaw her cradling tree would choose,
Singing her chant to hush her swart *pappoose*."

More careful researches have, however, led to the discovery that there is no such word in any Algonquin dialect, and that *pappoose* is nothing more than an imperfect effort to pronounce the English word, babies, as Yankee arose from English. It has, therefore, to take its place by the side of many such words, which owe their Indian origin to the imagination of the whites and not to the language of the natives. Such is also the word *Pale-face*, a great favorite with Cooper and many poets, which probably never was seriously used by an Indian in his own tongue, but makes quite a pretty appearance in such lines as these:

"The brave Tecumseh's words are good:
One league for terror, strife and blood,
Must all our far-spread tribes unite;
Then shall the *pale-face* sink to-night."
(*Tecumseh*, by Colton, XVIII.)

The word *Manitou*, which is generally held to mean God, has been the cause of much angry discussion. This arose from the fact that the early missionaries, from the zealous Puritan of the North to the pious Lutheran in Delaware and Virginia, used the word as representing the one great God of Christianity. The truth is, however, that *Manitou* is a word employed to signify the same thing by all Indians from the Gulf of Mexico to the Arctic regions, and this is simply spirit. Now, the Indians have good and bad spirits. Hence, it was at a great risk that the New England apostle, as well as the unknown author of the "Vocabularium Barbaro-Virgineorum," printed in Stockholm in 1696, could dare say: *Manetto:* "God." For, the Indians have a *Manetou* for every cave, waterfall, or other commanding object in nature, and generally make offerings to them at such places. Their bad *Manetou* differs in no way from our Devil. Hence, Judge Durfee was perfectly right, when he wrote:

"Praying for good, we to Cawtantowit bow,
And shunning evil, we to Chepian cry;
To other *Manittoos* we offerings owe,
Dwell they in mountain, flood, or open sky."
(*What Cheer*, Cant. II. *B.*)

When Father Marquette came to the Indians who directed his steps toward the Mississippi, "they answered," he writes, "that they were Ilinois, and in token of peace they presented their pipes to smoke. These pipes for smoking are called in the country the *Calumets*." It is not improbable that we owe to these words of the pious and energetic missionary the addition to our language of this word. And yet it is by no means an Indian word, as is frequently believed and quite as frequently stated. Their own word is simply a term meaning pipe. *Calumet*, on the other hand, is nothing more than the old form of the French word "Chalumeau," from the Latin "Calamus," and was the name given to a pipe by early French settlers, the colonists of New France. It is, therefore, a much more genuine

Americanism, than most of the Indian words which we have simply obtained from the Indians in common with all other nations. The term *canoe*, on the other hand, has probably a more legitimate Indian pedigree. Although it has reached us only through the same French agency in the diminutive form of *canot*, there can be little doubt that it is the Carib word *canaoa*; at least the natives of San Salvador are said to have called smaller boats thus, when Columbus first landed there. The Indian's *canoe* in the Northwest, it is well known, is made of the Paper or *Canoe Birch* (Betula papyracea), found in Maine and the whole North, but not in the South. Its thick, glossy, and pliant bark is used by the Indians for the manufacture of baskets, boxes, and trinkets of all kinds, which they ornament with beads and colored straws. It is this bark also which served their ancestors, as it serves them now, in some districts, for the much more important structure of canoes, for, taken whole from the tree, it can be spread open, fashioned into a graceful shape and lined with wooden ribs. They are still used wherever the Indians have an abiding place, and hunters are apt to speak of them briefly as *birches*. The short oar with a broad blade by which the exceedingly frail and nicely-balanced canoe is propelled, requires no mean skill and close attention; hence the slang phrase of *paddling one's own canoe* means to be skillful and energetic enough to succeed unaided, as the song says:

> " Voyager upon life's sea,
> To yourself be true;
> And where'er your lot may be,
> *Paddle your own canoe.*"
> (*Harper's Mag.*, May, 1854.)

Among the articles of personal apparel which distinguish the Indian there are two, which have been and still are so extensively used by the whites also, that their names have become household words and parts of our language. These are the *Mocassin* and the *Tomahawk*. The former, in the Massachusetts dialect written "Mocasson," in the Kenisteno dialect and some other offshoots of the Algonquin "Mockisin," is a shoe made of soft leather without a stiff sole, frequently ornamented more or less richly. These shoes have been largely adopted by Western hunters and all men who have hard work to do in winter. Thus we are told that "the loggers are obliged to take good care of their feet; one of them often wears three or four pair of socks, with a pair of *mocassins* over them—the mocassins, because they give the foot more freedom and thus render them less liable to freeze, are generally preferred to coarse leather boots." (Minnesota Pineries, *Putnam's Magazine*, July, 1857.) They are, however, no protection against cold or wet; hence S. Kercheval tells us that "in winter they were stuffed with deer's hair or dry leaves to keep the feet warm, but in wet weather it was usually said, that they were only a decent way of going barefooted, owing to the natural spongy nature of the leather of which they were made." (*Hist. of the Valley of Virginia*, p. 221.) A resemblance, more fancied than real, has given to a poisonous snake (Toxicophis piscivorus), which is brown with black bars faintly marked, like the black marks of wear and tear on the buff leather, the name of *Mocassin Snake*, while in the South a man made drunk by bad liquor is said to have been "bitten by the snake," or simply to be *mocassined*.

The *tomahawk* had in like manner become the familiar weapon of the frontiersman, who handled it with greater skill even than the Indian. In most Algonquin languages the word appears as *tahmahgan*, consisting of *otamaha*, "to beat," and *egan*, a term used in the construction of all verbal nouns, so that it literally means "a beating-thing." The name was given by the natives to every form of heavy war-club in use among them, though the most common form was that of a comparatively light axe with a hollow handle, so that it could serve as a pipe also. To the upper part the scalp of the defeated enemy was frequently attached. A favorite game of the early settlers is thus described by Kercheval: "The *tomahawk*, with its handle of a certain length, will make a given number of turns at a given distance; at five steps it will strike with the edge, handle downwards; at seven and a half it will strike with the edge, handle upwards, etc., a little experience teaches the eye and the hand, and the sport of *throwing the hatchet* is great." (*Hist. of the Valley of Va.*, p. 243.) As the Indians performed certain ceremonies with the tomahawk, burying it when they made peace, and digging it up again upon the breaking out of a war, the two customs soon became familiar to the early settlers, and the phrases, *burying the hatchet*, and *digging up the hatchet*, were soon used in conversation generally for the reopening or amically arranging of difficulties of every kind. Thus W. Irving says: "They smoked the pipe of peace together, and the colonel claimed the credit of having, by his diplomacy, persuaded the sachem to *bury the hatchet*," (*Washington*, I. p. 361,) and the backwoodsman gives his advice in the homely words: "now, shet up and don't bother talking about *digging up the hatchet*." (*Life on the Prairies*, p. 314.) The strange process of *scalping* seems to have been peculiar to the Indians of this Continent; at least it has not yet been found among other tribes; the Red man, it is well known, prepared himself for his fate by allowing his hair to grow in a long tuft on top of his head, which he called his *scalp-lock*. The victor would seize it with his left hand and with a sharp knife, the *scalping-knife*, by a single turn of the hand sever the skin in a circle on the crown of the head; then with a powerful jerk pull off hair and skin, and transfer it to his belt or tomahawk. The custom is still prevalent among several Western tribes, and the term of *scalping* so familiar to Americans, that it is not unfrequently used for "total defeat" or "utter annihilation in debate." The favorite term for the actual operation among Western hunters and frontiersmen was, however, the graphic phrase *lifting hair*, and thus a recent Army Report could still contain the words: "I saw at once that the Arrapahoes were not after stealing cattle but after *lifting hair*, and told the corporal so, but he would not believe me." (*Congressional Report*, August 17, 1868.) Before setting out on what they call the *war-path*—a word that has led to the use of the phrase, *he is out on the war-path*, for a man who is about to make a deliberate attack on an adversary or a measure—*a council-fire* is lit in the centre of the village, around which gather the *braves* of the tribe, as their fighting men are now-a-days officially described in the military reports from the Western Plains. The term itself is, however, of French origin, and was first used by the admirable missionaries of France, as when Father Hennepin says: "One of the *braves* accompanied me down to the river holding the precious vessel close to his heart." At this council-fire they sit, often for hours, smoking in silence their *Kinni-Kinnick* or *Killi-Kinnick*, as it sounds in some dialects, a term originating with the Dahcotahs or Sioux, and designating a mixture of dried sumac leaves turning red, and red willow bark, which are finely chopped and grated, and then mixed with a certain proportion of genuine tobacco. The true smoker from the East would probably appreciate the mixture as little as the Englishman relishes the tea of the Continent, improved (!) by spices or a few spoonfuls of rum, but Western trappers and hunters soon learn to prefer it to genuine tobacco. When the latter is mixed with the bark of the cornel-tree it is known as *Esquipomgole.* Then a *pow-wow* is held, a corruption of *powan,* which in the New England dialects meant a prophet, conjuror, or medicine-man, called in Ojibway *waheno* or *jossakeed.* The term was adopted by the early settlers for any great assembly called together by Indians to celebrate feasts, perform dances, or hold councils. S. Kercheval says: "Towards the latter part of February we commonly had a fine spell of open, warm weather, during which the snow melted away.. This was denominated the *pow-wowing* days, from the supposition that the Indians were then holding their war-councils for planning their spring-campaigns into the settlements. Sad experience taught us that in this supposition we were not often mistaken." (*Hist. of the Valley of Va.,* p. 190.) The term seems to have been suggestive enough to be fully adopted, and is still very generally used to designate any public meeting, perhaps with a sly suggestion, that there was more zeal than sense exhibited there. "Tammany held another *pow-wow* on the subject, but the meeting broke up in a row," said the New York Herald on February 2, 1867. The usual freedom is taken with the noun and it is changed into a verb, so that Dr Kane, a careful writer, could correctly say of the prophet of the Esquimaux: "He prescribes or *pow-wows* in sickness or over wounds, directs the policy of the little state, and is really the power behind the throne." (*Arctic Explorations,* II. p. 118.)

The family of the Indian is somewhat oddly called a *lodge,* from the French word *loge,* for hut, whenever not the braves only, but women and children are all included. "It was not pleasant to learn," says Governor N. S. Langford, "that twenty-five *lodges* of Indians had gone up the valley a few days before our arrival, and to be told by a trapper that he had been robbed by them, and, in common parlance, *set on foot* by having his horse and provisions stolen." (*The Wonders of the Yellowstone,* 1871.)

What most distinguishes the Indian in his external appearance, is the *Totem* he wears on his breast—a device of some animal, a wolf, a heron, or a turtle, which is drawn in paint, or engraven in the skin of his body. It serves to distinguish from generation to generation the particular class or subdivision of his tribe to which he belongs, and often furnishes the name of the whole. The word is of Algonquin origin, and sometimes derived from *dodaim*, a term signifying townmark, but unfortunately, there is no such word as *dodaim* to take it from. Longfellow speaks of it eloquently, thus:

> "And they painted on the grave-posts,
> Of the graves yet unforgotten,
> Each his own ancestral *totem*,
> Each the symbol of his household,
> Figures of the bear and reindeer,
> Of the turtle, crane, and beaver." (*Hiawatha.*)

This common custom of all the Indian tribes of the continent hitherto known, seems not to have reached northward beyond a certain line, for W. H. Dale tells us that the "*Totemic* system is not found among the Innuit." (*Alaska and its Resources*, p. 223.)

Besides these words, derived more or less directly from Indian terms and Indian customs, American English has borrowed from them a number of names in Natural History and in the kitchen. It is quite characteristic of this that the first mention ever made of Americanisms should be contained in the words: "Sed et ab Americanis nonnulla mutuamur ut *mais* et *canoa*." (Alex. Gill, cited by J. R. Lowell.) *Maize* is, however, rather of West Indian origin, belonging to the Carib language, and in Hayti called *mahiz* or *mahis*, of which the Spaniards at the time of the first discovery made *maïz*, and through the French *maïs*, we have obtained our term. The first origin of the grain is wrapt in as much mystery as that of most cereals; like all products of foreign, unknown countries, it appeared under the general name of *Indian Corn* in Spain, and *Turkey Corn* in Italy, just as the bird of this continent appears as *coq d'Inde* in French, and as a *turkey* in English. In America it is universally known as *corn*, since every country calls the staple cereal by this generic name, so that wheat (or all small grains) in England, rye in Germany, and oats in Sweden appear as corn in the idioms of these countries.

Its fertility and great nutritive power attracted early much attention, and from the first settlements to our day, it has been the staple food of man and beast. Beverley already alludes to some of the many varieties found in this country. "*Flint Corn*," he says, "looks smooth and as full as the early ripe corn, the other has a larger grain and looks shrivelled, with a dent on the back of the grain, as if it had never come to perfection; this they call *she-corn*. This is esteemed by the planters as the best for increase." (*Hist. of Virginia*, p. 127.)

Corn is not eaten raw, though there seems to be literally no stage at which the *ear* is not fit for food when suitably prepared. The *tucket*, as the green ear is called as long as it is soft and milky, is quite a delicacy to some palates, but generally its consumption is considered too great a waste, and time is given it to fill up, grow to full size, and harden. The imperfectly-formed ear, on the contrary, is called a *nubbin*, a term said to be of Indian origin, though the presumption is not improbable that it is nothing more than the English word *nothing*, which the negroes very uniformly pronounce *nuffin*, and *nubbin*. The modes of preparing the green and the ripe ear for the table are almost infinitely varied, from the simple ashcake of the Indian, to the elaborate pudding of the great city. Furnishing, at all times, a toothsome dish, it is perhaps most appreciated in the simple shape of *roasting-ears*, as the latter are called, when, still green, they are quite soft and pulpy, with just enough consistency to be roasted Indian fashion, before a fire or in the hot ashes. "Indeed, this is a very good and pleasing food," says Beverley, naively (*Hist. of the Valley of Va.*, p. 117), and P. Cartright, more plaintively: "The Methodist preacher of those days (before 1800), often slept in dirty cabins, on earthen floors, before the fire, ate *roasting-ears* for bread, drank buttermilk for coffee, or sage tea for imperial, and took, with a hearty zest, deer meat, or bear meat, or wild turkey, for breakfast, dinner, and supper—if he could get it." (*Autobiography*, p. 243.) When ripe, the grains become too hard for eating, and have to be ground into *corn meal*, which the negroes of the South invariably, and very judiciously, prefer to wheat flour. This meal is made up in various ways, the simplest of which was learned from the Indians. "Tempering this flower," says valiant John Smith, "with water, they make it either in cakes, covering them with ashes till they are baked, and then washing them in fair water, where they drie presently with their own heat; or else boyle them in water, eating the broth with the bread, which they call *Ponap*." (*Virginia*, I., p. 127.) The latter word was the term *apohn* in the Powhatan dialect, and hence comes the modern *pone*, a name invariably given in the South to a maize-cake. Hence even F. Olmsted could still write, "We all clustered around the fire, the landlady alone passing through our semi-circle, as she prepared the *pone* and fry and coffee for our meal." (*Texas*, p. 319.) The negro of former days, preparing his simple but savory meal in his cabin, would dab the roughly-kneaded cake down upon his hoe, and thus bake it before the fire; the result was a *hoe-cake*, unsightly to the eye, but palatable enough. Quaint old Barlow refers to it when he says: "Some talk of *hoe-cake*, fair Virginia's pride." (*Hasty Pudding*, 32.) In the New England States another, not less primitive method was pursued; here the dough was spread upon the stave of a barrel-top and thus baked before the fire; at times the irresistible pumpkin was mixed with it, and then it appeared as "Rich *Johnny-cake*, his mouth has often tryed." (J. Barlow.) From thence the precious dish spread westward with the restless Yankee, and already, in 1840, the Hon. Mr. Duncan could, on the floor of Congress, speak of life in Ohio as merry enough, when "The frolic consisted in dancing, playing, and singing love and murder songs; eating *Johnny-cake* and pumpkin pies, and drinking new whiskey and brown sugar out of a gourd."

In olden times the *johnny-cake* seems to have appeared occasionally in an odd disguise, if we recognise him in the following lines:

> "Then times were good; merchants cared not a rush
> For other fare than *jonakin* and mush."
> (*New England Crisis*. Benjamin Thomson, 1675.)

But while *hoe-cake* is dear to the South, and *johnny-cake* at home alike in the East and West, the *hasty pudding*—Indian meal stirred in boiling water into a thick batter, and eaten with milk and sugar, or molasses—is a favorite dish all over the Union. Joel Barlow's popular poem on the subject describes the primitive mode of preparing it thus:

"She learnt with stones to crack the well dried maize,
Thro' the rough sieve to shake the golden shower,
In boiling water stir the yellow flour;
The yellow flour, bestrew'd and stirr'd with haste,
Swells in the flood, and thickens to a paste,
Then puffs and wallops, rises to the brim,
Drinks the dry knobs, that on the surface swim;
The knobs at last the busy ladle breaks,
And the whole mass its true consistence takes."

The dish was a favorite of the Indians, and in fact their common food during the greater part of the year. They called it, to the ear of the early settlers, *supawn*, but this was probably merely a corruption of the Lenape or Delaware name *asapahn* and is, no doubt, the same as the *samp* mentioned by Roger Williams, as "a kind of meale pottage unparched; from this the English call their *samp*, which is Indian corn, beaten and boiled and eaten hot or cold, with milke or butter, which are mercies beyond the natives plaine water, and which is a dish exceedingly wholesome for the English bodies." (*Key to the Ind. Lang.*, p. 13.) Both words are evidently derived from the Algonquin *saphac*, meaning "soft gruel, or anything thinned," but early settlers fancied it a Dutch word, and hence honest J. Barlow could write indignantly:

"On Hudson's bank, while men of Belgic spawn,
Insult and eat thee by the name of *suppaum*."
(*Hasty Pudding.*)

Nor was he less patient with his Southern neighbors, of whom he speaks with equal scorn:

"E'en in thy native regions, how I blush
To hear the Pennsylvanians call thee *mush*;"

and yet, if he had lived long enough, he would have heard the name of *mush* given to the pleasant and extremely nutritious dish all over the South. It was almost universally known to the Indians, as seems to be natural from its great simplicity; it is probably the "*sagamity*, that is to say, Indian meal boiled in water, and seasoned with grease," of Father Marquette. In some parts of the West, another mush is frequently used, but as it is made of rye after the manner of a Hasty Pudding, it is called *Rye Mush*.

Besides the more aristocratic *batter-cake*, found to perfection in the South, there is another preparation of corn called *hominy*, or *homony*, an Indian dish, so called from an Indian word written by Roger Williams in his Key *ahuminea*, meaning "parched corn," and in the Powhatan dialect *ustatahominy*, while R. Beverley has it *rockahominy*. (*Hist. of Va.*, p. 155.) To prepare this dish, which is likewise eaten all over the Union, but especially appreciated in South Carolina, the corn is either coarsely ground or hulled, and boiled with water. S. Kercheval already calls "*hog and hominy* the standard dish of all early settlers" (p. 48), and to this day, pork and corn, in this shape, are relished alike by high and low. "That ar Jake," says Jim the Cracker, in an account of Georgia, "'ll never make a man, Cap'n; he don't take kindly to *hog and hominy*, no how, but ketches them no 'count birds and eats 'em. Yes, sir, he does;" while T. O. Richards, in his "Rice Fields of the South," tells us that "to be bidden to a planter's *hog and hominy*, is to be presented with the full, free hospitality of his house." From some fancied resemblance to a kernel thus hulled, a snapping-beetle, or Elater, of Pennsylvania, is called the "*Hominy-beater*." (S. S. Haldeman.) A more direct and more correct connection exists between the name of the cereal and that of the river which has become so famous during the late Civil War, the *Chickahominy*, which was so called from flowing through the fertile lowlands that bore King Powhatan's ample harvests, and thus became the great granary of his dominions. The name itself, *Checahaminend*, in the original, meant "land of much grain." A special variety of corn, with dark, small grains, serves to furnish a Yankee dainty, very popular in the New England States, and hardly known elsewhere. The grains are placed on a heated shovel or held in a wire gauze over a brisk fire, till they pop open, swelling to great size, and in the act of bursting, expose the snowy white inside, thus presenting a pleasing appearance in harmony with their attractive odor. This is called *Pop Corn*, and eaten with salt or sugar. The same tendency to *pop* is possessed by a variety of cake made of Indian corn, baked very hard, and called, from its disposition to jump about in the act of baking, and, as it were, to dodge, *Corndodger*. "*Corndodger* and fried bacon," says F. Olmsted in his pleasant book on Texas, "seem to be the universal food of the people," and a Western tourist assures us that "*Corndodger*, baked in the ashes, salt pork broiled on the end of a stick, and a little muddy tea, must, on the prairie, suffice for the hungry stomach." *Corn-juice* is the poetical name which Western men are fond of giving to whiskey, because it is frequently made of corn, and thus justifies the quaint quotation of J. R. Bartlett:—

> " Old Monongahela whiskey,
> Whiskey made of Indian corn juice."
> (*Pluribushta.*)

Nor must we forget to do honor to another combination of corn with kindred dainties, which we owe to the Indians, their *mesiccwotash* in the Narragansett dialect. In its Anglicised form it reappears as *succotash* or *suckatash*, and consists of green corn with beans boiled together, to which experts add, after the example of the Indians, a small allowance of venison. The palatable dish is held specially dear in New England, and hence appeared in due form at an Indian banquet held in 1836, in Providence, in honor of the two hundredth anniversary of the settlement of Rhode Island. "An Indian mat being spread out, a large wooden platter well filled with boiled bass graced the centre supported on one side by a wooden dish of parched corn, and on the other by a similar one of *succotash*." (Stone's *Life of Howland*, p. 262, *B.*) The word *nocake* with its ludicrous resemblance to English, but quoted in Wood's *New England Prospect*, 1634, as a true Indian word, represented a powder made of Indian corn parched in the ashes, and stuffed into a long leathern bag to serve as provender for long journeys. Although the preparation is of course no longer used, the word may still be occasionally heard in the New England States. Mixed with sugar the same powder appears under the name of *Rokage* or *Yokeage*.

Next to succotash the most important article of food with the Indian was probably *Pemmican*, which has ever since remained the main reliance of all explorers, hunters, and voyagers. The name consists of the two Kenisteno words *pemis*, which means fat, and *egan*, the general substantive inflection, so that the whole simply signifies "fat-substance." It consists mainly of buffalo meat—though other meat is sometimes used in the same manner —dried in flakes and then pounded between two stones. The powder is next put into bags made of the hide of the slain animal, with the hair outside, into which melted fat is poured till it is quite full. Then, the whole being pressed down, the top of the bag is closely sewed up, and thus the valuable provender can be easily carried and long preserved. Fifty pounds of meat and forty pounds of fat make a bag of pemmican, and will last a careful traveller several months. In this state it may be eaten raw, but the voyageurs generally mix it with a little flour and water, and then boil it, in which form it is known throughout the Northwestern territory under the elegant name of *robbiboe*. Travellers have always found pemmican good and wholesome food, though it would perhaps be more palatable without its unprepossessing appearance and a goodly number of buffalo hairs, which are apt to be mixed up with it through the carelessness of the hunters. The *pemmican* of Arctic explorers and hunters in other continents is made of any meat that is available, after the same pattern, and often, for good reasons, without the admixture of fat.

A plant of such universal usefulness and so familiar to a great nation could, of course, not fail to furnish in its various parts also a number of terms and phrases to the idiom. The *cob*, the spike or stipe, on which the seed of the plant grows, may have derived its name from the old English meaning of "head" attached to *cob* (the German Kopf); but Americans carefully distinguish between ears of corn, as they are called while the ears are yet attached to the stipe, and *cobs* of corn, when the latter are removed. They still furnish a certain amount of nutriment, when mixed with more valuable food; but their best use seems to be for pipe-heads, for which they are extensively used by the poor people of the South. There, it must not be overlooked, the *cob* or pithy placenta, which remains when the grains have been shelled off, is as large as the full *ear* of the Northern corn. Old smokers say that a Virginia *corn-cob* pipe surpasses all others in sweetness, lightness and endurance. The name of this part of the plant once gave rise to an unexpected witticism on the part of a negro, who, after the surrender of Lord Cornwallis at Yorktown in 1782, remarked to a friend: "He no *Corn*wallis now; he *Cob*wallis; Gineral Washington shell all the corn off him too slick." *Cornstalk*, on the other hand, was the name of a famous Indian chief, well known in the history of early Northwestern settlements. The leaves of the beautiful plant, which closely resembles the sugar-cane, and is often chosen in lawns and garden-plots as a graceful centre to tufts of smaller plants, are called *blades,* and when dried and stacked up for use, assume the name of *fodder,* furnishing with the top of the stalk most valuable food for all cattle. It is these blades, interspersed with the graceful *tassels,* as the flowers are called, and ripening ears, which were used for ornaments in the first efforts ever made at a style of American architecture. A variety of maize is known as *broom-corn,* since its top and dried seedstalks furnish the immense majority of brooms used in the Union. A *corn cracker* is looked upon as so low a person that he is simply called a *cracker;* he inhabits the low, unproductive regions near the sea-shore, and besides his generic name derived from the chief article of his diet, he appears as *Conch* or *Low Downer* in North Carolina, and as *Sandhiller* or *Poor White Trash* in South Carolina and Georgia. Even in Florida he is found occasionally, leading a wretched life in the woods, and resembling in his habits the worst of the old Indians. The *Crackers* of North Carolina, are, perhaps, the poorest of them all. "Their occupation is collecting turpentine, and they are said to possess an unnatural craving for a clay-diet. They are popularly known as *Crackers,* but their gaunt aspect and haggard, vacant countenances induce one to suppose that they might with greater truth be called *cracked.*" (*Blackwood,* Jan. 1860.)

Corn Rights, on the other hand, were in the earliest times of western settlements, rights to land acquired by cultivation, for: "In 1776 settlements were made on New River (in Virginia); the lands taken up in this region being held by what were known as *Corn Rights*—whoever planted an acre of corn acquired a title to a hundred acres of land." (Withers, p. 48.)

The outer husk, by which the grain is protected against the weather, is generally called *shuck,* and although a common saying has it that a man or a thing is not *worth a shuck* or not *worth shucks,* this shows only the relative merit of the latter in comparison with the more valuable ear. *Shucks* are very much prized at the South as fodder for cattle, and the *husking* or *shucking* (from *Shuck,* the husk of a walnut or shell of a bean.—Grose.) of corn is universally an occasion of merry-making, and one of the gayest of rural frolics known in the country. At the North the thrifty farmer, no longer able to enjoy the *Canticos,* as his fathers called their frolics from an Indian word, invites his neighbors, far and near, to help him, as he is expected and ready to help them another day, and then they set to work, lads and lasses, with many a merry custom inherited from their forefathers,

> " For each *red ear* a gen'ral kiss he gains,
> With each *smut ear*, she smuts the luckless swains."
> (Barlow's *Hasty Pudding.*)

and thus

> "In the barn the youths and maidens
> Strip the corn of *husk* and tassel,
> Warm the dullness of October
> With the life of Spring and May;
>
> While through every chink the lanterns
> And sonorous gusts of laughter
> Make assault on night and silence
> With the counterfeit of day."
> (*Helen Lee.*)

In the South the negroes used to have high times at *corn-shucking,* and gave especially full play to their quaint, but melodious songs, with which they lightened the labor and transformed the task into a frolic. The following portions of two such songs may serve as specimens of a class of songs which will soon have ceased to exist and be speedily forgotten:

> " Oh boys! Come along and *shuck the corn;*
> Oh boys! Come along to the rattle of the horn!
> We'll *shuck* and sing to the coming of the moon,
> And den we'll ford the river.
> Oh Bob Ridley O! O! O!
> How could you fool the 'possum so?"

The other used to be sung by one voice, the response being given in a chorus, and at each refrain the husked ear would be thrown on the rapidly-rising pile in the centre:

"Solo. Obadiah.
Chorus. Jumped into the fire.
Solo. Fire too hot.
Chorus. Jumped in the pot.
Solo. Pot too black.
Chorus. Jumped in the crack.
Solo. Crack too high.
Chorus. Jumped in the sky.
Solo. Sky too blue.
Chorus. Jumped in the canoe.
Solo. Pond too deep.
Chorus. Jumped in the creek.
Solo. Creek too shallow.
Chorus. Jumped in the tallow.
Solo. Tallow too soft.
Chorus. Jumped in the loft.
Solo. Loft too rotten.
Chorus. Jumped in the cotton.
Solo. Cotton so white.
Chorus. Stayed there all night!"

Of late a very brisk trade has sprung up in hackled *shucks*, and a Virginia paper said, "we saw a letter from Charleston, S. C. as to whether two hundred tons per month could be supplied," (Fredericksburg *Herald*, Dec. 10, 1870.) During the Civil War, on the other hand, the original *Blue Backs* of the Confederacy (so-called in opposition to the *Green Backs* of the Union) soon became known as *Shucks*, a name sufficiently significant of their evil repute as a circulating medium. Those were the days, when it was currently reported that ladies in the capital of the Confederacy could be seen in the streets, followed by a servant who carried the piles of money for the marketing, which they brought themselves home in their hands. It ought not to be forgotten, however, that this was by no means the first time in American history when paper-money had been reduced to such a low state. The same thing, precisely, had happened in the days of the Revolution, when General Washington had already said, (December, 1779,) "a wagon load of money will now scarcely purchase a wagon load of provisions."

A *Cornstalk Fiddle* is a toy familiar to every boy in the land: an outside fibre of a cornstalk is loosened, and, by placing a bridge under each end, it becomes a chord capable of producing a few dull sounds by each vibration. Among the many slang terms derived from the beautiful and valuable plant, none is probably more frequently heard than that of *acknowledging the corn*, with its more prosy variation of *acknowledging the soft impeachment*. The former means a confession of having been mistaken or outwitted, as the occasion may warrant, and is said to have originated, like many such phrases, at least twice in very different ways. The Hon. Andrew Stewart, Member of Congress from Pennsylvania, claimed in a recent speech to have caused its first appearance in public. In 1828, he was in Congress discussing the principle of "Protection," and said in the course of his remarks, that Ohio, Indiana, and Kentucky sent their haystacks, cornfields, and fodder to New York and Philadelphia for sale. "The Hon. Charles A. Wickliffe, from Kentucky, jumped up and said, "Why, that is absurd; Mr. Speaker, I call the gentleman to order. He is stating an absurdity. We never send haystacks or cornfields to New York or Philadelphia." "Well," said I, "what do you send?" "Why, horses, mules, cattle, hogs." "Well, what makes your horses, mules, cattle, hogs? You feed a hundred dollars' worth of hay to a horse, you just animate and get upon the top of your haystack and ride off to market. How is it with your cattle? You make one of them carry fifty dollars' worth of hay and grass to the Eastern market. Mr. Wickliffe, you send a hog worth ten dollars to an Eastern market; how much corn does it take at thirty-three cents per bushel to fatten it?" "Why, thirty bushels." "Then you put that thirty bushels of corn into the shape of a hog, and make it walk off to the Eastern market." Mr. Wickliffe jumped up and said: "Mr. Speaker, *I acknowledge the corn*."

The other popular account of the origin of the phrase ascribes it to the misfortunes of a flatboatman who had come down to New Orleans with two flatboats, laden, the one with corn, the other with potatoes. He was tempted to enter a gambling-establishment, and lost his money and his produce. On returning at night to the wharf, he found his boat with corn had sunk in the river, and when the winner came next morning to demand the stake, he received the answer, "Stranger, I *acknowledge the corn*, take 'em; but the potatoes you *can't* have, by thunder." (Pittsburg *Com. Advertiser, B.*)

Even the *cornfield* plays naturally a prominent part in Southern life, and as schoolhouses were apt to be erected in or near them, so-called self-made men are to this day fond of boasting that they never received any other education but in an *old cornfield school.*

Closely connected with the corn-shucking is the hunt of the *opossum*, (Didelphys virginiana,) that strange animal, which still preserves its ancient Indian appellation, though more frequently it follows the loyal Irishman's example, drops the O, and appears as *'Possum* simply. Captain John Smith, who may be said to have discovered it, describes it thus: "An *Opassum* hath a head like a swine, a tail like a rat, and is of the bigness of a cat. Under her bellye she hath a bagge, wherein she lodgeth, carrieth, and suckleth her young." (*Virginia*, I., p. 124.) Following his example, old authors in England and colonial writers spell the name *apassom*, till the more modern form superseded the Indian. The negroes are passionately fond of the very fat meat of the animal, which comes out only at night, and when hunted always takes refuge on a tree, hiding in some hollow. Thus it can be caught only by felling the tree, whereupon the cunning creature falls down apparently dead and often escapes by his power of simulation, which is so perfect as to mislead even the instinct of dogs. Hence the negro's song,

"A *possum* on a 'simmon tree,
With one eye winked right down at me,
Fust by his tail the crittur swung:
And this old chorus sweetly sung:
Get along hum, my yeller gals,
For the moon on the grass am shining."

As the poor animal is not supposed to be over-comfortable in his lofty position, with numerous enemies looking out for him below, his situation has given rise to the phrase, *to be up a tree*, expressive of being in a difficult situation. Some ten years ago, the English papers circulated a story taken professedly from an American paper, "in which this familiar phrase was said to have been made use of rather ingeniously by a preacher of the Spurgeon stamp, to attract the more worldly of his congregation. He announced as the subject of his next sermon: How to rise in the world—Zaccheus *up a tree*." The simulating power, which the opossum shares with the raccoon, has in like manner originated the very common expression, *to play possum*, used when a person pretends to be asleep; its meaning is, however, extended to cases of young ladies showing a little affectation of demureness, or of any one who affects to be unable to do what he ought to do or what he is presumed to be fully able to do. As the clever animal has, moreover, a trick of dodging the dogs in the treacherous moonlight and slyly jumping from one tree to the other, the phrase of *barking up the wrong tree* has come to be used when a person acts under a mistaken impression, very much as the English take the phrase of "being on the wrong scent" from their favorite, the fox. It ought perhaps to be added, that good authorities, such as Professor S. S. Haldeman, consider *Possum*—and not *Opossum*—the proper form of the name. To support this, they refer to two early quotations. The Penny Cyclopedia, 14,458, quotes: "*Possomes*, this beast hath a bagge under her belly, into which she takes her young ones, if at any time affrighted, and carries them away." (*Perfect Description of Virginia*, 1649.) The other, in which the animal is called *Possum* and described as above, is from Lawson's

4

Carolina, 1700, 1709, etc. It was certainly accepted as such by Gosse in his interesting letters from Alabama, who writes: "The initiated can tell a real dead *Possum* from one that is shamming; in the hypocritical state in which I saw it, the coil of the tail-tip was maintained, whereas in absolute death this would be relaxed permanently." (p. 234.)

The favorite tree of the opossum is the *Persimmon* tree (Diospyros virginiana), which owes its name likewise to the Indians, who called it *puchamin*. Captain John Smith has caught the sound fairly enough, for he tells us "The other (trees) which they call *Putchamins*, grow as high as a palmeta; the fruit is like a medler; it is first green, then yellow, and red when it is ripe; if it be not ripe it 'll draw a man's mouth awry with much torment; but when it is ripe, it is as delicate as an apricote." (*Virginia*, I., p. 122.) The fact is, that the plum requires to be exposed to severe frost before it is fit to eat; but then it becomes very sweet and luscious, with a decided vinous taste, which the opossum fully appreciates. How little even this common tree is yet known abroad, appears from the manner in which the clever writer on "Inroads on English," in *Blackwood* (Dec. 1870, p. 417), speaks of its fruit as *nuts*. Mr. Jefferson, the President, used to say, that with cultivation the fruit might be made valuable as a table-fruit and for preserves, while *persimmon beer*, as a kind of beverage made from it is called, might often tempt more fastidious palates than those of the negroes, who love it dearly. R. B. Beverley had evidently a good opinion of it, for he writes: "Of these (persimmons) some vertuosi make an agreeable kind of beer, to which purpose they dry them in cakes and lay them up for use." The familiar fruit has, like other Indian names of this class, given rise to many familiar expressions and slang phrases. To *rake up the persimmons* is a frequent term for "pocketing the stakes;" *the longest pole gets the most 'simmons* takes the place of the English "the longest pole knocks down the nuts," and the odd-sounding phrase, *huckleberry above the persimmons*, is used mainly in the South to express that something apparently simple and easy is far above the ability of the person who made the attempt.

The *raccoon* (Procyon lotor), an animal which has much in common with the opossum from its curtailed name of *'coon* to its fondness for persimmons, shares with it also the Indian origin of its name. The Algonquin (Virginian) *aroughcun* or *arocoun* (the scratcher), the name of the animal as quoted by Strachey and Smith, is evidently the ancestor of the modern form, and if there is any connection with the French *raton*, as is claimed by some writers, it is certainly not that of direct descent. In other Algonquin dialects similar names occur, and only among the Ojibways the animal was known as *aisebun*, "a shell it was," in allusion to the tradition prevailing among them, that the curious marks of the animal's furs were the traces of its former existence as a shell before it was transformed. Captain John Smith also quotes it thus: "There is a beast they call *aroughcun*, much like a badger, but uses to live on trees as squirrels doe." (*Virginia*, I., p. 124.) The *raccoon* is mentioned as such by Beverley, when he inveighs against animals that are fond of pilfering the settlers' beehives, and speaks of them as "bears, *raccoons*, and other liquorish varmine." (p. 122.) The shortened form, *coon*, is of comparatively modern origin, having been first introduced into polite language in 1840, when Harrison was elected President, and the skin of the animal was used as a kind of badge, in conjunction with cider and log cabins drawn about the country on wheels. The eccentric Davy Crockett is said to have used the word before, but it was certainly then first brought from the woods into good society, and speedily secured a footing. The whigs had no sooner adopted the emblem than they became known throughout the Union as *Coons*, their policy was denounced as "*Coonery*, which must fall with all its corruptions and abominations, never more to rise." (Boston *Post*, *B.*) The epithet was all the more forcible, no doubt, because so suggestive of the known character of the animal, which moves in a somewhat oblique and sidelong manner, and is up to all sorts of shifts in self-defence. Hence also the ludicrous corruption of *shecoonery*, for chicanery, not uncommon in the South, and expressive of a kind of mild and feminine whiggery. *A gone coon* represents a man in a serious or hopeless difficulty. This Western phrase is, of course, drawn from the idea of a *coon* which has been treed, and—like the one threatened by that famous shot, Captain Scott—is ready to say, "Don't trouble yourself to fire, Captain, I'll come down!" having no hope of escape. The amusing Slang Dictionary, published by J. C. Hotten, London,

1870, has, however, a novel and entertaining explanation. During the American War, it states, a spy dressed in a raccoon skin had ensconced himself in a tree. An English rifleman, taking him for a veritable coon, levelled his piece at him, whereupon the frightened American exclaimed: "Don't shoot, I'll come down of myself, I know I am *a gone coon*." That is the way history is read on the two sides of the Atlantic. Nevertheless the phrase is quite current in England, and the flavor of patriotism may have served to render it more popular. Why a coon should be presumed to be so long-lived as to make *a coon's age* a common expression in the South for any long period of time, is not quite so evident, but the "Cracker" who piloted Audubon through the marshes of Newtown, already exclaimed upon meeting his friend: "Wall, Pete, whar have you been? I hav'nt see you this *coon's age*." (*Life*, I., p. 178.)

A merry companion of the little bear is the *chipmunk* of the Indians, the *chitmunk*, or chit-squirrel of Canada (Tamias striatus), who loves to show its striped coat on the branches of a tree or the rails of a fence, and comes uninvited into gardens and orchards to pick up the pits in cherry-time. It makes a chattering noise, and hence:

> "Was it some *chipmunk's* chatter—or weasel
> Under the stonewall stealthy and shy?"
> (C. P. Cranch, *Summer Pictures*.)

It is not impossible, however, that the word is of later origin, as the term, to *chip*, from *chirp*, "to be merry," a provincialism in England, is quite common in America, and even the noun *chipper*, in the sense of "a lively, cheerful person," is frequently heard in New England. In some of the Eastern States the familiar name of the playful little creature, unknown in England, is *Hackee*.

A genuine Americanism, in every sense, is the *Moose*, (Alce americanus,) a deer of great size, peculiar to America, and so named by the Indians from his manner of feeding by stripping the young bark and the twigs from the lower branches. *Mooswah* is an Abenaki word, meaning the *stripper* or *smoother*, and is adopted almost without change in its Algonquin form *moos*. The animal excited the marvel of the early settlers, so that Lechford wrote of it in 1642, "There are beares, wolves and foxes, and many other wild beastes, as the *moose*, a kind of deare, as big as some oxens and lyons, as I have heard," (*Plaine Dealing,*) and Josselyn indulges in the quaint comparison, "The flesh of their fawns is an incomparable dish, beyond the flesh of an ass's foal, so highly esteemed by the Romans, or that of young spaniel puppies, so much cried up in our days, in France and England." (*New England's Rarities,* p. 19.) They are now comparatively rare, being constantly hunted for their meat, and the sport they afford, and retire more and more to the northernmost regions. They live in families of fifteen to twenty, each one of which confines itself to a certain part of the woods; this is called a *moose yard,* within which they often fall an easy prey to woodmen and hunters, blocked in as they are by the snow. The leatherwood (Dirca palustris), a small shrub with a tough, leathern bark, is a favorite food with these gigantic animals, and hence frequently called *Moose wood.*

Then there is the *Caribou* (Rangifer caribou), a small reindeer found in the northernmost parts of this as well as the older Continents, and so called by the early French settlers. One variety is known as the Barren-Ground, the other as the Woodland Caribou, but well-informed travellers tell us that they only represent the same animal at different seasons. It is curious that this name, so closely resembling a French word, should be of Indian origin, while another term used carelessly for Moose or Reindeer alike, should have been discovered to be of Basque origin! "*Orignal* is not Indian," writes the Hon. J. H. Trumbull, "but a slightly corrupted form of the Basque word for deer or stag. I discovered the origin of the name, some years ago, in Lescarbot's *History of New France*—but Littré has been before me in printing it, in his 'Dictionnaire,' with a reference to the very passage in Lescarbot." (Feb., 1871.) The poor animals have been ill-treated from of old: La Hentan, in his *North America,* calls them "a kind of wild asses," and other early French explorers, mention them as "vaches sauvages."

The *Wapiti* (Cervus canadensis), often confounded with the moose, is, on the other hand, a stag or perhaps an *elk* in the wider sense of the word. J. R. Bartlett is inclined to believe that the name comes from the Iroquois, but these Indian tribes have no labials in their language, and the same difficulty occurs here as in the derivation of "alewives" from an Indian "aloof." The Iroquois have, on the contrary, a proverb which says that the Algonquins and the whites "commence talking by shutting their mouths," as is necessary in order to pronounce the labials. The name is more likely to belong to the dialects of the Shoshone or Utah, which have a word *wapit*, meaning yellow, and as the yellowish or reddish color of the elk is quite peculiar, though dim, it may well have been called by them "the yellow deer." Even the hunters of the North are apt to call it "the red deer" or "the gray moose," to distinguish it from the common moose, which is black. This presumption is strengthened by the fact that the *wapiti* is very common in the Shoshone country and of great importance to the inhabitants. It is easily domesticated and has been frequently trained to harness.

Equally original, but very far from being as desirable, is another American animal, known by its Indian name. This is the *Skunk* (Mephitis mephitica), who was known as *seganku* or *secancu* to the Abenakis of Maine, and as *seecawk* to the Cree Indians, while the Mexican term conepatl has been changed into a more familiar-sounding name *conepate*, in some of the Southern States.

The small fetid animal is, of course, a near cousin to the English polecat, but surpassing it, if not in offensiveness of odor, at least in its far-reaching and penetrating power. Woe is the house to which it has, by chance or by the persecution of dogs, found its way! It has to be instantly abandoned by its inmates, and weeks of thorough purification often do not suffice to remove all traces. With biting irony the animal is called by the Yankees an *essence pedlar*, and as such was introduced to the reading public by no less an authority than the great poet Lowell. On the other hand, it has served to give its name to everything nasty and offensive, from the *skunk-cabbage* (Symplocarpus foetidus), the first child of spring in the New England States, but strong-scented and repulsive looking, to the *skunk* in politics or college-life, who earns his name by disgraceful deceit or dishonest acts, all of which are called *skunking*. Two poor birds, utterly innocent of any title to such a painful denunciation, are still apt to receive it at the hand of the vulgar: the *skunk blackbird*, whom the Rev. H. W. Beecher calls "the polyglot, who describes the way they talked at the winding up of the tower of Babel"—from its colors, black mixed with white; and the *skunkhead*, the pied duck of science, thus called all along the sea-coast. The slang phrase, *Let every man skin his own skunk*, which is due to Major Jack Downing, is a rather forcible version of the French proverb which recommends us "to wash our soiled linen in the family;" and however graphically it may paint the folly of meddling with other people's quarrels, the comparison is odorous almost beyond endurance. This genuine "varmin"—for no other animal deserves the name better—has been *improved*, after the manner of the American sense of that word, into an original maxim: "Vice is a *skunk* that smells awfully rank, when stirred up by the pole of misfortune." (*Blackwood*, April, 1861.) The phrase contains the very essence of modern social philosophy, and justifies the description of a proverb as the wisdom of a nation.

A kinsman in smells, if not in race, is the American *Muskrat* (Ondatra zibethicus), whose English name, derived from the strong musky smell of the beaver's first cousin, strangely resembles the more familiar Indian name: *Musquash*. Captain John Smith says of it: "The *Mussascus* is a beast of the form and nature of our water rats, but many of them smell exceedingly strongly of muske" (*Virginia*, I., p. 124), while the poet Lowell refers to its habitat in the line:

> "Forlorner than a *musquash* if you'd took an dreened his swamp."
> (*Biglow Papers*, II. 10.)

They are hunted for their furs, which are valuable, and become in sequestered places so bold that "these miniature beavers sit and eat clams on the steps of the boat-house." (*Harpers' Monthly*, August, 1847.) They give their name to the *musquash root* (Cicuta maculata), a poisonous plant growing in swamps.

Among imported animals at least two breeds of horses peculiar to America still bear the Indian names by which they were known from the first. One is the *Conestoga* horse, the probable result of a mixture of the Flemish cart-horse with an English breed, which takes its name from the Conestoga River, in the interior of Pennsylvania, where fertile lowlands and rich grasses are peculiarly favorable to the raising of stock, and where this breed was first produced. It is of large size and great power, and still much in favor in remote districts, wherever the introduction of railways has not destroyed the traffic carried on, as of old, by huge wagons, covered with white canvas and drawn by six of these magnificent animals. The other breed is known as *Narragansett* pacers, ponies said to be found only on the islands in Narragansett Bay, and very much valued on account of their powers of endurance and admirable pacing gait. The breed is, however, reported to be no longer what it was, which may well be the case, if the Rev. Dr. MacSparran was not actuated by a little enthusiasm when he wrote, in 1753: "The produce of this colony is fat cattle, wool, and fine horses, which are exported to all parts of English America. They are remarkable for their fleetness and swift pacing, and I have seen some of them pace a mile in little more than two minutes, a good deal less than three." (*America Dissected, B.*) The increasing fondness of Americans for fast trotting has naturally led to a comparative neglect of pacing horses, and hence much less is said now-a-days of the once famous Narragansett horse.

It is rather remarkable that among the birds so few Indian names should have become familiar to the whites, and even *Sora*, or, as R. B. Beverley writes it in true American style, *Saurer*, the name of a well-known luscious rail (Rallus carolinus), is not unanimously admitted to be of Indian origin. The bird is said to owe its plump appearance and much-praised flavor to the wild rice on which it feeds in the great estuaries of the Middle and Southern States.

Indian names of plants are more numerous. The *Cashaw*, or *Kershaw*, of the West, a pumpkin, may possibly be a corruption of an Indian name, though the relation to squash lies nearer. The *Oregon* grape has not yet had time to make its virtues known. The *Catawba* grape, one of the finest of the Continent, and so named from the Indians who dwelt in its native haunts, was, for a time, most relied on by the grape-growers of the Union, though at present hybrids obtained by crossing it with European varieties are generally preferred. It found early a formidable rival in the *Scuppernong* grape, which grows freely from Virginia to Florida, and covers often half an acre with the spreading branches of a single vine. It thrives mainly on the Scuppernong River, in North Carolina, from which it obtained its name, and is a great favorite with some, though the author of "American Wines" says: "The *Scuppernong* grape produces a wine naturally hard and dry, with little to recommend it but its peculiar flavor and aroma." (p. 615.) The *Chickasaw* Plum derives its name from an Indian tribe residing in the portion of Arkansas where the bush (Prunus chicasa) is found in great abundance along the banks of Red River. It bears a large and beautiful fruit, red in color, and of most pleasant taste. "The *Cohosh* displays its white balls and red stems," says A. B. Street, and thus picturesquely introduces one of the many plants that pass under the name of *Snakeroots*, from some fancied virtue as remedies for snake-bites. The *Cohosh* is the Actaea racemosa of the botanists, and the Blue, or White, or Black *Cohosh* of the common people, who prefer the old Indian name.

Gumbo is a word, which, Indian or not, is apt to recall most pleasant recollections in the minds of those who have learnt to know the excellent use Southern housewives make of the pod of the *Okra* (Hibiscus esculentus), in preparing a dish that also bears the name of *Gumbo*. Fredrika Bremer wrote in her quiet enthusiastic way: "*Gumbo* is the crown of all the savory and remarkable soups in the world, a regular elixir of life of the substantial kind. He who has once eaten *Gumbo* may look down disdainfully upon the most generous turtle-soup." The peculiar mucilaginous qualities of the plant lend new savor to the chicken, rice, tomatoes, and rich seasonings out of which cooks, especially in New Orleans, manufacture the popular dish. Far less valuable to the epicurean, but largely consumed by the masses, are the *peanuts* or *earthnuts* (Arachnis hypogaea), known in North Carolina and the adjoining States as *Goober* peas, so that during the late Civil War a conscript from the so-called "piney woods" of that State was apt to be nick-named a *Goober*.

Among trees bearing Indian names, we meet with the *Catalpa* (Bignonia catalpa, Linn.), a most noble and beautiful tree, so called by the Indians of South Carolina, where it was discovered in 1726 by Catesby. Its broad, large leaves and brilliant clusters of white and red flowers have made it a favorite in Europe also; its wood, however, is brittle, and the trees are short-lived.

Hackmatack is the old Indian name of the *Tamarack* of our day (Larix americana), a laurel peculiar to this Continent, and one of the most useful trees, which serves alike to build the houses of new settlers and the ships of our navy, its timber possessing very valuable properties. The most familiar among the trees which are called by their Indian names, is, however, the *Pawcohiccora* of Captain John Smith, our *Hickory* (Carya of several species). Ten years before Nuttall wrote his great work, it was known as the *Hicoria* of Rafinesque, and we read already in 1692 of "The strong *Hickory*, Locust, and lofty Pine" (Richard Frame), while W. C. Bryant sings of

"The *hickory's* white nuts,"

which in New York are called walnuts. The tree furnishes a valuable wood, largely exported for carriage building and other purposes, besides edible nuts. The former, possessing great toughness, combined with unusual flexibility, is much in demand for the manufacture of articles requiring these two qualities, while the name of the plant is constantly transferred to persons or objects notable for either. A *Hickory Catholic*, for instance, is free from bigotry and asceticism, while a *hickory armchair*, if not actually made of the wood, is a chair of more than usually yielding material. Occasionally the wood is split into thin layers, after having been thoroughly soaked, and then the splits are interwoven so as to make a pleasant, elastic seat for a chair. *Hickory* and oak both yield the necessary wood, and chairs of this kind are known, especially in the South, as *split-bottom chairs*, rough in appearance, but astonishingly comfortable for use. It is from the remarkable toughness and tenacity of hickory wood that General Jackson became, after the battle of New Orleans, familiarly known throughout the country as *Old Hickory*, a term as expressive at least of personal affection, as of a high appreciation of his character. In like manner a kind of shirts made of heavy twilled cotton, generally with a narrow blue stripe, which are much worn by hard-working men, are called *hickory shirts*, from their strength. General Brewerton describes his appearance during a "Ride with Kit Carson" thus: "I was attired in a check or *hickory shirt*, as they are called, a pair of buckskin pants, a fringed hunting-shirt of the same material, gayly lined with red flannel, and ornamented with brass buttons." *Hickory* trousers owe their name to the same good quality, while the famous nursery song, *Hickory*-Dickory-Dock, is said to contain a sly allusion to the hickory switch not unfrequently used instead of the classic rod. Mr. Strachey, in his "Historie of Travaile into Virginia," written in early colonial times, and recently published by the Hakluyt Society from a MS. in the Bodleyan Library at Oxford, states that *hickory* was also the name given by the Indians of Virginia to the white liquor made by them from the kernels of hickory nuts, so that when they saw the English at Jamestown use milk, they called that also *hickory*.

The *Shagbark* (Carya alba) is a variety of hickory, so called from the rough and shaggy appearance which its bark assumes in old age; as the latter peels off easily, the tree is also known as *Shell Bark*, and known all the better, since its timber is perhaps the most valuable, as its nut is certainly the most popular of all the varieties of hickory. The trees are, on that account, favorite resorts with all wood-animals, and of one of them Lowell sings:

> "The squirrel, on the shingly *shagbark's* bow,
> Now saws, now lists with downward eye and ear,
> Then drops his nut."
>
> (*Indian Summer Reverie.*)

A peculiar Indian name for the nut of the hickory is *Kiskitomas*, which is still occasionally heard in the West, where Indians are near, or in a poem like that which began with the words:

> "Hickory, Shellbark, *Kiskitomas* nut!"
>
> (*Literary World*, Nov. 2, 1830, *B.*)

The *Butternut* (Juglans cinerea) also belongs to this family, a beautiful tree with wide, spreading branches, turning in fall completely yellow, and thus proving its relation to the hickories. The juice of the fruit, rich in oil, serves as a dye, and hence the name of *Butternut* was applied to Confederate troops, dressed in uniforms of homespun cloth, that owed its color to the nut. *Butternut* is sometimes called the *Long Walnut*, from its shape, and the *White Walnut*, from the color of the wood.

There is a story told of Mr. Jefferson by his detractors, that in his desire to import valuable trees and plants into his native State, he ordered from abroad, among other shrubs, a number of dwarf chestnuts, quoted as *Castanea pumila* in botanical catalogues. They came, they grew, and turned out to be the *Chinquapin* of Virginia, a native tree, than which few are more common in the South. Captain John Smith already reported: "They have a small fruit growing on little trees, husked like a chestnut, but the fruit most like a very small acorn. This they call *Chechinquanims*, which they esteem a great daintie." (*Virginia*, I., p. 122.) The same Indian name is given to the shrub in Strachey's Vocabulary, the last syllable of which is the generic termination of words meaning all kinds of fruit, from whence also *mondanim*, in the Ojibway, "spirit-grain," which occurs so often in Hiawatha.

Under a borrowed name appears all along our Southern watercourses the *papaw*, so called from its fancied resemblance to the genuine papaw-tree of the Tropics. While the latter is a tree with a leafless trunk, and bearing fruit of the size of a melon, with a milky, acrid juice, the *papaw* of our streams (Asimina triloba), is only a fair-sized shrub, and its fruit, in the shape of long fleshy pods, is sweet and edible, so that it becomes quite important as food to the Indians. The twigs also prove useful in a case of emergency, since, being of a peculiarly supple and tough nature, they easily take the place of the willow-withes of the North.

The *Macock*, according to R. B. Beverley's Account of Virginia, "are a kind of melopepones or lesser sort of pompion or *cashaw*. Of these they (the colonists) have a great variety, but the Indian name is still retained by them." (p. 124.) The *Maracocks*, on the contrary, were, according to the same authority, the fruit of the passion-flower, which grows wild in Virginia, and bears an esculent seed-vessel, "about the size of a pullet's egg." The former name survives in its Anglicized form of *Maycock*; the latter is now believed to be identical with the word *murucuya*, the Spanish name for the same fruit, from which the French made *murucuca*.

The *Oswego* tea of the Shakers (Monarda didyma), owes its name, of course, to the Indian tribe from whom the first settlers learned its virtue, while the Indian names of *Pipsissewa* (Chimaphila umbellata) and *Pitahaya* (Cereus pitajaya) of New Mexico, are gradually disappearing to make way for the more familiar

English terms of Prince's Pride or Winter-green, and Indian Fig, under which the former is known as a popular domestic remedy, and the latter as the luscious fruit of a gigantic cactus. The *puccoon,* also, mentioned by Kercheval (p. 258), and long known under that name to early settlers, is now more generally called *Bloodroot,* and continues to be a favorite remedy with all who deal in simples.

A lowly plant, but one much appreciated in all the States of the Union, is the *squash,* presenting another remarkable instance of those cases of apparent identity, in different languages, which have so frequently misled amiable philologists. Malvolio says of Viola: "Not yet old enough for a man, nor young enough for a boy, as a *squash* is before it is a peascod" (*Twelfth Night*), and uses a good old English word, in the sense of "unripe or immature," which has its almost exact counterfeit in the Natic dialect of Massachusetts, where *asquash* means likewise "green or unripe." The Indians used to apply this word to all vegetables which were used while unripe or without cooking. The plants (Cucurbita) attracted early attention, and their relation to kindred vegetables seems to have even then been a puzzle to explorers. Beverley speaks of them in one place as "These *cushaws* are a kind of pompion, of a blueish-green color, streaked with white, when they are fit for use. They are larger than the pompions, and have a long narrow neck. Perhaps, this may be the above-mentioned *escushaw* of T. Harriott" (*History of Virginia,* p. 124), and in another place, "*Squash* or *Squanter Squash* is their name among the Northern Indians, and so they are called in New York and New England." It is now a favorite vegetable with rich and poor alike, and considered to possess certain properties peculiarly favorable for persons in delicate health. A variety is called *Cymblins,* which name R. B. Beverley thus explains, "The Clypeatae are sometimes called *Cymnels,* from the lenten-cake of that name, which many of them very much resemble." (p. 113.) His derivation was correct; for *cymnel* was really the ancient name for an oval cake, used primarily in the offices of the Catholic Church, and was so called from its vague resemblance to a wave of the sea (χύμα, a wave). Pegge's *Supplement* also furnishes: "*Simnel,* a rich cake, the outer crust colored with saffron. Shrops." *Simnel-bread* and wastle-cake graced Prince John's board at

Ashby when Ivanhoe went to its festivities. The inorganic *b* found its way there, as into "chimbley" and all words where it can creep in between *m* and *l*. That the *cymblins* of our day were as much esteemed of old, we may judge from a poem by Benjamin Thomson, written in 1675, in which he says:

> "When *Cimnels* were accounted noble blood
> Among the tribes of common herbage food."
> (*New England Crisis.*)

Lenten *simnels* are to this day quite common in many parts of England, and *Simblin* is even now the local pronunciation of the name in Lancashire, which comes nearest to Barclay's Saxon.

Squaw Root (Conapholis americana), and *Squaw* Weed (Senecis aureus) hold their place among the medicinal plants of the country, but owe their names to modern, not to Indian, usage. The *Tipsinah*, on the contrary, is a genuine native, and represents the wild prairie-turnip of the Northwest, which often constitutes an important part of the Indian's provisions.

Tobacco owes its name to a mistake: the early Spanish discoverors mistook the term by which the Caribs designated their pipe or vessel out of which they smoked, for the article itself. There is an opinion held by many that *Tabago* was also the name of a province of Yucatan, where the herb was first found growing; and still another, that the name is derived from *Tobago*, one of the Caribbean Islands. None of these theories, however, are as well authenticated as the first derivation, which is already quoted in Gilii's *Storia Americana*. The *weed*, as Americans are apt to call it, with a leaning to slang, is a native of their Continent (Nicotiana tabacum), and if not used more largely here than in any other part of the world, certainly constitutes at once a fruitful source of national wealth, and an almost universal cause of enjoyment to the people. There is probably no State of the Union in which the plant is not raised, and yet so little did the rulers of the land foresee its future importance, that in the instructions to Governor Wyatt of Virginia, dated July 24, 1621, we find the following order: "To put prentices to trades, and not let them forsake their trades for planting *tobacco* or any such useless commodities!" Now Virginia alone pays annually over four millions of dollars in taxes on this article into the Federal Treasury.

Tobacco is smoked in America as elsewhere; it is chewed perhaps more generally than abroad, a habit of which the poet Lowell says, "Our vile habit of *chewing tobacco* had the somewhat unsavory example of Titus Oates, and I know by tradition, from an eye-witness, that the elegant General Burgoyne partook of the same vice." For this purpose it is sweetened with licorice and mixed with every fair and foul ingredient that can give it color and flavor, and leads to the most offensive habit that strikes foreigners in their visits to this country—constant and copious expectoration. But even more disgusting is the purely American habit of *dipping*, which is said to have originated in the use of snuff for the purpose of cleaning the teeth. It seems that the acrid taste and narcotic effect of tobacco affects the system through the gums as well as through the nostrils, and this has led the women of the South especially, who constantly see all men and negro-women smoke around them, to use this method of allaying their craving for stimulants. A writer who had travelled through Virginia, described the process thus: "This neat, orderly, sin-exterminating woman rubbed snuff. She kept a snuff-box in her right pocket, filled with the strongest and most pungent Scotch snuff, and she went about all day, brandishing a dangerous-looking hickory stick with a mop at the end of it, which she was constantly *dipping* into this huge, black, horn snuff-box. Then she would fill her delicate mouth with load after load. At times she would invite her few friends to come over and take a *dip*." (*Putnam's Mag.*, February, 1853.) The *dipping-stick* is also called *snuff-swab*, as if nothing should be wanting to make the repulsive habit still more unpleasant. Fortunately it is rapidly going out of fashion, and only lingers still in remote districts lying far from railways and intercourse with the great world.

Besides *Appomattox*, from *Apomatox*, the Indian for "Tobacco-plant Country," and famous in history since the late Civil War, the plant has given its name indirectly to a fish that enjoys more different designations than probably any other dweller in American waters—the sunfish, who is often called *Tobacco-Box*—and to a plant which has, of late, attracted much attention. This is the *Tobacco Root* (*Valeriana officinalis*), called *Kooyah* by the Indians of Oregon, who bake the root for two days in the ground, to deprive it of its poisonous qualities, and then make it into a kind of bread, which they call *Supale,* and like much better than their *Wapatoo,* a dish early mentioned in W. Irving's *Astoria:* "He regaled them, therefore, to the best of his ability, with abundance of salmon and *wappatoo.*" (p. 194.) The word, representing the root of the Sagittaria sagittifolia," belongs neither to the Chinook nor the Chihali dialect, but is, as George Gibbs in his "Chinook Jargon" asserts, everywhere in common use. (p. 28.)

The term *Sums of Tobacco,* which is still occasionally met with in official papers, has its origin in the fact that for many generations, in old Virginia times, all taxes raised for the support of government officers, ministers, etc., were assessed in so many pounds of tobacco. A comparatively recent word connected with the use of the weed, is *Ambia,* a euphemism, mainly used in Virginia and the two Carolinas, for the expectoration which chewing makes necessary. The presumption is, that the word is a corruption of *Amber,* to which it bears a slight resemblance in color, manifesting certainly a delicacy of expression which borders upon the poetical.

The *Tumatl* of the Mexicans, our *Tomato* (Solanum esculentum), by Bartlett altogether ignored, and by Webster reported as "of American origin," is certainly not an exclusively American fruit, for although long known in Africa, and held there in high esteem by nations discovered but recently, it has become *familiar* to Americans only about two generations since. A competent critic, who wrote most pleasant and instructive things "Concerning Salads and French Wines," says of it: "The *tomato* is a noble fruit, as sweet in smell as the odors of Araby, and makes an excellent—and were I in France, I would say—an illustrious salad. Its medicinal virtue is as great as its gastronomical goodness. It is the friend of the well to keep them well, and the friend of the sick, to bring them back into the lost sheepfolds of Hygeia. The Englishman's travelling companion, the blue-pill, would never be needed, if he would pay proper court to the *tomato.*" (*Blackwood,* October, 1866.) It is a fruit universally used and esteemed in the Union, eaten raw with salt, as a salad, stewed and stuffed in various ways, and *canned* in immense quantities. Its name is gradually becoming Anglicised under the shortened form of *Tomat,* which is preferable—however objectionable to the eyes of purists—to the false new form of *to-may-to,* "invented to maintain a fancied analogy with potato, which indeed belongs to the same natural family—but so does nightshade and henbane." (S. S. Haldeman.)

Of more recent date, as far as its general introduction is concerned, is the *Yam* (Dioscorea alba) of the West Indies, so called from the Indian word *Ihame*. The very large and palatable root or tuber is now quite common in all the Southern States, so that a recent traveller could say: "To enter the piney woods of Mississippi is like returning to North Carolina, and to pass through them without eating roast *yams* and buttermilk, is like passing through North Carolina without eating hominy and chine of bacon." (*Putnam's Mag.*, June, 1867.) Nor must we forget the mysterious *Tuckahoe* of Virginia, in the opinion of many the only American variety of truffles of which we can boast. The peculiar plant (Sclerotium giganteum) excited the curiosity of the first writers on this country, by its growth underground, and the absence of all leaf or stem to connect it with the sources of light and heat on the surface. "Others," says already Captain John Smith, without explaining the matter, "would gather as much *Tockwogh* roots in a day, as would make them bread a weke." (*Virginia*, I., p. 228.) But R. B. Beverley adds more carefully, that it is "a tuberous root; which, while crude, is of very hot and virulent quality, but they (the Indians) can manage it so, as in case of necessity to make bread of it." (*Hist. of Virginia*, p. 153.) Hence it derives its name of *Indian Bread*, or *Indian Loaf*. Like the truffles of Europe, the *tuckahoe* also are sought for by dogs and hogs trained for the purpose, though little attention is paid to them in recent times. The term is now more frequently used as a kind of nickname given to the inhabitants of the poorer lands of Lower Virginia, whose poverty, it is implied, drives them to eat *tuckahoe*. "He is nothing but a poor *Tuckahoe*," was often heard during the late Civil War, when a peculiarly sad-looking conscript came in from the Lower James, apparently half-fed only, and shaking with "chills and fever."

Another underground product, known to us by its Indian name, is the *Coontie* of Florida, which designates the farina obtained from the so-called Arrow-Root (Tamia integrifolia), and which is said to be fully equal to the famous article from Bermuda. The root is, in its crude state, poisonous, and the Federal troops lost in the late Civil War a number of men by the want of precaution in first extracting its deadly properties.

Perhaps the Indian name of a town in Yucatan, *Sisal*, also, may be said to have become part of our commercial language, at least inasmuch as it is used for the prepared fibre of an Agave (not the Agave americana), very common on the Florida Keys, and well known in trade as *Sisal Hemp.*

Among fish the Indians have bequeathed to us but a few names, and their precise meaning varies so much in different localities, that it is not always easy to identify the species. Of those that are well defined we mention the *Barracouda* (Sphyraena barrocuda) of Tampa Bay and other Florida waters, a valuable fish of the pike-kind, taken with a spear by fishermen, who float with the tide so as to meet the wary animal with the sun shining directly in his eyes. More generally known is the *Chogset* (Ctenolabrus ceruleus), frequently called *Burgall* or Blue Fish, and found on the whole Eastern coast under a variety of designations, and the *Cisco* or *Ciscovet,* from the Indian *Siskiwit* (Salmo amethystus), which C. Lanman declares to be "unquestionably of the trout genus, but much more delicate, and seldom found to weigh more than a dozen pounds. They are a very beautiful fish and their habits similar to those of trout." (*A Summer in the Wilderness,* p. 219.) Unfortunately they are so fat, that they become eatable only after being salted.

The *Muskelunge* or *Muskalounge* (Esox estor), so called in Algonquin, is the largest pike known and peculiar to America. It abounds in the Northern lakes and rivers, reaching a length of five feet and a weight of eighty pounds in the upper lakes. "The *Muskalounge,*" says C. Lanman, "in the upper Mississippi, is somewhat of a sluggard, and owing to his size and hyena-like character, the very fish of all others for spearing by torchlight, one of the Esocida, of which Agassiz says America is the fatherland." (*A Summer in the Wilderness,* p. 139.) Perhaps more famous yet is the Indian name of *Menhaden* (Alosa menhaden) of the New England waters and as far south as Chesapeake Bay. Belonging to the herring kind and appearing at times in perfectly incredible numbers near the shore, they are caught and carted by hundreds of wagon-loads to the fields to serve as manure. Their popularity is so great in Massachusetts that a petition was recently (1870) presented to the General Court, as the Legislature of that State is called, in behalf of their friendly relations to the *Menhaden*! It set forth that the ancestors of the petitioners, when they landed in this country, fixed their abode upon the banks of the Neponset River, because of the abundance of fish therein; that the supply had never failed but proved an ever-present help "in the war of 1812, the Tariff struggle, the crises of 1837 and 1857," but that "when the troubles came on caused by the bombardment of Fort Sumter, the fish in the water of the Neponset quietly departed, and from that time we have been deprived of our hereditary luxuries." The loyal and fish-loving population, therefore, petition the General Court to cause the erring *Menhaden* to return to be eaten as of old! In the State of New York the same fish appear under the name of *Mossy Back* or *Mossbunkers*, a term much affected by W. Irving, who writes: "Here an old Dutch burgher related that he saw the duyvel in the shape of a huge *Mossbonker* seize the sturdy author by the leg and draw him beneath the waves. Hence, as to *Mossbonkers*, they are held in such abhorrence, that no true Dutchman will admit them to his table, who loves good fish and hates—the devil?" (*Knickerbocker History of New York*, p. 221.) The *Mummachog* is hardly known beyond the waters around Long Island; the small carp-like fish is more generally called the Barred *Killy*, (Fundulus.)

The *Porgy* (Pagrus argyrops) from the imperfect pronunciation of *r* by Americans also frequently called *Paugy* and *Poggy*, a fish of the gilt-head kind and much esteemed for its flavor, has a curious history connected with its Indian name. In the Narragansett dialects the latter appears as *Mishescuppaug*, the plural of *Mishescuppe*, which meant "large-scaled." Of this word the first part *mishe* seems to have been entirely lost, the next syllable *scup* has been retained in Rhode Island, while the last, a mere termination with the *p* of the word itself, *paug* has been lengthened into *paugie* or altered into *porgie*, and thus furnished the name by which the fish is known in New York. It is stated, however, upon J. R. Bartlett's authority, that "the entire Indian name is still common in many parts of New England." A fish much esteemed in Northern waters, and especially commended by Mr. Daniel Webster, as "an excellent fish, in its way inferior to none, unless it be the genuine sheepshead, for which I am told it was mistaken by

Roger Williams," (Letter to Mr. Seaton, Feb. 14, 1859), is the *Tautog*, (Labrus americanus.) The Indian word is the plural of *taut* and was really translated in the "Key to Indian Languages" as sheepheads, the name of a near cousin also caught in the same waters, though considered superior when caught in the South. In New York it is called *Black Fish* from its color. The *Tomcod* also owes its odd-sounding name—as if it were not a Tom Cat but a Tom Cod—to a corruption of the original Indian name, *Tahcaud*, an old Mohegan word, meaning "plenty-fish." This presumption is strengthened by the fact that Cuvier still calls it *Tacaud*, a word which naturally led by its sound to the conversion into a thoroughly English sounding name. The little fish (Morrhua pruinosa) appears in vast numbers with the first frost and is hence quite as well known as *Frost Fish;* thus we hear it said: "Here we met with large schools of *Frost Fish*, the *Tomcod* of our books, with hosts of hungry bluefish in fierce pursuit." (*A Whaling Cruise*, p. 119.) Nor must we omit mentioning the poor little *Weak Fish*, contemptuously so-called by the fishermen of Long Island Sound because of the feeble resistance it makes when caught by a hook. Its Indian name *Squeteague* is not only in use among the people of the neighborhood, but has found its way from the Narragansett dialect, in which it originated, to scientific works, where the fish appears as Labrus *Squeteague*.

Perhaps the most ludicrous corruption of an Indian name into a good English word is that of the Narragansett term *aloof* into *alewife*. The former is quoted by Winthrop in his essay "On the Culture of Maize" (*Philos. Trans.* No. 142, p. 1065), and by Baddam (*Memoirs*, II., p. 131), as stated in Webster's Dictionary. But as the Indian dialects of New England contain neither *l* nor *f*, the original word was more probably *ainoop*. Whatever may have been the true origin, there was enough resemblance in the term to tempt the English—for with them we are inclined to think the change arose—to convert it into their familiar *alewife*, and thus the little fish (Clupea serrata), resembling a herring, and used mainly for manure, appears at home and abroad in the ridiculous form of *alewives*.

While the common shellfish found in the sand of tidal rivers and known as *clam*, derives its English name very significantly from its resemblance to a clamp, and was so called for many centuries down to Captain John Smith, who writes: "You shall scarce find any bay or shallow shore or cove of sands where you may not take many *clampses* or lobsters, or both at your pleasure" (*Virginia*, I., p. 124), it is frequently still called by its Indian name *poquauhock.* This word, however, has shared the fate of other long Narragansett terms, and been made to do duty in parts: *pooquaw* being now the name of the Round Clam in Nantucket, while *quahaug* represents the same shellfish in New York, New Jersey, and Pennsylvania. (S. S. Haldeman.) The laws of Rhode Island use the term *quahog* in imposing a heavy fine on persons who take them between May and September from certain beds in Providence River, where, in common with several other places of like character, the luscious shellfish are regularly planted after the manner of oysters. The *clam* of Boston is the Mya arenaria of the *clam-banks,* and when salted for the fisheries it takes the name of *clam-bait. Hen Clam* is the name given in New England to the Mactra gigantea. It has already been mentioned that the *Quahaug* (Venus mercenaria) served in olden times to furnish the *Suquahock,* as Roger Williams calls it, of which the Indians made their currency: "After they have eaten the meat there (in those which are good) they breake out of the shell about halfe an inch of a blacke part of it, of which they make their *Suckauhock,* or black money, which is to them pretious." (*B.*) The *Soft Clam* is also still known by its Indian name *Mananosay,* suggestive of its long flexible snout from which it spirts water, so that on the sea coast: "even the toothsome *Manonosays* squirted water up through the sand what time the tides were out." (*Putnam's Monthly, May,* 1870.) Even the favorite method of preparing the clam has been taught us by the Indians, and is to this day known as a *Clam Bake,* from the fact that they are baked in an impromptu stove of stones and weeds. A hole in the ground of the proper size for the quantity to be prepared is lined with round stones and thoroughly heated by a continuous fire, then the hard clams are thrown in and covered with sea-weeds to prevent the escape of steam and flavor. The result is an unexpectedly savory dish, which is tempting enough to attract often large parties, and J. R. Bartlett mentions a political *Clam Bake* in Rhode Island in 1840, at which nearly ten thousand persons were present.

It requires probably a greater familiarity with the life of the clam to appreciate the force of the New England proverb: "*As happy as a clam at high water*," though at that time it certainly seems to enjoy the generous fluid that covers and feeds it at the same time. The vulgar use of the word *clamshell* is unfortunately more intelligible, and hence the expression, quite common wherever slang is heard, "*Shut your clamshell*, for: Keep your own counsel," is familiar even to English ears, and the poet Lowell uses it with great force in the lines:

> "You don't feel much like speakin'
> When, ef you let your *clamshells* gape, a quart of tar will leak in."
> (*Biglow Papers*, II. 19.)

In addition to these Indian terms derived from the former owners of our Continent, and more or less intimately connected with our social or domestic life, we have in our English a limited number of terms that owe their origin to Indians of Central and South America, or of the West India islands. Some of these are sufficiently familiar and important to deserve a place among American peculiarities of our idiom, although the great majority are probably as common in England as with ourselves.

Thus the *Barbecue*, the roasting whole of an animal by splitting it to the backbone and placing it on a rude gridiron of stakes, is a term—and a process—obtained from the Indians of Guiana, who used the word *Berbekot* for the wooden grills on which they broiled or smoked dried meats and fish. R. B. Beverley shows that the word was in use in Virginia before 1700, for he says: "By laying the meat upon four sticks, raised upon forks at some distance above the live coals," . . . which "they and we also from them call *barbecueing*." The word was adopted by the English in Guiana as early at least as 1665, and thus Pope was led to exclaim through Oldfield:

> "Lend me, gods, a whole hog *barbecued*."

There is no necessity, therefore, of resorting to the violent, if tempting, derivation from *barbe-à-queue*, words which in themselves bear no association with beardless hogs and oxen, and certainly would not be apt to be familiar to Virginia Indians. The convenience of thus preparing ample food for a number of persons in the simplest way, and the happy result of the process of roasting, have led to the preservation of the ancient custom, and down to the time of the late Civil War *barbecues* were frequent in the South and generally very happy occasions for neighbors and political friends to assemble in council. The merry scene in the shelter of a wood, the fragrant steam, the savory meat, and the lively interchange of wit and jest, all served to make the simple entertainment a bond of friendship and neighborly kindness among the assembled people, and spoke well for the simple habits and cordial feelings of what C. Lanman in his description of such a meeting calls "the yeomanry of Virginia." (*Adventures*, II., p. 259.)

The West India term *Cacique,* borrowed by the Spaniards from the *Cazic* of Hayti, has become so familiar to American ears, that it is often most absurdly applied, now to chiefs of Indian tribes and now to mayors of New Mexican towns, and any somewhat pompous and self-sufficient man is apt to be nicknamed the *Cacique* of his town. *Calico* is of course as familiar to our ears as to English, but the East India word, derived from the city of Calicut, does not denote the same material in America; while in England white cotton goods are still called *calicoes,* the name is here confined to *prints, i. e.* colored cotton cloth, coarser than muslin. The latter material, so called from Mosul in Syria, is, on the other hand, in New England never applied, as in England, to thick cotton cloths, which are there called *shirting* or *sheeting.* The difference in various States is so great in this respect, that a story is told of a gentleman in Philadelphia, who ordered muslin shirts in Boston, and although reminded of the unsuitableness of that material for the climate in which he lived, insisted upon his order, as he had always worn muslin, meaning cotton-shirting. When his shirts arrived, they were made of Swiss mull! The term muslin is, at the North, only used for thin, clear fabrics, and paper-muslin is known as sarcenet cambric.

The *Cassareep* of the West Indies, the name of the juice of the cassawa-root (Jathropha manihot), boiled down to destroy its poisonous properties, and much employed as a condiment, is as such well known, and has made the name more familiar to American ears than the *Chicha,* a fermented liquor made in the West Indies of Indian corn, and not unknown in the new States that were once under Spanish authority.

The Mexican word *Coyotl,* the Aztec name of the prairie-wolf

(Canis latrans. Say.), was adopted by the Spaniards in Mexico as *coyote*, and has been bequeathed by them to their successors in the ownership of California and other provinces of the former colonies. The word has come into general use now, not only for the disagreeable barking wolf, but more frequently even for the diggings which somewhat resemble the burrows in which the wolf lives. To *coyote* is a common expression there, meaning to sink small, shallow shafts. Hence we find an interesting account of the so-called *Colorado Desert*, giving us the following description of the animal: "I slept well, but the rascally *coyotes* awakened me at last by their yelping. Leaping up suddenly, I came within two or three rods of griping one by the tail. As they galloped away across the cool, gray gravel, in the dim light of the daybreak, it looked precisely as if they were skating away on ice." (S. Powers. *Afoot on Colorado Desert.*) Of the mines it is said: "All along the gulches *coyoteing* is going on at a great rate, and, to tell the truth, there is not always much choice between the four-legged and the two-legged *coyote*." (*Overland Mag.*, June, 1870.) The word is going Eastward, for a recent Chicago paper says: "One of the delights of Minnesota sleighing parties is being chased by *coyotes*." (February, 1871.)

Another Mexican name has survived and made its way into American nomenclature; this is the *Ocelotl* of Mexico, the *Ocelot* of Northern Texas (Felix pardalis), a large cat-like beast of prey, known also as *tiger-cat*, and extending Northward as far as Texas. It became known to us through early French settlers, who had given the name its present shape.

Guano, a word representing a fair, though not altogether successful, effort to pronounce the Peruvian *Huano*, which means "dung," is, of course, now well known all over the Union, and so largely prepared artificially, that the imminent exhaustion of the imported article will probably be viewed with indifference.

The *Hommocks* of Florida, islands in the everglades or lands under water, which are supposed by some to have once been coral islands in the midst of the ocean, before sand and mud filled up the regions around them so as to convert them into swamps, are presumed to have their name from a West India word familiar to the Spaniards. The derivation has, however, never been satisfactorily established, and it appears quite as likely that the term originated with the Seminoles themselves, who, as Bartram says, possess "this swampy and *hommocky* country." (*Travels in North America.*)

Hurricanes, also, more frequent in America than in Europe, have made their way into the language, and the word, familiar to English ears, appears already as *hericano* in Captain John Smith's account of Virginia, while no English dictionary mentions it before 1720, when it was quoted by Phillips. It is derived from the Carib *uracano*, fairly represented by the French *ouragan*, which the patriotic English naturalized, as usual, under the more familiar form of *hurry-cane!* The disguise seems to have been effective enough to lead learned men into temptation: some derived the word from a Quiche term which has never been discovered; others, like the learned Dr. Webster himself in earlier days, saw in it the root of the Latin *furio*. It is simply the common term of the dialect of Hispaniola for any high wind, and especially for the terrible tornado of the Caribbean Sea, the most sublime and awful display of power which nature affords.

It is a much mooted question whether the familiar term *Jerked Meat* arose from the familiar English word *to jerk*, or from the word *charqui*, which represents the same preparation in all Spanish-American countries except Mexico, where it is called *tasayo.* The custom itself, of drying beef and other fresh meats without salt in the open air, is quite as common now as of old, but the word was never met with in this sense before its employment in the "plantations." Kercheval says: "Their large wallets, well filled with bread, *jerk*, boiled ham, and cheese, furnished provisions for the drivers." (p. 224.) Wills De Hass also repeats: "As soon as daylight appears the captain started to where they left some *jerk* hanging on the evening before" (*Hist. of Early Settlements*, p. 389), and this use of *jerk* would seem to be in favor of its derivation from the Indian of Central America. A recent work by Mrs. Trail, however, shows the more recent use of the word: "Instead of cutting the meat into strips and drying it (or *jerking* it, as the lumberers term it)." (*The Canadian Crusoes*, p. 186.)

Even the Sandwich Islanders have given us some assistance in their word *Kanaka*, which with them means simply a man, but which has, since the intercourse established between their distant home in the Pacific and California, become quite familiar to our ears, so that we all know very well what is meant when we read of "The day that French Pete and *Kanaka* Joe shot each other to death over the bar in the front room." (*The Luck of Roaring Camp*, by F. B. Harte, p. 1.) In the same portions of the Union the once Mexican word *metatl*, in its Spanish form *metate*, has become well known to Americans. It designates the hollowed, oblong stone, used universally in those countries for grinding wheat or Indian corn for *tortillas*, or cocoa for chocolate. J. R. Bartlett himself, perhaps, introduced the word first to the general public in his excellent work on New Mexico, when he says: "For miles around the Casas Grandes the plain is strewed with broken pottery and *metates*, or corn-grinders," and since then every traveller has learnt and taught others to apply the word correctly. Its days as a living word are, however, numbered, as better methods of grinding supersede the imperfect, old custom, and soon *metates* will be known only in antiquarian writings. A longer lease of life may be predicted for *jacal*, another Mexican word, originally written *xacalli*, and meaning a straw-hat. It is now the name of a rough kind of dwelling, consisting simply of stakes, the interstices between which have been filled up with clay, such as are very common in Texas and the new States that were once Mexican. "To the left was the guard-house, part *jacal*, part tent-cloth." (*Overland Monthly*, March, 1871.)

The intercourse with British sailors, and the brisk trade carried on in the East Indies by numerous resident American firms, has brought the name of the disreputable suburb of Bombay, *Dungaree*, into common use in the United States. It was probably first the coarse blue cloth manufactured there, and named after the place, which made the name familiar to American ears, so that F. B. Harte could say of the motley crowd at the mines, which he so graphically describes: "Sometimes these appellatives were derived from some distinctiveness of dress, as in the case of *Dungaree* Jack." (*Luck of Roaring Camp*, p. 56.) Then the Anglo-Chinese war, in which American sailors took part, brought another term home to their mind, and hence we find a recent writer on Americanisms speak of "British sailors on the Chinese coast, who long ago learned to laugh at the clumsy *Dungaree*

Forts and Quaker Guns of their Celestial enemies," both of these inventions being largely used in the late Civil War. (N. S. Dodge.)

Captain Cook, in his "Sea Voyages," first noticed the word *Taboo*, employed by the Indians of Polynesia in a political and religious sense, for all that was forbidden to speech or touch, and we have obtained the term thus twice, indirectly from our English forefathers, and directly from the Pacific itself. The *Tamal*, or *Tamauli*, of our southernmost States, has, on the other hand, made its way with the Spaniards into our borders; they learnt to know the name from the Indians of South America, when they adopted the dish which it represents: a mixture of polenta and minced meat, wrapped in cornshucks and baked in the hot ashes. Mr. Olmsted says: "The mountebanks draw a crowd, and this attracts a few sellers of whiskey, tortillas, and *tamaules*, making a ruddy, picturesque group."

The *Tule* of Mexico is so widely spread over all the southwestern States, that the name, originally Indian, has become of universal use in designating the short Cattail (Scirpus lacustris), which, especially in California, covers plains where the eye finds no limit. The grass, insignificant in itself, and of no value save perhaps to cover the huts of shepherds and outlaws, affords refuge and breeding localities for immense numbers of aquatic birds. Occasionally, as "around Lake *Tulare*, it attains a larger size, growing to the height of eight to sixteen inches, and measuring three inches and a half near the root." (*Overland Monthly*, January, 1870.)

II.

IMMIGRANTS FROM ABROAD.

"When a score of nations, each with its own dialect, unite to make up our population, some effect must be produced on our language; some peculiar threads will be found after a while interwoven with the national web."

THE DUTCHMAN.

"The name of Hell Gate, which it continues to bear to the present day."
W. Irving.

On September 9th, 1609, a bold English mariner in the service of the Dutch East India Company sailed his little shallop *Half-Moon*, of eighty tons, into the beautiful bay of New York, and three days later entered the great river that here flows into the ocean. The latter took its name from the discoverer, Henry Hudson, and the land, claimed by Holland, was called New Netherlands. A few years later the island of Manhattan was purchased of the Indians for the value of twenty-four dollars, and the little town of New Amsterdam began to flourish, and became the chief town of a prosperous colony. But the English claimed the whole as part of Virginia, which belonged to them by right of a prior discovery by Cabot, and in 1664, already, there was an end of Dutch supremacy in New Netherlands, which fell into the hands of their formidable neighbors. New Amsterdam became New York with a facility which justifies the Fenian prophecy that it will soon be New Ireland, and the good Dutch burghers in the town and along the banks of the river up to Albany had to learn the language of their new masters.

The traces which their own idiom has left on the face of the country are here, as with the Indians, by far more important and permanent than the elements which it has contributed to our every-day language. Hills and mountains, rivers and lakes still bear their old Dutch names, though often sadly disfigured.

There are *Staten* Island, *Harlem* River, the towns of *Poughkeepsie, Flushing, Stuyvesant*, and *Blauvelt;* in the city of New York streets called *Cortlandt, Roosevelt*, or *Nassau;* outside of the city, *Coenties* Slip and Fort *Gansevoort;* and farther eastward

Spuyten Duyvel, Cape *May* (*Mey*) and Block (*Blok*) Island—almost all of them unaltered and forcibly recalling to us the days of the old Dutch dominion. But that crowded thoroughfare of New York, the *Bowery*, which for years reproduced all the fierce violence and reckless crime of ancient Alsatia, has little to remind us of the pleasant *Bouvery*, the garden-bower of old Dutch governors, who here enjoyed their fragrant flowers and luscious fruits in quiet rural retreats; nor would the ancient village of *Breuckelen*, seventeen miles from Amsterdam, which in May, 1676, gave its name to a small settlement within sight of the Bowery, recognize its godchild in the gigantic city of *Brooklyn*. The noble bay near by, in which the Navy Yard has long been situated, was once *Waale Boght*, a name hardly to be looked for under the thoroughly Anglicized *Wallabout*. The generic term *Kill*, a small stream or creek, has on the other hand remained faithful to many a small and large water of the North, from the lofty Kaats*kill* mountains, so-called from a picturesque brook arising in their bosom, to the broad *Schuylkill* (Hidden Creek) in the adjoining State. The *Fishkill* does still honor to its name, and the *Kill Van Kull* denotes the channel between Staten Island and Bergen, though it is, for brevity's sake, more commonly called the *Kills* simply. A small fish of the genus Fundulus, found only in these waters and used as a bait, is appropriately called *Killy Fish*.

This term *Kill* is one of a class of words which serve to mark the few traces of genuine provincialism existing in the United States; for the *Kill* of New York is a *brook* in New England, a *run* in Virginia, and alas! a *crick*, or creek, almost everywhere else.

The term *gat* also, meaning a hole, a pot, or a passage at sea, has survived in the names of many maritime localities. Barnes' Gate, as the English would have called it, thus continues to be *Barnegat*, but *Helle-Gat*, concise and rather too suggestive, has been softened and made proper by being changed into *Hurlgate*. W. Irving denounces the alteration thus: "Certain mealy-mouthed men of squeamish consciences, who are loath to give the Devil his due, have softened the above characteristic into *Hurlgate*, forsooth! The name of this strait, as given by our author, is supported by the map in Vander Donck's history, published in 1656—by Ogilvie's History of America, 1671—as also by a journal still extant, written in the XVIth century and to be found in Hazard's State Papers; and an old MS. written in French, speaking of various alterations in names about this city, observes: 'De *Helle-gat*, trou d'Enfer, ils ont fait *Hell-gate*, Porte d'Enfer.'" (Foot-note, *History of New York*, ch. iv.)

It was in the same way that the Dutch *hoek*, a corner, though generally modified into English-looking *hook*, is still found as part of the name of certain corners or angular points in the Hudson and the East Rivers, such as *Sandy Hook*, the first land sighted by the traveller from abroad, and *Kinderhook*, high up the river, made famous by the name of its owner, Martin Van Buren.

To these names may be added the Dutch term *overslaan*, to skip, to pretermit, which still survives in a few local names, where sand-bars suddenly interrupt the free navigation of rivers, as in the *Overslaugh* in the Hudson below Albany, the dread of all *skippers*. The same verb, it is well known, has given to English the familiar term of *overslaughing*, for the act of rewarding an outsider at the expense of the person entitled to the preferment by seniority in office. It is not unlikely that the term came into England under William and Mary; in America it is almost entirely limited to political language, and its technical meaning, inherited from Great Britain, in the army and navy. A prominent candidate for the presidency is thus said to have been *overslaughed* by his party if a man before unknown is nominated in his place, and army officers complained bitterly during the late Civil War when they saw themselves repeatedly *overslaughed* by civilians serving among the volunteers. "There is no danger that General Grant can be *overslaughed*," predicts the New York *Tribune* (Jan. 19, 1871), speaking of the next presidential election.

The Dutch word *Yonker* in the sense of the French Cadet and the German Junker, survives in the name of the town of *Yonkers*. The Right Reverend Bishop Kip states, in his charming sketches of former times, that he remembers visiting, in his early days, the old manor-house of the Phillipse family, still standing in Westchester on the Hudson. "When, before the Revolution, Mr. Phillipse lived there—lord of all he surveyed—he was always spoken of by his tenantry as the *Yonker*, the gentleman by excellence. In fact, he was the only person of social rank in that part of the country. In this way the town, which subsequently grew up around the old manor-house, took the name of *Yonkers*."

The *Knickerbockers* have been immortalized by the charming work of W. Irving, and a grateful posterity honors their many merits and kindly temper by calling all the descendants of old Dutch families after their time-honored name. Hospitals and banks, garments and games, all promise to preserve the old designation to distant posterity, and genial writers, from the famous brothers Duyckinck, whose Dictionary of Authors has made them known abroad as well as at home, to the eloquent divine on the Pacific Coast, Bishop Kip, unite in recalling the sterling virtues of their ancestors, while proving that nothing has been lost in transmitting them to their distant descendants.

It is a misfortune peculiar to patronymics in American hands that they suffer a sad perversion of meaning. As few journalists even care to distinguish the Scot from the Englishman, and are apt to call both alike English, so people throughout the Union are in the habit of confounding the Dutchman and the German, and call them all Dutchmen. It must be admitted that there is a good excuse for this confusion. Archbishop Trench tells us that, "Till late in the seventeenth century, *Dutch* meant (in England) generally German, and a *Dutchman* a native of Germany, while what we now term a Dutchman would have been named a Hollander." Quaint old Fuller says accordingly, "At the same time began the Teutonic Order, consisting only of *Dutchmen*, well descended." (*The Holy War*, II., c. 16.) It is evident that this arose not from a tendency to underrate, as when Frenchmen were dubbed Froggies and the like, but from a courteous effort to call the Germans by their own name "Deutsch," which being somewhat difficult to pronounce, readily changed into *Dutch*. Hence the American only follows the example of his forefathers in continuing to call the Germans who come to this country all *Dutchmen* and in speaking of their language as *Dutch*. He can, moreover, plead in his excuse that the German immigrants themselves but too readily acquiesced in the designation and adopted it themselves. Thus, *e. g.* the first English almanac ever printed in the German form was published by John Gruber, a native of Strasburg, under the title of "*Dutch*-English Almanac."

It is far less easy to explain why *High Dutch* and *Dutch Uncles* should be used so generally—the latter also in England—to express ludicrous sounds and undesirable relations. English slang uses *Dutch* for any gibberish or unintelligible sounds, and the *Dutch Uncle* is frequently introduced into conversation, when the last person one would wish to see is to be indirectly designated.

One would almost imagine that the *Dutch* of old must have been greater people than even the Knickerbocker Annals give them credit for—how else could the phrase: That *beats the Dutch*, have obtained such general currency? Mr. Bartlett met with it in a Revolutionary song of 1775 already, and to this day it is used whenever a peculiarly astonishing fact is announced.

It is much to the credit of the early Dutch *vrows* and their good works, that the majority of Dutch terms, which have been incorporated in our language, are attached to names of certain good things prepared in the kitchen, and a few articles of dress, in their day, no doubt, religiously made at home. Unfortunately the good people of New York have kept most of the good dishes to themselves, so that they and their names are rarely known in other States. Their *cookey*, a little cake so called from *Koekje*, and still a great favorite at Christmas and New Year, is apparently an exclusively Dutch tit-bit, and yet F. B. Harte makes one of his reckless California characters say: "Don't know whar he is! He lost every hoof and hide, I'll bet a *cookey!*" (*Luck of Roaring Camp*, p. 227.) If this dainty seems to be specially appropriated to great occasions, a *cruller* may, on the other hand, be found on many a cake-stand and in countless homes all the year round. Being made of a strip of sweetened dough, which is boiled in lard and then curled up at the two ends, it has received its name from a Dutch term *Kruller*, meaning a "Curler." Vegetables were evidently not much to the taste of the old burghers, for it seems they called Corn-salad (Valerianetta) with biting irony *Vettikost*, something like rich fare, and their descendants, still retaining the dish, have as contemptuously allowed it to appear half classically as *Fetticus* or in ludicrous English disguise as *Fatticows*. *Noodlejees*, an humble imitation of maccaroni and used like them for dumplings and in soup, retain in New York at least their old Dutch name, but are hardly known elsewhere. *Olycoeks*, on the other hand, have become more universally popular. Deriving their name from the Dutch *oly-coek*, oil-cake, because they are "balls of sweetened dough fried in hog's fat," as W. Irving describes them, they have become generally known as *doughnuts*. The latter were, of course, not unknown in England, for Halliwell already quotes them as being called *donnuts* in Herts, "a pancake made of dough instead of batter," but their popularity seems to have been increased by that of their Dutch cousins, and they have ever since maintained a strong hold on the New England palate. "*Doughnuts* and *pumpkin pies* seem to be the delicacies most held in esteem here," wrote Mrs. Trollope many years ago, and the same is true now. The West, however, does not seem to have appreciated the delicacy yet, if we may trust the account of an observant traveller who asked the waiter of a Western hotel, if he had any *doughnuts?* "*Dornoots*," said Pat, completely at his wits' end, "I'm a thinking them noots don't grow in this counthry." (*Putman's Mag.*, December, 1854.) They are frequently eaten at New York tea-gatherings, and this leads naturally to the recollection that the pronunciation of pump as *pomp* is in many cases due to the sound of the Dutch word. The good people in those days were very fastidious in the choice of the best water for their tea—as in fact conscientious tea-drinkers ought always to be—and certain pumps in the old city were renowned for their excellent qualities. These were called *tea-pomps*, and it is said that old inhabitants still remember some of the most famous, one of which stood in Franklin-street, where a boy was kept in the afternoon, pumping tea-water for the neighbors. *Rullichies*, once called *rolletjees*, little rolls, are small sausages stuffed with minced meat, cut into slices and then fried, a dish more palatable than wholesome. *Smearcase*, from the Dutch smeer-kaas, a preparation of curds spread on a flat surface to make into cheese, is the same as the more familiar cottage-cheese and as familiar to Germany under the name of Schmier-Kaese as to Holland. It occurs as early as 1842 in the Philadelphia "Price-Current." The same may be said of the famous *Spek en Apeltjees*, now commonly called *Speck and Applejees*, fat pork and apples cut up together and cooked; for the Germans and all their near kindred like fat and sweet things combined—a taste not unfamiliar to the New Englander, who loves his pork and molasses. Fat pork with haricot-beans, and thickly covered over with molasses, is a royal dish for seafaring men, and rarely long absent from the cabin of a whaling captain. The sweet condiment is evidently added to modify the richness of the fat, on the same principle which makes us use currant-jelly with mutton or well-larded venison.

It is somewhat remarkable, that of all these more or less tempting dishes to which the descendants of the Dutch settlers adhere with patriotic fervor and good taste, none should have become popular beyond the limits of New York and parts of New England, while the only preparation of theirs which can be said to have become national is one which can be but faintly praised. This is their *kool-slaa*, literally cabbage-salad, consisting of cabbage-leaves cut fine and dressed with vinegar and oil, pepper and salt, hardly equal to the much-berated *Sauerkraut* of the Germans. Persons who desire to be very correct, and are at the same time happily innocent of any knowledge of foreign languages, have, it is well known, an intense desire to improve unfamiliar words by twisting their shape till they assume a more pleasing, because more familiar, form. To this fate *kool-slaa* has nearly succumbed; it is now almost invariably written as in the following extract from a traveller's account of hotel-fare in Delaware: "A banquet of half-fried bacon afloat in grease, waxy potatoes, *coldslaw* apparently cut with a harrow, and coffee as weak as the butter was strong." (*Lippincott's Mag.*, Feb. 1871.)

The few names of articles of wearing apparel which the Dutch have bequeathed to us, are, like their dishes, almost entirely confined to the State, and often to the city, of New York, and may, as such, be fairly classed among the genuine *provincialisms* of America. There is something of old Holland naïveté in their *barraclades*, as napless blankets made at home continue to this day to be called; the word meant originally *baare klederen*, bare clothes (German Kleider), and graphically described the absence of the usual long staple. It recalls to our mind at once the picture of an old Dutch dame, so charmingly portrayed in W. Irving's loving description of Knickerbocker days, bending over her work in her *clockmutch* (klap-muts), a quaint though not unbecoming cap often seen in Gerard Dow's paintings, and still worn here and there by old-fashioned ladies of Dutch descent. No wonder that such a form, appearing suddenly among fashionable Biddies and brilliant Phoebes of ebony-color, should be hailed as a *Frowchey*, a well-nigh desperate attempt to render the staid old *Vrouwtje* (German

Frauchen), with which the wives of the good burghers used to be greeted. We have even heard the term applied to a poor little woman, looking, in her bright chintz gown and odd cap, her bent shoulders and deep-wrinkled face, like a picture of an old master, by boys who were as ignorant of its meaning as of the word *hoople*, by which they called their trundling hoops, and which they little suspected they owed to the *hoeple* of Dutch ancestors. Nor did their mothers think probably that they were using another such term when washing their children's dirty little hands, and calling them "too *mussy* in all conscience;" the word looks so like the Old English *muss*, and recalls so little the Dutch *morsig*, from which it is derived.

Very much in the same manner Americans are still occasionally heard to speak of a *logy* preacher or a *logy* talker in society, when they wish gently to insinuate that such persons are not peculiarly interesting, but approaching the character of "bores." The term is derived from the Dutch *log*, which means prosy, slow, or dull, and being by its very sound suggestive of its meaning, has maintained its hold on our language. This attachment to old words and old customs causes also the word *Paas* (Paasch) still to be used for Easter in many families of New York, and children especially are fond of calling their bright-colored Easter eggs by their venerable name of *Paas-eggs*, when merrily cracking them against each other in Russian fashion, trying to break their neighbor's and not their own. As, thanks to the resemblance of the German *Blumen*, the echo of a similar Dutch word in the form of *Blummie* and its diminutive *Blummachee* still survive among many people in the great city and along the banks of the Hudson River, *Paas-Blummachee* are well known in the flower-markets, and designate the common yellow Daffodill. The early azalea of our woods (Azalea nudiflora), is in like manner called *Pinxter Blummachee*, for the Dutch were faithful to ancient customs in celebrating after Easter their *Pinxter* (German Pfingsten), the Pentecost of our churches, the Whitsuntide of civil life. Nor do their descendants forget the habit of their fathers of extending the festival over the next day, and *Pinxter Monday* is a great day with their families and servants. "*Pinkster fields*," wrote F. Cooper, and "*spinkster frolics* are no novelty to us, for, as they occur at every season, and I am just old enough not to have missed one of them all for the last twelve years." (*Satanstoe*, I., p. 90. *B.*) There is, of course, no connection between this word and the familiar name of the little finger, also derived from the Dutch (*pink*), as it appears in the nursery rhyme, which accompanies the interlocking of the little fingers of the right hand:

> " *Pinky*, *pinky*, bowbell,
> Whoever tells a lie
> Will sink down to hell,
> And never rise up again."

It is very different with the name of the flower *pink*, which was originally derived from the German *Pfingsten* (the Dutch *Pinkster*), and owed its name to the season of its blooming. A similar confusion between two similar terms exists with regard to the Dutch word *pyl*, now used in the form of *pile* by New York boys to designate an arrow, and the good old English *pile* as applied to money. When we call the stone of a cherry or the hard kernel of any fruit a *pit*, we use unconsciously an old Dutch word (pit), by which our idiom has been enriched, so that the image of a "peach-*pit* put into the ground and rising in due time to grow into a beautiful tree" is an oft-quoted illustration of our own resurrection, employed in the pulpit. The *potty baker* of Mr. Bartlett, from the Dutch *pott-bakker*, has, however, entirely abdicated in favor of the shorter native *potter* himself, and retains only an antiquarian interest, like the once familiar *praatje* of Dutch burghers, which long survived in the painful corruption of *prawchey*, to designate a pleasant neighborly gossip. *To scup* instead of to swing, is still here and there a boy's term, and *terawchey*, made after the manner of *prawchey* from *te ratge*, "the little mouse," a familiar word in English, as well as Dutch nurseries, for the less poetical *creepmouse*.

Among the almost local terms of Dutch origin, which barely survive in districts inhabited by Dutch families, but which every now and then startle us by their sudden reappearance in poetry or in local description, are the following: *Brogues* (*brock* in Dutch) have entirely given way to breeches, but *Blauser*, from the Dutch *blazer*, is still the name of the Deaf Adder (Vipera berus), which blows up its neck and head, and therefore well deserves its graphic name. There is less poetry in the old term *blickey* from the Dutch *blik* (Germ. Blech), which is used in some parts of the States of New York and New Jersey for a tin pail, while *boonder*, originally applied to a brush, much in demand and in use by Dutch ladies, has lately derived a new lease of life from F. B. Harte's sketch of his *dog Boonder*. The word *feast*, a corruption of the original *vies*, and meaning "fastidious," can hardly be said to exist any longer; the Anglicized term *fyke* from the Dutch *fuik* is however still in use among fishermen for a large bow net, with which certain fish, like shad, are caught in New York harbor; and *hay-barrack*, a somewhat ludicrous corruption of *hooiberg* (hay-mountain), is in like manner locally applied to a thatched roof supported on four posts, under which hay is protected against the weather. *Bockey*, also, denoting a vessel made from a gourd, is derived from the Dutch, but limited in its use to the city of New York and its immediate vicinity.

There are, however, a few Dutch words in general use throughout the country. Among mariners, for instance, a *droger* or *drogher* has ever been well known, from the days of the old English *drugger* to our own cotton-*droger*, as a vessel built solely for the transportation of heavy loads. A *scow* also, a large, flat-bottomed boat, called originally *schouw*, is quite familiar to great cities, where it is employed as a dredger to clear the harbor or narrow basins, and to the Northern lakes, where they are often rigged so as to become fast sailers, a transformation, no doubt, little anticipated by their first builders. The word *school*, pronounced like shoal, and only provincial in England, but universally used in America, belongs to the Dutch, but of course long before their appearance on this continent. Hence Captain John Smith already reports, regardless of all orthography, of the bays of Virginia, "Here are infinite *skuls* of divers kindes of fishe more than elsewhere" (*Virginia*, I., p. 11), while the poet Saxe plays upon the resemblance to school in the lines:

> "No school to him was worth a fig
> Except a *school* of fish."
> (*The Cold-Water Man.*)

If the Dutch term *portaal* is in all probability only a Latin word, familiar to Holland as well as to England, and deserves, therefore, no place among Americanisms, the *stoop* of our houses is, on the contrary, a genuine addition which we owe to New Netherlands. The good burghers loved to sit on their *stoeps* (seats) smoking their pipes in peace and "lordly silence," and having wife and children on the *stoep bancke* by their side. The custom was pleasant and well adapted to our climate, and hence soon spread all over the country; with it the *stoop* became the common name for any covered or open porch with seats, in front of a house. Thus was Governor Peter Stuyvesant "found, according to custom, smoking his afternoon pipe, on the *stoop* or bench at the porch of his house" (Knickerbocker's *New York*), and thus in our day the traveller sees: "Piles of saw-mill slabs fortifying the wood-pile, which, paved with chips, the mangled remains of King Log, spread before the *stoop*." (*Conn. Georgics, Putnam's Monthly*, April, 1854.) In Canada the word is often written *stoup* and in the West occasionally *stowp*, but probably more from inattention than any purpose to naturalize it by a change of form.

The word *bush* has in like manner retained in America the original meaning of the Dutch *bosch* more faithfully than in England, where it generally designates a single shrub, while here, as in most British colonies, it means rather a region abounding in trees and shrubs. The term is at home in Canada; hence we read: "The farm-wood is cut off one mile from the river (St. Lawrence). The rest is *bush*, and beyond, the *Queen's bush;* old as the country is, each landholder bounds on the primitive forest, and fuel bears no price." (*Putnam's Monthly*, March, 1853.) During the war men "took to the *bush*" in the South as readily as at the North, and to this day Western papers report that the "Indians disappeared in the *bush*, when they saw the troops approaching." (*Cheyenne Chron.*, Aug. 17, 1870). It is a curious incident in the history of words, showing how two meanings of the same term may gradually become merged in one, that *bushwhacking* has thus of late received a new signification. Originally it was a harmless word, denoting simply the process of propelling a boat by pulling the bushes on the edges of the stream, or of beating them down with a scythe or a cudgel in order to open a way through a thicket. In this sense, which referred to the individual bush, W. Irving used it, when he described the Van Bunschotens of Nyack as "gallant *bushwhackers* and hunters of raccoons by moonlight." (Knickerbocker's *New York*, p. 110.) Afterwards, however, lawless persons and fugitives from justice, taking to the bush, were designated by the convenient name of *bushwhackers*, and during the late Civil War the deserting soldier and the unauthorized raider gave to the term a new and formidable meaning. They would infest public roads, plunder defenceless houses, and even invade peaceful towns, to return laden with their booty to safe retreats in the bush. "The general told us frankly," writes doughty Colonel von Borcke, "that we had more to fear from *bushwhackers* than from the enemy, but I trusted in my good old sword and bade my friends dismiss all fear." (*Blackwood*, Sept., 1865.)

The *bushwhacker* has unfortunately not disappeared in our days, although the term is probably often applied where another word would be more appropriate. Thus we read of a raid on illicit distilleries in Tennessee, that "in Smith County the government officials, with a squad of Federal soldiers, were fired upon by *bushwhackers*, but no one was injured. One man was shot in the thigh by the accidental discharge of his own pistol, and the remainder of the party is still in search of *contraband* distilleries." (Nashville *Banner*, March 7, 1871).

Among the words that may have come to our speech from more than one source is the word *span*, which we may owe to a German word *Gespann*, or a Dutch term *span*, familiar as *inspan* to all readers of works on South African explorations, or books like Gordon Cumming's Travels. In the United States the word is, however, generally used of horses only, and implies invariably a match in color, if not in all respects. "Commodore Vanderbilt drives a *span* of bays, which are said to have cost him ten thousand dollars, and Dr. Helmbold four in hand, which *span* admirably, of still greater value." (Philadelphia *Inquirer*, July 28, 1870.) Another such doubtful word is *spook*, which may be the Dutch *spook*, a spirit or a ghost, or the German *Spuck*, a phantom or a vision. The manner of writing it speaks for the former presumption, and so does the fact that the word is not only used in the British colonies, but even by classic writers like Lord Lytton. But, on the other hand, *spooks* prevail most in regions where Germans abound, as in the great Valley of Virginia and in the Northwest. A New York correspondent wrote recently of an old negro in Santo Domingo that "once he saw Toussaint L'Ouverture *spooking* about with an air of mournful majesty," (New York *Tribune*, Feb. 24, 1871,) and the "Acorn and Gem," a half-German half-English journal, published in Pennsylvania, says: "People near town firmly believe in the *spook*, and are afraid of going through that lane after sundown." (November 30, 1870.) In the Valley of Virginia there remains to this day a region called *Powell's Spook*, where a fierce mountain-creek breaks the silence of the night with its roar, and where Old Powell long ago coined money in defiance of the law. Growing rich in accordance with his compact with the devil, he barrelled up his treasure and buried it, but now goes about all night watching it carefully and frightening belated wanderers.

But of all Dutch words familiar to our ear, none has acquired a wider circulation and a stronger hold on our social system than the term *boss*, derived from the Dutch *baas*. It had, originally, with us as in its native land, the primitive meaning of "master," overseer, or superior of any kind, and retains it to this day in a large measure. Even now a *boss* shoemaker, or a *boss* bricklayer means the head of a gang of workmen, who deals their work out to them, and pays their wages, as an English master does to his workmen and apprentices. In this sense it is, even in England, now the cant term, if nothing more, with all mechanics, and can boast high antiquity for such a meaning, since as early as 1679, M. Philipse wrote: "Here they had their first interview with the female *boss* or supercargo of the vessel," (*Early Voyage to New Netherlands*), strangely foreshadowing the "Advanced Female" of the New World. For the proud Yankee, from the beginning, disliked calling any man his master, a word which, as long as slavery existed, he thought none but a slave should employ; and as the relation between employer and employed required a word, the use of *boss* instead of master, was either coined or discovered. Thus the word became early a part of the language in Northern and Western States, and Lord Carlisle could enjoy the naïve question propounded to him by his stage-driver: "I suppose the Queen is your *boss*, now?" In the same sense the slang-loving New York *Herald* said, in speaking of the Pope: "Rothschild refused to let him have any (money). The fact is, Rothschild is the real pope and *boss* of all Europe." It is curious that the word has actually found its way into French also, although only as a cant term; for M. Francisque Michel, in his *Dictionnaire d'Argot*, has: *Beausse, un riche bourgeois, terme des voleurs Flamands.* It made its way Southward, in America, but very slowly, and reached Pennsylvania only about 1852, with the construction of railways and canals. Since the emancipation of slaves in the South, the negroes also have become too proud to continue their old mode of address, and substitute for it the Northern *boss*, so that the word may fairly be said to be in universal use all over the Union. It has even been turned into a verb, and *to boss* is quite a common expression, meaning to direct anything, from *bossing a job*, that is, to contract and superintend it, to *bossing the house*, which means in the case of the husband or the wife, as Providence may direct, to rule and manage it. So familiar has the word become, that we are told of a child not five years old put into a corner for quarrelling, who wished to charge his sister with being the aggressor, and said: "I did not *boss the job*, it was sister." (S. S. Haldeman.) Thus the Dutchman is master in the land after all.

The word is occasionally grievously misunderstood at the South. There the negro has apparently not been able to catch the difference of sound in the Dutch *boss* and the English *bass*, and when he indulges in his favorite songs, he is quite sure to summon some skillful singer to lead, and promises to "*boss* him through." This meant, originally, nothing more than that he would sing the *bass* to the other's lead; but now it refers to the full chorus or refrain. This applies especially to the *shouting* songs, when the negroes form a ring, in which one half of the assembled company perform a shuffling dance, with a sort of ducking motion of the body, while the other half stand by and sing, one voice leading and stringing verse to verse, many of which are made up on the spot, and refer to the company present. These bystanders are said to *boss* the song.

The readers of W. Irving's delightful work on the *History of New York*, in which fact and fiction are so amusingly interwoven as to have deceived more than one acute critic, are familiar with his quaint and graphic description of the origin of *Moving Day*. He ascribes the curious custom which makes the first of May a day of horror in that city, on which every one who is not the fortunate owner of a house, vacates his lodgings and seeks new ones for the coming year, to the first great *move* made by the Dutch inhabitants of Communipaw to New Amsterdam "The anniversary," he says, "was piously observed among their sons, by turning their houses topsy-turvy, and carrying all their furniture into the streets; and this is the real origin of the universal agitation and *moving*, by which this most restless of cities is literally turned out of doors on every May-day." (Knickerbocker's *History of New York.*) The custom has certainly survived till now, and as Robert S. Coffin, the "Boston Bard," says,

> "Hurry, scurry—grave and gay,
> All must trudge the first of May,"
> (*The First of May.*)

but it is older than even the ancient settlement called Communipaw. The Dutch settlers evidently brought the custom with them from their transatlantic home, and to this day, in Bruges and its neighborhood, in Verviers and many other parts of Belgium and Holland, the first of May continues to be the general day of moving. It has not only become a characteristic institution of the City of New York, but the tendency to *move*, constantly to shift and drift from one place to another, is, by the home-keeping Scotch and Irish especially, not quite unjustly looked upon as a sign of instability in the national character. The marvellous facility of locomotion which this country affords by its net-work of railways, rivers, and canals, favors the disposition, to which must be added the temptation held out by countless openings for all in the newer States. The roving propensity subsides, however, in nations as in individuals, and already a strong tendency is perceptible in the United States to crowd the great cities at the expense of the open country.

The custom, also, to keep one room in the house as the *best room*, and to call it so, which still prevails in most of the Northern States, has been bequeathed to this generation by the first Dutch settlers of New York. The same name and usage may still be found in all the old towns of Holland, where these rooms are kept as dark as here, to preserve the furniture, and only opened on great occasions, when company is expected. A person entering a bed-room, also, in some out of the way New England town, would not fail to notice the chintz curtains and the puffy feather-bed with its bolster, not as in England, tucked in under the sheet, but with its own fair case of white linen; nor could he help being struck in the kitchen with the cheap but neat tiles on the hearth, and the delft-ware on the dresser, all features that prove the former presence of stout Dutchmen in these districts.

Nor must we, finally, forget, among the many pleasant things left us by our Dutch ancestors, the one Dutchman whom all American children hold dear and in great veneration. This is *Santa Klaus,* as the name is commonly though erroneously written, in reality *Klaas,* the abbreviation of Nickolas, a Dutch Saint of undisputed nationality, whose name is heard everywhere when his own day, Christmas, is drawing near.

THE FRENCHMAN.

"Can the leopard change his spots? Can the Frenchman lose his nationality?"—*E. About.*

OUR English contains, of course, a large number of French terms, which we owe, in common with our English cousins, to the supremacy which France has till recently exercised in war and in fashions. It might have been expected that large additions would have been made by the frequent and numerous streams of immigration, which have come to us from France itself and from former French dependencies. The French owned Acadie, and sent their missionaries throughout the whole West; they owned Louisiana, and thus met at the mouth of the Mississippi their zealous countrymen from the far North. Noble Huguenots, animated by a fervor and a constancy in no ways inferior to that of the Puritans, came over in large numbers and settled in the Southern States, where climate and national character seemed to be congenial, and the "charitable exhibition" of King William also sent in 1700 nearly a thousand more, who had left their native land on account of their religion. At a later period new arrivals came from home and from the colonies; the French Revolution sent many hundreds, the expulsion of the French from San Domingo added large numbers, and dissatisfied Imperialists came to find homes here after the banishment of their idol to St. Helena. French colonies were attempted in Michigan and in Florida; *Gallipolis* bore the name of its founders; even in the Great Desert a *Frenchtown* had a brief existence, and the Falls of the Kanahwa were once owned by a French company. French names still remain on the map of the United States as they were first bestowed: *Beaufort* and *Port Royal* in South Carolina, speak of the Huguenot and the scholar, as *La*

Moille River, *Calais*, and Mount *Desert*, in New England, remind us of the enterprise and zeal of the Jesuits in the very home of Puritanism.

There is no lack, in fact, of French elements in our population, and the grateful feeling long cherished throughout the United States for the efficient help rendered by France during the War of Independence, might, it seems, have given moral weight to the influence legitimately wielded by the representatives of a polished language, a matchless literature, and highest culture. But few and faint are the marks left by the French on our public life and our language. Their own character is too light and too fickle to impress itself forcibly on the sturdy, thoughtful Anglo-Saxon, as their frequent failures to adapt themselves to Republican institutions stand in striking contrast with the success of the latter among ourselves. There are, of course, a number of French words in use among Americans, whose fondness for Gallic words and things has laid them open to the charge that good Americans hope to go to Paris hereafter, but these terms are no more Americanisms than those borrowed by the English can be called Anglicisms. We shall content ourselves, therefore, with mentioning here only such as designate objects or institutions peculiar to this country, adding a few which have here a somewhat different meaning from that given them abroad.

Even the geography of the land retains but few traces of the brave French explorers, though Marquette and his brethren are recorded in many a town and river. All the more pleasing is it to find occasionally justice done, as in the case of that beautiful sheet of water now known as *Lake Champlain*. It was long called Lake *Corlaer*, after the great man of a Dutch settlement on the Mohawk River, who "for long years swayed the civic sword so potently and with such terror to evil-doers among the Indians, that they adopted his name in their language to signify a white governor. This doughty Dutchman, therefore, left his name to his successors, and the *Corlaers* went through their decline and fall with as much dignity, in a small way, as history ascribes to the Pharaohs and Cæsars. Like the founders of other dynasties, however, the original Corlaer came to an untimely end, being drowned, and as the catastrophe occurred in the lake, the Dutch stubbornly regarded their own hero as having the best right to it." But suddenly, and with her proverbial fickleness assigning no reason for the act, Dame Fortune declared for Samuel de *Champlain*, the brave servant of Henry IV., the father, as he was justly called, of *La Nouvelle France*, and henceforth the lake bore his name exclusively.

Other geographical names and terms in Natural History also are often met with, but the whole class of these words are generally of such exclusively technical meaning, that they can hardly be said to form part of our speech, except when they really become the common name of a whole class of similar objects. Such is, for instance, the case with *bayou*, meaning a stream—like the *Bayou la Fourche* in Louisiana or the Atchafalaya, connecting this bay with Red River—which takes a wide course, often on the largest scale, such as is, of course, possible only in low, alluvial regions. The English correlative is Gut, as the Gut of Canso—the *Gut* is a local offshoot of the Susquehanna. The word originally meant literally a gut, or leathern pipe, but in the Southern States is used to designate the outlet of a lake or river. That eccentric river, the Mississippi, with its bed higher than the surrounding country, instead of being sunk in it like other rivers, also boasts, below the mouth of Red River, of *bayous* running out of it, instead of rivers falling into it. It is of these broad channels that J. R. Lowell's hero says:

> " I had to cross *bayous* an' cricks (wal, it did beat all natur')
> Upon a kin' of corduroy, fust log, then alligator."
> (*Biglow Papers*, II., p. 13.)

Near the mouth of the giant river, its powerful current, at times of high water, frequently causes the caving in of a bank for long distances, and then on the opposite side a deposit of sediment accumulates rapidly to the extent perhaps of several acres of land. This is called *batture*.

The French word *butte* has in like manner become naturalized since it was first introduced by General Fremont, the Pathfinder, as he was then called. He stated in his report of the great expedition to the Rocky Mountains and Oregon, that the word applied "to detached hills and ridges which rise abruptly and reach too high to be called hills or ridges, and not high enough to be called mountains. Knobs is their most descriptive term in English, but no translation or paraphrase would preserve the identity of these picturesque landmarks." (p. 145, *B.*) The word has since become more and more familiar in California also, and furnishes the current term, *to butte*, meaning to chop off with a dull axe, used in the Northwest in laying out or recognizing an established logging camp. "Two of our company, who had lingered behind, came up with the information that they had seen several Indians making observations from behind a small *butte*, from which they fled in great haste upon being discovered." (N. P. Langford, *The Wonders of the Yellowstone*, 1871.) The word *coulee*, used in Oregon for a rocky valley with sloping sides (not precipitous as in a *cañon*), has not yet made its way beyond the new State.

It is very different with *crevasse*, from *crêver*, "to burst," a breach in a levee or embankment of a river, a word which represents such a terrible disaster and awakens such intensely painful recollections, that it is familiar to all Americans. Whenever the dam that holds the Mississippi in its uncertain bed is broken through by its turbulent flood, the cry of *Crevasse!* goes forth through the whole neighborhood, and unless plantations, homesteads, and cabins for many square miles are to be swept away into absolute destruction, gigantic efforts have to be made by the united efforts of one or more parishes to fill up the break and thus to stem the current. The *levee* has become so fully naturalized when meaning the high embankments on the lower Mississippi, that it is now generally known as *levy*. From the first settlement of Louisiana by the French the importance of protecting against inundation the rich alluvial lands on both sides of the river, which are actually at a lower level than the bed of the latter, has been felt and shown in vast earth-mounds, called *levees* by the old Creole word. The name has subsequently been extended to artificial embankments, like the famous *levee* of New Orleans, five miles long, and presenting an unparalleled picture of commercial activity and enormous wealth. The late Civil War played, sometimes for a purpose, sometimes by forced neglect, such havoc with the river-levees, that their restoration exceeds the financial resources of the riparian States, and the Federal Government is expected to make them a national work.

It would hardly be necessary to mention that the term *levee* is also used for the periodical receptions held by the President at his official residence, the White House, if it were not for the fact that the ridiculous word, derived from the *lever* or rising of the Grand Monarch, is in this case accented on the last syllable, whilst the embankment is pronounced like *levy*. The President's wife has, according to established usage, her days also on which she receives the sovereign people, but she is said to hold a *reception*.

The French word *arpent* also, a French acre, is still used in Louisiana as in the days before it was a State of the Union. "All that part of my real and personal estate, near Washington, in the State of Louisiana .... consisting of upwards of two hundred and eighty *arpens* or acres of land." (Will of Stephen Girard, 1832.)

But, perhaps, no French word in use among us is more generally known abroad than the *Prairie* of the West, a level or rolling tract of land, covered with coarse grass, and generally characterized by a rich soil of great depth.

> "These are the gardens of the desert, these
> The unshorn fields, boundless and beautiful,
> For which the speech of England has no name—
> The *prairies*.
>
> (*W. C. Bryant.*)

The *Level Prairie* is, perhaps, the exception, being found but rarely, and then mostly near, if not in, the valley of the Mississippi, while further west the *Rolling Prairie* prevails, with its gently undulating surface, resembling the great waters of the ocean, when the latter "is just undulating with a long groundswell," as Cooper describes it in his *Oak-Openings* (p. 237). New Mexico, Texas, and Arizona boast of vast prairies, often fifty miles square and more, which are covered with a whitish efflorescence of natron or soda, and these are known respectively as *Salt Prairies* and *Soda Prairies*. Their aspect is one of utter, almost unbearable desolation, and the thirsty traveller, who has to cross them, not unfrequently endures most painful sufferings. Even more terrible, and certainly more dangerous to life, is the *Trembling Prairie* of the Southwest, which is thus spoken of: "The land that first attracts the attention of the voyager—if indeed a few mud-lumps, a few almost floating isles, and a *trembling prairie*, into which one would sink as into quicksand, can be called land—is scarcely raised above the surface of the water." (*Putnam's Mag.*, May, 1869.)

It is to be regretted that the fair name of one of the most beautiful scenes of American landscape should have suffered, as most foreign words seem to be fated to suffer, in the process of naturalization. People living on the prairies themselves, or within sight, hardly ever speak of them otherwise than as *pararas* or *pereras*, and great is the variety of spelling by which authors have endeavored to represent the willful wanderings of the rebellious letter *r* in the word. "Mrs. Morpher," says F. B. Harte, "a womanly and kind-hearted specimen of southwestern efflorescence, known in her maidenhood as the *Per-rairie* Rose" (*Luck of Roaring Camp*, p. 156), and the clever author of *Los Gringos*, Lieutenant Wise, prefers it thus: "Looks lively 'nuff here Sundays: that are *perrary* 's fairly peppered with folks." (*Putnam's Mag.*, May, 1868.) The *prairillon*, or little prairie, is fast disappearing from our idiom.

The prairies have naturally given their name to many features in their appearance and to customs connected with the life of which they are the great stage. Some of these terms are hardly known beyond their own limits, as the Indian's free gift, which is professionally called *On the Prairie*, a phrase almost identical with the less diplomatic "nowhere;" and the *Prairie Bitters*, a horrible mixture of water and buffalo-gall, to which great medicinal powers are ascribed by hunters and border-settlers. The animal life on the *Prairie* is, on the contrary, well-known to the world of science, and to travellers and enthusiastic sportsmen. The *Prairie-hen* especially is looked upon as excellent game by the latter, and as a luxury now found in every market of the large cities on the seaboard, and a frequent visitor even to Covent Garden. It is the pennated grouse (Tetrao cupido) of the Western States, akin to the Scotch grouse of England and the Eastern cousin, of which W. C. Bryant sings:

> "I listened, and from midst the depth of wood
> Heard the low signal of the *grouse*, that wears
> A sable muff around his mottl'd neck;
> *Partridge* they call him in our Northern States,
> And *pheasant* by the Delaware."

Another dweller on the prairie that bears a false name, is the *Prairie-Dog* (Cynomus ludovicianus), a genuine marmot, and called a dog only in acknowledgment of his short, sharp bark, by which he warns his companions against an approaching enemy. As they live in large communities with their burrows in close proximity, western hunters speak of *Dog Villages*, and travellers say that "seen through the misty morning air the little conical huts and grotesque dark figures by their side looked, from a distance, not unlike a village crowded with people sitting idle at their doors." (*The Prairie Rose*, C. A. Murray, II., p. 19.) They number many thousands in each village, but we are told by an ancient traveller that "one arm of Red River is famous for the stupendous Village of the Dogs of the Prairie. The village is no less than twenty-five miles in length, and as many in breadth. It consists of subterranean galleries, sometimes nine feet deep and from four to five inches wide, and of a superstructure formed of earth, thrown up by these dog-voiced, but squirrel-resembling architects." (L'Abbé Em. Domenech.) In the West they are also known as *Gophers*, from the French *gaufre*, perhaps however through the English *to goffer*, to flute or crimp, because their countless holes literally honeycomb the soil in which they dig their villages. W. C. Bryant foretells a time when

> "the *gopher* mines the ground
> Where stood their swarming cities,"

but now-a-days the Western man, as well as the California miner, is content to *gopher* the ground wherever rich crops, or a harvest of gold and silver, may be found. With the usual carelessness of colonists, and owing in part to the ignorance of settlers of foreign origin, the term *gopher* has been applied to various animals, often entirely dissimilar in form and mode of life. That the little field-mouse of the West, a pouched, brownish-red rat with mole-like feet (Geomys bursarius), and a gray burrowing squirrel (Spermophilus franklinii), known also as the prairie squirrel, should have received the same name in Missouri and Mississippi, might not appear so far amiss; Kennicott thinks it has the best right to the name of *Gopher*. (*U. S. Agric. Report*, 1857, p. 75.) But there is no such excuse for bestowing the term upon a striped squirrel of Wisconsin (Spermophilus tredecimlineatus), which does not burrow, and still less a land-tortoise (Testudo polyphemus) of Florida. Even a large snake (Coluber couperi) is so called in Georgia. A ludicrous confusion of ideas has bestowed the name from a different source upon an entirely different object. Probably with a dim recollection that the word *gopher* occurs in Holy Writ, as the name of the wood of which Noah's Ark was built by divine command, a wooden coulter suitable for light sandy soil is in Florida sometimes called *gopher*, and thus an indignant "Cracker" says of a rival still lower in the social scale: "I've seen him pulling the *gopher* himself, harnessed to it like a d—d jackass, sir." (*Harper's Monthly*, Feb. 1859.)

The *Prairie Wolf* (Canis latrans) is an exclusively American species, about the size of a setter-dog, and lives like the fox in burrows, so that W. C. Bryant could say of him correctly:

> "the *prairie-wolf*
> Hunts in their meadows, and his fresh-dug den
> Yawns by my path."

They hunt in packs, and are much less afraid of man than European wolves. Further South they are better known under the Spanish name of *Coyotes*, a term borrowed from the Mexicans.

While the majority of prairies are treeless, every now and then an exception is met with, and of course eagerly sought for by settlers. "The sons of the forest," we are told by one of these emigrants to the Far West, "would seek the shelter of bordering groves for their dwellings, or else in the shade of those singular, but beautiful *islands*—groves in the midst of prairies—dense and dark within, but bending their graceful boughs over the pure sward of grass all around, bright with green and gay with flowers." (*Overland Monthly*, Feb. 1870, p. 148.) These *islands*, as they are poetically named, in the vast ocean of waving grass, were called *Mottes* by the early French explorers, and in many parts of the West still retain their old names. Thus Mr. Olmsted mentions them as striking features in the Southern landscape: "Before us lay beautiful prairies, with the smooth-grassed surface varied here and there by herds of cattle and little belts, *mottes* and groups of live oak," (*Texas*, p. 137, *B.*) while W. G. Simms quotes them in their corrupt form in the words: "In Western Texas a small clump of timber is called a *mot*." (The *Yemassee*, II. p. 110.) We can easily spare the word with its vague unsuggestive meaning, especially as the English terms of the prairie, almost all taken from the sea, are poetical and yet true to their meaning. Thus, besides *islands*, the prairie has also its *coves*, where small strips of grass-land run into a wood as if seeking for shelter against the blazing sun and the drenching rains, and its *bays* or large openings into a forest on its borders. Most graphically does the Rev. Mr. Cartwright describe how in the early days of his itinerancy as a Methodist preacher he had often to travel fifty and sixty miles a day in ceaseless rains, and how "there was no guide to be had, no road to follow, but the traveller's only resource was to sight a line from one *cape* to the other, and thus to cross the *bays*, no other landmarks being visible as far as the eye could reach."

Nor is travelling by water without its incidents and features, which still bear the names given them by early French explorers. There is the *sault*, a low waterfall or rapids, bearing its first name, eloquent of old age by the presence of the *l*, which has since left it in French, and the resemblance to Ben. Jonson's *salt*, employed by him in the sense of a leap, a jumping. The name, reduced in pronunciation generally to *Soo*, adheres firmly to rivers which, like the St. Lawrence and the St. Mary of Mackinaw, have been navigated by French missionaries and French boatmen and the familiar *voyageur* of our day, whether he paddles his canoe on Canadian streams or rises to the dignity of a fur-trader on the Upper Mississippi and in the great Northwest. If the waters rush hastily over obstructing rocks or just on the verge of a great waterfall, they form *Rapids*, first so called by French explorers on the St. Lawrence. The term was afterward applied to similar features in great water courses, especially the Niagara immediately above the Falls. The use of the plural in this sense is purely American, and the distinction thus made between a considerable descent in the river and a real cascade a very nice one. Lady Lyell, at Niagara, thought "the *Rapids* at times—especially in moonlight—a finer sight than the Falls themselves."

When *voyageurs* for their own purposes, or in the service of travellers, make their voyages in canoes, they are apt to avoid these rapids and falls by carrying their light *birches* over the intervening space, and where this can be done, the latter is called a *portage*. The term, now generally accepted as an English word, applies correctly to the strip of land between two navigable rivers or their head-waters; in fact to any break in a chain of water navigation, over which canoes and stores have to be carried on the men's backs. In the Eastern States, and especially in the Adirondack and White Mountains, the French term *portage* is exchanged for the more expressive English term *carry*. A traveller speaks of it thus: "The boat was taken out of the water, yokes hewn out with axes, and carried by the rapids. Imagine the delights of a *carry!* A path led by the Falls, but across it were big logs, blown down by some hurricane, and it wound up the sides of hills and through tangled thickets." (*Harper's Monthly*, February, 1860.) The process is, of course, very irksome to the voyageurs, and they prefer, therefore, *shooting* a river, that is to say, dashing over the rapids in the swift current. This is actually done in the St. Lawrence with large steamboats, which used to be placed under the direction of a frequently half-tipsy Indian pilot, and then, in his experienced and skillful hands, allowed to *shoot the rapids*, one of the most exciting scenes the traveller can witness in America. The bottom of the vessel actually grates the rocks in the bed of the river, but no lives have ever yet been lost. The word comes, of course, from the French *chute*, a term which is given extensively to places where a river, either from the nature of its surroundings or by the hand of man, is forced to contract within a narrow compass, and rushes through with great fury. The same word, frequently written *chute* or *shute*, is applied to an artificial plankway made on the side of a hill, down which the timber, cut above, is sent to a river in the valley. One of the most picturesque expressions of the West, also, is taken from this vehemence of motion caused by such a contrivance for wood or water: a man, passionately in love, is said to *take a shute* after his lady-love, and a young clerk may thus be heard saying: "To clap my eyes on her, and *take a straight shute* after her, was the work of a moment." (*The Country Merchant*, p. 221.)

The *voyageur*, when grown old, is apt to settle down into a *habitant* or *habitan*, as the humbler among the French settlers are still called in Canada and Louisiana, by a term which has come down to the former at least from the days of happy but short-lived *Acadie*. In the days of the Revolution they were not without political influence, and in one of General Washington's despatches they are called the "French Yeomanry." The term is, however, fast disappearing from Louisiana, and even in Canada it is rarely heard outside of the purely French districts on the St. Lawrence. One of their familiar terms survives yet, however, throughout the West; any special success they met with they were apt to call a *coup*, and in this sense the word is still used. "He followed closely on the trail of the savages, bided his time, struck his *coup*, and recovered a pair of packhorses, which was all he required." (*Life in the Far West.*)

On his travels and hunting expeditions the *voyageur* generally carries his most valuable property in curiously constructed saddle-bags called a *parflèche*. "The *teetsook* or *parflèche*," says General T. F. Meagher, "is generally made of dried buffalo hide, the hair of which has been beaten off with a stone, which softens it considerably; it is then put in the shape of an envelope. The articles stowed in it are kept secure and compact by thongs passed through holes in the flaps, and with one on each side, looped to the forks of the packsaddle, and lashed firmly together to keep them from slapping and pounding his ribs, the mule or the horse trots along pleasantly." (*Rides through the Rocky Mountains*, p. 576.)

The French word *caravane*, once very familiar to all the settlers of Western Virginia, Kentucky, etc., is still not unfrequently heard in the Southwest, and from the lips of emigrants who cross the Rocky Mountains. In former days *caravans* furnished the only means of communication between the new settlements and the Eastern cities. "In the fall of the year, after seeding-time, every family formed an association with some of their neighbors for starting a little *caravan*. A master-driver was selected, who was assisted by two or more young men. The horses were fitted out with packsaddles; a bell and a collar ornamented the neck. Every family collected what peltry and fur they could obtain during the year, to send them East for barter. They had no other stores of any kind, and needed salt and iron. The common price of a bushel of salt was a good cow and calf." (Wills De Hass, *History of Western Virginia.*)

The *caravan* is quite at home in New Mexico and Sonora, although frequently called there by its Spanish name, *conducta*, and the trade which it enables trappers and hunters, as well as distant settlers, to carry on, is often of considerable importance. The term itself is one which has, like many others, very nearly made the circuit of the earth: beginning in Persia as *Kârivân* or *Kirwân*, it entered Arabia as *Kairawân*, in the sense of "travelling through many countries," became French, as *caravane*, and is now on the shores of the Pacific, ready to be wafted back again to Asia, its native land.

In Western waters rafts were the first means of conveyance, soon to be followed by the *batteaux* of French traders; they have not yet entirely disappeared, and J. K. Paulding, in his Letters from the South, says: "The beautiful Shenandoah passes not far from this town, and is navigable for *batteaux*" (II. p. 71), and by a recent act of the Legislature of Virginia, a company is chartered for *batteaux* navigation on the Rivanna River (Jan. 17, 1871). The word *cache* (French *cacher*), on the contrary, now frequently disgraced into *cash*, is receding more and more to the West, where it still retains its first meaning of a hole dug in the ground *to cache, i. e.*, to conceal stores, and to protect them against thieves of all kinds. If properly made, these holes will preserve provisions for a year and longer, and great skill is manifested by Indians and Western travellers in effacing every trace of work that could betray the secret. Mr. Bartlett tells us how, on his expedition to settle the boundary line with Mexico, the "contents of a wagon were *cached* on the banks of the Gila, and camp-fires built over the openings, that the Indians might not discover it." The term is used in a wider sense, when a timid sportsman exclaims: "Do'ee hear now, boys, thar's sign about. This hoss feels like *caching*." (*Life in the Far West.*) The old English word *cahoot*, a slang word of the West and South for keeping company legitimately and illegitimately, is so little used and so far removed from its original in French (*cohorte*) that it does not deserve a place among Americanisms; *calumet*, on the contrary, the old, slightly changed form of the modern *chalumeau*, originated with the early colonists of New France, and has held its own mainly among the Indians, and in the intercourse between them and the whites.

It is to the French of Louisiana that the few words belonging to their language must be traced back which serve to designate shades of color in the descendants of colored people. Such are the *griffin*, from the French *griffon*, still frequently heard when applied to a mulatto, especially a woman, and the *quadroon*, from *quarteron*, the half-Spanish name of the offspring of a mulatto woman and a white man, among whom the very highest grade of beauty is not unfrequently found. The word is also occasionally written *cuarteroon*, with a leaning to the Spanish original, which, like the French, alludes to the one quarter negro-blood in the veins of the owner of the name. The offspring, in the next generation, of a quadroon and a white person, is called a *metif*. In the same State, as in all districts where sugar is raised, the term *bagasse* is one of great familiarity and importance. It comes from the low Latin *bagasea*, and designates the dry remains of the sugar-cane after the juice has all been pressed out. It is used as fuel under the sugar-kettles, and invaluable in those regions where other fuel is either not to be had at all or likely to be very expensive; occasionally also it serves as manure. Among the barely surviving words bequeathed to us by former generations are the *banquette*, the name of the sidewalk in some of the Southern cities, and the *barraque* or barrack, as applied to a roof on four posts for the sheltering of hay and other produce. In Canada, in the same manner, a small bedstead is still very frequently called a *bodette*, and an old-fashioned kind of gig a *calash*, from the French *calèche*, a name often applied also to that becoming covering for the head, familiar to English ears as "an ugly," and by no means improved under its new appellation. Another kind of carriage, of more pretension and greater capacity, is the *Carryall*, a corruption of the original *carriole*, so successfully carried out, that few are disposed to admit the French paternity, and stoutly maintain that its purpose is to express the capacity of the small one-horse vehicle to "carry all." The term originated, perhaps, in Canada, and thus came first to the Northern States, but while in the Dominion it now means a sleigh, its common use has extended throughout the country. "I once crossed Tennessee and Kentucky in a buggy," writes Professor S. S. Haldeman, "which the toll-takers were puzzled how to classify, as it had no place in the Table of Rates. At last it was determined to be a *Carryall*." It is a curious question how the terms *caveson*, quoted already as *cavesson* in Bailey's Dictionary, and meaning a muzzle for a horse, and *cuttoes*, a corruption of *couteaux*, should have maintained themselves so long in the New England States, where they are still used, when they have neither beauty of form or sound, nor pregnancy of meaning, to secure them so long a life-lease. We must assume that words have, like men, a providence which makes them occasionally long-lived for reasons incomprehensible to worldly wisdom. We can better understand how the term *vacher* connected itself with the almost innumerable herds of half-wild cattle roaming over Southern prairies, and how the extraordinary class of men, who keep the stock, brand the calves, catch the horses and break them, should have so long retained their original name. In the West and in California the term is fast giving way to a new word, *herder*, which is thus quoted: "It's well we've a good *herder*; they are not common. The first time I crossed the plains, I was a *herder*. I hadn't learned the trade at all, and a rough time we had of it." (On the Plains, *Putnam's Mag.*, Feb., 1869.) We cannot wish the same long life to the hideous name of *Vaudoux*, a French term, designating a certain form of worship and the object of this worship alike, introduced from the Island of Santo Domingo. The offspring of grossest ignorance and most barbarous impulses, accused of demanding human sacrifices and certainly accompanied by ceremonies of the most repulsive nature, the *Vaudoux* worship has, nevertheless, continued among the negroes of Louisiana, and an assembly was found engaged in it as late as the year 1862 in the State of North Carolina.

By some freak of public taste the word *vendue*, vulgarly pronounced *vandue*, in the sense of public sale, has continued to be used here, while it is but rarely heard in England. "His farm is soon to be sold at *vendue*, and I think of buying it," writes the author of the Letters from the South. (II., p. 127.) *Vendue-crier* is in constant use in Pennsylvania. Unjustifiable are the silly imitations of English ignorance in using French terms with meanings which have no existence in France; and still journalists will inform us that a great match is *on the tapis*, or that at such a ball Mrs. Grundy *chaperoned* two charming young ladies, although the *chaperon rouge* is the only chaperon known in France!

French words have, of course, not escaped corruption among us any more than in England, only we proceed perhaps with more recklessness while our foreign cousins act more from ignorance. We call the fine pear *Virgalieu* by the more convenient name of

Burgaloo, but make a great effort to give the Indian Turnip (Psoralea esculenta) its French name *pomme blanche*, while the *poteau*, a stake firmly set in the ground, to which wild cattle and horses are fastened, becomes a vulgar *putto* on the lips of Southwestern settlers, and the *poule d'eau*, a small black duck at home in the Gulf of Mexico, reappears as a *pulldoo;* and still even this is less grievous than the *Lave!* with which the guide or chief-hunter rouses his companions from their short slumbers, instead of saying *lève!* "How I hated the slow, steady *Lave! Lave!* of our old trapper, when his moccasined foot touched my side, and I had to rouse myself for another day's tramp through the endless wilderness!" (*Scenes in the Far West*, p. 97.) Nor can much be said in apology of the shamefaced prudery which dares not say *chemise*, and tries to conceal it under the disguise of a *shimmey:* much more pardonable are the *sherryvallies* of former days, the *chevalier's* or horseman's overalls, by which he protected his trousers against mud and thorny bushes on long journeys on horseback!

Names of places have not escaped this process of corruption. *Bob Ruly* in Missouri bears no resemblance to its French original *Bois Brulé*, nor does *Smack Cover* in Arkansas exactly represent *Chemin Couvert*, as it was first called by French settlers. One of the most striking cases of this class is probably a river in New Mexico, known as *Picketwire*, a name which was long a great mystery to all who had to use it. At last it was traced back, step by step, to the days of Spanish rule, when it had been regularly christened as *Rio de las Animas*, the river of Souls (of the departed). The French, who appeared next on the scene, translated this into *Rivière du Purgatoire*, and this the American conquerors, after the manner of Norman conquerors in England, changed into the River *Picketwire!*

A similar corruption has played havoc with a fair Indian name, and transformed it into a most absurd term of apparently French origin, by which not foreigners only, but even natives, have often been misled. On the Kennebec River, not far from the town of Norridgewook, the traveller sees a series of small but attractive falls, which he is told are called the *Bombazine Rips*. He is apt to marvel at the oddity of the name, if he has not seen much of the country yet, but he is sure to be still more astonished when he finds in Vermont, near Castleton, a second *Bombazine*, here applied to a lake. It has only been quite recently discovered—thanks to Whittier's Mog Megone—that the Indian tribe of the Norridgewocks, which resided in this neighborhood, once had a famous chief called *Bomoseen*, after whom they named both the falls and the lake. A Yankee trader, with more knowledge of dry-goods than Indian lore, no doubt, heard in Bomoseen nothing but Bombazine, and thus the poor chieftain was cheated out of his posthumous fame.

Bodewash would remind few hearers of its French derivation from *Bois de Vache*, as early voyageurs called the *Buffalo Chips* of the Western hunter and trader. On the treeless plains of New Mexico and Texas, the cow-dung gathered near springs, where cattle are apt to congregate, is often the only fuel, yet is even preferred to green brushwood, since it makes hardly any smoke and gives out a surprising amount of heat. Nor is the use of this strange fuel confined to the Southwestern States: in many parts of the Orient the same custom prevails, and even England is quite familiar with it, for Captain Grose has in his dictionary: "*Casings* or cassons; dried cow-dung used for fuel. Northumberland."

A still stranger disguise is worn by the beautiful shrub known as the *Osage Orange*. Its wood being specially well adapted for the bows used by the Indians, it was called *bois d'arc* by French settlers; the unfamiliar name became in the hands of English hunters *Bowdark*, in which form it was long familiar along the whole Western frontier, and finally it settled down into the still shorter *Bodok*, which is now the common designation in many parts of the Union. "The chief stopped under a beautiful *Bodok-tree*, and calling Ouachita to him with an imperious gesture, he bade her kneel at his feet." (W. G. Simms, *Tales*, I., p. 89.)

A few French words have entered our idiom either with greater force or a more special purpose than appears in English, and may, to that extent, at least, be looked upon as Americanisms. Thus the verb to *demoralize*, is, of course, not unknown to English authors, but Sir Charles Lyell tells us of his visit to Dr.

Webster, that "when the Doctor was asked how many words he had coined for his Dictionary, he replied, only one, to *demoralize*, and that not for his dictionary, but in a pamphlet published in the last century." (*B.*) Since then the word has become a great favorite in the United States, and is used on every occasion that will furnish a pretext for its employment. Hence the well-known anecdote of the Southern soldier in the late Civil War, who was found at the bottom of a ditch during the battle of Gettysburg, and when picked up for dead, piteously informed General Lee that he was not hurt, nor scared, but "terribly *demoralized*." The term *department* has here the special meaning of one of the principal branches of government, the Treasury, War, Navy, etc., with a Secretary at the head of each, corresponding to the ministers of continental monarchies. Here *departmental* business is transacted by a number of clerks, who for the sake of greater efficiency and method are distributed among so many *bureaux*, in each of which again a subdivision of departmental business is performed. In another connection we find the name of the royal *Bourbons* applied, now politically to any old-fashioned party which acts unmindful of past experience, and now as a trade-term to a superior kind of whiskey distilled in the county of *Bourbon*, in the State of Kentucky, or to successful imitations. *Pelage* is still heard in the West, as it was in the days when Bacon used it, to designate certain furs; thus sea-otters are described as having a "fur much lighter inside than upon the surface, and extending over all are scattering, long, glistening hairs, which add much to the richness and beauty of the *pelage*." (*Overland Monthly*, Jan. 1870, p. 25.) The French *robe*, on the other hand, is limited to the skin of a buffalo, while those of other animals are simply called *skins*. They are brought in *packs* of *robes*, ten being tied together, to the great fur markets, and thus a "coachman sat on the high box in splendid livery, with a costly *buffalo robe* thrown carelessly over his knees." (New York *Herald*, Jan. 9, 1870.)

Other French words, like *promenading*, instead of simply walking; *prestige* for a peculiar influence more felt than enforced; and *portemonnaie*, for a compact money-purse, are probably not more common in America than in England; and when a writer says of the mouth of the Mississippi: "Here and there, shaded by a graceful group of bananas, is a *latanier* hut with adobe walls, and a roof thatched with the fan-shaped leaf of the palmetto" (*Putnam's Mag.*, May, 1868), he would have been better understood in both countries by simply saying, "Bourbon palm," instead of *latanier.*

The abuse of *bouquet,* which is commonly pronounced and often even printed *boquet,* is "a corruption as dissonant to the ear as were to the eye the plucking a rose from a variegated nosegay, and leaving only its thorny stem." (George H. Calvert, *Popular Errors.*) Even *Boquet River*, in Essex County, New York, has been thus contaminated. The hope that it might derive its name from Colonel Boquet, who encamped on its banks with a British force in the colonial time, has failed; since it has been ascertained, from a letter written years before, that the correct name, *Bouquet* River, was given it from the flowers on its banks, which to this day make it one of the most lovely and romantic of American rivers.

Nor have proper names of persons been able to protect themselves against the overwhelming power with which the English language absorbs all foreign words, as the English character absorbs other nationalities. Frenchmen and French Canadians who came to New England, had to pay for such hospitality as they there received, by the sacrifice of their names. The brave *Bon Cœur,* Captain Marryatt tells us in his Diary, became Mr. *Bunker,* and gave his name to Bunker's Hill of famous memory; *Pibaudière* was changed into *Peabody, Bon Pas* into *Bumpus ;* and the "most unkindest cut of all," the haughty *de l'Hôtel,* became a genuine Yankee under the guise of *Doolittle.*

A curious form under which French still continues in Louisiana and some of the riparian counties on the Mississippi, is the *Creole-French,* a dialect or patois, consisting in the main of strangely disguised and disfigured French words, with an admixture of some English and a few genuine African terms. Its grammar has been written, and the learned librarian of Yale College, Mr. Van Name, has examined it philologically with great success. As it is rapidly passing away, a stanza of a popular *Coonjai* (congé), or Minuet, well known to Louisiana planters, may not be out of place here :

"Mo déjà roulé tout la côte,
Pancor (pas encore) ouar (voir) pareil belle Layotte,
Mo roulé tout la côte,
Mo roulé tout la colonie,
Mo pamor ouar grifforme là,
Qua mo gôut comme la belle Layotte."

THE SPANIARD.

"He has no Savey."
Mark Twain.

THE Spaniards have been so long masters in Mexico and Florida, that the acquisition of the latter State, and the formation of California and the territory obtained after the Mexican war into several new States, have made our people familiar with many terms belonging to their language. They remember with deep interest that the oldest town in the United States is *St. Augustine*, in Florida, founded in 1565 by the Spaniards, while venerable Jamestown, in Virginia, dates back only to 1607, and Plymouth, in Massachusetts, to Governor Winthrop in 1620. *Santa Rosa* and *Fernandina*, in Florida, retain with their ancient names many a relic and ruin of Spanish days, and California is almost altogether Spanish, as far as local names and the most familiar expressions are concerned. Spanish words, especially those relating to horses and mules and to their equipments, have of late come into general use in Oregon, owing to intercourse with California.

A number of these Spanish terms bequeathed to us by the former owners of the soil, are, of course, parts of the great English language, and as well known abroad as with us, but in the great majority of cases such words have assumed here either a new form or a special meaning, which makes them more exclusively part of our own speech. Known in England only to the few, they have become with us the common property of the people, and are understood not only by the dwellers in formerly Spanish districts, but quite as well by the general reader.

Thus we owe to Spanish distinctions, made at an early period of their dominion on this continent, several of the names by which shades of color are designated in the descendants of white and black persons who had intermarried. Their term *mulato*, from *mulo*, simply denoting a mixed breed, became our *Mulatto*, the name of a person whose parents were black and white. The name is in the United States given more loosely to any one who has white blood in him, though, strictly speaking, the offspring of a mulatto and a white man is a *quadroon*, or *cuarteroon*, as he is sometimes called by the Spanish term, and an *octaroon* (with an *r* in it which is inorganic, and has slipped in merely from a fanciful analogy to *quadroon*, while the proper form would be "Octoon"), is the offspring of a quadroon and a white. The latter is also sometimes called a *Mustee*, a term obtained from Cuba, but properly the Spanish *mestizo*, the child of a Spaniard and an Indian, which again produces *Mustafina*, the offspring of a mustee and a white, having therefore only one sixteenth of black blood in his veins. These nice distinctions have, since the emancipation, lost all the importance they had in the days of slavery, and the only interest that now attaches itself to the *mulattoes* especially, is the question how far they will show a superiority over the negroes, such as has been noticed in some of the West India Islands. So far two facts only have been established which bear upon this question. One is, that the *mulatto* is invariably a decided improvement on one of his producers, and not at all incapable of reaching the full stature of mental and moral manhood. The other is, that while an infusion of white blood thus beyond all doubt intellectualizes the black, it brutalizes the Red-man—a fact proven by the superiority of Brazil over other Spanish-American countries. In the Empire the mixture of Caucasian and negro blood has apparently not impeded progress of every kind—in the latter the fusion of European and Indian blood has produced utter and universal ruin.

The *negro* himself bears his first Spanish name, which simply means a black man, though the term is not often heard now in the United States, where a sickly philanthropy prefers speaking of *freedmen* and *colored* men, while contempt stigmatises them as *niggers*, and ludicrously as people of the "Fifteenth Amendment Persuasion," alluding to the amendment to the Constitution, which secured to them their rights of citizenship. The word *nigger* is, however, not to be charged to this country. In Wix's *Newfoundland Missionary Journal* we find: "Here we saw the wreck of the Royal *Nigger* (qu. Niger?), a fine vessel which had run ashore" (p. 79), and beyond all doubt of a possible mistake, in an article of the London *Telegraph*, written by W. G. A. Sala: "There seem to be as many negroes in Africa . . . full-blooded, black *niggers*." (Nov. 2, 1865.) The late Civil War procured for him a title, by which he was subsequently even officially known in many an Order of the Day and municipal proclamation. General Butler, when first stationed at Fortress Monroe, in Virginia, remembered his acuteness, so often shown at the bar, and drew the line between the negro as property held by a rebel, and the same man as property useful to the enemy. He saw that the moment had come when the status of such a person had to be legally defined, and declared in his official orders, that he should hereafter be considered as "*Contraband* of War." From that day the former slave was known as a *contraband*, a reality soon to be changed once more into the ghastly phantom of a citizen. General Butler's claim to the honor of having invented or originated this very happy designation, has subsequently suffered under the misfortune which has so maliciously followed other claims of his also. It was discovered that the term *contraband*, as applied to negro slaves, was not unknown in English literature; we certainly read in Captain Canot's amusing account of his life: "Scandal declares that while brokers are selling the blacks at the depot, it is not unusual for their owner or his agent to be knocking at the door of the Captain-General's secretary. It is even said that the Captain-General himself is sometimes present in the sanctuary, and after a familiar chat about the happy landing of the *contraband*, the requisite rouleaux are insinuated into the official desk under the intense smoke of a fragrant cigar." (*Twenty Years of an African Slaver*, 1854, p. 108.)

The *Negro* or *nigger* has lent his name to various other objects peculiar to American life. The *Negro-minstrel* is the artist who blackens his face, adopts the black man's manner and instrument, and recites his field and plantation songs, interspersed with laughable parodies of classic music. *Niggerheads*, again, are in the far South and Southwest the tussocks or tufts of grass and sedge standing out of a swamp, and bearing a faint resemblance to the woolly head of an African; while the same regions are familiar with the phrase of *niggering out land*, which marks the improvident and destructive method of working the same field, year after year, without manure. Among the cant words produced by the late Civil War, *nigger babies* also became very popular; the term originated with the veterans serving under the Confederate General Hardee, who gave that name to the enormous projectiles thrown into the city of Charleston by the *Swamp Angel* of General Gilmore, as his monster-gun in the swamps was ironically called.

The real *nigger baby* is known under the name of *pickaninny*, a word frequently derived, after the example of Boucher, in his Glossary, from the Spanish words *pequeño niño*, little child, but quite as likely of African origin; used in the West Indies to designate any young child, it is applied in the Southern States only to the offspring of colored parents, as J. R. Lowell says:

> "'Tain't quite hendy to pass off one o' your six-foot Guineas,
> An' git your halves an' quarters back in gals and *pickaninnies*."
> (*Biglow Papers, II.*, p. 25.)

The word has since made its way across the Atlantic, where it "is now completely naturalized among the sailors and waterside people of England." (*Slang Dictionary*, p. 200.)

The *Guinea* so pleasantly introduced by the poet, the small change for which is represented by the little ones, is the *Guinea Negro* of not many years ago, when the designation was quite common, though generally applied to a full-blooded negro, as if he had but recently arrived from his African home. The Rev. Mr. Cartwright says thus, with an energy which is, we hope, not often required in the pulpit, while speaking of an incident which occurred while he was preaching in the State of Tennessee: "Just then my fastidious preacher pulled my coat and whispered: 'General Jackson has come in, General Jackson has come in!' I felt a flash of indignation run all over me like an electric shock, and facing about to my congregation, and purposely speaking out audibly, I said: 'Who is General Jackson? If he don't get his soul converted God will damn him as quick as he would a *Guinea Negro*.'" (*Autobiography*, p. 192.)

The word *creole*, from the Spanish word *criollo*, meant originally nothing more than a child born of European parents in the West Indies, or on American soil; but it has long since been almost universally applied to any one born in the Tropics, without regard to race or color. In the United States, the meaning of the term is very vague, but a general feeling prevails, that the *creole* has some slight admixture of African blood in his veins—an impression probably imported from the West Indies, where negroes born on the islands are called *creole negroes*, in order to distinguish them from the African negroes, imported directly. In the Spanish colonies the *creole* was also often a man of color, as distinguished from the *gapuchin*—an Aztec word—the Spanish resident. In the South, on the other hand, the term is now most generally used for Americans of French descent, and this impression is strengthened by the existence of a dialect or patois, known as *Creole-French*, of which a sample has been given.

The Spanish word *Zambo*, originally meaning "bandy-legged," was by the Spaniards first applied to the offspring of a negro and a mulatto, and afterwards, in the South American colonies, to the child of a negro and an Indian woman. In the West Indies and the United States, the term has gradually come to be applied to all colored persons alike, and *Sambo*, as it is generally written, denotes simply a negro. It is of him Mrs. H. B. Stowe writes so enthusiastically: "No race has ever shown such capabilities of adaptation to varying soil and circumstances as the negro. Alike to them the snows of Canada, the hard rocky soil of New England, or the gorgeous profusion of the Southern States; *Sambo* and Cuffey expand under them all."

The word *peon*, from the Spanish term denoting first a foot-traveller and then a day-laborer, is of more recent date in our speech than in English, where it had become known through its use in India. We found the *peon* in the Spanish possessions, which now constitute California and the adjoining States, together with the system of *peonage*, as the peculiar relations were called, which existed in Mexico between the land-owner and his humbler tenants, or, worse still, between the creditor and his debtor, who, unable to discharge his obligations, voluntarily entered into a kind of serfdom to pay his debt by labor. The *peon*, in this sense of the word, is of course unknown to the territory annexed to the United States, but the term remains in use and is now applied mainly to humble laborers or small farmers of Spanish blood. Thus F. B. Harte says: "Leaving our horses in the charge of a few *peons* in the court-yard, who were basking lazily in the sun, we entered a low doorway." (*Luck of Roaring Camp*, p. 213.) Another Spanish term of the kind, the *juez del campo*, is now more generally used in the English form of *Judges of the Plain*. As such they appear already in the last code of California Laws, where they are appointed to attend the *rodeos* or great gatherings of all the cattle on a plain, for the purpose of separating, counting, and branding the stock belonging to each farmer; they have large powers in deciding all disputes concerning the ownership of every kind of cattle.

The *filibuster*, whether his name be derived from the Dutch *Vly-boot*, a sort of fast-sailing clipper, or from the German *Frei-beuter*, the familiar freebooter of the Low Country wars during the reign of Queen Elizabeth, obtained his unenviable reputation among us and with it the naturalization of the word among our words, during the unfortunate attack of Lopez on Cuba in 1851. The term, therefore, is an addition we owe directly to the Spanish word *filibustero*, as denoting first a small but swift vessel, and then a lawless adventurer, a pirate, landing in such vessels on a defenceless coast. Hence the Fenians also, in their unwarrantable inroad upon Canada, were called *land-filibusters*. It came prominently forward in the newspapers of the United States during the year 1852, mainly in connection with the ill-starred expedition against Cuba, but it must have made its way rapidly to England, as we find already in 1858 a work of high authority use it thus: "By connecting the maritime wars of the Etruscans with the piratical expeditions of the Lydians, and lastly by confounding the Torrhebian pirates with the *filibustering* Pelasgians, who roamed over every sea, plundering wherever they came, there has arisen one of the most deplorable confusions of historical tradition." (Mommsen, *Earliest Inhabitants of Italy*, p. 59.) Since then the word has come into general use among us to designate any process which attempts to achieve a rightful end by unfair means, and even in political slang it plays a prominent part. "The Democrats tried by every means to prevent the vote being taken; they *filibustered* for twelve hours, but the majority sat watching them with indifference, sure of success as soon as their hour should come." (*Debate on the Enforcement Bill*, Feb. 25, 1871.)

The *arriero*, the muleteer so well known to all travellers in

Spain, has of late become, in name and in duty alike, familiar to Americans; since Mexicans, who are the most expert in managing horses and mules, are universally employed in all the trains that cross the Plains. Now he is seen riding on his gayly caparisoned mule at the head of a picturesque *cavallard*, as the long strings of horses and mules, laden with merchandise, are called in the Southern States, from the Spanish *caballada*; and now he carefully leads a long *mulada*, "a drove of mules, hiding behind the swelling of the prairie, and watching the outline of the heights to see if no curious Indian is lying in wait there. If redskins or outlaws approach, the *mulada* is instantly collected in a body, and the drivers, under the direction of the *arriero*, stand ready for service with their pieces cocked." (Ruxton's *Adventures*, p. 65, *B.*) "The *caballada*," says, on the other hand, a more recent traveller, in purer Spanish, "contained not only horses and mules, but also here and there a stray *burro* (Mexican jackass), destined to pack wood across the rugged hills of New Mexico." (*A Ride with Kit Carson*, G. D. Brewerton.)

Certain features of the landscape in the South and West also continue to bear their original Spanish names, which are daily becoming more familiar as a part of our speech. The *alamo* (Populus monilifera) represents in Texas and all the formerly Spanish states the *Cottonwood* of the older parts of the Union, a most useful tree, so called from the cotton-like substance in which the seeds of this poplar are protected against the cold. Already in Lewis' and Clarke's *Explorations of the Rocky Mountains* we find it stated that: "During the cold weather the squaws cut down the *Cottonwood* trees as they are wanted, and the horses feed on the boughs and bark of the tender branches, which are also brought into the lodges at night." (I., p. 219.) They are found almost near all the bottom-lands and along the banks of streams and lakes growing wild, and carefully planted in the public walks of Southern and Western towns, which hence derive the name of *Alamedas*.

The *calabash* of the United States is not the tree generally known by that name, but, when at all applied to a plant, the Gourd (Cucurbita lagenaria), and more generally the drinking vessel, made from its bottle-shaped fruit, which procured for it the Arabic name, from which the Spanish *calabaza* was derived. By far the most frequent use made of the word is, as a cant term, for a weak and empty head, and thus employed in humorous language, as in the words: "Mind how you chuck, or you'll break his *calabash.*" (J. C. Neal, *Charcoal Sketches*, p. 223.) Far more generally in use is the Spanish word *chaparral*, from *chaparra*, an evergreen dwarf oak, which in its turn is derived from the Basque. The meaning of the word was, however, in the colonies extended to any thicket or succession of thickets, consisting not of oaks only, but of other plants peculiar to the district. In California, therefore, and the formerly Mexican states, *chaparra* with its collective termination *-al*, denotes a tract of land covered with shrubs and bushes, mostly armed with spines, but belonging to different classes of plants. The *chaparral* of Palo Alto, for instance, is described as being "defended by gigantic cactus here, sharp-pointed yuccas there, and cat-claw briars everywhere" (New York *Spirit of the Times, B.*); and we are told that a new town, "Middletown, on paper, flourishes like a green bay tree; on terra firma it is the dry *chaparral* and the forlorn hillside." (*Overland Monthly*, October, 1870, p. 322.) In other regions the *mesquite*, and some other shrubs of the family of the mimosæ, are most common, and still others, like the Creosote plant, and the *Greasewood* of the Americans, known locally under its Spanish name *chimisal*, predominate in the Northern parts of the State. F. B. Harte describes a man, in an inundation, rowing on the vast expanse of water and saying: "With my hands dipped listlessly over the thwarts I detected the tops of *chimisal*, which showed the tide to have somewhat fallen." (*Luck of Roaring Camp*, p. 229.) The origin of *Greasewood* is doubtful. Some derive it from the *Greaser*, the popular name of the Spanish Californian; others from the well-known fact that the *Grizzly* Bear gathers the leaves of the herb when he is wounded, and, his own surgeon, stuffs them into the wound tightly.

The *Mesquite* or *Muskeet* (Algarobia glandulosa), a bastard-locust, is frequently derived from an Indian word, simply because the Spanish term, *Mezquite*, from which we derive the name, is not an original word of that language. It represents in the South-western States not only the tree, which is thought by botanists to be identical with that which furnishes the Arabic gum of commerce, but also a fine, short grass, growing in great abundance, though only interspersed with other grasses, on the Western prairies. Of the former we read that: "By the roadside there was a Texan emigrant wagon, which had turned aside into the almost impenetrable *mezquite* brakes," and of the grass: "Now we come occasionally under the sweet influence of female angels, whose hoof-marked valley has no staple productions save jerked beef and *mesquite*." (*Overland Monthly*, Aug., 1870, p. 154.) The long, narrow pods of the tree, a mere shrub in less favorable localities, are not only a favorite food of all kind of cattle, but are ground by some of the more provident Indian tribes, and mixed with wheat-flour, giving their bread a peculiar and most palatable sweetness. The grass, also, has special virtues, among which the fact that it preserves its sweetness long after it is dried, is by no means the least important. Our kidney-beans form on South-western plains and in many of the old Mexican districts so constant an article of food, that they have become there universally known by their Spanish name of *frijoles*, while the *palmetto* (Chamærops palmetto), called *palmita* or little palm in Spanish, reaches up as far as the State of South Carolina, to which it has given its name and its flag, and is extensively used for thatching cabins, for making piles of wharves, and a number of similar purposes. A pine-tree, the Spanish *piñon*, has become quite naturalized also as *pinion*, since its edible nuts, long since appreciated by the animals of the forest, have become a favorite with the new settlers in Arkansas and the adjoining States. It is probably to the same language that we owe the term *ratoon*, used to designate the cuttings of sugar-cane of the second and third years' growth, which serve for planting new fields. Derived from the Spanish *retoño*, a sprout or shoot from a plant cut down previously, it has come into general use, and is even employed as a verb, so that planters will say: "the cane *ratoons* well this season, and everything bears a most promising look on the plantations." (New Orleans *Delta*, Feb. 21, 1869.) The prickly pear cactus, known also as Indian fig (Cactus opuntia) bears a purplish pear-shaped fruit, which in Southern countries becomes not only edible, but luscious, and is there generally known under its Spanish name *tuna*—a term which also serves to designate the pleasant beverage made from the fruit.

The features of the landscape in our formerly Mexican States are but rarely left in possession of their Spanish names; they either recall familiar objects at home, and then receive the same appellation, or they are new and suggest at once a special name. Some of the older terms have, however, stoutly maintained their right, and have thus become incorporated in our speech. Prominent among these is the *cañon,* often written *canyon,* to represent the Spanish pronunciation of the word, which originally meant nothing more than a hollow tube. It represents now a feature probably exclusively peculiar to the Southwestern States, gorges or ravines worn by violent watercourses, of such vast dimensions as to fill the beholder with feelings akin to awe. At times they are long, and so overhung by precipitous rocks as to resemble tunnels; at other times the sides rise to the height of several thousand feet, and the traveller riding along on a high table-land finds himself suddenly arrested by a rent in the rocks which allows him barely to discern the tiny watercourse at the bottom of the gigantic fissure. Where such narrow channels separate spurs or buttresses of the mountains, the Redwood generally follows the moist channel of the *cañon,* while in California there pour through these *gulches* the mountain torrents, the *wet diggings* of the gold regions. The word, but recently naturalized, has not escaped the common fate of being forthwith used as a verb, and hence already Captain Mayne Reid says: "I soon came to a bend, where the stream, after running parallel to the ridge, swept round and *cañoned* through it." The word *gulch,* which is so often found in connection with California matters, that it is largely believed to be of Spanish origin likewise, is of course nothing more than the good old English *gulch,* a "ravine," which after long neglect has come to new honor in the new States. They abound in the Southwestern States, and are quoted as "Steep *gulches,* where everything was absolutely and hideously naked" (*Afoot in Colorado Desert*), while new ones are formed continually, especially after earthquakes. "In places one side of the crevice was two feet higher than the opposite wall, and the long, straight *gulch,* from one to three feet deep, and nearly as wide, could be seen for several miles." (*Overland Monthly,* Aug., 1870, p. 161.) The word and its meaning are, however, well known to other countries also, for in Wix's *Newfoundland Missionary Journal* we find: "I have met with places in Fortune Bay, two or three miles only from each other, to visit which, in winter, it might be necessary to make a circuit of fifteen miles, to get round the deep precipitous chasms or *gulshes* and ravines." (p. 19.) As if to make amends for its homely origin, the word frequently appears in its Spanish form of *arroyo*, which is, at least in certain districts, as familiar as the former, while the *barranca*, another Spanish-American term for a ravine, is generally applied only to deep breaks, produced suddenly by heavy rains or swollen watercourses, and having steep and abrupt banks, like perpendicular walls.

The word *farallon*, meaning an isolated island or promontory, is at least of local importance, as the islands on the coast of California are so called, and hence the term is often misunderstood, and taken to be a proper name. The *Lagoons* of the South owe their origin quite as often to the French settlers, who certainly gave the name to the many bays and inlets of Louisiana, as to the Spaniards in the more southerly States. The *llano*, on the contrary, is the name of plains and prairies in the districts bordering on Mexico, unchanged as it was bestowed upon them by the first conquerors; the hills and long ridges with flat tops, which frequently border them, are, in like manner, still called *lomas*, and when very low, with the diminutive ending, *lomitas*. A high plain or table-land, on the contrary, is called a *mesa* or table, and hence, in a Report on the Pacific Railroad, it is thus introduced: "The *mesa* or table-land character is exhibited only along the line of the river-valleys, as high bluffs, the result of denuding forces, subsequent to the origin albasin-depositions." (Vol. I., p. 84, *B.*) Where they occur on a smaller scale, the diminutive form *mesilla* is used. Quite a poetical term survives yet in the lower plains, where occasionally a tuft of rank grass rises suddenly from amidst the arid waste, and cheers the parched and weary traveller with its promise of a spring. These springs, inexpressibly welcome in the vast deserts of those regions, were so heartily greeted by the first explorers, that they called them *ojos*, or eyes, and this name they still bear. A *picacho*, or pointed summit, is the term by which, in New Mexico and Arizona especially, the peaks are known, which rise abruptly from a level plain and serve as landmarks far and near.

The Spanish word *placer* has long since lost the primitive simplicity of its first meaning, whether it be derived, as some say, from *plaza*, and denoted nothing more than any particular spot, or really come from the word *placer*, a "pleasure," in allusion to the delight caused by the finding of gold in the shape of dust in certain localities. At all events, it was borrowed from the Mexicans in the latter sense, and for many years used to designate the deposits of drift-sand in which gold was found. The term became, however, soon so familiar to American ears through the astounding reports of gold-findings in California, that it was applied to the discovery of any good thing which promised a large reward. A careful writer in the *Atlantic Monthly* could, therefore, safely say: "The Homer of Chapman is so precious a gift, that we are ready to forgive Mr. Smith's shortcomings. It is a vast *placer*, full of nuggets for the philologist and lover of poetry" (April, 1858), and "Elegant Tom Dillar" in *Putnam's Monthly* says: "Because it is all I need. I think I have found a *placer*; I shall make money by it, and after this I shall be rich again." The word has even given a flourishing town the barbarous name of *Placerville!* The *plaza* itself, the public square, has become a familiar term with the acquisition of so many towns in which it formed a prominent feature, while *playa*, literally the "strand or seashore," finds in the Southwest an entirely new purpose to fulfill. It is there applied to those vast inland plains, known farther North as *salt* and *water* prairies, the surface of which is covered with a thick incrustation or nitrous efflorescence, known as *tesquite*, so as to give them the appearance of a large motionless lake. Mr. Bartlett himself describes them thus: "Emerging from the pass into the plain, our eyes were greeted with the sight of a white streak, which we would have taken for a lake, had it not been called the *playas*. This *playa* seemed to have an extent of twenty-five or thirty miles. The surface was an indurated clay, so hard that the wheels of our wagon scarce made an impression. After rain this basin receives a large amount of water, which seems to evaporate before vegetation gets a foot-hold." (*Personal Narrative*, I., p. 246.) The *presidio*, also, the name of a military post in the former provinces of Mexico, has been inherited from the Spaniards; and as many of these posts are now within the new States of the Union, the name is retained for the village, which generally occupies the place of the former fortifications. The same fate has been that of the *casa*, a word originally meaning simply a "house," but being by the Spaniards applied to country houses especially, the Americans have adopted it in that sense, and thus say: "His *casa* 's built too high up the foot-hills. O, thar ain't any water thar, you bet." (F. B. Harte, *Luck of Roaring Camp*, p. 228.) The term *pueblo*, also, in Spanish used to designate the village inhabited by Indians, under the care of a Spanish priest, and by him directed in worldly as well as in spiritual matters, still clings to the place. It has a peculiar interest in the case of the *Pueblo-Indians*, said to be the legitimate descendants of the ancient Aztecs, the former rulers of the country, who have given up their roving life and devote themselves to agriculture and domestic pursuits. But while they are thus semi-civilized and at least nominally good Christians, they nevertheless look piously and anxiously for the return of Montezuma, burning as of old his eternal fires, and celebrating his festivals in strictest secrecy. *Pueblo* itself is not unfrequently heard for a town or village that was formerly Spanish, and many of these continue to bear their old Castilian name. *San Francisco* alone seems to be in danger, at least colloquially, of losing its identity, as miners and others now very generally shorten it into *Frisco*. "They advised me to send him to *Fris'co* to the hospital, for he was no good to any one, and would be a baby all his life." (F. B. Harte, *Luck of Roaring Camp*, p. 51.) Nor must it be forgotten that the same term, *pueblo*, is applied also to the ruins in New Mexico and Arizona, peculiar erections, very numerous in the region between the Rio Grande, Colorado, and Gila rivers, which owe their origin to a partly-civilized race, differing from all others. "The *Pueblo Pintado* is one of the most remarkable. It is built of small flat slabs of grayish sandstone; between the stones are layers of small colored pebbles, the edifice at a distance resembling brilliant mosaic work. It is thirty feet high, and embraces three stories, the upper portion of each story forming a terrace. The building is one hundred and thirty yards long, and contains fifty-three rooms on the ground-floor. The *Pueblo Una Vida* is about three hundred and thirty yards long, while that called the *Chettro Kettle*, is four hundred and thirty-three yards long, and each story has one hundred and twenty-four rooms." (Charles Morris, *Monuments of Ancient America*.)

In like manner the Spanish word *sitio*, a square league of land, nearly equal to 4428 English acres, is perfectly familiar to all

Americans who either live or own land in the former Spanish possessions, as all ancient grants and charters mention this measure; the term occurs constantly also in the courts of law, and thus is brought to the higher courts in other States, also.

One of the few local terms taken from the Spaniards, which is used in the older States of the Union, is the word *Savannah*, well known as the name of the great seaboard city of the State of Georgia. The euphonious name has its very modest origin in the Spanish term *sabana*, a "linen sheet," which was applied by the followers of De Soto already to the prairies of the South. It became of general use in Florida, and when the State was incorporated into the Union, it was adopted into our speech. It was, of course, well known to English writers, and used by them also, as in Thomson's lines:

> "Plains immense,
> And vast *savannas*, where the wand'ring eye,
> Unfixt, is in a verdant ocean lost." (*Summer*.)

That its form and its meaning was not always quite clear, however, to English minds, we may presume from the *Salwanners*, which the old English innkeeper in Barnaby Rudge believed to be the name of a ferocious tribe of Indians, whose sole occupation was digging up tomahawks, and uttering unearthly war-whoops. When the savanna is a dry desert of considerable extent, it has the expressive name of *Jornada*, or the Day's Journey, and some of these terrible plains, which look as if they were forsaken by man and beast, and labored under a curse, are thus familiarly known. The *Jornada del Muerto*, the Plain of the Dead Man, as it might be translated, is ninety miles long, and requires several days to traverse; the trail is strewn with bleached bones, and early travellers, especially, used to look upon this part of the Overland Route as the most dangerous part of the whole undertaking. Efforts are, however, made to deprive these deserts of their terror by sinking Artesian wells, which would soon "change many dreaded *jornadas* from waterless deserts into cultivated plains." (Wislizenus, *New Mexico*.)

The *Sierra*, the suggestive name of a mountain-ridge resembling, with its numerous pointed peaks, the "saw" with its sharp teeth, seems peculiarly appropriate to the serrated mountain-chains of the Pacific coast. But Archbishop Trench, who first made this remark, was immediately taken to task by Alderman Moon, who destroyed the poetry of the resemblance at a blow, by declaring that *sierra* came from the two Arabic words *sah rah*, which simply means a desolate mountain-tract. Spanish authorities have, so far, preferred the *saw* doctrine. Two names of very special and peculiar localities will conclude this list. *Tinaja*, originally nothing more than an earthenware water-jar, is in the once Spanish districts very generally applied to small holes in the rocks on mountain-slopes, which, during the rainy season, are filled with water, and generally preserve a small quantity during the year. They furnish, in many regions, the only supply to travellers and hunters, and are hence most highly prized. The other term is the name of the State of *Texas*, literally meaning *tiles*, which, on the Mississippi and Western waters generally, is applied to the upper deck of steamboats. This is now a most desirable place, a light structure with glazed sides, in the very centre of the steamer, and immediately around the little glass house, from which the boat is steered, so as to afford ample room and a fine view. The cabins below this and above the grand saloon, where the officers of the boat are accommodated, also belong to *Texas*. Formerly, however, the space was open, without guards at the side or awning above-head, and frequented by the personal friends of the pilot and their associates, men of great daring, no doubt, and expert in the use of bowie-knife and pistol, but as little desirable company as the first settlers in the republic of *Texas*, which attracted all the lawless and desperate characters of the Union. It was then the name was given to this part of the boats, and the application was probably not altogether inappropriate.

The two Spanish terms, *hacienda* and *rancho*, have become so familiar to Americans in the former Mexican provinces, and all along the Pacific slope, that they have become incorporated in our speech. *Hacienda* is generally the name of a large and extensive plantation, with the mansion of the owner, while the *ranch*, as it is almost universally called now-a-days, is the small farm or peasant village, and the owner is called *ranchman*. The larger *rancho*, again, passes sometimes still under its old Spanish name of *estancia*, managed by a *mayor-domo* or upper butler. "The *hacienda* of Encarnacion, thirty miles south of Agua Nueva, was an *estancia* or *stock-ranch,* supplied with a bitterish but drinkable water from two deep wells worked by mules." (*Old and New,* June, 1871.)

The term meant originally nothing more in Northern Mexico than a hut rudely made up of a few posts and covered with branches, in which the *vaqueros* or herdsmen would sleep at night and seek shelter in bad weather. For with the Spaniards a *rancho* was a cattle-station or a hunting-lodge in a desert or a forest, far from the haunts of men; and it is from this meaning that the common tendency of corrupting words, and the national ingenuity shown in perverting their legitimate use, have derived the application of *rancho,* in Washington, to a place of evil report. (*Slang Dictionary,* p. 221.) In California a *rancho* sometimes means also the buildings on such a farm, while the lands put in cultivation for the purpose of raising corn or any other crop, are called a *labor,* pronounced like the Spanish word from which it is derived. All three names have been adopted, unchanged, and are in common use on the Pacific coast and in Arizona. The proper name for the buildings on a *rancho* used to be *rancheria,* but American carelessness dispenses with the word, and uses the shorter term for all it can mean. The owner or occupant of such a farm is the *ranchero,* a word long incorrectly pronounced *rankero,* if we may judge from J. R. Lowell's poems, who makes his hero, Hosea Biglow, say: "These fellers are very propilly called Rank Heroes, and the more they kill the ranker and the more heroick they bekim." (*Biglow Papers,* I., p. 122.) A *Milk-ranch* has of late become the familiar Californian term for a dairy.

The vast herds of cattle owned in those States are generally pastured all the year round; but where a dairy is attempted, the cows and their calves are every day driven into a *Corral,* as the large enclosure of cedar logs (*Redwood*) is called wherever it is used. The Spanish word, derived from *corro,* a circle, is quite as frequently applied to the ring formed by the wagons of an emigrant or hunter's train, into which all the horses and cattle are driven at night to graze, and to be protected against prowling Indians. On the outside the tents are pitched, with their flaps opening outward, and here the camp-fires are lighted. A traveller, therefore, writes: "The wagons were all *corralled, i. e.,* run together in the form of a horseshoe, so that the live stock, after feeding, could be driven into it." (*On the Plains, Putnam's Mag.*, Feb., 1869.) "On the 10th inst., sheriffs Morse of Contra Costa, and Harris of Monterey, *corralled* a party of Spaniards in the Pacheco mountains. One of them was of the party that murdered three Frenchmen in Suscal Valley. A desperate fight ensued, but the Spaniard was shot dead and his companions were captured." (*San Francisco paper*, January, 1871.) If the *corral* is near a house, it serves as stock-yard, and, as mentioned before, the cows are daily driven into it, to nurse the calves. The people of the ranch then crowd in with their milking-pails; the calves are caught by little boys with *lassos*, and their necks tied to the hind leg of the mother, who then, under a pleasing delusion, allows herself to be milked. The "cattle," on such occasions, often includes the *mustangs*, as the wild horses of the prairies are called, from the Spanish word *mesteño*, referring to studs and cattle-raising generally. "At sundown," G. W. Kendall says, in his lively description of the animals, "a drove of *mustangs*, or wild horses of the prairies, paid us a visit. When seen on a distant hill, standing with their raised heads toward a person, and forming a line as is their custom, it is almost impossible to take them for anything but mounted men. Having satisfied their curiosity, they wheeled with almost the regularity of cavalry, and galloped off, their long thick manes waving in the air and their tails nearly sweeping the ground. They are beautiful animals, always in excellent condition, and although smaller than our American horses, are still very compact and will bear much fatigue." (*Santa Fé Expedition*, I., p. 88.) They are caught with the *lasso*, the Spanish *lazo*, a long, slender rope, often made of rawhide, and having a loop at the end, which the Indians and the whites of the Plains know how to handle with amazing skill. Texans *twine* or *rope* a horse, instead of "catching" him, as it is called elsewhere, and then stake him out with a *stake-rope*. This may be either a *cabresto*, when it is made of hair, or—as is invariably the case in California—a *lariat*, of rawhide twisted. The word is derived from the Spanish *la reata*, and the rope is used to tie horses and mules together into a line, or to fasten them to a peg or stake driven into the ground. Hence J. R. Lowell makes his hero say, as he passes, on his return from the Mexican War, through parts of Texas:

"You see a feller peekin' out, an', fust you know, a *lariat*
Is round your throat, an' you a copse, 'fore you can say: wut air ye at?"
(*Biglow Papers*, I., p. 22.)

Occasionally the original word asserts its right, and then the word is more correctly used as *riata*, without the article. "I'm a coiling up my *riata*" (*Overland Magazine*, March, 1871) means, very graphically, I am preparing for my death. "There was a stake driven near its summit, with the initials L. E. S. Tied half-way down was a curiously worked *riata*. It was George's." (F. B. Harte, *Luck of Roaring Camp*, p. 230.)

With this *lariat* or a shorter rope also, a horse is *hobbled* out to grass, which consists in confining his two forelegs to each other, so that he cannot step more than six or ten inches at a time. Cunning mules, however, with their usual perverseness, soon learn to lift both forefeet at a time and gallop off; hence they are *lined*, that is, the forefoot is tied to the hindfoot on the same side, so that the step is very much shortened and their gait reduced to a kind of pace. As this rope is of the utmost importance, it is the invariable accompaniment of every horseman, and generally hangs from the *horn* of the saddle, as the pommel is here called from its horn-like shape. If the saddle should be a pack-saddle, it is known by its Spanish name of *aparejo*, and all saddles, for riding as well as for carrying burdens, are apt to have an *apishamore*, a saddle-blanket, made of buffalo-calf skins, under them, so as to protect the animal's back from being chafed.

The main purpose of forming a *corral* is to prevent a *stampede*, as a general scamper of the horses and mules of a *caballada* (contracted in Texas into *caballad* and pronounced *cavayard*), and of the cattle from their pasture-ground, is called in the Southwest from the Spanish word *estampida*. The word was first used of the herds of cattle and mustangs, which were so common in the North of Mexico, then applied to every drove, and to the horses, mules, and *bronchos*, as the packhorses are called (pronouncing the *ch* as in chocolate); but it is now employed to denote any sudden fright, which starts a drove of animals on a wild flight, or a start given them by thievish Indians and white outlaws, who wish to possess themselves of the more valuable part of the drove. The scene is full of terror, and yet not without grandeur: oxen, horses, and mules, all racing in various directions and at full speed across the plain, with eyes distended and glowing in wild fear, with tails on high, and strange sounds filling the air. If this happens at night, even the experienced hunter is rarely able to resist the panic, and thus Kit Carson himself, probably the coolest and most expert of Western hunters, was once carried away by the sudden surprise. "Some inexperienced traveller had given the alarm of Indians during his turn of guard-duty, or, as Western men express it, *stampeded* the camp. Kit Carson sprang to his feet, and, while yet half asleep, seeing some dark object advancing upon him through the long grass, seized one of his unerring pistols and shot, not an Indian, but his own particular riding mule, right through the head." (*A Ride with Kit Carson*, p. 237.) The term has, like many similar words, become so current as to find ready application to every kind of sudden start or fright. "The Virginia Legislature, becoming frightened at the approach of the cholera, have *stampeded* to the White Sulphur Springs, there to legislate in the ballroom of the principal hotel," says the New York *Tribune* of June 12, 1849; and in Blackwood we find it related of the Charleston Hotel, that "a shell had struck a house close by, and a sort of panic had been the result. Some had *stampeded* without waiting to dress, and had been seen with coats flying in one hand and pantaloons in the other, rushing frantically in the direction of the railroad-depot." (Jan., 1865.)

Another word which has, in like manner, obtained currency among us, and a meaning far beyond the original signification, is *fandango*, in Spanish the name of a popular dance and the appropriate tune. Certain authorities, however, claim for it an older date, and recognize in it an African word, believing that the dance and its name were both brought from Guinea to the West Indies by slaves, and that it had made its way from there back to Spain, which in its turn sent it to the American colonies. At all events, a *fandango* was found to mean in Mexico, where American soldiers first were initiated into its mysteries, any kind of nocturnal gathering, where the main entertainment consisted in dancing. In this form it is known in California and all the adjoining States. Miners and hunters delight in getting up an occasional *fandango* when they happen to be in town, and the Spanish residents are quite willing to attend, the men in their expensive *serapes*, Mexican blankets with an opening in the centre, woven by hand, and rich in gaudy colors, and the women with their *rebosos* drawn closely over the face, serving for bonnets, which they never wear. The men, on the contrary, seem reluctant to part with their *sombreros,* as the broad-brimmed hats are appropriately called in Spanish, from *sombra,* "shade," so that we read: "The old man extinguished his black-silk cap beneath the stiff, uncomely *sombrero,* which all native Californians affect." (F. B. Harte, *Luck of Roaring Camp,* p. 214.) Such is the *fandango* in its native land, but the term is used in the Eastern States also. Here, however, the idea of more than usual noise seems to be intimately connected with the term, and any very boisterous assembly, even a row, is familiarly called a *fandango.* "You must have had a real *fandango* last night," says the sleepless neighbor in a recent novel, "I heard your friends making merry till late in the morning, and not a wink could I sleep." (New York *Home Journal,* Dec. 14, 1850.) On such occasions, as well as at the somewhat more formal entertainments called *tertulias,* the refreshments are of the simplest, consisting mainly of *tortillas,* little flat round cakes made of corn-meal and cooked upon a sheet of iron, and a large supply of *aguardiente* or "fire-water," a kind of brandy distilled from the red wine of the country. The former constitute the ordinary bread of Mexico and its provinces. The grains are first soaked in ley till they are soft, and the outer covering peels off; then they are thoroughly washed in water and made ready for the mill, a flat stone, the upper surface of which is slightly concave, and a cylindrical crusher of the same material. A woman, by these simple means, crushes a handful of meal, which becomes soft and pulpy, and is then turned into a trough, kneaded, and made ready for the baking. In camp, men soon learn the mysteries of the artless process, and easily prepare the wholesome, palatable food, vastly preferable to the *atole,* a gruel of corn-meal familiar to all the regions which are or once were Spanish. The latter resembles in its simplicity, at least, the equally familiar *pinole,* parched corn ground and mixed with sugar and spices, which is much used by travellers, because of its compact form and extremely nutritious character.

After the morning's work every Spaniard and every dweller in the former Spanish possessions, yielding to the force of established usage, indulges in his *siesta,* a Spanish word derived from the name of the "sixth" hour after the beginning of day, our "noon." As the rest then taken is not necessarily confined to that hour, the term *siesta*, quite familiar to Europeans also, has become well known among Americans from two sources at once, and thus obtained so complete naturalization, that few persons using the word remember its foreign origin.

They here also learnt a word which seemed to come quite naturally to them, the Spanish *tinaja*, which they promptly declared to be nothing better than a Mexican effort to naturalize the familiar *tin* (tin-bucket) of the Americans. They had an opportunity of using the word in a complimentary sense, while admiring the Indian women, who carry these *tinajas* (earthenware vessels) of water gracefully on their head, when coming back from well or river, and thus acquire the same graceful, upright carriage, which is so striking in the women of Egypt and of the East Indies.

If the refreshments are simple, there is no lack of entertainment, for while part of the guests amuse themselves with dancing, others enjoy the favorite game of the Mexicans and American settlers, known as *Monte*, and taking its name, very graphically, from the "mountain" of gold which the banker piles up before him to attract customers. The very fact that it is a game of pure chance, and hence continually varying, makes it peculiarly attractive to gambling Mexicans and adventurous men of all nations, who stray and drift to California and the new States of the Southwest.

A few stray terms have, besides, found their way from the Spanish into our speech, and acquired there more or less perfect naturalization. Among these the most undesirable are probably the two vile companions, which we apparently shrink from naming in good English, the *chinch* and the *mosquito*. The former, mainly found in southern latitudes, bears its Spanish name of *chinche*, not only when it designates the common bed-bug (Cimex lectularius), but also when applied to an insect of similar offensive odor, which infests the wheat, and often does serious injury to a whole crop. The *mosquito* (Culex mosquito) seems to have been dreaded from of old, for even Bailey has already something to say of the *moschetto*, as he calls it after Italian manner. Our *mosquito* is, of course, a little fly only, but of most blood-thirsty nature, and even more intolerable in high northern latitudes than in the south. *Mosquito-nets* or *bars*, curtains of a light, transparent material, which are closely drawn over the bed, are therefore known and used almost in every part of the United States, and indispensable for those who would enjoy their rest at night. Nor does the word *garrote*, which we owe, of course, quite as much to England as to our Spanish neighbors, awake pleasant recollections within us in its various applications to tight collars, to robberies by means of partial strangulation, and to the Spanish mode of execution practised in Mexico; it is, however, much more generally used in America than in England. The word *adobe*, the Spanish term for a brick not burnt, but baked in the sun, has on the other hand become quite naturalized. The material of which they are made is abundant in California, and the bricks are hence, largely used in all the Southwestern States. "Some years ago," says a traveller in those regions, "I passed along a by-road in Alameda County, through one of these *adobe* fields, which had been sown in oats. The crop was in blossom, and, riding on horseback, the top of the grain had an average height somewhat exceeding the level of my eye sight." This *adobe* soil is found in parts of the State outside of the great Central Valley. "In the county of Santa Cruz it is largely diffused, and there is a rancho, adjoining a creek, both of which bear the same name, which was given by the natives with reference to the physical character of the alluvium, *Salsapentos*, which means, Get out of it, if you can." (*Overland Monthly*, August, 1870, p. 160.) The word has made itself so much at home with us, that J. R. Lowell says of the Red Robin:

> "Choosing out a handy crotch an' spouse
> He goes to plast'ring his *adobe* house."
> (*Biglow Papers*, II., p. 157.)

The common jail is, in Southern States, very frequently known as the *Calaboose*, a term which is probably a corruption of the Spanish *calabozo*, partly due to an intermediate French word, *calabouse*. It is quoted as sea-slang in the *Slang-Dictionary* (p. 93), but in America serves regularly, as, for instance, in the case of the common jail at New Orleans, which bears that name. "More than thirty men were last night confined in the *Calaboose*, and with the present imperfect arrangements there, their sufferings must have been well-nigh intolerable." (New Orleans *Picayune*, June 30, 1869.) Another word, similarly corrupted, but treated much worse, is the geographical name of *Key*, as applied to ledges of rock rising near the surface of the water, and low, flat islands in the West Indies. The word is derived from the Spanish *Cayo*, a name given, among others, to the small islands on the coast of Florida, which was retained after the acquisition of that State, but pronounced as it now is written. One of the best known among them, *Key West*, has suffered still further ill treatment; it was originally *Cayo Hueso*, Bone Island.

Where formerly Spanish coins were current the word *pieza*, a piece, may still be occasionally heard in the transactions between Americans even, when a small silver coin, the Spanish *real* (de plata), is meant. In other parts of the Union it is represented by a term which has come from the West Indies. There—especially in Jamaica—a *bit* meant the smallest silver coin current, worth about sevenpence ha'penny; from thence the Southern States obtained their *bit*, fully known as *fi'-penny-bit*, amounting to six and a quarter cents; a defaced twenty-cent piece being called a *long bit*. With the disappearance of the Spanish coins from the United States, the word has gone nearly out of use. In England, however, fourpence continues to be called a *bit*, at least in city slang. The *picayune*, on the contrary, originally a Carib word, or possibly akin to French *pécune*, has not only held its own but become a popular word in familiar language. It was long used to designate, in Louisiana, Florida, etc., the Spanish half-real, and was next transferred to the American sixpence. The coin no longer exists in currency, but the term remains to designate anything peculiarly small and pitiful. "The whole thing this year was a miserable *picayune* affair," says the New Orleans *Delta* of the Bœuf Gras of 1866, an expression exactly corresponding to the Northern phrase: "a one-horse affair." "A dozen *Picayune* Amnesty Bills," states the New York *Tribune*, "will do much to inflame and diffuse Southern discontent, nothing to allay it." (Dec. 12, 1870.) The only serious use made of the term is found in the name of a very clever daily newspaper, published under the name of the *Picayune*, in the city of New Orleans, and sold for that coin, a fact which strangely recalls the name of the very first of all newspapers, published in Venice, and called *Gazeta*, from the coin of that name, for: "If you will have a stool, it will cost you a *gazet*, which is almost a penny." (*Coryat. Crudities*, II., p. 15.)

Of ill-treated Spanish words, perhaps none has suffered more grievously than *piragua*, a word probably of Indian origin in the first place, but introduced into the world of letters in this form, and soon adopted by the French also as *pirogue*, which is most familiar to American ears. Meaning, originally, a canoe formed of a single large tree, or sometimes two such trunks lashed together, it is in the United States used promiscuously for any small boat or canoe, and even for a larger vessel carrying two masts and a leeboard, such as were formerly used as ferryboats in the neighborhood of New York. But the word was soon Americanized in a variety of ways, and, except in print, its true form is hardly ever preserved. It appears in the West as *periauger*, a form under which it is used by W. Irving (*Washington*, II., p. 272), as *periauga* in Virginia, and thus quoted from the Western papers (p. 13), and even as *pettiauger* in the Far West. A mere grammatical perversion, involving, however, no less violence, is the use of the Spanish imperative, *Vamos*, as an English verb, which has of late become so universal that it is actually often written: to *vamose*. The interjection, corresponding very nearly to our: Well! became familiar to the American troops during the Mexican War in 1847, and being uncommonly popular among them, it soon spread as a cant term all over the Union. Now it is a verb: "Before the speaker's voice could be heard every democratic member had *vamosed*, and since that day no quorum has ever been present," was said of the Indiana Legislature. (February 18, 1870.) Mr. Bartlett quotes from a book, "Southern Sketches," the phrase *vamosed the ranch*, and calls this process of appropriating words: "breaking Priscian's head with a vengeance." (*Dict.*, p. 496.) Since J. R. Lowell, however, has used *to vamose*, the word must probably be considered naturalized.

In a recent poem by John Hay occur the following lines:

> "The nigger has got to *mosey*
> From the limits o' Spunky P'int."
>
> (*Banty Tim.*)

This mysterious word *mosey* is, probably correctly, said to be nothing more than a mere variety of the Americanized verb *vamose*, with the final vowel sounded, and the first syllable lost. It certainly has the same meaning, of leaving suddenly, and generally involuntarily. "My friend, let me tell you, if you do not *mosey* this instant, and clear out for good, you'll have to pay pretty dear." (Louisville *Journal*, October 9, 1857.) In this sense it has crossed the ocean, and reappears in English slang, especially as a summons: "Now, *Mosey!*" Its derivation from a mythical *Moses*, warmly as it is supported by English writers, has no foundation in fact, and is "only a new instance of the tendency to mythologize, which is as strong as ever among the uneducated." (*Atlantic Monthly*, August, 1860.) The Celtic proves its usual readiness to supply an ancestor to the quaint word, and proves its claims by the habit of Cornish miners to say, *Moas*, for Go! The verb is, of course, an entirely different word from that which enters into the composition of *Mosey*-sugar, molasses-candy with the meat of nuts mixed up with it. The latter comes from *Mosaic*, which the kind of inlaid work produced by the two colors, white and brown, resembles in some manner.

Few would recognize the proud old Spanish word *cavar*, which denoted the haughty, impatient pawing of a spirited horse, in the half-ludicrous term: to *cavort*. It is true, its derivation is sometimes sought in the verb: to curvet, from the French *courbetter*, but the fact that the term is very frequently not only pronounced but also written *cavault*, seems to speak in favor of its Spanish origin. It is now used, especially in the South, for any very extravagant manner of speaking or acting, with an intention of ridiculing the action. Thus Judge Longstreet makes one of his heroes of "Georgia Scenes" say: "In they came, boys and girls, old and young, making a prodigious noise, and prancing and *cavorting* at a tremendous rate." A recent traveller in South Carolina describes a court-scene thus: "In the court, a judge in a black silk gown, and a jury of nine whites and three blacks, were trying a black, evil-looking, one-eyed negro, for disturbing a religious meeting. The witnesses were all negroes, and the gist of their testimony was that Tony, the accused, came to the meeting-house, and—jes kep *cavortin'* round." (New York *Tribune*, May 7, 1871.)

Spanish terms may appropriately come to an end with the word *Zombi*, a phantom or a ghost, not unfrequently heard in the Southern States in nurseries and among the servants. The word is a Creole corruption of the Spanish *sombra*, which at times has the same meaning.

THE GERMAN.

"I schpeaksch English."—*Hans Breitmann.*

Even that more remarkable than creditable propensity of the German, to assert his cosmopolitan character by abandoning his nationality, and by repudiating, after a few years' residence abroad, all attachment to his own language, his national views, and private convictions, has not prevented statisticians from finding more than five millions of Germans in the United States. They are, moreover, not limited, like the Dutch and the French, to certain circumscribed localities; they are not scattered and lost in the great Anglo-Saxon family, like the Irish and the Welsh. Far from it; they constitute a large proportion of the population of great cities, and own vast tracts of land in all the agricultural States; they have their temples to worship Gambrinus in Boston and in New Orleans, in Norfolk and in San Francisco. Their press is powerful and high-toned, their potent voice is heard in State Legislatures and in the national Senate. Their influence is felt in every State, and their vote is decisive in great crises.

And yet they have not enriched our language by a dozen important words! The very fact of their excessive readiness to adapt themselves to all the exigencies of their new home, their unwillingness to use their own idiom as soon as they have acquired sufficient English to converse in it freely, and their prompt admission of the superiority of American terms as well as institutions, have well-nigh neutralized the influence they might nave exercised by their numbers, their intelligence, and their superior education. They have, no doubt, powerfully affected the national mind in all that pertains to the realm of thought—

American churches, American letters, and even American manners bear more or less the impress of German teachings; but the marks are not visible, because the action has been too subtle and slow, too secret and silent, to leave its traces on the surface.

This is all the more true of our speech, as their own beautiful and highly improved idiom, so near akin to our tongue, has sadly suffered by the contact with English. Scholars coming over from Germany remark with deep regret how rapidly their beloved language is yielding to the might of American nationality. They point with ineffable pain to the jargon spoken, written, and even printed in Pennsylvania—a hopeless departure from the old standard, and shocking in its barbarous admixture of English terms, which it mutilates as savagely as its own. The lines:

> "My Mary cot one leetle sheeps,
> Hees flees so vite mit schnow,
> Und efry blace als Mary pin,
> Dat tam leetle sheeps will go,"

show the havoc the uneducated German, whose ear cannot distinguish between *b* and *p*, or *d* and *t*, plays with English; and the following will, in like manner, illustrate the injury done to the mother-tongue:

> "Mudder, may I a schwimming went?
> Nix, my grosse dotter!
> I bet twice more als foofty cent,
> Dat you get drowned in de votter."
> (*Acorn and Germ*, Millwood, Pennsylvania, Sept. 14, 1870.)

Hans Breitmann's Ballads (by Charles G. Leland), give an example of the process which, artificial in the poems, goes on naturally in the regions where uneducated Germans and the descendants of such come in contact with the superior English which is spoken throughout the United States. On the other hand, in cities and a few specially favored districts, where a higher class of Germans are brought in contact with each other, they still speak their own language, publish their own newspapers, almanacs, and light literature, and have their own schools and churches, where instruction is given and services are held in German.

The result is, that with the exception of one or two German

words of greater importance, our speech has been enriched only by a few terms, relating either to slang or to—eating. The word *standpoint*, a literal version of the German *Standpunkt*, is generally considered as having originated in America; its use, however, has met with such prompt and general success in the pages of English writers, that America would probably find it difficult to prove the paternity. A *Turner*, however, has become literally what Americans call an "institution." The word represents our "Gymnast," but being applied to members of clubs and societies who make gymnastics a subject of pleasure as well as of health, it is now universally admitted into our speech. *Turnerfeste*, as their annual festivals are designated, excite the utmost interest, and their performances the greatest admiration in the large cities, while their clubs, or *Turn Vereine*, as they begin to be called even by many who are ignorant of German, exercise a most salutary influence on the people by inducing them to bestow that attention upon physical exercise, the want of which has so seriously affected the health of Americans.

It is somewhat strange that the word designating the very opposite to the *Turner's* character, the *Loafer*, should, in like manner, come from the German. He is the vagabond or idle lounger, who so oddly contradicts the world's impression of American energy and irrepressible activity; who meets you at every corner and in every grogshop of a city; disfigures every village as he sits on empty boxes and windowsills, lazily whittling a stick, and spitting his villanous tobacco; who supports bar-rooms and ruins his prospects, disgraces his family, and destroys his own life. He is far worse than the lazzarone of Naples in his forced inactivity under a wretched government, and in a climate where life is possible without labor; worse than the Mexican lepero, cursed with an incurable malady, and helpless in all his efforts. In vain has he been painted in quaint humor by many a clever artist, in vain has Walt Whitman declared that the forte of his nation is "confessedly *loafing* and writing poems." Although R. W. Emerson tells us gravely that the poet's "Leaves of Grass" are "the most extraordinary piece of wit and wisdom that America has yet contributed," we believe better things of his nation.

The term, common as it is, has, like many other common words, given the learned much trouble. The Philadelphia *Vademecum* said: "It is a convenient word, much needed in language, but without etymology." Many are the sources, on the other hand, from which other writers have tried to derive the puzzling word, and the oddest suggestions have been made in good earnest. One claims it as a descendant of the Dutch land-*looper*, a vagrant; another traces it back to *loaf*, and sees in it a beggar for bread. Can it be a contracted form of *low-fellow?* asks a third, and still another is sure it owes its origin to Rabelais, who among his wonders of word-coinage speaks of a certain good-for-nothing person, encountered by Gargantua, as lipe-*lope*. The fact that *loper* or *loafer* was in general use as a cant term in the early part of last century, when *landloper* was a vagabond who begged in the attire of a sailor (hence no doubt land-*lubber*, *Slang Dictionary*, p. 172), would seem to speak in favor of the Dutch derivation. The true origin of the word must, however, be sought in German, where *Läufer* is a term applied by the steady and phlegmatic people to men who are irregular and unsettled in life. Half of Germany pronounces this word with the vulgar sound of *au* as *lofer*, and from this, in all probability, the German term *Lofer* and our *loafer* are derived. The usual freedom is taken with the word in forming derivatives: to *loaf* is quite frequent, as in J. C. Neal's *Charcoal Sketches*: "One night, Mr. Dobbs came home from his *loafing*-place, for he *loafs* of an evening like the generality of people," (III., p. 11,) and the Philadelphia *Mercury* actually had a word *loaferishly*. (Jan. 13, 1867.)

The word suggests almost logically the familiar *Lager*, as the famous *Lagerbier* of Germany is now called, since thousands of breweries furnish the favorite beverage to thirsty Teutons and Americans alike. Its popularity was unbounded, and the consumption perfectly amazing, till quite recently a formidable rival arose in the shape of *buckbeer*, the renowned *Bock* of Bavaria. Whilst *Lager*beer is so weak that judicial proof has been brought into a Court of Justice of its inability to intoxicate a man even when several gallons have been drunk, the *Buck*beer, on the contrary, is one of the strongest made in Germany, and hence represented by a he-goat, from which it derives its name, and whose effigy may be seen in countless *beer saloons* all over the country. The other extreme, an exceedingly weak and insipid beverage, *Shenkbeer*, the *Schenkbier* of Germany, is so called because it has to be put on draught (*schenken*) as soon as it is made, for fear of turning sour if not immediately consumed. Whatever may be the objections to the immoderate use of beer, there can be no doubt that it favors temperance by weaning foreigners especially from the habitual use of *Schnaps*, as almost any distilled liquor is called by the Germans, even in America; and all who know the sad effects produced in habitual tipplers of this country, or the still greater horrors produced by absynthe, will readily concede some advantages at least to comparatively harmless beers.

The German is accused of being unable to enjoy life without a dish, which is as frequently—and as correctly—called his national dish as frogs were considered that of the Frenchman: his *sour-crout*. The *Sauerkraut*, cabbage cut fine, pressed into casks, and frequently allowed to ferment, is certainly a favorite with many Germans here as well as in their native land, but by no means more frequently to be met with than the *coleslaw* of the New Englander and his descendants. *Apple-butter*, not unlike the famous *apple-sauce* of Yankeedom, and made by stewing apples for twenty hours or longer in cider, is a dish peculiar to Pennsylvania and the valley of Virginia, where it is produced in enormous quantities. Here it has been inherited from the first settlers through several generations; among recent immigrants it is comparatively unknown. The German word *Metzelsuppe* (from *metzeln*, to kill, to butcher) has, in Pennsylvania and the Western States, where Germans abound, acquired the naturalized form *Metzel-soup*. When the "killing season" arrived, it was—and probably still is—a common practice among farmers to send their friends and near neighbors as much of the puddings and sausages they made as was necessary for one meal for the family, at least, and as this was sure to be reciprocated, the practice was usually accompanied by no special sacrifice. Still, there were cases in which no return was expected, as when the savory morsels were sent to tailors, shoemakers, and other humble persons employed by the family. This gift was called the *Metzel-soup*, although the term originated in a kind of *soup* made out of the broth, in which the puddings were "boiled off." The *pudding* itself is, in the same districts, and especially in "Pennsylvania Dutch," called a *Leverworscht* (*Leberwurst*, *i. e.* liver-sausage), and thus distinguished from *Blootworscht*, (*Blutwurst*, *i. e.* blood-sausage.) The real pudding was called *pawnhost* by the negroes, with whom it was a great favorite. The German *Bretzeln* have been adopted, with only slight modifications, wherever the peculiar twisted kind of bread is known, but the *Schnitzel*, slices of dried fruit, are almost universally called *snits*. A schoolmaster in a public school in the interior of Pennsylvania was drilling his class in arithmetic. He said: "If I cut an apple in two, what will the parts be?" "Halves!" was the answer. "If I cut the halves in two, what would you call the parts?" "Quarters!" "If I cut the quarters in two, what will the parts be?" The answer was unanimous, "*Snits!*"

Noodles, also, derive their name from the German *Nudeln*, and differ from the vermicelli of Italy only in the addition of eggs. With the dish the term of reproach, *noodlehead*, has come over from Germany, where *Nudeln* and *Grütze* (grits) are apt to be considered as the favorite food of fools. Hence J. C. Neal says: "Be sassy, be anything, Mr. *Noodlesoup*" (*Charcoal Sketches*, I., 137), alluding to the German *Nudelsuppe*. Thus also *dummerhead* is not unfrequently heard in Pennsylvania and some of the Western States, where the German element is prevalent—an imitation of *Dummkopf*, our "blockhead." The first part of the compound, the adjective *dumm*, is often used as *dummy*, not only to represent the absent partner at cards, but also any stupid, silent person. In this sense it is an inheritance from the Scotch as well, claiming near kindred to our *dumb*, as used in Allan Ramsay's well known lines:

> "Auld Gabbi Spec wha was sae cunning,
> To be a *dummie* ten years running."

In the sense of stupid, it is employed by the great Seer, Andrew Jackson Davis, who says of a medium that "he was the laughing-stock of his brothers and sisters, who nicknamed him a *dummy*, whilst his father averred that he would never earn his salt, for he had not gumption enough to make a whistle." (*The Great Harmonia*, p. 339.)

Sagnichts is almost the only political term ever employed by the Germans in America and adopted as a party-cry. They had been roused to an unwonted degree of indignation by the offensive doctrines of Know-Nothings, who claimed all rights and privileges in a country peopled entirely by immigrants, for natives only, to the exclusion of all foreign-born, naturalized citizens. With a fine instinct of political irony the Germans changed the term into *Sagnichts*, or Say-Nothings. It is not certainly known whether a similar political allusion lies at the bottom of a peculiar feature in the popular game of *Euchre*, but if the latter is really, as many maintain, a German game, the explanation would be easy. In this game the knave of the trump-suit is called the *Right Bower*, and the knave of the suit of the same color the *Left Bower*, and these two cards trump king and queen as well as every other card. Now *Bower* is evidently the German *Bauer*, and here, therefore, as certainly in a very similar German game, the *Bauer* or yeoman is given the place and power of the king. The term has become so familiar that *Right Bower* is now a common though perhaps still a cant term of high praise; hence an occurrence, in a recent debate in Congress, was thus reported: "They threatened to filibuster to prevent the bill from being considered, and as their *Right Bower*, General Butler, was absent, the stratagem would have succeeded, had not help come from an unexpected quarter." (*Globe*, November 17, 1870.)

Among the corruptions of German terms introduced into our speech may be noticed two ridiculous terms: *Katoose*, used in the New England States for any sudden unpleasant noise, and said to have been derived from the German *Getöse* (?), and *Kriss Kingle*, the sadly mutilated form of the beautiful word *Christ Kindlein*. The latter is in Germany already quite frequently contracted into *Christ Kindel*, the "Child Christ," on whom German children rely for their gifts on the Christmas-tree, and this form has the more readily degenerated, as it was, after the manner of words, prone to follow the analogy of *Criss-Cross*, a game played on a slate by children, and derived from old-fashioned Primers. These almost uniformly began the alphabet with the sign of the Cross, which was called *Christ Cross*, from the first lesson learned by children; for one of the oldest authorities on the subject, "The Boke of Curtasye," directs children to give special attention to the seven initiatory lessons of the Christian child. 1. The *Cross Christ*. 2. The Lord's Prayer. 3. The Ave and Creed, etc.

Among the many evidences of the absurdities to which the

freedom of phonography, so warmly advocated by many earnest men, but happily abandoned even in Webster's last edition of his great Dictionary, must inevitably lead, few are more striking than the word *fillipeen*, bravely quoted in Bartlett's Americanisms. As the pleasant custom which the term designates, is not known ever to have been connected with the giving of *fillips*, this manner of writing seems to be inexcusable; it certainly recalls neither of the two favorite derivations of the puzzling word. Fortunately it concerns Americans very little, whether the term is derived from the Greek *φίλος* and *ποινή*, or from the German *Vielliebchen*, since they use it only as they have received it from their English forefathers; but it ought surely to be protected against such utterly lawless spelling. The *muley-saw*, a saw which is not hung in the gate, is almost as bad; few would at first recognize in the English-looking word, with its squint at a *mule*, the German word *Mühlen säge*, from which it is in reality derived. But what shall we say of German phrases which seem gradually to force their way into English, like the *hold on!* used thus: "When the police-officer saw him quietly walk out of the door, as if to leave the court-house, he called out to him, *hold on*, my good friend, you are wanted!" (Cincinnati *Inquirer*, July 17, 1865), or the *what for* (was für) of the New Englander, who had lived so long in Missouri that he could rise in the House and say: "Mr. Speaker, I demand to know who dared present such a petition. *What for* a boldness is that, to come here and ask us, who have fought against treason for four years, to honor the very traitors whom we have crushed?" (St. Louis *Democrat*, Aug. 21, 1866.) They are simple barbarisms which the genius of our language may endure for a time, but which ought not to be encouraged and endorsed by careful writers, even in the pages of a newspaper.

There is much less harm in the introduction of German phrases drawn from nature or local peculiarities. Thus, while the French and English draw their terms of contempt or pity for youthful inexperience from unfledged birds with green or yellow bills, etc., the German fancifully notices that newly-born animals are apt to be licked dry promptly everywhere except behind the ears, and hence their colloquial phrase: "The youngster is not dry yet behind his ears." The expression having become familiar to

American ears in Pennsylvania first, has from thence spread to other States also. "Rustic maidens rejecting the attentions of youths, whom they consider too young to be of special value as lovers, are fond of saying: You are not *dry yet behind the ears*, you had better wait!" (Professor S. S. Haldeman.)

THE NEGRO.

"Dark sayings, darkly uttered."

THE negro formerly occupied too subordinate a position in the social scale to influence the speech of his masters. His ignorance, his carelessness, his inability, with peculiar organs of speech untrained for many generations, to repeat certain sounds at all, and his difficulty in perceiving others by the ear, account amply for the havoc he played with the king's English. These impediments have made themselves clearly felt, since zealous and intelligent teachers of both sexes have devoted themselves in numbers to the training of freedmen's children. They have encountered almost insuperable difficulties, even where mental capacities were apparently fully equal to those of the white race, and the zeal to learn was almost irrepressible. The most successful among the well-educated negroes, who have risen to honorable positions at the bar, or earned distinction in other professions, men of eloquence often, and always forcible speakers, retain nevertheless certain peculiarities of sound, of utterance, and accentuation, which would mark them, even if they bore no trace of their origin in their appearance, at least as much as foreigners are marked who have mastered a foreign idiom perfectly. Did not even the elder Dumas in his speech as in his writings betray his descent unmistakably?

The habits of the negro in his pronunciation of English words must, however, not be judged, as is too frequently done, by so-called negro minstrelsy. As French and German characters in comedy have passed into a conventional mispronunciation, as no American ever spoke like the Yankee on the boards of minor theatres in London, so have these so-called minstrels done great injustice to the negro, whom they claim to represent. Foreigners, especially, believe in the conventional negro, as Englishmen believe in the long-legged, tobacco-chewing, bowie-knife-carrying Yankee in Punch. The bulk of American play-goers, we fear, are as frequently misled.

The error arises often from utter ignorance of the vast difference that exists between certain classes and varieties of negroes. The Virginia slave, for generations accustomed to the nicer functions of a house-servant, in daily contact with gentlewomen, and accustomed to hear at table and during long journeys on horseback or in private carriages, the conversation of intelligent men, was far above the average of the British laborer, to say nothing of the French peasant. He spoke fair English, infinitely better, at all events, than the Yorkshire yokel, or even the thorough-bred Cockney. The slave on a sugar or cotton plantation in the Southwest, on the other hand, was but a step removed from the African savage; his speech, largely intermixed with African terms, was well-nigh unintelligible. But even in the so-called Border States there was an immense gulf between the house-servant and the ruder *Field-hand.* Some of the former possessed not only knowledge, but even refinement; body-servants, as they were called, taken abroad by their masters, astonished European gentlemen by their politeness of manner and their inbred courtesy, and the Ex-President of Liberia, long a slave in Virginia, never once lacked the dignity and self-possession required by his high office, when presented at foreign courts, or on the far more trying occasions, when he returned to his native State and met his former masters. But the *field-hand* was, what Mr. Olmsted says of him: "on an average a very poor and very bad creature, much worse than I had supposed before I had seen him, and grown familiar with his stupendous ignorance, duplicity, and sensuality. He seems to be but an imperfect man, incapable of taking care of himself in a civilized manner, and his presence in large numbers must be considered a dangerous circumstance to a civilized country." (*Journey in the Back Country*, p. 432.)

Nevertheless, it cannot be denied that even the most intelligent of the race seem to have some difficulty both in their hearing and in their organs of speech, which prevents their perceiving the more delicate modifications of sound, which abound and are of such paramount importance in English, and of reproducing them accurately. As the German, whose native dialect has from childhood up accustomed his ear to an utter disregard of the difference between *d* and *t*, and *b* and *p*, never ceases to confound them in English also, so the negro finds it often utterly impossible to hear certain sounds, and can consequently not imitate them.

One of the most striking evidences of this inability is found in the unique and very interesting manuscript, in Arabic characters, made by a Mandingo slave, who belonged to a Mr. Maxwell, of Savannah. His American name was London, and having become a zealous Christian, he transcribed the Gospel with rare precision, using even the vowel-points—*harakat*—of the Arabic grammar, proving thus his careful training at home in making copies from the Koran. But in spite of all this training, and with all his intelligence, he could only write the English words as their sounds affected his ear, and thus his vocalization was in this wise: (First Chapter of John) "*Fas chapta ob Jon. Inde beginnen wasde wad; ande wad waswid Gad, ande wad was Gad.*" The manuscript caused a ludicrous mistake, such as had happened even to Mr. de Sacy, the great Orientalist, who states himself that having received an Arabic manuscript from Madrid, he examined it carefully, and failing to discover a single Arabic word in it, suggested that the book was probably written in the language of the Hovas of Madagascar. Subsequently he found that the MS. was in Spanish, and had been written, according to the ear, by a converted Moor. In like manner the MS. of the intelligent Mandingo slave was presented to Mr. W. B. Hodgson, of Savannah, who also looked for Arabic words corresponding to the Arabic letters, and abandoned the task of deciphering it in despair. A chance remark suggested the turning of the latter into Roman letters, and he discovered at once by the sound what the eye had failed to perceive.

Still, the very imperfect manner in which the writer had evidently only been able to catch the English sounds, accounts at once for the majority of peculiar forms and sounds, which are so often exhibited as Americanisms, due to the influence of the negroes in our midst, while they are in effect nothing more than unsuccessful efforts to speak correct English. It is a grave mistake to imagine that the language adopted by negro minstrels is that of the negro; the Englishman might as fairly be judged by the "Mylord Goddam" of the French stage; and the use of *hab* for have, *lub* for love, *massa* for master, is by no means universal, nor has it ever been common to all slaves.

Of genuine African words which have become sufficiently well-known to be considered Americanisms, there are probably but three in our speech. One is the term *Buckra*, which, on the African coast, is universally applied to white men, meaning originally "a spirit, a powerful being," and is used in that application throughout the Southern States. Hence, Mr. Bartlett quotes the negro song:

"Great way off at sea,
When at home I binny,
Buckra man take me
From de coast ob Guinea."

Its meaning is occasionally transferred to white objects, and negroes thus speak of *buckra* yam, with the understanding, however, that it is not only white, but peculiarly good also. The word is occasionally enforced by the addition of *swanga*, an African term, meaning elegant or bright-colored, so as to strike and please the eye. A *Swanga Buckra* serves, therefore, among negroes, to designate a specially well-dressed white man.

From this African term is, curiously enough, a word derived which has made its way to New England, and is now quite at home on the banks of Newfoundland. This is *Swankey*, the name given—probably as something very elegant in taste and effect—to a beverage consisting of molasses, vinegar, and water, the favorite drink of fishermen. "Roll along here, shouted the cook. Tumble up an' git your *swankey*, boys. It's as good as ever you cocked a lip at. And at the word each man, his face glowing with excitement and exercise, took his turn at the *swankey* pail." (*Newfoundland Fisheries*, p. 110.)

It is presumed, though not proven, that the *Moonack*, a mythical animal known to negroes only, is also of African origin. The beast lives, according to their belief, in caves or hollow trees, and the poor negro who meets it in his solitary rambles is doomed. His reason is impaired, till he becomes a madman, or is carried off by some lingering malady. He dare not speak of it, but old, experienced negroes say when they look at him: "He gwine to die; he seed the *moonack*."

Cuffy, which is often claimed as a negro term, is in all probability nothing more than a corruption of the English slang term, a *cove*, and quite as frequently heard abroad as in the United States. "The fine dash of Virginia upper *cuffyism*, it is gone, gone forever. Sambo has settled down into a simple bourgeois." (*Putnam's Magazine*, December, 1854.)

Nor is the number of words large which express the relations of master and slave, and to which ignorant negroes, dull of hearing, have given a new meaning. Even the familiar appellations of *Uncle* and *Aunt*, by which for many generations every colored man and woman was called, were not peculiar to America, as Pegge's *Supplement* to Grose distinctly states that the two words are "in Cornwall applied to all elderly persons." The house and stable servant, in like manner, went by the generic term of *boy*, irrespective of age.

A word as hideous in sound as of import, connected with the negro, is the famous *Black Code*, a collection of laws first made by Bienville in Louisiana, which was ever after the model for all legislation on the relations of master and slave. When the colony was taken possession of by the Crown of Spain in the year 1769, the provisions of the *Black Code* were retained with such modifications as the "Siete Partidas" made on the subject of slavery. This system of laws has ever since been the Blackstone of Spain and her colonies, and is still the authority in the parts of America settled by Spaniards. Its power continued long in Louisiana, and controlled largely the rights of negroes, even after the colony became a State of the Union.

It is comforting to turn from such a subject to the term of tenderness, by which the black nurse was, for so many generations, known to the children of the South. This used to be *Mammy*, the same name formerly given in England to grandmothers, and by some derived from the Gypsy word *Mami*, which means grandmother. Even now many a *Mammy* is spending her declining years in the family of those whom she has nursed and reared, and thus the name still lingers on in the Southern States. In South Carolina and some of the Gulf States, the word is sounded and written *Maumer*, and thus it is quoted by a recent writer:

"An old *Maumer* (the general term of Southern children for their nurses), whose gray hairs are still covered by the bright turban, which always gave such dignity to the appearance of the nursery ruler. Where are those *maumers*, whom the children loved only less than those who bore them, and with whom the friendship only ceased with life? They, too, belong now to the past."

Indirectly, at least, the negro has given us the verb, to *maroon*, from *maroon*, the name applied in the West Indies to runaway negroes, who lived as outlaws in remote and inaccessible parts of the country. The term is used in the Southern States, though now less frequently than formerly, to designate a pic-nic or excursion party extending over several days. A few families agree thus to go *marooning;* they take tents and cooking utensils, and spend their time away from the haunts of men, and more or less in Robinson Crusoe style.

America owes the negro no small gratitude for the only national poetry which it possesses, as distinct from all imitation of old English verses, and all competition with English writers of our day. We have no ballad and no song that can be called American. The nearest approach ever made to the creation of a new type was the dramatic song *Jim Crow*, brought out about the year 1835 by an enthusiastic Yankee on the boards of a theatre in New York; it created a sensation, for it was new in form and conception, and no doubt rendered still more attractive by the strange guise in which it was presented. It was quickly followed by several other songs of the same kind, such as *Zip Coon, Longtailed Blue, Ole Virginny nebber tire, Settin' on a Rail,* etc. Then came, in 1841, a variation in the form of a descriptive ballad, famous *Ole Dan Tucker*, and after that the vein was exhausted. For a time this African inroad drove nearly every other song from the publisher's store and the drawing-room. It is strange that they are almost all sad, touching, and resigned. Philanthropists have, of course, ascribed this to the sad fate of the race. This is a mistake, for the negro is by nature, and was even in the days of slavery, emphatically a merry creature, full of fun and endowed with an almost superhuman power of laughing. He has become sad only since the responsibilities of earning his livelihood and exercising the duties of a citizen have been so suddenly imposed upon him.

It may be, that in another generation he will recover the happy cheerfulness of his race, and with it the love of song and laughter, but at present he feels instinctively that his race is passing through a great and perilous crisis.

He is passionately fond, also, of religious music, and the good ear for music, with a fair endowment of voice, which have been vouchsafed to his race, enable him to perform creditably and to enjoy heartily all manner of hymn and psalmody. But he must be allowed to translate the words into his own familiar terms and to alter them at will, utterly regardless of their meaning, so they suit the metre and chime in with the cadence. The following hymn, a genuine native production, and sung in the churches of Baltimore, which appeared not long ago in that excellent paper, *Appleton's Journal*, will give an idea of their manner of treating religious subjects:

PHARAO.

Didn't ole Phay get loss?
  Get loss, get loss?
Didn't ole Phay get loss
  In de Red Sea?
Phayo say, I gwine across
  In de Red Sea,
So whip up horses an' gallop across,
  In de Red Sea.

Didn't ole Phay get loss,
  Get loss, get loss?
Didn't ole Phay get loss
  In de Red Sea?
Hebrews say, we get across now
  In de Red Sea,
At thy feet we humblie bow,
  In de Red Sea.

Didn't ole Phay get loss?
  Get loss, get loss?
Didn't ole Phay get loss
  In de Red Sea?
Phayo say, I gwine along home,
  In de Red Sea,
Oh, how I wish I hadn't come
  In de Red Sea!

JOHN CHINAMAN.

"The heathen Chinee is peculiar."—*F. B. Harte.*

THE *Heathen Chinee*, as he will, no doubt, be called for many a year to come, bearing the baptismal name bestowed upon him in F. B. Harte's characteristic poem of Truthful James (a character invented by John Phœnix), has only so lately appeared on our shores, that Chinese terms can hardly be said to have found their way yet into our speech. *Johnny*, or *John Chinaman*, for under both names is he known in California, has for years given rise to angry debates in legislative halls, and to vehement discussions in public journals; he has been victimized unmercifully in the mines and gulches in the up-country, and brutally ill-treated in trade and in courts in the cities. He has recently even found his way to Southern plantations and to Northern factories, everywhere proving useful, faithful, and intelligent. The announcement of large arrivals of Chinese laborers and servants threatened at a time to become a question of national policy, and Labor-Leagues as well as Congress became deeply agitated on the subject. So far, however, their number has been too small, and their mode of life, their manners, and their faith, are too far apart from those of the United States to admit of their exercising any influence. The few Chinese terms used in conversation and by good authors, have all come to us through the English, and it is only due to our more frequent and more direct intercourse with China, if these words are in more general use here than abroad. Thus we say perhaps more frequently than our English cousins that a thing is *first-chop*, using the Canton-jargon of the Anglo-Chinese, which employs *first-chop* instead of our American *first-rate*. *Joss-houses* with ample supplies of *joss-sticks* are now quite common in San Francisco and other parts of California, where Buddhism and

Chinese paganism are better represented than even the Greek Church. They consist, however, as yet mostly of small, insignificant buildings, no real temple having yet been erected. It need not be added that the word *Joss* is not a Chinese term, but only a corruption of the Spanish word *Dios*, which is made to stand generically for any kind of god.

The word *Kootoo*, or *Kotow*, Chinese bowing, is in like manner very familiar to American ears, and largely used by a certain class of writers like N. P. Willis, in their fondness for peculiar, odd-sounding words. It is, moreover, generally misapplied, being used to convey the idea of flattery rather than of grave courtesy, which it originally denotes. Thus the New York *Tribune* says of the American citizen: "Consequently he has *kootooed* and salaamed before every travelling scribbler or story-monger, fearful that he would be dismissed by them to the dunce's stool for some solecism in manner or pronunciation." (February 2, 1871.)

Perhaps the most familiar of Chinese words to all Americans is the famous *Ginseng*, a plant so called from the two Chinese words *gen-seng*, "first of plants," on account of the high appreciation in which it is held by the citizens of the Flowery Empire for its medicinal virtues. The herb (Panax quinquefolium) is found all over the North, and for many years its root formed a most valuable article of exportation, besides being largely consumed at home. Its name, being thus continually used, has suffered the common fate of such popularity, and has been curtailed for the sake of brevity. *Sang* became the familiar term for the valuable herb, and in Virginia and North Carolina, where the trade was especially flourishing, men and women would go a *sanging*, as they called the process of gathering the plant. Hence the name of *Sang* Run, in the State of Maryland, and of the *sanging* ground near the villages where ginseng used to be found in abundance.

The Chinese have given a new meaning to the term *Company*, which promises, so far, to become an Americanism. A San Francisco paper explains the meaning, when it informs its readers that "There are no Chinese beggars, for nearly all who come over belong to one of the five great *Companies*. Each of these has a building and acts in all respects as a benevolent institution. The word of their merchants is perfectly reliable." (*Bulletin*, Jan. 13,

1869.) In like manner the word *punk*, originally meaning "rotten wood," and applied mainly to the pithy substance found in dead pine-trees, and sought for by boys because it gives out a phosphorescent light when rubbed, has obtained a new use in Chinese hands. It represents now the material of which so-called *joss-sticks* are made, as well as the sticks themselves. "A Chinese lady of rank in San Francisco walks attended by three maids of honor, bearing lighted sticks of *punk* highly perfumed. Her face is painted with a reckless disregard of expense and her hair is saturated with oil. Running through the knot at the back of her hair is an iron dumb-bell; on her head, gracefully waving in the wind, is a flower, which, from the fertilizing effect oil is said to have, is judged indigenous. Her short highly-colored silk dress is beautifully embroidered, and her feet are encased in the customary canoe-shaped sandals." (*Sacramento* paper, 1870.)

"From 1852–1870, nine thousand Chinese emigrants arrived in San Francisco, and there are probably seventy-five thousand in round numbers in the United States at present. In the South they have proved as satisfactory as in the North, and it is probable that another year will see their employment in manufactories and plantations widely extended." (Frank H. Norton, *Our Labor System*, 1871.)

Of the contemptuous and injudicious manner in which the poor Chinaman is treated in the Western States, the following resolutions actually offered—but not passed—in the Legislature of Oregon, in 1870, may give an example: "Be it enacted by the Legislative Assembly of the State of Oregon:—Section 1. No Chinaman shall be allowed to die in this State, until he has paid $10 for a new pair of boots, with which to kick the bucket.—Section 2. Any Chinaman dying under this act shall be buried six feet under ground.—Section 3. Any Chinaman who attempts to dig up another Chinaman's bones, shall first procure a license from the Secretary of State, for which he shall pay $4.—Section 4. Any dead Chinaman, who attempts to dig up his own bones, without giving due notice to the Secretary of State, shall be fined $100."

III.

The Great West.

THE GREAT WEST.

"There is pleasure in the sight of a glebe which has never been broken."
Walter Savage Landor.

THE New England States have a dialect of their own, by far the most fully developed and the most characteristic of all the varieties of English spoken in America. It represents alike the effect which climate has upon the organs of speech in their favorite sounds—the nasal twang and the violent curtailment of words,—and the direction given to the choice of terms and the arrangement of sentences, by their favorite occupations and their leading lines of thought. But the Great West has impressed the stamp of its own life even more forcibly upon the speech of its sons. Everything is on such a gigantic scale there that the vast proportions with which the mind becomes familiar, beget unconsciously a love of hyperbole, which in its turn invites irresistibly to humor. Life is an unceasing fury of activity there, and hence speech also is racy with life and vigor; all is new there to those who come from older countries or crowded cities, and hence new words are continually coined, and old ones receive new meanings; nature is fresh and young there, and hence the poetic feeling is excited, and speech assumes unconsciously the rhythm and the elevation of poetry.

The language of Western men has been called high-flown, overwrought, grandiloquent—it may be so, but it is so only as a fair representation of the Western world, which God created on a large scale, and which in its turn grows faster, works harder, achieves more than any other land on earth has ever done. Nor must it be forgotten that the West has no severe critic to correct abuses, no court and no polite society to taboo equivocal words, no classic writers to impart good taste and train the ear to a love of gentle words and flowing verse. Speech, there, is free as the air of heaven, and moves with the impulsive energy of independent youth, conscious of matchless strength, and acknowledging no master in word or deed. It is an intensified, strangely impulsive language, just as the life's blood of the whole West throbs with faster pulse, and courses with fuller vigor through all its veins. There is no greater difference between the stately style of Milton and the dashing, reckless lines of Swinburne, than between the formal, almost pedantic echo of Johnsonian rhythm in Hawthorne's work, and the free and easy verses of Brett Harte. Hence, New England has wit, and what can be more caustic than Lowell's deservedly famous political squibs? But the West has humor, golden humor, full of poetry, dramatizing dry facts into flesh and blood, but abounding in charity and good-will to all men.

So it is with their sounds, that come full and hearty from broad chests, breathing freely the pure air that sweeps down from Rocky Mountains unhampered, across broad prairies, over a whole continent. Words are as abundant as food, and expressions grow in force and extent alike, till they sound extravagant to the more economical son of the East. Speech is bold, rejecting laws and rules, making one and the same word answer many purposes, and utterly scouting the euphemistic shifts of a sickly delicacy. If it becomes vulgar—and it will become so, as the sweetest milk turns sour when the thunder rolls on high—the vulgarism is still what J. R. Lowell so happily calls "poetry in the egg." Its slang, also, is as luxurious as the weeds among the rich grasses, but at least it is home-made, and smells of the breath of the prairie or the blood of the Indian, and is not imported from abroad or made in the bar-room and betting-ring.

Hence the student of English finds in the West a rich harvest of new words, of old words made to answer new purposes, often in the most surprising way, and of phrases full of poetical feeling, such as could only arise amid scenes of great beauty, matchless energy, and sublime danger.

There is a strange perfume about the very term *backwoods*, which brings up before our mind's eye at a glance the forest of primeval trees, those formidable giants which the *pioneer* has to encounter at once with his trusty weapon, the axe. For it used to mean—real *backwoods* no longer exist—the partially cleared woods on the Western frontiers of the Union, which were considered the *back* of the new country, as the coast of the Atlantic constituted the *front*. The *East* having been first settled, and having furnished, to a large extent, the sinews and brains for the new States, was naturally looked upon as the representative of wealth, intelligence, and progress; and the *back country* became, from that time onward, synonymous not only with regions lying back, *i. e.*, to the West of the seaboard States, but also with a state of civilization somewhat behindhand. The nearest districts became early known—and are still very generally designated—as the *Up Country*, a term, when used as an adjective, peculiar to this continent. It is employed all along the seaboard from Maine to the Gulf of Mexico, with varying meaning, but always suggesting a certain inferiority to the seaboard population, because up the rivers, toward the headwaters, population becomes scarce, civilization imperfect, and schools few in number. Of this peculiar belt, J. R. Lowell says: "I imagined to myself such an *up country* man as I had often seen at anti-Slavery meetings, capable of district-school English, but always instinctively falling back into the national stronghold of his homely dialect, when heated to the point of self-forgetfulness" (*Preface to Biglow Papers*), and the result of this imagination was one of the most brilliant creations of American genius. In Southern States the inhabitant of the large seaboard city speaks with ineffable contempt of the *up country people*, and formerly used to rank them with Crackers and mean whites, till they made their political influence felt at elections.

The *back country* seems to have receded back from the Eastern States as civilization advanced Westward, but it still retains the character of a region, where lands and living are cheap, and people simple and unsophisticated. An opulent family, reduced in circumstances, and compelled to remove to a place where social claims were unknown and wants few and easily supplied, is thus alluded to in the *Letters from the South:* "The family were in great distress, though we helped them on a little to get to the *back country*, where I hear they are doing pretty well again" (p. 127); and even in more recent days a traveller in the West says: "The hotel was a roomy log-house, commanding a view of the *back country*, a prairie stretching off into the western horizon." (*Putnam's Magazine*, November, 1868.)

In common language the one is the *East*, the other the *West*. The former, now more generally known as the *Eastern* or the *New England States*, still maintains its strong hold on the minds of men by many a familiar phrase. *Down East*, in the American's mind, is instinctively placed near the low coast of the Atlantic, as it were down toward the sea, and at the same time toward the East, *i. e.*, in Yankeedom. The emigrant, who has gone to the West, still remembers with delight how they spoke and how they did *Down East*, and looks forward, after years of hard labor and painful longing, to his visit to the *East*, while the Virginian, to the second and third generation even, speaks only of going *home*, and still more frequently of *coming in*, when he proposes to visit his relatives in the Old Dominion. The *Down Easter* is well known by his language, his costume, and his peculiar habits, smiled at for many an odd trick he has, but respected for his many solid virtues. With him all that is done in his native land is right, and hence what he admires, he simply calls *about East*. "There was not a Yankee," says J. R. Lowell, when Horace Mann regretted we had not the French word "s'orienter" in our speech, "whose problem has not always been to find out what is *about East*." The enthusiastic (though quaintly exaggerated) love borne the *East* by its sons is, perhaps, most strikingly illustrated in Major Jack Downing's oft-repeated phrase: "I'd go *East* of sunrise any day to see sich a place." (*Letters*, p. 21.)

The *West*, on the other hand, is as vast and undefined as the East is limited in extent, and sharply marked in character. First, it meant all the gigantic states, which were the generous gift of Old Virginia, lying between the *Mother of States*, as she was hence called, and the great river. Thus Edward Everett could say in his great speech: "The enterprising, ingenious and indomitable North, the substantial and magnificent Central States, the great balance-wheel of the system; the youthful, rapidly expanding, and almost boundless *West*, the ardent, genial, and hospitable South—I have traversed them all." (*Speech*, July 5, 1858.) At that time, the regions on the other side of the Mississippi were the *Far West* of America, and beyond it rose the impassable barrier of the Rocky Mountains. Since the snow-capped range has been traversed by a railway, and new, powerful States have arisen on its Western side, facing the ocean, there is no longer a West to the Union, the great Pacific itself bounding it toward the setting sun. Still, the States west of the Mississippi continue to be called the West, and what is done *Out West* is as frequently mentioned as what happens *Down East* or *Down South*.

It is to this *West* that annually thousands and thousands of brave young men, daring families, and numerous whole companies carry the banner of civilization and the power of the great republic. For the American worships the Almighty Dollar, but, with few exceptions, only in order to gratify his first and greatest of all desires—to live in independence on his own land, and to enjoy in freedom the fruit of his labor under his own vine and his own fig-tree. The millionaire and the porter, the proud descendant of the grim Puritan or the rollicking Cavalier and the immigrant fresh from the Emerald Isle or Imperial Germany, all share this desire. A Stewart buys half a county in the neighborhood of New York and lays out a city, a Greeley purchases vast tracts in the purified South, and almost every capitalist invests a part of his fortune in real estate, hoping, from the steadily rising value of all lands in the republic, a large and certain return for his capital. The poor man drifts almost instinctively to the West to seek a home, where land can be had for the asking. The skillful mechanic and the frugal servant, the bankrupt merchant and the adventurous youth, all press in one unceasing current Westward, to build up their own fortunes and with them the power and prosperity of new States.

The government of the United States has ever been blameably lavish in the disposal of the matchless domain which Providence has placed in its hands. First offering the rich lands of the Continent, without respect for the rightful owner, to all who would take it—for cultivation or speculation alike—they now squander them recklessly in so-called *grants* to railroad companies and *rings* of every kind. This is a continuation of the original process, by which the British Crown granted lands to all who were willing to *plant* colonies in the New World. Hence the latter were called *plantations* in the North as well as in the South; in New England the first settlers were known as *planters*, and distinguished select families as *Old Planters*, while the oldest and most dignified member of each family was honored with the title of *Landlord.* The same occurred in the South. "The *adventurers,*" says Captain John Smith, "which raised the stock to begin and supply the *Plantation,* were about seventy gentlemen, some merchants, some handicraftsmen, some adventuring great summes, some small, as their estate and affection served. The *planters* are not servants to the *adventurers* here, but have onely counceles of direction from them, but no injunctions or commands, and all masters of families are partners in land and whatsoever, setting their labours against the stocke, till certain years be expired for division." (*Virginia,* I. p. 251.)

Very early in the history of this country a distinction arose between these enterprising but more or less speculating *planters,* and the actual *farmers* of the land. "The yeomanry of Massachusetts," we are told, "hold their heads high to this day, as their fathers spoke proudly of themselves as *farmers.* They were the men who penetrated the forest in all directions, sat down beside the streams, and ploughed up such level tracts as they found open to the sunshine; so that in a few years the Salem *Farmers* rose to much prosperity. The *Farmers* formed an order by themselves—not by having peculiar institutions, but through the dignity ascribed to agriculture." (*Salem Witchcraft,* Charles W. Upham.) On these plantations they had certain officers, whose power seems to have been very nearly paramount, and whose name still survives in the *selectmen* of our day. They were, and still are, the chosen magistrates, in whose hand is placed the management of all communal affairs, and juries are still selected, and not indiscriminately chosen as elsewhere, according to their discretion. N. Hawthorne speaks of them as they were in 1635 thus: "Woe to the youth or maiden who did but dream of a dance! The *selectman* nodded to the constable, and there sat the light reprobate in the stocks, or if he danced, it was round the whipping-post, which might be termed the Puritan Maypole." (*May Pole of Merry Mount.*)

It was one of these plantations, the *Plantation of York,* which in 1641 became, under the name of *Georgiana,* the first city in the United States, in the legal sense of that word, a charter being solemnly granted for that purpose by Sir Fernando Georges.

At a later period, a broad distinction arose between a Southern *plantation*, on which tobacco, sugar, and rice were *planted*, and a Northern *farm*, where the cereals were *raised*, a contrast which was still further heightened by the slave labor engaged in planting, while free labor was used in farming. That in Newfoundland a person engaged in fishing should also be designated as a *planter*, is probably to be ascribed to the habit of speaking of a sea "harvest," and comparing the two branches of industry with each other. A *planter* in Western rivers means, on the other hand, nothing more than a tree or a piece of timber firmly planted in the bed of the river by the force of its current—one of the most formidable obstructions to navigation.

From these early settlements on land purchased or taken by force from the rightful owners, bold explorers and restless adventurers set out still farther westward in search of richer lands, larger domains, or simply ampler space for hunting. At times these movements were favored by the great *Proprietaries*, as the grantees of large districts were often called, such as the famous *Patroons* of New York, and the noble Fairfaxes of Virginia. The former, retaining down to the present day their Dutch title, derived their rights from the Dutch government, which wisely and liberally granted large privileges and the title of *Patroons of New Netherland*, to all who should, in a given term, plant colonies of fifty souls on the banks of some navigable river. Hence W. Irving, in his inimitable portrait of the days of New Amsterdam, speaks of a man who "indulged in magnificent dreams of foreign conquests and great *patroonships* in the wilderness." These large possessions and exclusive privileges proved, however, soon obnoxious to the republican tendencies of the Union, and led to much trouble, as in the case of the famous *Manor* of Rensselaerwyck, founded by Kiliaen Van Rensselaer—who never came out himself to look after his magnificent domain. In the course of a few generations the number of tenants on this grant had risen to more than a hundred thousand souls, who chafed under the burden of paying ground-rent, where everybody else held his land in fee-simple. Hence resulted refusals to pay dues, combinations among the aggrieved, and the so-called *Anti-Rent Troubles*, sometimes settled by compromises and judicial decisions, and at other times leading to actual strife, as in the *Helderberg War*, which could be quelled only by the presence of a large armed force.

In Virginia similar grants were made by the British Government, as in the famous Patent issued to Lord Fairfax by King James I. In those days the colony was known as a land of *necks* or strips of land between large rivers, and men naturally preferred settling upon the rivers in order to possess themselves of rich bottom lands for farming purposes and also to be near to a convenience for market. Of these necks there were four, and one of them, known as the *Northern Neck*, and containing all the lands between the headwaters of the Rappahannock and Potomac to Chesapeake Bay, was granted to the Lord Fairfax of those days. Early in the spring of 1736 an agent came over to lay out the manor and grant portions in fee-simple to tenants; another Lord Fairfax came then himself, established his headquarters at Greenway Court, in the heart of his magnificent domain, living there in princely, though somewhat barbarous, splendor, and rapidly *settling up*, as it began to be called, his lands, even in the famous Valley of Virginia. But here, also, the rights of favored monopolists were found incompatible with the levelling tendencies of growing republicanism, and the descendants of the proud nobleman now own an empty title, but not an acre of their former possessions.

With the exception of such special grants and patents, to which subsequently titles obtained from the Spanish government were added, all land in the Union was held by the Government in trust for the people and sold or awarded in fee-simple. The process was as informal as the peculiar circumstances required. Early settlers would go out in the wilderness and simply take possession of a tract of land by chopping a piece out of a tree here and there and thus marking all within these lines as their own. This was called to *blaze* a tree, whether it served to secure ownership or merely to mark a path through a forest. The term is derived from the French *blason*, which already in Shakespeare's time was shortened into *blazen*:

> "Thyself thou *blazen'st*
> In these two princely boys,"

and was in like manner applied to the *blaze*, or white spot, in the forehead of a horse, as all these marks bore some likeness to the *blason* or armorial bearing of the Normans. "Many settlers did not content themselves," as we are told by S. Kercheval in his

History of the Valley of Virginia, "with marking the trees at the usual height with the initials of their name, but climbed up the large beech-trees and cut the letters in the bark, often forty feet from the ground. To enable them to identify these trees at a future period, they made marks on other trees around them as *references.*" Thus the new-comer, having selected his future home, would, in the language of the day, "at once *blaze out* on the tree-trunks his pre-emption claim," and henceforth he was secured in his property. As soon as he had built a cabin and raised a crop, however small, the occupant was, by the laws of Virginia—then stretching from the Atlantic to the Mississippi—entitled to four hundred acres and a pre-emption right to a thousand more adjoining, to be secured by a simple *land-office* warrant. There was, however, at an early period an inferior kind of land-title, called *tomahawk-right,* which was made by deadening a few trees near the head of a spring and marking the bark of some one or more with the initials of the *improver.* The *deadening* consisted in cutting with a tomahawk, then as familiar to the white man as to the Indian, a narrow ring round the trunk of a tree; this scarcely noticeable injury, nevertheless, goes to the life of the tree, and the latter dies, not suddenly, but slowly, by the lingering process of starvation. Such *tomahawk-rights* did not exist in law, but were, nevertheless, often bought and sold. (S. Kercheval, *History of Virginia,* p. 214.)

Rights thus acquired secure at least what is called a *claim,* although the *squatter* also insists upon a like right. In the poetical language of the West, a man who unceremoniously took possession of new land was said to *squat* down on it; and "hence is derived," says W. Irving, "the appellation of *squatters,* so odious to all great land-holders, and which is given to those enterprising worthies who seize upon land first and take their chance to make good their title to it afterward." In the wild frontier portions of the West the "enlightened citizen" has naturally a very indistinct idea of *meum* and *tuum,* and when once fairly settled, he objects very earnestly to being removed. Hence laws and writs of ejectment avail very little. Nor is the evil apparently diminished by an increase of population; for in the year 1870 official reports stated that not less than seven or eight thousand *squatters,* with a town of over a thousand inhabitants, had been found on an

Indian reservation in a central State of the Union, and a requisition was made for a large military force to restore the lands to the rightful owners. It was, of course, found inexpedient to employ troops for such a purpose, and the squatters carried the day. They were not so successful, however, in the days of the so-called *squatter sovereignty*, a word coined by General Cass, and representing the right of the inhabitants of newly-formed territories, mostly squatters, to determine for themselves what laws and institutions they would prefer. The question was of great importance when Slavery still counted among the latter, but Thomas H. Benton of Missouri already stigmatized the claim as "an insane demagogical idea, as unreasonable as for a child to be independent of its father."

The almost boundless liberty with which Americans use the words of their language, was recently shown with painful impressiveness. In a fearful catastrophe which happened in February, 1871, on the Hudson River railway, all the horrors of the disaster and all the grief for the numerous victims could not efface the deep impression made by the useless but noble heroism of the engine-driver, who refused to escape, stood by his engine, and plunged with it into the abyss. It appeared afterward that in discussing with railroadmen the expediency of jumping from an engine in time of danger, Doc. Simmons had once said, "I would *squat!*" He meant he would *squat* down behind the boiler and trust to going through with whatever might obstruct the road, after having pulled the brakes, reversed the engine, and opened the throttle.

The word *claim* has of late obtained special importance in the gold *diggings* of California and the adjoining States. The former now means not only the small piece of ground claimed by the individual discoverer, but quite as often a whole mining locality, and men speak therefore of "riding out to the *claim*, and seeing if part of it was for sale," while the rough miner will say: "You see, stranger, gold is sure to come out 'er that theer *claim*, but the old proprietor wasn't of much account. He was green, and let the boys about here *jump* him." (F. B. Harte, *The Luck of Roaring Camp*, p. 134.) The word *diggings* is one of the fallacious class that look as new as California—it is as old as Jeremy Taylor! He says: "Let us not project long designs, crafty plots, and *dig-*

gings so deep" (*Holy Dying*, I., 2, 3), evidently using metaphorically a term familiar in practice to all his readers. Its free use, however, is unmistakeably American; for now it denotes, in cant language at least, any special locality or region, and often even a dwelling or home. "Were you ever before in these *diggings*?" is a phrase very often heard in the West upon first introduction, and in J. C. Neal's *Charcoal Sketches* we read: "Look here, Ned, I reckon it's about time we should go to our *diggings*; I am dead beat, and you don't look as if you could keep out of bed much longer." (II., 119.) The miner of California and Nevada has been known, in times of a *rush*, to speak of a place where he could stand leaning against a stout post, as his *diggings* for the night. Generally, however, he means in good earnest the piece of land on which he hopes to reach *bed-rock*, where gold is found in quantities, and to *strike it very rich*, as soon as he comes to the *pay-streak*, that is, the lode or vein which is to repay him for all his labors. To ascertain his probable success, he *prospects*, digging here a few inches and there several feet into the ground, throwing himself down and examining closely every particle of sand or soil, or actually sinking a shaft. But the immigrant in search of land is also said to be *prospecting*, and the term has, since the late Civil War, been applied with new force to the numerous Northerners who have gone to the South in search of cheap farms and promising plantations. A report of the new Greeley Colony in Colorado says: "Much cedar was found in the gulches, with plums and grapes at intervals; an exploring party is soon to *prospect* the country from Greeley down to Julesburg." (New York *Tribune*, January 19, 1871.) "We noticed quite a number of gentlemen yesterday on the Central train; they were substantial farmers from Pennsylvania, come to *prospect* in our State. We bid them welcome." (Richmond *Dispatch*, May 21, 1866.)

Claim and digging alike are subject to the danger of being *jumped*. For there is a kind of poetic justice in the fact, that where one bold man was defiant enough to take land without regard to law or ownership, another equally bold man was apt to be near at hand, and ready suddenly to seize, or, in the energetic language of the West, to *jump* upon the land on which the other had *squatted*. If they did not respect the right of the first occupant, they were naturally as little disposed to dread the law, and to abstain from ousting a lawful owner; hence they became known as *Claim-jumpers*. Many a poor settler, unable to meet the rough brutality of such men, has had to abandon his homestead and leave it in the hands of the robber; but many a *jumper* has also been tried by a self-constituted jury of neighbors, and graced a tree on the land he would fain have made his own by the mere right of the stronger.

All the land not owned by special grant or actual occupancy is apt to be called *Wild Land* in Western parlance. This is laid out by the agents of the Government Land Office into regular divisions based upon parallels of longitude and latitude, which, when surveyed by the official *land-surveyor*, are laid out into square *sections* of 640 acres each, which are again subdivided into *quarter-sections*. This process, which takes place before the land is offered for sale, is called by the barbarous term of *sectionizing*, and hence the laws of Texas of 1828 say: "So much of the vacant land of the republic shall be surveyed and *sectionized*, as will be sufficient to satisfy all claims" (*B*). It is peculiar to this term, *section*, that it is one of the few words which have come back to the Eastern States from the West; for now political discussion abounds in references to *sectional* interests, as well as to party feelings, and the growing division of the Union into four great *sections*, the North and the South, the Central and the Pacific States, is looked upon with grave apprehensions by all friends of the Republic. "*Sectionalism*," says Mr. Seward in one of his ablest state-papers, "has received a final blow," but the prophet who predicted the final battle in the late Civil War so often and so peremptorily, years before it took place, may well be doubted in this prediction also. Nor is the word *section* used in political language only; it has become a common term for any parcel of land, and of a once wealthy family it is thus said: "In the progress of a half-century they had sold, bit by bit, their *section* of land, which, kept intact, would have proved a fortune." (*Lippincott's Mag.*, March, 1871, p. 289.)

The *section* as well as the *claim*, and, in fact, every tract of land *blazed* by a claimant, are defined by what the surveyors call the *corners*, marks on the tree between which the boundary lines are run. "Most of the lands belonging to Washington in the West," says a biographer of Colonel Crawford, "were located by Colonel

Crawford. We have frequently heard the old surveyors along the Ohio say that they often met with his *corners.*"

The only lands exempted from legitimate occupancy by new settler are the so-called *reservations,* made for the Indians and certain purposes of public importance, such as schools, etc. Most of these are now near or beyond the Mississippi; a few, however, exist still in the very heart of some of the oldest States; this will explain the following article, contained in the New York *Tribune* of Jan. 23d, 1871: "The resolutions of the New York Legislature, relative to the Alleghany-*Reservation* of the Seneca Indians, in Cattarauga County of that State, were presented in the House to-day. It appears that white settlers occupy lands in the town of Salamanca (!), within the *reservation,* without any title. It is now asked that a title be given these squatters, and that a new treaty be made with the Senecas, by which they may be compensated for the lands of which they have been deprived." In the New Dominion the corresponding term, is *Reserves,* as, *e. g.*, the *Clergy Reserves.*

All other lands can be obtained by *entering* them, and hence the Rev. Peter Cartwright, the famous backwoods preacher, says in his quaint and graphic autobiography: "Money was very scarce—I saw little of it, at least—and what little there was, was generally kept to *enter lands,* when Congress should order a sale." (p. 254.) This is done sometimes by the so-called *Prëemption* Law of 1841, which, however, only regulates a process known now for more than a hundred years. It was enacted "to appropriate the proceeds of the public lands and to grant *prëemption rights,*" and granted 160 acres of land to every head of a family, to a widow, and to any man over twenty-one, who will file his intention in a land-office, to enter upon and improve the land, and to reside thereon long enough to make it his residence. He pays for it one dollar and a quarter per acre in gold or a land-warrant, and the fees. The "man over twenty-one"—who must, however, swear that he does not own 320 acres of land elsewhere—includes, by law of Congress, spinsters, provided they will build a house on their prëemption, and there reside, although, poor lonely things, we fear there are not many that will accept the offer. In the year 1870, however, a damsel of twenty-two thus entered a quarter-section, erected a log-cabin, fenced in two fields, and by her own labor earned enough to support herself and a younger brother at school. The process is so familiar to the American mind, that the word *prëempt* has been created for the purpose, and the Western hunter says to his visitor, when he invites him to lie down in his tent: "Well, I guess, if you can find a corner that is not *prëempted*, you may spread your shavings there" (W. G. Simms, *Wigwam*), while Fitzhugh Ludlow writes poetically: "Any man, who has married a lovely blonde, and sees himself reflected in two blue eyes, has thereby made himself sure of heaven, having *prëempted* two quarter-sections of it, and settled on the same."

The law has its adversaries, and Horace Greeley fiercely says: "In our judgment the whole *Prëemption* system is a nuisance and a nursery of fraud, which Congress ought promptly to abolish, the Homestead Law answering every good purpose, which Preemption was intended to subserve." (New York *Tribune*, February 1, 1871.) This *Homestead* Act of 1862 gives to every citizen, native or naturalized, a home-farm of 160 acres, which is not liable for debts contracted prior to the issuing of the patent. The condition is five years' residence, before the *General Land Office* in Washington will issue the patent, and this is too irksome for American impatience. Hence we find it stated that "so rapid is the appreciation in value of land, when once settled on, that it is found by experience that from forty to fifty per cent. of those who *enter* their lands under the provisions of the *Homestead* Law, expecting to receive a gratuitous deed, prefer to pay for the land, rather than to wait the five years necessary for the consummation of their titles." (Our Public Lands, *Harper's Monthly*, January, 1871.)

To soldiers who are by Congress rewarded with a grant of land for their services during the war, and to companies entitled, by Act of Congress, to alternate sections on the line of a proposed railway, *land warrants* are issued, which entitle them to *locate* or take up a tract of new or uncultivated land. This word—not known to English dictionaries before Todd—is so suggestive and useful that, though long resisted in England, it has forced its way into the best authors. It has, however, never attained abroad to the same latitude of meaning which it enjoys here. The first meaning, no doubt, was simply to define a particular spot, but it is a genuine Americanism in the sense of selecting, surveying, and settling the bounds of a tract of land, in which it is now universally used. The great freedom with which technical terms are made to serve countless other purposes besides the first, has led to some very quaint uses of the ugly word. In Gilliam's *Travels in Mexico*, we find that "the mate, having *located* himself opposite to me at table, began to expostulate with me," where it is substituted for the good English word "seated;" whilst even W. Irving half ironically says: "At the tail of these vehicles would stalk a crew of long-limbed, lank-sided varlets, with axes on their shoulders and packs on their backs, resolutely bent on *locating* themselves, as they term it, and improving the country." The Annual Report of the Secretary of the Navy in 1871, contains perhaps the most daring use made of the word, when it says: "A vessel has been sent out to *locate* a harbor on the Pacific." Perfectly natural, on the other hand, is the technical use made of the word by the Methodists, whose ministry is essentially itinerant, while a small number of ministers are *located, i. e.*, appointed to remain at a place permanently, whenever old age, infirmity, or special purposes to be fulfilled make such an arrangement desirable. "I never asked to be *located*," said the venerable Peter Cartwright, "till I had served the Lord for half a century in the ministry." The Methodist Church speaks, therefore, also of the *location* of certain ministers, as surveyors and land-jobbers refer to a place as a good or bad *location*. The danger of admitting such words is, however, shown by the fact that quite a number of words have been offered for public approbation, made after the pattern of *locate*, since this has forced its way into public use. Making a speech has been called to *orate;* bestowing a grant to *donate;* approving of anything to *approbate;* and good authors have tried their best to secure them a footing in American English. An excellent magazine, the *Overland Monthly* of San Francisco, speaks of a "young but inactive half Mexican, who smiled at Caleb's infrequent jokes and listened a good deal when Caleb *orated* and the boss of the schooner slept." (Oct., 1870, p. 335.) A Law enacted by the General Court of Massachusetts prohibits a certain class of men "being *approbated* to keep an inn or public house," (Nov. 17, 1851), and the religious newspapers of the Union vie with each other in long lists of men who have *donated* large sums to the churches and colleges of each denomination. Even to *mission-*

ate has been attempted, and led to another barbarism, which is found thus introduced in *Putnam's Magazine* for Nov. 1870: "the Missionary work held Lota by a double claim; it was a birthright and a vocation—that is, as far as other people can *vocate* for a girl."

When the immigrant looks around for the kind of land he would choose, he is generally guided by a preference for districts where neighbors of his own race or faith are found; but if he cannot indulge in this luxury and must go to what is called *New Lands,* he has to be careful in his selection. Fraudulent companies will sell him *water-lots,* tempting enough on the map, but found, upon reaching the place, to be swamp or morass, and half the year under water, while rascally *runners* will sell him tickets to the State of Virginia, which he may reach in twenty-four hours, instead of the town of Virginia, in Nevada, which he cannot reach under several days. He will, of course, prefer prairie-land, if it is to be had, and look out for an *island,* a grove in the midst of the prairie, or at least for a *bottom,* as the richest land is apt to be called. Their vicinity is generally marked by those high banks with precipitous fronts, which, from their resemblance to bold promontories jutting out into the sea, are in America called *Bluffs.* The term was already thus used by Lewis and Clark in their famous Travels to the Pacific Ocean (1804), and the bold, steep front is thus referred to by W. Irving: "The mountains were broken and precipitous, with huge *bluffs,* projecting from among the forests." (*Astoria,* II., p. 270.)

The *bottoms* are sometimes known as *Intervales,* when they consist of alluvial land enriched by overflowing rivers. (Belknap, *History of New Hampshire,* 1792.) They are generally meadows, smooth and level, covered with rich grass and interspersed with clumps of trees, having a creek or a river running through them. Often they rise in beautiful terraces along the valleys of Western rivers, and "are locally and perhaps accurately known as *river-bottoms;* they were the favorite site of the Indian mound-builders." (H. R. Schoolcraft.) The word is, of course, as old as Shakespeare, who speaks of "a sheepcote down in the neighboring *bottom,*" but the application is peculiar to the West. In his search after these he will have to cross many a *divide,* as hunters and settlers are fond of calling the long, low ridge, which acts as a watershed, sending the waters from the slopes in opposite directions. "At last we came to the *divide*," says Mr. Ruxton in his *Explorations*, "and here we stood by the side of the waters that flowed on till they mingled with those of the Pacific" (II., p. 11), and F. B. Harte says: "Then up and dusted out of South Hornitos across the long *Divide*." Here, near the upper part of rivers, the new settler may meet with *flats*, which Bailey explains as "low, flat grounds, exposed to inundation," but which in America rather mean the alluvial lands close to a river, or very large shoals in the river itself. Here, as well as on larger prairies in the South and Southwest, he will also meet with those curious little hills and valleys which appear on wet prairies, where the heavy annual rains wash the ground, cracked in all directions by severe drought, into regular, hexagonal hillocks and valleys a foot or two deep. These are called *hogwallows*, from the resemblance they bear to soft places where hogs have been rooting and wallowing. "These *hogwallows* are formations of pitfalls and elevations, hollows and hillocks of every variety, which succeed each other like cups and saucers turned topsy-turvy," says a traveller in Texas. "They relieve the monotony of an unbroken level." (*Putnam's Magazine*, February, 1854.) The *Alkali Flats* are now crossed by the Pacific Railroad, but had already become familiar to the reading public as the "old bugbear of the Great American Desert." They are still found to be unpleasant to the traveller by their annoying dust, but appear quite fertile and abounding in agricultural capacities. "The *alkali* consists of gypsum and the chlorite of potassium and soda—a combination in the highest degree fertilizing, when not in too great excess in the soil. Wherever irrigation is practicable, the vegetable productions of this region attain a size and perfection utterly unknown in the Eastern States. The organic elements, moreover, are not capable of being exhausted, as they ascend by evaporation from the underlying deposits. It is more than probable that Artesian wells may yet convert a large part of the arid wastes of Wyoming, Nebraska, and Montana into fertile fields, and open new resources to the hand of enterprise." (Western paper, 1870.)

In other *bottoms*, again, where limestone formations prevail, *sinkholes* are a characteristic feature; this is the name here given to low depressions in the surface, from which powerful springs suddenly gush forth, often forming large ponds on the spot, or flowing off in the shape of broad rivers, capable of turning mills and driving machinery. The *hammocks* of the South, on the contrary, are gentle hills of peculiar shape, most common in Florida and the adjoining States. "The ground which a Southern hunter best likes is that which is designated by the name of *hammocks*, undulating hills, covered with oak, hickory, and magnolia, threaded by a good number of roads and cattle-paths." (P. H. Gosse, *Letters from Alabama*, p. 267.)

In former years it was a matter of first importance for the immigrant to choose his new home in a *free-soil* territory, as the lands were called which were owned by the United States, and as yet free from slavery; since the emancipation the term has, of course, lost all its meaning, and is important only for its historical associations, which date back to 1848. In the States where the battle between *Freesoilism* and *Slavery* was most fiercely fought, as on the bloody ground of Kansas, the name still survives with the passionate recollections of days of terrible and relentless warfare.

If the settler find no home on an *island* or in a *cove* of a prairie, he prefers, especially if he be a German, a *Knob*, as from its resemblance to a knob (Germ. Knopf), any rising is called in the West. Originally the term was limited to certain peculiar, round hills in Kentucky, the result of the material, soft sandstone and shale, having been worn by wind and rain into a rounded form. The word, however, soon extended over the whole West, and a hilly region is very apt to be called a *knobby* country in Western parlance. Should he build his cabin in a forest, he will soon find his neighborhood designated as a *neck of the woods*, that being the name applied to any settlement made in the well-wooded parts of the Southwest especially. Should he dread the *bush*, he may choose one of those beautiful forest glades called *oak openings* and found in the Northwest. They are undulating plains, covered with close, rich turf, and dotted all over with groups of fine, well-grown oaks, looking for all the world like a well-kept English park, though apparently endless. It is they which have given Mr. Cooper a title for one of his latest, though not most interesting novels. They are very different from the *Barrens*, with which they are occasionally confounded. The latter are elevated plains of poor soil, either having no growth on them at all, or barely supporting stunted trees unfit for timber. Such waste lands abounded formerly in some of the Eastern and Central States even, but were soon brought under subjection to man by energy and ingenuity. Thus, when Ohio began to be settled, some seventy years ago, most of its territory outside of the rich valleys of the two Miamis, the Scioto and Maumee, was in *barrens*. No foliage could be discovered for hundreds of miles, save on the banks of a few streams; fires having consumed, year after year, the young trees which Nature had tried to bring forth there. To-day, land in that State, everywhere, has advanced a hundred-fold, and yet one of the most profitable uses to which it has been put, and can now be put, is the growth of timber! It is from a vast stretch of such barren lands in the Northeastern corner of America, known as the *Barren Grounds*, that a variety of reindeer (Tarandus arcticus), derives its melancholy name of *Barren Ground Reindeer*, which it bears also if found in Greenland and other localities.

Where trees at all succeed in growing on such neglected lands, the latter are known as *Oak-barrens*, straggling forests of poor, stunted oak-trees, which show by their low growth and gnarled branches the poverty of the soil on which they have to subsist. The Southern States have, in like manner, *Pine Barrens*, which are still more desolate tracts, covered with light, loose sand, and bearing a wretched growth of pine-trees; the people who live here are called *sand-hillers*, and belong, generally, to the lowest class of whites. In the Southeastern States a similar kind of land, but of somewhat better quality, is known as the *Piny Woods*, the resort of poor people who cannot obtain lands elsewhere; while in the North and Northwest the superb tracts of noble woodland, which furnish the finest timber in the country, are called *Pineries*. Here loggers and lumberers in great numbers congregate during the season, and a recent traveller says admiringly: "No stimulants stronger than tobacco and tea are allowed in the *pineries;* the woods had not yet received enough of the influence of civilization to admit a bar within their hallowed shade." (*Minnesota Pineries.*) Thus hill and dale, valley and prairie, are open to the new-comer, and soon filled; the mountain alone seems to be shunned, as the rains wash all the rich soil from top and slope into the valleys below, and thus it has come about that the words, *Over the Mountain*, are frequently used with a very sad meaning. "He had a great deal to say of the palmy days of Virginia," is said of an old gentleman in J. P. Kennedy's delightful book, *Swallow Barn*, "and the generation which in his time had been broken up, or, what in his conception was equivalent, had gone *over the mountain*." *Sloughs* also are dreaded, whether they are pronounced like "ploughs" or *slews*, since the sudden changes in the American climate, with alternate fierce droughts and terrific rains, make them dangerous neighbors to cultivated lands. California boasts of them in proportions which would elsewhere entitle them to a very different name, for we are told: "Passing from this summit, on a gently descending grade, we reached the *slough* which joins the upper lakes with Tulare. This *slough* is about forty miles long and two hundred feet wide. The stream has a sluggish current to the Northwest, and both of its banks, for nearly the whole distance, are covered with tules." (*Overland Monthly*, Aug., 1870, p. 155.) *Wild Lands* are by no means undesirable, as they are merely so called because not yet cultivated; they embrace all the land yet unappropriated, though generally meaning the forest, by preference. It is different with the *Bad Lands*, which border the Missouri for about twenty miles, and were called, by the first French settlers, *Mauvaises Terres*, because, as a recent explorer, General Cuvier Grover, says, "they present a picture of Nature's wild deformities, a masterpiece in its way, characterized by a total absence of anything which could, by any possibility, give pleasure to the eye, or gratification to the mind, by any associations of utility. . . Colonnades and detached pillars of partially cemented sand, capped by huge globes of light-brownish sandstone, tower up from the steep sides of the bluffs to the height of a hundred feet or more."

Even where the land looks fair and a stream promises comfort in times of drought, care has to be taken to ascertain if the latter is not, perhaps, in summer a *Dry Creek*. This apparent anomaly is very common in the Southern and Western parts of the Union, and rivers, which have no other name but that of *Dry Creek*, are found in nearly every State from Virginia to California. It is from these frequent periods of suffering that the two words *drought* and *dry* are so much used in the country. The former retains very frequently the sound, and quite as often the manner of writing, which were once considered orthodox in England; *drouth*, as even the verb to *dry*, reverts at times to its ancient form to *drow*. Sandys says : "As torrents in the *drowth* of summer fail" (*B.*), and Milton uses *drouth* as he writes *highth*. "The great but only drawback to these fertile regions (in Virginia) is the almost certainty of a *drouth* during the summer months." (Richmond *Enquirer*, August 7, 1866.) As the drying up of a river makes more or less efficiently an end to all agricultural operations, the verb *to dry up* has become synonymous with to make an end. "*Dry up!*" is a familiar slang term for the more considerate Hush! "*Dry up!*—no, I won't *dry up*. I'll have my rights, if I die for 'em, and I'll stand here until I get's 'em, too; so you had better *dry up* yourself." (*The Student's Speaker*, P. Reeves, p. 79.) In another sense it is used thus: "As the long dry summer withered to its roots, the school term of Red Gulch—to use a local euphuism—*dried up* also." (F. B. Harte, *Luck of Roaring Camp*, p. 82.)

Even the larger rivers, the Ohio, Mississippi, and Missouri, it is well known, are entirely dependent on these variations in the supply they receive from their tributaries, which are often very quaintly called simple *drains*. W. Irving thus spoke of them: "About noon, the travellers reached the *drains* and brooks that formed the head-waters of the river." (*Astoria*, II., p. 254.) The consequence is that navigation is often impeded for months, as far as vessels of some draught are concerned. This leads to a peculiar phenomenon, called the *June Rise* of the Missouri, when suddenly all the head-waters come roaring and rushing down from the high table-lands, from which the great river springs, and swell it to its full height. The rise begins generally in June, though it is sometimes delayed till July, and of course affects the Mississippi also. It is called "A name of grandeur, of joy, of activity, of wealth, of harvests to all the dwellers on the stream, from the Gulf of Mexico to the far-off British line in the Northwest." (*Putnam's Magazine*, July, 1868.)

The immigrant may be able to reach his new home in the Far West by railroad, thanks to the vast number of roads that intersect each other in all the States; but he may also have to travel many a weary day across desert plains and hostile regions. In that case he learns to *camp out,* that is, to spend the night in the open air on the plain or under some sheltering tree; his resting-place is always called his *camp,* even when he is quite alone; when several families join, they are apt to have a *half-faced camp,* which is on one side open to emit free egress to cattle and horses. It is the *corral* of the Southwest. "Here we suddenly came upon a *half-faced camp,* filled with women and children; all the men having gone out hunting, as the whole party had been without meat for several days, and their store of flour had given out long ago." (*Scenes in the Far West.*)

Occasionally *caravans* are formed, such as have been in use in the Western States from the earliest times, placed under the guidance of some experienced frontier's-man, who regulates all their movements, waking them up in the morning by his fierce *Lave! Lave!* (from the French *levez-vous*), or roars his stentorian *Catch up! Catch up!* to rouse all and make them ready for an early start. The same startling cry is heard when a prairie-fire threatens the camp, and all hands are called upon to *fight the fire,* which is generally done by burning a wide circle around the camp to meet the approach of the flames, unless the actual beating out of the fire by the men can be attempted with success.

Wherever he may select his future home, what he now wants is his *lot*—a word, which in its application to land is unknown to England, and universal in the United States. It has its rise in an old Puritan custom. The first settlers in the sea-board plantations of New England owned the extensive salt-marshes, which produce such excellent salt hay, in common, and every man cut and cocked, saved and salted as much of the latter as he wanted. When, however, the population increased and the first simplicity and harmony were no longer maintained, it was agreed to divide out these commons in equal parts to all the families. This was done after the biblical precedent in the election of a twelfth apostle, by *lot,* and the choice of every man, as his name was drawn and he became entitled to select his piece of land, was known as *his lot.* The firm belief of the Puritans in a special providence watching over them and their interests made them continually resort to this manner of distributing lands or other articles of value, held heretofore in common, and thus the term *lots* soon came to designate any great quantity. Cotton Mather in his *Magnalia* speaks, hence, grimly of the "*great lot* of evil spirits" that possessed a poor woman in Beverley, and "stories of *lots upon lots* killed by old hunters in the White Mountains are heard to this day at the fire-side," says N. S. Dodge.

But it was not among the Puritans only that the custom prevailed. The proud cavaliers of Virginia were as familiar with it as their rivals. In an old deed preserved at Flower de Hundred, once a magnificent plantation on the banks of James River, we read: "Two paper *lotts* were made and framed, in one of which was written these words, viz.,—the uppermost part, in the other was written—the lowermost part, and being so made and framed were put into the croune of a hatt, and be it further remembered that the said Ro. Lucy and his wife Sarah, and said Phil. Limbney and Elizabeth his wife, did then and there for themselves and their heirs mutually agree and consent each to the other, that said *lotts* so put into the croune of a hatt should one after another be drawne out by a younge child then present, and given by the said child one *lott* to said Lucy and his wife, and one *lott* to said Limbney and his wife." In 1768 Colonel Byrd laid off the towns of Shockoe and Rocky Ridge, the former now the city of Richmond, the capital of Virginia, the latter the town of Manchester. In the paper of that day, the *Gazette,* it is stated that they were sold by lottery, the *lots* numbered, and mills, ferries, and water-powers placed among the prizes.

By such means the term *lot* obtained general currency in the new country, and every generation added new applications of its meaning. Not only every kind of lands, from a *town-lot* in the city of New York to a *water-lot* on a prairie in the Far West, was thus designated, but the banker in Wall-street has his nice *lot of stocks* for sale, and the drover in Missouri his *lot of hogs,* and one man has *lots of friends,* while another is troubled with *lots of debts.* But the extreme freedom with which such terms are used here is, perhaps, best shown in the fact that even cemeteries are laid out in *lots,* and quite recently a case came up in a New York court of a man who had mortgaged such a piece of property, in which the judge held "that though the conveyance of a *cemetery-lot* was allowable, it was not within the range of financial or commercial affairs to suppose that a man designed to transfer the remains of any member of his family, even conditionally, which must be the effect of the mortgage of his *cemetery-lot*." (New York *Herald*, Feb. 2, 1871.)

The same word has given rise to the odd phrase *across lots*, which denotes a short cut in sparsely-built-up towns, where men can save distances by crossing over vacant lots. Brigham Young, the apostle and chief of the Mormons, is reported to have said that he "would send his enemies to h—— *across lots*," and J. C. Neal makes one of his heroes sneeringly say to a grumbler: "You would cut *across the lot* like a streak of lightning, if you had a chance." (*Charcoal Sketches*, I., 35.) J. R. Lowell improves upon it by making it an epithet in the line—

> "To all the mos' *across lot* ways of preachin' an' convertin'."
> (*Biglow Papers*, II., p. 100.)

Having secured his *lot* by one of the various processes mentioned before, of squatting, pre-empting or entering, the new-comer begins by staking out the ground for his cabin and kitchen-garden. The *stake* plays, hence, a prominent part in the Western man's speech, and serves to characterize his movements. Where he settles, there he *stakes* or *sticks his stakes*. "Indications were favorable," says an immigrant in Nevada, "so we *staked* a body of ground along the main creek, built cabins, organized a company, and went to work to open our claim." (*Southern Magazine*, January, 1871, p. 90.) "It is a rugged, arduous task," we are told by one who has tried it, "to make a Christian home out of either dense forest or bleak prairie to this day. He who *sticks his stake* far enough from settlements to find homestead-land, must not expect to see a brickyard, blacksmith's shop, sawmill, gristmill, wheelwright, etc., in his neighborhood very soon." (New York *Tribune*, March 1, 1871.) Does he desire to change, he *moves his stakes*. Thus the son of a lawless squatter says coolly of his father: "In fact, he built the shanty for the purpose, lest titles should fall through and we'd have to get up and *move stakes* farther down." (F. B. Harte, *Luck of Roaring Camp*, p. 211.) The more energetic form—and by far the older—is to *pull up stakes*, the earliest use of which occurs in a MS. letter (owned by the Hon. J. Hammond Trumbull, of Connecticut), written by Thomas Lechford, a London attorney, who lived three or fou years in Boston, and went home to publish "News from Engla in 1642. In 1640 he writes to an English correspondent: "I am loth to hear of a stay (in New England), but am *plucking up stakes* with as much speed as I may." Since that early day the expression has held its own in American speech, a vivid reminiscence of Western life, and always forcible by its touch of the picturesque.

Next begins his warfare against the trees, which he unfortunately must needs regard as his enemies, since they stand upon the ground he wants for his home and live upon the soil which he intends shall support himself and his family. Unconscious of the day, not so very far off, when he will begin diligently to plant trees on the very spot from which he now uproots them so painfully, he sets to work with his trusty axe to *belt* or *girdle* them. In either case he cuts a circular incision through the bark and alburnum of the tree, and leaves it cruelly to die of starvation; the following year, or as soon as it is dead and dry, he sets it on fire, and thus saves himself the trouble of cutting it down. The process is also often called *barking* in the Northwest, while *belting* is the Southern favorite. The forest itself is known to the West only as *timber;* people used to "go to the *timber* for shelter" against invading Indians, and even now, "men take to the *timber* as soon as the Comanches are seen at a distance." (*Official Army Report*, Jan. 11, 1871.) Hence is the term *Cross Timbers* derived, the name of two remarkable tracts, about twenty miles wide and several hundred miles long, which extend in a southern direction between Red River and Trinity River, and are covered with lofty trees in so singularly regular lines and cross lines, that they suggest irresistibly the idea of having been planted at some remote time by the hand of man. It is not without a poetical instinct that the skeleton of a whale is known as his *timbers;* hence a visitor to Nantucket says: "In several places we passed the *timbers* of a whale, the remains of two that had been harpooned off Napeague during the previous winter." (*Putnam's Mag.*, Sept. 1870.) These same trees, which the new settler looks upon with such bitterness of feeling, have often to serve him as refuge in time of need, and early settlers, as well as hunters of our day, have made us familiar with the term *to tree one's self,* in the sense of taking refuge behind a tree. Already, in S. Kercheval's *History of Virginia,* we read of one of the most famous heroes in early

Indian warfare, that "Wetzel, as before, loaded his gun and stopped several times during this chase; when he did so, the Indians always *treed* themselves." (p. 201.) At other times, *to tree* means simply to kill, and the same remarkable frontier's-man said, when asked on his return, "What luck?" "Not much," he replied, "I *treed* one Indian, but the other got away." (p. 202.) When animals *take to a tree*, the hunter is said to have *treed* them, and considers himself already sure of victory and capture. This has again given rise to the cant phrase of *barking up the wrong tree*, which originated, of course, in the dog's losing the scent, or the hunter's mistaking the tree in which he thinks his game has taken refuge, and thus leading to vain efforts to dislodge the latter by barking or shooting. But it has made its way, like many such picturesque expressions, into the language of daily life, and the man who vainly tries to accomplish a thing for which he is not qualified, or addresses himself to the wrong person for assistance, is said to *bark up the wrong tree*. "You didn't really go to old Bullion," said a politician to an office-seeker, "Why, he has no influence there, I can tell you. You *barked up the wrong tree* there, my friend, and you deserve to fail." (Richmond *Enquirer*, September 8, 1835.)

When the tree is at last cut down, there remains the hideous, obstinate *stump*, yielding neither to axe nor to fire, but only to powerful machines, especially adapted to the purpose of uprooting stumps. A hindrance to the settler and a blemish in the landscape, the *stump* has but one usefulness, and that is, the moderate elevation which it affords to a public speaker, who can here take his stand and overlook the crowd which he wishes to address. Thus the West has endowed our speech with a whole number of terms derived from this backwoods custom of using the broad, level top of a stump as a rostrum. The man who wishes to canvass a district for Congress or any other office obtained by popular election, is said to *take the stump*, whether he virtually ascends it in the woods and addresses settlers and squatters, or speaks in Faneuil Hall to select audiences of Boston men. He *stumps it* from the time of his nomination till the day of election, and if he proves able to engage the attention of his hearers, or, still better, to persuade, coax, or cheat them into supporting his claims against all rivals, he is said to be an excellent *stump-speaker*. Such a man was Thomas Corwin, of Ohio, the very "prince of campaign orators," as his friends called him, and he gave his testimony in favor of the curious fact that the same speech is repeated over and over again on such occasions. "A man," he says, "who should attempt a fresh speech on every *stump*, would never have any speech worth listening to." "The *stump*-orator," asserts a foreign expert, "is by no means unknown in the British islands, and the phrase might perhaps be adopted, in default of a better, to describe the kind of speech which tickles the fancy or pleases the judgment of a miscellaneous crowd. The late Daniel O'Connell, Daniel Whittle Harvey, and Thomas Wakley, the coroner, were excellent specimens of the *stump-orator*, while in our day Mr. John Bright may lay claim to a similar distinction, though it must be admitted that Mr. Bright is a true orator, and speaks to the refined as effectively as to the roughs." (*Blackwood*, October, 1867.) The addresses made on such occasions are, of course, *stump-speeches*, and of these it is simply said in Dow's *Sermons:* "When you see a politician extra full of patriotism and stuffed with *stump-speeches*, you may take it for granted he wants office, either for himself or for some particular friend."

Two expressions are connected with the term *stump*, which have no reference to politics. The verb *to stump* is often used in the sense of "to puzzle," or to "nonplus;" a disputant says, *e. g.*, "But I will *stump* you yet, doctor" (*Scribner's Monthly*, February, 1871), meaning: I will confound and silence you yet; but this word has nothing to do with trees; it is the intensified form of: to *stub*, as people say, not less frequently, they *stumped* than they *stubbed* their toe. The American, however, at once makes the term useful in every possible capacity, and speaks of a conclusive argument, or a difficult problem: "That is a *stumper*." Nor is the slang phrase: "To whip the devil around the *stump*," to be traced very clearly to the backwoods. It denotes the indirect manner in which something is done, as when men will not pay a militia fine, for conscience' sake, and leave its value to be taken by the officer, a method formerly often resorted to by Quakers in England, in regard to taxes they considered unjust.

"*I whipped the devil round the stump*,
And gave a cut at every jump,"

is a Pennsylvania ditty quoted by Professor S. S. Haldeman, who also states that so many Quakers *whipped the devil round the stump* during the late Civil War, by supporting the government morally, but stoutly refusing to share its perils, that one of their faith assured him "the war had killed Quakerism in Pennsylvania."

A short stump of a tree, or any other large and irregular piece of wood, is called here, as in some of the Southern shires of England, a *chunk,* probably a corruption of the Old English *chump.* In the West people apply it to anything short and thick, and speak, hence, of "a tolerable *chunk* of a pony." In the South the word is even used as a verb, and where there are no stones, as on the alluvial soil which borders on the Mississippi, they say: "I'll *chunk* him," meaning that they will throw a clod of earth or a stick of wood at some animal. It is not impossible that the odd expletive *kerchunk* may be in some vague way associated with the noise caused by the sudden falling of a *chunk.* "I looked up," says W. S. Mayo, "and there I saw a young catamount, scrambling up the little, old oak; he stretched himself out on the branch and looked down upon me so kind of impudent, I thought I'd take a crack at him; I raised my rifle and down he came, *ker-chunk,* right on the edge of the precipice." (*Kaloolah,* p. 27.) The term, however, is a very Proteus, and appears under a great variety of forms, as in J. R. Lowell's line—

> "They
> Would all come down, *kerswosh!* ez tho' the dam broke in a river."
> (*Biglow Papers,* II., p. 104.)

As soon as the trees are cut down or burnt, the settler's place obtains the name of *clearing,* irrespective as yet of cabin or field being visible or not. Hence J. R. Lowell quotes: "A man speaking to me once of a very rocky *clearing,* said: Stones got a pretty heavy mortgage on that." Then the land has to be *broken up*—not simply *broken,* as in England, perhaps because of the much greater difficulty in breaking new land—and put into corn. Speaking of the Scandinavians who flock in large numbers to Wisconsin, a writer says: "The essential difference between Norsk and Nomad was quickly seen. The rude huts or excavations in the sides of the bluffs, which often gave temporary shelter to the first Norwegian settlers, were soon exchanged for comfortable log houses, and wide spaces of *breaking* showed the tender green of young wheat." (*Putnam's Magazine*, May, 1867.) Besides his crop of corn or wheat, the new settler is sure to have, as soon as possible, his *truck-patch*, which often is made to hold his cereals also. The word came, of course, from England, but at first only with the meaning of "small produce, cloth or the like," in which sense it is still used mainly in England. Thus R. B. Beverley says: "In 1654 they sent out two vessels, which made good profit of Indian *truck*, which they bought for things of much inferior value, and then returned." (*History of Virginia*, p. 2.) Captain John Smith also relates that his men "went to trade with the Indians of Chickahominie, where making showe of a great quantitie of *trucke* they had, which the Salvages perceiving, partly for revenge of some friends, partly for their *trucke*, one of them with an English peece shot Killingbeck." (*Virginia*, II., p. 36.) In later days, the small produce of gardens was called *truck* in contradistinction to the larger crops raised in open fields, and then the word *truckpatch* came into use. S. Kercheval says: "Every family, besides a little garden for a few vegetables which they cultivated, had another small enclosure containing from half an acre to one acre, which they called a *truckpatch*, and in which they raised corn for roasting ears, pumpkins, and squashes, beans, and potatoes." (*History of Virginia*, p. 218.) The term continues to be constantly used, and is now frequently applied in the Atlantic States to market gardens: "Northern men, familiar with the best manner of raising early vegetables and with the wants of Northern markets, have come and established *truckpatches* in our neighborhood, which have given them, in some instances, a handsome fortune in a few years." (Norfolk (Virginia) *Argus*, August 11, 1870.) In the South the phrase *poor truck* is applied to any inferior person or thing, as expressive of great contempt.

The settler's next purpose is to build himself a *log cabin*, a rough house of unhewn logs, notched together at the corners, while the interstices are filled up with clay so as to make them nearly air-tight. If more is attempted, a regular frame is prepared, and the setting up of the timbers is called a *raising*. None of these operations are, of course, within the power of the new-comer unaided, and hence the custom of *bees*, which prevails throughout the whole country. "You see, sir," said a squatter, in explanation of the term, "when you wants to get anything done right away in a hurry, all at oncet like, whether it's flax beatin' or apple parin', or corn huskin', and the neighbors all around come and help work, that's a *bee*—and a *buildin' bee* or a *raisin' bee* is, when they want to set up the frame or the logs of a house or barn." (*Life in the Far West*, p. 257.) The duty of neighbors to help on such occasions is so universally acknowledged that in olden times "a man, who refused assistance, was called *Lawrence*, and when it came to his turn to call upon the neighbors, the idler felt his punishment in their refusal to attend his calls." (S. Kercheval, *History of Virginia*, p. 249.) Another method, characteristic of those early days, and still occurring in many parts of the West, is the *hating out*. "The punishment," says the same author, "for idleness, lying, dishonesty, and ill-fame generally, was that of *hating* the offender *out*, as they expressed it. It commonly resulted in the reformation or banishment of the person against whom it was directed. If a man did not do his share of the public service, he was *hated out* as a coward." A *chopping-bee* is thus described: "Once a *clearing* was attempted on a large scale. It was for the site of a public institution. The inhabitants within a radius of ten miles were invited to a *chopping-bee*. Each one brought his axe and day's provisions. No spirituous liquors were allowed. The work was ordered by an elected marshal of the day. The front rank of trees, ten rods in width, were chopped partially through on either side; then the succeeding ones in like manner, for a space of perhaps twenty rods. Then the last rank were felled simultaneously by the united force, when with a crash increasing to a thundering volume, it bore down on the next, till all lay prostrate. And thus for three days did this volunteer war against the forest progress." (*Western Magazine*, January, 1868.) "*Raising-bees*," says W. Irving, "were also frequent, when houses sprang up at the wagging of the fiddlestick, as the walls of Thebes sprang up of yore to the sound of the lyre of Amphion." (Knickerbocker, *Hist. of New York*.) A *stone-bee*, on the other hand, is arranged to clear a field of stones, and a *husking-bee* to strip the husks from the ample supply of corn to be stored away for the winter—scenes of much merriment, and adorned by many a quaint old custom, as when the finder of a red ear is rewarded with the privilege of a kiss all around, or, if of the fairer sex, is expected to make her election of some one to be honored. Hence Longfellow's allusion to it as an Indian usage, that

> "Whene'er some lucky maiden
> Found a red ear in the husking,
> Found a maize ear, red as blood is,
> Mushka! cried they all together,
> Mushka! you shall have a sweetheart,
> You shall have a handsome husband!"
> (*Song of Hiawatha*, Canto XIII.)

In the West, and in the East where old traditions have not yet come to be sneered at, these *bees* are the main festive occasions for young people, where, amid social laugh and gossip, fingers and tongues work together. Every excuse is, therefore, readily seized upon, and even *quilting-bees* are popular, where the young women sit around a large frame to make a patchwork quilt, and where the young backwoodsmen find their way in, on some pretence, perhaps only on the Irishman's principle, that

> "If all the young women was ducks in the water,
> It's thin the young men would jump in and swim ater."

The good people are willing to come from twenty and thirty miles around to enjoy the frolic, and when the husking or quilting is over, when the house is built or the harvest reaped, the woodpile is raised or the apples are pared, and the nuts gathered in, then the welcome "fiddle" is heard, and, in spite of hard work and late hours, dancing begins and continues till morning. Occasionally, after the peculiar manner of the pilgrim fathers, religious exercises are quaintly mixed up with the work and the fun. A corn-husking is announced, or a raising-bee is arranged, and the neighbors from far and near assemble, each bringing his provisions in a basket. From the latter feature these pic-nics derive their names of *Basket-Meetings*. The most determined polemical divine, however, could hardly venture upon a long harangue there, since the minds are bent upon hard work and gay frolic, the means of escape are open on all sides, and the tempting baskets at any moment ready to allure the audience away from every other thought. The worst harm would be some such mistake as that which befell a young man from Down East, who related the matter thus:

"There was a *corn-husking*, and I went along with Sal Stebbins. There was all the gals and boys sittin' around, and I got sot down so near Sal Babit that I'll be darned if I didn't kiss her afore I knowed what I was about!" (*Traits of American Humor*, p. 134.) The idea of these assemblies is not new, only the poetical name of *Bee.* They are known in the Old Country under various names, as, *e. g.*, the "Clay Daubin" of Cumberland, where the neighbors and friends of a newly-married couple assemble, and do not separate till they have erected them a rough cottage.

The *log-house* thus erected is, of course, of the utmost simplicity. The Rev. Mr. Cartwright describes the interior of one, which was neither better nor worse than the majority of those he found some fifty years ago in the now flourishing State of Illinois: "We had a hewed *puncheon* for a table, with four holes in it, and four straight sticks put in for legs; forks were driven down between the puncheons for bedsteads; cross-poles and side-poles put in these forks, and *clapboards* laid crosswise for cords." (*Autobiography*, p. 252.) The Hon. Mr. Duncan, of Ohio, described a better kind of *log-cabin*, in a speech on the floor of Congress, thus: "A house made of round logs, one story high, of dimensions suited to the size or number of the family who were to inhabit it, and sometimes with reference to an increase, a puncheon floor, a live back loft, and a clapboard roof. The industry of the matron and her daughters was displayed by the thick folds of linsey frocks, pants, and hunting-shirts that behung its walls; its top was underhung with strings of dried pumpkins." The *puncheon* mentioned in these descriptions is a split log, the upper side of which has been more or less carefully smoothed with a broadaxe or a hatchet; raised upon rough logs or sleepers, they furnish the floor of most backwoods dwellings. The *clapboards*, known in England as thin boards prepared to serve for staves, are here thin, narrow boards, three to four feet long, and thinner on one edge than on the other, which serve to cover the sides and roofs of houses, being placed so as to overlap each other. It has been suggested by a distinguished etymologist, Dr. Elwyn of Philadelphia, that the term may be originally derived from the thin, smooth boards called a *clapboard*, on which in the North of England a kind of bread is *clapped*, which, hence, is known as *clapbread.* The fireplace consists ordinarily of a few stones roughly arranged for the purpose, and the chimney of stout sticks of wood, about two feet long, which are piled up crosswise, and cemented with clay or mud. They are, hence, called *stick-chimneys*, and, strangely enough, answer their purpose so well, that they are common all over the West and the South.

In the next place the new settler makes a fence around his lot, which is to serve as a garden; commonly a few gigantic roots of trees, dragged near each other, or slim young pine-trees, with some brushwood between, have to suffice. When leisure admits it, rails are split, and laid in endless zigzag, which makes the famous *Virginia-fence*, or *snake-fence*, immensely costly in all districts where wood is not absolutely a cumbrance to the ground, requiring much land, always out of repair, and harboring in its corners boundless supplies of weeds and much vermin. The capital invested in these snake-fences is said to be larger than the value of all stocks and agricultural implements. Hence the *fence* plays a prominent part in the life of the Western man, who watches it jealously, as a single break and a night's inroad of his pigs may cost him a year's labor, and who loves to sit on it, surveying all that is his own. As a man thus situated can with equal ease jump down on either side, the phrase to be or to sit *on the fence*, has become a common cant phrase for persons—in politics mainly—who prefer what J. R. Lowell pointedly calls

> "A kind o' hangin' round an' *settin' on the fence*,
> Till Providence pinted how to jump an' save the most expense."
> (*Biglow Papers*, II., p. 97.)

These are emphatically men who, as he elsewhere states, "believe, with Dædalus, the primal *sitter-on-the-fence*, that *medium tenere tutissimum*." (*Biglow Papers*, II., p. 85.) Politicians of this class are said to be *fence-men*, being cautious men, who wait to see on which side victory will declare itself, to jump down and join in the shouts of the winning party; and while the state of uncertainty lasts, they are said to be *fence-riding*. "We shall give the minority no such right to impede legislation," said the leader of the Republican Party on the floor of Congress, during an angry debate on Reconstruction; "this question is one of clear right and wrong, and there can be no *fence-riding*, when the rights of four millions of men are at stake." (*Congressional Globe*, July 17, 1868.)

Although these fences are, in most cases, made of rails, to *ride on the fence* is a very different thing from *riding on a rail.* The latter is a savage punishment inflicted by an excited crowd upon a person who has exasperated a community by some real or fancied outrage; he is placed upon the sharp edge of a rail, and thus borne on the shoulders of his enemies through the village to a pond or even worse fate. For it is frequently only the beginning of a punishment often reported as significative of American inventive barbarity—the *Tarring and Feathering* of offenders. So far from being born here, it is an old English custom, brought to us by the early settlers from their own home. For in the Laws and Ordinances appointed by King Richard I., for the use of his navy, occurs this sentence as quoted in Hakluyt (p. 7): "Item, a thiefe or a felon that hath stolen, being lawfully convicted, shall have his head shorne, and boyling pitch powred over his head, and feathers or downe strawed upon the same, whereby he may be knowen; and so at the first landing-place they shall come to, there to be cast up." The lesson has been well learnt, the practice religiously bequeathed from generation to generation, and employed in Boston, as Grose tells us, on persons suspected or convicted of loyalty, as it is, in our day, carried out on the banks of the Mississippi on criminals whom the law cannot or will not punish.

His cabin built and his lot fenced in, the new settler provides for his simple costume, which must be adapted to his driving a plough or hunting a "painter." He has, of course, his *blanket,* though in his case that term has a very different meaning from that which it bears when applied to an Indian; in the latter case, the *blanket* represents the Redskins' general costume, which may be more than a blanket or not, and hence the familiar expression in the West, used with regard to a half-breed, that "his father or his mother *wore the blanket.*" As the island of Mackinaw was formerly the chief post at which the Indians received their annual payments and presents, part of which, it was stipulated, always consisted of a superior kind of blanket, these became known as Mackinaw blankets or *Mackinaws* simply. Being very thick and well made, they served not only for beds but also for overcoats, which were called *Blanket-Coats,* and really answered their purpose admirably. A *hunting-shirt,* made of deerskin, and abundantly covered with fringes and stitchings, is his only costume for all seasons and weathers, and so eminently serviceable as to be adopted by hunters, explorers, and travellers generally. The great Pathfinder, General Fremont, was hence addressed by the poet Whittier, when he was the candidate of the Anti-Slavery Party for President, in these words:

"Rise up, Fremont! and go before!
The hour must have its man;
Put on the *hunting-shirt* once more,
And lead in Freedom's van!"

As flannel is his constant wear, the backwoodsman calls the rarely-used linen which chance may supply to him, and which he vows is a *nuisance* beyond all others, the *biled shirt*, because—forsooth!—it is occasionally boiled to be washed. The more usual material is a checkered fabric of cotton, and goes by the simple name of *checks*, to which John Hay alludes, when he sings—

"How Jimmy Bludsoe pass'd in his *checks*
The night of the Prairie Belle."
(*Jim Bludsoe of the Prairie Belle.*)

His nether garments are his *leggins*—but rarely called leggings—as even W. Irving wrote the word after the Scotch manner: "Others had *leggins* and moccasins of deerskin, and buffalo robes, which they threw gracefully over their shoulders." (*Astoria*, I., p. 239.) Every other article of dress, worn by men in and near towns, comes under the general designation of *store-clothes*, and is out of the reach of the backwoodsman.

Two articles only he must have of prime quality, for on these depends his life: his axe and his rifle. Without the former he cannot cut down trees and plant his corn; without the latter he would starve, or soon succumb to his hereditary foe, the Indian. He hardly knows a greater disappointment than if axe and handle part company, and thus he has given to our speech the favorite phrase: to go or to *fly off the handle*. If a fair lady loses her temper, or, worst of all, if she breaks the tender promise, she is said to *fly off the handle*, and the disappointment is as serious to the unlucky lover as a lost axe to many a settler. The meaning is occasionally extended beyond that misfortune even, as when the New York *Home Journal* speaks of a poor man having succeeded to a large fortune from a distant relative, who "*went off the handle* in England rather unexpectedly." (July 21, 1867.)

His rifle is, of course, more important still, and hence he loves it with almost tender affection, cleans and caresses it, and speaks of it as a *shooting-iron* with that loving affection which makes many a husband speak of the partner of his joys and his sorrows as the "old woman." The more recent revolver, now quite common in the West, is, on the other hand, his *five* or *six shooter*, according to the number of barrels. The rifle, also, has given to our speech quite a number of terms and phrases full of picturesque meaning. The ramrod is familiarly called the *gunstick*, and the whole represented as *lock, stock, and barrel*, which has come to mean the whole of any important matter. "Take it all in all," said Colonel Benton, "it is rotten; *lock, stock, and barrel*, there is not an inch of it sound, and the sooner we throw it away the better it will be for the nation." (*Speech on the National Bank.*) Good sight, and hence also fair judgment in using the *sights* on the rifle, are, of course, indispensable in hunting as in warfare; hence the *hind-sight* or notch in the hind-sight of a rifle plays a prominent part in hunters' language, referring now to the rump of an animal, and then to the main argument of an adversary. Watchful observation is, in like manner, represented by the *trigger-eye*, and a servant engaged to take care of a well-bred dog, "promised to *keep his trigger-eye* on the dog." (J. C. Neal, *Charcoal Sketches*, II., p. 17.) The old-fashioned *priming*, now no longer known as in the days when breech-loaders, and even percussion locks, were still myths to the backwoodsmen, never was considered of much importance when compared with powder and ball, and thus the term came, colloquially, to stand for anything of small import or value. David Crockett thus said of ferocious foreign animals, that they "would be no part of a *priming* to a grizzly bear of the Rocky Mountains." (*Adventures, B.*) In taking slowly and cautiously aim, as is the custom of the Western hunter, he gradually raises the front-sight, which resembles a bead, to a level with the hind-sight, and the moment the two are in a line he fires; hence, to *draw a bead*, is with him equivalent to firing, and from him the expression has made its way into colloquial speech. The man who attacks another in his speech is said to have *drawn a bead* upon him. Two misfortunes may happen to the hunter at this critical moment: if his rifle be of the old pattern, the powder in the pan may flash and the rifle refuse to go off, or he may have forgotten to put the latter at full cock. In the first case the flash in the pan produces a noise, known as a *fizzle*, such as wet powder also is apt to cause. From the hunter's failure, the word has become a general term for any ridiculous failure after a great effort. "The speech was as complete a *fizzle*," said the *National Intelligencer*, "as has ever disgraced Congress, and we hope sincerely the honorable member from Massachusetts will take the lesson to heart." (Dec. 8, 1851.) When recently a lottery was attempted in Virginia for a most laudable purpose, and the unfitness of some managers, and the dishonesty of others, brought about a complete failure, "the enterprise *fizzled out* in the most contemptible manner." (Richmond *Enquirer*, Sept. 17, 1866.) Hence failures in College recitations also are called *fizzles*. (Hall's *College Words*.) The other phrase, to *go off half-cock*, is as familiar to English sportsmen as to our hunters. The term *plumb centre*, on the contrary, is a peculiar Western phrase, expressive of a crack shot at a shooting match, though commonly the word is written *plum* only. "*Plum* in the centre each barrel shoots." (*Life in the Far West*, p. 119.) The fact that on such occasions the improvised target is not unfrequently a rag hung on a bush, has suggested to Professor S. S. Haldeman the thought that the familiar phrase: "That takes *the rag off the bush*," may have likewise originated from the use of the rifle in the hands of the Western hunter. The latter is not apt to miss; the man who can *bark a squirrel*, that is, as Mr. Audubon told us first, strike with a rifle-ball the bark on the lower side of a branch on which the little animal sits, with such accuracy that the concussion kills it without inflicting the slightest injury, that man never wastes his powder nor attempts the impossible.

And yet to the inexperienced eye of the European traveller, he seems to attempt an apparent impossibility, when he offers to *crease* a deer or other animal. An expert Western hunter shoots a deer—and often a horse that is to be captured—so cautiously, that the ball cuts the skin at a precise spot of the upper part of the neck; the animal instantly drops down and remains quiet and stunned, till it is secured,: "We were so much afraid of shooting the pet of our kind hostess that we enjoined François to *crease* the pretty little deer; for we stood sadly in need of food, the terrible fire having left not a single trace of a human habitation for twenty miles all around us." (*Travels in Canada*, 1863.) If the unlucky deer had been the lady's pet, the hunter would have admitted, in his graphic language, that he had *fired into the wrong flock*—a phrase which has also crept into every-day language, and denotes a mistake made in the effort to overcome an adversary. "When Mr. Saulsbury rose and called the Speaker's attention to the alleged blunder in the Secretary's report, his own friends jumped up in great excitement and pulled him down; he soon found out that he had *fired into the wrong flock*." (New York *Herald*, November 9, 1858.)

Among the favorite amusements of Western men are naturally trials of skill with their rifles. At one time they will bet on *driving the nail*. A stout nail is driven into a post about half-way up to the head; the riflemen then stand at a great distance and fire at the nail, the object being to hit the nail so truly on the head with the ball as to drive it home. At another time it is *threading the needle*; an auger-hole is pierced through the centre of an upright board, just large enough to allow the ball to pass, and the best marksman is he who drives his ball through without enlarging the opening!

The new settler who ventures into new lands, soon finds that he has disagreeable neighbors. The Indians, whether on their own hunting-grounds or on their reservations, have not all yet forgotten their old enmity against the intruders, and even in 1870 many a scalp was yet *lifted* from whites. Hence, his language is full of allusions to Indians and Indian warfare, and as the latter is nearly as old as the colonization of the land, many of these terms have become incorporated in our speech. Caution was, from the time of the first settlements, so necessary a quality among frontiersmen, and is still so requisite, however far the frontier may be removed westward, that it has given us, in connection with the national character of Northern men, an intensely American phrase. *To be a caution*, means, to be a warning, a marvel, a stupendous thing. "The way in which he pitched into them *was a caution*, I tell you," says the reporter of Mr. Wendell Phillips' speech, at a recent meeting in Worcester. "Stranger," said Tom Nye, in *California Sketches*, "look a-here, and tell me, whar did you ever see such gold? Come, now, *ain't that a caution*, I axe you?" (San Francisco *Bulletin*, August 5, 1868.) The *sign* of the Western man is, ordinarily, any evidence, seen upon the prairies or in the woods, of the appearance, whether recent or not, of animals or men. If the marks appear recent, they make what is called a *fresh sign*, if they are old, an *old sign*. "This was the place where some fresh beaver *signs* had attracted their notice." (*Life in the Far West*, p. 127.) But of all these tracks, the often almost imperceptible *Indian sign* is most anxiously looked for, and most carefully studied. To perceive them the backwoodsman says, in his high-flown language, you must *keep your eyes skinned*; "*keep your eyes skinned* for *sign*, and listen to my horn." (*American Humor*, Vol. II., *B*.) The regular footpath of the Indian, who always goes single so as to leave but one man's footsteps as *a sign*, is his *trail*; the word is as old as Hakluyt, who speaks of "many wayes *traled* by wilde beastes," but the special application is purely American. Hunters next adopted the term for their own paths through the forests, and for the track of animals, till finally it became in the West the general name for any and every kind of road. "In consequence of the abrupt sides of the cañon, which made out toward the lake, it becomes necessary to seek, at times, a *trail* within the hills." (*Overland Monthly*, Aug., 1870.) Of a lonely miner's hut we are told by F. B. Harte, that "the only outlet was a steep *trail* over the summit of a hill that faced the cabin," (*Luck of Roaring Camp*, p. 3,) for, in California the word is now in common use for road or path. Woe is the single Indian that is suddenly met, in time of warfare, by the enraged backwoodsman! He is instantly *shot*, which in this case does not, as in ordinary life, simply mean shot at, but killed. For it is, perhaps, the effect of the American's familiarity with shooting-weapons that he loves to say he *shot* a man, when he, perhaps, only wounded him slightly. F. B. Harte, therefore, speaks very carefully of "the day that French Pete and Kanaka Joe *shot* each other *to death* over the bar in the front room." (*Luck of Roaring Camp*, p. 1.) The Western man rarely uses the word, but he is quite rich in substitutes. Sometimes he prefers an English slang word, said to be derived from the fashion of rubbing out the names of friends on the slate or visiting list (*Slang Dictionary*, p. 216), with a novel and somewhat awful application: "*Rubbed out* at last, they heard him say, the words gurgling in his blood-filled throat, and opening his eyes once more, and looking upward to take a last look at the bright sun, he turned gently on his side and breathed his last." (*Life in the Far West.*) Then again he will borrow a phrase from tavern-life, where scores of debtors are chalked on doors and shutters, and *wiped out* when settled by payment more rarely than by grim Death. Its primary meaning has not yet disappeared, and a recent poem, "Dobbs his Ferry," said quaintly, in complaining of the change of old Indian names into modern, unmeaning names:

"Down there, on old Manhattan,
Where landsharks thrive and fatten,
They've *wiped out* Tubby Hook.
That famous promontory,
* * * * *
Stands, newly christened, Inwood."
(*Putnam's Magazine*, January, 1868.)

But from the hunter's lips it means nothing less than death. "If the Arrapahoes will not keep the treaty," says a recent report made to the Indian Bureau in Washington, "the settlers and traders unanimously assure us the whole tribe will be *wiped out* in another season. We look forward with some anxiety to the first appearance of grass and the renewal of hostilities." (January 17, 1871.) In California, the hunter is, perhaps, more likely to be *snuffed out*, and thus explains the origin of the phrase, "The thought that I was fired into by some stranger, who wasn't a-takin' no hand, and came near having my *light snuffed out* by some one unbeknown to me, is not a good thought to die on." (*Overland Monthly*, March, 1871, p. 285.) A very odd expression, confined, however, mainly to the mountaineers in the wilder parts of the Southwest, is quite expressive; they say they send a man *up Green River*, when they have killed him. The phrase had its origin in a once famous factory on Green River, where a superior kind of large knife was made, very popular among hunters and trappers. On the blade the words "Green River Works" were engraved, and hence the mountaineers, using the knife to despatch an adversary, literally sent his blood *up Green River*.

It is a striking illustration of the destructive power of slang that the once poetical and pious phrase *to go up* has recently been so completely mixed up with the absurd expression to go *up the spout*, as to lose its force and character. Of old, to *go up* meant to go to heaven, a meaning ludicrously illustrated by a tombstone in Dixon, Illinois, on which, above the name of the deceased, a hand pointed heavenward, and the words: *Gone up!* were added. This beautiful and expressive epitaph, once no doubt deeply touching to all who read it, would now only provoke laughter or be looked upon as blasphemous.

It is quite interesting to notice how another popular Western phrase for death—*to go under*—evidently represents in the Indian's mind, from whom it is borrowed, the same process of reasoning as in the German's mind, who uses the same word *untergehn* for perish, whether the figure be taken from the vessel, that literally goes under, or from the body that is put "under the grass," as they are apt to call it in the West, or, finally, from the Redman's simple notion of being under the knee of his conqueror—the fundamental idea remains the same. "Poor Hawkeye felt," says one of his biographers, "that his time had come, and knowing that he must *go under* sooner or later, he determined to sell his life dearly." (*Hawkeye, the Iowa Chief*, p. 210.)

If the Western man hunts by water, he is not always able to provide himself with a canoe; often he must be content with a simple *dug-out*, such as is even now frequently seen on small creeks of the South as well as the West. It is nothing more than a large log hollowed or dug out; but the skill with which the Western men and Canadian voyageurs (who call them *dug canoes*) will manage these rude boats, is astonishing. The Rev. Mr. Cartwright had, in the Far West, very often to travel by water, and says: "If by chance we got a *dug-out* or canoe to cross in ourselves and swim our horses by, it was quite a treat." (*Autobiography*, p. 486.) It is propelled by a paddle, and when well built apt to be as swift as a canoe.

In his warfare against the Indians, the frontiersman has inherited from his predecessors for many generations a term which at first looks ridiculously unlike its true meaning. The Red men he kills, he boasts of having *saved*. "I calculate, Mr. Hossifer (officer)," says an old Western trapper, "that war the most decisivest and the most sanguinariest fight you ever seen in all your born days. We boys, we up and pitched in thar, and we give the yaller bellies the most particular Hail Columby. We chawed um all up; we laid um out colder nor a wedge; we *saved* every mother's son of um—we did that thar little thing, boss." (Col. Marcy's *Army-Life on the Border.*) The origin of the term must be sought in the importance which early hunters and settlers attached to even a single load of powder and shot, at times when the former's subsistence and the latter's life depended on his rifle. Every wounded animal that escaped was a shot wasted, and the Indian, whom he had missed, was still prowling about to take his revenge. Only what was killed was really *safe.* How the phrase has made its way into our speech may be seen from the boast of a renowned duellist, a Texan judge, who said: "I have shot three men, and two of them I *saved.*"

In the Far West the settler is, to this day, asked whether he is going out to *hunt for meat,* for skins, or for scalps. Any kind of animal food is to him *meat*—commonly pronounced *mate*—and this he earns by his rifle alone. *Bear-meat* and *deer-meat* alternate with wild turkey—the term *venison* is hardly known in the West. *Bear-meat* is quite popular with him, and, if he can have his choice, he is sure to prefer *grizzly-meat,* as he briefly calls it, to all others. The *Grizzly Bear,* peculiar to America, has fortunately a very wide range all about the base of the Rocky Mountains, where *his* favorite food, the buffalo, is to be found. Hunters do not hesitate to attack him single-handed, formidable as he is, to *get his meat,* which is so highly esteemed that it can be found even at the eating-houses of San Francisco. The term *grizzly,* commonly misunderstood as denoting a peculiar color, is nothing more than the old English *grisly,* meaning ugly, from *grise,* which once was a name of swine. Mr. Grose explains it as meaning also a mixture of black and white or gray, and hence the very natural error. When young they are easily tamed, and thus F. B. Harte introduces a young Californian lady who "opened the door and disclosed a half-grown *grizzly,* who instantly raised himself on his haunches, with his forepaws hanging down in the popular attitude of mendicants." (*Luck of Roaring Camp,* p. 47.)

Sheep-meat, as mutton is called, is very rare in the Far West, and *deer-meat* has a drawback not generally known: "It is a nutritious meat when eaten with other viands, but it is a remarkable fact that in an exclusive diet of *deer-meat* it will finally cease to afford any sustenance, and a person thus living, will present the phenomenon of actual starvation. Frontiersmen have been found in Texas in the last stages of exhaustion, wan, shrivelled, and at the point of death, who had been reduced to this condition while there was a plentiful provision of venison in the camp." (R. B. Thorpe.) S. Kercheval touchingly says of his own childhood: "The lean venison and the breast of wild turkeys we were taught to call bread, and the flesh of the bear was called *meat*. This artifice did not succeed very well, for after living in this way some time we became sickly, the stomach seeming to be always empty and tormented with a sense of hunger. How delicious was the taste of the first young potatoes! what a jubilee when we were permitted to pull the young corn for *roasting-ears!* Still more so, when it had acquired sufficient hardness to be made into *johnny-cakes* by the aid of a tin grater. We then became healthy, vigorous, and contented with our situation, poor as it was." (*Hist. of the Valley of Virginia*, p. 214.) The wild turkey has given rise to a playful phrase, originating in the tradition of a white and a Redman, who had gone out hunting together, sitting down to eat a roast turkey, which they were to share. The Indian waited with the stoicism of his race, till his turn should come, while the surly backwoodsman ate and ate, and, as the poor Indian afterward reported, "*never said turkey once.*" To this day an unfair division and want of hospitality, especially in the South, is characterized by the blamed persons "*never saying turkey once.*" If he *hunts for skins*, he is known as a *Trapper*, from the traps he sets to catch animals with valuable furs. The ideal *trapper*, familiar to us in the shape of Cooper's *Leatherstocking*, never existed in reality; he is rare even now, having been driven from the so-called West to snaring and capturing his game in the Rocky Mountain region. "The majority of *trappers* of the present day are either Canadian-French or half-breeds (French and Indian) by birth. They now find their quarry in Dakota, Montana, Idaho, Washington, and Oregon, in the Red River region, British Columbia, and Vancouver Island. They are active, patient under toil, exposure, and hardship, versed in all the mysteries of woodcraft and the arts of the trapper, ingenious and full of expedients, generous and reckless in their expenditures, helpful and kind-hearted." (*Appleton's Journal*, April 1, 1871.)

In trapping, he uses the usual variety of traps, but also one he calls the *deadfall*, because it kills the game. It is commonly made of a heavy plank with one edge held up by what is technically called *Figure Four* trap-sticks—three sticks arranged like a large figure 4. "I know'd it would be easy to catch one by making a *deadfall*." (Mrs. Trail, *The Canadian Crusoes*, p. 85.) "The most beautiful notions are all lost for want of a trap, an intellectual *Figgery Four*." (J. C. Neal's *Charcoal Sketches*, I., p. 38.) If the hunter is out after scalp, he calls it going to *raise hair*. A more innocent sport, which plays a prominent part in Western life, is the hunting of bees. The *bee-hunter*, as he is called, catches a bee in a little box with some honey in it; the bee, first alarmed, and struggling hard to go out, soon catches the smell of honey, forgets its captivity, and, like a true Yankee—for they all came from New England—determined to make the most of every mishap, falls to, taking its fill. The box is then placed upon a stump or rock, the lid gently withdrawn, and the hunter steps aside to see the bee take its flight, which it does in about one minute, that is, as soon as it is filled with honey. Rising a few feet in the air, it circles around two or three times, taking its bearings, and strikes a *bee-line* for home. The pursuit of the bee to its hive in a distant tree is called *lining bees*, and considered a valuable accomplishment throughout the West. Hence G. W. Kendall describes a man thus: "The Indian he could circumvent and outmanœuvre at his own games, and at killing every kind of animal known in the woods or on the prairies; at fishing and at *lining bees*, the oldest and best hunters acknowledged Tom's supremacy." (*Santa Fé Expedition*, I., p. 53). Hence the familiar term of *bee-line* for any direct line from place to place, such as the bee chooses to return home. "Now you make tracks," says a hunter in *Scenes from the Far West*, "and strike a *bee-line* for home, or if ever I catch you in these diggins agin, you won't git home any more, that's all." (p. 234.) "The boy, anointing his face and hands with a little tar, diluted with sweet oil, made a *bee-line* for the upper end of the meadow." (*Putnam's Magazine*, July, 1870.) A rich store of honey is often found in hollow trees, among which the bee seems to prefer the *gum-trees* (Liquidambar styræiflua), which grow to a large size both in swamps and in dry woods. It has its name from the fact that the bark, if wounded in summer, distils a fluid gum or resin in very small quantity, which has an agreeable fragrance, and is often chewed at the South. If the tree should be hollow, it is called a *bee-tree.* This preference of the bees has led to a curious process of retaliation. The large but short-lived trees, when they once begin to suffer, soon become hollow, decaying at the heart and leaving a shell of some few inches in thickness. Then they are cut in convenient lengths to make casks, and among other hollow-ware also beehives; hence the latter are frequently called *bee-gums* or *gums* simply, furnishing the captive bees the same home they chose in the free woods. The fruit of the *bee-hunter's* skill is highly appreciated in his lonely cabin where sweets are not abundant, and hence *honey* is a favorite word in the backwoods for real or verbal sweetness. A ludicrous application of the term was found in an advertisement in a Tuscaloosa newspaper: "Notice. Persons indebted to the Tuscaloosa bookstore are respectfully solicited to pay their last year's account forthwith. It is of no use *to honey;* payments must be made at least once a year or I shall run down at the heels. I have not spare change enough to buy myself a shirt or a pair of breeches. My wife is now actually engaged in turning an old pair wrongside-out, and trying to make a new shirt out of two old ones. Come, come, pay up, my friends! keep peace in the family, and enable me to wear my breeches right-side-out!" (September 21st, 1870.) But the worst use of the sweet word is probably made in the formation of *honey-fogle,* in the sense of swindling or cheating. Mr. Bartlett suggests that the curious word may have its origin in the Lancashire *coney-fogling,* mentioned by Halliwell, as meaning to lay plots. It was long confined to Louisiana and Kentucky, then went to the Great West, and with the general advance of refinement has found a resting-place in the lips of Colonel Susan B. Anthony—as Western papers call her in admiration of her courage — who uses *honey-fugling* for "kissing," in her lectures on Women's Rights. "What is *Honey-Fugling* (*sic*)?" asks a writer in *Harper's Monthly,* and receives the answer: "It is cutting it too fat over the left;" a suggestive if not very clear explanation. (July, 1858.)

This fondness of sweet things has led to the curious expression of *souring* on an unpleasant task or occupation. As the English swain is said to be "sweet" on his lady-love, so the Texas youth *sours* on the beauty that will not listen to his addresses, and the man who abandons his plantations to take up some other business, is said to have "*soured* on planting."

The backwoodsman finds at home, besides honey, the *long and short sweetening*, peculiar to the West; the former representing molasses, as in the early days of the colonies molasses imported into New England from the West Indies was known by that name; the latter meaning *store-sugar*, or sugar made from the cane. For the settler has also *tree-sugar* made from the *sugar-maple*, as it is called (Acer saccharinum), and is apt, when his farm is an old one, to own quite a *sugar-orchard*, *i. e.*, a collection of maple-trees, preserved and watched over in the forest, from which he derives the necessary supply. A mere clump of such trees near his house he is disposed to call only a *sugar-camp*. *Sugar-parties*, during which the sap collected in large vessels is boiled down in the still wintry woods, amid much merriment and innocent mirth, are common from Vermont down to Western Virginia, wherever the noble tree will grow that gives its sweet blood to man; and the gatherings of young people in the beautiful groves to eat the warm sugar are practically but very prosaically called *sugar-licks*. Even the verb to *sugar off* is derived from this custom of eating the maple-sugar as it is poured off in its hot state on the snow around, thus making a dainty compound resembling ice-cream; which at home is often produced by a similar mixture with *tree-molasses*. The latter enables his thrifty housewife, who is, however, always a "lady," to make him a plentiful supply of *sarves*, as he invariably calls the preserves, of which all Western men are said to be peculiarly fond—no doubt from the natural instinct which makes them choose saccharine substances as an offset to the large quantities of fat and meat they consume. This sweet tooth has evidently been carried to the West from the first settlers of the East, for even there still lingers a tendency to prefer pies and preserves to bread and meat, and *sugar* is a term used, like *honey* in other countries, for all that is sweet in taste, affection, or —wealth. To *sugar off* is one of those expressions the thorough-bred Yankee rolls as a sweet morsel under his tongue when speaking of a large fortune or a rich inheritance. Thus we find it in a recent notice of the humorous author: "Josh Billings, who comes of a wealthy family—Shaws of Lanesborough in Massachusetts—

and it is estimated that his estate would *sugar off*, as they say in Vermont, about $200,000. Joshua is now about fifty years old, tall, round-shouldered, and an oddity, always carrying about on his features an expression indescribably ludicrous." (*Harper's Bazar*, March 13, 1871.)

The backwoodsman's table is otherwise very modest, and knows no peculiar dishes save the very simplest. *Cold flour*, as he calls it, is a delicacy, though it consists but of parched and pulverized Indian corn mixed with sugar; a few spoonfuls are stirred in a tin cup with water, and make a good meal when other food is not to be had. On the Texan trail travellers are very apt to provide themselves with this compound, making it more palatable by the addition of spices; in this form it appears as *pinole* in all the regions where Spanish used to be spoken. His daily fare is designated as *common doings*, a term which is transferred from the log-cabin to the great marts of the West, and then denotes any ordinary transaction in contrast with those that are very large or peculiarly profitable. "What shall we do?" says a poor frontiersman's wife, when she hears of a Federal officer who is to take up his quarters at her cabin for a day; "I can't give him *common doings?* And thar Jim's gone away and I can't send him over to Billy's wife, or I might get up some *chicken-fixings* for him." (Colonel Marcy, *Army-Life on the Border*, p. 117.) If the latter dish, highly esteemed all over the West and South as a delicacy for great occasions, or a turkey, come to the table, they are sure to be accompanied with *piles of stuffening*, as the usual stuffing of herbs and some relish is called in the fullness of Western speech. A very curious term is connected with the fondness of Western men for coffee and tea: "I take my tea *barfoot*, said a backwoodsman, when asked if he would take cream and sugar," using as J. R. Lowell observes, in this very novel signification an old English term, written in precisely the same manner in the Coventry Plays. Lean meat he calls, in the same brief manner, simply *poor-doe*, without regard to the animal from which it was obtained.

Good-natured, and even kind-hearted, as the backwoodsman generally is, his language is full of extreme words and eccentric phrases, which do not always justice to his real character. His solitary life, however, begets not only sturdy independence, but also utter disregard of mere conventionalities, and the rough life he must needs lead in constant strife with nature and with rival claimants of the soil, soon makes its impress upon his speech also. Many a peculiar term is, of course, taken here, as in every profession and special pursuit of life, from the objects around him, with which he is most familiar. He *works like a beaver*, but in saying so only follows the usage established long ago, for already in 1747 there appeared in the Boston *Rehearsal* the following advertisement: "To be sold by the printer of this paper, the very best negro in this town; is as hearty as a horse, as brisk as a bird, and will *work like a beaver*." The phrase has become common property, and hence we find that "The Radicals *worked like beavers*, but they were so far outnumbered, that I should not wonder if the Democracy got at least half the votes at this point." (Savannah *Republican*, Nov. 14, 1870.) On the other hand, the English use of *beaver* for a hat has entirely ceased, giving way to "gossamer," or, in modern slang, "goss," while the term is still used in the South and among old-fashioned people. The *Beaver-tree* (Magnolia glauca), is so called in the West, while elsewhere it is more generally known as *Castor-tree*, in either case from the fact that the *beavers* (Castor americanus) use the bark as food and the wood for their *beaver-dams*. The great importance which a crop of grass has for all stock-raisers and the Indians, whose very life depends on the buffaloes finding food and their horses pasture, has led to the use of the peculiar phrase in which the youth, who is no longer a boy and not yet a man, is picturesquely said to be *between grass and hay*. The fire made in the woods consists of large logs piled one upon another, and hence in the West a *fire is built*, and very rarely *made* as elsewhere. The raccoon furnishes the suggestive idea of a *coon's age* for a long time, and of a *gone coon* instead of the English phrase, "a gone goose." The Hon. Mr. Giddings said, on the floor of Congress, in 1845, "Besides the acquisition of Canada, which is put down on all sides as a *gone coon*, other brilliant results are to ensue from the possession of Canada." The mountaineer is apt to modify the phrase to suit his favorite animal, and speaks of a ruined person as a *gone beaver*. The *buck* suggests to the hunter the idea of being *hearty as a buck*, and makes him speak of *buck ague*, or *buck fever*, when he wishes to describe the nervous agitation of the inexperienced sportsman; so that G. W. Kendall wrote: "There is a very c mon disease prevalent among young and inexperienced hunters in Texas, which is known as the *buck ague*." (*Santa Fé Expedition*, II., p. 321.) The *buck fly* is the insect which plagues the deer at certain seasons, so as not unfrequently to drive them from their favorite feeding-ground; but whether the *buck negro* obtains his name from the animal or from the general meaning of *buck* as a slang term for strong or lusty, is not so evident. "Cries of: there he goes! were heard, as the skirmishers advanced, and a big *buck negro* was found in a hollow laying (*sic*) on his face, playing possum, and he actually allowed himself to be turned over on the back and kicked several times before he would acknowledge that he was alive." (Nashville *Banner*, January 8, 1871.)

The raccoon's favorite resort, the gum-tree, furnishes him with another figure of speech. This tree, the Sweet Gum, as it is commonly called, grows up very tall, and begins to spread its branches only at a great height from the ground, a feature which makes it the place of refuge for opossums as well as raccoons, when they are hotly pursued. Up there in his leafy retreat the animal is well hid from dog and hunter alike, and frequently defies all their efforts. This is what the Western man calls coming the *gum-game*, and he applies the phrase with great shrewdness and force to any case in daily life in which he thinks he sees a desire to overreach him by concealment. "You can't come that *gum-game* over me any more," says a Kansas man to a squatter, whose farm he wished to purchase, when the latter claims to have some fictitious title, "I've been to the land-office, and know all about the place." (Kansas *City Advertiser*, May 7, 1869.) The word is not unknown to the Eastern States, for J. R. Lowell uses it in the same sense: "You can't *gum* me, I tell ye now, and so you needn't try." (*Biglow Papers*, I., p. 135.) The old English phrase, *as stupid as a coot*, quoted by Halliwell already as an "old proverbial saying," is quite at home on Western low grounds, and finds a companion in the local expression, "he is a *poor coot*." Of the same nature is the expression, "*straight as a loon's leg*," in allusion to the peculiar leg of the Northern Diver (Eolymbus glacialis).

From the cock's spur, not unfrequently, as in England, supplied with a steel spur, he derives the use of *heeled*, in the sense of armed with deadly weapons, and in California, especially, a man giving an account of a fight, is apt to be asked: "Were both men *heeled*?"

The turkey is to the Western man a *gobbler*, a name most likely to have been derived from the very peculiar noise made by the proud bird when, shutting his eyes and beating his wings, he dances like a madman on his branch, and calls for his mate to come and admire his out-spread tail and crimson adornments. There is a negro melody, familiar in Georgia, which in the refrain attempts to imitate this *gobble*—the only feasible method, it has been said, of *talking turkey* yet discovered:

> "Ole mars William he gone to legislatur',
> Ah! chocaloga, chocaloga, chocalog!
> Young mars John, he done come home from college,
> Ah! chocaloga, chocaloga, chocalog!"

A hunter in the Far West writes: "I had gone some fifty yards up the fork, when I saw one of the *gobblers* perched, with his bearded breast to me, upon a horizontal limb of an oak, within easy shot." (Ruxton, *Adventures in the West*, p. 347.) The war brought with its large stock of old and cant terms also the use of *gobbling up*, instead of "taking from the enemy," a meaning derived from the voracity which is generally conveyed by gobbling. A correspondent of the Chicago *Evening Post* is credited with the first experiment; he wrote: "Nearly four hundred prisoners were *gobbled up* after the fight, and any quantity of ammunition and provisions." (July, 1861.)

Even domestic animals appear in a new light in the Great West, and this gives rise to new meanings of familiar terms. California, for instance, forms its vast flocks of sheep into *bands*, of about a thousand each, and employs *herders* to tend its valuable cattle. The former is hence called *sheep-herder*, and not shepherd, because the keeping of sheep is considered unfit for man, and no one will own to it! Formerly the work was done by Indians; then by such immigrants as were utterly unable by any exertion of their own to earn a living; and finally the task has come down to the despised *greasers* or "vagrant miners, who gamble off their wages as soon as they receive them, or runaway sailors from Frisco, who sell their blankets for a pillow-case of biscuits, and then go two days without eating anything, or vagabond soldiers, who fall asleep at their post and let the coyotes pull away a sheep." (*Overland Monthly*, February, 1871, p. 142.) The *Stool-Pigeon*, also, as familiar to English ears as to ours, exists here—and even in the Eastern States—still in both its primary signification and its figurative extension. In the former it means the pigeon, with its eyes stitched up, fastened on a stool, which can be moved up and down by the hidden fowler, an action which causes the bird to flutter anxiously. This attracts the passing flocks of wild pigeons, which alight and are caught by a net, which may be sprung over them. The figurative stool-pigeon is, of course, only the decoy-duck in another form.

A very peculiar term, full of instruction in showing the origin of many similar words, is the name of *Maverick,* used in Texas to designate an unmarked yearling. It is derived from the Hon. Samuel Maverick, of San Antonio, who removed to Western Texas thirty years ago, driving with him some three thousand head of cattle, then the largest herd in all the country. He established a *ranche,* and placed an old negro there in charge of the cattle, to mark, brand, and see after them. Unfortunately this man was more given to the bottle than his business, and, as a natural consequence, many a calf and colt went unmarked. The neighbors, having much smaller herds, were very careful to mark and brand every one of their calves during the early spring and summer. The spring after the arrival of Mr. Maverick's large herd these *rancheros* noticed a number of unmarked yearlings, and, well acquainted with the habits of his steward, naturally concluded that they were the new-comer's property, and hence called them *mavericks,* so that the very absence of a mark and brand was taken as evidence of his ownership. As the number of cattle rapidly increased, there were, of course, many unmarked yearlings running about that belonged to other owners and were well known as such; nevertheless the name clung to every calf with long or unmutilated ears, and to this day every yearling without a mark is a *maverick.* Any owner of a large herd considers himself authorized to brand a *maverick* which he finds on or near his ranche, and this operation is called to *jack a maverick.* With this process of marking or branding young cattle, so as to show to whom it belongs, another term is closely connected, the word *counterbranding:* when marked cattle are sold the mark is burnt in a second time on the opposite side, thus destroying the force of the original brand, and this process is called *counterbranding* cattle.

The *crooked stick* that will not fit into the pile, becomes the familiar nickname of a cross-grained person who does not suit society, and has, as such, made its way back again to the East, where it reappears in J. R. Lowell's *Biglow Papers* thus:

> "So as I aint a *crooked stick*, just like, like old—(I swow,
> I don't know as I know his name)—I'll go back to my plough."

Snakes, whom the backwoodsman hates for a good reason and with intense bitterness, furnish him with several graphic expressions. He has his *snake*-fences and countless *snakeroots*, reputed to cure snake-bites, and mostly inherited from the Indians, from the *Seneca snakeroot* (Polyga Seneca) at the North, to the *Virginia snakeroot* (Aristolochia serpentaria) in the South, one of which at least was known to the French settlers as *serpent-à-sonnettes*, and is to this day looked upon as an infallible remedy. The horror with which he discovers a snake—or under a rock perhaps a whole so-called nest of snakes, containing hundreds closely interlaced and hissing furiously at the intruder—has suggested to him the picturesque phrase of *waking snakes* with a double meaning. In grim allusion to the wriggling, hissing crowd of hideous creatures, he speaks of a peculiarly noisy, boisterous frolic as a *waking of snakes*, such as J. R. Lowell refers to in the lines—

> "This goin' where glory awaits ye, hain't one agreeable featur',
> And if it warn't for *wakin' snakes*, I'd be home agin short metre."
> (*Biglow Papers*, I.)

The other meaning is derived from the sense of sudden terror excited by the discovery, and makes *waking snakes* equivalent to "running away quickly," "a highly probable result in a country where a traveller about to start in the morning, is pleasantly informed by the landlord, that there's a smart sprinkling of rattlesnakes on Red Run, and a powerful nice day to sun themselves." (Carlton's *The New Purchase*, I., p. 85.) Not many years ago, negroes living near the foot of the Blue Ridge would ask leave "to be gwin' *wakin' snakes*" for the professors of the University of Virginia, who wanted some specially fine specimens of rattlesnakes for friends abroad, or for the students, who had them pitted against each other on the great lawn of the institution, and heartily enjoyed the terrific combats which the snakes would continue sometimes for hours. Western men have a special dislike to any indirect, underhand proceedings, and term them *snaking*, so that even in politics a man is said to *snake*, if he tries to obtain an advantage by such influence. On the other hand, *snaking* means quite as frequently to catch or to draw swiftly from any place. W. S. Mayo describes a struggle with an Indian thus: "He made a spring at a rail-fence, and I believe would have gone over it at the first jump, but just as he cleared the ground I *wollopped* the hoop around him and *snaked* him back, head over heels; he gathered himself like a frightened deer and cleared the fence the next jump, easy." (*Kaloolah*, p. 17.) Major Downing, in his *Letters*, uses it as a political effort, when he says of his great hero, General Jackson: "We *snaked* him out of the scrape as slick as a whistle." (p. 14.) This phrase, however, comes not directly from the snake itself, but from the use which is made of the phrase to *snake it out*, when applied by settlers to the drawing out of stumps by means of a long chain.

That even railways cannot escape the snake, and had in former days *snake-heads*, which constituted one of the most formidable dangers in railway travelling, has already been mentioned elsewhere.

The tendency of all Americans to use high-sounding words of extensive meaning for comparatively small matters, is nowhere more fully developed than in the West. Here even small objects are not brought, but *crowded*, and thus the Rev. Mr. Cartwright even says quaintly: "God Almighty *crowded* me into the world bareheaded, and I think no more harm to enter Massachusetts bareheaded, than for the Lord to bring me into the world without a hat." (*Autobiography*, p. 473.) What elsewhere is great appears to him nothing less than *cruel*, although here also he only follows the example set him by his early ancestors, since Hakluyt already thus used the word. Mr. Bartlett tells the pleasant story of a man who, having been quite seriously ill, was asked by the physician who had calmed the paroxysm, how he felt, and replied: "Oh, doctor, I am powerful weak, but *cruel* easy." (*Dictionary*, p. 170.) On the other hand, the Western man takes the much debated word *cuss*, and employs it where he wishes to express anything but a curse, often even affection. There is a touching incident mentioned in F. B. Harte's *Luck of Roaring Camp*, where a rough, wicked miner, Kentuck Joe, goes to see a new-born baby, and finding his finger clutched by the little creature, breaks forth ecstatically in the words: "The d——d little *cuss!* he *rastled* with my finger!" holding that finger a little apart from its fellows and examining it curiously. The question is, whether the term comes really from a vulgar pronunciation of *curse*, as most authorities state, or is an abbreviation of *customer*, with the primary idea of what is frequently called a *bad* or an *ugly customer*. The latter theory might be supported by the fact that a *cuss* is, as has already been stated, by no means always a *curse*, and that a low, miserly person is very apt to be called a mean *cuss*, which may be nothing more than a *mean customer*. This would apply even to a case like the following, taken from the New Orleans *Picayune*: "I had oft heard tell of Yankees, but never knew what *mean cusses* they were, until I met a few of them at Washington." The noun *cussedness*, also, is by no means always used in utter condemnation. "He done it out of pure *cussedness*," means, of course, out of sheer wickedness and malignity, and in this sense the *Coventry Plays* already employ *cursydnesse*. But quite as frequently *cussedness* is intended to convey the idea of resoluteness and obstinate courage, as in John Hay's popular song of *Jim Bludsoe of the Prairie Bell*:

> "Through the hot-black breath of the burnin' boat
> Jim Bludsoe's voice was heard,
> And they all had trust in his *cussedness*,
> And knowed he would keep his word."

The term has even been traced back to a French origin, from the fact that the same term is used in France. St. Simon uses it and confesses its usefulness. Speaking of the Abbé Dubois, he says: "Qui était en plein ce qu'en mauvais Français on appelle un *sacre*, mais qui ne se peut guère exprimer autrement."

A fertile country, like the western part of Illinois, conjures up pictures of fat kine and at once receives the name of *Egypt*, from the productiveness of the soil, as the natives say, but, in the opinion of outsiders, from the Egyptian darkness prevailing there. This (mental) darkness is explained by the extreme ignorance of hard-working, but also hard-drinking, low Germans, who first settled there, and found as predecessors only a "ground-tier" of poor, shiftless, and ignorant outcasts from Kentucky and Tennessee. Railroads and immigration have since entirely changed the state of things, and *Egypt* can boast of intelligence now as well as of fertility. Besides such special terms, the West loves *big* words generally, and calls a week an *eternal* time, a good officer an *almighty* general, and a spell of rain an *everlasting* deluge, with a tendency to form gradually a Comic Bible, which is most seriously to be deprecated. Where other men simply stir, he *livens up*, as we are told that "Lucien's father hastened to *liven up* the fire, and then sat down near the boy, who, gun in hand, was bravely watching the enemy." (*Harper's Monthly*, December, 1870.) If he speaks to a friend he *hollows*, and where a Northern man burns to do a thing, the Southwestern hunter "*freezes* for buffalo-meat and mountain-doin's." (Ruxton's *Far West, B.*)

This tendency is naturally increased when drink comes to its aid; the backwoodsman, working hard and having few amusements, is not disinclined to *liquor*, as his forefathers long ago taught him to do, for J. R. Lowell tells us that he read in the *Puritan* already: "Call 'em in and *liquor* 'em a little." To *liquor-up* is his own improvement. But of all the rare compounds known to Eastern bar-rooms, few ever reach his secluded home. Nor would he appreciate the bewitching softness of "Long Linked Sweetness," or the ecstacy produced by a "Kiss me Quick"—he likes to *take it* strong and hot. He has not yet forgotten the old custom of his forefathers, and takes a *horn*, as they called the stout horn-cup by their side; and if it is filled to the brim with *Old Red-Eye*, he likes it all the better, for whiskey is his favorite drink, and the red eyes it marks for its own by no means rare on the frontier. "Salted provisions and *red-eye* to boot" is the refrain of many a rude song, and if the latter is fiery and raw it is none the less welcome. "Formerly *rum* was the favorite, and largely produced in the New England States. The word itself, little known in the early days of the Union beyond Yankeedom, was brought into the Middle States by Eastern temperance lecturers, who often use it as a poetic and objurgatory term, instead of the proper word, whiskey." (Professor S. S. Haldeman.) The peculiar and by no means prepossessing redness of face which it is apt to produce, first on the nose and gradually extending over the cheeks, is professionally known as *rum-bud;* while the victim, the habitual toper, has conferred upon him the name of *rum-sucker*. The State of New York alone, we believe, uses the term *rum-holes* for its smaller grog-shops. Western men, once upon a time, devised a quaint and by no means inefficient way to avenge themselves on a well-known zealous temperance lecturer, a Mr. Hawkins. They took his name and applied it, in bitter derision, to an inferior kind of *rum*, calling it *Hawkins' Whetstone*. The hunter and trapper is said to have no other reply to the question: How are you? than the expressive monosyllable: *Dry!* The statement is, of course, in the highest degree unjust to him, and the term is not even an Americanism; it occurs as long ago as the days when the Middleton Plays came out, and may be found in many an old English poet, where it is used, just as now, for thirsty.

When the Western man is not *dry*, he is accused of being apt to be on a *bust*, as they call, in California, a great drinking-bout, accompanied with dancing and gambling, or as the West generally says in its free and easy way, on a *buster*. The figure is, of course, taken from the idea of enjoying a thing to *bursting*, and as the latter word is very generally contracted into *busting*, the *buster* need not be sought for in the word *bustard*, an old form of buzzard. It means simply anything so large or unusual as to "look like bursting." In this sense it is used in England also, and the London boys used to call the small new-made loaves, two-penny *busters*, while the papers gravely stated, after Dr. Hassall's revelations of all the fearful adulterations of bread, that "a sensitive person would sometimes *burst*, if he knew what he was eating." A New England paper, on the other hand, said of a fashionable evening dress, that it "*bust* open at the top and all over the arms." The next step, calling any astonishing thing, person, or event, a *buster*, is perfectly natural. The familiar use of the term led to the following amusing scene: Two young midshipmen accompanied once Commodore Morris, of the United States Navy, to Court at Rio, and seeing two very odd as well as foreign-looking gentlemen playing écarté, they walked up to them and placed themselves behind their chairs to watch the game. After a while one said to the other, "Hal, whom will you bet on?" The reply was, "I'll bet on this little monkey-faced fellow." "All right," says the first, "I'll go this cock-eyed old *buster* in the red wig." The words were hardly uttered, when up jumped the odd-looking couple—a brace of Envoys Plenipotentiary—with fury in their faces, to the terrified amazement of the youngsters, who had had no idea they would be understood, a fair inference from the general amount of linguistic knowledge possessed by their national representatives. To the credit of their Excellencies, they soon joined in the laugh, only cautioning their photographers to look, for the future, before they leaped. (*Lippincott's Magazine*, February, 1871.) The verb is, of course, quite as popular as the noun, and a poor fellow, brought up before the Recorder at New Orleans, made this plea in his defence: "Because I was a good-natured fellow, I had to go with them, frolicking, teaparting, excursioning, and *busting* generally." (New Orleans *Picayune*, February 14, 1869.) To *buss*—also a Western term—is, however, a very different term, and quite as much English as American, in the sense of to punch. "I'll *buss* your head," is a popular threat in the West. When he is *dry* he is very apt to yield to the quite pardonable longing of a lonely man in the backwoods, to hear what is going on in the world, to see human faces once more, and to get some liquor. He finds a variety in name, if not in reality, for the West is as rich in epithets for pure liquor as the Eastern States are fond of devising daily some new names for cunning mixtures. Now he is asked to take a *Stone Fence*, and now a *Railroad*, but both are simple whiskey, so called, in the latter case, "because of the rapidity with which it hurries men to the end of their journey." (J. C. Neal, *Charcoal Sketches*, I., 117.) The worst of *lickers*, as the signboards often have it in unconscious irony, is called *Chain-lightning*, from its terrible strength and stunning effect. Even the word *rotgut*, used as far back as in Heywood's *English Traveller* and Addison's *Drummer*, for a poor kind of drink, and in England still often heard in speaking of small-beer, has here been revived and made to serve as a name for particularly bad and fiery whiskey. All these he finds at the *doggery*, the very expressive name of a mean grogshop in the West and South. The Rev. Mr. Cartwright alluded to them when he described a camp-meeting, saying, "There was a crowd from the floating population of the river and loose-footed, *doggery*-haunting, dissipated renegades of the towns and villages all around." (*Autobiography*, p. 376.)

It is generally on such occasions, and in such company only, that a "free fight" occurs, after the pattern of Irish frolics, and the old, now obsolete, practice of *gouging* was indulged in. S. Kercheval already refers to the "detestable practice of *gouging*, by which eyes are sometimes put out, and which rendered the mode of fighting frightful indeed. It was not, however, so destructive as the stiletto of an Italian, the knife of a Spaniard, the small-sword of a Frenchman, or the pistol of the American or English duellist." (*History of the Valley of Virginia*, p. 251.) Mr. Bartlett remarks with patriotic indignation that Grose, in his *Dictionary*, defines *gouging* as "a cruel custom, practised by the Bostonians in America!" The term is taken from the carpenter's shops, where it is in constant use, just as Ben Jonson employed it in the lines:

> "By *googing* of 'em out
> Just to the size of my bottles, and not slicing."
> (*Devil is an Ass.*)

The practice, consisting of a turning out of the eye from the socket by the thumb-nail, which was suffered to grow long for the purpose, is now nearly, if not wholly, extinct, but the word is still occasionally heard, as flaying alive and skinning are used to express very hard treatment, which is threatened but never carried out.

The same happy termination unfortunately can not be predicted of the abuses and villanies transacted under the shelter of so-called *Lynch Law*, since recent cases, by no means confined to the West, but (in 1871) extending even to New Hampshire, prove the strong hold which the idea of popular justice has on the American mind. Perhaps no term in the whole list of Americanisms has been more thoroughly examined than this, and yet no conclusive proof has yet been adduced in favor of any one derivation. The oldest date assigned to it is the year 1498, when an Irishman, "James Lynch, Mayor of Galway, hanged his own son out of the window for defrauding and killing strangers, without martial or common law, to show a good example to posterity." (Extract from *Council Books* of Galway.) *Lydford Law*, explained by the doggerel lines—

> "First hang and draw,
> Then hear the cause by *Lydford law*,"

and said to have been practised under Richard II., claims an even earlier date, but lacks the ominous name. Another ancestor is found in one *Lynch*, who, in 1687–8, was sent to America to suppress piracy. As the laws were not administered with much rigor or formality in the Colonies, owing to "the difficulty of adhering to the usual forms of law in the newly-fashioned territories," it is presumed that this Judge *Lynch* was empowered to proceed summarily against the pirates, and thus gave rise to the term. (George H. Bailey in *Notes and Queries.*) The opinion which traces the law to one *Lynch*, founder of the town of *Lynchburg*, in Virginia, is entirely unsupported by any authority, and rests solely upon the identity of the name. R. W. Emerson describes it thus: "Wild liberty develops iron conscience. Want of liberty, by strengthening law and decorum, stupefies conscience. *Lynch Law* prevails only where there is greater hardihood and self-consistency in the leaders." (*Politics*, p. 117.) The absurdly euphemistic way in which newspaper writers of the day occasionally indulge in speaking of very grave matters, was recently shown in an account of *Lynch Law* justice, thus described: "Mr. Lyon, of Georgia, who owned several horses belonging to other parties, recently dislocated his cerebral vertebræ while performing trying feats at a rope's end, held by said parties, for the amusement of a large crowd." ("Personal" in a Western paper, December, 1870.)

A local application of the same principle is to be found in the *Vigilance* Committees of California, whose name, originally in all probability derived from the familiar Spanish term *vigilante*, has since made its way to other States also. The French *vigilance* is, of course, the same word, but the connection with the custom is not so evident. These *Vigilance Committees* originated, like *Lynch Law*, in the inefficiency of the appointed authorities to execute the law—when judges were intimidated, juries partial and guilty of the same crimes as those they were called upon to condemn, and public opinion all on the side of the criminal. Men of standing and character, who had much at stake, then formed themselves into a *Committee* to watch over the safety of their home and to punish criminals. The first self-constituted body of this kind was formed in San Francisco; others in New Orleans have become quite famous, and even in the Northwest their interposition has been repeatedly tolerated. In the Eastern States they have never obtained the support of law-abiding citizens, and on several occasions have been very promptly suppressed. In the more remote parts of the Union they continue, however, to exist, and probably to do some good, in default of a regular and efficient administration of the laws of the country. A recent instance is thus described: "The *Vigilance Committee* in Los Angelos (California) has proved itself a reality by its large numbers and vigorous action. At 10 o'clock on the morning of the 19th, three hundred men assembled in Stearn's Hall, elected Mr. Signouret President, and at once proceeded to try Miguel Lachenai for the murder of Jacob Bell, and other murders which he is known to have committed. After a brief session it was unanimously decided to hang Lachenai. At 11 o'clock the *Vigilantes* were divided into three companies and marched through the streets to the jail; guards were stationed at different points to prevent interference with their work, and a party commenced battering down the door, which consumed quite half an hour. Entering Lachenai's cell, a rope was put around his neck and he was led out into the street. The *Vigilantes* surrounded him and conducted him to a corral some two squares away from the jail, and hung him at 11.40 A. M. In the words he was given time to speak, he confessed his crime, but expressed no regret. The sheriff and his men made all the resistance possible, but they were unable to raise a man to assist them, all believing in the justness of the *Vigilantes*' action." (San Francisco *Bulletin*, December 8, 1870.)

When the man of the Western frontier is not *dry*, he is very apt to be *slewed*. This term has been traced to two or three different sources, among which the word *slough*, in the West pronounced *slew*, is not the weakest claimant. But as the word is quite as common in England, where sloughs are scarcely known, it may there really be a sea-term, derived from the apparent disorder on board ship at the moment when she tacks; the sails flap and she heels over, in which condition she is said to *slew*. It may, however, also have been suggested by the resemblance which the *slewed* or half-tipsy man bears to a sleigh at the moment when it goes round a corner, and its peculiar sliding motion is conveyed by the New England term: It *slewed* round.

Great as the backwoodsman is in terms and phrases concerning every object around him, he is greatest by far in speaking of himself or his comrade. The outsider of all classes and colors is simply the *stranger* to him, and he sings out to the traveller he meets on the trail, "Halloa, *stranger*, whar' may you be bound to?" He speaks of himself in mock modesty as *this child*, or more self-asserting, as *this horse*, and his friend is affectionately greeted as "Wal, Ole *Hoss*, how are ye?" A common challenge, often given to a whole company, around the camp-fire or at the bar-room, in an out-lying settlement, is, "Who dare set *this hoss?*" (*Life in the Far West*, p. 171.) For the *horse* plays in many ways a prominent part in the dramatic manner of speaking in the West, and has thence found its way back to the Eastern States. The old feeling of rude force connected with the horse, prevailing so largely in English as to produce numerous words, like horse-laugh, horse-medicine, and others, has here been strengthened by the love of metaphor. A *horse* is the name of a man of energy, and a Western man says readily, "He wasn't loony on a bargain, sir, no indeed; and he had plenty of hard *horse*-sense, and took good care of his property." (*Putnam's Magazine*, January, 1868.) Hence, also, the two extremes of lowest and highest esteem are both conveyed by horse-terms. Anything strikingly small and insignificant, from a church to a bank, and from a governor to a constable, is a poor *one-horse* affair, a figure obviously drawn from the plough and the wagon. The indignant settler who has been ill-treated, as he fancies, in court, denounces his attorney as a "miserable, *one-horse* lawyer;" and the Yankee newly arrived in England does not hesitate to declare that "Liverpool is a poor *one-horse* kind of a place," a term applied by Mark Twain to no less a city than Rome itself. Dr. O. W. Holmes delights his readers by his "*one-horse* shay;" and a witty clergyman of Boston inveighed once bitterly against "timid, sneaking, *one-horse* oaths," as infinitely worse than a good, round, thundering outburst. The *wheel-horse* is the Western man's best friend, and the *wheel-horse* of a political party its main prop and support. On the other hand, the figure of speech swells up to a *whole team*, the highest term of approbation Western men are apt to apply to a special favorite, the "good fellow," of England, as well as the man of great wealth or marked energy. "I like the judge," said a man from St. Louis to Mr. Prescott, once, speaking of Dr. Story: "He is none of your *one-horse* lawyers; he is a whole *team*:" and the New

York *Herald*, not long ago, declared: "Grant is a *whole team*, a horse extra, and a dog under the wagon." Here the *ne plus ultra* of recommendation is graphically conveyed by a charming completeness of the original figure of speech. The slang term is used and abused with boundless license, and a respectable journal once said in sober earnest: "Fanny Fern continues to make one of Bonner's *team*" (*Lippincott's Magazine*, July, 1869), wishing to inform its readers that the well-known literary lady still contributed to Mr. Bonner's popular paper, the *Ledger*. A new meaning has quite recently been added to the word *team*, since the introduction of Chinese labor at North Adams in Massachusetts: a group of three or four Chinese shoemakers working at the same bench is called a *team*.

There can be little doubt that this fondness for horse-terms, strengthened by the American's matchless skill in driving heavy stage-coaches over roads that would appear impassable to other men, has led also to the use of the verb to *trot out*, in the sense of to *bring out*. The term has become quite familiar to politicians also; and in discussing the elections to take place two years hence, a writer said: "It is a whole year too early to *trot out* a candidate of our party for the presidency." (New York *Tribune*, January 23, 1871.) It is probably a pure Americanism, on the other hand, to apply the verb *to balk* to the action of horses when, in going up-hill, they suddenly stop, and refuse to move forward, showing, on the contrary, a disposition to go back. In the English sense to *balk* means simply to frustrate or disappoint, as in the sentence given in Bailey: "*Balked* are the courts, and contest is no more;" and as used by Spenser in his *Faery Queen* (V., v. 10.); its application to horses is, hence, by no means inappropriate, and quite expressive. Even the slang phrase to *cut dirt*, vulgar but very suggestive as to the effect of the rapid motion of a horse on a muddy road, must be traced back to this fondness for the popular animal, and fast driving. "Now, I say, old *hoss*, if you don't hurry up and *cut dirt* like streak-lightnin', this child goes arter you, and you look out for a windin' sheet, you hear?" (*Border Adventures*, p. 231.)

A fine *turn-out*, meaning originally, as in England, only a handsome carriage with showy horses, has in like manner come to be applied to any display; and even a man who builds a large house or delivers an eloquent speech is, in the West, said to have made a *fine turn-out.* It is not uninteresting to see how the phrase has been changed in the far South, especially in Texas, where the same meaning is conveyed by the term *lay-out.* It is probable that the term is a gambler's phrase, referring to the sum of money which the banker at monte "lays out" allure customers. Now, however, a man who appears well-dressed in the street, succeeds in business or in a venture, is said to have made "a splendid *lay-out.*" To *roll out,* on the other hand, means there to begin a journey or commence an enterprise. The phrase originated in the fact that for many years the ox-wagon was the only means of transportation in Texas, although a few short railways penetrated the State for a short distance. Hence the teamster says; "I *rolled out* at sunrise this morning," and the merchant asks his partner, consulting him as to the expediency of beginning business, "when shall we *roll out?*"

Nor is it so entirely out of the question, as has been maintained by some modern writers, that the familiar term *fast* has been derived from the same tendency. It is acknowledged to be an Americanism in its first origin, but it has long since made its way into England, ascending from the streets into the drawing-room, and from the slang of the gin-shop to the leading article of the high-toned review. Its meaning, however, has changed with its patrons; it no longer reproaches the man, to whom the epithet is given, with actual vice and debauchery, but, at the worst, designates him as a gay, unsteady, and thoughtless seeker of pleasure. The prevailing idea seems no longer to be the rapid rate to a certain bad place, as Fielding suggests, but merely the rapid wearing out of health and strength by late hours, high living, and continuous excitement. In this sense Mr. Dickens speaks of a *fast* young man in the Christmas Story of 1859. Unfortunately, the term has been extended to the other sex also, apparently without much reluctance or opposition. The *fast* young girl of the period affects masculine habits, talks slang, drives fast horses, and advocates Women's Rights. In England the judgment is harsher; the *Saturday Review* calls the *fast girl* "a young woman who has lost her respect for men, and for whom men have lost their respect also." (July 28th, 1860.)

It is commonly assumed, though with doubtful justice, that the odd extension of curt *Sir*, into emphatic *Sirree*, is an effect of the Western man's tendency to augment both form and meaning of the commonest terms. The extraordinary word, in the utterance extended to a length by no means represented in its form, is however quite as familiar to the South as the West. A Hard-Shell Baptist preacher in Georgia is reported to have criticised its use in this manner: "*Bretheren*, it won't do, this talk that ain't primitive; we must give up them worldly remarks—must we not, bretheren, must we not, sisteren? Yes *Sir-ree*, and no *Sir-ree*, is slang terms and forbidden. I don't like 'em nor no brother don't like 'em. I'm determined to set my face aginst them—ain't ye, bretheren?—Yes *Sir-ree*, hoss! replied his tripping brother behind him in the pulpit." (*Putnam's Magazine*, February, 1855.) That the term has found its way to the great cities, also, may be seen from the following police report: In a case tried at Baltimore, a juror was supposed to be intoxicated. "The judge, addressing the man, said: 'Sir, are you drunk?' The juror, straightening himself up, in a bold, defiant tone replied: 'No *Sir-ree, Bob*!' 'Well,' said the judge, 'I fine you five dollars for the *ree* and five for the *bob*.'" (Baltimore *Sun*, March 20th, 1857.)

An active young man or a bouncing lass is apt to be admiringly designated as a *roarer*, with an evident allusion to some powerful and formidable animal that roars in the forest or on the prairie. Here also an effort is made to intensify the expression by a curious epithet, having reference to the catamount: a specially fine fellow of great size and strength is called a *ring-tailed roarer*. Screaming seems to impress the Western man with the same sense of strength and valor, for a *screamer* is another favorite term of admiration. "Why, boys," said a Georgia Cracker to a colored soldier of the Federal Army, during Sherman's famous march, "if them's the kind your regimen is made off, I knocks under: them's *screamers*." (*Recollections of the War*, p. 217. By a Lady.) If animal spirits are a little too prominent, and assert themselves with vehemence, they procure for the owner the name of *snorter*, though here also the implied reproof is not unmixed with a certain degree of admiration for the dash and the daring. "I'm a *roaring* earthquake in a fight, sung out one of the half-horse, half-alligator sort of fellows, a real *snorter* of the universe. I can strike as hard as fourth-proof lightning and keep it up, rough and tumble, as long as a wild-cat." (Thorpe's *Backwoods*, p. 183, *B.*)

The *Mountaineer*, as the man was called who earned his precarious livelihood by "hunting for skins" in the mountains of the Far West, is fast disappearing before nomadic cities and railways crossing a continent. Here is his description: "*Mountaineers*, when divested of their hunting-coats of buckskin, appeared in bran new shirts of gaudy calico and close-fitting buckskin pants, with long fringes down on the outside seam, from the hip to the ancle, with moccasins ornamented with bright beads and porcupine quills. Each, round his waist, wore his mountain-belt and scalp-knife, and some pistols sticking in their belt." (*Life in the Far West.*) A *tow-head*, originally nothing more than a light-haired boy, or, in the Western rivers, a slight ripple caused by some barely perceptible obstruction, is not unfrequently applied to a city-man with *store-clothes* and carefully arranged hair, contrasting with the long matted locks which the backwoodsman generally affects. The *rouser* is not only a man who talks very loud and occasionally yells, but also any startling event or exciting sermon. "That ar dare (deer), I tell you, was a *rouser* and no mistake," says the old hunter in *Stories from the Backwoods*, while an accomplished gentleman is thus spoken of in a novel: "He is a *rouser* at making punch, I assure you, though he only sips it like a lady himself." (*Putnam's Magazine*, January, 1868.) The English *roughs*, common only in London and in small boroughs at election time, where they are often known as "lambs," abound unfortunately in the United States. They belong to a turbulent class, recruited largely from the laboring and commercial population; they drink, they swear, but they commit no crime, save an occasional deed of violence in times when excitement runs unusually high, and are for the most part affiliated with one or the other of the two contending parties. They are, however, not often designated as *roughs*, since they prefer generally some local name of more or less grotesque form and brutal import, as *Dead Rabbits* in New York, *Moyamensing Hounds* in Philadelphia, or *Blood Tubs* in Baltimore. The Western *rough* is frequently a *roustabout*—a term evidently derived from the old English *roust*, quoted by Jamieson as meaning to disturb. He is a favorite character in the West, noisy, but not necessarily a rowdy, and frequently a useful member of society in some capacity which requires hard work and constant exposure. "As the steamer was leaving the levée, about forty black deck-hands or *roustabouts* gathered at the bow, and sang a rude Western sailor's song." (On the Plains. *Putnam's Magazine*, September, 1868.) But the most curious of all Western terms for men, is probably the name of the city of Boston, which by some strange freak of language has become the generic name of all whites among the natives of Oregon. "With this force we marched out into the Indian country, trusting that although the savages were at war with the *Bostons*, the devil was dead, and we should elude the traces of his lineal descendants on this march." (Trail-Making in Oregon. *Overland Monthly*, March, 1870, p. 204.)

IV.

THE CHURCH.

THE CHURCH.

Much has been said, half-admiringly, half-sneeringly, of the simple, homespun manner of American religion. There are here no lofty cathedrals with costly carvings and glowing colors in window and vault; no stately deans with their canons; even the bishops have but quite recently adopted the silk apron and the gilt crozier, which they had found so attractive at the Lambeth Conference. The Catholic Church alone maintains a sober splendor, but the stern Presbyterian, with his Puritan abhorrence of all outward form and ceremony, the hard Baptist, eschewing alike refinement and culture, and the zealous Methodist, who has neither time nor inclination to think of anything but his holy errand, seem strangely devoid of all that makes religion attractive to Europeans. Perhaps piety is only the more earnest in its homespun garb, and the quaintness and simplicity of religious language is but a reflex, perhaps an heirloom, of the days when the older English divines also spoke plainly, even bluntly, and men generally faced the facts of spiritual experience more boldly than is done now, because they were more closely inwoven in their every-day life. All the rationalism and skepticism of the New World has not been able to work out the Puritan leaven of the men in the Mayflower, and if religion is less formal, perhaps even less orthodox here, it is neither less sincere nor less fervid than in the Old World.

The most striking feature in our religious life is, no doubt, the perfect freedom allotted to every one, old and young, high and low, to choose his own mode of worship. No law prescribes church-*membership*, as it is commonly called; no inquiry is made by high authorities after the religious standing of candidates for office; no control exercised over their attendance on church ordinances, as is done on the Continent of Europe. As the Constitution of the United States purposely abstains from the mere mention even of God and of divine things, the citizen also is held accountable to his conscience alone for his religious convictions. Society is perhaps less tolerant, and while petitions have in vain been sent to Congress year after year for an open avowal of the Christian faith in public acts, social standing is only exceptionally granted to men professing openly to be without religion. Besides, every shade and variety of faith and church organization finds itself protected here, and Mr. Jefferson prided himself as much upon being the author of the Statute of Religious Liberty as upon having written the Declaration of Independence. Hence names of new sects and new meanings of familiar terms follow each other in such rapid succession here, that even the initiated is often at a loss to account for their origin and precise signification. The language even has suffered from this reckless spirit of innovation, although far more yet from the peculiar independence of all American churches. While in England the ministers of the Established Church and the better-trained preachers among the Dissenters are the jealous guardians and principal disseminators of pure English throughout the country, in America no such influence is exercised by the clergy. The very zeal of the majority, unhampered by English phlegm and Oxford traditions, leads to a freer use of the language, and the frequency of extempore preaching prevents, as a matter of course, very careful composition. Methodist and Baptist preachers were, until lately, kept, partly from necessity and partly from choice, from obtaining a high grade of education, and being generally called upon to address utterly uneducated hearers, their language was naturally adapted to their own imperfect training and the ignorance of their congregations. Even the best-educated clergymen were apt to seek new forms for their new views, or ready to employ popular terms in times of public excitement, as when the disastrous fashion of political sermons was still in vogue. Thus they soon went far beyond their brethren in England, who have often been accused of allowing much slang and disagreeable vulgarism to creep into the pulpits, which should give forth pure speech as well as pure doctrine.

Thus the very word *religion* itself came early to be abused and to be forced to mean piety. Certain sects began by speaking of men who wished to *get religion*, so that the Rev. Mr. Cartwright could write of his own preaching: "It was remarked by many that it seemed the easiest thing here, of any place or time they ever saw, for sinners to *get religion*" (*Autobiography*, p. 27); and of a friend of his: "Her husband was a Methodist, and several of their children had *got religion* among the young converts. This lady got powerfully convicted and concluded that she had never had any *religion*." (p. 87.) A thoroughbred Yankee boy, of Keene, in New Hampshire, drew a nice distinction when he said: "Pa is the piousest man in the valley, but I enjoys the most *religion*." (*Putnam's Magazine*, Dec., 1869.) A person proposing to *join a church* is expected first openly to *come out*, that is to say, to *profess* his religion, and then he is admitted to membership in the form peculiar to each church, and ever after known as a *professor* of religion. The *church* is not only the building, but, contrary to English usage, the congregation, after the apostolic manner, as employed in the words: "When they had ordained them elders in every *church*." (*Acts*, xiv. 23.) To *join* it, application is made to the pastor or the deacon; hence the account given of "Mr. Fips, who wanted to become a *member* of Pilgrim *church*. It would have made him respectable. But Deacon Flagg replied to his application gravely, 'Very sorry, Mr. Fips, but the church is full. There isn't a single vacancy. If there should be one I'll let you know.'" (*Putnam's Magazine*, Aug. 1868.) In the Methodist church this open avowal is frequently made by persons who have *met with a change*, or have been *struck under conviction*—a favorite phrase at times of great excitement—or who have *experienced* religion. Thus the same excellent divine, whom we have repeatedly quoted, says: "When they were done preaching, they opened the way for persons to join the church by giving in their *experience*. If accepted, their *experiences* were declared good, and the right-hand of fellowship was freely given, and there was great joy in the camp; but it was death in the pot to me." (p. 67.) Any person who dwells much upon religious matters, or his own state of mind, is said to be *serious*, a term which perhaps originally was used with a sneer, but now is applied in all earnestness and approbation. In some localities, especially in the New England States, the church is also called a *society*, in others a *parish*, without referring in either case to the original meaning: the former is "a parish, but without territorial limits; the latter, a society of persons united for church purposes, but consisting of persons only."

The building itself is called a *church* only by some sects; others followed the opinions of the Puritans, who "held that a church was a body of Christians, and the place where they met was a *meeting-house*." (Elliott's *History of New England*, I., p. 131, B.) This was but one of the points on which the men of Plymouth determined to differ from their oppressors at home. "For," says an able writer, N. S. Dodge, "antagonism was their normal condition of life. To meet and pass an approaching vehicle on the left-hand was then, and still is, the custom in England; they changed it to the right. It had been customary, from time immemorial, to kneel in prayer to God; they changed it to the standing posture, whether in the family, the social meeting, or in public worship. Banns of marriage were in their native country proclaimed in church; they advertised them in the vestibule. The funeral service of the Rubric was read there at the burial; they bore their dead to the grave in silence. They abolished the sign of the cross in infant baptism, the prostration before the altar in receiving the holy communion, and the wedding-ring in marriage. The evangelists and apostles might not be designated as Saint Paul, Saint John, and the like, because it savored of Papistry; the Bible might not be read without comment in public worship, since it was improper conformity to hierarchical service; and of holy days none was recognized but Sunday, which they called Sabbath. Good Friday gave place to the annual Fast Day, always appointed on Thursday, and Christmas to Thanksgiving Day in the autumn. The most devout were never to groan aloud during prayer, nor to say amen; marriages were to be celebrated by civil magistrates, who not only gave the covenant to the parties interested, but made the prayers; and the melody of viols and organs in public worship was numbered with 'Nebuchadnezzar's idolatrous concert of the cornet, flute, dulcimer, sackbut, psaltery, and all kinds of music.' The church was called *meeting-house*, the service the *meeting*, and the priest the *minister*. Sunday began at sunset on the previous evening; thanks were returned after every meal as well as grace said before, and fish made the

Saturday's dinner instead of Friday's. Theatres were not permitted, and actors were flogged. Officers of the government were selected from among *church members* only, and the latter were known to have been converted by being able to name the day and the hour when they had experienced the new birth." This Puritan leaven is still as active as ever, and shows its strength nowhere so strikingly as in matters and terms of religion. With the Yankee, the *meeting-house,* with its *steeple*—the word "spire" is hardly ever heard in America—has found its way to every part of the Union; only the stately building of New England is in Georgia "built of hewn logs, unceiled and unplastered, with sliding window-shutters of planks, having low benches placed as in a schoolroom, for seats; it is situated in a grove not far from the village, near a pleasant spring of water." (*Southern Life,* p. 137.)

The inside of the meeting-house is, however, not always so simple as it was in the days of the Puritans. Even then the high *seats* were much in demand, and the yearly *seating,* as the assignment of seats according to rank and office was called in New England, gave rise to much silent envy and open controversy. The custom still survives in the annual renting of seats in certain churches, on which occasion the lively competition for choice pews induces ambitious members to pay often enormous premiums, and thus fills the treasury of the church without trouble and complaint. The system of pews made its way but slowly into some of the churches, and the word *seat* was long used and abused in this connection. Thus we are told that the Methodists in the West used "to erect a shed, sufficiently large to protect 5000 people from rain and wind, and cover it with boards, after which they would *seat* the shed, and collect there people from forty and fifty miles around." But "Since the Methodist Church," says the Rev. Mr. Cartwright, mournfully, "has risen in numerical strength and become wealthy, the system of *pewed* churches is fast becoming the order of the day," thus using one of the new words of the language. As if in derision of the custom, they speak in Nantucket of a *pew-cart,* "a kind of one-horse, two-wheeled, springless carriage, a sort of pew upon wheels, or a box without seats, simply to stand up in, and with high sides, around which runs a rope to hold by." (N. P. Willis, *Home Journal,* Oct., 1857.)

The word *meeting* gains a new significance in the compound

camp-meeting, a term not unfrequently used in ridicule or reproof, though without a shadow of excuse. "Somewhere between 1800 and 1801," says the father of Western Methodism, "in the upper part of Kentucky, at a memorable place, called Cane Ridge, there was appointed a sacramental meeting by some of the Presbyterian ministers, at which meeting, seemingly unexpected by minister and people, the mighty power of God was displayed in a very extraordinary manner. It was kept up day and night, protracted for weeks; there were from 12,000 to 25,000 people present at times. It was said by trustworthy witnesses that often more than a thousand persons broke out into loud shouting at once, and that the shouting could be heard for miles all around..... This was the first *Camp-Meeting* ever held in the United States, and here our *Camp-Meetings* took their rise." (p. 31.) The idea is not new. When St. Francis assembled 5000 of his followers on the plains of Assisi, and held, what has been called in the records of the Franciscan order, the Chapter of Mats, the people had no other shelter but rude tents made of mats, just as at *camp-meetings* simple tents and booths made of branches serve the purpose. Nor does the resemblance end here. The Saint had to moderate the excesses of fanaticism and penance in which his disciples indulged, in precisely the same manner in which even *backwood-preachers*, as they are called in the West, have now to repress the overwrought zeal of their followers.

In the West, specially large and long-continued assemblies of this kind are called *Big Meetings*, whilst in the New England States they are more commonly designated as *Protracted Meetings*. Notice is given a long time beforehand, renowned preachers are announced as coming to the help of local ministers, and the preaching, praying, and exhorting are *protracted* for a week and occasionally even for a longer period. At all of these various meetings, *revivals* are frequent, as is well known, but certain features of these extraordinary occurrences among the Methodists have led to the technical use of certain words. Thus, persons who are peculiarly excited to a consciousness of their sinfulness, and the necessity of seeking salvation, are called *anxious mourners*, and led by the minister or deacons to the *anxious bench* or *seat*, a bench near the altar, there to receive aid and comfort. In their intense excitement they are apt to become nervous and hysterical, and one of the symptoms of this state is known as the *jerks.* The Rev. Mr. Cartwright calls them a new exercise, overwhelming in its effects on the minds and bodies of the people. No matter whether they were sinners or saints, his hearers "would be *taken* under a warm song or sermon and seized with a convulsive *jerking* all over, which they could not resist, for the more they resisted, the more they *jerked.* More than five hundred people would be jerking at once. Proud young ladies and gentlemen, dressed in silks, jewelry, and prunella, from top to toe, would take the *jerks.* At the first jerk you would see their bonnets, caps, and combs fly, while their long, loose hair would crack like a wagoner's whip." At a large revival, where numbers of Arians attended, there was a wholesale exorcism; in that meeting the crowd *fell* by hundreds; *mourners* were grovelling on the ground in every direction; the cries of the penitents and the shouts of those who had gotten religion went up without intermission day and night, and amid them all danced, and whirled, and flew about in seemingly uncontrollable madness, countless *jerkers.*

In 1804, a revival occurred in Tennessee, Kentucky, Ohio, and other Western States, remarkable for another symptom, approaching in its character a regular malady. At the large, open-air meetings, almost as soon as the sermon commenced, numbers suddenly fell to the ground, deprived of bodily strength, and some were violently convulsed. These affections received the name of *Falling Exercises.* *Whirling Exercises* were still more grotesque affections, in which, during a sermon, persons spun round like a top for upward of an hour, without experiencing any fatigue, precisely after the manner of the dancing dervises of the East. Although these symptoms for many years accompanied almost all religious exercises held in the open air, and attended by large numbers, it need hardly be added, that they are quite rare now-a-days, and little encouraged by the majority of preachers.

A church wishing to obtain a minister, depute some of their number to invite him, and hence a reverend gentleman tells us: "He was at the head of a movement to give me what ministers term a *call,* for I then received a letter from the old pensioners, asking me to come and be their chaplain." (*Lippincott's Magazine,* Oct., 1869.) If the *call* is accepted, the minister is said to *settle,* so that the biography of Bishop Asbury mentions "his having been *settled* at the early age of seventeen" (p. 137)—a ceremony which in his case was simple enough, but in many churches is made the occasion of much ceremony and great rejoicings, giving occasionally rise to an old-fashioned *infare* or installation. He becomes what in some churches is called a *stated* preacher, and assumes now the *desk*, for the distinction made in England between the pulpit and the reading-desk is not observed by all the churches of America, and in New England especially, the words: "What we want for our security is that the voice from the pulpit may concur with the voice from the *desk*," would not be very intelligible to many pious readers.

As these *calls*, after the first, are very apt to be accompanied by the temptation of an increase of salary, sneerers have occasionally pretended to believe that ministers feel bound to see what is called a *Providential Call* in such an invitation. The sneer is, of course, utterly unfounded, although the offers thus made would probably prove irresistible to less unselfish men. Even where the *stated* salaries, as they are called, seem moderate, handsome perquisites are apt to come in with the rites of the church. New Year's *remembrances* are quite fashionable in large cities, while in smaller towns and rural districts preachers have to familiarize themselves with a custom peculiar to American churches, and founded upon true Christian humility: they learn to accept presents in money, in provisions, and even in clothes, which they would probably hesitate to accept in any other walk of life. It is by no means unusual for a liberal church-member to present his pastor with a supply of linen, a suit of clothes, a new hat, or even more modest gifts, though more frequently all the members combine and have a *basket-meeting*, as it is called in the West, or in the Eastern States, hold a *donation-party*. On such an occasion friends and parishioners appear suddenly—for it is generally a *surprise-party* at the same time—at the parsonage, request the owner to retire to his study, set his table in the dining room, loading it with good things, fill his pantry, lay out presents, and then invite their willing host and his family to join them at the merry feast. As the salary of ministers is small everywhere outside of the large cities, where it sometimes rises to twenty thousand dollars, as in the case of Mr. H. W. Beecher, and as the rules of the Methodist Church strictly limit the minister's income to a mere pittance, this method of supplying an addition is as welcome as suitable. Cases are, however, known in which the company was larger than the supply they brought, compelling the minister to contribute more than his parishioners had done; in this case his feelings must be akin to those of a poor housewife who is suddenly called upon to entertain a *surprise-party.* During the late war, especially, families were often unable to keep up the style of entertainment of former years, and it became a kind of fashion for their friends to *drop in* unexpectedly, with the tacit understanding that the use of the house was all the owner had to furnish. This was, however, but rarely taken literally, and hence it has been said of them, that "as to *surprise-parties,* there was a delightful freedom and absence of form in the notion, but the mutual friend's wife must be an angel if she can appreciate the joke."

In many churches the *minister*—a term which stands uniformly for the clergyman of the Established Church also, and not, as in England, only for the minister of a dissenting house of worship—is both supported and somewhat controlled by his *deacons.* The power enjoyed by the latter, especially in the New England States, has descended upon them from the days of the Puritans, among whom *deacons* were men wielding great authority and formidable powers, in worldly matters as well as in the concerns of the church. Among their duties was that of reading aloud the hymns given out by the minister, one line at a time, the congregation, having no hymn-books in those early days, singing each line as soon as read. Hence was derived the phrase of *deaconing off* at a meeting, which is explained by J. R. Lowell as meaning to give the cue and lead the debate. (*Glossary to Biglow Papers.*) As Yankees have a popular proverb that "All *deacons* are good, but there is odds in *deacons,*" the difference may have given rise to the phrase, to *deacon* berries, which, we are told by the same high authority, means, to place the largest berries on top—we trust without any sly desire to impose,

> "To funk right out o' p'lit'cal strife aint thought to be the thing,
> Without you *deacon off* the time you want your folks to sing."
> (*Biglow Papers.*)

But why the same word, when applied to a poor, new-born

calf, should mean to kill it, is a mystery to all but Yankees, among whom the phrase of *deaconing a calf* is said to prevail to the present day.

The minister is, by such and similar means, brought into close contact with his congregation, and this intercourse is barbarously called *fellowshipping*. Fortunately the term—of comparatively recent origin, and probably unknown before 1813, when it was first met with by Mr. Pickering—is still confined to ecclesiastical writings and discussions, and may soon—to use its ill shapen companion—be *disfellowshipped* (!) altogether. At times it begins to creep into humorous language, as when an indignant damsel is made to say: "No, thanky, Miss Randall, Dely Bligh aint such a fool as that yet; she hasn't never *fellowshipped* the minister, though he did court her, I say for't, considerably of a spell. I am glad on it, too." (*Atlantic Monthly*, Feb., 1861.) He now has a congregation, rarely a *parish*, a word which is generally used only in the Episcopal and Catholic Church, and in Louisiana has so far lost its original meaning as to designate simply the *district* of South Carolina and the *county* of other States. In his official duties he is, of course, guided by the rules of his church, only of a marriage he is asked to make a *publishment* of the banns, and in the case of *funerals*, two peculiarities may be noted here. The great distance at which the first settlers lived from each other, made it often impossible to obtain the services of a minister on such occasions; this led to the custom, still prevailing even in densely-settled districts, and especially among the freedmen of the South, to have *funerals*, *i. e.*, special funeral sermons preached some time after the death of the person. As the grief of a crowd is not expected to be very deep, and the year or two which may have elapsed since the burial may safely be presumed to have allayed even the sorrow of the family, such *funerals* are apt to become an occasion for merry-making. This is all the more likely to occur, as in many parts of the Union, especially in Pennsylvania, the custom still prevails—not of giving wine and cake as formerly—but of those who attend the services returning to the house of mourning and dining there. No liquor, however, is offered, and there is nothing convivial in the meal; it is simply a refreshment offered to those who have come from a distance to show their respect for the departed. This, however, is also called a *funeral,* apart from the religious ceremony, and while the duties performed during the latter have been barbarously called to *funeralize,* the former has escaped the corruption. A somewhat curious phrase has been made by the aid of this word *funeral,* which is apparently purely American. "This is *none of your funeral,*" is heard quite frequently as an indirect rebuke for intermeddling, with the ludicrous undercurrent of thought, that the troublesome meddler has no right to be crying at a strange man's funeral.

The word *platform,* in its frequent application to ecclesiastical constitutions, is by no means an Americanism. Lord Bacon speaks of "the exemplar or *platform* of God" (*Advancement of Learning,* p. 225), and Hooker mentions views "conformable to the *platform* of Geneva." "A *Platform* of Church Discipline," is the title of a book printed as early as 1653, in London. (B.) The use of the word in politics is more likely to be peculiar to America, and to speak of a *plank* of a platform, is a genuine and exclusive Americanism, "not yet naturalized in England." (*Blackwood's Magazine,* Oct., 1867.)

In his sermons, lectures, and discourses, the American minister uses better English than any other class of professional men; there are very few words which may be said to be either peculiar to the pulpit or objectionable to the purist. He rarely uses slang, with the exception of the occasional and unwarrantable introduction of politics; and on the whole escapes wonderfully well from the national fondness for big words and picturesque phrases. He will, perhaps, speak of *amenability* with the political orator, and of *accountability,* instead of the English accountableness, and quote Robert Hall as his authority. In the West he may *argufy* a point, and find support in Hallowell's Dictionary, where the word is referred to various dialects. In Virginia he notices with pleasure "one who listens well, a respectable, *assentatious* stranger" (J. D. Kennedy. *Swallow Barn,* p. 224), and encouraged by this silent assent given to his position, may forget his *curtitude* (Prof. S. S. Haldeman), and expatiate too long on the ways by which we may be *happified.* Thus he is in danger of becoming *lengthy,* a word admirably suggestive, though as yet not admitted to the sacred pages of an English dictionary. A Scotch critic says, however, forcibly: "This daring interloper has made good its way in the language. Expressive of a new meaning, the word must be accepted, whether or no the grammarians and lexicographers approve; and *lengthy*, whether of American or English origin, will probably remain English while the language lasts." (*Blackwood*, Oct., 1867.) And the master of American English, J. R. Lowell, says of the same word: "We have given back to England the excellent adjective *lengthy*, formed honestly like earthy, droughty, and others, thus enabling their journalists to characterize our Presidents' messages by a word civilly compromising between long and tedious, so as not to endanger the peace of the two countries by arousing our national sensitiveness to British criticism." (*Biglow Papers*, II., Pref.) It is probably not essential to Mr. Jefferson's fame whether he may or may not be credited with the invention of the word *lengthily*, as stated in Webster's Dictionary. If the minister *summarizes* his points, he uses but a phrase frequently met with in the writings of good authors, and will be readily pardoned for it; his listeners will thus escape from the favorite habit of many preachers, *renewedly* to impress their points, a word as repugnant to good taste as to patience. The word *solemnizing*, in the sense of making serious, was long condemned as a clerical fault, but like *lengthy*, it has forced its way, by its usefulness, into later English diction, and is now sanctioned by the best orators, and even an author, so sensitive to the delicacies of language as De Quincey. If he finally adds one or two *improvements*, in order to apply and enforce his doctrine, he may offend Mr. Webster, who refuses to give that meaning of the word in his unabridged edition, but he will, nevertheless, let us hope, *improve* his hearers. A quaint allusion to this part of the service is made in an account of a church at Windsor, in Connecticut, built in 1709, which had neither pews nor seats. "Where," says the chronicler, "during President Edwards' long sermons running on to a Tenthly, with a goodly number of *improvements* appended, could the people find a sitting-place? Where, indeed, but on the sills and sleepers? Soon, however, the society passed the liberal vote, that the young men should have the liberty to make a seat upon the beams." (*Putnam's Magazine*, August, 1869.) Should he conclude his sermon without saying, if he is a Southern man, "*Grant* to hear us," instead of "Vouchsafe to hear us," and if he is a Northern man, without asking his hearers to join him *prayerfully*, instead of devoutly, he may well be commended for having escaped the few objectionable words with which American preachers, as a class, can be charged.

The absolutely unlimited freedom enjoyed by every citizen, not only to connect himself with any church he may prefer, but, if he can, to found himself a new church, has naturally led to the rise of sects innumerable, generally known as *denominations*. It it, perhaps, not absolutely certain that Americans are really the most religious people on earth, because, as a young American lady once assured the Holy Father, to set him at his ease, upon being presented to him, "they have so many *denominations*."

Sometimes these rise within the bosom of a well-known church, as in the case of the Baptist Church, which counts quite a number of subdivisions, known occasionally under somewhat peculiar names. Such are the *Soft Shell* Baptists, so called on account of their less stern manners and less rigid principles, which allow them to be indulgent to certain worldly usages, and to educate their ministers carefully for the pulpit, while the *Hard Shell Baptists,* who call themselves *Primitive* Baptists, set their faces like flint—to use their own term—against an educated ministry, and especially against all foreign evangelical missions. Hence, a member of Congress in recommending a friend for the position of Chaplain to the House, could say of him: "Mr. Morris is a regular member of the *Hard Shell Baptist* Church, a very pious man, not of very eminent ability, but just the man to pray for such a crowd as this." (B.) The Presbyterian Church thus gave existence to a new sect, when in 1801 their Synod in the State of Kentucky censured and silenced preachers, who had taken part in revivals, which they thought a disorder. These ministers immediately renounced the jurisdiction of the Presbyterian Church and organized one of their own. "Here," says the Rev. Mr. Cartwright, triumphantly, "was the origin of what was called *New Lights.* They renounced the Westminster Confession of Faith and all church-discipline, and professed to take the New Testament for their church-discipline. They established no standard of doctrine. Every one was to take the New Testament and read it, and abide by his own construction. They adopted the mode of immersion, the water-god of all errorists." (*Autobiography*, p. 32.)

In other cases the new sects became known by the name of their founder. Most prominent among these, if not by their number, at least by the publicity of their proceedings, were the followers of William Miller, known as *Millerites*. Expecting the first judgment, when the dead bodies of the saints would rise, and the living would be changed, so that both should be caught up in the air to meet the Lord, to take place in 1844, they settled their earthly accounts, bade farewell to their friends, assumed their white ascension-robes, and prepared for the sounding of the last trumpet. The 23d day of October, 1844, was the appointed time, and in some parts of the Union, in Ohio, New Jersey, and Delaware, the astonished traveller could see the highways and byways thronged with anxious crowds of men and women, while the trees in the orchards and the roofs of houses were filled with the more impatient *Millerites*, who thus hoped to be nearer to their new home in heaven. The disappointment on that and several other days, which were announced subsequently, rapidly diminished their number, but they are by no means extinct, and Mr. Miller, like Dr. Cumings, continues to foretell the near approach of the Millennium. *Christians* (pronounced like the word Christ) has been a favorite name with several sects, of which some re-appeared as *Marshallites* or *Stoneites*, while the more pretentious *Restitutionists* of Massachusetts believe in an immediate return of all things to their original form and purity. The South has its numerous *Campbellites*, founded by a learned and zealous Dr. Campbell, and *Thomasites*, seceders from his creed, who believe in the annihilation of the wicked, and a second creation of the good. The *Cochranites* of the New England States held public exhibitions of so gross a character that the civil authorities were more than once compelled to intervene, for the vindication of public decency. They professed to be the successors of the *Puritans* of an earlier day, who derived their name not from the noble exiles at Plymouth, but from the fancy that they were perfectly pure in heart and conduct, and completely emancipated from human passions, a beatific condition which they attempted to prove by discarding all clothing at their public assemblies. Even the simple Quakers have their *Hicksites*, who adopted the name of their first leader, Mr. Hicks, and are Socinians.

The *Dunkers* or *Tunkers*, so called from the German word

tunken, to dip, are one of the oldest as well as one of the quaintest of American sects. Already in 1744, when Virginia sent her first Commissioners to Lancaster, in Pennsylvania, in order to make a treaty with the Six Nations, they went "the next day, being Saturday, to the *Dunkers'* Nunnery, and the Indians danced, drank, and shrieked." (*History of Early Settlements*, Wills De Hass, p. 97.) Branching off in 1724 from the so-called Seventh-Day Baptists, they adopted several new features, such as a new mode of immersion, by plunging the candidate three times into the water backward, love-feasts, and foot-washings, and a costume and mode of address of their own, and soon grew in numbers and wealth. Their farms, extending along the base of the Alleghany Mountains, from Pennsylvania through the fertile Valley of Virginia toward the South, are marked by careful location, great thrift, and abundant harvests.

By far the most remarkable of American sects are the *Mormons*, a name which the deluded *Saints*, as they call themselves, are said to owe in poetical justice to an imposition practised some two hundred years ago. A very clever French writer, the Abbé de la Mothe de Vayer, engaged, in 1650, in a spirited controversy with a famous scholar and wit, M. de Montmor. In a series of brilliant but whimsical attacks the Abbé plays countless variations on the name of his adversary, and repeatedly pretends to derive Montmor from Mormon, which he declares to be the Greek word μορμῶν, a scarecrow! Nor does the curious coincidence stop here; for the fictitious *Mormon* of 1643—a book pretending to have been written by M. de Montmor, but in reality a scurrilous parody—argued in favor of polygamy! Hence, argues the well-known Thomas Boys, in *Notes and Queries* (Jan., 1858), this early French work most probably furnished the author of the new book of Mormon, whoever he may have been, with the leading idea and many prominent features. The history as well as the shocking theology—if their creed can be honored with such a name—of this most gigantic of all impostures since Mahomet's days, have been so fully and so admirably described by recent travellers, that nothing need be added here. The *Latter-day Saints* may well be left to the just retribution by which they must sooner or later be overtaken. The *Gentiles*, as they contemptuously style all outsiders, are daily encroaching upon their territory, where, according to a recent President's message, "Brigham Young is at once spiritual head of the Church and governor of the Territory of Utah, so that all authority, secular as well as spiritual, centres in himself." They still sing their famous song of invitation at their *wood-meetings*, as they call their assemblies in the open air:

"Come wretched, come filthy,
Come ragged, come bare;
You can't look too horrid,
Come just as you air;"

crowds still come from distant lands, where wretched poverty and filthy crime rule supreme, in unison with ignorance and superstition, and dozens of women are still *sealed* or *scaled*—as the varieties of spiritual marriage are called by them—to one husband, in order to enter heaven through his agency—but their days are numbered. Mormon rule in Utah has evidently come to an end. "A free press has disputed Brigham's powerful influence over the minds of his ignorant followers. Honest Federal judges have refused citizenship to the Prophet's latest recruits, because of their polygamy, and a large influx of miners of *Gentile* morals, or no morals at all, has greatly lessened the overwhelming, political majority, by which the Saints have long controlled the territory." (New York *Tribune*, March 7, 1871.)

The *Shakers* deserve mention here only in as much as they are now confined to America, and the name may hence be considered an Americanism. Their doctrine also has essentially changed since they seceded about 1770 in England from the Quakers. They now derive their name and their worship from their solemn though *shaking* dance, and the importance they attach to shaking as mentioned in the Bible, quoting words like: "The Lord promised that he would *shake* the earth with terror,"—"In that day there should be a great *shaking* in the land of Israel,"—"He would *shake* the heavens and the earth,"—"I will *shake* all nations and the desire of all nations shall come,"—and according to the apostle: "Yet once more I will *shake* not the earth only, but also heaven, signifying the removal of things that are *shaken*, as of things that are made, that those things, which cannot be *shaken*, may remain." At the same time they declare that the word Desire in the verse, "And the desire of all nations shall come" (Haggai,

ii. 7), is feminine, that consequently salvation was announced to come to mankind through woman, the nuptial "Bride of the Lamb," and this female Saviour was Ann Lee, the founder of their sect! She is to them the "Desire" of the prophet, and their spiritual mother, and as thus redemption is completed in both sexes, the race must die out, and the *Shakers* are called upon to accomplish this extinction by preaching and practising celibacy.

It can hardly be presumed that the *Spiritualists*, not unknown to England, but abounding in America, claim any religious character; at least Mr. Perry, as quoted by Mr. W. H. Dixon, says: "As a *spiritualist,* I have yet to learn that we hold anything as sacred. I am opposed to any resolution that has the word sacred in it." Their terminology is as trite as their doctrine. "There is a dark, motley crowd of wizards, witches, and spiritual *rappers,* so called, that have sooner or later invested all lands, and are the common property of the devil," said that zealous divine, the Rev. P. Cartwright, long before the famous *Fox Girls,* of Rochester, in New York, revived the absurd theory of spirits in heaven or elsewhere communing with men on earth by knocking on tables and walls. Hysteric women and silly men serve as *mediums,* through whom the spirits have spoken much balderdash, but so far failed to make known a single fact of real usefulness; and their papers, such as the *Spiritual Age* of Boston, Massachusetts, advertise sedulously, that "a *Circle* is held for Medium Developments and Spiritual Manifestations at Bloomfield-street every Sunday, morning and evening, admission five cents; and every Sunday afternoon, admission free." The *naïveté* of these organs of misled enthusiasts may be judged of from the following anecdote told in the same paper (October 3, 1868): "A few evenings since, as a private *Circle* of Spiritualists were receiving communications from the other world from a little child, it ceased suddenly to communicate, but after repeated solicitations it came back, and in infantile language said: "There's a good deal of difference now, than when I was on earth. Then my dear mamma used to tell me little children should be seen and not heard; now little children must be heard and not seen." And upon the strength of such revelations, the Insane Asylums of the Union are filled with hundreds of victims of *Spiritualist visitations.* It would be difficult to understand how the practical sober mind of the American can be so easily led astray, if it were not for the insatiable curiosity of some, who are eager to know the secrets of the other world, and the satisfaction which free and independent spirits have always found in venturing upon forbidden ground for the sake of the risk, and in the confidence of their strength to conquer where weaker minds succumb. It is gratifying to think how energetically such errors are combated, and how triumphantly the fraternal love among all Christians has been proven by the *Union* Meetings held in all the States of the Union, where every sect is represented, and joint prayers are offered for national as well as individual salvation.

V.

POLITICS.

POLITICS.

"Than politics the American citizen knows no higher profession—for it is the most lucrative."

De Tocqueville.

THE political language of every nation bears naturally the stamp of the peculiar character of the laws and the constitution under which they live, and thus English conservatism is reflected in the steady maintenance of familiar names and terms, generation after generation, whilst the speech of the *mobile vulgus* in the great Republic changes almost from year to year. The active participation of the masses, and the extension of the right of suffrage to the very lowest and most ignorant classes have, moreover, favored the admission of so many vulgar and cant terms that in politics, above all, the line between slang and solemn speech is not always perceptible. Where appeals are made at every election to vast assemblies, not unfrequently consisting largely of so-called Mean Whites, and of Blacks but recently emancipated from slavery and all its blighting consequences, strong colors must be used to paint the adversary, and still stronger language to impress the dull minds. The newspapers join, as a matter of necessity, in the general hue and cry, and foster the taste for violent epithets and picturesque expressions. The very heroes of the day are recommended on the score of their humble origin and modest occupation—the *self-made* man is preferred to the accomplished son of distinguished parents, and to be a gentleman has well-nigh become an insuperable barrier to success in political life. From an early period in the history of the republic the people have felt the indirect flattery of the boast that its great men had once been among the lowest; it implied the prospect and the right of the lowest to rise, as self-made men, to the highest place of honor. They recollected with pleasure that Roger Sherman had been a shoemaker, Benjamin Franklin a soapboiler and printer, and Rufus Hatch a peddler. Henry Clay, the great Commoner, as his friends loved to call him, was spoken of during election-time as the *Miller boy of the Slashes,* and Abraham Lincoln as the *Rail-splitter* and *Flatboatman.* Under the presidency of Andrew Johnson, once a tailor, Congress boasted of Senator Wilson, a journeyman shoemaker, and of Representative Banks, a blacksmith. Vanderbilt, the owner of a continuous railway from New York to Niagara, loves to tell how he rowed a huckster's boat when a youth, and Dr. Helmbold, the millionaire, how he began life as a cabin-boy.

Hence also, the tendency to familiarize great men by their nicknames, and thus bring them down, as it were, to the level of the masses. General McClellan was *Little Mac* or *Young Napoleon,* Hooker became *Fighting Joe,* and Sheridan is still *Little Phil.* Sherman was known as *Mad Tom,* and Sumner as the *Bull of the Woods*—even the Orleans Princes, who made a campaign under General McClellan, had to submit to the universal fate, the Count of Paris becoming *Captain Perry,* and the Duke of Chartres *Captain Chatters.* Nor were the commanders of the Confederates spared on their side: General Lee was *Mas Bob,* Johnston *Old Joe,* and Longstreet the *War-Horse;* Jackson became immortal as *Stonewall,* and an unlucky namesake as *Mudwall;* the dashing Cavalry leader Stuart was known as *Jeb,* Early as *Crackers,* and poor old General Price, in the West, as *Old Dad.*

Even the name of the confederacy of States, the *Union* of the *United States* was, from the beginning, too formal for the good people, and the familiar letters *U. S.*, seen on all government property throughout the land, were soon universally read *Uncle Sam.* The story of its origin, in the year 1812, is generally told thus: A Mr. Samuel Wilson, invariably called Uncle Sam by kindred and friends, was an inspector appointed by the government to receive large supplies for the army, contracted for in New York, and to be delivered at Troy, on the Hudson. It so happened that casks and chests were all marked with the initials of the contractor, Elbert Anderson (E. A.), above and beneath those of the country, United States (U. S.) A facetious workman, being asked the meaning of the latter, in jest replied: "he did not know, unless they meant Elbert Anderson and Uncle Sam." The jest took, was repeated by the other workmen, and by them carried into the army, and recalled wherever articles marked with the familiar *U. S.* reappeared in their presence. Thus the name spread from the Commissary's barrel of beans throughout the land, and has never since lost its hold upon the public mind.

Now, J. R. Lowell sings:

"For I have loved my country since
  My eye-teeth filled their sockets;
And *Uncle Sam* I reverence,
  Partic'larly his pockets."

(*Biglow Papers*, I.)

In the army, it seems, even this designation was deemed too full and formal, and, as early as the year 1827, it became a familiar saying among soldiers, to *stand Sam*, whenever drinks or refreshments of any kind had to be paid for. As they were accustomed to see *Uncle Sam* pay for all their wants, to *stand Sam*, became to their mind equivalent to the ordinary slang phrase: to *stand treat.*

Whilst this is the familiar name of the national government at home, it is abroad, perhaps, better known as *Brother Jonathan.* The name is taken from Jonathan Trumbull, who was governor of Connecticut at a time when General Washington had come to Massachusetts to assume command over the army, in the War of the Revolution. He discovered here such a want of supplies, ammunition, and even good-will, that the cause seemed almost hopeless. In this difficulty he found great support in the energetic and wise governor, and thus contracted the habit of saying, in every emergency, "We must consult Brother Jonathan." The phrase became soon familiar to his aids and subordinates, and through them to his army; they took it up, and the by-word spread quickly over the country. *Brother Jonathan* became, henceforth, the familiar designation of this country, as John Bull is that of England, and "since that day," says a recent writer, "a great many people have found *Brother Jonathan* a very helpful relative in time of need." (*Overland Monthly*, March, 1871.)

Almost all of the technical terms connected with the government of the United States, were necessarily those long familiar to English ears, but many received here a very different meaning and use from their originals. The use of *Government* itself, without an article, and still more so of an adjective *governmental*, long condemned by English authorities as a barbarism, is peculiar to this country, while the term *gubernatorial* finds its local limits in the powers of a State governor, in contradistinction to the national government. Nor is the special meaning of *the Executive*, instead of executive officer, for the president of the United States, given abroad to the term; the *Judiciary* also, as denoting that branch of government in which judicial power is vested, is American. The third branch of the government of the Union, the legislative body, is in like manner known as *Congress*, consisting of the *Senate* and the *House of Representatives*. Formerly it was here customary to speak of *The Congress*, but the name became soon so familiar that the article was promptly omitted, and we are assured that "since the last thirty years in England also, a half-educated man may speak of The Congress as well as of The Parliament; but such is not even the conversational practice of well-educated Englishmen." Its labors, its powers, and practices, are all called *congressional*, and thus Mr. E. Everett distinguished between "*congressional* and official labor." The *Senate*, consisting of two members for each State, the general interests of which they represent, is presided over by the *Vice-President*, and it and the *House of Representatives*, who are chosen by a certain number of inhabitants, and represent the people more directly, constitute jointly the legislative branch of government. A *Congressman* is generally a member of the House, though some writers apply the term to *Senators* also. The *States*, which form the Union, have the same three branches, though under different names: the Executive is here styled *Governor*, the legislative branch a *General Court* (in Massachusetts), a *General Assembly*, or briefly the *Legislature* (in Virginia). Members are chosen to *sit on* the Legislature in many States: "In this year Governor Randolph was to be chosen to *sit on* the Legislature, but Mr. Jefferson was long violently opposed to such a plan." (Tucker's *Life of Jefferson*, I., 319.) This body generally meets or *sits* at the *State-House*, a term either specially made to serve the purpose, or possibly derived from the Dutch *Stadhuys*, but in either case peculiar to America, while the judiciary sit at the *Court-House*. The latter name is in some of the Southern States very generally given to the county town, and thus *Fairfax Court-House* and *Culpeper Court-House* have become famous in the late Civil War, while the real names of the towns are utterly unknown to history.

The States, it is well known, claim having given up certain rights of their own to the Federal Government, reserving, however, certain other rights necessary to their independence. These latter have become most fatally known of late as *State-Rights,* since the question as to their precise nature and extent was ostensibly the cause of the late Civil War. The tendency is here, as in Europe, toward centralization of power, and the Federal Government is daily growing stronger at the expense of the States. The *constitutionality* of every such so-called usurpation of power is necessarily much discussed, but has received a severe shock in the recent adoption of two new theories of government. The one was Mr. W. H. Seward's device of a *Higher Law,* first broached by him, in 1850, in a speech made in the Senate, on freedom from slavery in the Territories. He said: "The Constitution regulates our stewardship; the Constitution devotes our domain to union, to justice, to defence, to welfare, to liberty. But there is a *higher law* than the Constitution, which regulates our authority over the domain." Vast and vague as the authority is, that may be thus claimed, it is at least founded upon an alleged law; but another authority has been appealed to and successfully established in the government, and this is the *War Power,* a new word made to meet new exigencies. Mr. J. Q. Adams is believed to have first used it in some of his State papers, for the purpose of designating the scope of the martial law, which, in certain cases, necessarily supersedes the orders of the legislature. Its first actual application is generally attributed to General Fremont, when he availed himself of his military authority, as Commander-in-Chief in the West, to declare, that all slaves were free by the mere presence of the Federal army. The measure itself was not sanctioned by government, but the doctrine was adopted, and subsequently made to justify some of the very boldest steps taken by the Federal authorities.

By the side of the *States,* the Union contains within its confederation *Territories,* embryo States, as it were, not yet possessing the necessary population to entitle them to representation in Congress, and a share in the common government. The Executive appoints their officers, governor, etc., and they are represented by *Delegates,* having a voice, but no vote, on the floor of Congress. Each State is again subdivided into smaller fractions, which in the Eastern States are known as *towns* or *townships;* in Louisiana, from the former French régime, as *parishes;* in South Carolina, as *districts;* and in all the other States, as *counties.* In connection with the latter term, Mr. Pickering already notices the universal pleonasm used by Americans in speaking of the *County of Berkshire,* forgetful of the fact that *shire* (a share) means the same thing as *county.*

It has already been stated that in popular language the Union is, on a larger scale, divided into the *North* and the *South,* the *East* and the *West,* with a disposition to speak of each of these parts as of a *section,* and of its special interest or characteristics as *sectional*—a distinction which the strong tendency toward centralization is likely to efface more and more. A necessary political division, however, is that into *districts,* of which each contains as nearly as possible the number of inhabitants which are entitled to send one representative to the *House.*

For the purposes of an election, these districts, and often large cities also, are still further subdivided into *precincts,* within which polls are established. "The result of the election has not yet been ascertained, as the reports from the outlying *precincts* will not be in for several days." (Richmond *Enquirer,* November 8, 1870.)

As the proper arrangement of districts is of the very greatest influence on the result of the elections, the manner of *apportioning,* as it is called, their due share of representation to all, is often a political measure of vast importance, and, it is feared, not always carried out with undoubted impartiality. Whenever, for instance, a new *Census* is held, as the enumeration of all the inhabitants of the United States every ten years is called, and shows that certain districts have increased in their population, a new *apportionment* has to be made, and in doing this more regard is generally had to the interests of the party than the rights of the people. The word has become so familiar to American ears, that it is not unfrequently used for other purposes also, as when J. C. Neal speaks of "Those ladies who get too little in dame Nature's *apportionment* bill." (*Charcoal Sketches,* II., 87.)

The process of laying out the districts themselves, also, is one calling for much political ingenuity, and the *districting* new States, or *redistricting* old States, as it is technically called, is an occasion of intense excitement. It has even obtained a special name—*gerrymandering*—from a Mr. Elbridge Gerry, a prominent politician of Massachusetts, who in 1811 first proposed to *redistrict* that State in such a manner that those sections which gave a large number of Federal votes, might be brought into one district. From that time this process, by which one party may obtain a majority in an election, although the opposite party have a majority of all voters, has been called after the ingenious author.

The prevailing fondness for fancy names has, of course, not spared the Union and its great divisions also, and thus, among many that are merely local, three such terms, at least, are in universal use. The Western States, with their youthful vigor and daily increasing political power, are generally designated as the *Great West;* the New England States, that have so long ruled the country, are familiarly known as *Yankeedom,* and the Southern States—during the war, the whole Confederacy—as *Dixie;* a popular term most probably derived from the geographical line drawn by Messrs. Mason and *Dixon,* which formerly separated the free from the slave-holding States. It came first into use when Texas, a new State that had just joined the Union, was believed to be an Eldorado, where colossal fortunes could be made in a short time; and thousands went there, alone or with their slaves to begin a new career and accumulate treasures. Negro melodies used the shortened term, and from them *Dixie* passed into common use, as the name of the happy, abundant South. It ought, however, to be mentioned here, that another version exists of its origin. A Mr. Dixy is said to have lived during the last century, when slavery still existed in the State of New York, on what is even now known as Manhattan Island. He had large numbers of slaves, many of whom, in the course of his long life, he sent to the South, to cultivate broad tracts of land which he owned there. These poor people, torn from their home and their old associates, looked back with intense longing to the land of their birth, negroes having in those days a surprising attachment to localities, and in their memory *Dixy's* farms, and all concerning them, gradually assumed most charming colors. Thus they would talk and sing of *Dixy*, till negro-minstrelsy sprang up, fashioned one of these songs into a ballad, and *Dixie* was born. The version, if not strikingly probable, has at all events the merit of reconciling the Northerner to a term regarded with much dislike and political hatred.

Of really historic names which designate certain parts of the United States, the *Old Colony* and the *Old Dominion* are perhaps the only two that survive. The former designates the territory held by the original Plymouth Colony, which preceded by many years the establishment of a colony on Massachusetts Bay; in 1692 the two colonies were united in one, the State of Massachusetts, but the old name still survives, and is cherished by the descendants of the first settlers. The other name was earned for Virginia by her loyalty to the Stuarts during the time of the Commonwealth. The colonists on the James River refused to recognize Cromwell and the Protectorate, and strenuously maintained their allegiance to Charles II., who was then in exile on the Continent. They even wrote to him, through their governor, Sir William Berkeley, assuring him of their loyalty, and expressing the most earnest wishes for his health, happiness, and restoration to the throne. They also invited the king, who was then at Breda, in Holland, poor in purse and apparently poorer in prospects, to emigrate to Virginia. Cromwell sent a fleet to bring them into submission, and, as Bancroft states it, "they refused to surrender to force, but yielded by a mutual deed and voluntary compact." As soon, however, as news was received of Cromwell's death, Charles II. was solemnly proclaimed King of Great Britain, Ireland, and *Virginia*, and all writs and processes were issued in his name, so that he was virtually King of Virginia, in fact, before he had begun to reign at home, *de jure*. For once the Stuart-king was not ungrateful; he restored the governor, deposed by Cromwell's order, to his place, commanded the arms of Virginia to be quartered with those of Great Britain on the royal escutcheon, as they appear on coins struck as late as 1773 by order of George III., and authorized—at least by tacit consent—the use of the words *Old Dominion*. It has been asserted that, with a view to recognize and cherish similar loyalty elsewhere, the English Government has recently bestowed upon the remaining British provinces of North America the title of "The *Dominion* of Canada."

Another division, frequently found alluded to in books as well as in the daily press, and when tariff questions are discussed in Congress, of constant occurrence in political speeches, is that of *Atlantic*, *Pacific*, and *Gulf* States, according to their bordering upon the two great oceans or the Gulf of Mexico. The latter, especially, have always had interests and strong claims of their own, as they alone produce cotton, and long believed that *Cotton was King.*

The motto of the new republic, *E Pluribus Unum*, however appropriate to the confederacy of many States which constitute but one great Union, has still the disadvantage of being neither new in thought nor original in form. The fact is, it was taken from a modest, metrical composition in Latin, written by Mr. John Carey in Philadelphia, and entitled: "The Pyramid of Fifteen States," in which occurs the following verses:

> "Audax inde cohors stellis *e pluribus unum*
> Ardua pyramidos tollit ad astra caput."

The three famous words were, of course, here also but a quotation, and the same motto occurs already in 1731 on the title-page of the Gentleman's Magazine, published in London. (*Overland Monthly*, March, 1871.)

The flag of the United States, containing originally only thirteen stripes, alternately red and white, was adopted by resolution of Congress, June 14, 1777, with a Union of thirteen stars on blue ground "representing a new constellation." The concluding words suggested two facts. The number indicated the number of States in the new Union, and has, hence, been steadily increased with every accession of a new State. The Union itself was, however, added, because the stripes were in all probability but a modification of the first republican flag of Boston, which retained the colors of the old St. George ensign, though the cross had been abolished by Governor Endicott as a sign of antichrist. It is frequently stated that the coat-of-arms of General Washington, containing three stars in the upper portion, and three bars running across the escutcheon, may have suggested the new flag; there is, however, no authentic evidence of such a fact, and it seems in the highest degree improbable that a young republic, in the first flush of enthusiasm and liberty, would adopt as its ensign the heraldic blazon of a modest English house. The *Stars and Stripes* of the United States have since advanced to the front rank of flags among the nations of the earth, in spite of the poet Trumbull's bitter lines, complaining that they

> "Tore the azure robe of night
> And set the stars of glory there,
> Inscribed with inconsistent types
> Of liberty and thirteen *stripes*."

Sailors laugh at it good-naturedly, and seeing it hoisted, say: "There goes the *gridiron*;" while the Confederates in their day used to speak of it, in derision, as the *Stars* and *Bars*. *Stripes and Stars* is an unusual designation, popular perhaps only with poets for the sake of the rhyme, as in the well-known lines—

> "Hurrah for the *Stripes* and *Stars*,
> Hurrah for annexation;
> Hurrah for our Yankee tars,
> And our Universal Nation."

A national anthem the great republic has not yet achieved. The *Star-Spangled Banner*, written during the war of 1812 by Mr. Francis S. Key, when on board a ship lying opposite Fort McHenry, near Baltimore, over which the American flag was flying, is probably most generally accepted as such. Its concluding lines—

> "Oh say, does that *star-spangled banner* yet wave
> O'er the land of the free and the home of the brave?"

never fail to inspire the patriotic heart. It is, perhaps, but in keeping with the foreign extraction of the vast majority of American citizens, that the most popular song and the only tune that can be called national, from its universal popularity, is the foreign-born melody of *Yankee Doodle*, which was first printed in 1775, during the siege of Boston.

Congress holds its *sessions* after the precedent of the British Parliament; but the same term is applied in some of the States to special courts of justice, engaged in regulating merely local affairs, like the granting of licenses or the building of bridges. The members, who, after English precedent, are styled *Honorable*, but, with American fondness for titles, retain the prefix for life, here have, or try to get, the *floor*, in order to deliver their speeches.

These are said to be not unfrequently delivered for *Buncombe*, an expression which has made its way with a large number of American political terms to England, and is almost naturalized there. The imported term denotes there false sentiments in speaking, as pretended enthusiasm or fictitious sympathy. The term originated thus: "A grave member of the Lower House of Congress, from the venerable State of North Carolina, representing a district, which included the County of *Buncombe*, in which he resided, whose style of speaking produced the very common effect of driving the members from the Hall, was one day addressing the House, when, as usual, coughing and sneering commenced, and the members began leaving. He paused a while, and assured the House that there need be no uneasiness on their part, and that for himself it mattered not how many left, for he was not speaking to the House, but to *Buncombe*." (Richmond *Compiler*, August 17, 1841.) Henceforth *Buncombe* became the generic name for any constituency, and politicians, who speak not on what interests their audience, but what may influence those who have chosen them as their representatives, are said to be *talking Buncombe*. An English writer thinks "This parable, explaining the origin of *Buncombe*, would form a very useful text to set up, handsomely illustrated, over the Speaker's chair in Parliament." (*Blackwood*, April, 1861.) With us the word has suffered much by constant use, and already in 1856 we find: "That a great deal of all this (celebration of Washington's birthday) was *buncom* (*sic*) and bogus patriotism, is an opinion very possibly entertained by many of the judicious and grave of our readers." (*Harper's Magazine*, Editor's Easy-Chair, April, 1856.)

The work done by Members of Congress is very largely influenced by agents from without, and by certain established usages of their own. The former is collectively called the *Lobby*, a term which, originating in the German *Laube*, a bower or small summer-house, meant for many centuries nothing more than a small hall or entering-room, preceding a larger room. In America, the rooms and passages surrounding the hall, in which legislative bodies hold their meetings, soon monopolized the term, and in a short time the men who assembled there to exercise whatever outside pressure they could bring to bear upon the legislators, were themselves called the *Lobby*. All who had petitions to be granted, contracts to be given, or favors of any kind to be bestowed, either went themselves or sent well-qualified agents to Washington, to *lobby* their cause, as it was called. Capitalists used the power which wealth gives, even where no bribery was attempted; high social standing was made serviceable, and even beauty and the charms of a silvery voice were not wanting to secure the votes of susceptible members. "A committee," said the New York *Herald* recently, "has been sent to *lobby* a new appropriation for our Post-office through the House." (Jan. 13, 1871.) And a young lady of great personal attractions, but not equal artistic endowments, was thus held to account: "Oh, Miss Vinnie Ream, *lobbying* is all very well, and even *button-holing* has no harm in it; but to go and smile bewitchingly till green banks bring forth golden butter-cups—isn't that a *leetle* too much?" (Chicago *Evening Post*, Feb. 7, 1871.)

The members themselves are apt to have some favorite project which allows them to appear generous while they act from a selfish motive; in that case they are said to have *an axe to grind.* The incorporation of a trading company, the chartering of a new railway, the renewal of a valuable patent—all such schemes are *axes to grind.* The term is attributed to J. K. Paulding, but occurs before his time in a newspaper sketch in the style of Benjamin Franklin's "Too much for your whistle." It introduces a boy, who was induced by a clever fiction to turn the grindstone for another man to *grind his axe.* (Professor S. S. Haldeman.) "Special legislation in behalf of private interests is one of the curses of this country, otherwise so blessed by the smiles of Divine Providence. The number of *axes* which are taken to the various State Capitols, to be *ground* at the public expense, is perfectly enormous." (New York *Tribune*, March 23, 1871.)

As many members are apt to be in the same position, parliamentary usage has established a system of *log-rolling,* as it is called, by which they engage to help each other mutually. The term is taken from the habit of *loggers,* in the great lumber regions of the Northern States, to help each other in the hardest work they have to perform—the rolling of their immense logs from the place where the tree has been felled, to the water on which they are to be floated down. Each *logging-camp* thus assist the others in accomplishing a work which would be beyond the power of any single one. In like manner, one member of the legislative body, unable to command sufficient votes for his own purpose, says to another member in the same position: Vote for my bill and I will vote for your bill; and this is called *log-rolling.* The process is especially resorted to by a new class of men, that has lately come into prominence, applicants for large grants of public lands to companies chartered to build railways, lay deep-sea telegraph lines, or to engage in other great works of national importance. The frequent impudence of their demands and the pertinacity with which they pursue their end, have brought them the unenviable name of *land-grabbers.* They are thus referred to in a sketch characterizing a recent governor of California: "Haight has made, on the whole, a good governor. He has fought rigorously the *ring* of land and money *grabbers,* and his course on this question has made him feared and disliked by them; but with the people generally it has made him popular." (Boston *Advertiser,* January 7, 1871.)

In more recent times *log-rolling* has lost much of its former prestige, as now-a-days all schemes of importance are taken up and pushed through by *rings,* combinations made outside the House, by whose activity and ample means everything is prepared beforehand, and all interests are secured, before the matter is reached by the House. Men who are not in the ring, either from conscientious scruples or because they command no influence on the floor, are called *outsiders,* and are *left out in the cold.* *Wire-pulling* is not an American custom exclusively, as the figure of speech is as old as the Marionettes of Italy and France, on whose miniature stage the actors were set in motion by wires, which the exhibitor pulled from above; but *wire-working,* as it is also called, has probably reached a higher degree of perfection here than abroad. "You can have no idea of the extent to which *wire-pulling* is practised in the Congress of the United States," wrote already poor, querulous Miss Martineau; "every man of the floor seems but to move in obedience to some power on the outside." Great skill in this art is facetiously called *sculduggery* in the West. *Pipe-laying,* on the contrary, is an original term here, derived from a fictitious and treacherous correspondence, which pretended to give an account of the method by which voters from Philadelphia were brought to the polls in

New York, while the fraudulent scheme was concealed under the form of a contract for the laying of water-pipes from the Croton Aqueduct. The whole scheme was first denounced by the press, then examined in Court, and discovered to have been devised purely for the purpose of casting odium upon a political party. It made, however, so deep an impression upon the public, that the term *pipe-laying* was at once incorporated in the dictionary of political terms, and is still used to designate the employment of persons as voters, who are not entitled to vote, by fraudulent means. Two terms applied to special classes of bills are of very recent origin, but have already established themselves too firmly in political slang to allow any hope of their speedy disappearance. *Pincher* is the curious name applied—probably in the Legislature of Pennsylvania first—to a bill which promises to secure a pecuniary reward to those who are interested in its defeat! Of the other, Professor S. S. Haldeman says: "American demoralization and sentimental delicacy rivalling that of London thieves, who call a handkerchief a *wiper*, has carried *rooster* into the halls of republican legislation, where it indicates a bill, or proposed law, which will benefit the legislators—and no one else—for as the rasorial fowl scratches for his sustenance, so his figurative namesake is supposed to scratch the dunghill of modern legislation. The term was in 1870 extended from the bill or law to the proposer of it." (*Letter*, February 6, 1871.) A new word, not yet found in our dictionaries, is the name of persons delegated from the two Houses for the purpose of devising an agreement on some point in dispute between them; as they form a *Conference*-Committee, they are individually known as *Conferees*. "The Conference-Committee on the Appropriation Bill failed. The *Conferees* on the part of the House would not agree to the proposition of the Senate to raise the salaries of all the United States Judges." (New York *Tribune*, February 27, 1871.) To this class belongs also the *Floater*, a candidate representing several counties, and therefore not considered directly responsible to any one of them. The term originated in Texas and has never become very general: "J. W. Lawrence, Esq., requests us to withdraw his name as a candidate for *Floater* in the district composed of the counties of Fayette, Bastrop, and Travis." (Texas *State Gazette*, July 16, 1853.)

The English term *to rat,* as applied to members who suddenly *back out* from a position they have long maintained, is in America replaced by the equally suggestive term *to crawfish* or *crayfish,* derived from the peculiar mode of locomotion of the animal. The use of the word originated in the West, but has become quite general. "General Wise," said the Richmond *Enquirer,* "*crawfished* awfully; he has actually appeared in a United States Court, and, what is more, has complimented Judge Underwood on his courtesy and other good qualities." (May 13, 1870.) When a measure, odious to one party, is to be forced through by the strategy of the other party, the former are apt to attempt delaying the final vote by every available device, and this, as has been stated elsewhere, is called *filibustering.* One of the means employed for this purpose is to deliver long speeches, merely to consume time, and for this the expression *to gas,* has, of late, come into use. *Gas* itself has long been acknowledged to be an essential element of many popular characters, and R. W. Emerson says with rare candor and great severity: "'Tis odd that our people should have not water on the brain, but a little *gas* there. Can it be that the American forest has refreshed some weeds of old Pictish barbarism, just ready to die out—the love of the scarlet feather, of beads, and of tinsel? The English have a plain taste. Pretension is the foible especially of American youth."

If the *lobby* and the *rings* are said to be bent upon filling their purses at *Uncle Sam's crib,* as the National Treasury is often called, the members are sometimes accused of providing for their own interests not less eagerly. While in Congress they receive, besides their regular salary, *mileage,* a somewhat extravagant compensation for their travelling expenses from home to Washington and back again. *Constructive mileage* is paid when the members are only supposed to have gone home, and to have returned to the seat of government, without having actually been absent. This is the case, for instance, when one *Congress,* as it is called, expires on the 3d of March, and the next Congress begins its sessions on the 4th of that month: all the members who *hold over, i. e.,* are re-elected for a new Congress, are paid their full mileage as if they had returned to their home and then came back to Washington. The matter is trifling as far as the majority is concerned, but in the cases of members from distant States, as from the Pacific coast or New Mexico, the sum assumes gigantic proportions. It was thus that "Dr. Miller, the new Senator from Georgia, who had been kept out of his seat since 1868, and only sat four days in the last Congress, was allowed fourteen thousand dollars back pay." (Washington *Patriot*, March 7, 1871.) It is a painful fact that, besides this compensation, members are frequently accused of enjoying, like other officials of the government, certain perquisites of their position, which are known by the offensive slang term of *pickings and stealings.* The figure of speech is taken from the habit of loafers and thieves to loiter on the wharves of seaport towns, and of picking out flakes of cotton from the bales that are there lying about in great numbers, or of stealing even larger quantities. The *sweepings* are more exclusively the side-earnings of lucrative offices, of which a humorous writer says: "*Sweepin's*, they tell me, is quite a circumstance in New York; the *sweepin's* of the Post-Office is about three thousand a year, and they say the *sweepin's* of the Custom-House keep eighty-nine 2.40 horses agoing night and day." (Josh Billings' *Sayings.*) A curious term has, of late, sprung up in the South, to designate the necessary expenses for purchasing legislative votes and newspaper influence, in order to get even routine-business safely done. These are called *Chicken-pie.* J. G. Tracy, State Printer of the State of Texas, having failed in obtaining a partner's share in a Galveston paper, was accused by the owner of the latter, that he had offered him, besides the purchase-money required, "slices of *chicken-pie*," thus fastening upon him an unenviable notoriety. When the *term* for which a Member was elected, expires, he returns into private life, but frequently is rewarded for his services by an office, in proportion to his merits or his political influence. Some of these offices in the gift of the administration are peculiar to the United States, as, *e. g.*, that of *Surveyor*, an official who surveys all the inspectors, weighers, gaugers, and other employés in a United States Custom-House, and enjoys a very large income and patronage. Another such office is that of *Naval Officer*, whose duty it is to receive copies of all manifests and entries in the Custom-House, to estimate duties, examine accounts, and perform other responsible duties, for which he receives a liberal salary and enjoys large perquisites.

It is well known that the political doctrine of rotation in office prevails in the United States. Few offices are held "during good behavior," outside of the Judiciary; all others change with the result of the presidential elections every four years. General Harrison is generally credited with having first used the phrase and applied the principle that *To the victors belong the spoils,* meaning by the latter word all the offices in the gift of the government. By this rule the President becomes the head of an army of several hundred thousand office-holders, who depend entirely on his will, and whom he can at pleasure deprive of their position, from the humble light-house keeper in Maine to the great minister at the Court of St. James. J. R. Lowell explains, therefore, pointedly, in his Glossary, the term *spoils* as meaning "the object of political ambitions!" while his hero, Hosea Biglow, spells it, of course, never otherwise than *spiles.* When the poor office-holder, whose tenure is at best limited to four years, is superseded by a successor, he is, in political language, *beheaded* or *decapitated.* "The axe," wrote a correspondent from Washington, "is still doing its bloody work, and heads are flying off in all directions. The clerks in the Treasury Department begin to feel anxious, as the work of *decapitation* will soon make an end of them also." (New York *Herald,* August 5, 1869.) Not even the ministers, here called *secretaries,* are exempted from this rule, as they are not, like their English namesakes, responsible to Congress, but simply advisers of the President, whose *Cabinet* they are by courtesy said to form. In this capacity they are called upon, for instance, to furnish periodical reports of what has been done in their respective departments, and upon the basis of these papers the President founds his official communications to Congress, known as *Messages.*

In the process of electing those officers which are chosen by the people—a class including unfortunately even the Judiciary—and its representatives in the legislative bodies of the Union and the individual States, many words occur, either entirely new, or used in a modified sense, as compared with their meaning in England. *Popular sovereignty* is naturally the fundamental doctrine of the republic, vindicating for the people the right of self-government, and consequently of choosing its own rulers and officers of every kind. A few of the latter are, however, still elected, not by the masses directly, but by proxy, as it were; thus the President is, at least nominally, not chosen by the people, but by *Electors*, who are voted for at the *presidential* election. But whenever an election is to take place, from the *Chief Magistrate*, as the Executive is frequently called, to the town-constable, a regular *campaign* is inaugurated. This is the grandiloquent name for the simple English term "contest," the time between the *primary meeting* and the election itself; sharply but not unjustly criticised by James Grant White as "bloated, army-bumming bombast." (*Words and their Meaning.*) As soon as the time approaches for an election, the friends of the different candidates for office meet first in private to discuss their chances, *i. e.*, their popularity, and their usefulness for the party. As to their qualifications for the office, they are considered a matter of course; the German proverb: "to whom God gives an office, he gives the sense for it," finds here its fullest application; besides, the American never doubts his ability to do everything, from keeping a ho el to ruling a nation, and, what is more, he generally does it better than one would expect. The whole of the candidate's life is ransacked to find events, successes, or votes, out of which may be made *political capital*, a term purely American in its origin, though long since transplanted to England, and naturalized there in the political slang dictionary. "*Political capital!*" exclaims an indignant writer of Tory principles; "one might just as well speak of a man's moral capital!" (*Blackwood*, October, 1867.) If he has been in political life before, his *record* is carefully searched to find out if he is *sound*, that is, if he has always voted strictly with his party, and can, therefore, not be reproached with inconsistency by his opponents, since that is the unpardonable sin of the politician. Often it is not enough to ascertain the *soundness* of the candidate; it must also be proven that he has on all occasions come out *flatfooted* in behalf of his party and all party measures. The term is of Western origin, and derived from the manner in which men place their feet firmly and "flatly" on the ground, when engaged in a tussle or personal combat. "Now the committee of the vestry . . . put their *foot flatly* down on auricular confession and priestly absolution." (The Row at St. Clement's Church. Philadelphia *Bulletin*, March 23, 1871.)

Should he be found wanting in this aspect, he is called *shaky*, as not being firm and resolute in his principles; or he is denounced as *weak in the knees*, that is, unsettled in his political convictions and infirm of purpose. " General Butler is setting a good example to his *weak-kneed* brethren, which will do them good." (New York *Times*, Sept. 7, 1870.) The *shaky* and the *weak-kneed* politician is quite sure of being *dropped* by his inexorable party, as soon as he ceases to be useful. Should the candidate prove to have always stood up bravely for every measure adopted by his party, and to have resisted with energy every effort to overthrow or thwart it, he is said to have *backbone*. " Men do not know how to resist the small temptations of life, from the same deficiency in their *dorsal arrangements* (!). *Backbone* is the material which makes an upright man, and he must be firm on all points, if he would pass scathless through the struggle of life." (*The Republic*, March 17, 1859.) The abolitionists of former days affected the term especially; thus Mr. Wendell Phillips said, that " General McClellan cannot end the war. He has no *backbone*;" and Miss Anna Dickenson even spoke disparagingly of the President, saying, that " if Mr. Lincoln had *backbone* enough, which he has not, he would not tamper or treat with slavery, but abolish it at one stroke, at once and forever." At times this *soundness* refers to a particular tenet, as in the days when the whole country was in great excitement about the question, whether the new State of Kansas should enter the Union as a free State, or admit slavery within its borders. Thus a man in favor of the latter alternative was, half-humorously, half-contemptuously, said to be *sound on the goose*, as J. R. Lowell sings—

" Northern religion works wal North, but its ez suft ez spruce,
Compar'd to our'n for keepin' *sound*, sez she, *upon the goose*."
(*Biglow Papers*, II., p. 88.)

Was it because slavery was looked upon at the South as the goose that laid the golden eggs, which was accordingly killed in due process of time? Now, *sound on the goose* means simply to be stanch on the party question, whatever that may be for the moment.

A politician of the *right stamp*, unmerciful to his adversaries, and inexorable in exacting every inch of his followers, is called *dyed in the wool;* and even poor General Taylor, whose success in Mexico led to his death at the *White House*, as the President's modest mansion is called, was at one time claimed by the party "as a democrat *dyed in the wool*, as a democrat of the Jeffersonian order of 1798." (New York *Commercial Advertiser*, May 24, 1847, B.) The great Daniel Webster once illustrated the origin of the phrase, by relating an adventure of his own. Students in his time of college-life were in the habit of riding on horseback to Dartmouth College, where he was bred, and rented a pasture there for their horse till the end of the term. So he went also, in his homespun clothes, and with his books in a pair of saddle-bags. He "had the *blues* for many days after his arrival," he would add, with his hearty laugh, "because a drenching rain had washed the indigo from his new suit *dyed in the wool* at home, into his skin, coloring it deeply, darkly, beautifully blue." (*College Courant*, January 21, 1871.)

When these general questions are satisfactorily settled, a *caucus* is called, to decide on the men and the principles which are to be presented to the people in public meetings and through the press. This word, it is well known, has been traced to various sources, and it can hardly be said that the mystery is yet fully explained. Classic scholars, with that enthusiastic love of antiquity which admits of nothing good that is not ancient, claim the ancestry of the term for the Latin-Greek "scyphus," the name of the cup which Joseph used for divination (Genesis, xliv. 5, 15), and which was carried off by his brethren in their bag. More liberal linguists have raised the question, if *caucus* might not be connected with the Latin *joculare*, or the German *gaukeln*, in both cases referring to the fact that the *caucus* predestinates by apparent, if not actual, chance what is to be done hereafter. The only historical basis is the authenticated fact that, in the year 1763, a *caucus* was held, since such a meeting is mentioned by that name (Caucus-Club) in Adams' *Diary*. Dr. Gordon, in his *History of the American Revolution* (1788), traces the term still farther back into antiquity. He says: "The word is not of novel invention. More than fifty years ago (1735), Mr. Samuel Adams' father, and twenty others, one or two from the north end of town (Boston, Massachusetts), where all ship-business is carried on, used to meet, make a *caucus*, and lay their plans for introducing certain persons into places of trust and power." (I., p. 240.) Hence it has been generally supposed, and not without good reason, that the word was originally derived from meetings held by ship-*caulkers* on strike, or with a grievance, and that it gradually assumed its present meaning. The word has crept slowly into English parlance, and is now used in Great Britain in the sense of a private assembling of politicians before an election, where candidates are chosen and measures of action agreed upon. In America its privacy is not an essential feature, and even the Senate of the United States holds its *caucus* meetings in public, at least so far as the press is concerned. R. W. Emerson, in his *Essay on Politics,* says: "If a man found himself so rich-natured that he could enter into strict relations with the best persons, and make life serene around him by the dignity and sweetness of his behavior, could he afford to circumvent the favor of the *caucus* and the press, and covet relations so hollow and pompous as those of a politician?

Here, in these preliminary assemblies, the great principles of the party are laid down in a compact form, to which the candidates are expected to swear allegiance, and to devote all the influence of their official position. They are embodied in a *platform,* a word new only in its application to purely political principles, while it has long been used in matters of church discipline or faith; a *plank* of a platform, meaning one of the principles of which the latter is constructed, is, however, a pure Americanism, and hardly yet naturalized in England. The tendency to carrying out such figures of speech to its last extremes, is well shown in the phrase: "every *plank* and *splinter* of the *platform,*" used by an energetic writer in the Providence (Rhode Island) *Journal.* After the platform, which in our day is generally expressed in sufficiently vague terms to allow great latitude, the caucus will generally agree upon a *Ticket,* a word taken from the actual ticket or ballot which is dropped into the ballot-box at the time of election, and on which the names of the candidates are written or printed. It means, in this case, the whole list of candidates agreed upon, which are to be presented to the people for ratification. It undergoes, however, often before its actual use, many changes, and only when a man adopts the whole list as made up by his party, is it called a *clean* or *straight* ticket; but if he takes off one or more names to substitute others which he prefers, the ticket is *scratched.* At times the party itself is divided into fractions, each one of which rejects some candidates of the others, and the result of such a split in their own ranks, is a *split* ticket, while a man voting for some candidates of his own party and for one or more of his opponents, would deposit what is known as a *mixed* ticket. *Sticker* is the familiar name of a candidate printed on a slip of paper with the back gummed, to be pasted over the name of another candidate by those who wish to vote a *split* ticket; the term originated in 1860 in Pennsylvania as a *mixed* ticket. The candidates thereupon begin the campaign; they *run* for an office, with American haste and energy. Hence the Rev. Mr. Cartwright says: "The first time I *ran* for office in Sangamon County, I was on the North side of the river, as they say in England, electioneering." (*Autobiography*, p. 262.) Generally he begins *canvassing* the county or the State, and to *stump it*, as the indispensable electioneering tour is now very generally called—only the candidate for the *presidency* being considered exempt from the duty of presenting himself in person before the people to solicit their suffrages. Sometimes, however, a *mass meeting* is previously held, such as were known as monster-meetings in Ireland during Mr. O'Connell's agitation. The term was first used in America during the famous Hard-Cider Campaign for and against General Harrison and Mr. Tyler; now it is universal, even the French and the German languages having adopted and fully naturalized the word in their scanty, political dictionary. When the great Radical, Mr. Beales, summoned the people to assemble in Hyde Park, August 5, 1867, London was placarded all over with the announcement of the proposed *Mass Meeting*, and German papers abounded with similar advertisements, when the victorious troops were expected to return from France. In the meeting, or on the stump, the candidate is expected to *define his position*, a phrase probably invented by Virginians, who became accustomed to it in the halcyon days of democratic supremacy, when eloquent members were in the habit of making unanswerable speeches of a day or two in the Legislature, or filled with their definitions the columns of the then famous paper, Mr. Ritchie's Richmond *Enquirer*.

On the floor of Congress, during his visits home, when addressing his constituents, and above all on Fourth of July orations the Member of Congress vies with the politician generally in kind of exaggerated patriotism, which is designated as *Spreau*

Eagleism. It consists, mainly, in boundless praise of the greatness, power, and glory of his native land, and is, therefore, rather too severely denounced by the North American *Review* as "a compound of exaggeration, effrontery, bombast, and extravagance, mixed metaphors, platitudes, defiant threats thrown at the world, and irreverent appeals flung at the Great Being." (October, 1858.) The Eagle of the United States, on such occasions, is made to spread its wings and to soar high—hence the term. The same bad taste, when found in oratory not confined to political subjects, is commonly called *high-faluting*, a term variously traced back to a corruption of *high-flighting, high-floating*, or even to a Dutch word *verlooten*—to flay by whipping. While *Spread-Eagleism* pleases all enthusiastic patriots, the cultivated dwellers in cities, as well as the plain-spoken multitudes who delight in the oratory of the stump, *high-faluten*, as it is frequently written, is almost always addressed to educated or half-educated audiences, who are supposed to appreciate bombast, big words, and high-sounding phrases, with or without meaning. An after-dinner *high-faluting* speech, attributed to the great Daniel Webster, reads thus: "Men of Rochester, I am glad to see you, and I am glad to see your noble city. Gentlemen, I saw your falls, which, I am told, are a hundred and fifty feet high. Gentlemen, Rome had her Cæsar, her Scipio, her Brutus, but Rome in her proudest day had never a waterfall a hundred and fifty feet high! Gentlemen, Greece had her Demosthenes, her Pericles, her Socrates, but Greece in her palmiest days had never a waterfall a hundred and fifty feet high! Men of Rochester, go on! No people ever lost their liberties, who had a waterfall a hundred and fifty feet high." That the vein has not run out, we may rest assured after reading the following extract from the Report of Legislative Proceedings in Indiana: "The American people—and we are proud to call ourselves that—are rocked in the bosom of two mighty oceans, whose granite-bound shores are whitened by the floating canvas of the commercial world; reaching from the ice-fettered lakes of the north to the febrile waves of Australian seas, comprising the vast interim of five billions of acres, whose alluvial plains, romantic mountains, and mystic rivers rival the wildest Utopian dreams that ever gathered around the inspired bard, as he walked the Amaranthine promenades of Hesperian gardens, is proud Columbia, the land of the free and the home of the brave." (Mr. Heywood's Speech on *Gravel Roads*, January 21, 1871.) A writer on the "Good Looks of Americans" closed his article with the modest assertion: "It is even easier to come into this world of America, say the midwives, than into any other world extant." (*Putnam's Magazine*, March, 1853.) And yet the word—and perhaps the substance, if substance it can be called, with the shadow—has found its way to the Old Country, and the *Slang Dictionary* (p. 154) assures us that *high-faluting* is now quite common in Liverpool and London, East, while the London *Times* uses it soberly, in the sense of "fustian, high-sounding, unmeaning eloquence."

When the election at last approaches, the excitement, fanned by all these preliminary measures, runs, of course, very high, and violence is not rare; but only one feature in the process of voting is known by an American term. This is the *ballot-box stuffing*, a crime which consists in filling the boxes intended to contain the votes deposited during the day, previous to the election, with a number of ballots, so that when the whole is examined by official *judges of election*, the majority is securely established. The term is not yet used in England, because the ballot has not yet been introduced; but as this is impending, the *stuffer*, as the criminal is called, will no doubt soon be known there also.

Among the great questions that have divided the nation, and hence have occupied the public mind more pre-eminently, some, dating from the time before the late Civil War, have become known by special names. Already in the earliest days of the Republic, the *Blue Laws* of New England excited uncommon interest at home and abroad, and recent publications of great value have once more directed public attention to this remarkable feature in American history. Connecticut is still often mentioned as the *Blue State*, unquestionably from its being the original stronghold of the Presbyterians, who were once known by the contemptuous name of *Blueskins*, as Butler says:

"'twas Presbyterian *true blue*,
For he was of the stubborn crew
Of errant saints, whom all men grant
To be the true Church Militant."
(*Hudibras*, I., p. 26.)

Even generations afterward, when the inhabitants of the *land of steady habits* were accused of having made signals along the coast for the benefit of the British, during the war of 1812, these lights on the coast of Connecticut were called *Blue Lights*, adding a new word to the vocabulary of treason. The charge, it is said, was utterly unfounded, but the term has survived to this day, and is frequently used in political controversies. The famous laws of New Haven, also, perhaps the most striking illustration of the innate tendency of the human heart toward intolerance, are known as the *Blue Laws*, thus joining them to the *Blue Laws* of all the colonies of New England, among which they were the last to secure a sad pre-eminence. Their authenticity has often been denied, and Dr. Peters' well-known book on the subject has been declared a libel; as, for instance, by a well-informed correspondent of *Notes and Queries* (Vol. XI. p. 321), writing from the State Library at Hartford, Connecticut. They are, however, repeatedly quoted by good authorities, as by Judge Haliburton (*English in America*, I., p. 314), and are confirmed beyond any doubt by the reprint of the "Abstract of Laws of New England," in Governor Hutchinson's *Collection of Papers*, London, 1655, where the identical provisions may be found. They fully illustrate the characteristic words of the melancholy lawgiver of Shawmut, that "he had left England because he did not like the Lord Bishops, but that he could not live under the Lord Brethren."

It is a question more curious than important whence the term *blue* originally came. A patriotic "Antiquarian of Hartford" claimed, in 1838, that it was applied to the New Haven code, from the simple fact, that the first printed laws of that colony were sent out on blue-colored paper. As he fails to adduce any proof for his statement, the conclusion can hardly be admitted; for there is abundant evidence that the term *blue* was known in England long before, and used in a very similar manner. It is not improbable that, quite accidentally perhaps, an allusion was made to the extreme Puritan zeal of the Presbyterians for a literal following of Scripture, by referring to the "ribands of blue," enjoined upon the Israelites. (Numbers, xv. 38.) Or it may be, that the annotator of Gray's *Poems* explains the matter, when he states that the poet's *blue aprons* had reference to the preachers in blue aprons, of those times, when persons were admitted to preach who wore blue aprons in their trade. This is evidently the meaning of a cotemporary political squib, in which a visit to a church is called a going

> " to a lecture,
> Where I a tub (pulpit) did view,
> Hung with an *apron blue*,
> 'Twas the preacher's, I conjecture.
> His use and doctrine, too,
> Was of no better hue,
> Tho' he spoke in a tone most mickle."
> (*Loyal Song.*)

The same term of *blue apron* had, in the mean time, been applied to the Parliamentary party also, as a reproach, because it consisted so largely of men in humble situations of life. Thus it was especially used after the Restoration, as a term of ridicule and contempt, as in Butler's lines:

> " Can fetch in parties (as in war
> All other heads of cattle are),
> From the enemy of all religions,
> As well as high and low conditions,
> And share them, from blue ribands down
> To all *blue aprons* in the town."
> *Hudibras*, p. 3, c. III. 1, 870.)

This species of ridicule was, almost as a matter of course, carried over to New England, and used in the colonies, as it had been at home, by those who wished to bring the institutions of the early Puritan colonists into disrepute and contempt. The term *blue* was perhaps even more extensively used there than in the mother country, and was more especially employed to characterize the laws as brutally strict and bloody, and yet not without their whimsical oddity. It is certainly not without a quaint and almost ludicrous air that an article like the following could appear, little more than a hundred years ago, in an English newspaper, printed in the colonies:

" Milford, Connecticut,
"Nov. 21, 1755.

"After perusing a false and scurrilous letter, printed at New York, signed Edward Cole, it was thought proper that the same should be publicly whipt, as tending to beget ill will, and brushing a disunion in the several governments in America, the contrary of which, at this time, and present situation of our affairs, is much wanted; accordingly it was here, at 4 of the clock this afternoon, after proper notice of drum, publicly whipt, according to *Moses' Law*, forty stripes, save one, by the common whipper, and then burnt." (Connecticut *Gazette*, Nov. 29, 1755.)

It must, however, not be concluded from these suggestions that *Blue Laws*, in this sense of the word, were strictly confined to the New England States. The early settlements in Virginia, with all their abhorrence of Puritanism, enacted very similar regulations. Here also swearing was severely punished; here also the church required attendance on all its services, under heavy penalties, and here also domestic discipline was enforced by public laws, only the church was the Established Church of England, and the fines were all paid in tobacco.

Captain Grose gives still another version, which may account for the strength derived by the epithet *blue* from an additional meaning. He states that Coventry was formerly famous for dyeing a *blue* that would not change its color, and could not be discharged by washing. Therefore the epithets of *Coventry Blue* and *True Blue* were figuratively applied to persons who would not change their party or principles on any consideration. As the Presbyterians were equally famous for their stern and sturdy adherence to their own convictions, the term was perhaps as generally as deservedly applied to them in this sense also. Whatever may be thought of these stern Puritans as lawgivers, their memory is dear and sacred to all New Englanders; they celebrate the day on which they landed at Plymouth, the 22d of December, as *Forefathers' Day*, and they love to speak of them reverently and affectionately as

"The *Pilgrim Fathers*—where are they?—
The waves that brought them o'er
Still roll in the bay, and throw their spray
As they break along the shore;
Still roll in the bay, as they roll'd the day,
When the Mayflower moor'd below,
When the sea around was black with storms,
And white the shore with snow."

(*John Pierpont.*)

During the war of the Revolution the term *continental* acquired a new meaning in America, being applied to all that concerned the colonies as a whole, even before they were united into a Confederacy. Hence their troops and their paper-money were both *Continental.* "Delaplace," says a recent writer, "had about as much respect for the *Continental* Congress as Allen had for Jehovah, and they respectively relied upon and feared powder and ball more than either. In fact, the *Continental* Congress was then but a shadow, for it had no existence till six hours afterward, when it assembled in Carpenter's Hall in Philadelphia, and its authority was hardly acknowledged in prospect, even by the armed patriots in the field." The slang term, *Continental Damn,* almost universally applied to the utterly valueless Continental paper-money of those days is, nevertheless, traced back to a very different origin by an acute and positive scholar, James Grant White. "The phrase seems to me a counterpart, if not a mere modification, of others of the same sort—a tinker's damn, a trooper's, etc., and as the troops of the colonies were called *Continentalers* or *Continentals* during the war, and for many years afterward, it seems to me probable, that the phrase in question was at first a *Continental's* damn, from which the sign of the possessive was gradually dropped." (*Words and their Uses,* p. 396.) A political doctrine of much notoriety, and likely to gain in importance, is called the *Monroe Doctrine.* Mr. J. Q. Adams first originated one part of this famous doctrine: that which declares the American Continent, even where not yet actually occupied by settlers, as no longer open to colonization by European powers. The second part dates only from the year 1823, and originated with Mr. Monroe, who was then President of the United States. As the former State-paper was directed against certain reputed interferences of Russia in the Northwestern part of the continent, so this manifesto was intended to meet similar presumed intentions on the part of the Holy Alliance. It declared, in substance, that any extension of the system of government, as it prevailed in Europe, to any part of this hemisphere, would be looked upon as "dangerous to our peace and safety." The doctrine has been strictly maintained ever since, and found its last practical illustration in the successful effort to relieve Mexico from a foreign ruler and French armies.

Among the later sources of political excitement which have deeply agitated the public mind, and seriously threatened even a disruption of the Union, were the three doctrines of *Free Love, Free Soil,* and *Free Labor.* The first-mentioned is not peculiar to America in name or in principle, and having failed in spite of being never in any way impeded, so that even the "right of suffrage, and a husband every four years," do not promise content, is likely to be entirely merged in the more comprehensive question of *Women's Rights.* The principle of *Free Soil,* on the contrary, American in form and in practice, as opposed to Slavery, has led (it need not be explained how) to a terrible war, and the utter extinction of the *Peculiar Institution,* as Slavery was long called. The question of the day, full of import here as in the Old World, is that of *Free Labor,* as far as it involves the impending conflict between Capital and Labor, the term itself having been transferred, from its first use in opposition to *Slave Labor,* to the independence of the workman as regards his employer.

American politics abound in catch-words, the great majority of which pass away with the accident that gave them birth, while others please the fancy of the populace, or acquire, by an unexpected success, such a hold on the public mind as to secure to them a longer lease of life. One of these is as ludicrous in its origin as tenacious in its persistency in the slang of the day. The story goes that General Jackson, better known in American history as *Old Hickory,* was not much at home in the art of spelling, and his friend and admirer, Major Jack Downing, found therefore no difficulty in convincing the readers of his "Letters," that the President employed the letters *O. K.* as an endorsement of applications for office, and other papers. They were intended to stand for "All Correct," which the old gentleman preferred writing *Oll Korrect,* and hence they are used, to this day, very much in the sense of the English "All Right." To the question how a convalescent is, the answer comes back: "Oh, he is quite *O. K.* again!" The term has found its way to England, and is quoted in the *Slang Dictionary* (p. 191), though without explanation.

A far more serious phrase is the *Manifest Destiny* of Mr. Webster, which fairly represents the mischievous power of such slang words. Designed originally for the expression of a perfectly justifiable doctrine, that America was intended by Providence to be a republic, and a refuge for all who wished to be free, it was soon found to be a convenient cloak for every measure of aggrandizement or violence. It was *Manifest Destiny* that conquered part of Mexico and purchased Alaska; it is *Manifest Destiny* that Cuba should be annexed and Canada ceded to the United States. J. R. Lowell terms it justly a phrase characteristic of "that national recklessness as to right and wrong," of which Mr. Birdofredum Sawin, in the *Biglow Papers*, is the very incarnation. Before the abolition of slavery the *Underground Railway* had become quite an important feature in Northern efforts to aid escaping slaves, and to provide for their future, and a grievous cause of complaint on the part of Southerners against the Abolitionists. The substance having passed away, the name, no doubt, will soon be forgotten.

Nullification, another term full of weighty meaning, will, on the other hand, probably retain its place in the national speech as long as the Union lasts, though its meaning changes with the different phases through which the country passes. The term was transplanted into American politics as early as 1798, when, on the passage of the *Alien and Sedition Acts*, the Legislatures of Virginia and Kentucky adopted certain resolutions, drawn up chiefly by Jefferson and Madison, one of which declared that, when the Federal Government assumed powers not delegated to it by the States, a *nullification* of the Acts was the only rightful remedy. But the word and the idea had a very different and far more serious significance as used by Mr. Calhoun. As interpreted by him, *nullification* was an exclusively Southern principle, amounting to open and absolute defiance of the laws of the land and the constituted authorities. Its legitimate fruit, *secession*, was denounced as treason long before it led to civil war, even so far back as the dark days, when Non-Intercourse and Embargo Laws seriously threatened the prosperity of the country. Since then, the ominous word has every now and then been heard in faint murmurings, now in one, now in the other section, but the horrors of the late war will do more than all policy and legislation can do to lay the grim spectre.

Mr. Calhoun has often been credited with another such phrase, very popular at one time, and often revived as the occasion offered—*Masterly Inactivity*. It was by him employed in speaking of the acquisition of Cuba, which he deprecated, alleging that when the proper time came the island would gravitate to the United States, and in the mean time the policy of the government was a *masterly inactivity*. The term, however, was not new, having been used in the British Parliament repeatedly, and attracted much public attention during the first French Revolution. It has been suggested that the idea originated in the prophet's words, "their strength is to sit still." (Isaiah, xxx. 7.)

Difficulties which were grave enough to call for the use of arms had as yet but rarely disturbed the peace of the Union. A *Whiskey War* in Pennsylvania, arising from troubles connected with illicit distilleries, survived long in the memory of men, and was in 1838 followed by the so-called *Buckshot War* in the same State. The well-known statesman, Thaddeus Stevens, was accused of a desire to retain Joseph Ritner as Governor of the State of Pennsylvania for a second term, after he had been defeated at the election. This led to serious disorders; the troops were called out, and orders were issued that they should have their cartridges loaded with "buckshot and ball," from which circumstance the short and unbloody war received its name.

The late Civil War has produced a smaller crop of political terms, and even slang words, than might have been expected. The *Peculiar Institution*, as Slavery had long been called, because it was peculiar to the Southern States, was, of course, one of the principal causes of the calamity. The word arose in connection with the abuse to which the term *Institution* has been subjected in all its uses. Whatever is looked upon as a permanent and essential part of any system, is apt to be so designated by careless writers. "Garroting, as an *institution*, may be said to be almost extinct in New York." (*Tricks and Traps of New York*, p. 47.) Even the usually careful writers of the New York *Tribune* once said: "Woman cannot be counted out and classified as a mere appendage. She is an *institution*, and hereafter must receive the most general culture and recognition." (August 11, 1858.) The buzzards of Charleston are gravely described as an "*institution* of the city;" and when Mr. Seward visited China, a correspondent wrote: "On that morning the visitors were, for the first time, made acquainted with an Eastern *institution*, which, though doubtless entertaining as a topic for future narrative, is seldom amusing as an actual experience. At an early hour a typhoon of great severity swept over the bay, destroying a vast amount of property, and causing the death of hundreds of natives." (New York *Times*.)

The evils of the Peculiar Institution brought about finally the *Secession* of one Southern State after another. They *seceded*, that is, they broke the compact into which they had entered when the Union was formed, and went out. Hence, the *Union-men* on the other side, or *Federals*, as they long preferred being called, fought for the Union against rebellion. The soldiers soon learned to bestow nicknames upon each other; the Southerners were *Secesh* or *Rebs*, or, more good-naturedly, *Johnny Rebs*. "There was a notion about that the leading *Rebs*, that is, the *Rebs* who had property, would have to forfeit, and that the leading patriots would find that loyalty was not only beautiful, but also profitable." (*Once a Week*, May, 1871; p. 506.)

Even the more expeditious *Johnny*, familiar already in many a word, as in *Johnny-cakes*, had to answer the purpose, and a recent writer was very well understood when he wrote: "Just enough of excitement and peril was there in hunting these cattle, wild almost as the buffaloes on the prairies, and in bringing them safely in, in spite of the vengeful pursuit of the enraged *Johnnies*." (*Putnam's Magazine*, October, 1868.) The Northerners were *Yanks*, or *Bluebellies* (from their blue uniform), or *Boys in Blue*, a term which has since become the official name of certain half-military associations, frequently consisting of negroes. Nor were names wanting for the different fractions of political parties, though at the South not much diversity of opinion was allowed. The North had, besides the familiar party-names, its *Doughfaces*, Northern abettors of Slavery, perhaps deriving their names from an appreciation of the kneadable character of dough. J. R. Lowell explains the term in his *Catalogue Raisonné* as meaning, "A contented lickspittle, a common variety of Northern politicians," and alludes to it again in the lines—

"Each hon'rable *doughface* gits jest wut he axes,
An' the people—thur annual soff sodder and taxes,"
(*Biglow Papers*, I., p. 51.)

It is said that John Randolph, of Roanoke, in denouncing the famous Missouri Compromise as "a dirty bargain," also branded the eighteen Northern Congressmen, who helped to displace

Mason and Dixon's Line, as *doughfaces*, and that the epithet at once passed into the slang dictionary of politics. Then, there were *Copperheads*, so called from the contempt entertained for the snake that bears that name, or from the poor Redman, who used to be thus stigmatized; they were Democrats, and retorted upon violent Union men by calling them *Niggerheads*. *Butternuts* were the sympathizers with the South in the North and the Middle States: the term was derived from the color of the uniforms worn in the early part of the war by Confederate soldiers in the West, which, being homespun, were dyed brown with the juice of the butternut (Juglans cinerea). The most advanced among the republicans, who were willing to sacrifice every constitutional right rather than give up the Union, were called *Radicals*, or from the lips of their adversaries contemptuously *Rads*. "Burrell is a good *Rad*, and has as much right to embezzle a little as Reed had." (*New Era*, April, 1871.) The third party in the strife, the slave, who had before been a chattel, and called a *nigger*, became gradually, as his importance was more clearly perceived, and finally made itself portentously felt at the polls, a *negro*, a *contraband*, and a *freedman*. In familiar intercourse, he appeared suggestively as *darkey*, a term not unknown in England (*Slang Dictionary*, p. 117), or humorously as an *unbleached American*. The *Colored Man*, once popular at the North as well as at the South, has almost disappeared, since the difficulty of deciding in the use of this euphemism between the quadroon and the "negro so black that charcoal makes a chalk-mark on him," has become manifest. It is said that the freedmen, in the first glow of their new rights, proposed to call the Whites *Plain People*, in return for the term *Colored People*, by which they were designated themselves.

Among the terms brought out by the war is the old Scotch word *raid*, so well known to all readers of Scott's poems, from the lines—

> "Widow and Saxon maid
> Long shall lament our *raid*."
> (*Lady of the Lake.*)

The word, meaning a warlike invasion on horseback into the enemy's country, and derived from the verb to *ride*, assumed new life and new force by the brilliant *raids* made on both sides, and often producing unexpected results. Officials, who were not expected to expose themselves to the fire of the enemy, like quartermasters, commissaries, etc., were nicknamed *bombproofs*, while the long-forgotten *bummer* reappeared on the flanks and in the rear of the two armies. The *bummer* may be a cousin of the *bumble*-bee, as far as his erratic movements and pilfering propensities are concerned; but he is, far more likely, descended from the German *Bummler*, a man who goes about without aim and purpose, and lives on the fruits of other people's labor. In German, the term is used good-naturedly, and has nothing offensive in its meaning; here, however, the practice of stealing is inseparable from the word. Hence, Major Nichols makes the *bummer* give this account of himself: "Look hyar, Captain, we ain't so bad after all. We keep ahead of the skirmish-line allers; we lets 'em know when an enemy's a comin', and then we ain't allers away from the regiment. We turns over all we don't want ourselves, and we can lick five times as many Rebs as we are any day." (*Sherman's Great March.*) J. G. Leland's Hans Breitmann, who, having himself been a *bummer*, as he has since become an "Uhlan," reports that the old original bummer was "a man named Jost, belonging to a regiment of Pennsylvania cavalry, whose proficiency in *bumming*, otherwise *looting*, in swearing, fighting, and drinking lager-beer, raised him to a pitch of glory on the Federal side, which excited at once the envy and the admiration of the boldest bushwhackers and the gauntest guerrillas in the Confederate host." Occasionally, the bummer was called a *buffalo*, a term peculiar at first to North Carolina, and thence spreading over the South.

The *Jayhawkers* were a more offensive class of men, combining murder with marauding, and were famous before the war already, during the bloody strife carried on in Kansas. The term is not American, but an importation from Australia, where it is said to have been coined by convicts, and came to us by way of California. They fought in Kansas often side by side with the equally ill-famed *Border-Ruffians*, a term invented by the New York *Herald* to designate the bands of lawless men who infested the borders of some of the Western States, but especially Kansas, waging relentless war against all parties alike. The terrible state of things there led the New York *Tribune*, some time previous, to speak of *Bleeding Kansas*, and the expression conveyed so exactly the feeling of thousands of sympathizers with the *Free-soil* movement, that it was at once adopted, and became a rallying-cry, which will not soon be forgotten.

The *Mossybank*, on the contrary, was the man of the South, who secreted himself in a remote forest, or an inaccessible swamp, in order to escape conscription. His name was derived from the quaint fancy that he was determined to keep in hiding till " the moss should grow on his back—" as German students used to call the oldest veterans at the university, *Bemooste Häupter* (moss-covered heads).

The immense bounties paid at the North to volunteers led to a new trick and a new term: men would receive in one State a bounty of many hundred dollars, enlist, join their regiment, and run away after a few days; they went into another State, enlisted once more, receiving a second bounty, and sometimes repeated the experiment several times in succession. They obtained the title of *bounty-jumpers;* while at the South, a man who dared not return after the war was over, and left his country to escape the consequences, was called contemptuously a *rat.* The *Musical-Box* of the Confederates was also known as *Jeff Davis' Box:* it was the humorous name given by the men to the lumbering, ill-built army-wagons, which were apt to creak horribly for want of greasing; but their *Wooden Horse*, which was at one time thought at the North to be an infernal-machine, to be sent into New York or Boston Harbor, was a secret society, organized for political purposes, and dissolved as the latter ceased to exist. The old *Bastille*, and its painful memories, were revived in American speech when the term was applied to the secret military imprisonment of suspected sympathizers with the South, a measure silently deprecated but passively consented to by the *Hickory Unionists* of the Border States, a large and influential class of men, who, like Dante's fallen angels, impaled upon some of the iciest spears of his terrible irony—

> " non furon ribelli,
> Nè fur fedeli a Dio, ma per sè foro."
> (Edward Spencer, *Eclectic Magazine*, December, 1870, p. 662.)

It is curious that the same term has recently been revived in England also, where it is used as a slang term to denote a prison or lock-up, its abbreviated form *steel* being, however, the favorite expression with the lower orders. (*Slang Dictionary*, p. 71.) The poor prisoners were rarely said to have been "captured;" but like personal property that was taken swiftly, seized and thrust into a bag, soldiers also were *bagged.* "We stole upon the Secesh unawares, on the other side of the creek, and by pouncing upon them all of a sudden, we *bagged* the whole lot." (Louisville *Journal,* September 7, 1864.) A more cruel word, in the true sense of that term, was during the war but too frequently applied to the disposal of peculiarly obnoxious prisoners. They would be intrusted to a guard to be conveyed to the nearest headquarters; but when the latter reached the place to which they were sent, the report was usually, "Prisoners were *lost,*" and no further inquiry was deemed necessary. "The two horse-thieves were escorted to the county-town by some forty or fifty gentlemen, most of whom had been aggrieved by the robbers. But as they approached the wood near Vandalia, all fell back except five or six, who soon disappeared in the forest. When they rejoined their friends on the turnpike, they simply declared that they had *lost* their captives, and thereupon all returned to their homes." (St. Louis *Democrat,* July 14, 1863.) Even the battle did not escape the tendency to give to all things nicknames. The "boys," with a witty turn of the military significance of the word, were in the habit of terming a battle a *brevet-hell!*

Two much discussed terms are *shebang* and *skedaddle.* The former, used even yet by students of Yale College and elsewhere to designate their rooms, or a theatrical or other performance in a public hall, has its origin probably in a corruption of the French *cabane,* a hut, familiar to the troops that came from Louisiana, and constantly used in the Confederate camp for the simple huts, which they built with such alacrity and skill for their winter-quarters. The constant intercourse between the outposts soon made the term familiar to the Federal army also. "Many a poor fellow," says an old soldier, "who enlisted to do hard fighting, lost the number of his mess, and was carried out from his *shebang* to his long home." (*Overland Monthly,* March, 1871.)

The word *skedaddle* even crossed the Atlantic, and was once gravely discussed in Parliament. It appeared in print, probably for the first time, immediately after the battle of Bull Run, and was at once caught at and repeated all over the country. In answer to inquiries about its origin, some Irishmen at once claimed it as their own, deriving it from their *sgedad-ol,* which means "scattered all," and naively suggested that one of their valiant countrymen might have uttered the words while running away from Bull Run. It cannot be denied that in an old Irish version of the New Testament the word is used thus: "I will smite the shepherd and the sheep of the flock shall be *sgedad-ol.*" The soldiers, at all events, were tickled by the sound of the word, which served to give a humorous appearance to a somewhat ignominious act, and thus it spread, appearing in the reports of correspondents of London journals. The *Times* noticed it particularly, and repeated the phrase, "A Northerner, who retreats, *retires upon his supports,* but a Southerner is said to *skedaddle.*" Thereupon Lord Hill wrote a letter to prove that the term was excellent Scottish, well known in the North of England also. It is true that in Ayrshire and Dumfrieshire people use it quite frequently to describe the spilling of milk or water from a pail. Milkmaids are heard to say, "Mind, you are *skedaddling* all your milk," and farther North the dropping of coal from the bucket is also called *skedaddle.* The probability of this derivation is much strengthened by the fact that the word exists in the kindred Scandinavian dialects, as Swedish has a term *skuddadahl* and Danish its *skyededehl,* with exactly the same meaning: what therefore the Scotch may not have done—importing the word into the army—may have to be credited to the numerous Scandinavians from Wisconsin. A facetious writer in the Louisville *Journal* was probably the first to trace the word to a still more ancient form. He derived it "from the Greek verb σκεδάννυμι, to scatter or disperse tumultuously," and its infrequent aorist σκέδασα, used by Herodotus and Homer, the latter of whom employs also the noun σκέδασις in the sense of an emphatic scatteration. (*Iliad,* XIX. 171—XXIII. 162; *Odyssey,* I. 113, as quoted in Crusius' Lexicon.) The English *Slang Dictionary* endorses this view, declaring that Lord Hill and the *Times* were both in the wrong, and attributing the odd word to some professor at Harvard, who may have set it afloat, utterly unconscious that the bantling would meet with such unexpected success. For whatever it may mean or wherever it may originally come from, there is something so descriptive in the term, that it is likely to maintain itself in our speech in spite of all grammarians, and will probably be proof against all attempts to remove it. Its very success in the two armies speaks in its favor; for at the time when General McClellan was making his vain efforts to reach Richmond (in 1863), even the French princes on his staff had picked up the novelty, and it was gravely quoted in some French publications abroad.

Short phrases also became, at times, very popular, and have not lost the prestige yet, which they acquired during the war. Such was poor Mr. Lincoln's naive expression, when he was asked why he did not make an end to the war, and replied, that few knew what a big job it was, but, with his marvellous cheerfulness and implicit trust in the nation, added: "If we just keep *pegging away* it 'll all turn out right." The term may possibly be taken from the shoemaker's patient work, but to *peg* means at the same time to *strike*, and Mr. Halliwell already quotes: "I gave him such a *pegging*," meaning such a beating. The phrase *All quiet on the Potomac*, since repeated in many a song, and familiar as a common expression for an undisturbed state of things generally, became stereotyped on the nation's mind by its constant repetition in the War Bulletins of Mr. Cameron, then Secretary of War. The fact that almost every Federal Commander-in-Chief, when disappointed in his efforts to break through General Lee's lines and to enter Richmond, professed in his official reports to have —not fallen back—but *changed his base*, made the phrase quite a by-word at the North as well as in the South. To this day, therefore, it is used as a humorous way of admitting a defeat, or at least the necessity of trying once more in some other way. Thus an enthusiastic writer, recommending to the public his new invention of a Gentleman's Pocket Spittoon, writes thus: "For years my attention has been called to the necessity of a *change of base* in the matter of tobacco-spitting, from the public floor, under the public eye, to some more private receptacle, under the individual care of the devotee." (New York *Tribune*, February 2, 1871.) It is well known, that as far as the war was concerned, the final conqueror at once superseded the phrase by adopting the new resolve: "To fight it out on this line." Of more humble meaning, but infinitely diversified is the term, to *flank*, which, from the strategy of the generals, descended in the mouth of privates to very lowly and not always honorable meanings. When the men wished to escape the attention of pickets and guards by slipping past them, they said they *flanked* them; drill and detail and every irksome duty was *flanked*, when it could be avoided by some cunning trick. Soon, however, honesty itself was thus treated, and the poor farmer was *flanked* out of his pig and his poultry, and not unfrequently even the comrade out of his pipe and tobacco, if not his rations. The height of strategy was employed in these various *flank manœuvres*, when the Commissary could be made to surrender some of his whiskey, and thus it came about, in the South at least, that to *flank the whole bottle* was a phrase expressive of superlative cunning and brilliant success.

Among the minor details of the war that produced new terms, may be mentioned the word *sorghum pulling* or tugging, as found in the line: "We hear in this county of several marriages, one or two hops, some *sorghum-tuggings*, and any number of gum-suckings, for the holidays." (Richmond *Dispatch*, December 20, 1870.) The curious term has its origin in the name of the Chinese sugar-cane (Sorghum saccharatum), which was very largely cultivated in the South during the Civil War; syrup was made from it in large quantities, and became soon the general substitute for sugar, which could not be obtained. Hence *sorghum* became not only itself a favorite with soldiers and all classes of society, but soon acquired a general meaning, denoting anything specially pleasant or desirable. As the people of the South had always been fond of *molasses stews*, in which the boiling molasses was *pulled* or *tugged* out into long strings, the same was now done with the sorghum-molasses, and hence the name.

Since peace has been restored, the great work of *Reconstruction* has gone on uninterruptedly for six years in the South, apparently unsuccessfully, although the formal restoration of the Union was accomplished. This process, also, has given rise to some peculiar terms. To secure the loyalty of conquered Southerners a multitude of oaths were exacted of them, and among these two assumed new names: the *Amnesty Oath*, which secured pardon according to the terms of an amnesty granted by the President, and which was irreverently called "Damnasty-Oath" by those who swallowed it, and the still more hateful *Iron-clad Oath*. General B. F. Butler, sometimes considered the author of all those peculiarly harsh and severe measures, nicknamed *Iron-Clad*, spoke of these oaths in 1870, thus: "Oaths have become odious in this country by reason of their frequency and their *iron-clad* character. They have become as cheap as *custom-house oaths* or *dicers' oaths.* Nobody seems to care much for them." In 1871, he said, however: "Every giving way that Congress had so far allowed, had been the death-knell of some black or white friend of the Union. He hoped that the *iron-clad oath* would never be repealed. It was a patent of nobility for royalty, referring to the Ku-Klux outrages." (New York *Tribune,* February 2, 1871.)

The necessity of providing loyal officers for the States, whose citizens were almost all disabled from taking these oaths, without which they could not hold office, required the employment of a number of men from the North, who flocked to the South in search of employment and emoluments. Some performed their duty faithfully and wisely, and rose rapidly in the confidence and esteem of Southerners, being by them chosen to fill high places, as governors, senators, etc. But a large number, also, sought only their private interest, and having entered the South poor, quickly became rich; these the suffering people soon began to designate as *Carpet-baggers,* from the only piece of luggage which they had brought with them on their arrival from the North. Colonel Joseph Hodgson, editor of the *Mail,* a paper published at Montgomery, in Alabama, is said to have invented, or at least to have first used in print, the opprobrious term, which quickly became popular as a name for all adventurers in search of fortune in the South. "The general drift of public sentiment is, that the *carpet-baggers,* scalawags, ex-slaves, ex-slaveholders, rebels reconstructed, rebels unreconstructed, and Southern loyalists should be left, for a brief period at least, to fight out their own battles, in their own way; and that if the nation is ever again to become a party to their quarrels, it shall be on no slight pretext and for no trivial purpose." (New York *Post,* April, 1871.)

The evidently dishonest among the Southerners, who went over to the dominant party, and unblushingly lived on their conquered friends and neighbors, were called *Scallawags* or *Scalawags,* from an old variety of wags described by Mr. Bartlett as a "compound of loafer, blackguard, and scamp." (*Dictionary,* p. 382.) "That *scallawag* of a fellow ought to be kicked out of all decent society." (*Western Sketches, B.*) It was one of this class, rather than the eloquent advocate of Women's Rights, often charged with the crime, who first publicly used the illshapen word *miscegena-*

tion, and openly dared to advocate the expediency of favoring, by every agency of State and Church, the mingling of the black and white races. It seemed hard to make a word that could be worse, and still even this has been accomplished by American genius, for we read that "A *Miscegenationist,* named Williams, was tarred and feathered, and dumped into the river at Grenada, Mississippi, the other day." (Richmond *Dispatch,* March 15, 1871.

The word *loyal* itself, one of the noblest words in the language, though of foreign birth, had to answer new purposes. *Loyal Leagues,* as well as *Union Leagues,* were formed all over the country, to aid in re-establishing and firmly consolidating the Union that had been so near to disruption, and *Loyalty* became the test of all who sought preferment, or wanted aid from the restored powers. But as the sacred thought expressed by the word was abused by flatterers and hypocrites alike, the term itself also suffered curtailment in its sonorous sound, and the *loil* man, as he was often called, inspired the upright at once with a suspicion of lip-service or selfish zeal. No such doubt hung, on the other side, at any time over the meaning of the word *Ku-klux* (written Ku-Klux, Ku Klux, and Ku-klux), a meaningless name of an abomination, the sad result of lawlessness on one side, and tyranny on the other side, such as results almost invariably from an imperfect pacification. The *Ku-Klux-Klan* was or pretended to be a secret political organization, "the original purpose of which was, by their ghastly apparel, in which they traversed the country, to appeal, to negro superstition, and prevent devastations at night. But Radicalism raised such an infernal howl, and thieves at length assuming the *Ku-Klux* garb, the organization was finally abandoned." This is the explanation given at the South, through one of its organs. (Memphis *Appeal,* January 17, 1871.) At the North the *Ku-Klux* are looked upon as men who, under some specious pretext, but always under the shelter of night and disguise, perpetrate political outrages, terrify some, murder others, prevent the freedmen from enjoying their newly-acquired rights and from pursuing their labors in peace and safety, and seriously endanger the republic itself. It is certain that whatever may be said in defence of such secret, irresponsible organizations, they can, in their best aspect, aim no higher than to substitute Lynch-law for equity and justice. No well-ordered State, no conscientious government can, tolerate them for a moment; fortunately their reign in the South is limited to very few and very small districts, and as peace and order are restored by a wise administration of the laws, they will disappear with other evils engendered by the war. We have called the *Ku-Klux* as unmeaning as unwarranted. It ought, perhaps, to be mentioned that some ingenious suggestions have been made to explain the absurd name, among which the following is the least improbable: "On the borders of Texas, near the Rio Grande, there lived a Mexican by the name of Nal. K. Xulkuk. He, like the Bowies, who invented the *Bowie* knife, was a desperado, but, unlike them, he fought against and depredated upon the American settlers. He is still remembered in Texas by many who have seen and heard of him, as well as dreaded him. His motto was to seek unceasingly to avenge a real or fancied wrong to himself, his followers, or his country. His name spelled backward gives us, as it gave to the founder of the new order, its name of *Ku Klux Klan*." (Correspondence of Chicago *Republican*, March, 1871.) Another theory derives the odd name from "*Kruked Kluks*," the Scottish for "crooked clutches," ascribed to the Evil One, and thus mentioned in an old poem, written on the death of John Peney, a Welsh non-conformist:

"The Welshman is hanged,
Who at our kirke flanged,
And at the state banged,
And brened are his buks;
And tho' he be hanged,
Yet he is not coranged,
The de'il has him fanged
In his *kruked kluks*."
(From Weever's *Funeral Monuments*, ed., 1631.)

The many absurd attempts at explaining the odd term, led an indignant English writer to exclaim: "Why, Sir, the word *Ku-Klux* is an invention, just letters shot together promiscuous... Presently a learned party will trace *Ku-Klux* to the Indians or to the Feejee mermaid, and get a medal for his discovery." (*Once a Week*, May, 1871.) "But the general cause of dispute with the *Ku-Kluxers* has been some action on the part of the carpet-baggers through the niggers." (*Ibid.*)

As the government of the United States reserves to itself the usual prerogative of coining money, it may not be amiss to mention the few peculiar terms that are connected with the currency. A truly national coin is the *Eagle,* so called from the emblem of the republic, which it bears; it is of gold, and of the value of ten dollars; double eagles, as well as half and quarter eagles, are in existence, though rarely seen. The only other coin peculiar to the United States is the *dime,* a silver coin of the value of ten cents, and the *half-dime,* both also very generally known as *ten cent pieces* and *five cent pieces.* Copper-money is represented by *cents.* In Texas at least the words *dime,* bit, two bits, etc., are still exclusively heard in shops and stores. The Spanish silver coins, which were long current in some parts of the Union, have nearly all disappeared, and with them their local names, as the *fip* and the *levy,* coins representing six and a quarter, and twelve and a half cents, the former a contraction of five pence through the English fippence, the latter the scant remnant of eleven pence. "A *fip's* worth of dinner and a *levy's* worth of sleep," were the words of a loafer of Philadelphia, where the names remained longest in use. (J. C. Neal, *Charcoal Sketches,* I,, p. 58.) The sixteenth part of a dollar is, in like manner, still frequently called a *picayune,* in New Orleans. Since the war a few new coins, of the value of a few cents, have been issued, mainly of *nickel,* and hence often so called, constituting what is known to the laws a *Fractional Currency,* or copper and *nickel tokens.* As the United States have, since the war, had exclusively paper-money, the cant name given to it from the green color of the back, *Greenbacks,* has become universal. "The word *Greenbacks* has become entirely domesticated as a respectable and generic term for an all-pervading species of evil, than the presence of which nothing can be worse, except its absence." (I. N. Spenser, *Eclectic Monthly.*) The confederate notes bore, for the same reason, the name of *Bluebacks,* which was, however, soon exchanged for the slang term of *shucks.* Nor have the solid gold coins escaped entirely the contamination of slang. When the Hon. T. H. Benton, of Missouri, put his whole strength forward on the floor of Congress and through the press to introduce a gold currency, he accidentally called the latter mint-drops, with a slight attempt at a pun. The word, however, became popular, and for many years gold coins were very largely known as *Benton's mint-drops,* while the author of the phrase was called *Old Bullion.*

VI.

Trade of all Kinds.

TRADE OF ALL KINDS.

"Fair weight, fair measure, fair speech."

B. Franklin.

It cannot be denied that if the English are a nation of shopkeepers, and have never proved the truth of Napoleon's charge more fully than during the last years, the Americans are not unmindful of the same source of wealth, and *shop-slang*, as their British cousins call the terminology of the counting-house, forms no insignificant part of our peculiar speech. Much, however, is here also looked upon as American, that has long been in use as good—or bad—English, and among these terms, wrongfully imputed to us, stands naturally foremost the *Almighty Dollar*. How often have English authors cast the unlucky word, first coined in its modern form by W. Irving in 1837, in his *Creole Village*, into our teeth, and tried to make the world believe that none but Americans knew the "almighty" power of money! We hope they will recall the first lines of Ben Jonson's Epistle to the Countess of Holland, which read thus:

"Whilst that for which all virtue now is sold,
And almost every vice, *almightie gold*;"

and substituting the dollar for the guinea, they may safely claim the authorship of the phrase. It may even be doubted whether the dollar is as powerful in America as gold is in England, although a sarcastic writer speaks severely of the "unrelenting and desperate onwardness of the great Yankee dollar-chase." (*Putnam's Magazine*, April, 1855.) It is certainly remarkable that, with all this veneration for the Dollar, the sign by which it is represented in writing ($) should still be an unexplained mystery. The most plausible explanation among the many that have been offered, is, that it represents the letters U. S. (United States) drawn in one, for brevity's sake, so as to distinguish the American currency from the Spanish coins, which were largely used before the young republic could establish its own coinage. It is equally unjust to charge Americans with the invention of the phrase, to *make money*, much as they may be addicted to the practice. Dr. Johnson already rebuked Boswell sharply for using it, and said: "Don't you see the impropriety of it? To *make money* is to coin it; you should say, to *get money*." Moreover, if Americans are fond of *making money*, they are also able to make a good use of their earnings, as England has seen in the benefactions of Mr. Peabody. They may well be pardoned, therefore, the almost endless variety of terms they employ in designating large sums, speaking of a *mint*, an *ocean*, a *mine*, a *sight*, and a *power* of money.

Money itself has in the United States, as in England, probably more designations than any other object—liquor alone excepted—many of which are purely whimsical, while others may be traced back to the material of which coins are made. Among the less generally known terms are *John Davis* or the *Ready John*, sometimes simply *John* or *Ready*, *spondulics*, *dooteroomus*, often shortened into *doot*; *tow*, *wad* (both of them evidently tailors' slang); *hardstuff* or *hard*, *dirt*, *shinplasters*, or simply *plasters*; *wherewith*, *shadscales*, or *scales*, "for short;" *dyestuffs*, *charms*, and also the more modern designation of *stamps*; all of which are missing in the list given in the English Slang Dictionary, and may therefore be considered as Americanisms.

Unfortunately, the skill in making money is sometimes illegally employed after the manner of Dr. Johnson's suggestion. False coins, the makers of which are curiously called *coniackers*, abounded as long as specie was in use, and since *greenbacks* are the only currency, counterfeit paper-money is quite as plentiful. The great success of one of the earlier counterfeiters has made his name a byword, as that of the great resurrectionist in England has become familiar to all readers. Burke abroad has his counterpart in *Bogus* at home. The latter is, however, a vile corruption of a most noble and romantic name, the Italian *Borghese*. In the year 1837 there passed through the Western and Southwestern

States a man calling himself thus, who drew large numbers of fictitious checks, notes, and bills of exchange upon the principal traders and bankers, and succeeded in swindling the public out of large sums. His transactions were so extensive, and the distrust in commercial circles so very great when his forgeries were discovered, that his name, pronounced, with American freedom, first Borges and then *Bogus*, spread over the whole Union. It soon became synonymous with any doubtful money transaction, and as it took the fancy of the people, its meaning rapidly extended to everything suspected of being unreal, spurious, or fraudulent. Thus a member of a Legislature supposed to be unfairly elected, was called a *bogus* representative; a woman with false hair and teeth, painted, or otherwise gotten up to look young, when she was old, was a *bogus beauty;* and famous—or infamous—Mrs. Cunningham, who, like Joanna Southcote, pretended to have had a child, without such being the case, was declared to have been delivered of a *bogus child.* The fondness of Americans for such terms, full of suggestive force, and yet avoiding the unpleasant directness of a charge, is strikingly seen in the almost endless variety of meanings to which the term has since been bent: ladies are accused of wearing *bogus diamonds;* overdressed, assuming upstarts are called *bogus gentlemen;* maimed soldiers wear *bogus*-legs, blind men *bogus eyes,* and even in courts of justice *bogus charges* are of constant occurrence. J. R. Lowell proposes, in spite of the almost historical descent of the word from this source, another derivation of *bogus* from the French *bagasse,* the worthless refuse of sugar-cane, which he thinks gave the name to other worthless things, and travelled gradually up the Mississippi from its birthplace, New Orleans.

Another term of similar character was the *Wild-Cat Money* of the last generation, which took its name from the notes of a bank in Michigan, bearing a Wild Cat or a panther on its face as a vignette. The bank proved utterly insolvent after having sent out a large number of notes, and for many years afterward all irresponsible banks, which then abounded, were designated as *Wild-Cat* Banks, and their notes often very curtly and severely as *wild cats.* "Does the honorable member in good earnest mean to revive the disastrous times, when thousands and tens of thousands were ruined by *Wild-Cat Banks?*" was asked on the floor

13*

of Congress in March, 1865. Other efforts at cheating are designated as *chiselling*—not as some have believed from the practice of *chiselling,* that is, opening by means of cold chisels the *safes* of banks and merchants, since the term is much older than the introduction of safes. "When the books were overhauled by the Committee, it was found that their late Cashier had appropriated to himself nearly two hundred thousand dollars, and that the stockholders would be *chiselled* out of a pretty considerable sum." (Savannah *Republican,* May 17, 1858.) A somewhat stronger term for the same operation is *gouging,* the figure of speech being evidently drawn from the carpenter's shop, where it means to scoop or chisel out with a hollow, cylindrical tool. An American lady wrote recently from Germany to the New York *Tribune:* "I should like to be informed in what sense the Germans can be called a suffering people; I look upon them as eminently prosperous. Between plundering and *gouging* France, as they will in the indemnity, they will pay the expenses of the war a dozen times over." (March 22, 1871.)

Very general in use, and, like *bogus,* applied to an infinite variety of uses, is the term *shoddy,* which we have obtained from England in more recent times. Meaning originally cloth made of a new warp filled with *shreds* (hence the name *shred-dy,* shoddy) of old and wornout cloth, it soon became synonymous with the poor material largely furnished to Government during the late Civil War by the class of contractors whose desire for riches was greater than even their patriotism—or their honesty. "The Pennsylvania regiments, who plead the Statute of Limitation against the debt of doing duty at the battle of Bull Run, were said to have been equipped for the field by certain ardent friends of the cause, with contract coats, that would not bear the strain of buttoning, and contract boots, the glued soles of which deserted the uppers in the first rain. As *shoddy* was very cheap, those who substituted it for real cloth became suddenly rich, and this, very naturally, led to the use of the term generally, as applied to all who acquired wealth by contracts. *Shoddy* became the name, more especially, of those who aped the aristocracy of other lands, and of all kinds of hollow schemes and nefarious undertakings." (Mr. Spencer.) We have now *shoddy*-men as well as *shoddy*-manufacturers; unprofitable preachers, unwise politicians, and unsafe merchants are all *shoddy*, and the same author, quoted above, suggests that the weaving in of so much cast-off material from the shores of Europe and Asia, into the fabric of American society, may ere long end in producing a great *shoddy nation*. It is certain that art has become *shoddy* to a high degree, and New York especially can boast of a marvellous *shoddy architecture*, brown-stone fronts with nothing behind them, and grand structures so flimsily built that they fall before they are finished. There is even *mental shoddy*, such as J. R. Lowell sings of when he says—

> "I call it *shoddy*,
> A thing, sez he, won't cover soul nor body,
> I like the plain all wool of common sense,
> That warms you now and will a twelvemonth hence."
> (*Biglow Papers*, II., p. 67.)

A verb, even—to *shoddyize*—has been made to supply an apparent demand.

Peter Funk, who also plays a prominent part in a certain class of commercial transactions, is, in all probability, a myth like William Tell, although tradition speaks of a person of that name having once been famous, by his skill in exciting buyers at an auction, to raise their bids till they often exceeded the value of the article they wished to purchase. The name is perhaps a simple manufacture, from the vague and unsatisfactory meaning of the word *funk*. It now designates the person who aids in getting up so-called *mock auctions*, sales held for the sole benefit of inexperienced countrymen, at which more or less worthless articles, imitation jewelry, watches of gilt copper and the like, are offered; where unwary purchasers are forced to take a large quantity while they only bid for a very small portion. The whole establishment is a cheat, and *Peter Funk*, one of the confederates, plays the *by-bidder* or *puffer*, as it used to be called in England. (Grose's *Dictionary, sub voce.*) "The Mayor has once more ordered a police sergeant to be stationed at the door of every *Peter Funk* auction-room in Broadway and the Bowery, but in spite of their warning voice, greenhorns will walk in and be fleeced." (New York *Herald*, November 14, 1859.) A peculiar feature at genuine auctions is the so-called *upset price*, a price mentioned by the auctioneer before beginning the sale, as the lowest sum at which the article offered will be disposed of. "He says: Business before soup. Between fish and pudding he will sell a prairie. The *upset price* is knocked down with a knife-handle, and the bargain is clinched by the help of the nut-cracker and the sugar-tongs." (*Putnam's Magazine,* December, 1854.)

A less mythical personage has imported his name from England to these shores, and established himself in commercial circles with surprising success. This is the Arab messenger, or *Chiaous,* who was sent in 1607 by the great Signior, as the Sultan of Turkey was then called, to England, and availed himself of his position in London to commit gigantic frauds upon the Turkish and Persian merchants of the great city. The transaction became known at 'Change in all its details, and the extent as well as the notoriety of the facts led to the formation of a verb, to *chouse,* as synonymous with cheating or defrauding. The word *Chiaus* is, of course, well known from of old: in Sandys' Travels (p. 48) it is defined as meaning "one who goes on embassies, executive commandments, etc.," and in our days thousands have flocked to admire the French painter Boulanger's admirable picture of "Algerine *Chaouses.*" Nearly all the great poets of England use the word, though with varied spelling, from the *chowse* of Halliwell and Ben Jonson's *chiause* to the simpler *chouse* of Landor, Browning, and Foster. The word is quite familiar on this side of the Atlantic also, and by no means limited to money matters, as in the lines: "Dr. Dore should have consulted his beloved Germania, before he *choused* her out of her hoped-for Kaiser, and substituted an archangel so fat and scant o' breath in his place." (New York *Tribune,* January 19, 1871.)

The man who is not liable to be *choused* on a large scale, is nevertheless apt to fall into another danger, that threatens strangers in the large cities. A man walking before him, pretends to find a well-filled pocketbook, and either offers it to him, minus a certain sum for immediate need, for advertising, with the expectation of a liberal reward, or, with more cynicism, downright suggests a division of spoils. In either case his greed is justly punished by finding himself the owner of a roll of counterfeit bills, and out of pocket for the sum of good money he has given the finder, who goes rejoicing to try again and again his successful *drop-game,* as the cheat is called.

The man who means to employ his capital and his labor in commercial enterprises is not, as in England, said to go into trade, but he either connects himself with a *Moneyed Institution,* as chartered companies are generally called, like banks, insurance companies, and the like, or he devotes himself to *merchandizing,* a barbarous euphuism; the offspring of American grandiloquence.

A *trade* is only a single transaction, and often employed to designate an exchange; hence, small country shops express in advertisements their readiness "to *trade* for anything, meat, eggs, oats, and all kinds of country produce." When an agreement as to price and time of delivery has been reached, the question is apt to be asked: "Well, is it a *trade?*" and if replied to in the affirmative, the contract is binding, as far as verbal agreements have any force. The *tradesman* is consequently more or less than the retail-merchant of England, and to *trade* is by no means confined to regular commercial business. It includes, on the contrary, every similar transaction in daily life, and hence a traveller could report that "The Southerners are not nearly as commercial a race as the Yankees, but still they are much giving to *trading* amongst each other, and the other day, at a hospital in Gettysburg, an artilleryman, whose leg was to be taken off, no sooner knew that amputation was decided upon by the doctors, than he turned to another wounded man in the next bed, and before the operation was performed, had *traded* the boot which was henceforth to be of no use to him." (*Blackwood,* December, 1864.) Perhaps they remember too well the prophet's praising words about Tyre: "Javan, Tubal, and Meshech, they were thy merchants: they *traded* the persons of men and vessels of brass at thy market." (Ezekiel, xxvii. v. 13.)

Different branches of commerce have peculiar names in America, which are only very slowly becoming known in England. Such are *Drygoods,* cloths, stuffs, laces, etc., referred to in the following description of the greatest establishment for their sale: "Here an army of young men encounter the flood of women with their greedy, anxious eyes; they keep them at bay by piling up barricades of *drygoods* of every shade and pattern ever produced. This is Stewart's, a spot better known to the female mind of America than the graves of the fathers or the shrines of the saints." Among *Drygoods* one branch plays a specially prominent part in all public discussions on Tariff and Protection; this contains the so-called *Domestics*—used only in the plural—or goods manufactured in the country, as distinguished from imported goods. The word *goods* itself has its American meaning: a stock in trade is *goods*, and hence *drygoods* are so called, but although the word is used in the sense of the English term "stuff" also, it is never applied to the dress of a lady. In the West alone the use of *goods* for a single piece of material occurs occasionally; a clerk will recommend "that *goods* as an excellent fabric; sure to retain its color." *Drygoods* are kept carefully apart from *Groceries*, a word used here in the plural for the articles themselves, while English usage limits it to the singular, as denoting a grocer's shop or the grocer's ware. As among tea and coffee other stimulants readily find a place, the *grocery* has in America very speedily become a name for a groggery also, and from Pennsylvania southward *groceries* are apt to include, if not actually to mean, ardent spirits. "Families ought always to lay in their stock of *groceries* at the beginning of the year, as they thus reduce the cost, and are sure not to run out at an inconvenient time." (*Housekeeper's Manual*, p. 28.) The use of *Hardware* for articles made of metal, is now probably as common in England as with us, but it includes the "iron-monger," and all the subdivisions of this branch of trade known to English merchants, and ignored here. Of these various kinds of goods the merchant is expected always to have a large stock *on hand*—a phrase which in America is strangely abused, being applied to persons as well as to merchandise. "Be *on hand* early and vote the Republican ticket!" is the earnest summons of radical newspapers at the time of election. "A broker from Wall-street was *on hand*, and tried to pray, but he broke down half-way in the Lord's Prayer, and there seemed to be no one able to assist him." (New York *Express*, August 11, 1856.)

In no point does commercial language, however, differ more, as far as English and American usage are concerned, than in the terms *shop* and *store*. The English *shopkeeper* is unknown to us: the day of small things has long since passed for the Great Republic. To go *shopping* is perhaps the only phrase in which the humble word yet survives; everywhere else it is disdainfully put aside. The smallest cobbler's stall is a shoe or *boot store*, and the shoemaker's workshop a *Boot and Shoe Manufactory*, and every village of a few houses has its *Variety-Store*, where country people purchase anything they may want. The *shop* is so haughtily ignored that the zealous Temperance lecturer gathers his whole indignation into the contemptuous term of *grogshop*, where alone it seems to be in place. Nor does the American *merchant*—for no other title is thought suitable for the owner of the smallest establishment—condescend to "open a shop;" he *sets up a store*, a grocery, or a bazaar, at once. Quite as frequently, perhaps, he proposes to *run* it, a word applied with reckless freedom to every possible enterprise, from *running* the machine of the government to *running* a little grocery "round the corner." The following advertisement appeared in the leading New York papers: "The two largest retail bookstores in New York will be *run* by Sheldon & Company during the coming holidays, first, their present *store*, 498 Broadway, second, the elegant new *store* under the Grand Central Hotel." (December 20, 1870.) Even to *run one's face* is a frequent phrase, meaning to obtain money upon credit, in return for the borrower's name being placed on the *face* of a promissory note, which is then *run*. The kindred term to *circulate*, which originally applied to *bank-bills*—as the English bank-*notes* are still very generally called in America—is now applied to a variety of movements, and gentlemen *circulate* in good society, as if they were promises to pay themselves. By a similar process the fact that bank-notes may be *above par* or *under par* has led to the application of these terms to articles of other kinds, and even to man's conduct. Certain silks or laces are offered for sale with the recommendation that they are *above par*, or far superior to the common run of such goods, while a mean man's conduct is stigmatized as *under par*. "He was popular, but did not get money enough to support him, so he located and went into land speculations and got *under par* as a good man." (Rev. Mr. Cartwright, *Autobiography*, p. 114.) A man who has thus *gone under*, as commercial slang has it, and finds himself unable, for want of capital, to begin a new "business," has nothing left but to *clerk it*, that is, to engage himself as *clerk* (never pronounced *clark* as in England) to some more fortunate man, who owns a store. A kind of limited partnership is, in the West, not unfrequently called *to go on lays*. The term is evidently derived from the slang term *lay*, which means some, a piece, etc., and is thus used in the North of England. (*Slang Dictionary*, p. 169.) Ordinarily the term is restricted to operations in which many participate and work jointly, as in whaling-voyages and gold-diggings, where all labor alike and each receives a share of the profits. "Who is going to dig gold on the hundredth or two hundredth *lay?*" (*Overland Monthly*, March, 1870, p. 236.) From this use the word is transferred to meaning the right proportion, and the right thing generally, as in the phrase, "I'm goin' back and p'raps I may meet Canvas in heaven, ef I keep my word, which the preacher says is the right *lay*." (*Overland Monthly*, January, 1870, p. 88.)

If the young merchant is, on the other hand, successful, the world says that he *makes his pile*, a term taken, no doubt, in the first place, from the actual pile of coins, but soon used to mean simply a man's available means, his fortune. In the first sense it still serves the gambler, who really *piles* up his stakes and his winnings, as in the lines, "Three days ago I came down the river to sell my goods and furs. I made a pretty good trade, but that very night I lost my whole *pile* at poker. I was dead-broke, and hadn't a confounded cent left." (*A Trapper's Adventures*, p. 227.) In the sense of a large amount of money it is used by J. R. Lowell, when he says, "The government owed me quite a *pile* for my arrears of pension," (*Biglow Papers*, II., p. 23,) and meaning the available resources of a merchant in a creditor's words: "We never go over a party's *pile*, nor higgle, nor do anything small in these matters. Give us what you've got, and we'll take the balance when you are flush." (*Putnam's Magazine*, November, 1868.) If he does not succeed, he may at first be merely *hard pushed* or *hard run*, and means may be found to extricate himself; but if that is out of question, his business is *wound up*. It depends, of course, upon the state of his assets, whether he can *settle* with his creditors, or is found to be *dead-broke*. The use of the former term in such a case is unknown in England, where *settling* means simply *arranging* a matter, and also an account, by payment or otherwise. In America, however, to *settle* is generally intended to mean paying a debt, although evidently accounts may be settled and yet not paid. A man called upon to settle a bill is expected to do nothing less than to pay it; and even Mr. Howell, in his carefully written *Italian Journeys,* uses the Americanism, "When we came to *settle* for the wine." It is in this sense, also, that passengers on board steamboats are commonly summoned by a fearful ringing of bells and shouting of colored porters, "to please walk up to the captain's office and *settle.*" If he cannot arrange matters amicably he is *dead* or *flat broke,* in the far more energetic than elegant language of the trade, meaning that he is utterly ruined, and left without any resources whatever. "When he left the gambling-house, he was observed to turn toward a friend with the words, *Dead-broke!* and then to disappear round the corner. A moment after a shot fell, and upon hastening to the spot, he was found lying dead on the pavement, a revolver by his side." (Cincinnati *Enquirer,* July 17, 1866.) It may be that, before the crisis is reached, he has tried to help himself by getting his *paper shaved.* A *shaver,* in the American sense of the word, is a person who buys up another man's note at a heavy discount or more than legal interest—a practice formerly not unknown to banks even, which were then called *shaving banks.* The term is said to have originated at sea, where a *shaver* has long been the sailors' name for a sharp fellow, derived very naturally from the delicate but cruel operation of shaving on board ship. "May I be hanged myself," says N. Hawthorne, "if I believe Mr. Higginbotham is unhanged till I see him with my own eyes, and hear it from his own mouth; and, as he is a real *shaver,* I'll have the minister or some other responsible man for an indorser." (*Mr. Higginbotham's Catastrophe.*) In his efforts to obtain money he has probably had much *shinning* to do, as slang calls the running about to friends and acquaintances, regardless of all obstacles in the way that endanger the safety of the borrower's shins. In England the same meaning is attached to the term in city slang, but in America it has been largely extended, and is applied to any eager search after help. "'*Shin it,* good man!' ejaculated a good-natured urchin, '*shin it* as well as you know how!' The qualification was a good one, Berry not being well calculated for a *shinner* of the first class." (J. C. Neal, *Charcoal Sketches,* II., p. 13.) A political song in praise of the Whig Party, of the year 1840, speaks of the delectable associates—

"Coxcombs and dandies, loafers and nibblers,
Shavers and *shinners,* peddlers and scribblers,

> Bankers and brokers, and cunning buffoons,
> Thieves that steal millions and thieves that steal spoons."

This process of *shinning* is resorted to whenever the merchant or banker is *short,* that is, in want of the necessary means to comply with his obligations. The meaning of this term differs, likewise, from that which it receives in England, where, for instance, the conductor of a 'bus is *short,* when he does not give up all the money he has received. In America, *short* has to cover the absence or want of everything that ought to be on hand; hence, "a common practice is to withhold a little of a poor sewing-girl's pay from week to week, on the plea of being *short,* and when a handsome aggregate has been reached, to boldly deny the debt." (*Putnam's Magazine,* April, 1868.) When the express companies fail to deliver parcels at the right time, the agent is apt to say, "The box is on the way-bill, but it is *short* to-day; it will reach here to-morrow." In this sense the term is a genuine Americanism. Finally, the merchant *winds up* his business, using thus a term familiar wherever English is spoken, but the same verb is also used intransitively here, and of a National Bank, which had suffered severely by defalcation, it was said: "A receiver has been appointed, according to law, and the bank will *wind up,* probably without serious loss to the stockholders." (Philadelphia *Ledger,* May 7, 1867.) His property is, of course, sold, including both his personal property and what is here called *real estate,* a term which, when not taken in the strictly legal sense, is nothing more than a big-sounding, vulgar phrase for houses and land; hence the newspapers abound with columns headed, Real Estate Transactions, where Land Sales would have been quite as expressive. The *avails,* as the proceeds of all sales, or of rents, profits, etc., are apt to be called, in New England especially, remind us of the *vails* given to servants in old England, two terms which J. R. Lowell maintains are identical.

If the poor bankrupt is not set up again by his creditors, he is very apt to become a *drummer,* an agent of other houses of commerce, represented in England by the "touting bagsman," or the more ambitious "commercial gent." The larger houses of the North especially, employ, often at high wages, numbers of such drummers, who travel through all the Southern and Western States, soliciting orders, informing themselves of the standing of customers, and collecting outstanding debts. "Look at that man, he is *drummer* for A. T. Stewart, and carries blank checks in his pocket-book which he is authorized to fill up to the amount of fifty thousand dollars." (*A Country Merchant out West*, p. 217.) He carries with him, probably, not such fabulous checks, but careful extracts from the *tickler*, as the great book is facetiously called, in which all debts and notes falling due are recorded, because it is used to tickle the memory of the debtor, as well as of the creditor. The business of the *drummer* is probably not esteemed the most distinguished, even in the trade, but the peculiar qualities necessary for success in this line, great tact, a pleasant address, a persuasive tongue, and a keen eye to business, give to the class of superior *drummers* a character of its own.

Among the varieties of trade, two appear under special names. *Dickering*, or bartering in small articles, is probably a word of Dutch origin, and explains the line in Whittier's poem,

> "For peddling *dicker*, not for honest sales,"

although Cooper speaks very much in the same manner of "*dicker* and swap." The minuteness of the ware in which this kind of trading is generally confined, is shown in the fact that "Sam Jones called at the store of a Mr. Brown, with an egg in his hand, and wanted to *dicker* it for a darning-needle." (*Sam Jones*, p. 127.) The other way of trading is, also, not unknown to England, though often, by English writers, represented as peculiar to America. This is the *swapping*, or, as it is more frequently written and almost always pronounced, the *swopping*. J. R. Lowell says very pointedly: "The fallacy that *swop*, as a New England word, is describing accurately the New England propensity to barter or trade anything, from jack-knives to horses, is shown by the line of Dryden:

> 'I would have *swopp'd*
> Youth for old age;'

and Ray in his *North Country Words* has: "*To Coup:* To exchange, or *swap*." Ben Jonson, Dean Swift, and a host of classic writers, were in the habit of using it, and even the *swopper* was not unknown in England, for—

"The headlong fool who wants to be a *swopper*
Of gold and silver coin for English copper,
May in 'Change Alley prove himself an ass
And give rich metal for adulterated brass." (*Old Poet.*)

The word is said, however, to have fallen among low company. The South Sea stockjobbers damaged its reputation, and it has since lost all character by becoming a household word with horse-jockeys. In this country the term is universally used, even Mr. Lincoln often employing it as an illustration of his policy, when he assured wise counsellors that "when a man was swimming across a river was not the time for *swopping* horses;" and the very Indians on our Western plains have become familiar with the word as well as with the transaction. "As soon as he saw me, he cried out: Well, Mark, what do you say? Will you *swop* your mare for my mule, if I give you a twenty-dollar note to boot?" (J. P. Kennedy, *Swallow Barn.*)

Perhaps the only commercial term that ever became a universal favorite in the army is the *going up the spout*, which was used, in the Confederate army almost exclusively, for any disastrous conclusion of an enterprise, as well as for the loss of an article. A man's mule, that had strayed away from camp, was said to have *gone up the spout*, and the Confederacy itself, after the surrender of Richmond, had simply *gone up*. The figure of speech is taken from the spout, or tin-tube, up which pawnbrokers send the ticketed articles to be kept till redeemed, and which generally runs from the ground-floor to the wareroom in the upper part of the house. (*Slang Dictionary*, p. 204.) That the term was not unknown to the Federal army, also, may be seen from the following account: "Dr. B., Assistant Surgeon in the army, was very fond of milk, and on a march in Virginia rode up to a mean-looking house by the roadside, and, cap in hand, addressed a slatternly-looking girl, standing arms akimbo in the doorway, while the men of the column were listening and watching the negotiation: 'Madam, can I purchase a canteen of milk and a loaf of bread of you?' Slowly and loudly the answer came: 'We haint got no bread. We haint got no milk. We haint got nothing. We're clean done *gone up the spout*. So ye can tote yourself away from hyar.'" It is not quite clear why the Southern States, which are naturally much more given to agriculture than to commerce, should so specially affect the phrase *of no account*, evidently borrowed from the ledger. But the wealthy planter and his humblest field-hand both know hardly a stronger expression of utter contempt than to say that a man is of *no account*, or, as the negro is sure to say, of *no 'count*. A warning friend says, therefore, to a gentleman: "It is not fit for such as you to concern yourself with Miles Rutherford; the man is half in liquor, and of *no account* if he was not." (J. P. Kennedy, *Swallow Barn.*) Pretended ghosts in Virginia are thus spoken of in a Northern paper: "They are delightful fellows, these ghosts; they possess, in common with other more celebrated ghosts, a tendency to be extremely frank—making no bones at all of informing the said hosts that they are *no-account* people." (New York *Tribune*, January 17, 1871.) "Lur a'Mussy!" cries Tom Brooks, the clever house-carpenter; "Pete! he *no 'count* nohow, he poor fiel'hand nigger!" (*Flush Times of Alabama*, p. 117.)

A stern old Puritan has left his name to his far-off descendants, to be held in esteem here as Cocker is in England, and in those parts of the Union where New England rule is not supreme. It seems that a worthy inventor, called *Gunter*, brought out in 1623, about the time of the great Puritan exodus to this country, his famous Rule of Proportion. This became then familiarly known as Gunter's Proportion or Gunter's Line, and the term has ever since remained a popular standard of appeal in cases of doubt and dispute. (*Slang Dictionary*, p. 104.) Since that time the phrase *According to Gunter* has held its own in Canada almost exclusively, and in the New England States at least very largely, instead of the old-fashioned "According to Cocker," being frequently used without the slightest idea as to whom the debt of gratitude ought to be paid. In the West the name is rarely heard except in jocular application; in the days of specie currency, for instance, *coppers* was quite a common term for the cents then in circulation, and if any difficulty occurred in counting up a small sum, *Gunter* was appealed to for assistance. In the same happy days, *dimes*, ten-cent pieces in silver, were apt to represent all the money-property of a person, and a young lady was said to *have the dimes*, when she was reputed rich. The English sixpence, on the other hand, survives in a phrase that has come down to us from Indian times. Conrad Weiser, a famous trader among Redmen during the last century, relates that an Indian arrived on a Sunday with his furs, and found the trader unwilling, either to give him more than two-and-sixpence a pound, or to close the business on that day at all. The Indian had, of course, to submit, and was asked to go to church with the trader, where, he was told, the white people went once a week to *learn good things*. He got along quite well till the sermon began, when he fancied the clergyman was looking at him angrily, and speaking of him to the congregation. So he retired, and smoked his pipe upon the steps till the meeting broke up. He then went round to the other traders in the town, but as they all offered him only the same price, he swore a little at the *same old two-and-sixpence*, and concluded that the whites attended church, not to learn good things, but to cheat poor Indians in the price of skins. (*Notes and Queries*, March 6, 1838.) From that time the phrase, the same *old two-and-sixpence*, has remained a part of our speech, and may be still heard in every part of the Union. Paper-money, in like manner, early earned its slang-name, and has ever since been familiarly known as *shinplaster*, the ludicrous term being professedly derived from the times of Continental paper-money, which was of little value, so that old soldiers, wounded in the leg, dressed their wounds with the worthless notes, which thus became literally *shinplasters*. "If you have no brass and no tin, give us a *shinplaster* then—them's my terms." (J. C. Neal, *Charcoal Sketches*, II., p. 23.)

The process of *paying* what is due enjoys its own list of terms, since the verb to *pay* is used in America in the very largest sense. In familiar language the *cui bono* of olden times is rendered by the practical: Does it *pay?* and hence men complain, that literature does not *pay*, if it does not secure a liberal reward, and that it does not *pay* to try and be friends with a man who is an obstinate enemy. *What's to pay?* means simply, What is the matter? Of attractive mountain scenery in Maine, it is said: "The rocks are very beautiful at those falls of Ammonoosuck. A drive anywhere in these hills *pays*, to borrow the slang of this bank-note world. It is pure enjoyment." (The White Hills, *Putnam's Magazine*, October, 1853.) To *foot a bill*, by paying the amount at the bottom of the account, is a phrase equally well known abroad and with us; but why we should borrow from the thieves' language the old cant term for picking pockets, to *fork over* or *fork out*, to represent an honest payment of a bill, is not quite evident. The stiff fingers, slyly inserted into a pocket, and seizing its contents as with a fork, explained the phrase well enough, so long as theft was contemplated, but in America *forking out* means nothing more than paying money. There may be occasionally a threat concealed in the words, as when an indignant creditor says, "Now, sir, you will please *fork over* that money to me, and pay your bill, or I'll have the law out of you, as sure as you are born." (Albany *Argus*, September 5, 1867.) Such a process, by which a man is made to pay under threats, is here, as in England, expressively called *bleeding*, a term quoted already in Bailey's Dictionary. (*Slang Dictionary*, p. 76.) If all cannot be paid, there remains what in American phraseology is called a *balance*, the term being transferred from money-transactions, where its use is, of course, perfectly legitimate, to almost every kind of remainder that may be suggested. "We listened to Wendell Phillips for about half an hour, and having an engagement elsewhere, we were forced to leave, and so lost the *balance* of his oration." (Boston *Transcript*, December 27, 1861.) "Most of the respectable inhabitants held commissions in the army or government offices; the *balance* of the people kept little shops, or cultivated the ground." (*Words and their Uses*, R. G. White.) The word is thus used very much like the Scottish *lave* (what is left), as already quoted by Grose, and used by Burns in the line—

"I'll get a blessing with the *lave*,
And never miss it."

In some parts of Virginia the word *shank* is quaintly used for the same purpose, and one friend will say to another, "Suppose you come in and spend the *shank* of the evening with me?" The *balance* has, moreover, made its way into England also, and in *Once a Week* we find the advice: "Whoso wishes to rob the night to the best advantage, let him sleep two or three hours, then get up for two hours and work, and then sleep out the *balance* of the night." (*Words and their Uses*. R. G. White, p. 94.)

Wall-street, in New York, represents 'Change in London, and, like the latter, abounds in technical terms, which are, however, of such strictly professional character and ever-changing nature, where they do not belong to commerce generally, that they cannot in justice be called Americanisms. *Bulls* and *bears* strive here as elsewhere for the mastery, by means of *longs* and *shorts*, trying to make a *corner*, selling or buying *call-loans*, which have to be repaid whenever the debt is called for, despising *kite-fliers*, who try to rise by means of fictitious paper, as long as they are unsuccessful, and pitying a *lame duck*, a stock-jobber who is unable to meet his engagements.

Among colloquial terms derived from Commerce, and more directly from book-keeping, few are more frequently heard than *posting* and *posted up*. The former has gone through various transformations; its first meaning of going by *post*, that is, with great speed and safety, has then been applied to the transfer of items from one column or one ledger to another, and finally serves in the phrase of *posting books*, to express the satisfactory closing of accounts generally. "My books are *posted*, and I shall give up all official duties, to enjoy a little leisure, which I hope to be able to employ with advantage." (W. H. Seward, Letter, May, 1870.) To be *posted up* means, by a natural transition, to be well informed, primarily, of course, as to commercial transactions of the counting-room and the Exchange, and is probably derived directly from the prevailing custom of *posting up*, literally on post and pillar, slips of paper containing the latest intelligence. A man is, however, said to be *well posted up* on any subject, if he is found to be in possession of the newest facts and latest dates, such as involve all recent changes. "Miss Fudge has kept a close eye on equipages, caps, cloaks, and summer recreations. She is well *posted up* on these matters." (Ike Marvel, *Fudge Doings.*) The phrase is known in England, and quite recently even the London *Times* was pleased to say that "American papers were remarkably well *posted up* on European affairs during the war." (January 19, 1871.) The *post-note* of commerce retains the old word *post*, for which *mail* is now almost universally substituted; it means a note, payable to order (not to bearer), and intended for transmission by mail. In like manner a *Memorandum Check*, so named because it has a *Mem.* on its face, designates a check not to be presented immediately for payment, but at such a time as may be mentioned in the *Mem.*

Certain branches of commerce are peculiarly fertile in cant and slang terms, of which a few at least have become actually parts of our speech. Such is the fate of boot and shoe makers, who pass, with all the cobblers of England and the brethren of Hans Sachs, for men of eccentric habits and quaint genius. *Sons of wax* is neither an uncommon nor an uncomplimentary name for them, although the address, "How are you, my *son-of-waxes?*" quoted by Professor S. S. Haldeman, can hardly be excused. Since they have formed themselves, however, into a most formidable association, called the *Sons of Crispin,* they are universally known and quoted by the name of their tutelary Saint, who stole leather to make shoes for the poor. A late "strike," in which they indulged, led to the importation of a number of Chinese into Massachusetts, who took the place of the rebellious men, and soon excelled them in neatness, though not in quickness of work. To this fact a paper referred, saying: "The same spirit protests against the despotism of the *Crispins,* which the gentleman, who means to be master of his own business, has, by his Mongolian battery, effectually demolished in his own town (North Adams). It was diamond cut diamond. For a large and influential element of the *Crispin* organization was brought into the country by capital, in the same way in which it now complains that capital is bringing the Celestial shoemakers." (*Appleton's Journal,* September 21, 1870.) Like so many other American terms, this also has already become well known in England, where we find it used thus: "Away went the customer after his hat, and *Crispin,* standing at his door, clapped his hands, and shouted, 'Go it, you'll catch him.'" (*Slang Dictionary,* p. 105, foot-note.) Even a *local Crispin,* meaning the one cobbler of a little village, appeared recently in the *Home Journal* of New York.

An almost ludicrous slang term, possibly of negro manufacture, is the expression *Forty-'leven.* The first part is in all probability the familiar number used, like other round numbers in Hebrew, as an indefinite expression, as boys say, "You have scared me like *forty,*" and teamsters boast of a powerful horse, that will *pull like forty.* The addition of *eleven* is the element of incongruity added to the humorous exaggeration already expressed, and thus "a *forty-eleventh cousin,* for instance, expresses an infinitesimal degree of relationship, one too small to be stated accurately, and hence stated in fictitious numbers." (Professor S. S. Haldeman.) J. R.

Lowell does not fail to make good use of this Americanism, also, and says:

"Nor don't want *forty-'leven* weeks o' jawin' an expoundin'
To prove a nigger hez a right to save him, ef he's drownin'."
(*Biglow Papers*, II., p. 106.)

Another ludicrous exaggeration of this kind is taken from the violence and noise with which ordinarily bricks are dumped out of carts; a thing done vehemently and with much display is said to be like a *thousand of bricks.* "When Mr. Nye had finished, Mr. Stewart rose, and with his irresistible logic and impressive language came down upon him like a *thousand of bricks*, till he was utterly crushed and demolished." (*Western World*, March 5, 1864.)

Of all trades, however, the trade in liquors abounds most in more or less grotesque terms, and phrases of the greatest variety, some few of which only are genuine Americanisms, and others mere applications of familiar words to new purposes. As a matter of course, no man acknowledges frankly that he "drinks liquor;" that would apparently shock the sensitiveness of a man laboring under delirium tremens, so numerous are the substitutes for the plain truth. He may be disposed to *liquor*, when he is perfectly free and easy among friends and associates, and, as nearly two hundred years ago (April, 1699), an Englishman would exclaim: "When we had *liquored* our throats" (London *Spy*, p. 15), he now roars out: "Come, boys, let's *liquor*—what'll you have?" (J. C. Neal, *Charcoal Sketches*, I. p. 36), but generally he condescends only to *smile.* This oddest of all euphuisms ever invented to hide a hideous thing, is now almost universally in use in all parts of the Union, though it was at first confined to the West. "There are many fast boys about, some devoted to the fair sex, some to horses, some to *smiling*." (Baltimore *Sun*.) An Englishman tells us that "an American lady, Mrs. Christie, having sent some fine old rye-whiskey to him, he, unconscious of the pun, said to his travelling companion, an American: This cannot be called Lacrymae Christi, suppose we call it the Smiles of Christie! Good, said the American, I see you are learning our language." (*Blackwood*, October, 1867.) Nor is the noun less frequently used, and Mr. Bartlett quotes an account of a wedding, at which the alderman who performed the ceremony invited the company to *smile* with him, and "one general *smile* entirely absorbed the fee." (New York *Tribune,* January 31, 1855.) This invitation, a universal custom in America, has naturally also its own name, to *treat,* an abbreviation of the original *to stand treat,* which is not quite obsolete yet. A man *treats,* when he invites his friends to go to a place where ardent spirits are sold, and to order whatever they like, volunteering at the same time to pay for all that is consumed. The custom is peculiar to this country, and considered imperative in certain classes as an act of common courtesy. The casual meeting of two men, who may never have exchanged a word with each other, is a signal for both instantly to exclaim, "Come, let's have something," and down they dive into the nearest subterranean *bar.* The one who spoke first insists upon paying the *shot,* not without the reasonable assurance that at the next meeting his new friend will return the compliment, as a matter of course. If two friends meet, the phrase is: "Let's drink to old times." To *Do as I do* is nearly obsolete. "Come, gentlemen, *do as I do?*" was once the polite request of one who wished his friends to join him at the bar. If a man has a large number of friends, and wants "to do the thing princely," or if he runs for an office, and knows where to meet the independent voters, he has only to take them to a saloon, and order some complicated beverage *all around,* to secure their good-will for the day. The disastrous effects of this almost universal custom, which produces an endless chain of visits to such places, can easily be imagined. Besides its fatal consequences, it has its ludicrous side also, and a writer in the Chicago *Evening Post* very pertinently asks: "If a man, upon meeting an old friend, were to pull out a handful of postage-stamps and say, Let's have some stamps, I pay! or if several persons happening to meet in a store were invited by a generous patron to 'come and help themselves to a few suspenders and socks;' what would be thought of it? And yet, why can liquor be offered thus, and nothing else?"

The same fanciful phraseology surrounds the places where these scenes take place. *Groggeries* or *Doggeries* are only found near the shanties of Irish laborers or in remote Western and Southern settlements, where things are still occasionally called by their true name; in the cities *Shades* are perhaps most numerous, suggesting cozy retreats, secure from the bright light of day. *Saloons* abound mainly in the West, at least in this sense, for everywhere in this country the term is applied to any room from a parlor to a cookshop. "The eminent pioneer of American sculpture, brilliant talker, and accomplished gentleman, the lamented Horatio Greenough, we are told, was indignantly eloquent against the American abuse of this graceful importation from the French, applied as it is in the United States to billiard-rooms, oyster-cellars, *grogshops*, and railroad cars!" (G. H. Calvert.) A more recent euphuism yet is the *Sample Room*, where, under the pretext of allowing customers to judge by samples, any number of small glasses of liquor are sold behind a transparent screen, which protects the *samplers* from the eye of the public.

It is in these places, known besides by a number of equally fanciful but less general names, that an important personage, the *bar-keeper*, rules supreme. It is he who distributes the simple and manufactures the compound drinks called for by the imaginative and thirsty American, the odd names of which have excited so much wonder and amusement in the minds of all travellers. It was probably after having practically tested the matter that N. P. Willis wrote of one of these heroes at the St. Louis Hotel in New Orleans: "The gracious and gentlemanly master-*barkeepers* stood braiding rainbows across their firmament of decanters, as they flung the ice and the rosy liquors back and forward into fragrant contact with the mint." The usual small glass of simple spirits is technically known as a *smaller*, though the term is also used in derision, as in the order, "Bring us one of the largest kind of *smallers*, a tumbler full of brandy and water, without no water in it." (J. C. Neal, *Charcoal Sketches*, III., 23.) Of artificial compounds, most of which have ephemeral renown only, and change names as well as elements, only a few are genuine Americanisms, and have almost attained to the dignity of what is in cant called an "institution." Such is the *egg-nog*, the indispensable beverage taken at Christmas all over the South, derived from *Nog*, ale (Grose), and consisting of eggs, cream, and brandy, beaten up together; the *mint-julep*, made of brandy and water, iced, and flavored with aromatic mint. The *Julep* is, of course, the old word familiar to us from Milton's Comus, the same *julep* which in Arabic already meant a sweet potion, and thus was adopted in English; the mint, however, is an American invention, and since pounded ice has been added to the compound, it has been asserted that

> "*Juleps* the drinks of immortals became,
> When Jove himself added a handful of hail."
> (*C. F. Hoffman.*)

A *julep*, however, is not limited to this meaning; in Virginia, at least, the word has from the first settlement of the colony continued in the same sense in which the word *dram* is used at the North. The English early borrowed it from the French. Two centuries and a half ago it was customary to make juleps by the gallon, ready for immediate use without the trouble of present preparation. Pepys, in his Diary, June 22, 1660, says: "Thence to my Lord's and had the great walk to Brigham's, who gave me a case of good *julep*."

Cobblers and Sherry *Cobblers* are known to have been old favorites with our forefathers, though nearly forgotten when they were revived in this country, but the practice of sucking in leisurely the delicious beverage by means of *straws*—not unfrequently represented by slender glass tubes—is earnestly claimed as a genuine Americanism. The excessive fondness of Americans for these and a thousand other strange but always very palatable compounds, may be judged by the simple fact that, in spite of the high duties on wines and ardent spirits, and the large salaries demanded by skillful, experienced *barkeepers*, the bars of most of the large hotels suffice, by their own profits, to pay the annual rent of the building.

The *Ring*, as unfortunately not only the P. R., familiar to English ears, but every combination of politicians, speculators, etc., is called here, has naturally contributed its share of cant terms to our speech. The American is, on the whole, far less fond of sport itself than the Englishman; he hardly knows sport as a national pastime, however excellent a sportsman he may be individually, and, with the exception of racing, public sport is little known away from the large cities. But he is, on the other hand, passionately fond of excitement, loves to risk much in order to gain much, watches the ventures of others with keen interest, and loves, therefore, the use of all sporting terms for the sake of the flavor they bear. He is perfectly familiar with all the phraseology belonging to English sport, and fond of applying it to the ordinary occurrences of life. The *chalk* of the pugilistic ring, which marks the limits that bind the two contestants, reappears in many a phrase of his daily life. The President, in whom he is disappointed for one reason or another, does not *come up to chalk;* when he dismisses an official, he is made to *walk the chalk;* and if an antagonist or a competitor declines to meet his rival in open discussion, he is denounced as not having *come up to the scratch,* as the chalk-line is called, which divides the ring fairly. Even the *tavern-keeper's*—not as in England the *inn-keeper's*—chalk must lend itself to such figurative language. "You can't do that *by a long chalk,*" is a common expression for a man's inability to accomplish his purpose, derived from the chalk-marks of credit on the owner's door or shutter. It is thus often literally applied to the fact that a speculator, for instance, cannot succeed by *a long chalk,* in other words, by all the credit he may be able to command. The phrase is one of the oldest in the English language, from the familiarity of the people with inns and their customs, and appears under a great variety of forms, from A. Smith's pun—

> "And if you want fresh liquor, you must pay,
> For *chalks* too often walk themselves away—"
> (*Alhambra.*)

to the more modern expression of, To beat by *long chalks,* which is also not unfrequently heard here. (*Slang Dictionary,* p. 97.)

The word *strike* is quite a fruitful source of colloquial terms, from the combination of workmen for cessation of labor till higher wages are paid—a word of comparatively recent origin in America, but already quite naturalized in England, to the *striking* a lead in a gold-mine. *Tenpins,* as the old-fashioned Ninepins are uniformly called since a pin was added in order to escape from the penalties of a law which prohibited Ninepins, have furnished the expressive phrase, for an unexpected success, to *make a ten-strike.* "I tell you what, my son, if you have really bought that plantation, you have made a *ten-strike* of it; it is worth a hundred thousand any time you bring it into market." (*Flush Times in Alabama,* p. 217.) The miner literally with his pickaxe *strikes* a vein, while he is hard at work prospecting, and from his luck the phrase is transferred to any sudden discovery of good fortune. "It was thought in the mines and gulches that Mliss has *struck* a good lead." (F. B. Harte, *Luck of Roaring Camp*, p. 153.) But the greatest success of all was made by the fortunate owners of sterile lands in Pennsylvania, who *struck ile* (oil), as it is called in common cant; the petroleum-wells thus opened were a source of immense wealth to them, and colossal fortunes have been amassed in an incredibly short time in the so-called Oil Regions. This phrase also has made its way into the language of the day. "We are told Mr. Harte has *struck ile* in Chicago. At a dinner given in his honor, each guest brought five thousand dollars as his contribution to Brett Harte's new magazine." (Philadelphia *Ledger*, February 15, 1871.) In the West a *striker* is not only a shoulder-hitter, as might be suspected, but a runner for gambling establishments, who must be as ready to strike down a complaining victim as to ensnare an unsuspecting stranger. "He was one of the most accomplished *strikers*, or barkers, as they are called, in the employ of the hells." (*The Country Merchant*, p. 317.) *Cappers* they are called, when the game is the famous *Three-Card Monte.*

Striking is, however, by no means a favorite word for such acts of violence; it has too many figurative meanings. *Kicking* seems to be more popular, if we may judge from its frequent application to other purposes. The disturber of the public peace is said to *kick up a row,* and so is the man who brings discord into a public body or party. "The ill-treatment of Mr. Sumner will not be borne patiently by his friends and the New England States; it is sure to *kick up a row* in the Republican party, the effects of which will be felt at the next Presidential election." (Louisville *Courier-Journal,* March 19, 1871.) More ungracefully still, an unfortunate lover, who is simply "jilted" at the North, is more violently *kicked* at the South—a phrase marking most characteristically the contrast between the free and easy manners of our day with those of past days, when the strongest term used for the painful occasion was to give and to get the *mitten.* The latter word ought, however, always to be *mittens,* as the phrase is derived from the same use made of the French *mitaines,* which had to be accepted by the unsuccessful lover instead of the hand, after which he aspired. If a combat really takes place, it may be a simple wrestling, which is often pronounced *rassling,* not without good reason, since *wrast-*

ling is good old English, and so used by Chaucer, whose Miller "at *wrastling* bore away the palm." It is rather a curious taste which led Mr. Motley, in his admirable work on the United Netherlands, to use a very familiar phrase, and to state that "Howard determined to *wrestle no farther pull.*" In fighting, a horrible contrivance is sometimes used, called in savage irony *knuckle-dusters,* an iron instrument contrived to cover the knuckles so as to protect them from injury when striking a blow, adding force at the same time, and with knobs or points projecting, so as to disfigure and mutilate the person struck. It is stated, upon English authority only, that "this brutal invention is American, but has been made familiar in England in police cases between the officers and sailors of American vessels." (*Slang Dictionary,* p. 168.) A *knock-down* is familiar wherever English is spoken, both in the sense of actual prostration and of an argument which completely *floors* the adversary. "That was a clincher; I don't know when I have heard a *knock-down* argument which left the opponent so little life and breath. Governor Walker skinned him alive." (Richmond *Whig,* July 7, 1870.) *Knocking off* means to stop work, and has been a common phrase with workmen of every kind for more than two hundred years, though but of late admitted into good company. "I have a great mind," says an operative employed by the day, "to *knock off* and call it half a day." (J. C. Neal, *Charcoal Sketches.*) A similar term, derived from the slang of operatives, is to *knock out the wedges,* which is used to express a painful embarrassment in which a man is left by his friends, after having been led into it by their agency. . The figure is taken from the danger threatening a woodchopper, who has driven wedges into a log, and in helping to remove one, may have his hand caught by the carelessness of his companions. To this, J. R. Lowell refers in the lines—

"I don't approve o' givin' pledges;
You'd ough' to leave a fellow free,
An' not go *knockin' out the wedges,*
To ketch his fingers in the tree."
(*Biglow Papers,* I., p. 90.)

To *knock up* is likewise a familiar term, but is not unfrequently applied in the United States to a very curious purpose, characteristic of the false prudery of the people. An English traveller relates, with comic distress, how he inquired after a lady's health, and was told by her sister that she was *knocked up*. He insisted upon knowing what had brought on the excessive fatigue—as he understood the term—and was only more embarrassed than the lady, whom he fairly put to flight, by learning afterwards that the phrase was used in speaking of ladies when in an interesting condition.

The purpose of such a tussle need, however, not necessarily be a regular fight; it may be the result of a simple desire to inflict punishment. The good old English word to *lam*, quoted already in Bailey's Dictionary, as meaning "to beat or bang," still does good service in our country. Its derivation from the same root as the verb to *lame*, was long considered good, and strengthened by Grose's spelling of the word *lamme;* but less credit was given to those who saw in it the remnant of the Latin *lambere*, as J. R. Lowell, perhaps with a facetious smile, suggests, and to the followers of Sir W. Scott, who gave the parentage to one Dr. *Lamb*. The presumption is, that the word is the direct descendant of the Old Norse *lam*, a hand, which happens also to be Gaelic. (*Slang Dictionary*, p. 169.) A curious addition has extended the modest word into *lambasting*, evidently combining the two effective agencies of *lamming* and *basting* into one formidable operation. "I can't hide," says a braggadoccio, "when anybody owes me a *lambasting*." (J. C. Neal, *Charcoal Sketches*, II., p. 79.) Other *fast* characters prefer to *larrup* unruly and troublesome youths, employing a word well known as an English provincialism (Forby), and said to be a corruption of the sailor's *leerope*, from which he suffers on board ship. If the sufferer be a child, it is *spanked*, that is, punished by slapping with the open hand. Moor gives the word as in use in Suffolk (England), and as denoting a mother's punishment. Bailey also has it, and derives it from an old Saxon term; and to this day it is in constant use in the South, where many old English words still survive and flourish, that have long since become obsolete everywhere else. As we call remarkable excellence *striking*, it is perhaps not unnatural that very showy things should be called *spanking*, and hence, here as in England, it is no uncommon expression to speak of "a pair of *spanking* bays." (*Slang Dictionary*, p. 240.)

Happy, however, the fight that ends without more serious consequences, since the habit of carrying arms is almost universal in America, and nothing is held cheaper than human life. The very readiness with which the American risks his own life, now bravely battling in war, and now venturing wantonly across the Atlantic in a nut-shell, makes him think of the life of others as little as of his; and since everybody entertains the same fatal view, life seems to need more immediate protection than the laws can afford. Hence the numerous *Bowie-knives* of the South and West, formidable weapons, over a foot long and two inches broad, which derived their name from two or more brothers, desperadoes, called *Bowie*, who figured in Texas during the time of Davy Crockett and Sam Houston. In Arkansas they prefer a variety which can shut up into the handle, because it is more easily worn on the body, and call it, with savage irony, an *Arkansas toothpick*.

> "Straightway leaped the valiant Slingby
> Into armor of Seville,
> With a strong *Arkansas toothpick*,
> Screwed in every joint of steel."
> (Ben. Gaultier, *American Ballads*, *B.*)

Hence, also, the still greater number of *revolvers*, as all revolving firearms are called, from the heavy Navy Revolver with its long range to the diminutive Derringer, little over two inches long. The professional *rough* is almost always thus prepared for mortal fight: the term *roughs* is, however, less familiar in America than in England, its place being largely taken by the *rowdy*, a word made in this country by legitimate descent from the *row*, in which he loves to engage. A recent Boston paper said sadly but frankly: "*Roughs* and *rowdies* are multiplying fearfully in our borders; this Commonwealth is not properly policed, and we want a patrol, day and night, of gensdarmes." (Boston *Courier*, March 19, 1871.) The *row* was probably at first an Oxford term for any noisy disturbance, but soon spread throughout fast society, and has lately emerged from the Bohemia of slang into the kingdom of good English. The word *rowdy*, however, has but quite recently crossed the Atlantic, and will probably wait for the *row*, before it also takes its place in English parlance. A *rumpus* —perhaps from the same root as the German *rumpeln*—denotes any great noise, not necessarily connected with deeds of violence, after the manner of the English *shindy*, but when the rowdy is in earnest and his blood is up, he has a terrible term by which to designate the nature of his action: he *raises Cain*. "He had been knocking around all day in every grog-shop and bar-room in town, and when evening came he was seen swaggering down Main-street, his head bare, his eyes bloodshot, and his revolver in hand, shouting: Who'll hinder this child? I am going to *raise Cain!* Who's got anything to say agin it?" (*Scenes in the Far West*, p. 117.) A *spree* is a very innocent amusement in comparison, hurting generally no one but the merry fellow who pays for his frolic with a bad headache; and yet there are those who will derive the word, like the kindred *spry*, from the French *esprit*, which they say produced the two bantlings in Louisiana! The English, in like manner, hold their Canadian brethren responsible for the two words, of which *spry*, much used among us, has not yet been admitted into careful writing. Grose has already *sprey*, which he says means ingenious, spruce, and in this sense the word is much used in conversation; with us it means, besides, quick motion and prompt action, so that people say, "Come, be *spry!*" when they wish to urge others to haste. "He was the *spryest* chap I ever saw," is high praise from a Yankee's lips, and J. R. Lowell makes it serve a good purpose when he says, "Hosy sez he sed suthin a nuther about Simplex Mundishes or sum sech feller, but I guess Hosea kind o' didn't hear him, for I never hearn o' nobody o' that name in the villadge, and I've lived here, man and boy, seventy-six year cum next tatur digging, and thar aint nowheres a kitting *spryer* n' I be." (*Biglow Papers*, Preface.)

In his outward appearance the *rowdy* of America differs little from his brother in the Old Country, except, perhaps, in the one point of wearing frequently a *soaplock*, a lock of hair which he makes to lie smoothly by means of soap. It is the descendant of the Cavalier's *sidelock*, of which Sir W. Scott says: "The gauntlet is speedily drawn off, that he may adjust his *sidelocks*;" but it has sadly degenerated in the wearer, and now as often designates the latter himself as his absurd ornament. "The police took up in the Bowery, last night, a number of men and women, who were engaged in a grand mêlée near Thomas' barroom; the majority of the former were well-known rowdies and *soaplocks.*" (New York *Herald*, June 11, 1857.) The female ornament, corresponding to the soaplock and worn by the *g'als* of the Bowery as the latter is worn by the *b'hoys*, is the *spit-curl*. This is the descendant of the bow-catcher (*sic*) or kiss-curl of England, just as the aristocratic love-lock of the days of Puritanism was the ancestor of the republican soap-lock. The name, given in derision to the short hair at the side of the head, curled into little volutes and gummed to the skin, is happily fast going out of fashion. When poor Mrs. Trollope was a refugee in this country, in 1832, this was one of the features in our social life that caused her such poignant sorrow. "Indeed, Mamma, said Miss Maria," she reports, "arranging her *spit-curl* in that particular manner, which at once explains the meaning of the rather particular appellation given by American ladies to the captivating little lock which adorns their temples."

As long as the rowdy is thus at work in comparative harmlessness, *on a spree* or *in a rumpus*, he is very fond of designating his peculiar proceedings as *cutting up* something, apparently desirous to convey the idea that some mischief, some *cutting* must be mixed up with it or there would be no fun in it to him. He *cuts capers*, he *cuts up shines*, he even *cuts didoes*, as if he would imitate famous Queen Dido in her cunning device by which she received her magnificent "hide" of land. Such at least is Professor Mahn's interpretation of an expression which so far has baffled all research. "If you go to *cutting up shines* in court, I shall fine you or send you to the Tombs for a fortnight." (Police Report, New York *Herald*, March 28, 1859.) "This 'ere Frenchman has been *cutting up didoes* in my house now for several days; he ain't sober onst a week, and breaks all my cheers and tables, Mr. Recorder." (*Pickings from the Picayune*, p. 147.) The transition from the innocent amusement to the serious fight is, however, a very slight one, thanks to the tendency of Young America to *pitch in*. The term originated probably with Western settlers, to whom the familiar expression of *falling to* did not seem strong enough to convey their superabundant energy, and thus changed the falling into a *pitching*. "I had no one to help me," says a new settler, "so I concluded to *pitch in* and do it myself." (*A Trip to the West*, 1853.) *Pitching it strong*, is perhaps best illustrated in American humor, which is not content with small measure or modest criticism, and to *pitch into* a person is expressive of its application to some rival or adversary. "Grace Greenwood, supposed to be buried somewhere in the West, recently gave signs of remaining vitality by *pitching into* a younger pseudonyme, the sparkling and saucy Gail Hamilton." (*Lippincott's Magazine*, July, 1869.)

A special kind of *rowdy*, known only to America, is "the b'hoy that runs *wid de machine*," as he is called in his own slang language. The particular *machine* in this case is the fire-engine, with its hose, ladder, and other paraphernalia, that he delights in literally *running* through the streets amid deafening shouts and yells. He loves the din and turmoil, he loves the excitement of the fire itself, and—to his credit be it said—he loves fearlessly and recklessly to risk his life a thousand times in order to save that of others, or even property only. In our day, however, the phrase has become a favorite expression for the management of any great enterprise, and it was in this sense that Mr. Lincoln once told a friend, in return for a liberal amount of advice and admonition about his administration, "Now look here! If I have to *run this machine* I shall *run it* my own way, and be accountable to God, my conscience, and the people, but not to you!" In the same manner people *run a bank*, a store, and anything they undertake—even their own *face*, when they obtain credit solely on account of their respectable appearance. It ought to be borne in mind, however, that this cant use of the word *machine* is by no means an Americanism. England has its bathing-*machines* now, stage-coaches used to be generally called *machines*, and as late as 1858, municipal reports in London spoke of the horses employed in stage-coaches and omnibuses as *machines*. We find in *Notes and Queries* this early evidence of such use:

"E'en tho' I'd the Honour of sitting between
My Lady Stuff Damask and Peggy Moreen,
Who both flew to Bath in the London *machine*."
(Anstey's *New Bath Guide*, 1766, p. 93.)

The *rowdy* may be at the same time a *bully*, if he is given to ruling others by threats and acts of violence. This term, however, has of late acquired a new meaning—it is not quite sure whether first in England or in America—of a more harmless character, though decided slang in its nature. *"Bully for you,"* was a phrase which became very popular during the late Civil War, and everything remarkable for strength or efficiency has since been designated as *bully*. The term is such good old English, that there would be no objection to its revival, but for its modern allegiance to slang. Shakespeare asks: "What says my *bully* rock?" (Merry Wives of Windsor); Sir W. Scott makes his Friar Tuck sing—

> "Come trowl the brown bowl to me,
> *Bully* boy, *bully* boy!"

and in his Lady of the Lake he sings—

> "Yet, whoop, *bully* boys! Off with your liquor,
> Sweet Marjorie's the word, and a fig for the vicar!"

It is in precisely the same humor that *bully* is used in America. A Mississippi boatman's song has the lines—

> "Now is the time for a *bully* trip,
> So, shake her up and let her rip;"

and it has been suggested by a prophetic critic that a Bohemian version of the Bible would probably speak of the "great hunter" as "Even Nimrod, the *bully* shootist before the Lord."

The corresponding modern term—for a few years are often a long life-lease for a popular cant word—is the phrase, "How is that *for high?*" borrowed from a low game, known as Old Sledge, where the *high* depends, not on the card itself, but on the adversary's hand. Hence the phrase means, What kind of an attempt is that at a great achievement? It is of Western origin, having made its appearance in some of the Northwestern journals, but has spread, as weeds do, rapidly, all over the Union, and will no doubt soon find its way to England also. A familiar nursery-rhyme is thus altered to "suit the times:"

> "Mary had a little lamb,
> It jumped up to the sky,
> And when it landed on its feet,
> Cried: *How is that for high?*"

while an editor, overcome with difficulties, made this touching though indirect appeal to his subscribers:

"I had a dream the other night,
When everything was still;
I dreamed that each advertiser
Came up and paid his bill;
Each wore a look of honesty,
And smiles were round each eye,
As they handed over the stamps.
They yelled: *How's that for high?*"
(Pennsylvania paper, February, 1871.)

Besides this favorite game, known under a variety of names, as Seven Up, etc., *Monte* is most generally known in the South and Southwest; a sad inheritance of the former owners of the soil, and passionately indulged in by the mixed population of those regions. The fact that players at *Three-Card Monte,* as it is most commonly called, are said to *buck* at monte, causes the familiar phrase of *bucking* at anything, in the sense of putting forth one's whole energy. "You'll have to *buck* at it like a whole team, gentlemen, or you won't hear the whistle near your diggings for many a year." (San Antonio paper, 1870.) Far more generally, however, than these games, the *fast* and the *rough* American like two or three others, which have become almost inseparably connected with their favorite resort, the bar-room of the city or of the Western steamboat. One is known as *Euchre,* said by Professor Mahn to be of German origin, and proving its ancestry to some extent by designating its two highest cards as *Right* and *Left Bower,* evidently the German Bauer or peasant. The universal popularity of the game, which is not unknown to the ladies of the South especially, has led to the use of many a phrase drawn from its peculiarities. The verb to *euchre* is thus pressed into the service to denote a defeat, not at cards only, but in any rivalry. "I'll *euchre* him if I can, and I think I can. I've got a little money to put up on it, anyhow, and I'll put it up, too." (*Putnam's Magazine,* November, 1868.) The game of *Loo* furnishes in like manner a verb, to *loo,* meaning to defeat. "Douglas was *looed.*" Another such game is known as *Poker,* evidently a distant relative of *poke* and the French *poche,* representing what in other games is called a pool. Like its near cousin, suggestively called *Bluff,* poker is a mere hazard game, with which, however, is combined great skill in bragging to a purpose. One man offers a bet on his hand, another doubles the bet, and "goes one better;" then the first tries to *bluff* him off by a still higher bet, and thus the stake rises rapidly to often enormous sums. When finally the hand has to be shown, it often turns out to have amounted to nothing, and the whole has been a *game of bluff* or of *brag*. In making a bet, the player says: I'll *see* it (that is, your hand), and go two (or more) better. Hence again various phrases used colloquially all over the Union. *I see it,* is now as common in England as with us, and generally ascribed to the old use of the word, as it occurs already in Cibber's *Careless Husband,* "I don't *see it* ;" but there can be little doubt that the great number of uses to which the verb to *see* is now-a-days put in slang phrases, have more recently been obtained from the popular game. "In street parlance, *to see* is to know or to believe, and *I don't see it* means, I put no faith in what you offer, I don't believe you." (*Slang Dictionary,* p. 223.) "The matter was presented to Mr. Lincoln by Mr. Seward and several other gentlemen; but he simply said, I can't *see* it as you *see* it, gentlemen, and there was nothing more to be done." (Washington paper, July 29, 1861.) *Poker,* when played by betting before looking at one's hand, is called *Blind Poker,* and this has given rise to the very common phrase, to *go it blind,* used whenever an enterprise is undertaken without previous inquiry. J. R. Lowell in speaking of Jefferson Davis, praises ironically his great skill and power

> "to impress on the popular mind
> The comfort and wisdom of *goin' it blind.*"
>
> (*Biglow Papers,* II., p. 118.)

When a lady in California is threatened by her husband, furious at having been betrayed by her, and aiming a rifle at her head, she suddenly presents two small revolvers and cries out, "I can play a hand at that game, and *go one better.*" (*Overland Monthly,* March, 1871.) The latest invention seems to be a chance game, called *keno,* very popular in New York, and played in public places of amusement by one or two hundred persons at a time. The ordinary Faro is generally veiled under the euphuistic term of *Ye Tiger,* a curious name, quite adequate to express the destructive and voracious nature of the game, but recently attributed to a Chinese deity! "A favorite figure of one of the Chinese gods of gambling is a *tiger* standing on his hind-feet, and grasping a large *cash* in his mouth or his paws. Sometimes the image is made of wood or clay, or drawn on a piece of paper or board. The title of the beast, 'His Excellency, the Grasping Cash *Tiger*,' is frequently written on a piece of paper, and placed in the gambling-rooms between two bunches of mock-money suspended under the table or on the wall behind it. This figure is the sign for a gambling house: 'The Fighting *Tiger*.' It is curious that we should have to look to China for the origin of this phrase." (*Appleton's Journal*, January 7, 1871.) A technical term is the *sweat-cloth*, a cloth marked with figures, and used by gamblers with dice; while the generic name of *hell*, derived from England, is quite as frequent here as in its native land.

Such occupations, drinking, fighting, and gambling, are, of course, sure to lead to crime, and the rowdy is apt to find himself some unlucky day on his way to prison, which in New York bears the melancholy name of the *Tombs*, though built in the heaviest Egyptian style of architecture. His fate there presents nothing peculiar to the locality, with the exception of an undesirable acquaintance he is likely to make there; this is the *shyster*. Lawyers are hanging continually about the Tombs, in which certain courts are held, and some of these ill-reputed men offer their services to the new-comer, compel him to pay a fee in advance, and then—do nothing. On the contrary, they *fight shy* of him, and hence they have obtained their name. "A *shyster* indicted and locked up," is the heading of an article, which states that "E. J. Anderson, the lawyer who is charged with having taken $50 from two seamen to defend their case, and not going near them afterward, was, in default of $6,000 bail, summarily committed to the *Tombs* to await trial." (New York *World*, March 8, 1871.)

VII.

Afloat.

AFLOAT.

"Think of our schooners, our clippers, and our monitors."
Hon. Thaddeus Stevens.

A NATION so eminently successful in all matters pertaining to navigation, having built the fastest clipper, the first monitor, and the largest river-boat, and owning a continent bordering upon two oceans, while gigantic streams and countless watercourses traverse it in all directions, and the largest lakes on earth afford ample sea-room within its own bounds,—such a nation cannot but have numerous terms and phrases referring to the life on the water and in the waters. Her sailors are found in every part of the globe, her fishermen on every bank and in every sea where daring energy and unconquerable perseverance find a reward, and throughout the whole land there is scarcely a district where boats are not handled, and fishing-lines thrown, by the boy already.

Nevertheless the number of new words coined, or of old words used in a new meaning and form, for things connected with the sea and its tributaries, and the life in the waters, is but small. English terms, used for such purposes, are so abundant and so well suited to all the details of the profession, of sport, and even of accidental variations, that there arises but rarely a necessity for a new name. American sailors—not often of American birth in our day—and American fishermen, use almost exclusively the language of their British cousins, and Isaak Walton is perhaps more generally read and known and quoted in America than in his native land. It is only where names have been supplied by French or Spanish settlers before the time of American rule, that words like *Canoe* or *Pirogue* have made good their place in our speech; these and their kindred have been mentioned under their appropriate head. Of English forms a few refer to the peculiar shape or use of vessels. Such are the *bankers*, vessels employed in fishing on the Banks of Newfoundland, and deriving their name from the locality. J. Q. Adams, in his report on the fisheries, speaks in high terms of their value in a pecuniary aspect, and their usefulness in training admirable seamen; while a recent work on "Newfoundland Fisheries," tells us that "the crew of a *banker* is generally composed of twelve men, including the skipper or captain, who exercises no direct control over the others, but is recognized by them as the principal personage on board." The name must not, however, be confounded with the *bankers* of North Carolina, people living near that part of the Atlantic coast which there also is called the "banks," and who used to be wreckers of doubtful repute. They now combine the vocations of farming, fishing, and wrecking, but it is said that their kindness and hospitality to wrecked seamen is unfailing and unlimited. The *Chebacco* boat, bearing the old Indian name of a town in Massachusetts, now called Essex, where they were formerly built, is another class of vessels engaged in the Newfoundland fisheries, and characterized by a very narrow stern, from which feature they also derive the name of *Pinkstern*, after the Dutch *pink*, a vessel with such a stern.

These and similar boats are often propelled by a *Setting-Pole*, a pole much heavier than the canoe-pole, and hence used very differently. It is a stout pole, shod with a heavy-pointed "socket," and has on the other end a knob, to place against the shoulder. "The poles are *set* upon the bottom by the boatmen standing on each side of the bow, and as the boat advances the men move along the running boards with the stationary poles at their shoulder, sometimes walking bent almost on all-fours, until they have arrived at the stern, when they draw the poles up and *set* them again, the headway keeping the boat from receding. In more rapid water, the men *reset* alternately." (S. S. Haldeman.)

A *battery* is the odd name given in Chesapeake Bay to a heavy boat, not unlike a coffin in shape, and hence also known as *coffin-boat*, used in duck-shooting. Its peculiar build enables the hunter to float gently down upon his unsuspecting game, lying below the surface of the water, while the heavy calibre of his gun, and the fact that he fires it from a kind of miniature embrasure, have, no doubt, led to the use of the word *battery*. The *Monitor*, finally, a word beyond all question belonging to America, as well as the formidable vessel to which, under various forms, it has since given the name, is well known as the famous invention of Captain Ericsson—the first ship built with a revolving turret. The principles of her construction were altogether new in the history of naval architecture, and, after the signal victory of the first *monitor* in Hampton Roads, the name became a household word at the North. The great inventor has not made it known what induced him to choose the name: hence etymologists have evolved it out of their inner consciousness that he must have borrowed it from Gray's *Monitor Dracæna*, a large lizard covered with impenetrable armor. Irreverend Confederates called the hideous-looking vessels *cheese-boxes*, and apparently one designation is, etymologically, though not æsthetically, as good as the other. Their own unsuccessful imitations they still more disrespectfully called *Tinclads*.

In speaking of the proceeds of deep-sea fisheries, at least one new term has become sufficiently familiar to the general public to take it out of the class of merely technical terms, and entitle it to the honor of an Americanism. This is the *dunfish*, cod prepared so as to give it a dun-color, from which the name is derived. For this purpose the fish are salted, and then laid in piles in a dark room, covered with salt-hay or some similar substance. After two or three months the piles are opened and the fish examined, after which they are piled up once more in a compact mass and left to ripen for another two or three months. In July or August they are ready for use, and command a high price, being far superior to ordinary codfish. J. G. Whittier describes an old puritan's outfit thus:

> "They had loaded his shallop with *dunfish* and ball,
> With stores for his larder and steel for his wall."

Another term connected with the cod is the name of the scaffolding on which they are dried, the *flakes*, as the long poles are called, which are laid upon crotched posts and covered with brush, so that the codfish can be spread upon the platform and dried. But the word is not American; it is found in the singular, at least, in Wright's *Collection* as in use in the north of England, and meaning a hurdle or a paling. In Whitbourne's *Discourse and Discoverie of Newfoundland,* London, 1622, we find, moreover, "Some teare down *flakes,* whereon men yeerely dry their fish, to the great hurt and hinderance of many others that come after them." (p. 66.) These *flakes* are referred to on the following page as "stakes that are fastened in the ground, with rayles on them," thus fully establishing the antiquity of the term.

The *clipper,* also, a cutter or schooner built for fast sailing, with a long sharp bow and raking masts, can hardly be claimed as an Americanism, but the *clipper-built ship,* a vessel of large tonnage, but of the same model, originated here, in consequence of the eager competition for the new trade which sprang up between the Atlantic seaports and the Pacific coast, after California had been incorporated in the Union.

The primitive form of a *raft,* seen on the large inland waters, of gigantic size, and requiring not unfrequently several months to accomplish the enormous journey from the headwaters of a river, in frozen regions, to its mouth near the Tropics, has given its name to an object peculiar to American navigation. These are the stationary *rafts,* consisting of large numbers of trees and timber, which have been arrested, as they floated down the river, by some sand-bar or shallow flat, and there lodge for years, to the great annoyance of flatboat and steamboat captains, and causing grave injuries to trade and commerce. The *Great Raft* in the Red River of Arkansas had become so serious an obstacle to navigation, as to excite even the attention of Congress, and as its dimensions—it extended over twenty miles—made its removal impossible to private enterprise, it was undertaken at national expense. The first improvement upon the raft were probably the *flatboats,* long used for transporting produce on the great western rivers. They are described as "simply an oblong ark, with a roof slightly curved from the centre, to shed rain. They are generally above fifteen feet wide, and from fifty to a hundred feet long. The timbers of the bottom are massive beams, and they are intended to be of great strength, and to carry a burden of from two to four hundred barrels. Great numbers of cattle, horses, and hogs are conveyed to market in them." On the tributaries of the Mississippi, as well as on the great river itself, they used to be known as *Broadhorns,* because they were square at both ends; built during the summer and fall, as soon as harvest was over, they received their vast freight and were swept down the stream.

"We have seen family boats of this description, fitted up for the descent of families to the lower country, with a stove, comfortable apartments, beds, and arrangements for commodious habitancy." (*Mississippi Valley*, Flint.) Arrived at their destination, they discharge their cargoes, and are then sold as lumber, often leaving a handsome profit to the lucky owner. These *arks*, as they are familiarly called, are now-a-days but rarely seen on the Mississippi, the steamboat having almost entirely superseded them; on the more remote watercourses, however, where time is of less vital importance, they are still quite common, and the race of *flatboatmen*, a peculiar class of Western men, powerful, good-natured, and rough, will long survive. They are not a little proud of their quondam companion, who once floated with them down the great river, far from anticipating the high honor and the historic renown he would earn as President and as a martyr.

The *keelboat*, formerly as often seen on the Mississippi and its tributaries as the old-fashioned *flatboat*, differed in every respect from the latter. It was long and slender, of graceful build, too small to carry more than about thirty tons at the utmost, but admirably adapted by its light draft to pass over shallow places and other obstructions, which would delay larger vessels. It is still frequently found in Western waters, propelled by all the various means employed for the purpose, from "bushwhacking" to steam. *Wharfboats*, also, are probably found more generally in America than in any other country, and hence the term is almost an Americanism. It designates a large, solid float, often covered in, on which merchandise, lumber, etc., can be stored, for loading or for inland transportation, and which is generally moored to the shoreside to take the place of a regular fixed wharf. The latter would be useless in rivers which, like most of the Western waters, are subject to frequent and serious changes of level, now suddenly rising so as to overflow the banks, and then again falling low enough to leave vessels aground.

Schooners are generally believed to be an American invention, named by an American word, the first vessel of the kind having been built by a Captain Andrew Robinson at Gloucester in Massachusetts, in the year 1713. When she was launched, it is said, a bystander exclaimed, "How she *scoons!*" This word *scoon* was then much used in the New England States, as it is still used in Scotland, to denote the skipping of stones thrown so as to skim over the surface of the water. The builder, hearing the exclamation, at once said: "A *scooner* let her be!" and from that time vessels masted and rigged in this manner have been known as *schooners*. The origin of the term rests, as Dr. N. Webster says, on abundant and unimpeachable evidence, and is endorsed by the high authority of Professor W. D. Whitney.

A small fishing-vessel is known in the New England States as a *jigger*, but the term is purely local, and not suggestive of any peculiarity of rig or build, though subtle inquirers have been disposed to notice a resemblance in its peculiar manner of moving through the water to that of the ill-famed *jigger*, a sand-flea. *Liners*, on the contrary, are well known as the noble ships, belonging to regular *lines* of packets, which sail at regular dates between American and English ports, and are thus distinguished from other vessels which make the same voyage only as their interest may demand. Although no longer in the hands of American owners, their high reputation, established in former days, still secures to them a large patronage, in spite of the daily increasing competition of fast steamers.

A few of the terms used on board ship may be regarded as belonging to our speech exclusively. Such is the *flummadiddle*, a holiday-mess of New England fishermen, who lick their chops at the very mention of this oddly-named delicacy. It consists of a number of ingredients, the most important of which are stale bread, pork-fat, molasses, cinnamon, allspice, and cloves; by the aid of these materials a kind of mush is made, which is baked in the oven and brought to the table hot and brown. If two whalers should happen to meet upon the whaling grounds when such a dainty mess is served, they would be apt to have a very long and merry *gam*, as the conversation is called under such circumstances. "The *gam*," says H. Melville, "was long, but sober and serious; the two sea-dogs knew nothing of each other, and hence were cautious not to let out any of their secrets; they compared reckoning, hoped for whales, and discussed the weather in no complimentary manner." It is on such occasions that the flag of the approaching vessel is most anxiously scanned to see what news may be obtained, and great is the satisfaction of the Britisher even, when he sees the *Gridiron and Doughboys*, as he half contemptuously, half good-naturedly, calls the Stars and Stripes of this country. (*Slang*

Dictionary, p. 147.) The captain in American merchant-ships is almost universally known as the *old man*, and even the gravity of a high court could not resist the extremely ludicrous contrast, when, a few years ago, the case of a vessel was discussed before that tribunal, which had been brought home, after the master's death, by his brave widow, and the latter, a comely young woman, was gravely alluded to by one of the sailors, in his evidence, as the "*old man* down below." The same sea-slang calls the quadrant a *pig-yoke*, from a more fancied than real resemblance to that simple contrivance. It speaks certainly very eloquently in favor of *pork and beans*, that this national dish of the New Englander, unknown in the land of his pilgrim fathers, should have continued such a favorite for two hundred years. It is, of course, the descendant of the well-known English dish of "boiled pork and pease-pudding," a great favorite abroad in provincial towns; but the dried pease are here replaced by beans, as the latter are more prolific and of better quality in the United States. No whaling captain, it is said, ever allows the toothsome dish to be long absent from his table, and the vessels on the great lakes always lay in a goodly store of *pork and molasses*, when they undertake a longer voyage. The latter term, also, has on board American vessels not unfrequently a new and special meaning: sailors on board of whaling boats call their share of the proceeds of their cruise a *voyage*, as this share is paid them instead of money-wages.

In the pursuit of fishing, both at sea and in inland waters, a few terms are peculiar to this country, though many are only in local use. The *dipsy*, for instance, the sinker of a fishing-line, is only known in Pennsylvania; the name, of course, arises from the *dip* the little weight takes as soon as it touches the water; the *dobber*, on the other hand, the float of the line, is peculiar to New York. An *eel-spear*, a kind of trident used in catching eels, is the American substitute for the English "eel-shear," and *gigging*, in the sense of catching fish with a *gig*, is in Virginia still used to denote night-fishing with a three-pronged spear, as it was done in the days of Captain John Smith. The word *gurry*, used by sailors and fishermen for the slime and blood of fish adhering to their hands, is, in all probability, an inheritance from the old English, though a connection with *gory* might, perhaps, be established. *Kibblings* are the small fragments of fish used as bait on the banks of Newfoundland, and *kid*, a large box into which fish are thrown as fast as caught—a term, however, local in the New England States. The *leader* is a small line of hair, gut, or grass, by which the angler's hook is attached to the line itself, also called a *snell*; and a *lig*, in Maine, the hook, to which a little piece of lead is cast to serve as a sinker. From the word *line*, American daring has at once made a verb, and it is a very common phrase to say, "I shall go *lining* this evening," or "I *lined* this fish." "The squeteague," says Dr. Smith, "is taken both by *lining* and *seining*, and because it makes such feeble exertion and resistance in being drawn in by a hook, it has received the appellation of *weak-fish*." (*Fishes of Massachusetts, B.*)

A mysterious term, probably originating in mispronunciation, is the word *scrod*, meaning a small cod broiled; its legitimate form is *escrod*, but in its shortened form, which is largely used by fishermen, it applies to any kind of small fish, fit for boiling. An analogy with *shreds* (of fish) has been suggested, which would be quite probable but for the existence of *escrod*.

Sharking is the convenient way of calling an expedition undertaken to take *sharks* in a harbor, while the evil habits of the fish have given occasion to name a lean hog, with its insatiable voracity, a *shark* in the West, and to form a verb, *sharking*, which denotes the habit of preying upon others. W. Irving thus says: "He was one of those vagabond cosmopolites, who *shark* about the world, as if they had no right or business in it, and who infest the skirts of society like poachers and interlopers." (Knickerbocker, *History of New York*, p. 231.) *Still-baiting*, on the other hand, is used in distinction from "trolling," for fishing with a line at one and the same spot.

Oysters are raised from their natural or artificial bed by *oyster-tongs*, a ferocious hybrid between an iron-toothed rake and a pair of scissors, having two long handles, crossing each other, so that at fifteen or twenty feet depth the iron teeth bite between each other, and, like fingers of clasped hands, gripe firmly whatever is in their clutches. "It is a sight to watch the men pull up the heavy *oyster-tongs*, and shake out bushels of luscious bivalves." (*Connecticut Georgics.*)

Two very beautiful words, used and perhaps invented by our

coast-people, are *moonglade* and *grayslick*. The former denotes the soft, silvery track which moonlight traces on the waters, and has come down to sea-faring folk from the days of the pilgrim fathers, among whom both *sunglade* and *moonglade* were used. The so-called Old Colony people, retaining jealously much of the speech of their forefathers, still employ these terms to embody in language the falling of light aslant hillside or glen by night and by day, and sometimes the track of light leading apparently from the observer to sun or moon, is also called thus. The other word, belonging more properly to the fishermen of Maine, means a state of the sea when the wind has died away, and the water, unbroken by waves, assumes the familiar "glassy" appearance. The men will, hence, say: "We may just as well take to the oar, for we have gotten into a *grayslick*." While the first part of the word refers to the dim but beautiful color, *slick* (sleek) fully expresses the quiet, oleaginous condition of the sea in such places.

American sailors use the word *handsomely* in rather a peculiar meaning; instead of ordering a sail to be furled carefully, the captain is very apt to shout out, "*Handsomely*, my men, don't hurry, *handsomely* for'ard there!" Nantucket fishermen, besides, have a way of using the words *on the coast*, even when on shore, in the often very ludicrous meaning of "near at hand," and a gallant lover will assure his lady-love that if she will only fix the day, "he'll be sure to be *on the coast* with the parson." *Slack water* navigation, also, is probably an Americanism; it means a kind of inexpensive canal in the river itself, in which, by means of dams and locks, a sufficient supply of water is maintained at all seasons. Almost all the larger rivers, in the Eastern States, are thus made navigable high above their original limits.

If there are few nautical and fishing terms that can be called genuine Americanisms, the number of slang words and slang phrases, originating with sailors and fishermen, is, on the other hand, not inconsiderable. The majority of such expressions may, of course, be found in England also, as the sailor is emphatically a cosmopolitan, and his speech the same in every harbor of the world. Some of them, however, can be distinctly traced to this country, if not in their first creation, at least in the special meaning which they have acquired.

Thus the familiar designation of ships at Lloyd's in England, by letters, and a series of numbers attached to them, has led in America to the use of the phrase *A No.* 1, for men and things generally. "She's a prime girl, she's *A No.* 1," said already Sam Slick, and since Judge Haliburton's day, the term has become more common still. J. R. Lowell sings:

> "He was six foot o' man, *A* 1,
> Clean grit and human natur',
> None could quicker pitch a ton,
> Nor dror (draw) a furrer quicker."
>
> (*The Courtin'.*)

A No. 1 *and no mistake* is the intensified form the phrase assumes here, while in England it is amplified into "First Class, letter A, No. 1." (*Slang Dictionary*, p. 17.)

The two words, *ahead* and *aboard*, are in like manner transferred from sea-life to shore-life, and used in America with a frequency which can only be excused on the plea of their extreme usefulness. Railroad conductors and stage drivers, coachmen and cabmen, all urge you to "get *aboard*, and be quick, or you will be left," and *ahead* is used for every possible forwardness that can be imagined. Schoolboys are *ahead* of others, the American press is *ahead* of the English, and one church is *ahead* of another in the liberality of its creed. To *go ahead* is commonly regarded as a genuine Americanism, and even if the phrase should not be original—which there is good reason to doubt—the tendency to restless and energetic progress is certainly a characteristic feature of the nation. The impatience of the term is well defined by Mr. Howell in his attractive *Venetian Life*, where he speaks of a "Sharp, bustling Yankee, who rushed into the Armenian Convent on the island near Venice, one morning, rubbing his hands, and demanded that they should show him all they could in five minutes." The *goaheaditive* American, as he alone of all men would ever dare to say, is the type of the man of the period; and when the Franco-Prussian war broke out, a New York journal once more ventured upon the invariable prophecy, that "in this complication of European difficulties, a favorable opportunity was afforded to American *goaheaditiveness*." (*Times*, Aug. 17, 1871.) Hence the English term: All Right! has disappeared here, and its place, at sea and on land, is usurped by the national *Go ahead!*

The familiarity with boating, which the unsurpassed number of watercourses all over the country naturally produces everywhere, has led to the use, not only of *paddling one's own canoe,* as has already been mentioned, but also of *bailing one's own boat,* in the sense of "minding one's own business," independently and without waiting for help from others. To *bear a hand* is a similar term borrowed from the sea-phrase, and means, even in the Far West, to be active and not to delay.

Gunboats and *Floating Batteries* are well known everywhere in these days of naval warfare and armor-ships, but it was reserved for the soldiers of the late Civil War to bestow the name of *gunboats* upon the contract shoes furnished them, which were apt to be as clumsy and awkward as gunboats appear to sailors. There was in the fancied resemblance a ludicrous correspondence with the manner in which the ladies of Lima, famous for the extreme smallness of their feet, look upon the less favored women of other countries. It is related that some very beautiful English ladies once created quite a sensation among the men of Lima; but when the ladies were asked how they liked the foreign beauties, the answer was, that they were well enough, but looked as if they were walking in *canoes.* The term *Floating Batteries* was, in like manner, applied in bitter irony to the army-bread furnished by the Confederate Government. The word *bogus,* as applied to an American beverage consisting of rum and molasses, is probably only an impatient abbreviation of the *Calibogus* of Captain Grose, whose humor omits none of these pleasant compounds, and who takes care to inform us, in his *Classical Dictionary of the Vulgar Tongue* (ed. 1823), that in his day it was a nobler, though hardly a healthier mixture of rum and ale! The ship's *caboose,* better known as the "galley" or shelter on deck, where the cooking is done, has lent its mutilated name (*camboose,* from Dutch *kombuis*) to a small railroad-car, used for various special purposes, and not known on English railways. Even the manner of speaking to vessels at sea, by *hailing* aloud or through a speaking-trumpet, has been transferred to land usage, and a man is familiarly said to *hail from* his native State, or a stranger is accosted with the words, "Well, sir, and where did you *hail from* last?" The *hounds,* also of a ship, the projecting parts of the mast, which serve as shoulders for the top or trestle trees, have been transferred to land, designating the parts projecting from the front axletree to form a support for the tongue or pole. The word is, in this latter use, not unfrequently written *houns* simply.

Chowder also seems not to have been unknown to our ancestors, for Grose speaks of it as a "sea-dish," but the very indifference with which he, a man of infinite taste, mentions it, proves that it cannot have been the famous dish produced by the inventive genius of the venerable and pious pilgrims of Plymouth. A new halo has since been shed around the time-honored term by the masterly manipulations and majestic name of the "mighty man of Marshfield," for it is well known that Mr. Webster excelled in his *chowder*, which he did not disdain to make himself, as he had caught the fish for it with his own hands. It is described as "a many-sided dish, of pork and fish, potatoes and bread, onions and turnips, all mixed up with fresh chequits and seabass, blackfish and long clams, pumpkinseed and an accidental eel, well peppered and salted, piled up in layers and stewed together." Cider and champagne are not unfrequently added, and the "matelote," as the French would call it, is a most tempting dainty—to very hungry people. It seems almost an insult, after that, to call a dunce a *chowderhead*, but J. R. Lowell uses it, and he cannot fail to be high authority in all matters concerning New England. It has already been stated that sea-coast people have vulgarly transferred the *clamshell* to the lips of their friends on shore, but the power of slang is most strikingly illustrated by the fact that even the Government of the United States condescends to allow its patent locks on mail-bags to be officially designated as *clamshells.*

A *dock-walloper* denotes a trifling, idle fellow, who loiters about the docks, and is an object of great contempt to Jack, probably not unknown to British ports, though, it may be hoped, less numerous there than in America. The term is applied also to the frequent crowds of unemployed emigrants in every large seaport. To *go a cruise* seems to be such a natural expression for the man of Nantucket and most of his neighbors on the coast of New England, that even when he goes inland, he is sure to *go a cruise*, whether he ride on horseback to have an airing, or engage a seat in a stage-coach to visit a distant neighbor.

In what the great bliss enjoyed by clams—salt-water vegetables, as the New Yorker derisively calls them—really consists, has never been ascertained, but a very general impression of their great happiness is evidently prevailing, for coast people—and after them inland people likewise—are very fond of envying others who, they say, are *as happy as a clam*. The expression appears strangely inappropriate, in a notice of a newly-married couple who "left the church and immediately set out on a two years' wedding tour to Europe, *happy as two clams!*" (Baltimore *American*, January 19, 1871.) Occasionally greater happiness yet is conveyed by adding to it the words *at high-water*.

The *keel* of the vessel, of the utmost importance to the sailor, has hence given rise to many a homely but not unpicturesque expression in our language. The *keel* itself serves, in regions along the sea-coast, to name any broad, flat vessel, used for many a domestic purpose; it is the *keeler* or *keeler-tub* of the New England States, the vessel in which the dishes are washed, and to which J. R. Lowell refers, when he says:

'And greasy Joan does *keel* the pot."

Hence also the common phrase of *keeling over*, in nautical language denoting the complete capsizing of the vessel, by which the keel comes uppermost, and in social life used to express an entire overthrow of a man's hopes or circumstances. "We may safely say," writes the New York *Tribune*, "that the whole (Fenian) enterprise has *keeled over* and shown bottom; there is not a grain of hope left to the leaders." (Sept. 14, 1867.) Even the nautical phrase *keel up* has been forced to do ordinary work in the language and to accept the duty of a verb: "As I was not in the habit of using spirits at all," writes the Rev. Mr. Cartwright, "I knew that a little would *keel me up;* so I forbore, but with all my forbearance presently I began to feel light-headed. I instantly ordered our horses, fearing we were snapped for once." (*Autobiography*, p. 205.)

It is a curious evidence of the facility which cant terms have, like weeds, to grow up from a stray seed, and to take the place of better words, that a long-extinguished custom, dating back to the days when slaves were employed in river navigation, should have given us one of the most familiar, colloquial phrases. In those times slaves, who had been delinquent in their work or disrespectful in their manners, were frequently punished by being sent on board the heavier keelboats that went up the Western rivers; here they had to work very hard against the powerful current, and hence to *row up* became soon identical with severe scolding or actual punishment. "We hope," says the New York *Herald*, "the President gave his Secretary a good *rowing up;* he certainly deserved it for his imbecility." (May 7, 1856.) This process of *rowing up* seems, in early days, to have been especially difficult and painful in a small tributary of the Ohio, which winds its tortuous and unsafe channel through a part of Kentucky. A happy allusion to the hardships connected with the navigation of this river, made by a member from Kentucky on the floor of Congress, took the fancy of his audience, and, after its publication, of the people generally. Since then it has become a universal cant phrase to say, that an unlucky wight, who has failed to be elected to some public office, was *rowed up Salt River*. If the candidate, or his party, should have been very grievously defeated, they were apt to be *rowed up to the very headwaters of Salt River*. It will be seen that by a strange confusion of ideas, not unfrequent in the use of metaphors, it was not the poor oarsmen condemned to the hard work, but the passengers in the boat, to whom the unlucky aspirants to honors were compared.

"We thought . . . .
That Sag-Nichts and strangers would tread o'er his head,
And we up the *Salt River* billows."

(*Burial of Uncle Sam.*)

The importance which the *shad* has gained in American fisheries and in commerce, has led to the use of its name for various purposes. The good people of New England are prosaic enough to call the beautiful service-berry, with its beautiful sprays full of delicate white blossoms, the *shadbush*, because, forsooth, it blooms about the time when the fish ascend the rivers in early spring! Hence W. C. Bryant writes:

"the *shadbush*, white with flowers,
Brightened the glen."

(*The Old Man's Council.*)

The peculiar shape of the Quakers' drab-coats, which slope,

without the usual break, from the front gradually toward the tails, has suggested, to eyes familiar with the shad, a resemblance to the outline of that fish, and in coast-slang, therefore, the Friends are apt to appear as *shad-bellies.* It is not quite so evident why landsmen should take their revenge by subjecting Jack, when he has indulged too freely in drink on shore, to the disgraceful process called *shanghai.* The long-legged bird, with his ridiculous strut and mock splendor, had long bestowed his Chinese name upon a dandy, and became, from its striking appropriateness, as popular a nickname as the English "swell." But when the verb to *shanghai* is applied to sailors, it refers not to the bird, but, according to a seaman's statement, to the town of *Shanghai,* where the process so called is said to have been once very common. The latter consists in drugging the unlucky sailor, when he enjoys himself after a long cruise, on shore, and carrying him, while in a state of insensibility, to a vessel about to depart, where he finds himself upon his recovery, entered in all forms on the book. "No doubt the men were to have been quiet till the following morning, and before that time they would have been drugged, *shanghaied,* and taken away from all means of making complaint." (New York *Tribune,* March 1, 1871.)

The American who hesitates not to speak of himself as a *gone coon,* or a *live hoss,* or an *alligator,* occasionally varying the phrase and making himself out to be *half-horse half-alligator,* in Kentucky, does not neglect the life on the waters any more than that on the prairie and in the swamp. "I am a she-*steamboat,* and have doubled up a crocodile in my day," said a damsel who came to the rescue of famous Colonel Crockett, as he lay caught in the crotch of a tree, with a number of eagles pulling out his long hair for a lining in their nests. "Wait till you have *steamboated* it for a while, as I have done, and if there is more than an ounce or two of you left, I'll pay the damage," was the warning an old gambler gave a youngster who had begun life very fast, and was showing the effects. (*Southern Literary Messenger,* June, 1854, p. 117.) While the modern steamboat, with its noisy paddle-wheels, represents thus the fast or energetic man of our day, the old-fashioned vessel, with its small wheel at the stern, still found in Western waters, and as a ferry-boat in all parts of the Union, suggests to the picture-loving mind of the American the slow progress of former days. Hence, J. R. Lowell describes an inefficient "old-timey" place as having

> "Many social priviledge, but a one-hoss *starnwheel* chaplin."
> (*Biglow Papers,* II., p. 20.)

The sailor's legitimate dread of *squalls* in places where he has not sea-room enough, has led to the adoption of *squally,* in the sense of "dangerous," under almost all circumstances. Anything looks *squally* to the Englishman as well as to us, which is threatening; hence, Major Downing wrote: "The times are now getting pretty *squally,* and if we don't look out sharp, things will go all to smash." (*Letters,* p. 95.) Another sailors' term has, curiously enough, made its way to the Far West, and, from the analogy of cases, obtained currency there. The ship which is in danger on a lee-shore, or a narrow channel, may still escape if she can *swing clear*; and so may the canoe, entangled in the brakes of a swamp or the closely-matted grass of a river; hence the phrase *to swing clear,* is often used in the sense of "obtaining elbow-room," or, "room to spread," as landsmen would say. The Rev. Mr. Cartwright thus characterizes one of his brethren: "He was an ordinary preacher in common, yet at times, as we say in the backwoods, when he *swung clear,* there were few that could excel him in the pulpit." (*Autobiography,* p. 324.) Sailors return the compliment by borrowing the name of the lower part of a flail, the *swingle,* which falls on the grain in threshing, and giving it to a shark known as *swingle-tail,* since his long and flexible tail is wielded somewhat in the same manner, and certainly as effective in thrashing his enemies. A similar mixture of sailors' names with landsmen's notions has led to the cant terms by which sturgeons and herrings are apt to be known on shore. The former coming up the Hudson River as far as Albany, and being highly esteemed there, especially when roasted in the form of steaks, are popularly known as *Albany Beef,* while the common herring, caught in great abundance near Taunton, in the State of Massachusetts, is called there a *Taunton Turkey,* half in derision and half, no doubt, for the sake of the alliteration:

> "Our fisheries o'er the world are famed,
> The mackerel, shad, and cod;
> And *Taunton Turkeys* are so thick,
> We sell them by the rod."
> (Allin, *Yankee Ballad, B.*)

"Let's *up jib*, and say no more," is a phrase often heard on the Eastern coasts, but not very intelligible to those who are entire strangers to ships and their main parts. Others will, of course, know that the hoisting of the jib is a signal of departure, and hence the sailor's phrase has become synonymous with "let us be gone." That the huge size of a whale should have led sailors, and after their example others also, to speak of any man or event of unusual and imposing proportions as a *whaler*, seems natural enough; but it is not quite so certain whether the verb to *whale*, used in the north of England and with us, instead of "to beat," is not rather a corruption of the more familiar term to *wale*, i. e., to strike so as to raise *wales*. The confusion may have all the more readily arisen, as the animal is called *wale* not only very largely in the United States, but also "at home," for instance in Harwich and other ports familiar with whaling. A Mississippi paper, relating a somewhat marvellous story of an alligator floating up, after receiving many shots, "with a sort of grape-vine twisted round his head, to hide it," adds that "the captain found, on opening the 'gater's body, two pigeons inside, whole and undigested. Oh, he was a regular *waler*, says the captain. On this immortal occasion of shooting such a *waler*, the captain had recourse to the old lure of all 'gater hunters, to a dog trained to yelp and so attract the 'gaters, who like dog above all other meats." (Mississippi *Clarion*, January 17, 1865.) It is the same word used with happy effect by J. R. Lowell in the lines—

> "Their masters can cuss 'em, and kick 'em, and *wale* 'em,
> An' they notice it less 'an the ass did to Balaam."
> (*Biglow Papers*, I., p. 13.)

The enormous steamboats of the Ohio and the Mississippi require such vast supplies of fuel for their long journeys, some of which extend to weeks, that in early spring, upon the opening of the navigation, detachments of men are set on shore at convenient places, whose duty it is to cut wood, pile it up on shore, and carry it on board the boat that has engaged their services. These men, a rough and roysterous but not vicious race, lead here wretched lives, consumed by low fevers and devoured by musquitoes, but receive enormous wages. The boats necessarily stop often to *wood-up*, as the term is, and *tie up* to such a *wooding-place*. The passengers avail themselves of the opportunity to take a stroll on shore, to examine the snakes and vipers which are apt to accumulate beneath the huge woodpile, and to take a drink; hence, unfortunately, *to wood*, has in the West become a popular euphemistic term for "to take a dram." A distinguished British nobleman, recently connected with royalty, was hence not a little puzzled when a Western member of Congress, in a moment of hilarity, invited him to leave the Minister's house, where they met at a large party, for the purpose of *wooding-up*.

On the Eastern coast another ship-term has made its way inland, and even usurped a meaning for which it was probably never intended. It seems that when horses were first brought from England to the colonies, no vehicles came with them, and would, in fact, not have been available, as there were no other roads, then, but bridle-paths through the forest. Boats, on the contrary, were numerous, and furnished the principal means of transportation, but had to be laid up during the winter, when their tackling was carefully stored away. As soon as the ice was thick enough for the purpose, sledges were made, and as the colonists had no harness for their horses, they very ingeniously used the boat-tackling instead. Thus it came about that *tackling* was continually used in speaking of fastening a horse to a vehicle, and when the rude contrivance gave way to real harness, the term remained unchanged for two hundred years. *Tackling* a horse, is, hence, to this day the common term for harnessing, all "the way up from the Old Colony to Hampton Beach, and along the banks of the Merrimac River, through a country as thickly populated and as highly civilized as any of equal extent in the United States." (C. Dodge.) "You had better *tackle* the horse at once," said Prudence, "or we shall be late." (*Atlantic Monthly*, October, 1867.) "My friend promised to send my *tackling* to town to be mended, so that we might go down to the beach and enjoy a nice drive in the afternoon." (Letter from Newport in New York *Herald*, August 17, 1863.)

Another Americanism connected with steamboats is the *smoke-stack*, as the chimney is universally called. Hence, after an explosion, we are told that

> "Sure as you're born, they all got off,
> Afore the *smokestacks* fell."
> (*Jim Bludsoe of the Prairie Belle*. John Hay.)

The navigation in Western waters has its peculiar dangers, and among these none are more dreaded than the *sawyers* and *snags* of the Mississippi, and some of its tributaries. The former are trees washed away by the current, either during a high flood or after their roots have been completely undermined, and then so imbedded in the river-bottom as to impede navigation. As they constantly change their places, steamboats often come unawares upon them, and are sunk or at least seriously injured. *Snags* derive their name from the old English *snag*, defined by Halliwell as "a tooth standing alone," whilst its meaning on our Western waters is more like that in Gill's proverb: "A bird in the bag is worth two on the *snag*," quoted by J. R. Lowell. The *sawyer* has the advantage of moving to and fro with a sawing motion, as the current tries to dislodge it; the *snag* is too firmly imbedded to move. "*Snags* and *sawyers*," says C. Lanman, "abound throughout the whole extent of the Mississippi; they are taken from the shore by a rushing tide and planted in the channel quite as rapidly as the *snag-vessels* can extricate them from their dangerous position." (*Summer in the Wilderness*, p. 124.)

A somewhat technical term, perhaps, is the *hugging-frame*, the arched truss-braces which span the length of the majority of American steamboats. (*The Engineer.*) To this class belongs, likewise, the *spreaderstick* of the person who drives horses on the towpath, which pull a canal-boat. "The captain had started on his downward trip, and had tied up his boat near Oldtown, when he was attacked with a *spreaderstick* (a piece of wood used as a swingle-tree on the tow-track), and was brutally murdered by Howard." (Cumberland *Journal*, February 10, 1871.) The name is evidently derived from the use to which the stick is put, in *spreading* and holding apart the traces or ropes by which the horses pull the boat. A like term is the *Fish-Basket* of Pennsylvania, which designates a structure for taking fish, and is figured in Eli Bowen's *Sketchbook of Pennsylvania* (II., p. 83). "Various species," says Professor S. S. Haldeman, in a Memoir of 1844, "are abundantly caught . . . in *fish-baskets*, made of lathwork, with diverging walls of stone." The fact that the plural of the word *wharf* differs in England and here, is characteristic of the manner in which words generally are treated by us and by our English cousin. Here we say *wharves*, although Bancroft writes,

"Commerce pushes its *wharfs* into the sea," while in England *wharfs* is considered alone admissible, although there also we find—

> "Out upon the *wharves* they came,
> Knight and burgher, lord and dame."
>
> *Tennyson.*

The English are, however, following our example very largely, and ere long, no doubt, both nations will use *wharves* alike.

VIII.

On the Rail.

ON THE RAIL.

RAILROADS, as they are now uniformly called in America by the public, although some companies owning large leading lines prefer the English name of *Railways*, have contributed, on the whole, fewer words and expressions to American-English than might be expected, from the enormous extent of their widespread network, the number of persons to whom they give employment, and the ingenuity which they stimulate. The fact is partly accounted for by the perfect identity of the systems prevailing in England and on this continent, and their almost simultaneous introduction in both countries. Besides, so many of our railroads are built by British capital, and therefore, in part at least, under foreign control, that the terminology has not yet become quite independent of that of the Old World. And yet the very elements of nomenclature, so to say, are different: railways abroad are *railroads* here, stations there are *depots* here, and English carriages and coaches have become American *cars*. The preference for *Road* lay probably in the greater familiarity with the term generally; highways were rarely known to the people here, as they are in England, and everything was called a road, from the National Road crossing the Alleghanies on its way West to the *roadside* inns, along the corduroy-roads of the South. Why we should ever have exchanged the sensible *station* of the English for the absurd *depot* of the French, is perfectly unaccountable; all the talk about the old friendship for France, dating from the days of Lafayette and Rochambeau, will, we fear, not explain the absurdity. And if we but gave it either its French sound, which is not hard to acquire, or anglicized it at once, like men! But no, we must needs call it *dee-po*, and thus add to the absurdity. Justly, therefore, does R. G. White, in his clever book on *Words and Their*

Uses, call it "the height of pretentious absurdity to give the name of dépôt to a little lonely shanty, which looks like a lodge outside a garden of cucumbers, a staging of a few planks upon which two or three people stand like criminals on the scaffold." (p. 149.) But then, the American loves big names, and ere long, he is quite sure, the depot becomes what the name indicates, so rapid is the growth of the country, and so marvellous the power of railroads in developing its resources. He makes amends, moreover, by calling the coaches of England simply *cars,* though the increasing demand for comfort has quickly led him to seek compensation in naming the truly superb carriages which now, virtually though not in name, represent the first-class coaches of foreign railways, *Palace-Cars,* and even *Silver* Palace-Cars! It is the same unfortunate tendency which makes him adorn his magnificent steamers with that outrage on decency, *Bridal Chambers,* and tempts writers for the press to dub every comfortable town-house a *palatial* residence. It is to be hoped that the introduction of *Stock Palace-Cars* on some of the Northern roads will speedily lead to the adoption of more appropriate names, for surely all the sensible and most praiseworthy improvements in cattle-trains would not justify the name of palaces for their stalls. A special car is, on all the more important *routes,* as the Post-Office Department calls the lines, provided for a mail-agent, who performs his duties there, and receives letters dropped in an outside box on the way. This is called the *Mail-Car,* of one of which the following terrible story was recently reported: "Two sons of Governor Miller of Minnesota were arrested in January for robbing a *mail-car* on the Central Pacific Railway. One of them turned State's evidence against his brother, and the other committed suicide. So they both obtained acquittal." (New York *Tribune,* March 23, 1871.)

The *sleeping-cars,* introduced a few years ago on American railways, and an inestimable comfort on long journeys, which often extend through a whole week on a continuous line, have given rise to a new form—the *sleepers,* as they are briefly designated. In an account of a fearful accident in the State of New York we read: "In front was the Buffalo *sleeper* of the Chicago Lightning Train; it had twenty-seven passengers, and not a soul was saved." (New York *Tribune,* February 6, 1871.) This tendency to shorten words, most pardonable perhaps in the haste engendered by rapid railway travelling, has also led to the use of *rail* as a noun and a verb. No one answers the question, How are you going to travel? by a fuller reply than by saying, "I'll go by *rail*," or still more briefly, though in language as yet bordering upon slang, "I'll *rail* it all the way."

The train, as it appears in sight, introduces us at once to an Americanism, the *cow-catcher*, the well-known, triangular fender of iron, placed in front of the locomotive, to clear the line of cattle, sheep, pigs, and such like trespassers—an instrument unknown to the well-guarded railways of Europe. Here they are eminently useful, often saving stray animals from destruction and preventing serious accidents. Not long ago a runaway horse with a sleigh and its owner was met by a locomotive on a branch-road near Philadelphia; the fireman, in the moment of contact, passed forward and seized the horse by the bridle. "The train continued for some distance with a man and a horse on the *cow-catcher*, and when it was stopped, both were found to be uninjured; the sleigh was entirely demolished." (Philadelphia *Ledger*, Dec. 19, 1870.) Next to the locomotive comes another feature peculiar to American trains—the *express-car*; since the business of great Express Companies has become so immense as to require a special car of the largest dimensions on almost all the great railroads of the country. Since Americans have given up the word *luggage*—except perhaps in Boston and Boston-dependencies—the car which here is exclusively used for its conveyance is, of course, called the *Baggage-Car*. It generally follows the tender, and is quite a place of interest to foreigners, with its simple but most effective system of *checks*—which are by means of a leather-strap fastened to the trunk, while the stamped marks are entered into the *baggage-agent's* books—and its countless variety of portable and not portable trunks. This system of *checks*, an exclusive peculiarity of American railways, is apt to strike travellers from abroad as the greatest improvement devised for the purpose, and thus elicits praise like the following: "Luggage is the pest of the traveller, but the Americans have a way of lessening the evil. When you come to a railway-station, an official receives your luggage, and learns your destination. He then brings a bunch of brass-tickets, each fitted with a looped strap, and each furnished with a tally.

Handing you the tally, he at the same instant loops the ticket on to the article by its most prominent handle. The articles are thus *labelled* for their destination, and you have been supplied with a record of the deposit. At no intermediate stage, change of carriage, ferry, or any other stoppage, need you be under the least anxiety. The articles are sure to appear at the proper place. Moreover, as you approach the end of the journey, a porter or omnibus-conductor comes forward, who, for a small fee, undertakes to collect your baggage, and bring yourself and it, or the baggage by itself, to any hotel, or other house you may name." (London *Athenæum*, September, 1870.)

In this sanctum of the baggage-agent you see *hand-trunks*, containing in an incredibly small place the supply of the experienced and self-denying traveller for many months, who finds it cheaper to purchase collars and socks, and other small articles, whenever he wants them, than to have them washed. By their side you see colossal *Saratoga-trunks*, as they are called from the most fashionable of American watering-places, in which ladies' dresses find ample room for expansion. Some are iron-shod on the sides, others are protected by gutta-percha knobs at the corners, still others stare at you with broken locks and gaping rents, for the *baggage-smasher*, as the porter is commonly called, handles his burdens with appalling recklessness, and responsibility there is none. The long, roomy cars of the American train are, of course, not set directly upon their wheels as English coaches are—the latter would not stand our rough, cheap structures. They are, on the contrary, built so that they rest upon two separate and independent centre-bearing *trucks* of four, six or eight wheels each, which secure to them both safety and great elasticity. The English buffer, a cushion resting upon strong springs, to meet and deaden the shock with another car, appears, in this country, as a *bumper*, and the stoker as a *fireman*; but for this unusual simplicity ample compensation is found in giving the driver, as he is called in England, here the proud name of *engineer*. The most important official on the train is, of course, the *conductor*, whose functions on the whole resemble those of the guard abroad, but on whose shoulders rests the entire responsibility for the promptness and safety of the train and its entire contents. While this is his official title, he is universally addressed as *Captain,* for Americans insist upon carrying the analogy with the steamboat, with which they were universally familiar long before railroads existed, through all the details. The passengers are summoned by loud calls of, "*All aboard* for Chicago!" or whatever the place of destination may be. The train is started, not by the English phrase, All right! but by the usual *Go ahead!* and persons walk from car to car to see what friends they may find *on board.* They are called upon to *settle their fare,* precisely as they are summoned to do on board a Western steamboat, and in the new Palace Cars they pay more, if they engage a *state-room,* while *sleeping-cars* have their upper and lower *berths.* The usual Express Train is not half fast enough for the impatient traveller; he must have his *Lightning* Express Train, and in the Far West improves still farther by calling it *Greased Lightning,* after a favorite Yankee term.

The road-bed, and especially the space between the rails, is called the *track,* but a train is said to be *off the track* when the wheels have, by some accident or other, lost their hold on the rails. As American railroads are not generally ballasted, and thus liable, in sandy regions, to be enveloped in unbearable clouds of dust, *track sprinklers* are frequently employed to water them. This process must, however, be carefully distinguished from another kind of *watering,* to which railroads, or rather railroad companies, have of late become liable. "To *water* stock," says an indignant writer, "is necessary on a stock farm, but I question if it be wise in running a railroad to *water* anything but the engine, and perhaps the track." (*Every Saturday,* Dec., 1870.) "This process consists in creating fictitious stock, without its being a representative of industry expended or work done, and thus resembles very much the debasing of coins practised by former sovereigns. Upon such increase dividends are secured by the imposition of rates far in excess of the cost of transportation. The difference between charge and cost is the measure of the gains. These spoliations have been carried on to such an extent as to embarrass, most seriously, the industries and commerce of the country. A competent writer affirms that in two years the capitals of twenty-eight Northern railroads have been *watered* to the extent of nearly two hundred millions." (New York *Tribune,* December 17, 1870.)

The word *track* has lent itself very naturally to the formation of several cant phrases, of which, however, perhaps but one belongs legitimately to the railroad-track, all the others being of older date than the earliest use of the latter. This is the favorite admonition to *clear the track*, when persons are summoned to get out of the way, either literally or figuratively. "When the *track was thus cleared* of all obstructions, Mr. Bingham introduced his bill, and announced at once that at one o'clock he would call for the previous question upon it." (*Congressional Proceedings*, January 17, 1870.) To *make tracks*, on the contrary, is a metaphor drawn from Western life, and refers to the importance attached to trails, tracks, and signs of every kind, in all regions where Indians and wild beasts have still to be encountered. It is said that in a camp of United States troops on Staten Island, near New York, in the year 1862, an officer was heard to call upon a private in these words: "Pat Doolan, *make tracks* right off, and slant into your position!" (*Once a Week*, February 15, 1862.) To catch a man *in his tracks* is a phrase of the same nature, and suggested to J. R. Lowell the Latin *e vestigio*, and the Norman French *enes les pas*, both of which have the same meaning as the Americanism, immediately. Even to be on the *right track* must be referred to the hunter's language, but the new phrase, just coming into use, You are *off the track*, promises, if adopted, to add another contribution to railway slang. Even here, however, the *track* of the race-course comes into serious competition with the railroad, and in the case of the cant phrase, He has the *inside track*, which means that he has luck on his side, and great advantages over his competitors, there can be no doubt that it originated with jockeys, and has sole reference to the race-course.

The railway officials have borrowed from nautical language the word *run*, to denote the distance which their engine or the whole train has run in a given time. First they speak of *running* one or more trains, and then they state that the *run* will be made in so many hours. "Engineers and firemen often arrive at the end of their *run* somewhere among the small hours of night, and from that or other causes have to spend considerable time about the round-house." (*Rail-Road Gazette*, 1870.)

Even the *flag*, with which the watchmen signalize in the daytime, has been verbalized, and a train is now said to have been *flagged* before a collision. An awful catastrophe occurred early in 1871 on the Hudson River Railway, and an influential paper said, "The trains were to be *flagged* from the tank instead of the bridge, and at night the white light, indicating All-Right! was left permanently at the post, seventy rods from the nearest watchman!" (New York *Evening Post.*) An ominous word, verbalized with like freedom, is *telescope.* The frequency with which trains collide on American railways, has led to the use of the word for the purpose of designating the manner in which, on such occasions, one train is apt to run right into the other, as the smaller parts of the telescope glide into the larger. Hence the following article: "Two through-trains on the Erie Railway came in collision yesterday, near Paterson. One of the trains had stopped, and the locomotive of the other train, which was following, *telescoped* into the rear cars of the first. The smokestack of the locomotive and several cars were smashed. We append the list of the wounded. The brakeman, Sol. Collins, was instantly killed." (New York *Herald,* September 17, 1859.) The important *signal*-flag of the railway-guard has in like manner, been converted into a verb, and persons who wish to hail a passing street-car or to stop any conveyance, are very apt to say that they mean to *signal a car.* "The lady was standing on the sidewalk, and with her parasol *signalled* the next car just coming in sight." (Philadelphia *Ledger,* June 7, 1861.)

In the Western States, with their level surface and vast unbroken prairies, railroads could often be built in straight lines, avoiding all curves and *bays,* as they are apt to be called there, steep *grades* (*vice* English *gradients*), and expensive windings. In that case, a railroad was frequently called an *Air-Line Road,* or, in common parlance, a *Straight Shoot.* Since the number of such roads has increased in the more thickly settled parts of the Union, the advantages of direct lines between two great centres over others which meander from town to town, have become very manifest, and for a few years a tendency to build such *air-lines* has agitated Legislatures, from whom help was asked, and financial circles at home and abroad. An air-line road from New York to Washington is warmly advocated, and others have been actually built, not unfrequently running for long distances by the side of older lines.

On the track, American railroads show us of things peculiar to them—*frogs*, or iron plates placed where two lines intersect, and, as J. R. Bartlett suggests, so called from the resemblance they bear to the frog in a horse's hoof; *switches*, where the English *shunt* their trains, and above all *snakeheads*, pieces of rails thrown up in front of a train and passing through the bottom of the cars with fearfully destructive power. Fortunately, the flat rails, which alone made such formidable accidents possible, have now gone entirely out of use, and this danger at least is no longer to be apprehended. Alas! that it should only have given way to far graver and more frequent accidents, which have made articles under the head of *Railroad Disaster* almost a standing paragraph in every journal of the Union! The mortality on American railroads is frightful; careful statisticians compute that to every one who perishes on French railways, twenty-nine perish in America. But a graver evil is yet behind—the utter absence of all responsibility, which increases the recklessness of companies, and the indifference to the loss of human life in the public.

It must not be forgotten, finally, that the Americans had an *Underground Railway* long before London bethought herself of this remedy for her overcrowded streets; only it was so far underground that it was never beheld by human eyes. Mrs. H. B. Stowe said in her famous work that "nothing has awakened more bitterly the animosity of the slaveholding community than the existence, in the Northern States, of an indefinite yet very energetic institution, the *Underground Railroad*." (*Dred*, II., p. 302.) If that be so, we may be grateful that the abolition of slavery in the Union has made an end to this secret conveyance, by which fugitive slaves were enabled to escape from their bondage to the Free States and Canada, and that thus one more of the great causes of irritation has been removed, which have so long prevented cordial friendship and true union between the North and the South.

Among the passengers *on board* the train, but one class enjoys a special name, and they are known by the painful title of *Deadheads*. Whether the term originated in theatres, where it is well-known to box-keepers, or on railways, the meaning is always the same: the *deadhead* enjoys whatever may be had for money without paying. Hence the class of *deadheads* is almost endless, every favor being returned, every adverse criticism averted, and every service acknowledged by a *free ticket.* The *deadhead* receives his newspapers without subscribing, travels free of charge on steamboat, railroad, and stage, walks into theatres and shows of every kind unmolested, and even drinks at the bar and lives at the hotel without charge. While similar favors are not unknown in Europe, where journalists and critics, officials and the managers' friends, enjoy their privileges, the custom of allowing ministers of the gospel to travel free of charge, which prevails very largely in the United States, must be looked upon as a genuine and praiseworthy Americanism. The word has even been made into a verb, and is used thus: "Elder Knapp, the noted revivalist, is exciting a theological fever in the towns of Massachusetts. In Pittsfield, recently, he is reported to have advertised that he would furnish a 'free pass to glory,' but very few of the unrighteous population seemed anxious to be *deadheaded* on this train." (New York *Tribune,* May 2, 1871.)

IX.

Natural History.

NATURAL HISTORY.

"In America, Nature's children are grand and grotesque, in form and in name."

De la Condamine.

In the nomenclature of the various departments of Natural History little that is truly and originally American can be expected, since the most prominent objects classed under that head, are well known in Europe, and have long since been named there, while the few that were first discovered here, received their names generally by the first settlers, Frenchmen and Spaniards included. Where this was not the case, they are of such rare occurrence and limited usefulness, that their proper designation is known only to men of science. We have endeavored to give elsewhere those terms which are clearly traceable to foreign idioms, and shall here content ourselves with mentioning such names only as deserve consideration for some special reason.

Among *Animals* peculiar to this continent, the American *Buffalo* stands naturally foremost, both on account of the vast numbers which still are found in the West, and for its vital importance for the preservation of the Indian race. The name is a very ancient one, given by Pliny, as βούβαλος, to the wild ox (Urus), then attributed to various wild animals of large size, and finally transferred to our *Bison* (Bison americanus), a near kinsman of the German Auerochs. The immediate ancestor of that name is, no doubt, the Spanish *bufalo* (Bos bubalus), as the French *buffle* could not well have lent itself to such an enlargement. The animal, too well known to require a description here, lends its name to a number of other objects. *Buffalo-Cider* is the ludicrous name given to the liquid in the stomach of a buffalo, which the thirsty hunter drinks, when he has killed his game at a great distance from water. The name is, likewise, given to several plants, of which the buffalo was formerly believed to be particularly fond, such as the *Buffalo-Grass* (Sesteria dactyloides), which has the remarkable property of giving, every spring, new life to the winter-killed blade, without casting its stubble or sending out new shoots. The *Buffalo-Clover*, on the prairies most frequented by the animal, and the *Buffalo-Berry* (Shepherdia argentea), found only on the upper Missouri, are named in the same manner. A fish even bears the same name as the gigantic bison, on account of its remarkable shape, which has in science also procured for him the title of *Taurichthys* (S. F. Baird). The hide of the buffalo alone is called a *robe*, but where it is most used as a cover, it is never known otherwise than as a *buffalo* only. "I put my blanket over my head, drew my *buffalo* close around me, and let the snow fall upon me till I was fairly buried, my breath alone making an opening through which I could breathe." (*Adventures in the Rocky Mountains.*)

The *Elk*, constantly confounded with the Caribou, the Wapiti, and the Moose, has been mentioned elsewhere. The *Catamount* (Felis concolor), is an animal peculiar to this continent, and occurs in different parts of America: as the *Cougar*, from the *couguar* of the French, which they themselves again took from *cuguaracu*, the name of the animal among the Guaranies of South America—as the *puma* from Mexico to Cape Horn, so called by the Quichuans of Peru—and as the *painter* or *panter*, the familiar corruption of panther, found in the everglades of Florida, where it hides in the high grass or crouches on the branches of the live oak to spring upon its prey. "'*Painter*-meat can't shine with this,' said a hunter, to express his delight at the delicate flavor of an extra cut of tenderloin." (*Life in the Far West*, p. 311.) In the Chippewa dialect, it re-appears as *missi-pezhew*, the Great Cat, and this is the animal found in Canada and Maine, the only one in the latter State that man need fear. As for the name *Catamount*, it may have been derived from the Spanish words *gato*, a cat, and *monte*, a mountain, as many maintain, but, if this be so, the derivation is, of course, older than the American usage; for Beaumont and Fletcher have already the English combination, which seems to be, far more justly, the true ancestor of the modern word—

"Would any man of discretion venture such a gristle,
To the rude claws ot such a *cat-a-mountain*."

Pope and Arbuthnot call it by the same name, and nothing is more probable than that *catamount* is simply a shortened form of the fuller and older name.

"The blinded *catamount* that lies
High in the boughs to watch his prey,
Even in the act of springing dies."
(*W. C. Bryant.*)

The *Chickaree* is the red squirrel (Sciurus hudsonius) of the North, from the Atlantic to the Missouri, named so, no doubt, from the peculiar noise he is fond of making; as a tiny bird has, in like manner, received the name of *chickadee* from its peculiar note. "I woke up to find myself the subject of discussion of a troop of *chickarees*." (The Adirondacks, *Putnam's Magazine*, August, 1868.) The same squirrel is, in North Carolina, known by his Indian name of *Booma*. The Ground-Squirrel, on the contrary, is a name erroneously given to the Striped Prairie-Squirrel (Spermophilus tridecemlineatus), mentioned elsewhere as Gopher. The *Cross Fox* (Vulpes fulous, var decussatus) so called from the black cross on the back, is dear to the trapper for its fur; a cross between silver-gray and the common reddish is highly prized by peltry dealers. A very curious animal, peculiar to this country, is the *Ground-hog*, as it is commonly called in the South, or the *Wood-chuck* (Arctomys monax), familiar to Northern farmers. It is a species of the marmot tribe, very destructive to grass and growing crops generally. Like other marmots, it lies hid in its burrow, and dormant during the winter, emerging in early summer. "As I came home through the woods, with my string of fish, trailing my pole, it being now quite dark, I caught a glimpse of a *wood-chuck* stealing across my path, and felt a strange thrill of savage delight, and was strongly tempted to seize and devour him raw—not that I was hungry then, but for that wildness which he represented. (*Walden*, H. D. Thoreau.) One of the few superstitions found native in this country is connected with this animal. Candlemas is known as *Ground-hog Day*, for on that day the ground-hog comes annually out of his hole, after a long winter nap, to look for his shadow. If he perceives it, he retires again to his burrow, which he does not leave for six weeks

—weeks necessarily of stormy weather. But if he does not see his shadow, for lack of sunshine, he stays out of his hole till he can, and the weather is sure to become mild and pleasant. "It is feared," says a distressed Low-Churchman, "that the introduction of ritualism and candles on that day may have thrown this year undesirable light and shadow on the emerging *ground-hog*, and brought confusion upon the weather." (New York *Tribune*, February 7, 1871.) The negroes of the South are keen hunters of the poor creature, who, in winter a mere ball of fur, during the summer grows into a perfect ball of fat, and is considered a great luxury at the "quarters." The second part of *wood-chuck* is used as *hog* is in *ground-hog*, for pigs are almost universally summoned to the feeding-trough by the word *chuck! chuck!* repeated several times, evidently the descendant of the old English *sug! sug!* which Grose says is a word used in Norfolk "to call pigs to eat their wash."

A curious but by no means inappropriate name is that of a tiny rabbit, which is called *Jackass-Rabbit*, in honor of its very large ears, and long, slender legs (Lepus callotis). It is found only in Texas and the neighborhood of the Rocky Mountains, and known to hunters under a great variety of other names also, such as Texas-hare and Mule-rabbit. The *Lucyver* of Maine, a wild-cat or lynx, has, on the contrary, no right whatever to a name so nearly akin to Lucifer; the word is a corruption of *loup-cervier*, the name given it by the early French settlers. The *Mink*, sometimes called a miniature otter, and then again an aquatic weasel, haunts all the streams and lakes of the United States, harboring under roots and hollow banks, from which it darts forth to prey upon fish, craw-fish, and all the tenants of the water. It even makes occasional predatory excursions into the poultry-yard, and is a great lover of fresh eggs. Its fur, very popular among ladies, is one of the most beautiful of American peltries, and brings a good price in the market. Hence it is much persecuted, and needs not the poet's suggestion to

"Mind the *mink*
Paddling the water by the quiet brink."
(*J. G. C. Brainerd.*)

The *Musk-Ox* (Oribos moschatus), and the *Musk-Rat* (Fiber zibethicus), owe their names, of course, to the powerful odor which they exhale under peculiar circumstances. The former is only met with in the country around Hudson's Bay, the Barren Grounds of Arctic America; but the latter, closely allied to it in form and habits, abounds near all our lakes and streams. In the Northern States it is generally called *Musquash*, from its general Indian designation, which has in science also given it the name of *Ondatra*, from the Huron dialect of the Iroquois tongue. Another animal, peculiar to America, and found on the plains west of the Missouri River, is the *Bighorn* (Ovis montana) the Rocky Mountain sheep. "The *Bighorn* is so named from its horns, which are of great size, and twisted like those of a ram." (W. Irving, *Astoria*, I., p. 253.) The *Pronghorn* (Antilocapre americana) is not a true antelope, because it sheds its horns, and has its name from the fact that each horn has a prong jutting out of it. It is called *Cabrée* by the Canadian voyageurs, and the *Goat* by the fur-traders. The hunters of the West value its meat very highly, and travellers on the Pacific Railway are eloquent in their praise of the animal's swift and graceful motions. The *Mule-Deer* (Cervus macrotis), the largest deer found on this continent, derives, in the same way, its less poetical name from its unusually long ears, while the variety found on the Pacific coast (Cervus columbianus), is more commonly designated as the *Black-tail Deer*, from the black tip to its tail. (S. F. Baird.)

Birds suffer in America more, perhaps, than in any other country, from the general want of instruction in Natural History, which leads to profound ignorance of all that concerns them, except, perhaps, local habits. The same bird appears often under half a dozen different names, in different parts of the Union; and again, distinct varieties are considered as one, because they are all called by the same name. Such is, for instance, the case of the *grouse* and the *bobolink*. The *partridge* proper (Perdix cinerea) does not exist at all in America; the name is usurped by a *quail* in Pennsylvania and the South a *pheasant* (Ortyx virginianus) and a *grouse* (Bonasa umbellus); hence, W. C. Bryant sings:

"I listened, and from midst the depth of wood,
Heard the low signal of the *grouse*, that wears
A sable ruff around his mottled neck;
Partridge they call him, by our Northern streams,
And *pheasant* by the Delaware."

From its cry it has obtained here, as well as abroad, the additional name of *Bobwhite.* The *bobolink* (Dolichonyx oryzivora), so called from the peculiar notes of its song, also Bob of Lincoln, is the same bird as the *Reed-bird* on the banks of the Delaware, and the *Rice-bird* still farther South. His quaint pied garb, his busy, active manner, and his inimitable song as he flutters across a meadow, have made him a pet with the farmer and a favorite of American poets.

"Meanwhile that devil-may-care, the *bobolink,*
Remembering duty, in mid-quaver stops,
Just ere he sweeps o'er rapture's tremulous brink,
And 'twixt the winrows most demurely drops,
A decorous bird of business, who provides
For his brown mate and fledglings six besides,
And looks from right to left, a farmer 'mid his crops."
(J. R. Lowell. *An Indian Summer Reverie.*)

Their cheery, laughing manner is well reproduced in the lines:

"One day in the bluest of summer weather,
Sketching under a whispering oak,
I heard five *bobolinks* laughing together
Over some ornithological joke."
(C. P. Cranch. *Summer Pictures.*)

In another place J. R. Lowell describes his song, thus:

"June's bridesman, poet o' the year,
Gladness on wings, the *bobolink,* is here.
Half hid in tip-top apple-bloom, he swings,
Or climbs against the breeze with quivering wings,
Or, giving way to it in mock despair,
Runs down, a brook of laughter, thro' the air."
(*Biglow Papers*, II., p. 158.)

The merry bird is also known by the spurious name of American Ortolan, but is a very different bird from the European ortolan; the transfer of the name being a literary perversion like that of *peewee* into *peewit,* the name of a European water-bird. Its saddest name is the common one of *Skunk Blackbird,* not unfrequently heard in the South, and due to the coloring, which remotely resembles that of the ill-smelling animal. It has a formidable rival in the *Cat-bird* (Mimus carolinensis), who earned his name from his cat-like cry when alarmed, as well as from his inimitably sly ways, in slipping stealthily through the bushes close up to your feet and away again, before you are quite sure he was there. This thrush possesses great imitative powers, and in spite of its plain, gray costume, and often very discordant cries, the result of fear or anger, is a great favorite in almost every part of the country. It is of him F. Cozzens wrote with a certain enthusiasm: "Hush! The musical monologue begins anew; up, up, into the tree-tops it mounts, fairly lifting the leaves with its passionate effluence; it thrills through the upper branches; and then, dripping through the listening foliage, in a cadenza of matchless beauty, subsides into silence again." (*Sparrow-grass Papers.*) The master, universally acknowledged as matchless in his powers, is, however, the *Mocking-Bird* (Mimus polyglottus). Plain in color and unattractive in form, so common as to be found through the whole length of this continent, from the frontier of Canada to the Empire of Brazil, there is still no bird more highly prized, none more eagerly listened to, than the little brown mimic, often called the Long-Tailed *Mocker*, who has in his marvellous throat every song and every sound that can be heard by the ear of man. In the forest and in the garden he mocks every bird, from the musical strain of the thrush to the ludicrous gobble of the male turkey, and, hung up in his cage in town, he imitates with equal success the cries of itinerant merchants, the rumbling of heavy drays on the pavement, and the shrill whistle of idle boys. And ever and anon there come in between a few notes of ineffable sweetness and great pathos, as if he were, after all, not unmindful of his home in the country, and bethought himself of his mate and his brood. It is all the more unjust to confound him with the butcher-bird of the North (Lanius septentrionalis), whose popular name is *Nine-killer*, a name derived from the prevailing notion that the number of his victims, which he actually impales and hangs up as a butcher does his meat, never exceeds the number nine at a time. In Canada and some of the Northern States they bestow upon this ignoble, almost songless bird, the name of *Mocking-Bird.*

Similar confusion prevails here about the name of *Buzzard*, which is commonly misapplied, being given to a vulture instead of a hawk, since true buzzards bear at least some resemblance to the two American *Henhawks* (Butes borealis and Butes lineatus), the latter known as the red-shouldered hawk.

> "Silently overhead the *henhawk* sails
> With watchful measuring eye, and for his quarry waits."
> (J. R. Lowell. *Indian Summer Reverie.*)

Even the oft-quoted *Bald Eagle* (Haliaetus leucocephalus), or *Baldheaded Eagle* and *Whiteheaded Eagle*, are only spurious book-names, and perhaps on this account the poor bird has so readily been adopted as the emblem of the United States. He does not seem to have always kept good company, for Richard Frame spoke already in 1692 of

> "The Turkey-Buzzard and the *Bald Eagle* high,
> Wild Ducks, which in great companyes do fly;"

and Benjamin Franklin wrote almost plaintively: "For my part, I wish the *bald eagle* had not been chosen as the representative of our country."

A double blunder is committed in giving the name of *Turkey Buzzard* to a bird that is neither a turkey nor a buzzard, but a vulture (Cathartes aura), and bearing but a very faint resemblance to a turkey, while he is remarkable for his graceful flight in the higher regions of the air. "Mr. N. P. Willis had vultures before his eyes, but because the vulgar name of *turkey-buzzard* suggested the name of an English hawk, called buzzard, this was sufficient to cause him to turn an ugly, unclean, filth-devouring scavenger, into a splendid-looking, proud, handsome bird of prey, capable of being married to falconry!" (S. S. Haldeman, *Southern Review*, January, 1868, p. 216.) It is this bird which acts as health-officer in the Southern cities, and may, therefore, be seen stalking through the streets or perched on roofs and awnings, unmolested and absolute master, as the special pet of the authorities. To kill one of them is a high misdemeanor; and the negroes used to look upon them as little less than sacred animals.

The *Oriole* deserves a place among American birds only as far as the variety peculiar to this continent differs slightly from the European, having a rich orange where the other has pale yellow, and deserving therefore, best of all, its name, derived from *aureolus*, the golden. It is also known as *Baltimore-Oriole* (Icterus baltimore) from the numbers found near that city, and as *Hangbird* from its peculiar nest, of which C. F. Hoffman sings—

> "Where the *Oriole's* pendant nest, high up,
> Is rock'd on the swaying trees."

The name occurs already in Bailey's Dictionary (1730), under the Mexican word, "Xochaitotl, a bird in America . . . called the Hang Nest or Hang Bird," and hence J. R. Lowell says correctly;

> "The six old willows at the causey's end,
> Striped here and there with many a long-drawn thread,
> Where streamed, through leafy chinks, the trembling red,
> Past which, in one bright trail, the *hangbird's* flashes blend."
> (*An Indian Summer Reverie.*)

The *Whip-Poor-Will* (Antrostomus vociferus) is, on the contrary, a genuine American bird, and, with his sad, monotonous cry, a striking element in Southern nature as soon as the sun has set. Its utterance is so peculiar, that already the Indians tried an imitation by which to name the bird; they called it *Waw-o-naisa,* while the first Dutch settlers, with a similar purpose, named it *Quok-koree.* Thus also *Whip-poor-will,* universally pronounced *Whipperwill,* is an adaptation rather than an imitation of the original sound, like the Wish-ton-wish, Willy-come-go, and Who-are-you, all names applied to various species. W. Irving already complained of the sound, when "ever and anon was heard the melancholy plaint of the *Whip-Poor-Will,* who, perched on some lone tree, wearied the ear of night with his unceasing moan" (Knickerbocker, *History of New York,* p. 231), and J. K. Paulding speaks in like strains of

> "The lonely *Whip-Poor-Will,* our bird of night,
> Ever unseen, yet ever seeming near,
> His shrill note quaver'd in the startled ear."

Audubon used another name, familiar to the Southern States, and said: "No sooner has night fallen and the nocturnal insects emerged from their burrows, than the sound *Chuck-Will's-Widow,* repeated with great clearness and power, six or seven times in as many seconds, strikes the ear." (*Ornithology,* I., p. 273, *B.*) The only vulgar name of the poor, solitary bird is *Bull-Bat*—the large bat—and this may have instinctively led to the adoption of a similar term, *Cow-bird,* or *Cowpen-bird,* for another bobolink (Molothrus pecoris); the former in allusion to the prevailing notion, that the bird loves to seat himself on the backs of cattle and to rid them of vermin; the other from the preference they show to *cowpens* (pronounced coppen) as the enclosures for cattle are frequently called in the South. Another far more respectable relative is the *Brown Thrush* (Harporhynchus longicauda), an American thrush endowed with fair musical talents, and hence popularly known also as the Ground or Mountain Mocking-Bird, from its habit of slipping stealthily through the bushes, close to the ground. It has curiously enough, in addition, the name of *Thrasher* (probably a variation of Thrush), and it appears as such in many authors: "I love the city as dearly as a *brown thrasher* loves the green tree that sheltered its young." (*C. Mathews*, p. 125, *B.*) Less loved, but hardly less pleasing, is the song of the thrush, which is popularly known as the *Veery* (Turdus wilsoni), common in Massachusetts and in autumn in Virginia, mentioned thus: "The singular, quaint, and musical song of this querulous species." (Nuttall, *Ornithology*, I., p. 397.) The *Bull-bat* is a night-hawk (Caprimulgus americanus), marked by its wide and capacious mouth, and called *bull-bat* by the common people because of its nocturnal habits, in which it resembles bats, and its large size and fierce movements.

Our *Robin* (Turdus migratorius), a useful bird, destroying incredible numbers of grubs, is not to be confounded with its English namesake, which it resembles slightly. "The Red-breasted Thrush, which in New England we used to call the *Blackbird* (the English blackbird being also a thrush) and in Canada the *Robin.*" (P. H. Gosse, *Letters from Alabama*, p. 295.)

Another bird, the English name of which is an imitation of its peculiar cry, and which we frequently find misapplied in this country, is the European *Pewit* or lapwing, which is not at all known in America, and yet often quoted. Even W. Irving seems to have been so little mindful of the birds of his beautiful home as to write: "The *Pewit* or *Pe-wee* or *Phoebe*-bird, for he is called by each of these names." (*Knickerbocker Magazine*, May, 1839, p. 434.) He evidently fancied that the familiar fly-catcher, which calls itself and which we call *peewee* (Contopus virens), must be a water-bird, because the English lapwing or green plover calls itself *pewit*. Nor is it much more easily understood how the name of a bird with so marked a cry—whom even the French call on that account familiarly *Dix-huit*—could have been used in rhyming by the Poet-Laureate of England, as if his name sounded *Pu-et.*

Its quaint, jerking motions have procured for it quite a number of popular nicknames, such as *Tilt-Up*, from the tilting of the tail, and *Teter*, pronounced here *teeter* and not as in England *titter*, the see-saw amusement of children on a balanced plank. Here, however, the word is used more extensively for a mental process of the kind, approaching to fretting, so that when Mr. Peabody was to be buried at his native place, a member of the Maine Legislature said: "Mr. Speaker, I am disgusted with the conduct of this House. This funeral at Portland is going to be a grand affair, but when I see this house *tetering* and sea-sawing as if it didn't know its own mind, I declare I wish Mr. Peabody had not died."

The *Humming-Bird* is peculiar to this continent, but strangely diffused over every part of it, so that Professor John Gould could journey from Hudson's Bay to Patagonia and collect numbers everywhere, capturing in all two thousand specimens of two hundred and thirty species. The tiny *Mango* Humming-bird (Trochilus colubris), with its brilliant plumage, sudden, almost ecstatic flight, and inexhaustible energy, is one of the most characteristic as well as most pleasing features of American landscapes, and known familiarly, from the sound caused by the marvellously quick beat of its wings, as *Hum-bird* or *Hummer* simply.

The *Chewink* is only the ground-robin under a more proper name, derived from its note, which in some parts of the Union is reproduced in its equally familiar name of *Towhee*, while the French of Louisiana, in appreciation of its plumpness, call it *grasset*. It is the Pipilo erythrophthalmus, and thus described by P. H. Gosse: "The *Towhe*-Bunting is a prettily marked bird, black above, with white bands on the wings; the sides are chestnut-red and the underparts white. His note resembles the word towhé." (*Letters from Alabama*, p. 297.)

The *Chickadee* (Parus atricapillus), elsewhere known by the quaint title of *Hoary Titmouse*, bears its name also from its utterance: it is the tiny, black-cap titmouse, of which J. R. Lowell says—

"Far distant sounds the hidden *chickadee*,
Close at my side; far distant sound the leaves. . . .
(*An Indian Summer Reverie.*)

The same fate has befallen an aquatic bird, peculiar to this continent (Oxiechus vociferus), whose very sharp and piercing note is represented in the name of *Killdee*, or still more strangely corrupted *Killdeer*, while the harassing sound of a small owl (Ulula acadia), has procured for it the popular name of *Saw-Whet*, from the resemblance it bears to the sharp rasping or filing of a saw.

Dippers are small birds (Hydrobata mexicana; Baird), so called in Europe also, because they dip under water in search of their food; like so many of their class, they also re-appear in different parts of the country under different names, now poetically as *Water Witches*, from the quickness with which they dive after the flash of a gun, and now more energetically than gracefully as *Hell-Divers*. Among such vulgar names is found also *Mud-Hen* or *Marsh-Hen* for the Virginia rail (Rallus crepitans), although the common bluish-black wading-bird, the *Corn-crake* (Fulica), shares with it the name, and deserves it better. Even a tall, likely crane has been dragged down into the mud, as W. Irving tells us: "Squatting himself down on the edge of a pond, catching fish for hours together, and bearing no little resemblance to the notable bird of the crane-family, ycleped *Mud-Poke*." (Knickerbocker, *History of New York*, p. 317.)

In the Far West we meet with one of the most singular birds peculiar to the New World, the *Burrowing Owl* (Pholeoptynx cunicularia), a species of day-owl, well known for its abnormal habits. It lives on the prairies, in the "villages" of the Prairie-dog (Arctomys ludovicianus,) residing in the forsaken burrows. Audubon says of it, "The burrow selected by the *Burrowing Owl* is usually at the foot of a wormwood bush, (Artemisia,) upon the summit of which the owl often perches, and stands for a considerable while. On being approached, they utter a low, chattering sound, start, and skim along the plain. When winged, they make for the nearest burrow, and when once within it, it is impossible to dislodge them."

The *Prairie-Hen* (Cupidonia cupido) has so many names, that Americans themselves will speak of them, not unfrequently, as if there were as many different species to be found in the West. It is quite common to hear them called *grouse*, a family to which they undoubtedly belong, and hence are, even by men of science, occasionally quoted as Pinnated Grouse. In *Heath-hen*, the more familiar heath of Scotland has simply been substituted for prairie; but the *Sage-hen* (Centrocercus urophasianus) of the Northwest, though of the same species, has a much longer tail than the Prairie-hen, carries it differently from the latter, and grows so large that strangers are apt, at first sight, to mistake it for a turkey. "Near Fort Laramie we saw the first *Sage-hens;* they were hard to get at, but Kit Carson soon had two or three hanging at his side, and they made us a feast." (*A Ride with Kit Carson.*) *Sap-suckers* (Picus varius and others) are absurdly so called in the United States, from a belief that they suck the sap of trees, and thus cause them to die—one of the few utterly groundless superstitions peculiar to this country, and in all probability brought here by ignorant foreigners. The *Sora* (Porzana carolina,) so quaintly called *Saurer* by R. Beverley, (*History of Virginia,* p. 135,) has already been mentioned.

The proud name of *King-bird* is very fairly given to the bravest of birds, the *Scissor-tail,* (Tyrannus carolinensis), who comes to us in summer from the far South, and excites the admiration of all, who, in earnest or in sport, attempt to trouble his young. He flies at the intruder with marvellous energy and intrepidity, and does not shrink from attacking even hawks and eagles in defence of his young. The Narragansett Indians and other tribes called him, in appreciation of his bravery, the *Sachem,* while in some parts of the South he is known as *Fieldmartin.* The *Yellow-Hammer* or *Flicker* (Picus amatus), the most beautiful of American woodpeckers, with bright, golden wings, is universally known as *Clape,* from a name bestowed upon him by the first settlers. In western New York he is called characteristically *High-hole,* and in Louisiana as *Pique bois jaune.* The *Yellow-Throat* (Sylvia) derives, in like manner, its name from its golden throat, which utters most pleasing music during pairing-time, while the *Yellow-Bird* (Chrysomistris tristis), also called *Thistle-Bird,* is quite yellow, with black wings. "The *Yellow-bird* begins to occur in restless flocks, flitting from weed to weed with alternate openings and closings of the wings, twittering all the way, very much like our English goldfinch." (P. H. Gosse, *Letters from Alabama,* p. 295.)

In addition to such popular names bestowed upon the more familiar or more striking birds, similar terms are also frequently heard in connection with domestic fowl. The *Pea-Hen* or *Guinea-*

Fowl, for instance, appears often as Guinea-*keet* or *keet*, simply from its peculiar and unpleasant note; a tailless fowl is in Pennsylvania called a *bunty*, and a small speckled kind a *creepy*. (S. S. Haldeman.) But the manner in which the common dung-fowl is treated, deserves special mention and—reprobation. There is little harm, perhaps, in calling a hen a *biddy*, a term already mentioned by Halliwell, and frequently used abroad and with us in calling chickens to feed; but to make from it a *he-biddy* for the cock, and *chickabiddy* for the little ones, is a somewhat violent proceeding. Much better, however, to do this, than in absurd prudishness to shrink from the good old English word *Cock*, and translate it into the unmeaning *Rooster*, as if it were not known that almost all birds are roosters, and hens certainly, quite as much as cocks. Dr. Hyde Clark, perhaps too severely, calls the term *rooster* "an American ladyism for cock," and a recent English writer professes even to have heard a *Rooster* and *Ox* Story in the United States!

It is probably only the effect of carelessness in writing, and the fondness of a certain slipshod style, which introduced the use of *Barnyards* for the fowl most frequently found there; still even a poet, like Fitz G. Halleck, could write to a friend, "I recollect his (Dr. Banks) discovery of an ale-house at Brooklyn, where the English mistress was superior in her choice of *barnyards*, and their cooking." (Mount's *Memoir of F. G. Halleck.*)

Ocean-birds and coast-birds are, of course, not as familiar to the eye of the people at large, and hence comparatively safe from nicknames; but, on the other hand, the want of knowledge concerning them has, especially in the United States, led to a great confusion of names in the case of many varieties. The *Broad-Bill* (Fulix marila), for instance, which in October appears in large numbers on the Eastern coast, is called a *Black-Head* on the Chesapeake Bay, and a *Raft-Duck* in Virginia, while the most highly prized of all ducks, the pride of the American kitchen, is known from its color as the *Canvas-Back* (Aythya vallisneriana) wherever it appears on the coast of the Middle States. The *Lawyer* is the little, black-necked stilt (Himantopus nigricolus), whom the people of New Jersey are reported to have wittily nicknamed thus "on account of its long bill" (*B*), although Stilt and *Long-Shanks* are far more obvious names.

The *Loon* (Colymbus torquatus), generally called the *Black Swimmer*, deserves mention here only because of the many terms and phrases derived from its peculiarities which have been transferred to our speech, more even than to colloquial English. Thus the phrase, "straight as a loon's leg," has already been suggested, and to call a man a *loon* is a common term of contempt, though it must not be overlooked that the word has repeatedly been explained as a corruption of a *low one*, probably upon no better ground than the fact that Grose, in his Vocabulary, writes it also *lown*. The *Old Wives*, of our coast, are probably of two different kinds, for Sonnini gives that term as the name of sea-gulls in South Carolina, while other authorities state that the Brown Duck (Harelda glacialis) is popularly known by that name. It has also the still more equivocal title of *Old Squaw* in some of the New England States. The *Whistler* or *Whistle-Wing* (Bucephala americana) is, on the other hand, a duck well known on the Susquehanna and in Canada, though generally quoted as the *Golden Eye*. "The silence of the forest was unbroken save by the whirring sound of the large white and gray duck called by the frequenters of these lonely waters the *Whistle-Wing*." (Mrs. Trail, *The Canadian Crusoes*, p. 230.)

If the names of birds are not always easily traced, owing to their diversity in different parts of the Union, the difficulty is still greater in the case of *fish*, which are bound to certain localities, the seashore, the great lakes, or a few rivers or brooks, and hence are apt to appear under a variety of names. Only such will, therefore, here be mentioned as are more generally known, and whose names may be said, to some extent, to have established their claim as being considered a part of our speech.

One of the most ill-treated of the kind is perhaps the *sunfish* (Pomotis vulgaris), whose name is borne alike by a shark and a sea-monster, looking more like the dissevered head of a fish than an entire animal. The little perch, however, deserves its name, for it is a beautiful, glittering creature, although J. R. Lowell sneers at him under two other names which he likewise bears:

"Lazy as the *bream*,
Whose only business is to head up the stream,
(We call him *punkin-seed*.)"

(*Biglow Papers*, II., p. 38.)

The latter name the fish earns from the curious spots on its sides, which to a lively imagination look somewhat like pumpkin-seed; but to the name of *Bream*, used in New England, it has no title whatever. In other States it re-appears even as a pond-perch, a tobacco-box, and as a roach. (S. S. Haldeman.)

The most remarkable of sweet-water fishes, known by an odd English name, is the *Stone-Toter*, mentioned thus by J. K. Paulding: "The most singular fish in this part of the world (the Valley of Virginia) is called the *Stone-toter*, whose brow is surmounted with several sharp little horns, by the aid of which he *totes* small flat stones from one part of the brook to another more quiet, in order to make a snug little enclosure for his lady to lie in in safety." (*Letters from the South*, II., p. 4.) This is probably the Stickleback (a Gasterosteus), who builds his nest in the manner indicated by the author, though a mullet also is occasionally called by that name.

One of the most common fish of the United States is the *Cat-fish* (Pimelodus, of several species), which hence enjoys a number of aliases; its popular name being simply *Cat*, or *Catty*: "He'll fetch you up like a *catty* on a cork-line—jerk!" (J. C. Neal, *Char-coal Sketches.*) Its thick head, with its long feelers, has procured for it the names of *Bullhead* and *Horned Pout*, while a species is known also as *Mudpout*, from its preference for the mud of rivers and creeks, and irreverently, from its black color perhaps, as *Minister*.

The Catfish of the Mississippi sometimes grows to a length of three or four feet, and strikes with great force any object that comes in its way, endangering even the safety of a canoe. The *Chub* and the *Blackfish* are but local names for the *Tautog*, of whom mention has been made under the head of Indian words.

The *Gar*, so called from the resemblance its long, slender body and sharp-pointed head bear to a spear or dart, called *gar* in Anglo-Saxon and old English, is represented in American waters by several species, the *Banded garfish* (Belone truncata) of the coast, also known as *Bill-Fish*, and a pike-like fish (Lepidosteus), found in fresh waters. The latter is a formidable animal, half fish, half reptile, having rhombic scales, and found only in the lakes and rivers of Western America. It has, besides, an air-bladder that serves almost the purposes of a lung, and it can thus live longer out of water than any other fish. He is, as they described him to Sir C. Lyell, "a happy fellow, and beats all creation; he can hurt everything and nothing can hurt him." Growing sometimes to a length of ten feet, he is said not to shrink from encountering an alligator even, although his name of *Alligator Gar* refers less to these hostile meetings than to his resemblance to the reptile. The *Blue Perch,* also known as *Nibbler,* from the wicked delight he seems to take in nibbling off the fisherman's bait, and as *Conner* on the coast of New England, is the *Burgall* mentioned elsewhere, as the *Bony Fish* is the famous *Menhaden,* called *Hardhead* in the State of Maine.

The *Bubbler* deserves his name well, for when drawn from the waters of the Ohio, which he frequents, he makes an extraordinary bubbling noise, as if protesting against such ill-treatment, just as the *Croaker* does, in his way, when caught in the bays and inlets of the Gulf of Mexico. Among fishes, as among birds, we meet with a *Lawyer* (Lota), so called in Canada, we are told by the fishermen there, "because he ain't of much use, and the slipperiest fish that swims." (J. Hammond, *Wild Northern Scenes, B.*) The *Lake-Lawyer* (Amia) is the Mud-Fish of Western waters, so called from its "ferocious looks and voracious habits" (Dr. Kirtland, *B.*), while in the lakes the same qualities have procured for him the name of *Dog-Fish.* The *Red-Horse* (Catostomus duquesnii), a sucker, found in the Ohio and its tributaries, derives its odd name from its red color and large size.

Among saltwater-fish, the *Sheepshead* (Sparus ovis), is probably the most highly esteemed for the table; the name is not improperly derived from the resemblance of his head and teeth to that of a sheep. *Rock-Fish,* also not unfrequently called *rock* simply (Labrax lineatus), is highly esteemed; it is caught in American rivers, which it ascends, and differs from the *sea-bass,* which abounds in the Atlantic, and belongs to the perches. The *Rock* is beautifully marked with seven or eight black lines on a silver-bright ground, and hence is generally known as *Striped Bass,* a great delicacy in the opinion of connoisseurs. The *Sea-Robin* has its strange name from the striking resemblance it bears to a bird, as with long, outstretched, pectoral fins it floats along under water as if poised upon two broad wings. This peculiarity has also procured for it the name of *Flying Fish,* while a very strange grunting noise, which it makes when caught, has led to its being called the *Pig-Fish* on other parts of the coast. The *Rusty Dab* (Platessa ferruginea) is the popular name of one of the flat-fishes, caught on the coasts of Massachusetts and New York, where also a small mackerel is called a *tinker*, while a small shad of inferior quality is contemptuously dubbed a *tailor*—the Blue-fish (Temnodon saltator) of the Lower Potomac being a *Saltwater-Tailor*.

The *Rudder-fish* (Palinurus perciformis) abounds on the southern part of our Atlantic coast, and is thus referred to: "That splendid creature, the coryphene or dolphin of mariners . . . the spotted *rudder-fish* and the purple-banded pilot were often seen beneath the stern." (P. H. Gosse, *Letters from Alabama*, London, 1859, p. 11.) Another fish with remarkable spots is the *Groper* (Serranus erythrogaster), which is found near Florida. "The most numerous kind was a thick-set fish of considerable size, called a *groper*, covered with olive-colored irregular spots; the inside of the mouth and throat was of a brilliant vermilion." (P. H. Gosse, *Letters, &c.*, p. 18.) It does not clearly appear how the *Yellow-Tail* obtained its name, since this remarkable creature, which is only occasionally seen on our coasts, has a pale, crimson tail, which contrasts beautifully with the long bands of delicate pink and yellow marked alternately on its body.

The *King-Fish* (Umbrina alburnus), a sea-fish four or five feet long, and thus called at New York, re-appears as *Whiting* in South Carolina and Florida, while the familiar *Halibut* in many parts of the United States recovers its original name *Holibut*; for Phillips in his *World of Worlds* takes great pains to make us aware that the proper name of the fish is *Holy But*, and Bailey also quotes it as *holibut* in his Dictionary.

The *Clubtail* is nothing but a shad, whose tail is swollen with the great amount of fat which he is apt to accumulate at certain seasons of the year; the name is nearly limited to the Carolina coast, where the fish is taken in large numbers. *Coverclip* is the curious name by which the sole is known in the waters of New York; but even more mysterious is that of *Calico*, which may be heard quite as frequently. One of the most remarkable of American fishes is the *Angler* (Lophius americanus), so called from its long feelers, which it protrudes from its hiding-place in the mud for the purpose of attracting the smaller fry on which it feeds. A more popular name is *Devil-Fish* or *Sea-Devil*, a name to which it is not entitled, as that belongs to the gigantic ray (Cephaloptera vampyrus), which has earned it by its hideous form and cunning devices. This is the *stingray*, or, as it is often mis-named, *stingaree*, which excited the utmost amazement among the early settlers. Captain John Smith writes: "Our captaine taking a fish from his sword (not knowing her condition), being much of the fashion of a Thornback, but a long tayle like a riding-rodde, where on the middest is a most poysoned sting, of two or three inches long, bearded like a saw on each side, which she strucke into the wriste of his arme neare an inch and a half; no bloud nor wounde was seene, but a little blew spotte; but the torment was instantly so extreame, that in 4 houres we all with much sorrow concluded his funerall and prepared his grave in an Island by. Yet it pleased God by a precious oyle Dr. Russell at fyrst applyed to it, his tormenting paine was so well asswaged that he eate of the fish to his supper, which gave no less joy and content to us than ease to himself, for which we called the Island *Stingrai*-Isle, after the name of the fish." The huge creature grows in the waters of Florida to such a size that Dr. Stover, of Boston, once captured one eighteen feet broad and seventeen feet long, with a tail of the same length.

One of the remarkable family of fishes, whose skin is granulated like a file, and which are hence known as File-Fishes (Balistes), has in addition the uncomplimentary name of *Fool-Fish*, because of the extremely odd manner in which it swims, the body being sunk below the surface and the open mouth on a level with the water—a position which gives to the poor, wriggling creature an appearance of extreme stupidity. The *Frost-Fish* is the Tomcod, mentioned elsewhere, and so called from its appearance on the coast during the winter months.

There are few more splendidly-colored creatures in the world than some of our American fish, and among them the Southern *King-Fish* (Lampris guttatus), or *Opah*, stands foremost. Its steel-blue back contrasts strangely with its bright green sides, while the remaining parts are of delicate rose-color; its flesh is as palatable as its appearance is gorgeous. On the coast of New Jersey the fish is known by its more modest name of *Hake*.

"Fish of all kind inhabit here
And throng the dark abode;
Here haddock, *hake*, and flounders are,
And eels and perch and cod."
(Joseph Green. *Burlesque on M. Byles*, 1788.)

A peculiar name is that of the *Lafayette* (Leistormus obliquus), which arose from the fact that this delicious sea-fish one summer arrived in the waters of New York precisely at the same time when General Lafayette paid his last visit to this country. (Dr. S. F. Baird.) It abounds mainly on the coast of New Jersey, and, as people there appreciate the delicacy fully, it is also called *Cape May Goody*.

Herrings appear in America under such a variety of names that it is often very difficult to identify the precise species. Besides the common *American Herring* (Clupea elongata), which differs from the European species, this name is applied to various genera, which have no other claim to it but a distant resemblance. Such is the *Moon-Eye* (Hyodon tergisus), also known as lake and river herring, and as toothed herring, the *Shad-Herring* (Chatoëssus signifer), sometimes called thread herring, or threadfish, and the *Herring-Salmon* (Coregonus clupeiformis), which appears often as Shad salmon, and even White fish. The *Pencil*-Fish, a small fish of the Pacific coast, also loses its identity not unfrequently in the same manner, while the genuine herring has given its own name to the well-known *Herring Gull* (Larus smithsonianus) of the Atlantic coast.

Oulachan (Mallotus pacificus; Richardson), is the native name, often misrepresented as Hoolikan, and even Eulachon, of a small salmonoid fish of the Pacific coast, thus described by good authority: "*Hoolikans*, sometimes called *Eulachons*, very delicious fishes of the size of small herring, come in April in shoals as far south as the mouth of the Columbia. Flocks of sea-gulls herald their march by hovering over the column and swooping down on it. Up the rivers they follow the fish, screeching and swooping. The *hoolikans* are so fat as to baffle ordinary methods of cooking them for the table. Oil is expressed from them by the Indians in large quantities and sold up and down the coast." (S. Wilkeson, *Christian Union*, March 22, 1871.) W. Irving reported the same fish as "about six inches long, called by the natives the *Uthlecan*, and resembling the smelt." (*Astoria*, II., p. 79.)

The *Toadfish* (Batrachus tau), allied to the fishing-frog and resembling it in repulsive ugliness, appears also as *Oyster-fish* on the coast of New Jersey, where it is found to frequent the oyster-beds, and as *Grubley* on the coast of New England. A rival in appearance at least is the *Horned sucker*, also known as *Chub-sucker* (Catostomus storer), sucking with the lips, and thus distinguished from the *remora*, which sucks by means of a remarkable disk upon the head, and thus fastens itself to other large fishes or the bottom of vessels.

The lower animals are either not sufficiently known to the people at large to obtain correct or even significant names, or they have, when referred to by well-informed persons, the names they bear in England. The most characteristic of this class, as is best known abroad, is probably the *Rattlesnake* (Crotalus durissus; Linn.), which was at an early period of the republic chosen as the national emblem. For when the first fleet of the United States sailed on the 17th February, 1776, from the Capes of Delaware, the vessels bore a yellow flag containing a rattlesnake in the act of striking, with the motto, "Don't tread on me," and under the same emblem the troops of South Carolina fought for some time. It was more than a year before the unpleasant flag was superseded by the Stars and Stripes, "representing a new constellation." (Act of Congress, June 14th, 1777.)

The rival of this formidable snake is the *Copperhead* (Trigonocephalus contortrix), which rejoices in nearly a dozen names, having apparently a different one in every part of the country. It is known as Copperbelly and Chunkhead, as Red Viper, Adder, and Deaf Adder, even as Dumb Rattlesnake, because it does not give the warning before it strikes, on account of which chivalrous challenge the Indians call the rattlesnake a Brave. The *Cotton-Mouth*, probably the same as the famous *Moccasin* Snake, is an equally dangerous snake of Arkansas, while the true *Copperbelly* (Nerodia erythogaster) is perfectly harmless and of aquatic habits.

Turtles also and tortoises abound, especially in the Middle and Southern States, the land-tortoises appearing under the fanciful shape of *tortles* in Pennsylvania, to distinguish them from turtle-doves, which are never thus designated.

Swam Bo-si-ka-do the turtle,
Swam behind him with the baggage,
Zhin-ga-den-i-quan the *tortle*.
Old Mik'nâk was drown'd quite early—
Mikenâk—terrestrial tortoise,
Whose ancestral home is standing
Where Mishinimâkinong lies.
(*MS.* additions to Ward's *Higher Water*.)

Hence the verb to *tortle*, to move off in the awkward manner of a turtle, which J. C. Neal uses in the phrase: "Now, you two hook to one another like two Siameses and mosey. . . . *Tortle* off, it's slick going, 'specially if you're going down." (*Charcoal Sketches*, I., p. 77.) The *Turtle* ordinarily is the marine tortoise, and is said to have received its name from the French *tortue*, Latin *tortus*, from its crooked feet. In old writers it is frequently written *turkle*, and may, after all, be nothing more than a corruption of the word tortoise. The *Mud-Turtle* (Sternothuerus odorata), is a common variety, found in swamps and marshes, while the *Snapping Turtle* (a Chelonura), also called simply *Snapper*, is a ferocious kind, snapping at everything, and inflicting a painful bite. "Yesterday, much amusement was created at 'Change by a pickpocket, who investigated a gentleman's pocket and found his hand suddenly caught by a fierce snapping-turtle. It appears the gentleman had recently been robbed of his pocketbook, and adopted this method to catch the thief." (Philadelphia *Ledger*, June 17, 1851.) Another tortoise of greater size and equal ferocity is the *Softback* (Trionyx ferox). *Terrapins*, said to be so called from the French terrapène (?), are salt-water turtles, highly valued by epicures for their delicious flesh; they are most frequent in the salt-water marshes of the Middle States, and Baltimore, especially, was long famous for its terrapin stews.

The innumerable hosts of lizards, living in the water and on land, which are found in the United States, pass in the same manner under such a variety of names in different States that it is often impossible to identify the precise species. It is curious, however, that water-lizards especially should be so often compared to dogs. One large species, a salamander, with smooth, naked body, appears thus as *Water-Dog* in the West, while others are indifferently called *Water-Puppies* and *Ground-Puppies*. The smaller kinds are known in the Eastern States as *Spring-Keeper*, from a boyish notion that they guard the springs in which they are generally found. They even enter the *spring-houses*, small buildings erected over a spring to keep milk and fresh meat, by placing the vessels in shallow troughs, through which the water runs; a term not mentioned even in Loudoun's *Encyclopædia of Agriculture.* (S. S. Haldeman.) The term *Salamander* is, on the other hand, without any ostensible reason, transferred from the real owner to a pouched rat (Geomys pinetis), common in some of the Southern States, while the name, as bestowed upon safes, *Salamander Safes*, is quite appropriate, being suggestive of the ability of these huge iron boxes to withstand, like the fabled salamander of old, the action of the fire. *Fast-Runner* is the well-deserved name of a lizard (Tachydromus sexlineatus) which combines with great beauty wonderful swiftness of motion.

In Virginia, and the Southern States generally, almost all active wood-lizards are called *scorpions*. "There are three or four species," says P. H. Gosse, "the most common of which is called, by a strange misnomer, the *scorpion* (Agama undulata), and it is this species which so rapidly scuttles along under the crisped leaves." (*Letters from Alabama*, p. 48.)

Hellbender is the energetic name of the American Salamander (Menopoma alleghaniensis), an aquatic reptile, often eighteen inches long, and so called on account of its extraordinary hideousness.

Reference has already been made to the curious variety of crabs, known here as *Fiddlers*, small, gray, one-armed crabs, who scuttle and dodge about as jerkingly and nimbly as a fiddler's bow, whence their familiar name. At the time of their annual marches they proceed, each male with his large claw raised in front like an immense club; the poor females have no such large arm, and march under the protection of the males. These little creatures are, however, under Providence, made useful, for we learn that "the ditches in the land near the Mississippi would not suffice to carry off the fresh water during the high water of spring and early summer, were they not aided by the myriads upon myriads of *fiddlers*, everywhere boring into the soil and honeycombing it with innumerable chambers and passages." (*Putnam's Magazine*, May, 1869.) When the poor crab is undergoing the painful process of changing its armor, and hides its sensitive naked body, it is called a *Shedder*, and eagerly sought after to appear as a great delicacy on the table under the name of *Soft Crabs*, or *Soft-shell Crabs*. The King-Crab of England is known here as *Horsefoot* (Limulus polyphemus), having somewhat the form of a horse-shoe; it is so common on the Atlantic coast from Canada to Virginia as frequently to be used for manure. The *Bullfrog* (Rana pipiens) excited at a very early period of American history the greatest amazement abroad, for John Josselyn reported in 1672 already, that in Virginia not only barley changed readily into oats, but "frogs were found on river-banks and edges of ponds, a foot high." (*New England's Rarities Discovered*, p. 73.) Another writer recently spoke of his amazement when he first heard, "mingled with the batrachian chorus, an occasional dissonant croak, deep, heavy, and of such roaring volume as to deceive Taurus himself;" for the *bullfrog's* potent voice at times really resembles the low roar of a bellowing bull.

The American *Locust* is not the same insect as that which is so called in Europe, but a cicada or harvest-fly, instead of a grasshopper, of which J. R. Lowell says,

> "The *locust's* shrill alarum stings the ear."

The genuine locust is, of course, not unknown to this continent, and there are several allied species found here, one of which is very numerous and terribly destructive in Utah, so that it is only kept in abeyance, "thanks to the beneficial gluttony of the gulls, those beautiful birds of a bountiful God," as Brigham Young once said in one of his sermons. A variety, very different indeed (Cicada septendecim), which appears only every seventeen years, and ought not to be confounded with the former, struck already the first settlers with surprise; an anonymous description of Bacon's Rebellion, dated July 13, 1705, says: "The third strange appearance were swarms of flies, about one inch long and big as the top of a man's little finger, rising out of spigot-holes in the earth, which eat the new sprouted leaves from the tops of the trees, without doing other harm, and in a month left us."

A species of grasshopper (Cyrtophyllum concavum) has obtained the quaint name of *Katydid*, in imitation of the peculiar noise which the male makes in autumn toward evening, by means of the membranes of his wing-covers. The harsh, grating sound is nevertheless almost articulate, and hence easily interpreted as meaning *Katy did*, the answer being, in children's views, *Katy didn't.*

" The nights grow cool,
And see-saw *Katydids* foretell the chill
Of leafless forest and of icy pool."
(C. P. Cranch. *Summer Pictures.*)

An English traveller heard the concert differently: "A large species of gryllus," he writes, "called provincially *Katedid*, fills the air with its nightly music, such as it is. Fancy a score or two of people with shrill voices, divided into pairs, each pair squabbling with each other, I did!—You didn't!—I did!—You didn't! the objurgation maintained with the most amusing pertinacity, and without a moment's intermission, on every side." (P. H. Gosse, *Letters from Alabama*, p. 183.)

Another variety shares with a species of Dragonfly the name of *Devil's Darning-Needle*, provincially known in England as the Devil's Needle (Wright), while the common Mantis is at the South graphically designated as the *Rearhorse*, from its odd way of rising on its hind-legs.

Yellow-jacket is the familiar and descriptive name of a small hornet (Pelopsus), and of the Sand-wasp (Ammophila), one of whose cousins is familiarly known by the name of *Dauber*, from the manner in which he builds his nest, literally daubing it all over, so as to make it waterproof, and quite a strong structure. "I watched," says P. H. Gosse, "with much interest the proceedings of a *Dauber* in building her mud-cell; it is a pretty species" (Pelopsus flavipes). (*Letters from Alabama*, 1859.) Both of these insects are endowed with formidable powers of stinging, and yet but little more dreaded than the *Gallinipper*, a very large mosquito, quite common in the South and West. The term is usually derived from *gall* and *nip*, but it seems more likely that the first part of the word originated, like the *gallibagger* of the Exmoor dialect (Grose), from the provincial expression *gallier*, which means to fight, and *galliment*, a great fight. An English traveller relates how a huge, brawny deck-hand, on board a Mississippi steamer, once offered to lie naked on deck, and endure the stings of all the mosquitoes that might settle on him, without wincing, if the traveller and his friends, who had wagered large sums on the question, would keep off the gallinippers. He lay there several minutes, covered with ravenous insects, and among them several of the latter species, when the narrator, to test his powers of endurance, applied the burning end of his cigar to the poor fellow's back. He jumped up with a terrific oath, exclaiming: "Did you not promise to keep off those *gallinippers?*"

The *Hessian Fly* (Cecidomyia destructor; Say), a small midge, very destructive to young wheat, is said to owe its name to the popular notion that it was first imported into America in the straw-beds of Hessian soldiers, enlisted by the British Government during the Revolutionary War. It is certain that the insect first appeared on Staten Island, and in 1796 in Virginia, thus making its way gradually over the whole country; but its precise mode of introduction can now no longer be positively ascertained. The *Midget* of Canada and some of the Northern States, is the *Sand-fly* of Europe, as *Moth* is in the United States commonly restricted to the domestic pest, while the night-flying Lepidoptera are erroneously called *Butterflies*, and the Coleoptera *Bugs*. English writers are apt to amuse themselves at the American habit of calling their beetles *bugs*, but forget their own great poet's lines:

> "Let me flap this *bug* with gilded wings,
> This painted child of dirt, that stinks and stings."
> (*Pope.*)

We speak thus of May-bugs and June-bugs, of Golden Bugs and even of Lightning-Bugs, instead of fireflies, and the only bug of English usage (Cimex) passes, in the South especially, under its Spanish name of *Chinch*, brought from the West Indies. "*Chintses* (so buggs are by the Negroes and by some others called, in Jamaica)." (John Southall, *A Treatise of Buggs*, London, 173–.)

Persons of great wealth and distinction are irreverently called *Big Bugs*, and "I-street, in Washington," is thus said to "be inhabited by the foreign ambassadors and other *big bugs*." J. C. Neal makes a nice distinction when he says of a rich man without social importance: "He is one of your *big bugs*, with more money than sense." (*Charcoal Sketches*, III., p. 117.)

The word "stag" is very rarely used in America, *deer* being almost universally employed for the purpose; the Stag-Beetle (Lucanus) of England also re-appears here as *Hornbug;* the small beetle which lives and feeds upon pease as *Peabug*, and the German Petz Keffer (Petz-käfer) of Pennsylvania has been Americanized by a third metamorphosis into *Pinchbug*, while the larva of the ant-lion is, in Virginia, called *Hoodlebug*.

The honey-bee is, of course, a European importation, and was early known to the Indians as the *white man's fly*, because it generally preceded even the first settlers of the new race. The only truly native honey-makers are the burly, dozing *bumble-bees* of several species, of which R. W. Emerson sings:

"When the Southern wind in May-days
With a net of shining haze
Silvers the horizon wall,
And with softness touching all,
Tints the human countenance
With a color of romance,
And, infusing subtle heats,
Turns the sod to violets,
Thou, in sunny solitudes
Rover of the underwoods,
The green silence dost displace
With thy mellow, breezy bass."

Etymologists generally see in the name the Greek *Βομβύλιος*, and refer it, moreover, to the name of the genus *Bombus*, to which the insect belongs. In Scotland, the sound of the bee is called bumming, and hence the insect was first called *Bum-bee*, and then *Bumble-bee*, the second *b* having been produced by eduction. The name thus written occurs already in Barham in the line, "Black Beetles and *Bumble Bees*, Bluebottle Flies" (*The Knight and the Lady*), and the German verb *bummeln* strengthens the theory. Nevertheless, a fallacious opinion is entertained that the name is a corruption of *Humble Bee*, connected with the German word for it, which is *Hummel*, and derived from the Scotch hummel, which originally means hornless, and makes *hummel-cow* a cow without horns, but in this case implies the want of a sting. Both terms are in use in the United States, the latter especially in the South.

Another native insect is the *Squash-Bug* (Coreus tristis), a common species, so called because of its destructive power in eating the vines of squashes and melons; the *Tumble*-bug (Canthon

17*

lolvis) akin to the sacred scarabæus of the Egyptians, who so industriously rolls his balls of dung on dusty roads and lonely paths; the *Sand-flea* or *Sand-hopper* (Orchestra), dwelling on the seacoast of Long Island and other sandy places, where he diverts children by his sudden and energetic leaps, by which he tries to escape pursuit; and the *Seed-tick*, a minute and noxious Ixodes, which burrows in the skin, and produces often very serious inconvenience. The whole company is designated by the poet above as "sandfleas, junkies, and greenheads." The Seed-tick is, in all probability, the same insect as the hated *Jigger* or *Chigre*, of Kentucky, which has derived its name from the genuine *Chico* of the West Indies (Pulex penetrans), but does not, like the latter, cause torment by depositing its eggs under the skin of the feet, particularly the toes, which often produces quite formidable sores. They are so numerous and perpetually present in the South, that they have their changing nomenclature according to age. "The first season they are called *Seed*-ticks, the next year they become *Yearling*-ticks, and the third, *Old*-ticks." (P. H. Gosse, *Letters from Alabama*, p. 220.)

Plants have the privilege in every country on earth of appearing in a double character: with a scientific name, useful, but known only to the botanist, and with a homely name, familiar to all, and generally derived from some peculiarity of form or color, or some medicinal virtue, ascribed to them from experience, or, more frequently, from superstition. This is, perhaps, more generally the case in America than in Europe, because the first settlers were rarely acquainted with botanical names, and, on the other hand, very careful observers of every new tree or shrub, flower or root, they met, always expecting to make some valuable discovery, when they did not apprehend a new danger. Thus they were naturally led to name new plants from those features in their appearance that struck them most forcibly, or from the manner in which they could make them useful in the field or the house.

The *herbs* of the land suffer under the unfortunate tendency Americans have to soften initial vowels by an additional *y.*; as they say *year* for ear, and even *yere* for here, chiefly in Maryland and southward, so they also say over a wider region, *yarb* very generally for herb, and *yarb-tea* is a very common article, especially in the New England States. "Then we had an Erie Railroad 'splendid breakfast:' bean-coffee, *yerb*-tea, leather-steak, and rain-water milk." (New York *Tribune*, January 23, 1871.) That article of *tea* is altogether a great mystery in the United States. While their fast clippers bring fresh teas in enormous quantities, and the new railway from the Pacific enables the best qualities to reach the great markets in still shorter time after the crop has been gathered, Americans drink perhaps a greater variety of decoctions under the name of tea than any other nation. It was a great puzzle to benevolent ladies, who, at the beginning of the late Civil War, tried to make themselves useful in tending and nursing the wounded soldiers. The question, "Will you have a cup of tea?" was very apt to elicit the counter-question, "What kind of tea have you got? sage- or sass- or store-tea?" It was soon discovered that *store*-tea was all over the interior of the country the name for genuine tea, or at least such as is sold under that title in "stores." *Tay*, however, they pronounced it, the Irish of Swift—

> "And sneers as learnedly as they
> Like females o'er their morning *tea*,"

whenever they were Southerners, following here also the good old English custom, derived from the Chinese—

> "Here, thou great Amra, whom three realms obey,
> Dost sometimes counsel take, and sometimes *tea*."
>
> (*Pope.*)

Sage-tea and *Mint*-tea were, of course, familiar to all nurses, and *Sass*-tea made itself known as *Sassafras*-tea, a decoction made of the tender shoots and the roots of a laurel (Sassafras officinale), the bark of which has an exceedingly pleasant taste and fragrance, and valuable medicinal properties. *Spice*-tea is, in like manner, made from another laurel common at the South, the *spice-bush* (Laurus benzoin; Linn.), the bark of which is very spicy and much valued in fever, whence it is also known as *Fever-bush*. Under the former name it appears in W. C. Bryant's lines—

> "This tangled thicket on the bank above
> Thy basin, how the waters keep it green!
> There the *spice-bush* lifts
> Her leafy lances." (*The Fountain.*)

Jersey-tea (Ceanothus americana) is known to New Jersey only, and *Bohea*-tea means a dark tea made of every other plant and herb in America—only not of the Chinese shrub known by that name. *South-sea*-tea or *Yopon* (Ilex vomitoria) occurs North and South, and, in spite of its formidable, scientific name, makes a pleasant and slightly intoxicating tea—at least so say the people of North Carolina, in whose State it is indigenous. They dry the leaves by a slow heat and then make an infusion of it, which may be quite palatable, as the plants belong to the same-family from which, in Peru, the famous Maté-tea is prepared. Even distant Labrador is called upon to aid in furnishing a variety of the favorite beverage; at least in the Northwest they have a tea called *Mash*-Tea, and another called *Labrador*-tea, made from two plants (Ledum palustre and Ledum latifolium), the leaves of which possess moderate narcotic qualities, and are said to furnish a pleasant infusion. At the other end of the Union, in Texas, New Mexico, and the adjoining territories, *Santa Fé*-tea is popular, made of the leaves of a plant which has the modest merit of looking like the tea-shrub (Alstonia theaformis), although the likeness does not extend to taste or flavor. In the Far West, at the foot of the Rocky Mountains, grows a shrub known as *Red Root*, which produces a tea not unlike the genuine article, and is said, like the latter, to "cheer and not inebriate." The *sarsaparilla* of the United States is not the Mexican plant (smilax) with its tea and other far-famed preparations, but a variety of the ginseng plant, an Aralia and other herbs, used as substitutes. Teas are made, besides, from balm and elder blossoms, catnip and pennyroyal, horehound and snakeroot (ludicrously written *snecrut* by Signor Boccone, Rayo, 1698). *Dittany* (Cunila mariana) also furnishes a tea, and, as it is apt to grow plentifully in its localities, there is a popular notion that, when one has been found, its leaves will point out the direction of others.

Another preparation of vegetables appears in almost as great a variety of forms, and certainly contains as many different products; this is the famous *sauce*, pronounced generally *sass*, but in Pennsylvania *saas*. The term itself is old, and already in Forby and other glossaries quoted as meaning, vegetables eaten with flesh-meat. But America has given it a far more extended usefulness than it ever had in England, and whilst at home it has almost everywhere, except in Norfolk and a few outlying districts, given way to the modern terms of "garden-stuff" and "garden-ware," it has held its own altogether in the New England States. In the Southern States it is, on the other hand, almost unknown, and its place supplied by *greens*. R. Beverley, nevertheless, used it in speaking of Virginia: "Roots, herbs, vine-fruits and salad-flowers, they dish up in various ways, and find them very delicious *sauce* to their meats, both roasted and boiled, fresh and salt." (*History of Virginia*, p. 217.) Beaumont and Fletcher use *Green Sauce* for vegetables, and hence the Southern usage, which permits, even in the best society, the appearance of *Bacon and Greens*. "You shall have horse to ride and weapon to wear," wrote John Randolph of Roanoke to J. K. Paulding, the novelist, "*bacon and greens*, Virginia fare, and help me make hay in the finest meadows in the world." The *Sass* of New England is scientifically spoken of as *Long Sauce*, when beets, carrots, parsnips, and the like are referred to, and as *Short Sauce*, if onions are meant, and other bulbs; but the variety of *sauces* generally far eclipses even Ude's historic boast, that he could invent a new sauce for every day of the year. W. Irving, therefore, already speaks admiringly of a venerable dame, "deeply skilled in the mystery of making apple-sweetmeats, *long sauce*, and pumpkin pies." (Knickerbocker, *History of New York*, p. 234.) The word is used as a verb also, so that N. Hawthorne could write, "He was a bright-eyed man, but wofully pined away, which was not more than natural if, as some people affirmed, his ordinary diet was fog, morning mist, and a slice of the densest cloud within his reach, *sauced* with moonshine, whenever he could get it." (*The Great Carbuncle.*) Then arose the noun *sauceman*, the green-grocer of other lands, of whom the same author speaks thus: "Behind comes a *sauceman*, driving a wagon full of new potatoes, green ears of corn, beets, carrots, turnips, and summer squashes." (*The Toll-Gatherer's Day.*) By a natural transition the sharp, spicy character of ordinary sauce, with its origin in the Latin term for *salt*, was transferred to an impudent, sharp reply, and the person gifted with the power of readily giving them was called saucy. Thus *sauce*, or in Yankee speech, *sass*, has the same meaning of abuse or impudence of speech, which Halliwell already gives to the term in older times. J. R. Lowell writes it his own way in the lines—

"Of all the *sarse* that I can call to mind,
England does make the most unpleasant kind—"
(*Biglow Papers*, I., p. 58.)

while J. C. Neal uses the more common form: "I've a good mind to strike and be *sassy*," and "Don't give me none of your *sass*, for I don't mind *sass*." (*Charcoal Sketches.*) The term is, of course, not of American origin; *sauce* is to this day used in Essex (England) not only in precisely the same meaning of garden-stuff, but also corrupted there into *sarce* and *sass*, with the meaning of impudence.

The American continent abounds in a number of underground plants, which are frequently made available for some useful purpose, as the early settlers learned it from the Indians. Such is the common *Putty-Root* (Aplectrum hyemale), more generally known by its familiar name of *Adam and Eve*, which it owes to the pair of tuberous roots always found together, though belonging to the growth of different years. The plant is an ὄρχις in Greek, and was in Arabic called khusjut-al-salib (Testiculis vulpis), from which the English *Salep* is derived. The latter, a beverage made from the powdered root of the Orchis, called in England the Red-handed Orchis, with sugar and milk, was formerly much sold in stalls at London at an early morning hour. It is now almost forgotten, having been entirely superseded by the cup offered at modern coffee-stalls, but even Charles Lamb still mentions the bowl of *salep*. (*Slang Dictionary*, p. 218.) The *Alum*-root (Heuchera americana), so called on account of its astringent qualities, used to be formerly much used by herb-doctors, and has not yet entirely been abandoned, as the *Pleurisy*-root (Asclepias tuberosa) is used as a mild tonic and stimulant. The *Blood*-root (Sanguinaria canadensis) has its name from the blood-red juice of its root, but is perhaps more generally known by its Indian name of *Puccoon*, of which R. Beverley already reports: "They have the *puccoon*, with which the Indians used to paint themselves red, and the sumach and sassafras, which make a deep yellow." (*History of Virginia*, p. 238.) The *Bowman's* root (Gillenia trifoliata) is in like manner better known as *Indian Physic*, "a species of American ipecac, and frequently used as a vomit" (S. Kercheval, *History of the Valley of Virginia*, p. 238); "though," he adds, "more frequently a decoction of walnut-bark, which, when used for a purge, was peeled downwards, when used for a vomit it was peeled upwards."(!) *Bread-root* (Psoralea esculenta) is the well-deserved name of a beet-like plant growing abundantly in the Rocky Mountains, and exceeding not unfrequently twenty inches in circumference. The white pulpy substance within is full of farinaceous matter, and furnishes a most palatable and nutritious bread. It has also the name of *Indian Turnip*, having been long used by the Sioux and other tribes of the neighborhood, and a variety of it (Camassia esculenta) that of *Kamas-Root*, the support of the Digger Indians, while the early French hunters called it *Pomme Blanche*, or *Pomme des Prairies*; but it must be held carefully distinct from another *Indian Turnip* (Arum triphyllum), the root of which is acrid, and, when fresh, highly poisonous. One of the thousand pretended remedies for that dread affliction, the cancer, is drawn from a yellowish plant (Orobanche) found in almost all parts of the Union, and hence called *Cancer*-root. The *Pink*-root (Spigelia marilandica) is by no means limited to Maryland, as the name would seem to indicate, but grows far to the South, and is quite generally known as *Carolina Pink* also—a plant bearing very beautiful flowers, and having great medicinal powers as a purgative and a vermifuge. The various plants which furnish, in so-called *Snake*-roots, an antidote against snake-bites, have already been mentioned in connection with snakes. The *Stone-Root* (Collinsonia canadensis), the flowers of which have an odor like lemons, is also known as *Rich Weed* from this fragrance; it is much used in family practice as a diuretic, and is said to enter largely into the manufacture of fashionable stomachics. The *Whiskey*-root suggests its purpose by its name. It is a cactus, growing on the sandy hills along the Rio Grande, and similar districts farther South, and known to the Indians as *Pieoke*. The latter dig up the root, slice it, chew the pieces, and swallow the juice, which has a powerful intoxicating effect. "Our men had found some *Whiskey Plants*, and Jack, having long been with the Indians, taught them at once how to use the delightful treasure: in a few hours they were not only merry, but wild as devils, and we had to guard the corral ourselves all night, for they were utterly unconscious of what they were doing." (*Across the Isthmus.*)

The *Mandrake* of Europe has a namesake on this continent,

which, however, is a very different plant (Podophyllum peltatum). H. T. Tuckerman tells us that there lived in Medford (Massachusetts), more than a hundred years ago, Jane Turrell, who wrote:

> "The blushing peach and glossy plum there lies,
> And with the *mandrake* tempt your hands and eyes."
> (*America and her Commentators*, p. 33.)

The same plant is, outside of New England, generally known as May apple, and thus described in the lines of an American poet:

> "Mysterious plant, that nurse a luscious fruit,
> The star, transformed by summer's sultry air,
> And in the fibres of the long, slim root,
> A potent medicine bear;
> While in each shield, which the pure blossom hides
> So carefully, a poisonous death resides."
> (*W. L. Shoemaker.*)

The same term of *May-Apple* is not unfrequently applied to a large, globular excrescence produced by the sting of a wasp on the miniature flowers of the Swamp Honeysuckle (Azalea mediflora), and, on account of its frequent occurrence, occasionally to the shrub itself.

It is not impossible that the word *Goober* or *Guber* may be connected with the geographical division of the country, as *Guber* is the name of a district in the Haussa (How-sa) country, where the nut abounds, and the Haussa language is in extensive use in trade. In some parts of the United States a kind of chocolate is made of the nut; in others it serves, when parched and beaten with sugar, as a dessert-sweetmeat; while in England it is not only eaten, but used to furnish a valuable and palatable oil.

The potato, from the Spanish *batata*, appears in the United States almost uniformly as the *Irish Potato*, to distinguish it from the native *Sweet* or *Carolina* potato (Batatis edulis), akin to the convolvulus, and so called by Linné. It has, however, given rise to the familiar phrase of *Small Potatoes*, applied in derision to anything mean or petty. It is the agricultural slang-word opposed to *Some Pumpkins*. "Give me an honest old soldier for the Presidency—whether Whig or Democrat—and I will leave your *small-potato* politicians and pettifogging lawyers to those who are willing to submit the destinies of this great nation to such hands." (New York *Herald*.) "All our American poets are but *small potatoes* compared with Bryant," says an enthusiastic admirer of the poet, in the New York *Tribune*. In New England, where potatoes are not as easily raised as in more favored regions, the phrase is occasionally strengthened by an intensifying addition. A Yankee says: "*Small potatoes*—few in a hill—the hills fur apart—and a gra-ate way to go and dig 'em." (Hon. J. H. Trumbull.)

Among peculiar plants of this kind must be noticed also the *Groundnut* (Arachis hypogaea), which has the strange habit of burying its pods underground after flowering, in order to ripen its nuts. Hence it is also known as *Earthnut,* while its most common name at the South, where it is extensively cultivated, is *Peanut,* from the pea-like pod and seed. Among the negroes in Florida it is, moreover, known as *Pinders,* while in Virginia and North Carolina it re-appears as *Goober,* or Gooberpease, and is as such even quoted in market reports.

The *Cowpea* is a genuine pea, and cultivated largely for the same purposes as clover. In Oregon the Chinook Indians live largely on an edible bulb called *Wapatoo* (Sagittaria sagittifolia), which is called *Tuk-hat* in their native dialect, while another root of the same distant region is the *Thistle*-root, mentioned by George Gibbs.

By the side of these underground plants peculiar to the Union, there are numerous berries known here under new or newly-applied names, of which some assume quite an importance as commercial articles. Such are, for instance, *Cranberries* (Oxycoccus macrocarpus), a different variety from that common in Europe, and largely cultivated for the market. They were noticed already by Captain John Smith, though not approved of; for R. B. Beverley tells us that *cranberries* "are of a lively red when gathered and kept in water, and make very good tarts. I believe these are the berries which Captain Smith compared to the English gooseberries, and called *Raw comens,* having perhaps seen them only on the bushes, where they are always very sower." (*History of Virginia,* p. 114.) The *Tree-Cranberry* (Viburnum opulus), also known as *Cramp-Bark,* is not equal to the former, but much relished by lumberers in Northern regions, who cook them with molasses; they played quite a prominent part in the accounts of Arnold's expedition. A third cranberry (Viburnum lentago) gives only a small, shrivelled fruit, which is known as *Cowberry*, and brought to the market in Massachusetts and Canada, mixed with many little stems, very much like raisins, and quite insipid. The French Canadians, however, are fond of them, and call them *cérises*. The *Service-Berry*, called by Sir George Simpson "a sort of cross between the cranberry and the black currant," is the fruit of a shrub (Amelanchier canadensis), which is also called *Shadbush* (see *Shad*), and eaten either alone or mixed with pemmican. General T. F. Meagher says of it: "The *teé-amp*, or *service-berry*, abounding in the Rocky Mountains, has a dull, sweet taste, the richness of which makes most people in this region fond of them. The Indians gather and dry large quantities, and when properly prepared and cooked, they are very palatable and wholesome. They grow upon a bush varying from two to twelve feet high, but seldom exceeding two inches in diameter. The wood is very hard and tough, and is much used by the Indians, who display great skill in straightening it out for arrows and ramrods." (*Rides through Montana.*) In the Southern States, where the *Service-Berry* is quite common, the shrub grows to the size of a respectable tree.

The *Partridge-Berry* (Mitchella repens and Gaultheria procumbens), is the name of two very different plants, of which the former (Mitchella) is tasteless, while the latter is equally bright in color but pleasant to the palate. In the New England States and in Canada it is often called *twin-berry*, from its uniformly double scarlet-berry, while in Eaton's *Botany* this name—and fly-honeysuckle—is given as the English name of Xylosteum ciliatum, and the Xylosteum solonis is called the swamp twin-berry. (S. S. Haldeman.) N. Hawthorne says of it, that "The forest offered her the *partridge-berries*, the growth of the preceding autumn, but ripening only in spring, and now red as drops of blood upon the withered leaves." (*Scarlet Letter.*) It has a rich aromatic flavor and odor, which is made use of in the manufacture of odor, though it is curious that in such cases the odor of the inner bark of the black birch (Betula lenta) can hardly be distinguished from that of the partridge-berries. It is also known as *chequer*-berry, and in New England occasionally as *chick*-berry.

Dew-berries (Rubus canadensis) differ from the English variety in color, being black, and utterly unlike dewdrops, which the English berries represent by a white, wax-like covering; they grow on a low, trailing blackberry, while the black raspberry itself (Rubus occidentalis) is more generally known as *Thimble*-berry, from its resemblance to a thimble. *Bilberries*, a corruption of blueberries, are here as in England only another name for whortleberries, and the same to which Shakespeare refers in the line—

> "There pinch the maids as blue as *bilberry*."

It is, however, maintained, that here also the variety is not the same as the English, but belongs to the division *Euvaccinium*. They are great favorites with American poets, and R. W. Emerson sings of them:

> "Aught unsavory or unclean
> Hath my insect never seen,
> But violets and *bilberry* bells,
> Maple sap and daffodils."
> (*The Humble Bee.*)

With this exception the term *huckleberry* has entirely superseded the old form of *whortleberry*, even when the latter spelling is still retained. This is quite natural, as the old English term *whort*, meaning a small blackberry (Halliwell), is now quite obsolete. Fields in which they grow abundantly are in New England frequently called pastures, and to this custom J. R. Lowell alludes when he says: "The greater part of what is now Cambridgeport, was then, in the native dialect, a *huckleberry pasture*." Very different is the so-called *choke-berry*, in reality the fruit of a low apple-tree (Pyrus arbutifolia), and deserving its name as fully as the *choke-cherry* (Prunus borealis), with which it shares remarkable astringent qualities.

Bayberries are gathered from a plant called wax-myrtle (Myrica cerifera), because its fragrant leaves, resembling those of the myrtle, have an odor like that of the bay; when boiled down they give a fragrant green wax, which is used in making candles and for other purposes. *Hack* berries or *Pompion* berries, on the contrary, are obtained from a shrub, which at times reaches nearly the size of a tree (Celtis occidentalis), and are sweet and edible, not unlike so-called bird-cherries. The queen of them all is said to be the lovely, creeping *snowberry* (Chiogenes hispidula), whose long delicate sprays trail over the bare rock and moss, bearing a fresh white berry, larger than the small, pointed leaves; although others give the prize to the *spice-berry*, the "little, creeping *wintergreen*, with its scarlet berries." (Mrs. Trail, *The Canadian Crusoes*, p. 175.)

Among the so-called *weeds*, we meet with the familiar *Bindweed* of England, referred to by Tennyson in the line—

> "The fragile *bindweeds'* bells and bryony rings"—

which, here as in England, designates the varieties of Convolvulus, while the Black Bryony (Tamus) is called *black bindweed*, and the Smilax *rough bindweed* (Loudon). *Bugle-weed* (Lycopus virginicus) is the name of a plant more commonly known as Virginia hoarhound, and, in the South especially, highly esteemed in affections of the chest; it is taken as a tea or made up in candy. The *Carpet-weed* (Mollugo) is appropriately so called, as it covers the ground, even in cultivated fields, with its small, spreading branches as with a close carpet, while the *Iron-weed* (Vernonia noveboracensis) is, on the contrary, the tallest weed found on the rich blue-grass soil of Kentucky; at the North it is more generally known as *Flat-top*. Perhaps the most familiar of all these plants is the *Jamestown-weed* (Datura stramonium), in the South uniformly called *Jimson-weed* or *Jimson* simply, deriving its name from the ancient town of Jamestown, where it was first observed to grow after its introduction from the West Indies; since then it has spread over all parts of the country, and its beautiful flowers, with their nauseous smell, are seen on every river-bank and in every low place. R. Beverley says of it: "The *Jamestown-weed* is one of the greatest coolers in the world. It being an early plant, was gathered very young for a boiled salad by some of the soldiers, to pacify the troubles of bacon, and some of them eat plentifully of it, the effect of which was a very pleasant comedy; for they turned natural fools upon it for several days." (*History of Virginia*, II. p., 110.) Like all the Daturas, this plant also has certain poisonous properties, which medicine employs as a remedy against asthma and similar diseases; it is a favorite drug with wise old women among the negroes, *Jamestown-weed* being justly held to be one of the most cooling applications known to botanists. R. Beverley derives from this "coldness" a quaint hope of counteracting its poison: "Perhaps," he says, "this was the same herb that Mark Anthony's army met with in his retreat from the Parthian war. . . Wine, as the story says, was found a sovereign remedy for it, which is likely enough, the malignity of the herb being cold." (*History of Virginia*, p. 122.) *Hardhack* is the unpoetical name familiarly bestowed upon a lowly plant (Spirea tomentosa), growing in low grounds and bearing a modest but comely flower, which J. R. Lowell mentions, when he says, "Our narrow New England lanes, shut in by bleak stone walls on either hand, and where no better flowers are to be gathered than goldenrod and *hardhack*."

Briers is the familiar name of all creepers with thorns or prickles, among which ranks the wild raspberry, as well as the trailing spinous brier (Schrankia uncinata), which is so irritable, that the slightest touch makes the leaflets close instantly. It is also known as the *Sensitive Brier*.

The *Pickerel Weed* (Pontideria cordata) owes its fishy name to the superstitious belief, once quite general in England, that it bred pickerel: its arrow-headed leaves and spikes of blue flowers are very attractive in standing waters throughout the Middle States. The *Poke-weed* or *Poke* simply (Phytolacca decandra) is one of the most useful plants of the South, where all its parts are profitably employed: the root for medicinal purposes, the young shoots for the table after the manner of asparagus, and the berries as a favorite dye of rich purple with poor people. *Poke-juice* is occasionally used in beverages, and the *Poke-berry* as food for birds, and other animals. From its great popularity the weed is known by a variety of names, such as *Po-can*, the Indian name in Virginia, from which Poke is derived, as Cocum at the North, and as Garget and *Pigeon-berry* in New England. A peculiar usefulness is that of the *Rosin-weed* (Silphium laciniatum), the leaves of which are supposed to point nearly North and South, and are hence constantly consulted, especially by French voyageurs in their journeys across prairies without landmarks. The weed is on this account also called *Compass-plant*.

To the same class of plants belong a few others not designated as weeds, such as the pretty little *Bluets* (Oldenlandia caerulea), a delicate little herb, which in early spring fills the wood with its tufts of pale-blue flowers, each having a small yellow eye in the centre, known also as *Quakers*. The *Blazing Stars*, on the contrary, represents both a Colchicum and a medicinal plant (Aletris farinosa), which, under the name of *Devil's Bit*, is highly esteemed in the West for its virtues, known to the Indians from of old. The *Boneset* is the familiar name here of the English Thoroughwort (Eupatorium perfoliatum), with its medicinal properties, like the *Fleabane* (Erigeron canadense), which is similarly endowed and largely used by the Shakers in their well-known preparations. Its name is derived from the English fleabane, used for the purpose indicated by the word, and as such mentioned already by Bailey. The Shakers use, in like manner, large quantities of the *Coolwort* (Tiarella cordifolia) and of the *Frostwort* (Cistus canadensis); it derives its peculiar name from the beautiful crystals of ice which late in autumn shoot forth from the cracked bark near the root, and give it the appearance of frostwork. *Horse-nettle* (Solanum carolinense) is the familiar name of a troublesome nettle, a low weed, which in the Southern States is almost universal, and in fall and winter covers the fields with its bright yellow berries, that are often eaten by children, and cause grave inconvenience by their poisonous qualities. The English name *pennyroyal* has in America been transferred to a plant resembling the original mint, but different in kind (Hedeoma pulegioides), which has not only a similar appearance but also the same very peculiar taste and odor. Another plant resembling the pennyroyal of the Union, is known as *Blue Curls* (Trichostema dichotomum), from the peculiar clustering shape and deep blue color of its flowers. They resemble in this the *Ladies' Tresses* (Neottia tortillis) of the Southern States. *Albany Hemp* (Urtica canadensis) derives its name from the fact that in Albany (New York) its fibrous bark was once quite largely used in the manufacture of hemp; while a nettle with succulent, semi-transparent stems is called *Clearweed* (Pilea pumila). The *Everlasting* (Gnaphalium), or *Cudweed*, is the American representative of the Immortelle of Europe in name and peculiarities; "herb-doctors" alone ascribe the name to a pretended virtue of the herb to prolong life indefinitely. *Lamb's Quarter* is the equally quaint name of an herb (Chenopodium album) once supposed to be of special excellency for young lambs' food, making them rapidly fit for the table. *Mad Dog*, on the other hand, was in the same early days believed to be a cure for hydrophobia, and hence so called; a more general name is *Skull-cap* (Scutellaria lateriflora), from the shape of its flowers, the calyx of which, when inverted, looks like a helmet with the vizor open. The *Bitter-Sweet* (Solanum dulcamara), recently chosen as the title of a volume of excellent poems by J. G. Holland, deserves its name well, as the taste is first bitter and then sweet; it is a beautiful plant, often large enough to become almost a shrub, and famous for its clusters of orange-colored shells in winter, opening like a corolla around the crimson berries.

Grasses abound naturally in a country of which so small a part is as yet under cultivation, and even springs up voluntarily in richest abundance on certain soils. Some of these varieties, known under French or Spanish names, have already been mentioned; others are called by some suggestive term, not always meaning the same thing as in England. Thus *Bear-Grass* (Yucca filamentosa), common by the side of little streams and shady places, is not a grass at all, but a lilaceous plant, and has a much better claim to its other name of *Silk-Grass*, from the silky filaments that appear on the edges of its leaves. *Blue-Grass* (Poa compressa), on the contrary, is a well-known and most valuable grass, growing richly in several varieties on limestone soil, and springing up voluntarily all over the States of Pennsylvania, Tennessee, and Kentucky. It remains green for the larger part of the year, and serves to raise the enormous herds of superior cattle for which those States are famous. Both the region where it grows naturally and the settlers there are known as *Blue-Grass* simply, and hence the State of Kentucky especially is often thus designated. "The Postmaster-General has restored the mails on the route between Louisville and Lexington. It does not speak well for the condition of the *Blue-Grass Region*, that he has felt warranted in doing this only on assurances from the Secretary of War, that troops have been placed along the line for the protection of the mail-agents." (New York *Tribune*, April 6, 1871.) A distinction is sometimes, quite unjustly, made between lands producing Blue-Grass, and the comparatively poor land, on which grapevines grow wild, and which is hence called *Grapevine* Land. *Buffalo-Grass* (Sessleria dactyloides) and *Buffalo-Clover* have already been mentioned, in connection with buffaloes, from whom they derive their names. *Grama* or *Gramma*-Grass (Choudrosium), abounds in the Western borders, and is excellent food for cattle. "In the middle of the day the cattle leave the high ground and go to the river-bottoms for water. About four o'clock they go back to the high ground and graze on the rich *gramma* and bunch-grasses until night, when they lay down on the warm, sandy soil and sleep until next morning." (*Grazing on the Colorado*, 1870.) *Bunch*-Grass (Festuca) is limited to the plains of New Mexico, and the *Cow*-Grass is a plague of the South, being a very free grower and quickly overrunning fields in which it has once taken root, in such a manner as to defy all efforts at destruction. An equal nuisance, as far as crops are concerned, is the so-called *Crab*-Grass (Digitaria) of Louisiana and Texas, but it makes at least amends by its usefulness as hay, in which form it cannot be surpassed as fodder. Even the favorite *Clover* yields to it in nutritive qualities. The white or *Wild Clover* is of indigenous growth, and abounds on the banks of nearly all rivers. The red was introduced into the Valley of Virginia by John Lewis, the father of that General Lewis to whom Washington wished the general command of the Continental Armies to be entrusted. "It was currently reported by their prophets, and believed by the Indians generally, that the blood of the red men, slain by the Lewis's and their followers, had dyed the trefoil to its sanguine hue." (Wills de Hass, *History of the Valley of Virginia.*) *Cut-grass* (Leersia oryzoides) has its name from the manner in which careless hands or bare feet are cut by the sharp edges of its leaves. *Eel-Grass* is again not a genuine grass, but a seaweed (Zostera marina), which is thrown on shore in large quantities, and derives its name from its inhabitants. *Guinea-Grass* (Panicum maximum) has only lately made its way into the United States, having been imported from the West Indies, where it has long been cultivated mainly to furnish fodder for horses. *Salt-Hay*, a very important product of salt-marshes, is of two principal sorts, called *salt-grass* and *black-grass*. They are the fine, short grasses growing upon the level surfaces called *salt-meadows*, alluvial deposits of a strange, unctuous mud, stretching along the New England coast in recesses, and up the river-valleys. A twenty-foot pole may often be thrust down into it, finding no bottom; and yet these dangerous meadows are regularly mown, and rich harvests gathered from the ever-trembling surface. The *Toothache-Grass* (Monocera aromatica), is a curious grass of Florida and a few adjoining districts, growing in a bare stem to considerable height, and injurious to the milk of cows who eat it when young and tender. The root, when eaten, affects the salivary gland; this has led to its being looked upon as a remedy against toothache, and hence its odd name, which it shares, however, with the *Toothache*-Tree, the common name of two shrubs, the prickly ash and an avalia. But perhaps the most highly valued of all cultivated grasses is one which gratefully bears the name of the earliest propagator. It is the Herd's Grass (Phleum pratense), known universally as *Timothy*, after Timothy Hanson, who carried it, about 1780, from America to England.

It would not seem improper to mention among the grasses some of the wild-growing plants of this class, which are peculiar to our continent. Such is, for instance, the variety known as *Wild Oats* (Avena fatua), which grows wild upon the more elevated parts of California, and furnishes admirable forage. "With a little care," says a local paper, "any amount of stock may be maintained all the year round upon our *wild oats*, which will spring up wherever moisture helps it, even after the seeds have lain a long time dormant in the ground." The *Wild Rice* (Zizania aquatica) also, although a water-plant, resembles the grasses, and especially oats, so that the early French settlers used to call it, after their home-fashion, *folles avoines*. The Indians of the Northern regions, especially around the headwaters of the Mississippi, depend largely upon the scanty produce of this perennial plant, from whence it is also known as *Indian Rice*. It serves at the same time to fatten the waterfowl that leave those regions for the South, so as to enable them to perform safely their long, weary journey. To this class belongs, in appearance at least, the *Chess* (Bromus scalinus), a troublesome weed growing up among valuable wheat, and not unlike oats, which has given rise to the common error that it is a degenerated wheat; hence its frequent name of *Cheat*. If reaped and ground up with the wheat, it is said to produce narcotic effects. The poorest of grasses, almost approaching the nature of a moss, is the *Poverty Grass* (Hudsonia tormentosa) of New England, which will grow in scanty bunches on soil that refuses to produce anything else.

Among smaller plants a few are known in America under special names when becoming useful for household or other purposes. Such are the beans, known in England as Kidney-beans or French-beans, while here they are called *String-beans*, from the strings or fibres which are pulled off from the pods in preparing them when green for the table, or *Snaps*, and occasionally *Snap-beans*. The *Wild-bean* (Phaseolus diversifolius) is also known as the *Wild Potato* of several Indian tribes; it grows on all the rich bottoms of the West, and is very useful as food. This is a very different plant from the *Wild Potato Vine* (Convolvulus panduratus), also known by its Indian name of *Mechoacan*, which grows in sandy soil all over the United States, and has a root possessed of certain medicinal virtues. The so-called *Oyster Plant* (a Tragopogon) is the familiar name of salsify, derived from the resemblance which the plant has in taste, when cooked, to the oyster; hence it is also called the *Vegetable Oyster*. The *Cantaloupe*, named so by the French, is the same variety which is elsewhere known as *Musk-melon*, and so easily raised in the South that every negro used to have his own *melon-patch*. *Bull-briars* are, however, limited to the Southwest, where the Indians make bread from the farinaceous root; another name for it is *Bamboo*-briar, and not improperly, because the very large briar attains, in the rich alluvial bottoms which it prefers, at times the size of the bamboo. *Alonsenel* is a Mexican name, familiarized to American ears on the Western prairies, where the remarkable plant (Cowania stansburiana) is highly prized as a styptic in hemorrhages, and for other medicinal virtues.

Of very different usefulness are two other plants, the *Creosote* Plant (Larrea mexicana), which covers vast districts in the sandy parts of California and extends eastward as far as Arkansas. Its odor, exhaled from the resinous matter it contains, fills the air to a great distance, and makes it utterly unfit for food of cattle; it is said, however, to possess certain properties beneficial in rheumatic complaints. The *Soap*-plant (Phalangium pomeridianum) belongs to the same regions and is there known as *Amole;* its pulp, when stripped of the bark, and rubbed on wet clothes, produces an abundant lather, and even smells somewhat like new brown soap. The Spanish inhabitants used, besides, to make saddle-cloths of the plant. They also gave to one of the many varieties of Yucca, peculiar to that country, the name of *Spanish Bayonet*, from the resemblance borne to that weapon by its stiff, sharp-pointed leaves. In like manner the name of *Maguey*, by which they designate the plant, known in America familiarly though incorrectly as Century Plant, has become quite common in the Southwestern States, and with it the *pulque*, the well-known intoxicating beverage prepared from its sap. Even *Coontie* (Coontie Adka), the name of a preparation obtained from the root, known more familiarly as *Arrow-Root* (Zamia integrifolia), is now quite frequently used, since the plant is largely cultivated in Florida and produces a valuable return. Cotton has given at last two special names to our speech: the *Sea-Island* Cotton, grown only on the islands along the coast and on the coast itself of South Carolina and Georgia, once celebrated as having the longest and finest fibre of all varieties, but now no longer cultivated with success; the other, *Upland Cotton*, a variety often grown quite near the former, but of shorter fibre and inferior value. It is in all probability the peculiarly soft and pleasant touch of the *cotton-wool* which has, from time of old, led to the expression, to *cotton* to a person, as if to make one's self as pleasant and agreeable as cotton to him, which is still very frequently heard in the South and West. The phrase is so old that Halliwell already terms it an Archaism, and quotes Halliday and Laurance, saying—

> " Her heart's as hard as taxes and as bad;
> She does not even *cotton* to her dad."
> (*Kenilworth Burlesque.*)

In Congreve's *Love for Love* we find also the phrase: to *cotton* together.

The *Long Moss* or *Spanish Moss* (Tillandsia usneoides) forms one of the most striking features in the Southern landscape, as it waves in long, graceful festoons from the branches of live-oaks and cypresses. It is, of course, no moss, though at first sight it resembles the Tree-moss (Usnea) of the North; but that is a lichen, while this is a phenoganeous plant. It grows, like a true epiphyte, upon these trees, but without deriving any nourishment from them. Having no roots that bind it to any one place, it hangs in rich clusters, as if it had been thrown by accident over the branches, and adds much to the impressive though melancholy appearance of the noble groves of live-oaks, such as are seen to perfection in the neighborhood of Savannah. Even in winter these long, dense garlands cover the bare stems and branches as with a curtain, and give them a weird, fictitious appearance of life. The *Virginia Creeper* (Ampelopsis quinquefolia) is, on the other hand, one of the most graceful woody vines known; it is also called *American Ivy,* though it has nothing to entitle it to such a name, and the *Woodbine.* The *Bermuda* Vine (Vitis riparia) is the *Chicken Grape* of Southern States, famous for its fragrant blossoms, but bearing no fruit. The *Fox-Grape* (Vitis labrusca) was noticed by R. Beverley as growing "upon small vines and in small bunches, and of a rank taste, when ripe, resembling the smell of the fox, from whence they are called *fox-grapes.*" (*History of Virginia,* p. 116.) Another explanation of the name is derived from the foxy pubescence which characterizes the surface of the leaves. In the South a kindred grape (Vitis vulpilia) is known by that name, which bears larger berries and is less acid than the former. But there is still another source from which the name has been traced: the old English word to *foxe,* in the sense of to intoxicate. For in the year 1640 Beauchamp Plantagenet wrote of a wine in Delaware (Uvedale), and praised its intoxicating qualities in these quaint words: "A second draught, four months old, will *foxe* a reasonable pate," and hence, it is asserted, arose the name of *Fox-Grape.* They abound in the Southern States: Sir John Hawkins spoke of drinking a wine made from American grapes in Florida, in the year 1564, memorable as the birth-year of Shakespeare, and a high authority on the subject says, in 1870: "The woods of Louisiana, Mississippi, and Arkansas abound in varieties of wild vines, that yield masses of fruitage, renowned as raccoon, bear, bull, chicken, and *fox-grapes.*" (*American Wines,* p. 625.) The reddish color of the first-named variety re-appears in a little phosphorescent moss, known as *Fox-fire.* "The little catadid (*sic*) pierced the air with his shrill music. The *fox-fire*—as the country people call it—glowed hideously from the cold and matted bosom of the marsh." (J. P. Kennedy, *Swallow Barn,* p. 173.) It is a kind of rotten wood, which at night resembles a mass of glow-worms, and owes its brilliancy to the decaying micelium of a fungus. The *Mustang*

Grape (Vitis rotundiflora) is a native of Texas, bearing small bunches with large berries, and capable of furnishing a very superior wine, resembling Burgundy.

The so-called *Supple Jack* (Berchemia volubilis) is a creeper very much resembling the muscadine vine, but with a deeper color; the name is derived from the very peculiar manner in which it twists and curls around the shrubs to which it clings, so as to produce very curious shapes and curves, which are made use of in the manufacture of *supple-jack* canes. All these plants which climb up trees are, in America, indiscriminately called *Vines.* "There is among the *Vines* one called *Cross Vine,* from the singular circumstance of its stem, on the stripping off of its bark, spontaneously dividing into four parts, as if it split crosswise into quarters." (P. H. Gosse, *Letters from Alabama,* p. 114.)

Among the shrubs peculiar in name and nature to America, the *Alder* deserves a place only in so far as its name is recklessly transferred to a number of other shrubs, that resemble the original in the form of their leaves. The people thus call a buckthorn (Rhamnus aldiflorius) the *Dwarf Alder,* the Sweet Pepperbush (Clethra alnifolia) the *Spiked Alder,* and even a Winter-Berry (Prinos verticillatus) the *Black Alder.* In like manner they appropriate the name of the tropical Pimento to a sweet-scented shrub (Calycanthus floridus), the bark and wood of which have quite a spicy flavor. At times, a more careful distinction is attempted, by calling it the *Carolina Allspice,* from the State, in which it is quite abundant. The *Button-Bush* (Cephalanthus occidentalis) has its name from the resemblance of its globular catkins of flowers to round buttons, just as Buttonwood is the popular name of the so-called Sycamore-tree (Platanus occidentalis), from the curious ball-shaped seed-vessels which hang by a long slender thread, the peduncle, from the branches, and do not drop till the following spring. J. R. Lowell sings of it:

"Beneath a bony *buttonwood*
The mill's red door swings open wide;
The whiten'd miller, dust-imbued,
Flits past the square of dark inside."
(*Beaver-Brook.*)

The tree is known also as *Sycamore* and *Plane-Tree.* *Calfkill* is the absurd name given in the North to one of the most beautiful flowering shrubs of North America (Kalmia angustifolia), from a foolish notion that its poisonous leaves were apt to kill calves that browsed on them. The poison is there, no doubt, as in all the laurel-family, to which the bush belongs, and owes its frequent name of *Laurel*, but in so small quantities as to be comparatively harmless. The plant is, in the South, more generally, though equally erroneously, known as *Ivy*. The Northern States have a *Hobble-Bush* (Viburnum lantanoides), with long, straggling branches, which impede progress, whence it is also called Tangle-Legs; while in the South the *Tear-Coat* (Aralia spinosa), also humorously called *Shot-Bush*, rises almost to the dignity of a tree, its prickles being quite formidable to hunting-shirts and Indian blankets. With the usual objection to the correct sound of *tear*, Western men, however, almost uniformly speak of it as *Tar*-Coat. The *Honeysuckle* of the South has nothing in common with the shrub correctly so called; the name is given to a curious woody plant (Azalea viscosa), the brilliant flowers of which are surrounded by a viscous secretion. It is not quite clear why a most ornamental evergreen shrub, which not unfrequently attains the size of a small tree (Gordonia lasianthus), should be afflicted with the insipid name of *Loblolly Bay;* it grows wild in all the maritime parts of the Southern States, and is largely planted in parks and pleasure-grounds on account of its beauty; its usefulness is limited to a moderate fitness for tanning which the bark possesses. There is a dash of poetry in the name of *Nine-bark*, which is given to a low shrub (Spiraea opulifolia) growing in the Northern and Western States, from the fact that its bark is quite loose and easily peels off, layer after layer, though the number Nine has probably no more to do with it than with the lives of cats. An exceedingly handsome, flowering shrub is a variety of the Judas-Tree, familiar to the East, and so called from the legend that on a branch of it Judas hung himself; the American species (Cercis canadensis) is more simply called *Redbud*, from the profusion of bright pink flowers with which it is covered in spring, before the leaves have appeared.

Another beautiful but fleeting flower, is that of the so-called *Tree-Primrose* (Oenothera fruticosa), a large flower flaming in brilliant yellow. Another family is represented in some of the

States by the little *Smell-Lemon* (Cucurbita ovifera), the fruit of which is about the size of a small orange, bright glossy red, with stripes of yellow running round, like the meridian lines on a globe. The smell is very fragrant, and hence the name.

A few plants, not before mentioned, are familiarly known from their connection with the aborigines. An *Indian Currant* (Symphoricarpus vulgaris), more generally called *Coral Berry*, and a native of Missouri—*Indian Hemp* (Apocynum cannabinum), a medicinal plant—*Indian Tobacco* (Lobelia inflata), occasionally used instead of tobacco by virtue of its acrid leaves; and less important Indian grasses, cresses, and strawberries.

The trees of America bear, with few exceptions, names given them by the first settlers, which were very generally taken from those they were familiar with at home. Hence the number of those who appear either under new names or under old names, differently applied, is quite small. Among the latter are a few fruit-trees, with which some peculiar terms are connected. Apples, for instance, appear here in the shape of *Apple-Butter*, a thick sauce made by boiling apples a long time in cider, which is then put away, like butter, in tubs and firkins, and keeps for nearly a year. Thrifty housewives in New England know it as *Apple-Sauce*, while the frugal matrons among the Germans in Pennsylvania and the Valley of Virginia call it by the former name. *Apple-Jack* and *Apple-Brandy* furnish a genuine brandy made from fruit—unlike the Russian brandy or brandy-wine, which is a whiskey or grain spirit. Known even in the pretentious form of *Apple-John* in New England, it has the terrible name of *Jersey Lightning* farther south, and in Virginia rules supreme as *Apple-Brandy*, although here a few peach-kernels are generally added to give it the flavor of peach-brandy. "We had no sooner scrambled out of the sleigh than a huge bowl of *Apple-Toddy* made its entrance; the bowl was of solid silver, an old family-relic, with the crest of the old Huguenot family as handles, and in the golden liquid danced the roasted apples, which are here substituted for the usual lemons." (W. M. Thackeray.) *Apple-Slump* is the odd name of a favorite New England dish, consisting of apples and molasses baked within a bread-pie in an iron pot. It is also known as *Pandowdy;* and the good people of those States claim, with their usual assurance, that this *apple-potpie* is the true father of the phrase, *in apple-pie order*. This may very well be, as the latter was as well known to their ancestors in England as the dish, Halliwell quoting the term as quite common in various provinces. The *Apple-bug* (Conotrachelus nenuphar; Herbst, 1797) is thus described by J. P. Kennedy: "The *apple-bug*, as the country people call the black, beetle-shaped insect which frequents summer pools, and which is distinguished for the perfume of the fruit that has given it its name, danced in hazy masses over the surface of the still water." (*Swallow Barn.*) The insect above mentioned is also known as Plum-weevil, and destroys plums and peaches, cherries and apples, by puncturing them to insert its eggs, which causes the fruit to fall prematurely. (Harris, *Insects of Massachusetts*, p. 66, 351. S. S. Haldeman.) The *apple-worm*, on the contrary, is the larva of the European Coddling-Moth (Carpocapsa pomonetta), now at home in America also.

Castañas is the Spanish name for chestnuts, quite frequently given in Texas and the Southwest to the palatable pinecones of a screw-pine there (Pandanus). The *Coffee-tree* (Gymnocladus canadensis), often called *Kentucky Coffee-tree*, or *Kentucky Locust*, derives its name from the fact that in the days of early settlements the seeds were frequently used as a substitute for coffee, a practice renewed during the late Civil War. The *Hickory*, mentioned elsewhere, bears an edible nut, which is not unfrequently dignified by the name of *Walnut*, especially in the Northern States, where the real walnut does not thrive, while a larger kind of hickory-nut is known as *Bullnut;* the *Butternut* (Juglans cinerea) deserves its name by the large quantity of oil its fruit contains, on which account the latter is also often called *oilnut*, and the *Mockernut* (Carya tomentosa) is a variety of the hickory-nut. The *Pecan* Nut (pronounced *pecawn*) is the fruit of another variety of hickory (Carya olivaeformis), so called from the French *pacane*, and often so written, which is a great favorite throughout the Union. Part of its popularity is, no doubt, due to the facility with which the soft shell of the nut yields up the meat, which lies in two lobes and can be easily taken out; but the nut is, besides, by far the most pleasant of all to the taste. *Pecan* trees are, hence, very carefully managed, and a recent traveller says very justly: "There is not a richer sight than to see a noble *pecan* tree, as tall as the tallest hickory, full from bottom to top of the oval nuts growing in dense clusters, a shade darker in color than the leaves." The smallest of the family and the least palatable is, from that circumstance, called the *Pig-Nut* (Carya glabra), though the same name is often applied to the root of an earth-nut (Bunium).

The *Honey Locust* (Gleditschia triacanthus) is popularly so called because it bears a large pod containing a pulp of honey-like sweetness. It produces probably the most formidable of all thorns, as remarkable in size as in number, and is, hence, in the South and West quite as well known under the name of *Thorny* Locust. The common *Locust* (Robinia pseudacacia) is the same as the European acacia, and considered a very valuable tree for its timber, which makes the best posts for fences and gates that can be procured. The *Mango* is mentioned here only because the name is borrowed from the delightful fruit of the West Indies, to designate a pickle, consisting of a green muskmelon stuffed with a variety of seeds and spices.

The *Sand-Cherry* (Cerasus pumila) is the name of a reclining shrub, growing on sandy soil in the North and West, and of its black fruit, which it bears in profusion; they are, however, not pleasant to the taste. The *Wild Cherry* (Cerasus virginiensis) bears a fruit entirely unfit to eat, but its wood is considered very valuable, especially for cabinet work. The *Black* and the *White Spruce*, both American trees, deserve mention here, because from their branches is extracted the flavoring material for a beverage known as *Spruce Beer*, very popular in Canada, where it is sold in immense quantities, and of late manufactured quite largely in the United States also.

Oaks abound in America, not only in numbers, but quite as much in varieties, of which some are known by names peculiar to this country. The *Black Jack* (Quercus nigra) is the barren oak of botanists, and mingles with dogwood, cedar, and tall pines on the seashore, where it thrives most freely. The *Burr-Oak* (Quercus macrocarpa), one of the noblest and largest of the family, is very numerous in the rich bottom-lands of Western States, and frequently called *Overcup* White Oak, from the peculiar form of its acorn. "The trees, with few exceptions, were what is called the *burr-oak*, a small variety of a very extensive genus; and the spaces between them, always irregular and often of singular beauty, have obtained the name of openings." (J. F. Cooper, *The Oak Openings*, p. 27.) But the most beautiful of all is the *Live-Oak* (Quercus virens), so called because it is nearly an evergreen; a tree which loves the salt-air of the ocean, and furnishes a highly-prized wood, admirably adapted for ship-building. It is thus described:

> "With his gnarled old arms and his iron form,
> Majestic in the woods,
> From age to age, in the sun and storm,
> The *live-oak* hath stood;
> With the gray moss waving solemnly
> From his shaggy limbs and trunk."
> (*H. R. Jackson.*)

All the smaller, and some more or less dwarfish, varieties, are comprehended under the familiar name of *Scrub Oaks*, such as cover the sandy plains and sterile ridges of the Western Deserts, where vegetation can barely maintain itself.

Next to the Oaks the Maples are probably most prominent among American trees, both by their great variety of form and their general beauty. In autumn especially some species assume those gorgeous colors which have made the American Fall so famous among painters. The most remarkable among them is the *Sugar-Tree* or Sugar-Maple (Acer saccharinum), a beautiful tree in trunk and branch and leaf, from whose sap sugar is made by boiling. Its praise was once quaintly sung thus:

> "We'll hang by our own staples;
> Three cheers we'll raise for Indian Corn,
> And nine for *Sugar-Maples*."
> (*Putnam's Magazine*, October, 1851.)

They are generally preserved when the forest is cleared, and such a collection of trees is known as a *Sugar-Bush* or *Sugar-Orchard*, while the place where the sap is boiled in huge kettles during the winter months is, in like manner, known as the *Sugar-Camp*. Here farmers obtain the vast quantities of sugar which the generous tree affords them every year, and great is the merriment during the process, till the time comes when all ends in uproar, thanks to "the boys enlivened by rye-whiskey, whiskey and water, whiskey sweetened with *sap-sugar*, and small beer, all graduated to the tastes and ages of the company." (*General Ogle.* A Character.) Two other varieties of maple are the *Bird's Eye* and the *Curled Maple,* which furnish peculiarly beautiful wood for the purposes of the builder and the cabinet-maker. Among other trees peculiar to this continent, we may notice the *Arrow-wood* (Viburnum dentatum), which obtained its name from the fact that almost all the Indian tribes roving over the plains between the Mississippi and the Rocky Mountains make their arrows from its long, straight stems, as the Osage Orange (Maclura) received its common name of *Bodok* from its fitness for bows (bois d'arc). The *Balsam Fir* (Abies balsamea) and the *Balsam Poplar* (Populus balsamifera), owe their names to the balsam which the former furnishes from certain blisters under the bark, and the latter from the resinous matter covering its buds. Only the former, however, can be collected for practical purposes, and appears as *Canada balsam,* while the tree is also known as *Balm of Gilead,* in imitation of the Eastern terebinth. *Basswood* (Tilia americana) resembles the genuine linden tree of Europe so closely in all but the size of its leaves and flowers as to be fairly entitled to its botanical name; the term *bass* means *bast* (German, Bast) the inner bark of the tree, which was formerly much used for making mats or cordage. J. R. Bartlett quotes from one of Brigham Young's sermons a graphic allusion to this pliant material: "I say, as the Lord lives, we are bound to become a sovereign State in the Union, or an independent nation by ourselves; and let them drive us from this place if they can—they cannot do it. I do not throw this out as a banter. You Gentiles and hickory and *basswood* Mormons can write it down, if you please, but write it as I speak it." (*Dictionary, sub voce.*)

The Black or Sour Gum is familiarly known in the Northern States as *Pepperidge* (Nyssa multiflora), a name strangely illustrating the tendency which common people have to force a meaning upon words which to them are unintelligible. Its ancestor is the Latinized *berberis* (from Arabic barbârîs), which in the first place became *Piperidge,* and as such was applied to the proper owner, the barberry, but subsequently, in a second metamorphosis, re-appeared as *Pepperidge,* for one of the most beautiful American trees, equally well known in New England under its probably Indian name, *Tupelo.* "The woods," says J. R. Lowell, "were not wanting of pine, of oak, and maple, and the rarer *tupelo* with downward limbs." It is curious, that while the name *pepperidge* is thus transferred, the term *barberry* (berberis) is properly applied, although it has suffered from the belief that *berry* formed part of the original—an idea to which the berries of the plant were suggestive. The same false impression prevails in the corruption of asparagus into sparrow-grass.

These two trees, Black Gum and Sour Gum, are, however, different varieties of the same family (Nyssa), the former more common in the North, the latter very abundant in the South. The resinous gum exuding from these trees and the Juniper is much used for chewing in North Carolina, Virginia, and the Western States, where *gumsuckings* are quite a festive occasion for the votaries of that amusement. The ludicrous facility with which American speech-terms are interchanged, has led to an utter confusion, in many minds, between the terms *gum* and *rubber*. The great philologist, Dr. W. D. Whitney, tells us in his admirable work on Language, how a Philadelphia gentleman, entering a friend's house without his wife, explained her absence by stating that "she was cleaning her gums upon the mat"—meaning her India-Rubber shoes. And in return, gum-trees are not unfrequently called *Rubber*-trees, and hence J. R. Lowell, in a different sense of the term, speaks of the false notion—

"That *rubber-trees* first began bearin'
When p'litickle conshiences come into wearin'."
(*Biglow Papers*, I., p. 49.)

As *Black Wood* is, in the Northern States, used as a generic term for the evergreens, hemlock, pine, spruce, and fir, so the term *cedar* is there rarely applied to the genuine cedar; it is more frequently applied to a cypress (Cypressus thyoides), and then called *white cedar*, which fills the famous *Cedar Swamps* of the South, or, as *red cedar*, to a Juniper (Juniperus virginiana.) The *Cedar Swamps* are not, as in England, merely wet, marshy places, often found in uplands even, but in the South are uniformly low grounds under water, and filled with cypresses, as is the case in the numerous bayous, known as *Cypress Brakes*. This *Cypress*, however (Taxodium disticha), is a Southern tree entirely distinct from the European tree of the same name, and thus described by P. H. Gosse: "It is a tree of noble stature, being occasionally seen 120 feet in height, and very valuable for the durability of its timber; hence it is much in request for building. Its root generally swells in a great cone or beehive-shaped protuberance, several yards in circumference, from the summit of which the tree springs." (*Letters from Alabama*, p. 261.) From the very dangerous nature of the swamps in which they grow, slang has derived the expressive verb to be *swamped*, instead of to be ruined. "To say the truth, if they hold me to the price I have agreed to pay, I'm afraid they'll *swamp* me. (*Adventures of a Country Merchant*, p. 241.) The *swamper*, however, is a very harmless and useful laborer; it is the man who, in Maine and the Northwest, breaks roads for lumberers through the great pine-forests.

Another mis-named tree is the maple with ash-leaves (Negundium americanum), which is universally known as *Box-elder*. The *Tulip-tree* (Leriodendron tulipifera), on the contrary, deserves both that name and its alias of *white-wood* well, from its beautiful white wood and its tulip-shaped, honey-filled blossoms. Although very common in the South, where it is simplv called the *Poplar*, it is one of the finest of American trees, and fully entitled to W. C. Bryant's praise:

> " the *tulip-tree*, high up
> Opened, in airs of June, her multitude
> Of golden chalices to humming-birds
> And silken-winged insects of the sky."
> (*The Fountain.*)

Among the peaches, Americans distinguish *Free-stone* Peaches, in which the stones lie loose, while in *Cling-stones* they adhere firmly to the flesh of the fruit. The distinction was made early after the first settlement of the State, and R. B. Beverley already wrote: "The best sort of these (peaches) cling to the stone, and will not come off clear, which they call Plum Nectarines and Plum-peaches or *Cling-stones*. Some of these are twelve to thirteen inches in girt. These sorts of fruits are raised so easily here that some good husbands plant great orchards of them, purposely for their hogs, and others make a drink of them, which they call *Mobby*; they sometimes distill it off for brandy. This makes the best spirit next to grapes." (*The History of Virginia*, p. 179.) Real plums are, when growing wild, frequently called *Snells*, and hence a recent traveller through the Northern States, says: "When *snells* were mentioned, they went out in the dark and plucked some; they were pretty good. They said they had three kinds of plums growing wild—blue, white, and red."

All the Magnolias are, in the South, familiarly designated as *Laurels;* the Big Laurel (M. grandiflora), as well as the Southern Cucumber-tree (M. cordata). Another variety of this noble family of Magnolias is known as the *Umbrella-Tree* (Magnolia tripetala), from the likeness which the large leaves, radiating from the end of its branches, and expanding over a surface of three feet diameter, bear to an open umbrella. The *Sweet Bay* is the familiar name of a much humbler relative (Magnolia glauca), and not to be compared to the *Swamp Magnolia* (Magnolia grandiflora), while the *Cucumber-tree* (Magnolia acuminata), changes its snowy-white blossoms into a fruit, not unlike green cucumbers, which afterward turns a bright red.

One of the noblest of American trees, which, from its magnificent proportions and cherished associations, has almost come to be considered the emblem-tree of the New England States, the *Elm*, is in its very home sadly ill-treated, as far as its name is concerned. The term is so generally corrupted into *ellum* that it is often actually confounded with *alum*. J. R. Lowell, with his keen ear for Yankeeisms, and his subtle appreciation of their force, says, therefore,

"In *ellum* shrouds the flashin' hangbird clings,
And for the summer vyage his hammock swings"—
(*Biglow Papers*, II., p. 158.)

while Edward Miller reports that "the Mushroom Rock is an extraordinary freak of nature in Kansas, in the Valley of *Alum*, or more probably *Elm* Creek, for in Western parlance the latter is pronounced as if it had two syllables, and it is difficult to distinguish between the two words." (*Proceedings of the American Philosophical Society*, March, 1868, p. 382.) The *Nahoo* is a common species of elm (Ulmus alata), of peculiar beauty of form and foliage.

A beautiful variety of horse-chestnut (Aesculus glabra), is known by the picturesque name of *Buckeye*, given by the early settlers in the West, on account of the resemblance which the dark-brown nut bears to a buck's eye, when the shell first cracks, and exposes it to sight. As it used to abound in Ohio, that State, as well as a citizen of the State, is apt be called a *Buckeye;* but so merciless has been the war waged against trees in those regions, that not a single tree is found growing naturally near Cincinnati, and very few in the State at large. *Mahogany* (Swietenia mahogani), found in Southern Florida in great abundance, deserves a place here only on account of the strange transposition of vowels which has changed the original South American name of Mahagoni, retained in German, into the modern form. The common *pines,* found in many varieties in almost every State of the Union, furnish at least one peculiar name, the *Pinion,* derived from the Spanish *piñon;* the term is applied to the tree which grows abundantly in the Southwestern States and the regions at the foot of the Rocky Mountains, and to the nuts, which are sweet and palatable, a favorite with birds and bears, and welcome to Indians and travellers, when short of provisions. Hunters and experienced travellers know how to find them, not only in their natural places on the tree, but even in hidden storehouses—deep holes in certain other trees, in which a Mexican woodpecker is in the habit of depositing them with rare foresight, long before he lays his eggs, that they may serve as food during incubation. It may not be amiss to mention, in this connection, that the fallen leaves of all the evergreen trees are familiarly known as *pinetags* or *pinestraws.* "He was treading on a mat of *pinetags,* which soon shall crisp beneath his tread no more." (*Virginia Country Notes.*) "*Pinestraw,* as the yellow sheddings of this tree are called." (J. P. Kennedy, *Swallow Barn.*)

A strange confusion of names has thrown two trees, entirely different in family and features, into the same class, as far as a common designation can produce such a result. *Dogwood* is the name given to the *Cornel-tree* (Cornus florida), and to the *Poison Sumac* (Rhus venenata). The former, a beautiful though small tree, covers American woods in early spring with a profusion of large, snowy-white flowers, and adorns them in autumn with scarlet berries, while its wood is useful for many a purpose. The latter, an inmate of swamps, and well known by the beauty of its semi-tropical foliage, hides a violent poison in its leaves, and even affects susceptible persons who approach it too nearly.

American rocks have almost uniformly been first examined by English geologists, and bear, therefore, with very few exceptions, names familiar abroad as well as with us. Among the exceptions may be mentioned the three varieties of limestone, which are known as *Bird's Eye* in New York, as *Cavern* in Kentucky, from the numerous caves or *sinks*, as they are locally called, with which the hard strata of this carboniferous formation abound, and as *Cliff* in the West, from the bold cliffs or bluffs found upon the banks of streams. The latter is partly Silurian and partly Devonian, and form a very striking feature in American landscapes from the State of Ohio, westward. The local pronunciation of the word is *Clift*—found thus already in Spenser—from a natural confusion with the *cleft* in a rock, such as is mentioned in the lines, "And it shall come to pass while my glory passeth by, that I will put thee in a *cleft* of the rock." (*Exodus*, xxxiii. 22.) Hence, also, the adjective *clifty*, designating rivers and creeks on the banks of which these limestone-cliffs abound, and the region generally in which they are found. "The valley was of that character which is here called *clifty*—numerous bold bluffs, overhanging beautiful bottom-lands, now clad in rich verdure, and now picturesquely baring their snowy sides to the golden sunlight." (*Scenes in the Far West.*) Another variety of limestone is known as *Cotton Rock*, probably because its light gray or buff color, when first bared to the light, somewhat resembles fresh-gathered cotton-wool; it is a Magnesian limestone, abounding in Missouri, and valuable as a building material, because of its softness when first quarried. The unpleasant name of *Stink-stone* —often changed into *Swine-stone*—is not altogether undeservedly borne by a carbonate of lime which emits a very offensive odor on being struck. The term *sulphur* is altogether erroneously given to bituminous rocks occurring in Kentucky and Tennessee, even when no sulphur is present, from the mere fact that generally this formation abounds in sulphurous springs. *Wall-Rock* is the homely name given to granular limestone, used largely in building walls.

X.

Old Friends with New Faces.

OLD FRIENDS WITH NEW FACES.

"Ideas which filter slowly into English soil and abide there for a generation, flash like comets into the elastic atmosphere of America."
(*North British Review*, 1867.)

THE largest part of so-called Americanisms are nothing more than good old English words, which for one reason or another have become obsolete or provincial in England, while they have retained their full power and citizenship in the United States. Thus all the provincialisms of the Northern and Western counties of England have been naturalized in the New England States, thanks to the Pilgrim Fathers, who had left the banks of the Trent and the Humber, and subsequently by new colonists, who followed from Norfolk and Suffolk. They brought not only their words, which the Yankee still uses, but also a sound of the voice and a mode of utterance which have been faithfully preserved, and are now spoken of as the "New England drawl," and "the high, metallic ring of the New England voice." (Charles Wentworth Dilke.) The former is nothing but the well-known Norfolk "whine," the proverbial annoyance of visitors from the "shires." From New England words and sounds alike were carried westward, and speedily extended through the neighboring States, even to the Mississippi. Precisely the same happened in Virginia, which also received through her cavalier-settlers and the countless indenture-colonists a strongly-marked vocabulary of her own, which she faithfully and with Southern conservatism preserved, while at home and all around her everything changed, and which she at a later period transmitted to those vast new territories, that looked up to her as the Mother of States.

When these settlers were cut off from constant intercourse with the mother-country, their language ceased, of course, to be influenced by the court, the great writers, and the press of England; it retained the familiar forms and sounds, undisturbed by fashion and the effects of close intimacy with other nations. But greater results yet were effected, when the colonies threw off the political restraints that had heretofore attached them to England; the language became as independent as the republic, and refused any longer to be guided and controlled in any way by English authorities. At the same time, an unbroken stream of immigration poured into this country vast numbers of persons, mostly of humble origin and without education, who brought with them the local words of English counties, and the provincialisms of the sister kingdoms of Scotland and Ireland.

During all this time great changes had taken place in England. At a very early period, already, a large number of good old Saxon words were banished from polite society, and continued to exist only as far as they were used by the peasantry or a few families belonging to the upper classes in remote country districts. Puttenham, in his *Art of English Poesie* (ed. 1582), teaches (eleven years before Shakespeare): "Our writer, therefore, in these days shall not follow Piers the Plowman, nor Gower nor Lydgate, nor yet Chaucer, for their language is now out of use with us; neither yet shall he take the terms of Northmen, such as they use in daily talk, whether they be noblemen or gentlemen or their best clerks, nor in effect any speech used beyond the river Trent; *though no man can deny that theirs is the purest English Saxon at this day.* Yet it is not so courtly, nor so current as our Southern English is, no more is the far Western man's speech. He shall, therefore, take the usual speech of the Court, and that of London, and the shires lying about London, within sixty miles and not much above." The English writers obeyed his behest, and the English people followed their example; but not so the colonies. In America the "purest English-Saxon" of Puttenham's day was carefully preserved, unaffected by court, or town, or shire, and hence the curious result is obtained that by many an humble fireside in the Low Country of Virginia, the pines of New Jersey, or in the shadow of the mountains of New England, words are heard pronounced as they were in the days of Alfred, and with meanings unknown to England. Moreover, whenever America has needed a new word for new wants and new discoveries, it has gone to that immense mine of treasure in the early English days, from which to borrow—as William Hamilton eloquently expresses it—

> "Ancient words
> That come from the poetic quarry
> As sharp as swords."
>
> (*Letters to Allan Ramsay.*)

"Into this treasure," says a Scottish critic, "the Americans are dipping more deeply than we, and so far the influence of their example upon the mother-tongue must be recognized as both legitimate and beneficial." (*Blackwood,* October, 1867.) Hence, nothing is more common than to hear English writers blame Americans for adopting a new word; then the word is found in English writers, and we are scolded for claiming the honor of producing it! Such was the case, as Mr. Pickering shows, for instance, with the word to *advocate,* which was first censured as an Americanism, and then, having been found repeatedly in the pages of Milton and Burke, was made the basis for a charge of "unfounded claims to discovery."

Nor must it be forgotten that the strange revolutions which are stated to have taken place in the meaning of many common words are, in most instances, nothing more than the result of the preservation of an old sense, which, if carefully traced, may still be found existing in remote districts of some of the English counties. This is occasionally acknowledged even by British travellers; thus Waterton, after his fourth journey through this country in 1824, said of the American as he found him: "He has certainly hit upon the way (but I could not find out by what means) of speaking a much purer English language than that which is commonly spoken on the parent soil. This astonished me much, but is really the case." (*Wanderings in South America.*) The nomadic character of the American, the ubiquity of the newspaper, and the diffusion of knowledge throughout all classes of society, have, subsequently, given a uniformity to this pure English which is unknown in other countries; and if really better English is not spoken here than in the mother-country, the American idiom is at least free from provincialisms, and the masses speak it better than the people of England.

It has, hence, been the purpose of the compiler to collect, in the following pages, mainly words which are obsolete in England, while still preserving here their former power; such as have changed their meaning to adapt themselves to new purposes and altered circumstances, and a few entirely new forms, unknown to the Old World.

A.

Abergoins, a Western corruption for *Aboriginal*, frequently used for *original*. "That is an *aboriginal* idea; I never heard it before." Also instead of *Indian:* "Bolling Robertson, equally a descendant of Pocahontas, had the Indian eye, and the whole cast of his countenance was *aboriginal;* his temper was quick, but his heart kind and excellent." (*Letters from the South,* I., p. 23.)

Academy, used with grandiloquence for school; as every college of some pretensions must needs be a "University." "Schools no longer exist in the towns and villages, rarely in the fields; *academies* and colleges supplant them." (*Putnam's Magazine,* February, 1855.) A custom denounced with great scorn by Boswell's father, the old Laird of Auchinleck: "Whose tail do you think he has pinned himself to now, mon? Dominie, mon—an auld dominie; he keepit a schule and call'd it an *acaademy!*"

Accommodate, to, is in New England especially used in the sense of providing for travellers, from the meaning of *accommodation* as applied to public houses. "The question (where is the hotel?) invariably called forth the response: Thar ain't nun, but farmer Smoot *accommodates.*" (*Putnam's Magazine,* January, 1870.)

Admire is mentioned by J. R. Bartlett as being "often and absurdly used in New England," in the sense of a lively, eager wish. "I should *admire* to see the President." He seems to object in like manner to the use of the word, when it means to wonder at, to be affected with surprise; and yet this use has the highest authority for it.

"The undaunted fiend what this might be *admired*,
Admired, not fear'd."
(Milton. *Paradise Lost,* II., v. 677.)

"The more I *admire* your flintiness."
(Beaumont and Fletcher. *Nice Valor.*)

And Pepys, in his Diary, besides numerous other instances, says, February 22, 1663–4: "He, that is, Charles II., is so fond of the Duke of Monmouth, that everybody *admires* it, that is, wonders at it."

Ad is the printer's usual abbreviation for "advertisement," adopted not only in newspaper-offices, but also in the daily expanding advertising business of the country. "*Ad* means exactly as much as advertisement, and is two letters instead of thirteen." (*Putnam's Magazine*, August, 1868.)

Advanced Female is one of the most distasteful pet-terms of the day, generally bestowed sneeringly upon women who claim all the rights and privileges of men, in addition to those already willingly granted to their sex in appreciation of its peculiar claims. "One of the oddest instances of the shortsightedness of the *Advanced Female* to the interest of her own cause, was given in the petition recently offered to our State Legislature, for the appointment of young girls between the ages of fourteen and eighteen in the place of boys, as pages in the two Houses at Albany. Now, even if those petitioners, who seem to be in earnest, were blind to the impropriety of thrusting young girls hardly past childhood into such a position, it is strange that common sense did not suggest to them, that a man with ordinary respect for decency, or with daughters of his own, had no object in becoming equally blind, nor would ever be likely to consent to such an arrangement." (New York *Tribune*, February 2, 1871.)

Advocate, to, a word once much objected to by English critics as an Americanism, is not only good English—"whether this reflect not with a contumely upon the Parliament itself, which thought this petition worthy not only of receiving, but of voting to a commitment, after it had been *advocated* and moved for by some honorable and learned gentlemen"—(Milton, *Animadversions*, § 1.)—but has established itself beyond controversy in modern writers on both sides of the Atlantic.

Afeared, still in use in the Southern States, especially in Virginia, is, of course, only the once familiar word preserved, while elsewhere the modern form *afraid* has superseded it. The old verb *fearan* and old English to *fear*, were constantly used in the transitive sense of "to frighten or terrify," and hence *afeared* came to mean "frightened," as in Shakespeare's well-known lines:

"Though with his breath the hinges of the world
Did crack, we should stand upright and *unfeared.*"

Afore and *aforehand,* both generally supplanted by "before" and "beforehand," still survive in remoter regions of the New England States, and are supported by J. R. Lowell on the plea that "Spenser and his Queen, neither of them, scrupled to write *afore,* and *'fore* was common till after Herrick."

After night is a local expression, peculiar to Pennsylvania and some of the Border States, where *night* is very commonly used for the hours of the afternoon, and hence, "Court will open again *after night,*" means simply "after candlelight," as it is expressed everywhere else.

Aggravate, to, in the sense of irritating or ill-treating, is not an Americanism, nor used improperly. "This arose partly from a belief that the quarrel was final, and that, therefore, there would be no danger in *aggravating* Violet by this expression of doubt." (Trollope, *Phineas Finn,* ch. 73.) This is precisely the meaning with which it is used by J. C. Neal: "One may be as philosophic and as splenetic as he likes, when he is fishing, without risk of being *aggravated.*" (*Charcoal Sketches,* I., p. 118.)

Ague, frequently mis-called *aguy, agy,* and in the South even *ager,* while in the North *ague,* pronounced like plague, is not unfrequent, is rarely used without its companion, fever, and the two form the familiar *fevernagy* of the West. The varieties of this very common and often fatal disease are thus designated: "On my way I was suddenly taken ill with a real *shaking-ague* in a large prairie, ten miles across, and shook so severely that I could not sit in my sulky." (Rev. P. Cartwright, *Autobiography,* p. 433.) "He himself had been troubled with a *dumb-ager* since last conference." (F. B. Harte, *Luck of Roaring Camp,* p. 166.) "The old proverb, 'An ague in the spring is physic for a king,' wouldn't be highly appreciated in these diggings, whar *agy* is rayther objected to." (*Southern Lit. Messenger,* March, 1857, p. 27.) "Lansing, Michigan, is a very healthy locality for the *ague.* It comes creeping up a fellow's back like a ton of wild oats, goes crawling through his joints like iron spikes, and is followed by a fever, which prohibits the patient from thinking of anything but the Independent Order of Good Templars. It isn't the every-other-day kind, but gets up with a man at daylight and sleeps in the small of his back all night. His teeth feel about six inches long, his joints wobble like a loose wagon-wheel, and the shakes are so steady that one can't hold any kind of conversation except by putting in dashes." (Philadelphia *Age. Correspondence,* April 3, 1871.)

All along, another so-called Americanism, in the sense of "all this time," is in use in England, for instance in Sheffield, where, as we read, "She has been ailing *all along.*" (*Sir Richard Phillips' Tour.*)

All Hallow's Eve, anciently the vigil of All Saints' Day, is one of the few festive days still known in some parts of the Union. In Pennsylvania the usual amusements of dipping for apples floating in a basin, and other sports familiar in the north of England, are well known. The boys pass through the streets throwing shelled corn at the windows, transfer vegetables from the garden to the porch, and indulge in other less harmless pranks. (S. S. Haldeman.)

Alley, the name given by boys to a choice taw made of alabaster, and probably an abbreviation of the latter word, even when made of inferior material. (Dickens, *Pickwick Papers,* p. 358.)

Allow, to, is constantly used in the Middle and Southern States in the sense of affirming a statement. "I *allow* that's a good horse," in Southern parlance means, I assure you. "Mother is perfectly ridiculous," a young South Carolina lady said; "she *allowed* she'd switch me if I didn't go home, and she picked up a bit of brush. I up with another, and told her to come on." (*Putnam's Magazine,* June, 1868.) It is frequently, also, used in a more vague sense, corresponding with the "guess" of the East and the "reckon" of the South, as in John Hay's recent lines:

"But I come back here *allowin'*
To vote as I used to do."
(*Banty Tim.*)

Alter, to, when applied to animals, as is constantly done in the South, means to geld—the transition from a general change to a special one of this kind being very natural. A pupil translating *Taurus* by *ox,* the teacher asked him: "Haven't you *altered* that animal?"

Amalgamate, to, generally used only of metals and other substances and of abstract ideas, is in America applied more particularly to the mixture of the black and white races. The corresponding noun, *amalgamation*, has of late given way to the horrible compound, *miscegenation*, a term as little to be commended as the idea it represents.

Amazing, in the sense of wonderful, is a melancholy evidence of the prevailing bad taste which loves to deal in superlatives. It is, however, quoted with the same meaning in Bailey's Dictionary already, and hence not to be charged to this country.

Ambition, oddly and perhaps ignorantly used instead of grudge or spite, is limited to Virginia and North Carolina, and those parts of the West to which it has been carried from thence. "He brought an action against me for *ambition*." (*Virginia Literary Museum*, 1829, p. 418.) The use of

Among for between, when only two persons are referred to, is of course unwarrantable, but of frequent occurrence, and by no means unknown in England. "What can we do *among* us? We are but two, and they are ever so many." (*Scenes in the Far West*, p. 317.)

Anent survives in the New England States, and is frequently written *anend*, as in J. R. Lowell's line: "The Yankee still uses familiarly the old phrase, *right anend* for continuously." *Anan*, so constantly met with in J. F. Cooper's novels, is now-a-days heard only in New Jersey, and occasionally by old-fashioned persons, meaning precisely what Halliwell says: "*Anend:* How, what do you say? By lower class of persons to higher, when they do not understand what is said to them." (*Sub voce.*)

Applicant, in the sense of diligent student, is already noticed in Pickering's Vocabulary, but can hardly be said to be thus used any more. It means now, as in England, a petitioner.

Appreciate, to, has in this country, besides other meanings, the peculiar sense of, raising in value: "These improvements will *appreciate* the farm immensely." (*Rural Register*, 1860, p. 29.) It has, with its noun, *appreciation*, the more common meaning of, increasing in value, likewise. "His Pennsylvania lands have not *appreciated* as he had hoped, and when he left the cabinet he was a poor man." (Bishop Kip, *Life of Thomas Pickering*.)

Argufy, to, a vulgar word used to signify, to argue and to import, is perhaps less frequently heard in this country than in

England, though not unknown here. Halliwell mentions it as found in various dialects, and the biographer of the Lord Chancellors of Ireland, J. R. O'Flanagan, says: "He (Lord Clare) doesn't speak a word, but when the counsellors are done *argufying* he leans over the desk and gives a nod to Jack Dwyer, who tells him what to do."

Armory is, in the United States, the name of a place where arms are manufactured, as well as the house in which they are kept—the latter meaning alone being known in England.

Around, like *about*, is constantly used adverbially with the meaning of, in the neighborhood; the most violent abuse of which liberty is mentioned by J. R. Bartlett, in the case of a minister who was reported to have said of one of the Saviour's apostles that "he stood *around* the Cross." "I was standing *around* when the fight took place." (New York *Police Gazette.*) "Gail Hamilton is rather small, has a round, fresh, and happy-looking face, blue eyes, and brown hair, worn short and sort of curled or frizzed. She is animated in conversation, talks as she writes, is witty, fond of jokes, and must be pleasant to have *around*. She doesn't look a bit pedantic or blue-stockin'-ified, and should pass nicely for twenty years old." (Washington paper, December, 1870.)

At is one of the particles most abused in American speech, though here also much allowance ought to be made for ancient usage still surviving among the descendants of early English settlers. Thus the old custom of saying *at* hill and *at* wood in designating a place on a hill or near a wood, from which so many proper names like Atwood and others are derived, gives it the meaning of *by* in many cases. "I bought it *at* auction" is correct English, but, "It is to be sold *at* auction" is American only. It is in like manner a provincialism, at least, to say, *At* the East and *at* the West, instead of *in* the East and West; and it is somewhat curious to notice that this is not promiscuously done, but the better-known New England States are generally spoken of as *in* the East, while the remoter South is designated as *at* the South. *At* is used also instead of about or after, as in the familiar phrase: "What is he *at* now?" meaning, "What does he propose to do now?" *At that*, added as an expletive to strengthen an expression, may be considered as an Americanism. "He is a Down-East

Yankee, and a smart one *at that.*" It seems to have here precisely the same force as the German "und zwar." "He has a scolding wife and an ugly one *at that.*" (J. C. Neal, *Charcoal Sketches*, II., p. 17.) J. Durand, in his translation of Taine's *Art in the Netherlands*, says of the complexion, "Ordinarily, among the laboring classes and in advanced life, I have found it wan, turnip-hued, and, in Holland, cheese-colored, and moldy cheese *at that.*" As a mere expletive *at* plays a prominent part in Southern speech, well illustrated in the remark of a recent traveller in the South: "There is nothing so curious in the whole Southern vocabulary, colored and white, as the use of this preposition. It seems the indispensable finish of every sentence. Where is it *at?* Where have you been *at?* Where are you going *at?* Where's my lesson *at?* Where does she live *at?* It is universally used in this way by negroes and whites, except the best-educated classes of the latter."

Attackted occurs in America, as in England, in the speech of the illiterate, the result of an apparent misapprehension of its being formed like *transact* and similar words. It is quoted by J. P. Kennedy:

> "From there we left nine hundred men in the Western Territory:
> Our militia was *attackted* just as the day did break."
> (*Swallow Barn*, p. 213.)

Authoress, like poetess, condemned by W. C. Bryant, seems to become more popular as the number of female authors increases in the United States.

Avail, to, is beginning to be used actively instead of reflectively, and men say: "He *availed* of the offer," without the usual "himself." The construction is not unknown in English, for Pope has the line:

> "Explore
> What means might best his safe return *avail.*"
> (*Quoted by Bailey.*)

A recent telegram in the Northern newspapers ran thus: "New York, Feb. 7, 1871. To the Press of the United States. Gentlemen: *Availing* of the courtesy of the Western Union Telegraph Company, I send you, by wire, the annexed appeal in behalf of the suffering people of France."

Awful, in the sense of ugly and unpleasant, instead of its legitimate meaning of, full of awe, is generally regarded an American ism, and it must be admitted that its use here is unwarrantably frequent and incorrect. "The brightest speaker of the (Women's Rights) Convention has been Mrs. Adele Hazlett, the small, slender, wiry little woman from Michigan, who has an indefinite amount of snap in her eyes, and, in the words of a feminine admirer, an *awfully* cunning, little, turned-up nose, and is dreadfully saucy." (New York *Tribune*, January 13, 1871.) But this use of *awful* is at least as much of a Scotticism as an Americanism, and "an *awful* swell" is heard as constantly in English slang as similar expressions with us. The Cockney even improves upon it and makes it *orful*. But to employ *awful* as an adverb and to say, as in England, "She is an *awful* fine woman," (*Slang Dictionary*, p. 68,) can in no way be excused. Still, it is constantly done. "They couldn't get Bill into a row, for he is afeard of hisself, when he gets *awful* mad, and he allers lef his shooting-irons in his room, when he went out." (*Story of Wild Bill.*) "A hot and dusty day! cry the poor pilgrims as they wipe their begrimed foreheads and woo the doubtful breeze which the river bears with it. *Awful* hot! *Dreadful* dusty! answers the sympathetic toll-gatherer." (Hawthorne, *The Toll-Gatherer's Day.*)

Axe, instead of ask, survives with astonishing vitality in Southern speech, and is almost uniformly used by the negro population. It has, of course, the warrant of great antiquity and noble patronage, for, coming unchanged from the Anglo-Saxon, it was used as the legitimate form by the highest in the land down to Queen Elizabeth. "*Axe* not why," says Chaucer's Miller, and in the Frere's Tale we read: "*Axe* him thyself if thou not trowest me." After that period it was abandoned by the Court, but the common people continued its use and brought it to this country. The Cockney and the Norfolk hind use *axe* as exclusively as the poor white folks and the freedmen of the South. It has, besides, been well said that "for purposes of lyric poetry and musical compositions *axed* would be infinitely preferable to the harsh sound *asked,* which no vocalist can pronounce without a painful gasp." (*Blackwood*, October, 1869.)

B.

Back is often used instead of ago, as in the familiar phrase, "Why, that was a long time *back!*" It is the remnant of *back-*

ward, which was formerly so employed by good English writers. "Look upon it some reigns *backward*." (Locke.) The latter word has frequently, as an adjective, the meaning of bashful, and, in the West especially, that greatest of rarities, a modest, timid youth, is called "a *backward* colt"—no doubt from an instinctive appreciation of the contrast with "forward." *Back* again is substituted for *backward* in the phrase *back and forth*, which, in New England at least, is universally used instead of "backward and forward."

Bad is used for ill in familiar style, where *badly* ought to be employed, as when a man says: "I feel quite *bad* to-day." In sentences like "I wanted to see him *bad*," which may be heard every day, its use is, of course, unpardonable.

Bagging, in the majority of cases, does not mean the material for making bags generally, but the hempen bags made specially for packing cotton.

Ball, as far as it relates to games, is found in America as Foot-Ball, Base-Ball, Town-Ball, Corner-Ball, Paddle-Ball, and a great variety of other names. Of these, *Base-Ball* is looked upon as the national game, cricket being comparatively unknown, and found only in some of the Catholic Colleges. Its predecessor was the "Old Cat" of former generations; in 1825 the first *Base-Ball Club* was formed in the City of New York, and of course named the Knickerbocker Club. Now the numerous Clubs are united in a "National Association of Base-Ball Players;" they consist, in the main, of professional players who receive large salaries, often amounting to several thousand a year, and meet each other during the summer, contesting for prizes. They assume odd names, as the Kickenepawlings of Philadelphia, and the Kikiongans of Indiana. The Esculapeans of Brooklyn are all physicians, and the Malta Club of New York contains nothing but milkmen.

Bamboozle, to, means here, as in England, to perplex or mislead; but although it has been used here as long as in England in familiar and popular language, its true origin has never been ascertained. The *Slang Dictionary* quotes it simply as "Modern Gypsey," whatever that may be intended to mean; others propose seriously to trace it back to *bamboo*, and Swift says it was invented by a nobleman in the reign of Charles II. Probably it existed long before, and was only then first used in polite society, as even Arbuthnot condescends to use it.

Bang-up, the old word for a heavy overcoat, now superseded everywhere else by newer names, still survives in some parts of the Union. "He was clothed in an old *bang-up*, black vest, grey pants, and straw hat." (Philadelphia *Ledger*, June 11, 1853.)

Banjo, often represented as an African word, is simply the corrupted and softened form of the old *bandore*, a descendant of the Greek *πανδοῦρα*, a musical instrument invented by Pan. Thomas Jefferson speaks of it as an instrument "proper to the Blacks, which they brought hither from Africa, and which is the original of the guitar, its chords being precisely the four lower chords of the guitar." (*Notes on Virginia*, p. 47.)

Bannock, in Scotland a round cake of oatmeal, kneaded in water only, and baked against a stone, called bannock-stone, while the same cake is called a girdle-cake if baked on an iron plate, means in America a cake of Indian meal, fried in lard.

Banter, to, in the West, means not merely to joke and jest good-humoredly, but also to challenge to a match, and to provoke a wager. "We had a fine *banter*, but the match was postponed till spring."

Barm, or *barme*, is used in New England instead of yeast, the initial letter of which, although persistently dropped (east), seems to be a rock of offence to American organs of speech, so that there are quite a number of substitutes for the unlucky word. It has the sanction of Beaumont and Fletcher, and of Shakespeare, who uses it in his Midsummer Night's Dream, while Chaucer already sings:

> "Of tarte, alum-glas, *berme*, wert, and argoils."

Batter cakes are the familiar cakes of Indian meal, made with buttermilk or cream, and seldom absent from a Southern breakfast-table.

Bay not only designates an inlet from the sea, but very frequently also any low, swampy region in the South, perhaps so called from the bay-trees which are apt to abound in such localities. "They found themselves on the edge of a very dense forest of pines and scrubby oaks, a portion of which was swallowed up in a deep *bay*, a swamp-bottom, the growth of which consisted of mingled cypresses and *bay* trees, with tupelo, gum, and dense thickets of low stunted shrubbery, cane-grass, and dwarf willows, which filled up every interval between the trees, and to the eye most effectually barred out every human intruder." (W. G. Simms. *The Wigwam and the Cabin.*) *Bay-Galls* are large, gloomy, almost impenetrable swamps in Florida, full of deer, bear, and catamount.

Bazar is a word for which America is indebted to Mrs. Trollope, who established the first in Cincinnati—an enterprise which unfortunately did not succeed, and was thought to have contributed largely to her bitter animosity against this country.

Be, instead of am or are, as frequently in the Bible, is still quite popular in New Hampshire and Massachusetts, as it survives in like manner in some of the provincial dialects of England. "*Be* ye content now, deacon?" asks a woman in Mrs. H. B. Stowe's recent novel.

Beat, to, retains here the meaning which is given in Bailey's Dictionary, to surpass, excel. "Who *beat?* Why, of course, Highflier *beat* the mare all to pieces." (Louisville *Courier,* May 17, 1854.) A further extension of this meaning has led to the use of *beat* instead of *beaten,* as when people say, "We felt dead *beat,*" meaning that they felt quite overcome. The verb is rendered intensive by the addition of *all hollow* (instead of *hollow,* as in English). "In this matter we *beat* the English *all hollow,* and we mean to do the same in everything else." (New York *Herald,* December 13, 1867.)

Beau, to, a verb used by the uneducated instead of "to escort."

Beautiful, like elegant, is a much misused term, being applied indiscriminately to anything pleasing or good. The butter on the breakfast-table is quite as often called *beautiful* or *elegant* as the finest lady on Broadway. "That was *beautiful* conduct," said the New York *Mirror,* of a heroic act.

Becaise, instead of because, often made a matter of special reproach to the South, since it is common to the Whites there, is almost unknown to the Blacks. It is not a corruption, or at least a corruption of old date, and sanctioned by usage at the time when Virginia was settled, and the word was brought over from England; for Pepys, in the Appendix to his Diary, quotes a letter of the Earl of Leicester to Cumnor Hale, requiring a strict investigation into the sudden death of Amy Robsart, "*becaise* of my thorough quietness and of all others hereafter." (Vol. IV., p. 339.)

Beef is often applied in the South to an ox, and the butcher calls on the planter to see if he has any *beeves* to sell. "She'll make a fine *beef*," is said of a cow giving no milk, which is to be fattened.

Beer, without the addition of a descriptive noun, is very rarely heard in America, *ale* being generally used where an Englishman would say *beer*. The first small-beer of the country, made in 1630, is thus described by an anonymous poet:

> "If barley be wanting to make into malt,
> We must be contented and think it no fault,
> For we can make liquor to sweeten our lips
> Of pumpkins and parsnips and walnut-tree chips."

Bellowses, for lungs, not unknown in English slang (*Slang Dictionary*, p. 72), is actually in use in New England and Pennsylvania. J. R. Lowell says, "His *bellowses* is sound enough." (*Biglow Papers*, I., p. 23.)

Belly-guts is the unæsthetic name given in Pennsylvania to molasses candy, and, in New England, by a corruption of belly-cutter, to low sleds on which boys slide down-hill in winter, lying flat on their bellies. (*B.*)

Belongings, in the sense of gentlemen's shirts and drawers, is a euphemistic term, by no means found only in Washington newspapers, where it seems to have been first discovered, for we are told that, "We observe that this substantive appears in the *Philological Society Dictionary*, under the sponsorship of Mr. Ruskin." (*Blackwood*, April, 1861.)

Ben, the uniform Yankee manner of pronouncing *been*, is thus justified by J. R. Lowell, in his enthusiastic apology for Yankeeisms, and with a special view to justify his brother poet Whittier, who seems to affect the word particularly: "It has the authority of Sackville, Gammer Gurton (the work of a bishop), Chapman, Dryden, and many more, though *bin* seems to have been the common form." The Yankee only follows the old custom of Kent.

Bench, in the New England States, supplies the English term *form*, when applied to a long seat without a back.

Better, for more, prevails in the East as in Herefordshire, England, and in familiar language everywhere. "It is *better* than ten bushels, I warrant you." *Bettermost*, a redundant superlative, is in like manner common to both countries, though not admitted into good society anywhere. *Betterments*, the legal term for improvements, as explained by Bouvier, is a word hardly ever used now-a-days, the latter word having taken its place.

Big, instead of great, can hardly be called an Americanism, however common its use may be, since Jeremy Taylor, in his noble sermon On the Return of Prayer, speaks of him "whose spirit was meek and gentle, up to the greatness of the *biggest* example." (Quoted by J. R. Lowell.) But the over-energetic combination of *great-big*, which is constantly heard in the South, may well be regarded as a native extravagance. "I saw a *great big* snake in the road." The *Big Drink* is an equally intensive term for the Mississippi River, full of droll humor, after the manner of Western extravagance.

Bile for *boil*, almost universally regarded as a most reprehensible vulgarism, has, in like manner, high authority for its use by those who have bequeathed it to the present generation. "*Bile;* this is generally spelt *boil*, but, I think, less properly," says no less an authority than the great Johnson himself. Thus endorsed, *bile* has maintained itself throughout the country, and the *biled* shirt of the late Civil War has anew proved its indestructible vitality. "Pigs will be ketched by steam and will be *biled* fit to eat before they are done squealing." (J. C. Neal, *Charcoal Sketches*, II., p. 27.)

Bindery, as a place where books are bound, is a new word, and, according to Webster's *Dictionary*, an Americanism. "Before long the Mercantile Library will have a *bindery* of its own." (*Scribner's Monthly*, February, 1871.)

Biscuits, in England representing our "crackers," a hard, dry bread, mainly baked for ship-use, here designate a peculiar kind of hot tea-roll, usually fermented.

Birdie, a frequent name in the United States, especially in the South, derived from Bird or Burd, a Scottish term of endearment, applied to young ladies,—

"And by my word, the bonny *bird*
In danger shall not tarry."

(*Thomas Campbell.*)

Blackmail, originally the money paid to the agents of robbers to secure protection from the latter, in Scotland, has in the

United States obtained a wider signification, and designates any money extorted under threat of exposure, public attack, or ill treatment in the public papers.

Blackstrap, a mixture of molasses with some spirituous liquor, and commonly distributed to the hands during harvest. "I am carried back to long-ago noonings in my father's hay-fields, and to the talk of Sam and Job over their jug of *Blackstrap* under the shadow of the ash-tree, which still dapples the grass whence they have been gone so long." (J. R. Lowell.)

Blather and *blatherskite*, probably fanciful derivatives from blatant, are frequently heard in the West to designate blustering, empty threats. Bailey quotes it as meaning loud talking or disputing, and says that Skelton has it, that it is still known in Northamptonshire, and adduces the phrase, "None of your *blatheration*." It seems to be of Irish origin; at least J. R. O'Flanagan gives a curious etymology of the word: "Lord Redesdale was speaking of people who learnt to skate with bladders under their arms to buoy them up, if they should fall into a hole and risk being drowned. 'Ah, my Lord,' said Toler, 'that is what we call *bladderum skate* in Ireland.'" (*Lives of the Lord Chancellors of Ireland.*)

Blickie is, in New Jersey, a common term for a tin-bucket.

Blizzard, a term referred back to the German *Blitz*, means in the West a stunning blow or an overwhelming argument. "A gentleman at dinner asked me for a toast, and supposing he meant to have some fun at my expense, I concluded to go ahead and give him and his likes a *blizzard*." (*Crockett's Tour*, p. 16, *B.*)

Block, besides its ordinary meanings, serves in America also to designate a connected mass or row of buildings, and even a whole portion of a town, enclosed by streets, whether it be built upon or not, and in this sense is a genuine Americanism. "The terrible conflagration destroyed an entire *block* and a large portion of the adjoining streets." (Leavenworth paper, June, 1869.) The word has been adopted in England, and is often met with in newspaper-language. Occasionally it is substituted for *block-house*: "I reckon it was a joyful surprise to Betsy, when we broke into the *block*." (W. G. Simms, *The Two Camps*.)

Bloomer designates both a costume devised by a Mrs. Bloomer for independent ladies, and the wearer of such a costume. A well-known damsel, who, during and after the late Civil War, appeared very frequently in the press of England, as well as of her native land, was thus described: "Doctor Mary Walker appeared before the audience in a charming *Bloomer*-costume, much improved upon the original, in bright colors, and very short on top and no longer at the other end." (Philadelphia *Ledger*, January 27, 1865.)

Bobbery, a cant term for a noise, is generally used here in a more good-natured sense, as differing from the objectionable row. The etymology of the word is much disputed. S. S. Haldeman derives it from the Hindoo haṛbaṛî; other authorities also call it "Anglo-Indian" (*Slang Dictionary,* p. 79), and still others connect it with the verb to *bob,* from which *bobbing around* is derived, and Chaucer's famous town "yclept *bob* up and down." "You are a pair of impertinent rascals; what do you mean by kicking up such a *bobbery* at this time of night?" (J. C. Neal, *Charcoal Sketches.*) "People who declare themselves responsible only to Nature's God, are very apt to kick up a tremendous *bobbery* and to make long scolding speeches." (New York *Tribune,* February 6, 1871.)

Bogue, probably from the same root as bogy, is in frequent use in New England in the sense of coming suddenly upon men. "I don't git much done 'thout I *bogue* right in along 'th my men." (J. R. Lowell.)

Bogus, the name of a beverage consisting of rum and molasses, well known to sailors, is occasionally heard in the Eastern States, especially among fishermen. It is probably an abbreviation of the more familiar *calibogus.*

Bonny Clabber, quoted already by Ben Jonson in the lines—

> "It is against my freehold, my inheritance,
> To drink such balderdash as *bonny-clabber,*"

and by Swift—

> "We scorn for want of talk to jabber
> Of parties o'er our *bonny-clabber,*"

means in Pennsylvania and the South not ordinary fluid milk, turned or soured by long standing or a thunder-storm, which is there called *Sour Milk,* but thick milk, from which the whey is drained to get the curds out, of which afterward *smearcase* is made. The following verse seems to be an unprinted part of Yankee Doodle—perhaps even unwritten before—

"*Baughnaugh claughbaugh* all the week,
Sour milk on Sunday,
Pretty girls on Saturday night,
And go to work on Monday."

(*S. S. Haldeman.*)

The word is frequently shortened into *clabber* simply.

Book, to, is very common in the sense of to engage a seat in a stage or other public conveyance.

Bookstore, a place where books are sold, is the American term for the English "bookseller's shop."

Boosy, or more frequently *boozy,* originally a vile gypsy word, but now very largely used, even by careful writers like G. W. Curtis. The origin is the Dutch *buysen,* to tipple, and it came with many other drinking-terms over from Holland in Queen Elizabeth's time. A "*bouzing* ken" was the old cant term for a public house, and so it is still in modern days. "*Bousing* and belly-cheere" are frequently coupled by Elizabethan writers. It is barely possible, that the word may have been introduced into the United States twice: once by the English settlers, and again by the Dutch colonists.

Bound, the participle of to bind, is frequently used for obliged. "She felt herself *bound,* in American phrase, to prevent Prussia from acquiring an accession of territory." (London *Quarterly,* January, 1871.) It is, like so many similar words, only restored to its legitimate use; even in some parts of England, and especially in the English districts of Southern Wales, it is heard frequently with the same meaning: "He is *bound* to do it."

Boughten, an old participle with the adjective termination, still survives in parts of New England and New York, and serves to distinguish articles bought at a shop from those manufactured at home. "Is this a home-made carpet or a *boughten* one?" The term is evidently due to Scotch settlers, who also say, "I have *putten* on my coat," and "I have *casten* a stone."

Boy, used, before the Civil War, to designate any (colored) man-servant, without regard to age. Gray-haired men would be addressed thus: "*Boy,* bring my horse up, I'm going now," and at a dinner-table the servant would be told, "*Boy,* where is the bread?" It is, after all, but the same tendency which in French calls the waiter "garçon," and in English, gave to *knave* (German, Knabe, a boy) the meaning of follower, so as to induce Wiclife to speak of "the Lordes knaves."

Branch is the generic name of every stream, large or small, in the South, a large river and a mere bayou being the only other designations. Bailey already defines it so, and shows how the term has been preserved in this country: "If from a main river any *branch* be separated, then, where the *branch* doth first bound itself with new banks, there is that part of the river where the *branch* forsakes the main stream, called the head of the river." (Sir W. Raleigh, *History.*) While New England knows only *brooks* and rivers, in other States it is the *run* and the *creek* that prevail, forming finally a great *river.*

Brandywine is once more heard in parts of the United States where the German element prevails, and where, hence, their own "Branntwein" is easily understood by all. The river of that name also recalls the cry: "Buy any *brandewine?* buy any *brandewine?*" in Beaumont and Fletcher's *Beggar's Bush.*

Brash is in America much used for brittle, and applied to wood and to vegetables. This originates, no doubt, with the use of *brash* in some parts of England for broken twigs and refuse boughs. The same idea underlies the meaning of *brash-ice:* "When from the effects of abrasion the larger blocks of ice are crumbled into minute fragments, this collection is called *brash-ice.*" (Hugh Murray, *Polar Seas,* 1829.) The word is also used with the meaning of *harsh,* probably from its former meaning of, hasty in temper, impetuous, as quoted by Grose. "See here, you are playing this a little too *brash.*" (*Putnam's Magazine,* August, 1868.) In Southern New Jersey and in Pennsylvania, an acid rising taste in the mouth is frequently called *brash,* and an indisposed person is said to be *brashy.* It has the same meaning in the North of England. (Brockett.)

Bravely is still, as of old in England, used in the sense of, very well, excellently. As Bacon wrote: "Swart, with his Germans, performed *bravely,*" our newspapers report: "The paving of Pennsylvania Avenue is going on *bravely,* and all will be ready for the great carnival." (Washington *Chronicle,* February 27, 1871.)

Breadstuff, a most useful word, designating all the cereals which can be converted into bread: corn, wheat, rye, etc., and occasionally bread itself. "One great objection to the conduct of Britain, was her prohibitory duty on the importation of *bread-stuff*." (Marshall, *Life of Washington*, V., p. 319, *B.*) Now-a-days the plural is more generally used: "*Breadstuffs* have declined, although farmers hoped for a rise in prices, in consequence of the Franco-German war." (New York *Herald*, October 21, 1870.)

Break, to, is in Virginia, and other tobacco-raising States, applied to the opening of the hogsheads, as they are sent from the plantations, previous to a public sale. The *breaking* is a process watched with much interest by buyer and seller.

Breakdown, is here, as in England, the term for a noisy dance, deemed violent enough to "break down" the floor; the "flare-up" of Ireland; in the South universally applied to the violent performances of the negroes.

Brewis, in England, a broth made of bread with broth poured over it, represents in New England crusts of rye and Indian bread, softened with milk and eaten with molasses.

Brief is used in the South very often, as in some parts of England, for prevalent, and has been regarded a corruption of "rife." A traveller in Virginia hearing the driver say "The wind is *brief*," asked what that meant, and received the answer, "The wind is a sort of peart."

Bring, to, takes in America almost altogether the place of the English, to fetch. Bailey says the two verbs differ in this, that we fetch things by another, but bring them in our own hand, and refers to the verse: "As she was going to *fetch* it, he called to her, *Bring* me a morsel of bread." (1 Kings xvii. 11.)

Brown bread designates bread made of a mixture of two parts of corn-meal with one part of rye-meal, once almost exclusively used in New England, but now very common throughout the country.

Brown stone, a dark variety of red sandstone, and highly esteemed as a building material in New York, where a *brown stone* front is apt to be looked upon as a sign of gentility. "The *brown stone*, now so fashionable, is perhaps the most perishable of all materials used in New York house-building. It is laminated and unequal in density, particularly absorbent of water, and susceptible to the chemical influences of the atmosphere." (New York *Tribune*, January 19, 1871.)

Buggy, in England, a light one-horse chaise, on two wheels, means in America a single-seated, four-wheeled vehicle, with or without a top, drawn by one or two horses.

Bull is used by Americans in good society only as a financial term, connected with "Bears," or as an Irish bull. At least it is commonly believed that *ox* is the only respectable term by which a bull can be safely designated, and even "gentleman-cow" has been attempted by very bashful prudes. There is a story current and quoted abroad, that a gray-headed American gentleman was seen to doff his hat reverently, and apologize to a clergyman for having inadvertently used in his presence the plain Saxon term.

Bundle, to, a custom still prevalent in Wales, and not unfrequently practised in the West, of men and women sleeping with all their clothes on, when there is not house-room to provide better accommodation. "Among other hideous customs, they (the Yankees) attempted to introduce that of *bundling*, which the Dutch lasses of the Nederlandts, with their eager passion for novelty and for the fashions, natural to their sex, seemed very well inclined to follow, but that their mothers, being more experienced in the world and better acquainted with men and things, discountenanced all such outlandish innovations." (W. Irving, *Knickerbocker History of New York*.)

Bun, recalling the English *bunn*, the familiar name of the rabbit (Halliwell), is, in America, frequently applied to the squirrel.

> "The mountain and the squirrel
> Had a quarrel,
> And the former called the latter, Little Prig!
> *Bun* replied :
> You are doubtless very big."
>
> (R. W. Emerson. *Fable*.)

Bureau is the name in America commonly given to a chest of drawers.

C.

Calculate, to, a word generally looked upon as an Arch-Americanism, and inseparable from the fictitious type of the Yankee, may be more frequently heard in the New England States, where trade and barter thrive, so as to make calculations familiar to old and young, but has made its way over the whole North and West. "You all know, though neighbor Vale has the best heart in the world, he hasn't a mite of *calkerlation*, and none of the Vales never had, as ever I heerd on. How he's gittin' on! and all for nothin' under the sun, only for the want of *kalkerlate*." (*Putnam's Magazine*, January, 1870.)

Can, to, a verb of recent origin, since the process of putting up fruit in air-tight *cans* has been adopted.

Caney, an adjective made from *cane*, is often met with in the West to designate places where cane is either still growing, or once grew in abundance; hence, numerous names of *Caney Branch*, and the like, in Kentucky.

Cant, to, in the sense of to turn over, is in common use with us, while in England it is rarely heard. Bailey, however, explains it thus: "In carpentry, signifies to turn, as when a piece of timber comes the wrong way, they say, *Cant* it, that is, turn it about." The same meaning is evidently attached to Grose's quotation: "He was *canted* out of the chaise." Hence, also, *cant-hook*, a useful instrument in the shape of an iron hook, attached to the end of a wooden lever, by means of which heavy weights can be easily *canted* over and moved. It is American in design and name.

Caption, originally a legal term, has been adopted by the American press to designate simply a title, a "heading:" "Under this *caption* I propose to consider two questions." (Rev. H. W. Beecher.)

Captivate, to, instead of to capture, has been called an Americanism, but has at least very good English authority for this meaning: "He deserves to be a slave, that is, content to have the rational sovereignty of his soul and the liberty of his will so *captivated*." (King Charles I.) It is, however, rarely ever heard now in this sense.

Carry, to, a verb constantly used in Virginia and the South, instead of to lead. "*Carry* the horse to water." The very opposite custom prevails in parts of England, *e. g.*, in Sheffield, where "they *lead* hay, corn, coals, and almost everything which elsewhere they *carry* or cart." (*Sir Richard Phillips' Tour*, p. 304.)

Case, in, is said, in the Southern States, of tobacco, when it is soft and pliant, or in a condition to be packed away in casks without loss.

Catch is almost universally pronounced *ketch* in the New England States, and frequently as far South as Virginia. This is, of course, only the old English sound and mode of spelling, retained from early days, without change; for we read in Chaucer—

> "Lord! Trowe ye that a coveitous wretche
> That blameth love and hath of it despite
> That of the pens that he can muche and *ketche* . . .
> (*Troilus and Cressida*, III., B. 75.)

The Cockney and the Virginian alike modify it still farther, and call it *kotched*. "I be *kotched* cold."

Cater-cornered, a very common term in Virginia and the South, is evidently derived from the French *quatre*, as in "Cater," the four of dice, etc.; and in "Cater-cousin." The word occurs in Carr's Craven *Glossary*, and Grose has a similar word, *cater-cross*. "You must go *cater-cross* the field, Kent." (*Sub voce.*)

Catstick, in England the bat for playing certain games at ball, is an Americanism as far as it is used for any unsplit stick of wood with the bark on, which is small enough to be grasped by the hand. This is probably the English provincial use of the term. (J. R. Lowell.) A *cat's nap* is, in New England, a short doze.

Catsup, the more common way of writing *catchup*, as quoted in the dictionaries, has Swift's authority in its favor:

> "our homebred British cheer,
> Botargo, *catsup*, and cavier."

Cattle, in England, used generically for all animals that serve for food or draught, is in America rarely used for any other beasts but those of the bovine genus—perhaps because horses were of much later introduction.

Centrical has, in Virginia especially, maintained itself in spite of its more popular rival "central," which has elsewhere completely usurped its place. It was much used by Sir W. Scott: "It is time to draw our party to a head, either at York or some other *centrical* place." (*Ivanhoe.*) "The State Papers of the Revolution use *centrical* continually." (Hugh Blair Grigsby.)

Certain belongs to a class of adjectives which Americans constantly use as adverbs. "He's done it sure and *certain*." It is frequently strengthened by the addition of *for*. "We shall be burnt out *for certain*." (*Harper's Weekly*, February 28, 1871.)

Chain-lightning, the Western term for "forked lightning," is generally rendered more redundant by being changed into *chained* lightning. In both forms it is constantly applied to inferior whiskey.

Chair is in South Carolina uniformly pronounced *cheer*, as stairs become *steers*, and *ai* is generally transformed into *ee*, with a system of strict retaliation, by which, e. g., *deer-meat* becomes *dare-mate*.

Champ, on the other hand, has its peculiar sound of *chomp* in New England as well as in the South, where *stomp*, in like manner, takes the place of *stamp*. To *chomp* means here to eat greedily, though it has also the meaning given to it in the *Spectator* already: "The pieces of a tobacco-pipe left such a delicate roughness on my tongue that I *champed* up the remaining part."

Chance is used in the South to express a certain amount or supply: "He lost a smart *chance* of blood."

Chaw, to, once the legitimate word, has, in England and here, given way entirely to the modern form, to *chew*. "I saw here the spruce-wax which the Canadians *chaw*, done up in little silvered papers, a penny a roll." (*Putnam's Magazine*, January, 1853.) The older form, however, re-appears quite frequently yet, and is especially retained for the quid of tobacco, which is called a *chaw*. "He said he didn't give me nothing; never even gave me a *chaw* of tobacco." (*Sketches of Southern Life*.) "Sparrowgrass, it don't hurt a tree a single morsel to *chaw* it, if it's a young tree. For my part, I'd rather have my trees *chawed* than not. I think it makes them grow a leetle better." (F. Cozzens, *Sparrowgrass Papers*.) *Chaw* is still the favorite word in Virginia and the whole South, as it came in the seventeenth century from England, where it was in common use. Pepys writes, June 7, 1665, in his *Diary:* "It put me into an ill conception of myself and my smell (it was in the time of the plague), so that I was forced to buy some roll-tobacco to smell and to *chaw*, which took away the apprehension." Thus it remained unchanged. "The late eloquent Watkins Leigh was asked by a friend what he thought of James Buchanan (the President), and answered, that he had one serious objection to him, and when pressed to name it, said that once, when he and Mr. Buchanan were sitting together in the United States Senate, the latter asked him for a *chew* of tobacco instead of a *chaw*." (Hugh Blair Grigsby, private letter, April, 1871.)

Check is in Pennsylvania the name of an impromptu meal of cold provisions. (S. S. Haldeman.)

Checkmate, to, in its secondary meaning of defeating any effort or adversary—not on the board—has become very popular in America since Morphy and Paulsen, in 1857 and 1858, made chess a favorite game throughout the country. "To *checkmate* means to baffle or obstruct." (*National Quarterly,* December, 1860.)

Cheek has, in America, retained the old English meaning of a door-post, as quoted in the Craven *Glossary:* "She threw up her hands against the *cheek* of the door and prevented me from putting her out." (Rev. P. Cartwright, *Autobiography,* p. 188.)

Chills and Fever is the common expression in malarious regions for fever and ague.

Chimley, for chimney, as used by Sir W. Scott: "A kirk with a *chimley* in it was fitter for them" (*Rob Roy,* I., ch. 120), is very common in all parts of the United States, though the fuller form, *chimbley,* is perhaps even more general:

"Agin the *chimbly* crooknecks hung,
An' in amongs 'em rusted
The ole Queen's arm that gran'ther Young
Fetched back from Concord busted."
(J. R. Lowell. *Courtin'.*)

Chirp, to, frequently enlarged into *chirrup,* and considered a mispronunciation of cheer up, but quoted as *chirp,* by Johnson, is in both forms in common use in America. Insects are here said to *chirp,* and the noun is substituted for the English *crick.*

Chist is the common New England pronunciation of *chest,* as *kittle* of kettle, and justified, as J. R. Lowell pleads, by the fact that both Bishop Hall and Purchas in his "Pilgrims" have *chist,* as well as by the derivation of the word from the Latin cista (German, Kiste).

Chivalry is a term often applied to Southern gentry and their peculiar social views. "The *Chivalry* of the South differs from the Yankee precisely as the Cavalier differed from the Puritan." (*Southern Literary Messenger,* June, 1849.)

Chock, to, in the sense of to fill up, as used in Fuller's *Worthies,* continues to be used in America. "What made the trunk so awful heavy, I couldn't see; but I found afterward she had all her clothes and mine, and then she'd *chocked* in all 'round with maple-sugar, and that's as heavy as the ten commandments to a horse-thief." (*Putnam's Magazine,* June, 1868.) Hence, also, *chockfull,* of which Halliwell says: "*Chockfull* is still in use in various counties." It is an open question, whether the term derives its meaning from the old English *chekkefulle,* quite full, or from the verb, to *choke,* or from filling the scales till they come down with a *shock.* (*Slang Dictionary,* p. 100.) "The house was *chockfull,* and when Forrest appeared, their shouts were terrific." (Philadelphia *Ledger,* January 21, 1851.)

Choose, to, is used by low-bred people, with the peculiar meaning of to choose not to take what is offered. A dish offered at table is declined with the words, "I don't *choose* any."

Chore, a task or small work of domestic nature, generally used in the plural, is in all probability the old English *char,* from which the modern *charwoman* is derived. J. R. Lowell states, however, that *chore* occurs already in Ben Jonson, and humorously derives it from the French *jour,* as a day's work. Its origin is more likely to be sought in the Anglo-Saxon caer, our word *care,* with the French softening of the initial, especially as the gradual transition from caer to char and chore, can be distinctly traced. Shakespeare speaks of

"the maid that milks
And does the meanest *chares*"—
(*Antony and Cleopatra.*)

while J. R. Lowell sings:

"I love to start out arter night's begun,
An' all the *chores* about the house are done."
(*Biglow Papers,* II., p. 51.)

"As daylight began to glimmer, I crowed very loudly several times, hoping that the old darkey who did the *chores* would think it was morning, and get up to light the fires." (*Atlantic Monthly,* November, 1870.)

Chuckfull, an unwarranted but frequent mode of spelling *chockfull.* "These prairies are nature's banks, stuffed *chuckfull* of cash, which any man can draw out if he will only present his check. The funds are deposited to the credit of Labor, Pluck & Co. It is the poor man's savings' bank." (*Putnam's Magazine*, December, 1868.)

Chunk, in the sense of a short, stout piece of wood, is not unknown to English provincials, but *chunky* is probably a genuine Americanism, first used by Dr. Kane, of North Pole celebrity. "A tolerable *chunk* of a pony," means, in Southern and Western parlance, a cob.

Circumstance is not unfrequently used half-humorously, and almost always negatively, to indicate a matter of more or less importance. "Yes, as you say, this fish is first-rate, but it ain't a *circumstance* to what can be done in the cooking way." (W. S. Mayo, *Kaloolah*, p. 37.)

Claybank, a word not found in English dictionaries, is in America often used to denote the color most common to a bank of clay. "I mounted a *claybank* colored nag and rode to the hunt." (*Putnam's Magazine*, February, 1855.)

Clean, used as an adverb for, entirely, is so far from being an Americanism, that Shakespeare uses it continually, even saying *clean gone* in the sense of, out of sight. "The old mare, summoning all her mettle, rose at the fence and went *clean* over it, not a single horse daring to follow her." (*Rural Register*, May, 1847.)

Clerk, in the North generally pronounced *clurk*, is in Virginia and some parts of the South still called *clark*, as it was not only sounded, but even written, at the time when that colony was settled. Pepys writes, July 30, 1662: "So we got a dish of steaks at the White Hart, while his *clarkes* were feasting of it in the best room of the house."

Clever, one of the most disputed words in our speech, seems to have been undeservedly criticized, as its meaning varies almost infinitely, with the locality in which it is used. Bailey says of it: "*Clever* is in all senses but a low word, scarcely ever used in burlesque and conversation, and applied to anything a man likes, without any settled meaning." If Northern people among us, therefore, choose to employ it in the sense of good-natured and obliging, there seems to be no ground whatever for objection. Even now this troublesome word, a favorite with our race wherever they are, can neither be traced back to an undoubted derivation nor defined in its meaning beyond cavil. Used in England, generally, for good-looking, or handy and dexterous; it means in Norfolk, rather, honest and respectable, and sounds there like *claver*. In some districts of Southern Wales it indicates a state of good health; in a few southern counties perfect clearness and completeness, and in other parts, as with us, courtesy and affability. The American pet-word, *smart*, has, however, largely superseded it in our speech, and only in Virginia and some parts of the South *clever* is still much used in its old English meaning of skillful at work and talented in mind.

Climb, to, is occasionally used in the extraordinary sense of *climbing down*, as in the account of the Rev. H. W. Beecher:— "I partly *climbed down*, and partly clambered back again, satisfied that it was easier to get myself in than to get the flowers out." (*Star Papers*, p. 41.)

Clip, to, in the sense of to give a blow; and the noun, a *clip*, meaning a blow, must be looked upon as Americanisms, though Bailey has *a clop* for a blow, and Halliwell (p. 255, No. 6) the same. "He ran up to him, hit him a severe *clip*, and dashed through the window." (*Police Gazette*, November 17, 1860.)

Clothier, besides being the ordinary name of a tailor and draper, is here also used to designate a person who makes and fulls cloths, which is not done in England.

Coast, to, means, in boys' parlance, to slide down a frozen or snow-covered hill on a sled. The term, used in New England and New York only, is not improbably derived from the French *côte* of their Canadian neighbors.

Coincidence, although quoted by J. Angus as an Americanism, is not unknown to English authors.

Collide, to, designates the sudden and violent meeting of two persons, trains, vessels, etc., in motion. Although the English generally use to *collision*, as in "Wave *collisions* wave" (Royston Pigott in Trans. *Royal Microscop. Society*, December, 1870, p. 298), the term is not, as has been sneeringly stated, the "happy result of frequent railway collisions," but a good English word. (*Notes and Queries*, March 28, 1868.)

Comical has in the South the peculiar meaning of strange, extraordinary. "Dr. White, who discovered the Puncheon Run Falls, said to a mountaineer that they were a great curiosity. 'I don't see nothing kewrus about 'em,' replied the man disdainfully, 'when the water comes over the top, it is bound to run down to the bottom, and der ain't nothin' kewrus or *comical* in that. Now,' —adding meditatively—'if the water was to run up, you see, then I'd allow it to be a kewrosity.'" (E. A. Pollard, *Southern Scenery.*)

Company has recently acquired a new meaning in California, where it represents five societies, respectively called "Yung Loo," "Si Yap," "Sam Yap," "Yan Wo," and "Ning Yeung," and forming the connecting link between the Chinese immigrants and their native land. "Maintaining a sort of intelligence-office on a large scale, they effect engagements for the Chinamen, look after their interests here and at home, are their bankers and brokers, and return their embalmed bodies to their families in China. For these services they are paid by a percentage on wages received, acting, in fact, as a sort of general assurance-office for the benefit of their clients." (Frank H. Norton, *Our Labor System,* 1871.)

Concern means here, more frequently than in England, what Grose already gives as its signification, "a small estate;" and then is extended to all that belongs to a certain business without regard to size: "General Sherman having ordered a certain depot to be discontinued, the removal of the large amount of stores produced delay; after several reports, he blurts out thus: Better burn the whole *concern* down than go on this way." (*Putnam's Magazine,* January, 1870.)

Conduct, to, is in America frequently used without the reflexive pronoun, and the unpleasant form seems to creep into the pages of English writers also. "Castor and Pollux in their famous Argonautic expedition *conducted* with great gallantry." (Alden Bradford, *The Wonders of the Heavens.*) "Mr. Schutt said to him, How strangely you have *conducted!*" (Binghamton *Republican,* January 17, 1871.)

Connection, in America, points out the distinction between persons united by common descent, who are called "relations," while *connections* are related only by marriage. In England, "relations" is the common designation of all; the beautiful words, "kinsman and kinswoman," are but rarely heard here, and the latter especially, but very imperfectly represented by, female relative. (R. G. White.) *In this connection* is a favorite phrase of some American writers, which Fitz Greene Halleck advised Mr. Gould, the author of *Good English*, to doom to what Sir W. Scott's daughter called, unquestionable fire.

Considerable, used as an adverb or noun, is an unwarrantable abuse, but of common occurrence, even with careful writers. "That was *considerable* of a battle, wasn't it?" (Lucian Minor. Diary. *Atlantic Monthly*, July, 1870.)

Constable, in America, designates no other officer but the city or town official, whose duty it is to preserve peace, carry out the orders of the sheriff, attend juries, etc.; while in England the *constable's* duties and powers extend over a whole district.

Contemplate, to, is constantly used here for the simpler word, to propose, to intend, and, still worse, frequently enlarged into, to *have in contemplation*. These are evidences of that "habitual showiness in language, as in dress and manners, which denotes lack of discipline or lack of refinement. Our American grandiloquence, the tendency to which is getting more and more subdued, comes partly from youthfulness, partly from license, the bastard of Liberty, and partly from the geographical and political greatness of the country, which Coleridge says is to be 'England in glorious magnification.'" (G. H. Calvert.)

Convenient has assumed a new meaning in the United States, probably due to Irish influence. It is used to denote what is near at hand, within easy reach; a farm will thus be advertised as having "wood and water *convenient* to the house."

Corduroy, the name of a ribbed stuff, has in new clearings and sparsely populated districts of the South given its name to a rough kind of road, consisting of loose poles or logs laid across the swamp, which resembles somewhat the ribbed appearance of the velvet. "Here we made our first acquaintance with those formidable instruments of torture called *corduroy*-roads; the jolting was terrific, but we were told it was the only road possible in these low grounds." (*Letters from the South*, p. 217.)

Cornwallis, the unfortunate commander of the British troops, survives sadly in the memory of New England by the name of a mock-muster held annually, to take the place of the old Guy Fawkes procession, and to commemorate the surrender at Yorktown. J. R. Lowell says: "It was a masquerade in which the grave and suppressed humor, of which the Yankees are fuller than other people, burst through all restraints and disported itself in all the wildest vagaries of fun." "It allowed some vent to those natural instincts which Puritanism had scotched but not killed."

> "There is fun to a *Cornwallis*, I ain't agoin' to deny it."
> (*Biglow Papers*, I., p. 26.)

> "Recollect wut fun we hed, you 'n I an Ezzy Hollis,
> Up there, to Waltham plain, ahavin' the *Cornwallis*."
> (*Biglow Papers.*)

Corp takes in Pennsylvania, very frequently, the place of the fuller form, corpse.

Corporosity, for the living body, belongs to the same part of the country, and is still in common use. "His *corporosity* touches the ground with his hands in a vain attempt to reach it." (J. C. Neal, *Charcoal Sketches.*)

Cotbetty, an American compound of the English *cot*, which English glossaries quote as meaning an effeminate, troublesome man, and the term *Betty*, used very much in the same sense, is occasionally heard to denote a man who meddles with woman's special duties in a household.

Coverlid, instead of the legitimate English coverlet, is so generally used that it must be considered a genuine Americanism. J. R. Lowell defends it on the ground that it "is nearer its French original than the diminutive coverlet, into which it has been ignorantly corrupted in politer speech"—its ancestor being *couvre-lit*, the cover for the bed.

Cow, heard as *k-yow* in the New England States, is the inheritance of early settlers from Essex, Norfolk, and Sussex, where the same pronunciation is still prevalent among the laboring classes. It cannot be doubted, however, that the nasal twang of the early Puritans, also, has left its indelible impress upon Yankee speech, precisely as it is heard to this day in conventicle prayer-meetings in Norwich and Boston, Colchester and Harwich. The word *cow* was once made a shibboleth in the following manner: "During the Kansas excitement, a stalwart but illiberal Missourian was the owner of a ferry on the main-track of immigration. Dreading the effect of an influx of New England innovators, he established a test which was satisfactory to himself, though one cannot but doubt its universal applicability. He kept tied by the horns to a tree on the river-bank one of the 'milky mothers of his herd,' and on the arrival of a customer, was wont to inquire, whether 'he saw that thar brute,' and what he 'mought call her?' If the applicant *reckoned* it was a *cow*, he could go on his way rejoicing; but should he *guess* it to be a *keow*, or in a moment of hapless impudence asked the questioner if he 'didn't spose everybody knew a *keow*,' he must needs seek some other crossing-place, as well as depart under a heavy weight of malediction." (*Overland Monthly*, February, 1870, p. 189.)

Cowcumber, also, is universal Yankee, and quite common all over the United States—excused as "coming nearest to the nasal sound of the original *concombre*." (J. R. Lowell.)

Cracker, meaning a small firework, has in America entirely superseded the English *squib*, which is only heard in political slang. It designates, also, a small hard biscuit, as is the case in the North of England.

Cracklings, a favorite toothsome dish of the Southern States, consisting of pieces of the rind of pork roasted, which are baked into the bread of negroes, and make one of their greatest luxuries, known as *goody-bread.*

Creature is frequently used in the South for an animal, especially a horse. Its more common form is *critter*, with a nice distinction between the two, when applied to men, as explained by General Squash of Connecticut in the *Gouty Philosopher:* "The word *creature*," said the General, "implies a certain amount of goodness, beauty, respect, and love, as when we talk of God's *creatures;* whereas *critter* is always associated with some idea of inferiority in the person so designated, and of good or even ill-natured contempt on the part of the speaker. Thus when I tell you that Mrs. or Miss A—— is a *creature*, you'll learn, if you do not interrupt me, that I consider her lovely either in mind or person or both. But were I to call her *critter*, and no more, you'd be justified in believing that, in my opinion, she was either a slut, a scold, a scandalmonger, a fool, or a flirt, and that I had no respect for her. If I said to you in the street: 'Look at that lovely *creature!*' it would probably be to direct your attention to a fine woman or a beautiful child. But if I said: 'Look at that pretty *critter!*' the words might apply to a pet-poodle or a prancing horse. Ours is a great country, sir, a very great country, but it swarms with *critters*, as you'll see if you travel much among us and open your eyes as you go. They are the unwholesome growth of our over-ripe civilization and of our too much liberty." (*Blackwood*, October, 1867.)

Creek, in New York and the Western States a small stream, such as in New England is called a *brook*, and elsewhere a *run* or *branch*. Its familiar pronunciation is *crick*, as it is written by Captain John Smith and in the dedication of Fuller's *Holy Warre*. "Neare their habitation is little small wood or old trees on the ground, by reason of their burning of them for fire. So that a man may gallop a horse amongst these woods anyway, but where the *creekes* or rivers shall hinder." (Captain John Smith, *Virginia*, I., p. 131.) "It was a dark and stormy night, when the good Antony arrived at the *creek* (sagely denominated Haarlem River), which separates the island of Manhattan from the mainland." (W. Irving, *Knickerbocker History of New York.*)

Cruel, used as in Hakluyt for great, is one of the intensive expressions much affected by uneducated Americans, but not an Americanism. It was brought over from England in the early part of the seventeenth century. Thus Pepys, in his *Diary*, July 31, 1662, writes: "Met Captain Brown of the Rosebush, at which he was *cruel* angry." And again, February 21, 1666–7, he says: "W. Batten denies all, but is *cruel* mad."

Cry, to, had in former days, in the New England States, the special meaning, to publish the banns of marriage in church. "They shall be *cried* three times in church, before they can be married." (*Laws of Connecticut.*)

Curious, in the sense of nice, excellent, as used by New England farmers, is not an Americanism, as it occurs continually in old English writers, and has only been preserved here, while other terms are substituted for it in England.

Curfew—the name and the ceremony—were both in use in Pennsylvania (Northumberland County), in 1835, and perhaps later.

> "The shivering wretches at the *curfew* found,
> Dejected, shrunk into their sordid beds."
> (Thomson. *Liberty*, IV., 755.)

Curtitude is occasionally found for shortness. "German market women, who, in skirts of convenient *curtitude,* carry their loads in large, convenient baskets." (S. S. Haldeman, *Notes.*)

'Cute, instead of *acute,* has become almost a word of its own, being stronger in its peculiar meaning than the fuller form, and almost exclusively applied to Yankees. "What became of the particularly *'cute* Yankee child, who left his home and native parish at the age of fifteen months, because he was given to understand that his parents intended to call him Caleb?" (N. Hawthorne.) The word is, however, not unknown in England also. (*Slang Dictionary,* p. 115.)

D.

Daddock, an old English term, rarely heard abroad, even in provincial dialects, is quite common in the rural districts of the New England States, and not unfrequent in the West, where the great long trunks of fallen trees, slowly rotting away and turning into mould, are thus called.

Daffa-down-dilly, a combination of "Sapharoun," or Saffron-lily with Asphodelus, the old English affodilly, which became, on a mutual compromise, not rare in popular names, daffadown-dilly, the old English enlargement of daffodill, and was thus used by Spenser, in his "Shepherd's Callendar." It has been revived or maintained its vitality in Virginia.

> "Diaphenia, like the *daffa-down-dilly,*
> White as the sun, fair as the lily,
> Heigh ho! how I love thee."
> (*Henry Constable.*)

So also:

> "*Daffa Down Dilly* came up in the cold
> Thro' the brown mould."
> (*Southern Magazine,* January, 1871.)

Daft, from Chaucer's *daffe,* a fool, and in Scottish and North of England dialects meaning a lunatic, or one that has been befooled, is likewise quite frequently heard in the South: "are you *daft* to do such a thing?"

Dander, instead of *dandruff,* in the phrase, "to get one's *dander* up," is supposed ludicrously to substitute the dandruff for the hair itself. (?) "He was as spunky as thunder, and when a

Quaker gets *his dander* up, it's like a Northwester." (Major Jack Downing's *Letters*, p. 75.)

> "What will get your *dander* riz?"
> (J. R. Lowell. *Biglow Papers*, I., p. 10.)

Dansy is used, in Pennsylvania, of persons who are failing from old age. It is the same word which Grose quotes as *dansy-headed* in Norfolk and Suffolk, meaning giddy or thoughtless.

Dark Moon, the time between the old and the new moon, is used in the West as in some parts of England.

Daze, an ancient form of *dazzle*, and used by Spenser, Drayton, and others as a verb, is here often used as a noun, to represent a state of utter bewilderment—"She sat like one in a *daze*, as if stunned by the strangeness of her surroundings." (*Putnam's Magazine*, January, 1870.)

Deaf is frequently pronounced *deef*, as was done in olden times, and still continues to be done in Westmoreland, Cumberland, and other parts of England. In Scotland, soil and vegetables are both called *deaf*, when they are sterile; and thus in America, also, nuts are said to be *deaf* when they are decayed or empty.

Dearborn is the name of a light four-wheeled carriage, like the Brougham called after its inventor. "At last the stage was ready —a three-seated *dearborn* with one white and one brown horse." (*Lippincott's Magazine*, March, 1871, p. 245.)

Deck, the name of a pack of cards, repeatedly charged as an Americanism, is so thoroughly English that it is used in Hoyle's famous *Book of Games*. It is, however, in the Western States almost exclusively employed instead of *pack*, which is rarely heard there.

Declension, very rarely used in England for the act of declining, is not unfrequent here. "He asked me to drive with him to-day, but I was forced to send him a *declension*." (*Southern Literary Messenger*, July, 1859.)

Deed, to, meaning to transfer by deed, is a genuine Americanism in its use as a verb. "I fear he has already *deeded* away all his property, and his wife will have nothing when he dies." This is generally done by *deed of trust*, as the hypothecation of landed property is uniformly called in the Middle and Southern States.

Deputize, to, in the sense of to appoint a deputy, is occasionally heard, as it was in the days of Bailey, who mentions it as a term just coming into fashion when he wrote his great work.

Desperate is, in like manner, used now and then for exceedingly. "He was *desperate* glad to see you, I vow." (W. G. Simms, *The Yemassee.*) It is commonly pronounced *desprat*, or even *desput.*

Dew is the common pronunciation of *do* in New England, for the Yankee, "innocently unconscious," ignores all difference between *oo* and *u* in a number of words; and his great advocate, J. R. Lowell, pleads with much force in his behalf, that in this he only follows faithfully the example of the common people of Norfolk and Cambridge in England, who are descended from the same stock with himself. Why he should distinguish, however, between some words and others is not quite clear; but while he says *noo* for new, *Joo* for Jew, and *stoo* for *stew*, he never changes *few;* he speaks of *destitoot, institoot*, and *Toosday*, but leaves *depute* as it is.

Dickey, a gentleman's shirt-collar in New England, means a false shirt-front in England. It is said to have originated with the students of Trinity College, Dublin, who at first styled it "Tommy," from τομή, a section, which the servants changed into "Dicky." (*Slang Dictionary, sub voce.*) "My soul swells till it almost tears the shirt of my buzzum, and even fractures my *dickey.*" (J. C. Neal, *Charcoal Sketches*, III., p. 34.)

Dining-room servant, the name given especially in the South to the English "butler," in the North generally represented by the "parlor-maid."

Dirt is in America generally used for soil, as *rag* is used for any piece of linen or cotton. A Southern lady will order her servant to "fill a flower-pot with *dirt* and bring it to her." An unpaved road is carelessly called a *dirt-road*, and the foreigner is apt to be surprised at hearing people speak of *clean dirt.* "We walked on *dirt-floors* for carpets, sat on benches for chairs, ate on puncheon tables, had forked sticks and butcher-knives for knives and forks." (Rev. P. Cartwright, *Autobiography*, p. 486.) "The love of *dirt* is among the earliest passions." (C. D. Warner, *My Summer in a Garden*, 1871.)

Disremember, to, now entirely out of use in England, still survives in the South and West.

"He fou't us game, somehow, I *disremember*
Jest how the thing kem round."
(F. B. Harte.)

Dodger has, besides the ordinary signification, the meaning of unleavened corn-bread in Virginia and the West, though its more frequent form is *corndodger*.

Dogs is the name still given to andirons in Virginia, and current also in New England. "In Walter de Bibleworth I find *chiens* glossed in the margin by andirons." (J. R. Lowell.) "Brailey's Graphical and Historical Illustrator says that some years ago they dug up, in a Roman camp (in England) a pair of iron *dogs*, so that they are a piece of ancient furniture" (*Idem*). They are also called *fire-dogs*, probably from a faint resemblance to dogs, and the frequent occurrence of dogs' heads on their front part. In New England a thrifty housekeeper speaks of "going out to buy a pair of *dogs*."

Dominies—with a long *o*, not *dŏminies*, as in Scotland, for schoolmasters—is a title still used for their ministers by the so-called Dutch Reformed Church in portions of New York and New Jersey.

Dove, the old form of the past tense of *dive*, is still much used by seamen, and in some parts of the United States by landsmen also.

"Straight into the river Kivasind
Plunged as if he were an otter,
Dove as if he were a beaver."
(H. W. Longfellow. *Hiawatha*, Canto VII.)

Down, to, in the sense of to humble, as in Sidney's "to *down* proud hearts," is utterly forgotten in England, but well preserved in America. "I drew my horsewhip and told the negro if he attempted to close the gate, I would *down* him." (Rev. P. Cartwright, *Autobiography*, p. 206.)

Dozy and *dozied* are said in Pennsylvania of timber beginning to decay and unfit for use, while the decay is yet hardly perceptible, but the timber already brittle. (S. S. Haldeman.)

Dreadful belongs to the large class of words with strong meanings, like awful, terrible, horrible, excessive, etc., which Americans love unfortunately to use on all occasions for the sake of creating a sensation, or at least attracting attention by the form, which they cannot gain by the substance of what they have to say.

Dress has in America entirely superseded the word *gown*, as a part of a lady's costume; the latter term being but rarely heard, except among very aged persons.

Driver, in like manner, is the universal name for the man who drives the horses, whether the latter pull a plough or draw an elegant carriage. The English *coachman* is comparatively unknown.

Dud, in the singular, is an Americanism; the plural form being at least known in England, though not much used. The latter means, however, not only rags and old clothes, but all moveable property. "The three (Railway) Commissioners, in whose appointment you had no voice, decide that you must get out, leave your house, bundle out your *duds*, and be off." (New York *Tribune*, January 23, 1871.) "Think of her? I think she is dressed like a *dud;* can't say how she would look in the costume of the present century." (*Putnam's Magazine*, February, 1870.)

Dump, to, in the sense of unloading a cart by tilting it up, is peculiar to this country. It is in all probability an imitative term, made from the sound, the heavy thud or knock which that operation produces. "It is no joke to go on all day *dumping* loads of dirt down that steep embankment, and each time you tilt your cart to fancy mule and cart all going overboard." (*How to get Rich*, p. 117.) Open lots, where "rubbish may be shot," as the English say, are here called *dumping-grounds*.

Dutiable, liable to duty, a term which in the United States never represents the tax levied on real estate or farmers' stock. The word, which came into use with the first tariff, has proved eminently useful, and is universally adopted. "The following articles shall be *dutiable* hereafter at the fixed rates." (*Act of Congress*, 1865.)

Dyspeptic, an unfortunately frequent word in American conversation, has long lost its special meaning, and is now used to denote all the various forms of weakness of the digestive organs, which lead the citizens of the republic to appreciate with special bitterness the force of the old saying, that "God gave us meat, but the Devil sent us cooks."

E.

Eat, to, is one of a class of verbs, which boundless license has led to apply to persons, instead of, give to eat. A Western steamboat is thus said to be able "to *eat* four hundred passengers and to *sleep* at least two hundred." "Hoosier: Squire, what pay do you give? Contractor: Ten bits a day. Hoosier: Why, Squire, I was told you'd give us two dollars a-day and *eat* us." (*Pickings from the Picayune*, p. 47.)

Eccentric has in Western parlance obtained a curious meaning, which threatens to spread in spite of its absurdity. "I want my land down to the *eccentric*," said an illiterate man in Illinois, objecting to the reservation of mining rights under his purchase.

Edibles and *Bibibles* is a similar innovation, used for food and drink. "The table was spread and loaded with *edibles* and *bibibles* of every possible kind." (Pittsburg *Dispatch*, August, 1860.)

Editorial, used instead of the English leader or leading article, is in this sense a genuine Americanism. The term used elliptically for Editorial Article, arose from the custom of inserting in each day's paper only one or two articles, written by the editor himself, while the others were furnished by contributors or irresponsible sub-editors. It has, however, firmly established itself in our speech, and found a companion of still worse character in the *Local*, which designates either the articles of local interest only, or the reporter whose special duty it is to collect local news. In trying to find an article in a newspaper, a man will therefore say: "It is not an *Editorial*; you must look among the *Locals*."

Educational, often quoted as a new word, occurs in Burke, and has only been revived in our day. *Educator*, also, used more than once by English writers, has only recently obtained that currency among us which it had never been able to secure before. As there is need for a word which shall comprehend every kind of person who devotes himself to the education of the young, from the children's governess to the renowned professor, the term will probably become more and more popular.

Egg, to, in Pennsylvania pronounced to *agg*, and all over the country confounded with the verb, to *edge*, is used in America in its ancient meaning of inciting and pushing forward, as well as in the more recent sense of pelting with eggs. "The drede of God is that we turne noghte agayne tille oure and yure thurghe any ille *eggyng*." (*MS. Lincoln*, A. I., 17, fol. 196.) "The man, a black abolitionist of the deepest dye, was *egged* out of town last night, and will find it safer, we venture to say, not to show himself again." (Kansas paper, 1860.)

Emptyings, commonly pronounced and written *emptin's* in New England, means there the lees of beer, etc., and yeast; but even J. R. Lowell, the master of Yankee speech, professes to be utterly at a loss to divine its origin.

> "And it's jest money throwed away to put the *emptin's* in."
> (J. R. Lowell, *Biglow Papers*, II., p. 11.)

End is in the same regions very generally pronounced *eends*. "Stingy enough to skim his milk at both *eends*."

Engine, the common abbreviation of Fire-Engine, though generally pronounced *injine* (so as to rhyme with *mine*), has in popular speech become almost hopelessly mixed up with *Injin*, the Indian, and *injens*, little seed-onions. Even persons who speak of the full-grown seed as *onions*, will call the small ones *injens*. J. R. Lowell says with humorous pathos, in his indefatigable efforts to justify Yankeeisms: "In one of Dodsley's Old Plays we have *onions* rhyming with *minions*—I have tears in my eyes while I record it." (Preface to *Biglow Papers*, p. 37.) "What do you call this when 'tis bil'd and the skin's tuk off? what's this without *injens?*" (J. C. Neal, *Charcoal Sketches*, II., p. 42.)

Enthuse, to, in the sense of filling or being filled with enthusiasm, is considered by R. G. White so exclusively a Southern word, that he says he "never heard or saw it used, or heard of its use, by any person born and bred North of the Potomac." Since those words were written, the word—bad as it is—has proved too useful to be so strictly confined any longer, and found its way even to England. "It seems that this State, so quickly *enthused* by the generous and loyal cause of emancipation, has grown weary of virtuous effort, and again stands still." (Baltimore *American*.)

Esquire, a title in England still given only to certain classes of men, and long reserved in the United States also to lawyers and other privileged persons, is now with republican uniformity given alike to the highest and the lowest, who does not boast of a military or other title; the result being that it is strictly limited to the two extremes of society.

Evening, in the South and West, takes the place of the afternoon—the time between dinner and supper being *evening*, and after supper *night*. Persons meeting at two or three o'clock, wish each other "Good *evening*," and speak of a "fine *night*," or promise to "come to-*night*," although the sun may but just have sunk below the horizon.

F.

Factory-Cotton designates in America unbleached cotton goods made at home, in contrast with those imported.

Fair, to, generally used in the form of to *fair* off, or to *fair* up, is a Southern term denoting that the weather is clearing up slowly.

Fall, for Autumn, by no means an Americanism, is a term which had only become unfamiliar to English ears. It has been used nearly by every writer of mark, and almost always in picturesque contrast with the corresponding name of *Spring*, since the green verdure which *springs* forth in the early season, *falls* to the ground again in autumn.

> "A honey tongue and heart of gall,
> Is fancy's spring, but sorrow's *fall*."
>
> (*Sir W. Raleigh.*)

> "What crowd of patients the town-doctor kills,
> Or how last *fall* he raised the weekly bills."
>
> (*Dryden.*)

Middleton also plays upon the words: "May'st thou have a reasonable good *spring*, for thou art like to have many dangerous foul *falls*." (Quoted by J. R. Lowell.) The beautiful word, thus enjoying poetical honors and prose-dignity in every century, is a word peculiarly dear to Americans, as the season itself is peculiarly beautiful in their country. There is nothing to be said, on the other hand, in excuse of the word *fall* as used to designate a fall of rain. "He thought there would be a *fall* soon." *Falling* weather is, in this sense, almost universally used in the United States to designate, if not absolute rain, any kind of damp, misty, or drizzling weather.

Family. A *man of family*, in England, almost exclusively denotes a man of *good* family; in America it means a man who has a family—wife and children. "Has he any *family?*" means, therefore, "Has he any children?"

Fancy, denotes in America everything fantastical and unusual, not only, as is the case in Macaulay's "*fancy*-prices" paid by the Prussian king for his giant soldiers, but also things and persons more ornamental than useful. "*Fancy*-men and *fancy*-women" are spoken of as congregating at fashionable watering-places, and *fancy*-stocks are such as exist only on paper. "For a few weeks Crystal-palace stock was one of the most active *fancies*. No one denied that it was very fanciful stock." (*Harper's Monthly*, November, 1853.) "Near one of the busiest points of the city a little *fancy*-store, in a modest wooden house, nestled between two pretentious marble-fronts." (*Putnam's Magazine*, October, 1868.)

Favor, to, resumes frequently its ancient meaning, mentioned by Grose when he says: "*Favor*, to ease, to spare." It is used of horses and other animals, rarely of men, when they limp slightly, sparing one foot. "The off horse *favors* his right foot."

Fay, to, the ancient word, rarely used since Swift, and curtailed from *fadge*, is still often heard in New England, with the meaning of to fit. "That *fays* nicely."

Feather, to, is in like manner still found in the same locality to designate the rising of cream on the surface of a cup of tea or coffee.

February loses, in the South, its first *r*, and sounds *Febuary*, as it does among illiterate people in England.

Feaze, or *feeze*, or even *pheeze*, to be in a state of excitement, a very common expression in Virginia and the Southern States, is not original in America. Nall's Glossary of Yarmouth words already contains a long note on the term, and Chaucer has

> "And thereat came a rage and such a *vese*
> That it madd all the gates for to rese."
> (*Knight's Tale*, *MS.*)

Wiclife also speaks of a placid pool of water that "gaderid togider having no *fyss*." (*John V.*, v. 4.) It comes from the Anglo-Saxon *fysan*, used to denote the rapid and noisy movement of water.

Female is one of the unfortunate words which have of late obtained very general currency among Americans, merely because it may be used safely and conveniently for all members of the fair sex indiscriminately, from the first lady in the land to the lowest outcast. It was once before in general use—in the reigns of Elizabeth and James—as part of the affected language of the court, and satirized unmercifully by the dramatists of that period. Shakespeare uses it frequently and often with all respect. Hume, we are told, calls Joan of Arc a *female*. Sir W. Scott says *female* twice as often as *woman*. Few persons certainly can entirely dissever the word from its instinctive association with animal life, and no idiom of our day and land is probably more offensive to good taste. It was quite natural that the same tendency should lead to the employment of the corresponding term *male*, and hence the press—the New York *Tribune* leading—teems with advertisements in which professors, servants, and errand-boys are all promiscuously offered as "*Male Help*," and governesses, companions, and cooks as "*Female Help*." The last agitation in the republic, in favor of extending the right of suffrage from the negroes to women, has led to the introduction of the additional horror of an "Advanced *Female*."

Fetch, to, in the sense of performing, as in South's: "He *fetches* his blows quick and sure," is still in use in the South. "Since, with an arm no bigger than the round of a chair, you *fetched* the old schoolmaster the famous lick, plump in the black of his eye." (*Putnam's Magazine*, February, 1853.) But in the sense of bringing, the word may be said to be almost unknown there: on the other hand it is, curiously enough, used for bringing up: "How you were the child of a missionary, and from your cradle had been *fetched* up for the work." (*Ib.*, November, 1870.) The very old participle, *fotch*, still continues in use among low people, and is very general among the negroes of the South. "They are almost all on 'em, sir, straight down from old Diomed, that old master Hoomes had *fotch* out from England, across the water, more than twenty years ago." (J. P. Kennedy, *Swallow Barn.*) Nor is the hybrid *fotched* wanting: "I was soon *fotched* up in the victualling line." (J. C. Neal, *Charcoal Sketches.*)

Fice or *phyce*, and an almost endless variety of spellings, designates very generally in the South a small worthless cur. "De debbil's in that 'ar *fice*, Jefferson would say a dozen times a day, and shake his gray head doubtfully." (*Putnam's Magazine*, August, 1868.) It is evidently the last small remnant of the old English *foisting* cur, quoted as *foisting* hound in Wright's *Provincial Dialects.* Nares gives nearly the whole process of gradual corruption: foisting—foisty—foist—fyst—fyce, and Grose already has it, fyst. Halliwell describes the foisting dog as a kind of lap-dog, so called from its bad habits, which often have to serve as an excuse for the sins of the owner. A *fisting* hound, also, is mentioned as a kind of spaniel, in Harrison's *England*, p. 230.

Finding-store, the English "Grindery-warehouse," in which shoemakers' tools are kept for sale, is considered an Americanism.

Finnikin, finniking, and even *finnicky,* are American corruptions of finical in frequent use. "You are too *finnicky* to kill yourself." (*Putnam's Magazine,* September, 1870.)

Fire, to, a term very generally used for to throw. "The boys were *firing* stones at the house at a great rate, and, after a while, the negroes began *firing* back with rocks, chunks, and broken bricks." (Charleston *Courier,* September 19, 1870.)

Fireworks is the quaint substitute which New Englanders not unfrequently use for matches. "'Wal,' said our host, 'that's easy enough. Got any *fireworks?*' '*Fireworks?*' I queried back again. Our friend answered, in seeming surprise: 'No! Haint none. Wait a minit!' So he entered the house and speedily returned with a box of matches." (*Putnam's Magazine,* September, 1854.)

Fish-skin, used in New England to clarify coffee. (J. R. Lowell, *Glossary to Biglow Papers.*)

Fisticate, to, severely censured as an American vulgarism, is found in Captain John Smith's *Account of Virginia:* "There are so many *fisticating* tobacco-mungers in England." (II., p. 38.)

Fix, to, may be safely called the American word of words, since there is probably no action whatever, performed by mind or body, which is not represented at some time or other by the universal term. It has well been called the strongest evidence of that national indolence which avoids the trouble of careful thought at all hazards, and of that restless hurry which ever makes the word welcome that comes up first and saves time. Whatever is to be made, whatever needs repair, whatever requires arrangement—all is *fixed.* The farmer *fixes* his gates, the mechanic his workbench, the seamstress her sewing-machine, the fine lady her hair, and the schoolboy his books. The minister forgets to *fix* his sermon in time, the doctor to *fix* his medicines, and the lawyer to *fix* his brief. At public meetings it is *fixed* who are to be the candidates for office; rules are *fixed* to govern an institution, and when the arrangements are made, the people contentedly say: "Now everything is *fixed* nicely." Americans must have had an early weakness for the word, for already, in 1675, the Commissioners of the United Colonies ordered "their arms well *fixed* and fit for service." (Quoted by J. R. Lowell.) It is not to be wondered at, after this, that Americans should be so continually *in a fix*—an expression which, in England only slang, is here used in serious language.

> "A poor woman and her orphan chicks,
> Left without fixtures, in an awful *fix*."
> (Planche's *Good Woman in the Woods.*)

"Even the President will find himself *in a fix* sooner or later, if he goes on alienating his friends by making injudicious appointments." (New York *Herald*, April 2, 1871.) *Fixings* very naturally abound, moreover, in American speech, from the "Railroad *Fixings*, required for the equipment of the new branch to Warrenton," (Richmond *Examiner*, July 16, 1860), to the *Chicken Fixings*, the universal dish of the West and the South. "An extraordinary sight were the countless waiters, held up to the car-windows at Gordonsville by turbaned negro-women, filled with coffee-cups, eggs, and the inevitable *chicken-fixings*, which it was henceforth our fate to meet at every railroad-depot, till we reached New Orleans." (*A Trip to the South.*)

Flap-jacks, in England occasionally called *slap-jacks*, are, in the West, generally eaten together with chicken-fixings. The term is used by Shakespeare, whose Prince is shipwrecked, and falls among some honest fishermen, one of whom invites him heartily to his house, and says: "Come, thou shalt go home, and we'll have flesh for holidays, fish for fasting-days, and, moreo'er, puddings and *flap-jacks*, and thou shalt be welcome." (*Pericles*, II. 7.) In New England *flap-jacks* are large pancakes, generally eaten at supper.

Flashy is used in the mountain regions of Virginia for everything that is not sweet and fruitful. "The peaches are *flashy* on account of the drought." (1864.)

Fleshy, disused in England, still continues to be heard constantly in America, meaning stout, in the same sense in which it was used by Ben. Jonson, and is quoted by Bailey. "You must have recovered entirely; you look quite *fleshy*, now."

Flip, from the Swedish flepp, a drink of brandy and sugar mixed with beer, and heated by plunging into it a red-hot iron, upon which it is handed round, foaming, was formerly a general favorite in village bar-rooms and at the farm-house fireside. It was considered as productive of sore ankles and shins, so that old gentlemen in knee-breeches and long stockings would frequently wear handkerchiefs tied around their legs. A place called Porter's, near Cambridge, was a favorite resort of Harvard students, who fully appreciated his excellent flip. There is a tradition of a benign President who one day went to the tavern, ordered flip, drank it, and said: "So, Mr. Porter, the young gentlemen come to drink your *flip*, do they?" "Yes, sir, sometimes." "Ah, well, I should think they would. Good-day, Mr. Porter!" and then went quietly home, wisely making allowance for the existence of a certain amount of human nature in ingenuous youths.

Flouring-mills, an American name for grist-mills.

Flunk, to, a verb denoting the backing out from fear; now obsolete in England, and surviving only in the well-known "flunky," is still used in the West.

> "A keerless man in his talk was Jim,
> And an awkward man in a row;
> But he never *flunked*, and he never lied,
> I reckon he never know'd how."
> (John Hay. *Jim Bludsoe of the Prairie Belle.*)

Flutter-wheel, in the West, means a very small wheel, requiring but little water, and often not moving steadily, but, as it were, with a flutter.

Fly, to, is used constantly, even in otherwise careful writers, instead of to flee, as *sit* takes the place of set, and *lie* of lay, in conversation.

Fogy, well known in England, and thus used quite recently,

> "Ay, though we be
> Old *fogies* three,
> We're not so dull'd as not to dine,

And not so old
As to be cold
To wit, to beauty, and to wine"—
(*All the Year Round*, 1868.)

means, in the United States, mainly an ultra-conservative in politics. It occurs in Scotch as *fogie*, a dull, slow, old man, unable or unwilling to reconcile himself to the ideas and manners of a new generation; in English as *fogey*, a singular, old-fashioned person—popularized by Thackeray. The origin of the word is evidently *fog*, and *fogy* means a man *befogged* with regard to the demands of the present time, whose intellect is, hence, *foggy* and hazy, unable to see things as they really are.

Folks, used in England only provincially, is, in New England especially, used very generally for people. Sidney said: "Discourses of their own and other *folks'* misfortunes," and Bacon speaks of "old *folks* and sick *folks*." Lord Herbert of Chertbury even has, "The Emperor's *folks*." In America, neighbors especially are *folks*:

"There's punning Byles, provokes our smiles,
A man of stately parts;
He visits *folks* to crack his jokes,
Which never mend their hearts—"
(Sam Kettel. *Specimens of American Poetry*, 1750.)

and in the sense of company:

"When strawberries seemed like red heavens,
Terrapin stew a wild dream,
When my brain was at sixes and sevens,
If my mother had *folks* and ice-cream." . . . .
(Fitzhugh Ludlow. *Too Late*.)

White folks have of late come into consideration, this being the common name given the whites by the negroes, though in the South they are generally calling themselves now *poor folks*. Even an adjective, *folksy*, has been made, which is used in Virginia and the South.

Foolery and *fooling* are both promiscuously used where a much stronger term of condemnation ought to be employed, and even the taking of life has more than once been called "mere *foolin'*" in the West.

> "An' turnin' quite faint in the midst of his *fooleries,*
> Sneaks down-stairs to bolt the front door of the Tooleries."
> (J. R. Lowell. *Of Louis Philippe, Biglow Papers*, I., p. 58.)

"Perhaps *foolin'* is nateral to some women, and there is no great harm done 'cept to fools." (F. B. Harte, *Luck of Roaring Camp*, p. 102.)

Force is a common name for a gang of laborers, whether they are Irishmen at work on a railway, or negroes employed on a plantation. "The crop of Colonel Harris was of this description. It far exceeded the ability of his *force* to pitch it in; but instead of buying additional slaves for the purpose, he conceived the idea of turning to account the lazy Choctaws by whom he was surrounded." (W. G. Simms, *Oakatibbe.*)

Forehanded, which means in England nothing more than early, timely, has in America the additional meaning of well off, comfortable in circumstances. "I'll work and board with you. I know there is no need for it. Father is *forehanded;* he says I can go to school, but I ain't going to try it." (*Putnam's Magazine,* January, 1870.)

Fork, in the singular, is one of two roads into which the main road divides at a place which is called the *forks.* A traveller arriving in Albany and calling for a bootjack, astonished the servant so much by the size of his foot, as to call forth the exclamation: "If you want them are boots off, you'll have to go back to the *fork* in the road to get them off."

Fornent, the old Scotch word, has been carried by immigrants, from southern Ireland especially, to Pennsylvania, and is there quite common, though generally pronounced *fernent* and *fernenst.* "He lives *fernent* the big house in the village."

Freeze, to, is used in almost all parts of the country as an extravagant term for wishing something ardently. "I tell you I *froze* for meat before the week was gone." (*A Ride with Kit Carson.*)

Freshet, is used very generally in the United States instead of *fresh,* in the sense of an overflow. "We had another *freshet* in the Noble Jeames yesterday, and fear the canal has been seriously injured." (Richmond *Whig,* October 21, 1867.) The word *fresh* has, however, often to serve the two purposes of denoting an inundation and a small tributary of a larger river. Milton already uses it to denote a pool of fresh water, and so is quoted by Bailey, while R. Beverley writes: "There are the Mawborn Hills in the *freshes* of James River, and the ridge of hills of Stafford County in the *freshes* of Pawtomeck River." (*History of Virginia*, p. 110.)

Frump, to, quoted by Bailey as meaning to frizzle up the nose as in contempt, and used so by Beaumont and Fletcher, has, like so many old words, survived in New England, where people still speak of a cross, ill-tempered person as "an old *frump*."

Full, an old participle, is often heard in the South for filled, and almost exclusively used by the negroes, who sometimes improve it in their way by saying *fulled*.

"Gen'el Jackson fin' de trail,
Whaw, my kingdom, fire away,
He *full* um fote (filled them fort) wid cotton bale,
Whaw, my kingdom, fire away."
(*Georgia Negro-Song*.)

Furr, oddly used by Yankee and negro alike, is a remnant of olden times, for Sidney also uses it instead of far.

G.

Gab, and the gift of the *gab*, seem to be considered universally genuine Americanisms. Originally *gab* meant only mouth, and hence a clergyman at Paul's Crosse, we are told, thought nothing of bidding a noisy hearer to "hold his *gab*" or "shut up his *gob*." (*Slang Dictionary*.) Chaucer, however, uses the verb already as meaning to talk idly; and Grose actually explains "the gift of the *gab*" as a "facility of speech." It is in this sense that the word is almost exclusively used in the United States, denoting especially a great command of words without an over-abundance of ideas. In the South the word is strengthened by being lengthened into *gabblement*, but only in its lowest sense.

Gal, for girl, also is an inheritance derived from emigrants from Essex, where it is still heard. A *gal-boy* is in New England used occasionally for the more familiar tom-boy.

Gale is in New England and in the South not unfrequently used to denote a state of pleasant excitement. "The children were in such a *gale*, it took us nearly an hour to get them to bed, and then they could not sleep for a long while." (*A Summer in the Country*, p. 221.)

Gallantry, as shown to ladies, is a custom of which Americans are justly proud, and hence probably the many forms under which the word appears. "One day I took a solitary ride there, while Oliver was *gallantizing* the ladies, a vocation for which his invincible good-humor and unfailing vivacity eminently qualify him." (*Letters from the South*, II., p. 174.) "More than half the Lima beans, though on the most attractive sort of poles, which budded like Aaron's rod, went *galivanting* off to the neighboring grape-trellis, with a disregard for the proprieties of life which is a satire upon human nature." (C. D. Warner, *My Summer in a Garden*.) "*Gallivanting* was never my forte, and I was quite willing to be sent away whenever ladies came." "*Gallavanting*, waiting upon the ladies, was as polite in expression as in action." (*Slang Dictionary, sub voce.*)

Gall, to, has in parts of the United States transferred its peculiar meaning of excoriating, injuring a surface, to a noun, which designates a certain class of low land, consisting of a treacherous matted soil of vegetable fire, producing little that is worth the trouble of harvesting it at the risk of life. In Florida such lands are generally called *Bay-Galls*, which see.

Gallowses, for suspenders, is not unknown in England also.

Gambrel-roof, so called from its hipped form, which makes it not unlike the hind-leg of a horse, called by farriers *gambrel*.

Gander-party is the modest name given occasionally in New England to what is more familiarly called a "stag-party," consisting of men only.

Gap, from its denoting any breach of continuity, is in the South generally applied to a pass in the mountains, through which a river or a road runs. Rockfish Gap, Brown's Gap, and other *Gaps* in the Blue Ridge of Virginia became thus famous in the late Civil War.

Garrison, in the West, designates not only the military force occupying a fort, but quite as frequently the place thus held, and even old forts and posts, long since abandoned, continue to be known there as garrisons. "It was late at night when we returned to the *garrison*, and the ominous silence, the absence of a sentinel, and the strange appearance of everything around us, sent a shudder through our hearts." (*Scenes in the Far West.*)

Gas, for moonshine or idle boasting, is quite frequent.

Gaum, obsolete in England, is still used here to denote soiling. "Don't let the child *gaum* herself all over."

Gavel, formerly used to denote a small heap of wheat, etc., not tied up, as in Chapman's line, "Their corn lies on the *gavel* heap," has found a new application in the amount of wheat, etc., cut by the reaping-machine and shaken out by one motion.

Gee, to, the term employed in driving a wagon, has been transferred to other transactions also, and people say in Pennsylvania, "That won't *gee*," when they wish to express that something will not serve the purpose. (S. S. Haldeman.)

Gentle, to, in the sense of Young's line, "To *gentle* life's descent" (*Night Thoughts*), is still quite frequently heard in America, and received a new application when Mr. Rarey practised and taught the art of *gentling* horses.

Gentleman and *lady*, as has already been stated, have in America no longer any distinctive meaning. The millionaire's porter is a *gentleman*, the schoolboy is a *young gentleman*, and the half-witted negro is facetiously hailed as old *gentleman*. This abuse has struck all travellers in the United States. The Duke of Saxe-Weimar was, in Alabama, asked the question: Are you the *man* that wants to go to Selma? and upon assenting, he was told: Then I'm the *gentleman* that is going to drive you. Precisely the same thing occurred to Sir Charles Lyell: "I asked the landlord of the inn at Corning, who was very attentive to his guests, to find my coachman. He immediately called out in his bar-room, Where is the *gentleman* that brought this *man* here? A few days before, a farmer in New York had styled my wife, *woman*, though he called his own daughters *ladies*, and would, I believe, have freely extended that title to their maid-servant." Under the head, "Help Wanted," a Philadelphia paper lately published, "Wanted. Two competent sales-*ladies*, at Newman's, 48 North 8th Street" (Philadelphia *Ledger*, December 16, 1870), and a distinguished writer says frankly: "I admit that our abuse of the word is villanous. I know of an orator who once said in a public meeting, where bonnets predominated, that "The *ladies* were the last at the Cross and the first at the Tomb!" The vulgarity of entering a traveller's name on the register of the hotel, as "Mr. —— and *lady*," is only surpassed by placing the same words on visiting-cards.

Get, to, one of the convenient words of the language, which Americans use, like *fix*, as maids of all work, seems nevertheless to be so well adapted to many purposes, that even English writers and orators begin to use it in ways which formerly were made a cause of grave reproach to our people. To speak of "*getting* religion" may not be exactly correct, and to "*get* corrected," conveys no clear meaning, but to "*get* money" has received the sanction of the best writers. "The Yankee notion that the *getting* of money is the chief end of man." (*Atlantic Monthly*, August, 1858.) To *get on* has become domesticated in English. The Earl of Derby, delivering recently the prizes to the successful pupils of Liverpool College, said, "We are a little too apt to look upon ourselves as mere machines for what is called *getting on*," and in another place, "he had *got* as much as he or anybody belonging to him." (December, 1870.) Even the shortened form *got* instead of *gotten*, long made a special reproach and considered an objectionable Americanism, has now its advocates in English. Wordsworth says:

"But then he is a horse that thinks,
And when he thinks his horse is slack;
Now, tho' he knows poor Johnny well,
Yet, for his life, he cannot tell
What he has *got* upon his back"—
(*The Idiot Boy.*)

and Lord Lytton goes so far as to use *forgot* in his last brilliant novel. To *get up on one's ear*, is regular slang, meaning, to rouse one's self to a great effort:

"They called me bully boy, altho' I've seen nigh threescore years,
And said that I was lightning, when I *got up on my ear*."
(*Words and their Uses.* Galveston *News*, May 4, 1871.)

Gird, to take a, has in the Northwest the peculiar meaning of to make an effort: "I'd just like to take one *gird* at Globe City, and if I couldn't fetch settlers, I'd cry co-peevi (peccavi). Will you let me try it?" (*Putnam's Magazine*, November, 1858.)

Given name, represents mainly in New England, but quite frequently throughout the United States, what in England is called the Christian, or first name—a designation said to have originated with the Puritans, who objected to the many saints' names used as Christian names.

Glade, the name given originally to a part of the water which is not frozen over, though surrounded by ice—from the analogy to the *glade*, an opening in the woods—has been subsequently applied in New England to smooth ice also. In the South the term is often used as a shorter substitute for *everglades*, the tracts of land covered with water and grass, which are so called from Maryland down to Florida.

Glass, to, used for to glaze, as was done in England in the times of Boyle, who quotes it, continues thus to be employed in the West and the South. "The windows were sashed and *glassed*, and hung with the whitest curtains of cotton, with fringes fully a foot deep." (W. G. Simms, *The Last Wager*.)

Glaze, on the other hand, is in the East transferred from the finish of pottery, etc., to the similar state of the ground after a hoar-frost.

Glut, a large wooden wedge, has been preserved in New England. It is, after all, but a special application of the general sense of *glut*, which means the complete filling up of a passage, in this case accomplished by the wedge.

Gondola, frequently corrupted into *gundalo*, is used in the New England States and along the Atlantic Coast to designate a low, flat-bottomed boat, in which produce is carried to market. The use of the word for a peculiarly shaped railroad-car is not unknown in England. J. R. Lowell says: "I find *gundelo* in Hakluyt and *gundello* in Booth's Reprint of the Folio Shakespeare of 1683."

Goney, the old English term for a stupid fellow, is not unfrequently heard yet in the New England States, while *gonus* is said to be the Latinized form used in colleges. "A stupid fellow, a dolt, a bootjack, an ignoramus is here called a *gonus*." All freshmen are *gonuses*. (*The Dartmouth*, Vol. IV., p. 116.)

Goodman and *Goody*, in the early days of New England settlements titles of honor, signifying heads of a household, continue to be used in more remote parts of those States, and Goody Simpkins may be heard, without the slightest intention to speak in any but the most respectful way of Mrs. Simpkins. *Goodies*, on the contrary, are, as in England, sweetmeats and nice things given to children.

Graft, to, is one of the many words by which the Sons of Crispin love to express the different modes of repairing boots. This term is generally applied when new soles are added, and new leather is sewed on all around; when a new bottom is made and the boots are renewed half way up, it is called *goosing* boots, and *foxing*, when a new foot is made to old "uppers." The names are, however, not kept equally distinct in all the States.

Grass Widows are, in the United States, wives separated from their husbands for a time only, and without incurring the slightest reproach. The great familiarity with American society which the English are so fond of assuming is shown in the veracious statement that "during the gold fever in California it was common in the United States for an adventurer to put both his wife (termed in his absence a *grass widow*) and his children to *school* during his absence." (*Slang Dictionary*, p. 146.)

Grain is used in America, as *corn* is in England, to designate the produce of all cereals, rye, wheat, oats, etc., and the papers quote therefore daily an account of the *Grain Market*.

Grand, used indiscriminately for anything great or large, is, like many similar terms, grievously abused. Every army during the late Civil War became a "*Grand* Army;" the Freemasons have nothing but "*grand* turn-outs," and when girls discuss an evening party, each boasts of what a "*grand* time" she has had.

Graveyard is a word rarely used by Americans, who prefer the more euphemious Cemetery. There is, perhaps, some excuse for this custom, as they have wisely chosen the most beautiful spots near their large cities, laid them out in shrubbery and forest, and made them so attractive, that every visitor to a large town is almost sure for his first and main entertainment to be driven out to the "Cemetery." The only well-known *Graveyard* in the country is a melancholy place in the Mississippi River. "On your right is a series of rocky bluffs, covered with a stunted growth of trees, before you an expanse of water, ten miles long and two wide, on your left an array of sand-bars and islands, where lie imbedded the wrecks of some fifty steamboats, and in the remote distance a belt of thickly wooded bottom land. This is the famous *Graveyard*." (C. Lanman, *A Summer in the Wilderness*.)

Gravy, in New England used for any liquid accompanying certain dishes, as, the *gravy* of a pie, a pudding, etc.

Great is, in the South especially, almost constantly coupled with big, and anything of considerable size is qualified as "a *great big* thing." In Pennyslvania the influence of uneducated Germans has corrupted the first word into *grade*, aided by the tendency to assimilation before the initial *b*, and as such *grade big* has been gravely quoted as meaning, "big by an additional grade or degree,"—a solemn warning to superficial linguists.

Griddles are not only the utensils for baking cakes, but also the cakes themselves. "Shovel-cakes are still to be had by a hungry generation, and the *griddles* of Mrs. Durfee in the Tea-House at the Glen, shall not want an historian as they have not wanted troops of lovers." (*An Account of Newport*, 1858.)

Grit and *gritty* are favorite terms, at the North especially, for that quality which a grindstone should have in order to make it serviceable: hardness and firmness combined. "He has the true *grit*," is considered high praise, while Meta Lander complains very justly that "womanly *grit* is not consistent with womanly grace."

"Thought I, my neighbor Buckingham
Hath somewhat in him *gritty*,
Some Pilgrim stuff, that hates all sham,
And he will print my *ditty*."
(J. R. Lowell. *An Interview with Miles Standish.*)

Clear Grit is thus defined by a high authority: "*Clear Grit* is that sterling manhood and womanhood that is always true to its own nature, and therefore in some sense to that highest nature in whose image we are made, no matter what may befall; as a diamond is a diamond all the same, you know, whether it blazes on the brow of an emperor or is hid under the mountain peaks." (Rev. Robert Collyer.)

Guess. There is, probably, no word in the Dictionary that has given more occasion to animated discussion than this. Quoted almost by every writer in America as one of the most obtrusive and repulsive Americanisms, considerable pains has been taken to prove its English orthodoxy. There is no lack of evidence that the word has been used in England from time immemorial, and by the best writers, in precisely the same sense in which it is now employed by Yankees. Selden, in one of his notes to Polyolbian, as quoted by J. R. Lowell, writes: "The first inventor of them (I *guess* you dislike not the addition) was one Berthold Swartz." Spenser says, "Amylia will be lov'd as I mote *ghesse.*" (*Faëry Queen*, Bk. III, c. viii, v. 57.) "If I were, I might find more cause, I *guess*, than your mistress has given your master here." (Vanburgh, *The Mistake*, Act I, sc. 1.) Chaucer sings:

"Her yellow hair was braided in a tress,
Behind her back, a yard long, I *guess.*"
(*Heroine.*)

"He whose design it is to excel in English poetry would not, I *guess*, think that way if it was to make his first essay in Latin verse" (Locke), and Milton says: "Already by thy reasoning this I *guess.*" (*Paradise Lost*, VIII, p. 85.) The only difference between the English and the American use of the word is, probably, that the former denotes a fair, candid *guess*, while the Yankee who *guesses* is apt to be quite sure of what he professes to doubt. As he only calculates when he has already solved his problem, so he also *guesses* when he has made sure of his fact. "I *guess* I do," is with him an expression of confident certainty. He is, however, quite as prone to go to the other extreme and to use the word without any other meaning than mere "thinking," as when he says: "I *guess* he is well," or, "I *guess* I won't go to-day."

Gumption, little more than a vulgarism or a cant word in England, is in America used very freely for understanding and discernment, and considered much less objectionable on the score of good taste. Burns wrote:

"Nor a' the quacks with all their *gumption*
Will ever cure her."
(*Letter to John Goudie.*)

O'Connell also tells how an Irish priest introduced the veto-question to a rural meeting by saying: "Now, ma boughall, you haven't got *gumption*, and you must, therefore, be guided by those who have." It is in this sense that it is constantly used here. "I assure you he was not lacking in *gumption*; what he wants is tact." (J. M. Buchanan, private letter.) The term is evidently derived from the old verb to *gaum*, to understand, which is still current in the North of England, and from which the noun *gumption* has been obtained after the manner of similar words—the *p* being inorganic, but never failing between the labial and the dental. There is no excuse, as there is no need, for the corruption *rumgumption*, common in England, where (in Yorkshire) even *rumgumptious* exists for pompous, or forward, which is comparatively rare in America.

> " They need not try thy jokes to fathom,
> They want *rumgumption*."
> (*Beattie.*)

Gut, in the sense of a narrow inlet or strait, filled with salt-water, is used here as in England, wherever its place has not been usurped by the French *bayou*.

H.

Hack, in England generally used for a hired horse, denotes in America mainly a hired carriage. To call a short, hard, cutting cough, a *hacking* cough, a term sometimes heard in the South of England, is quite common here.

Half-saved is a similar provincialism, found in certain localities in both countries, and denoting a half-witted person.

Halves, in Pennsylvania corrupted into *havvers*, is an exclamation heard by the person who happens to witness the finding of a valuable object, in order to claim half of the treasure-trove. People also propose to "go *halves*" when each is to pay half of the expense, and land is let out "on *halves*," when the owner and the tenant share equally in the proceeds. The latter term, used by Urquhart and Matthews in their Translation of Rabelais (Bk. IV, c. 23), is now obsolete in England, but still continues in use here.

Hand is made in America not only the representative of a person's ability to work, but even of his skill; and while the English say, "he *has* a good *hand* on the violin" (Addison), it is here said, "He *is* a good *hand* at whistling." "I have never seen a man who *was* a better *hand* at cradling, but he knows nothing else." (*Farmers' Gazette*, 1867.)

Handkerchief has here, as in England, much to suffer from the tendency to corrupt an absurd word (hand-cover-chief), the meaning of which is naturally hid to uneducated persons. This ill-treatment is so general, and especially the pronunciation, *handkercher*, so old and so constant, that serious doubts have arisen as to the true origin of the word. The derivation from *couvre chef* can, of course, not be denied, but it has been asked, if there may not be here, as in many similar cases, a double derivation. Shakespeare certainly writes, "Good Tom Drumme, lend me a *handkercher*" (All's Well that Ends Well), and *kercher* occurs already previously. In an official report on Bacon's Rebellion, dated July 13, 1705, we find: "Had Bacon in the paroxism of phrentick fury but drawn his sword before the pacifick *handkercher* was shaken out of the window." Pepys writes, September 2, 1667, "The king at this day having no *handkerchers*, and but three bands to his neck;" and three months later, December 12, again, "Here only, I saw a French lady in the pit, with a tunique just like ours, only a *handkercher* about her neck." There can be no doubt that the word was, in the 17th century, written by good authors exactly as it was pronounced, and thus imported from England into Virginia, where it has maintained itself unchanged to the present day. In Pennsylvania, *hankitcher* is quoted by Dr. Elwyn, and *hangcatcher* by S. S. Haldeman.

Handround, the name of an entertainment in the West, thus described: "We do dance, of course, but a *handround*, out here, is where we don't sit at table, but hand round the vittels. The table can't be set, you know, on 'count of its clutterin' up the dancin' room." (*Putnam's Magazine*, December, 1868.)

Happen in, to, in the sense of to happen to come in, is a use of the word not known abroad, but quite common here. "I *happened* in one fine day, and found them all fast asleep before ten o'clock." (J. P. Kennedy, *Swallow Barn.*)

Hard is a favorite word in the United States, applied universally to things or persons, from "*hard* money," in contrast with paper-money, to "*hard* times," for evil fortune. "Bob is what is technically called a *hard* customer; he drinks *hard*, he eats *hard*, for he is often *hard* set to get anything to eat, and he sleeps *hard*, for his bed is frequently a *hard* flag in the market." (*Pickings from the Picayune.*)

Hardwood comprises all woods of solid texture which decay speedily; elm, oak, ash, beech, basswood, and sugar-maple. *Hardtack*, sea-bread and army-bread alike. "Since the Rebellion broke out, some luckless wight stationed thereabout, munching his pork and *hardtack*, had named it the Parker House, in memory of better days." (*Putnam's Magazine*, August, 1868.)

Haul, to, weeds is common in many States instead of to pull up weeds. To *haul over the coals* is not an Americanism; it occurs as early as the times of the Reformation in the title of a controversial book, and in the modern sense of "to take to task." Jamieson traces it back to the ordeal by fire.

Haze, to, a term used on board ship and in public institutions of learning, is quite common in the United States. "Every shifting of the studding-sails was only to *haze* the crew." (Dana, 1840.) "The deeply-rooted custom of *hazing* the new cadets has been successfully suppressed, and no instance of ill-treatment has been brought to the knowledge of the superintendent." (*Official Report of West Point Academy*, 1870.)

Heap, once used in many parts of England to denote not only a quantity, but also a number of animals or men, as in Hakluyt: "Seeing such a *heap* of their enemies ready to devour them" (quoted by J. R. Lowell), and in Chaucer's well-known line,

"The wisdom of a *heap* of learned men"
(*The Prologue.*)

is still universal in the West and South in the same sense. "I saw a *heap* of old friends in town, but still felt sad at the many changes that met my eye everywhere." In like manner the old use of a *heap* or an *heap* for a large quantity has come down to us unchanged from Piers Ploughman, who says: "And other names an *heap*." "I began to feel myself mightily at home, and, as Virginians say, felt a *heap* of regret at bidding the excellent lady and her family good-by." (*Letters from the South*, I., p. 30.) Even the Indians have caught the infection, and we are told that "an Indian is always a *heap* hungry or thirsty, a *heap* brave or willing to do a thing." (*Life in the Far West*, p. 115.) "He is a big man, *heap* big man." (*Speech of Hole-in-the-Sky at Washington*, 1868.)

Hearn, the old adjective-participle for *heard*, is quite frequently heard where old English most prevails, in New England and in Virginia. "I have *hearn* master say so many a times." (*John Randolph's Body-servant at the Funeral.*)

"It's thinkin' everythin' you ever knew,
Or ever *hearn* to make your feelin's blue."
(J. R. Lowell. *Biglow Papers*, II., p. 161.)

Heft, to, which in England means—true to its derivation from heah, heave, heaved—to lift, is used in the United States in the sense of trying the weight of a thing by raising it, and hence the noun *heft* derives its meaning of weight, and, still more idiomatically, the greater part of a thing.

> "He was tall, was my Jack,
> And as strong as a tree,
> Thar's his gun on the rack,
> Jest you *heft* it and see—
> And ye come a-courtin' his widder. Lord! where can the critter, Sal, be?"
> (Penelope. *Overland Monthly*, August, 1870.)

> "Constitoounts air hendy to help a man in,
> But arterwards don't weigh the *heft* of a pin."
> (J. R. Lowell. *Biglow Papers*, I., p. 151.)

"No, that won't pay. We will be gone the *heft* of the afternoon, I reckon." (*Lippincott's Magazine*, March, 1871, p. 284.) "You see there's such a *heft* of snow, and no path broke." (E. S. Phelps, *A Woman's Pulpit.*) Even an adjective, *hefty*, has been derived from the word in New England. "Then, it must be confessed that he is, as a Yankee would say, a little *hefty* for the ideal lover." (New York *Tribune*, January 21, 1871.)

Heifer is not uncommon in the West for wife, and used with all kindness and respect. "Now, git out, I says, or the ol' *heifer* 'll show you whar the carpenter left a hole for you to mosey." (*In the Backwoods*, p. 71.)

Heir, to, instead of to inherit, is in use in New Jersey and Pennsylvania. "He *heirs* the property, and she *heirs* the farm." "A little boy is now the sole survivor, and *heirs* an estate which, a gentleman informs us, is worth some five or six thousand dollars." (New York *Times*, January 27, 1855.)

Help, often considered a genuine Americanism, is only an extension of the original word from an instrument to a person. Pepys already writes, March 18, 1662: "What a *help* he was to us!" and Mrs. Trollope fell in so readily with the use of the word, that she wrote in 1832: "A black *help* ushered in a young man," a phrase probably quite unknown to Rochester, in New York, from which place she dates her letter. The use of the word originated in New England, where perfect social equality has prevailed from the oldest times, while the "redemptioners" of New York and the

Middle States, and the "slaves" of the South, divided society elsewhere; nor has the term yet made its way into the interior of Pennsylvania. (S. S. Haldeman.) A variety is the *hired man*, a term very generally used North and South. "The Irish girls have found their way into the New England farmer's kitchen," complains a *laudator temporis acti*, "and the Irish laborer has become the annual *hired man*." (*Atlantic Monthly*, August, 1858.)

Hendy is Yankee for handy. "*Hendy* as a pocket in a shirt."

Herbs is the term used for the English "simples," which are so unknown here, that nothing is more common than an utter inability of young readers to understand the allusion to a perfumed garment, which is said to smell "like Bucklersbury in *simple* time." (*Merry Wives of Windsor.*) The *herb* doctor plays a prominent part, in a country where no restraint whatever is placed upon ignorant men who assume the functions of a physician, and simple men who entrust their lives to such hands. The word is, however, generally pronounced *yerb* or *yarb* by the multitude.

Hide, to, in the sense of "tanning one's hide" by severe blows, is as common here as in certain districts of England. J. R. Lowell thus refers to a habit of Louis Philippe's, when a schoolmaster in this country, "how he often had *hided* young native Amerrikins." (*Biglow Papers*, I., p. 57.)

Hity-tity, as the English *hoity-toity* is more frequently sounded and written in America, is here also used as a verb. "She expects to be *hitied-titied*, that is, to be made much of." (S. S. Haldeman.) The word arises from the obsolete English verb to *hoit*, which means to leap, to caper; if not from the noun *hoit*, which Grose quotes as meaning "an awkward boy." The American verb-transitive implies the doing of that which will call forth the exclamation, as the Greek ἐλέγη meant ἒ λέγειν, to say ε, alas!

Hoarding means, in America only, accumulating—never an enclosure, as in the English notice so often met on commons and vacant spaces: "No bills may be stuck on this *hoarding*." *Fence* is substituted for the latter.

Hockey-stick, the stick with a "hook," or curved bend at the end farthest from the hand, and used in playing ball, is occasionally written *Hawkey*-stick (J. R. Abbot, *Caleb in Boston*), and in the South, as in England, replaced by *bandy-stick.*

Hog takes almost exclusively the place of the English *swine*, which is rarely heard. "Mean enough to steal acorns from a *hog*," is the Yankee's extremity of meanness.

Hoist, to,—vulgarly called *hyst*,—means very often what an Irishman might call an "elevation downwards," a sudden, serious fall. J. C. Neal thus makes a merry toper say: "I can't see the ground, and every dark night I am sure to get a *hyst*—either a forrerd or a backerd *hyst*, or some kind of *hyst*, but more backerds than forrerds." (*Charcoal Sketches*, I., p. 74.)

Holden, the old participle, still survives in many parts of this country. The Rev. P. Cartwright says in his *Autobiography*: "A camp-meeting *holden* this year in the edge of Tennessee" (p. 144), and the official report of the Methodist Episcopal Church North (1870) says: "The first Methodist Conference *holden* in the West was *held* in Kentucky in 1789." R. W. Emerson writes: "The other element of friendship is tenderness. We are *holden* to men by every sort of tie, by blood, by pride, by fear, by hope, by lucre, by lust, by hate, by admiration, by every circumstance and badge and trifle, but we can scarcely believe that so much character can subsist in another as to draw us by love." (*Friendship*, p. 187.)

Hollow, to, a verb already in England from of old written in various ways, occurs in America, in like manner, under the different forms of *hollow*, *halloo*, and most commonly as *holler*. J. R. Lowell says: "Herrick writes *hollow* for *halloo*, and perhaps pronounced it (*horresco referens*) *holla*, as the Yankees do. Why not, when it comes from *hold*?" Shakespeare, it is well known, uses it—

"And in his ear I'll *hollow* Mortimer,"
(*I. Henry IV.*)

and Byron does not hesitate to say,

"To *hollowing* Hotspur and the sceptred sire."

The Yankee pronunciation is introduced into the characteristic account of a bluff old farmer, who said: "If a man professes to serve the Lord, I like to see him do it when he measures onions as well as when he *hollers* glory hallelujar." "The more I *hollered* the more the customers would come." (J. C. Neal, *Charcoal Sketches*, II., p. 157.)

Holpen, the old participle, like *holden*, is still often heard, especially in Kentucky, while in Virginia and by the negroes of the South a mongrel form, *holped*, is made for the Preterite of *I holp*, which there takes the place of *I help*.

Holt is occasionally used here, as in England, as a noun, the surd *t* marking the noun as the sonant *d* marks the verb. (Compare breath and breathe.) "Then let me have a *holt* of some of the fellows that made it." (J. C. Neal, *Charcoal Sketches*, II., p. 28.)

Homely, in England used for homelike, here serves mainly to express a want of comeliness. "She is certainly very *homely*, but so bright and cheerful as to appear positively lovely at times." (*Home Journal*, July, 1849.)

Honorable is, like Reverend, unfortunately more and more generally used without an article, in speaking of persons—a vice which F. G. Halleck stigmatized as "denying the Hon. John Smith the benefit of the definite article." "Yesterday, Hon. R. T. W. Duke, of Virginia, delivered his speech on the Enforcement Bill." (Richmond *Enquirer*, April 2, 1871.)

Hood is in America not the monk's hood nor that familiar to Oxford and Cambridge, both of which are unknown here, but a covering for the head, of bright-colored worsted, much worn by the ladies on the way to the theatre.

Hop, in the sense of an informal dance, at which full-dress is not expected, is a recent importation from England, where, in the slang of the upper classes, this use of the word has long prevailed.

Horse-Milliner, sometimes objected to as an absurdity, has high and ancient authority for its use. A newspaper recently observed facetiously: "They call a harnessmaker a *horse-milliner* out in Chicago." The editor had evidently never read Motley's admirable work on the *Rise of the Dutch Republic*, or he would have found the word quoted from a MS. of the sixteenth century. Sir W. Scott, also, in his *Heart of Mid-Lothian* (ch. xii.), makes Bartoline Saddletree say: "Whereas, in my wretched occupation of a saddler, *horse-milliner*, and harnessmaker."

Hospital is used in the United States to the exclusion of the English term *Spital*, which is here unknown. The "*Spital* Sermon," as the annual sermon preached before the Blue-coat School in London is still called on the title-page, would be almost unintelligible to many readers in America.

Hot, an old preterite of the verb to hit, is still occasionally heard in Virginia and the South. The negroes are apt to say, "He *hot* me a great big blow."

Housen, another old form brought to the South by the early

English settlers, survives there and in New England alike. "No one shall tarry at his (the Indian king's) *housen* longer than one night." *Householdry* is a new word attempted by a few ambitious writers in the sense of "household employment;" but

Housekeep, as a verb, has firmly established itself in American speech. "We went and *hired* (!) a house, determined never again to board, but to *housekeep*, whatever might be the expense." (*Southern Magazine*, January, 1871.) The new word, *to roomkeep*, arising from the exigency which forces impoverished Southern families to content themselves with renting a few rooms and keeping house in them, has not yet obtained currency.

Hove, the old preterite of "heave," still continues in many parts of the country. An old woman on the Isle of Shoals, complaining how ill her house was built, said: "Lor, 'twasn't never built, 'twas only *hove* together." Fishermen along the coast of New England, when trying the sailing capacities of a vessel in a heavy sea, melt a quantity of lard in a frying-pan on the tiny stove in the cabin, and if, in the act of plunging, "the fat is *hove* out of the pan," as they say, and the pan remains on the stove, she is considered a first-rate sailer.

How do? or, *How de?* is the common salutation in the South, instead of "How do you do?"

Hub, in the sense of the nave of a wheel, is common to America and England alike; and in this country, perhaps, most familiar as the name claimed by Bostonians for their city: "The *Hub* of the Universe." But *hub*, as meaning a protuberance in the road, or a projection on a mountain, is believed to be American only.

Hull is Yankee for whole, as

Hum is for home. "He aint to *hum*," says the New Englander, in his dialect, for "He is not at home."

Human, for human being, has been fiercely criticised as an Americanism, and yet Chapman uses it habitually in his translation of Homer, and his example is followed by a host of English writers. Americans, however, use it now more frequently than formerly, perhaps for brevity's sake. "I did not expect to meet a *human* in such a place." (Hammond, *Wild Western Scenes.*) "Parson Brownlow is just as fierce upon dogs, when they annoy him, as he is upon *humans*, when they cross his path." (*Harper's Magazine*, January, 1868.)

Humbug, however successfully developed in this country, is not a new term, but at least as old as Lord Chesterfield, who uses it in his letters. Halliwell mentions the term, and explains it as meaning a false alarm, a bugbear. The only native use is probably the name of a town in California, *Humbug Flats,* eminently suggestive of the "'cuteness" of the first settlers.

Hunk, not unknown in the provinces abroad, means here a large piece of bread and butter or cheese. It occurs occasionally in the sense of a place of refuge, a homestead; and is used by boys in play, when they have reached their "base;" they call it "being *honk.*" This term is derived from the Dutch *honk,* a place, a home, and has led to the political slang term of *Old Hunkers,* which means persons clinging to their homestead, and opposed to innovators. Hence, also, the familiar *Hunky Dory,* a term originating among the Virginia mountaineers, who used it to express very emphatically that they were "well, and in good spirits." It is said that the poor little Japanese who had become famous in England by his cry *Olrite* (all right), and derived his name from it, here adopted this word as the most characteristic of the American people, and used to cry, *Hunky Dory!*

Hunt, to, is in the South especially used for search: "Have you *hunted* through your drawers, Kitty? I have *hunted* all over the house." (*Southern Literary Messenger,* June, 1851.)

Husbandhood is a new word, recently coined. "The man is educated, not for *husbandhood,* but for manhood." (Miss Anna Dickinson, January, 1866.)

Hwish, an exclamation used in parts of New England, to turn men or cattle back. "In such expeditions I took my first lessons in the ox-compelling art. The mysteries of 'haw' and 'gee,' of 'hwo' and '*hwish*'—the last an outlandish Vermontese barbarism, signifying 'back!'—were duly explained." (*Connecticut Georgics.*) The word is known in parts of Yorkshire.

Hyper, to, a New England word for to be busy. "I must *hyper* about and git tea." (J. R. Lowell.)

I.

Icarian, as everything relating to Mr. Cabet's socialistic system is called, is a familiar term in America, where many efforts have been made to carry out his views.

Ilk is a much abused word, being constantly substituted for stamp, class, or society. "Men of that *ilk* are seldom good for anything." "We want to have nothing to do with Governor Swann, and men of that *ilk*." (Washington *Chronicle*, January 27, 1869.)

Illy, frequently charged upon American writers as an unpardonable sin, is used by some of the older English writers, though sparingly. It has excited much controversy, and while there is no well-founded objection to the use of the word, it has not been sanctioned by the consent of the people. In Texas the word *ill* has the curious signification of immoral, and "an *ill* fellow," means a man of bad habits.

Immediately, instead of as *soon*, is often met with; the press and numerous writers using it in this sense. "I knew it *immediately* I saw him enter the room." (New York *Ledger*, April 12, 1871.)

Improve, to, was remarked upon as early as 1789, by Benjamin Franklin, as an "old perversion of the word in New England, when applied to persons." We are told that it was thus used in the Colonial Laws of New Haven, about the middle of the seventeenth century, when it was ordered to read "the Scriptures and other good and profitable printed books in the English tongue, by *improving* schoolmasters or other help." Later it was used in the sense of use or occupancy of houses, and it sounds very odd to our ears to hear it said that "such a use of the word was common at the beginning of the century, but we do not remember to have seen or heard it in this sense for many years." (*North American Review*, January, 1847.) Now, the word is employed in the same way when speaking of things, land, or men, and the noun *improvement* means as much amelioration generally as the stock, buildings, fences, and other additions to the value of a farm or homestead. "I bought some stock and rented out the *improvement*, with a view to have something to live on." (Rev. P. Cartwright, *Autobiography*, p. 246.)

In for *into*, is general throughout the country, but the latter is gradually gaining ground.

In'ards, a new application of the word *inwards*, is thus explained by R. G. White: "Now-a-days a man who used, in general society, the simple English word (gut) for which some New

England females elegantly substitute *in'ards*, would shock many of his hearers." (*Words and their Uses*, p. 387.) "The *inner* man" is not much better.

Independent, applied to lifeless objects, as "an *independent* fortune," for one which makes the owner independent, is unwarrantable.

Interfere, to, is used in the North and West instead of troubling and using ill. "You'd better not *interfere* with my rousters, they don't like outsiders,—was the warning the captain gave these roughs as they scrambled on deck." (*Wild Western Scenes*, p. 23.)

Interview, to. The verb has been called an Americanism, and its origin ascribed to the brevity exacted by telegraphic communications; but it is as old as Hall's *Chronical*, printed in 1542. "*Interviewing* is nothing new; it existed in Cæsar's time; for did not great Julius ask: Who is in the press that calls?" (Richmond *Dispatch*, March 17, 1871.) "Everybody is *interviewed* now-a-days; Emperor William on his throne, the murderer Ruloff in his cell, and the man whose wife has just run away from him—all fall into the hands of the merciless newspaper reporter." (New York *Herald*, April 13, 1871.)

Invite, instead of invitation, a corruption of uneducated men, is an imitation of English slang, which has recently crept into our speech.

It, added as an expletive to verbs, is declared by Mr. Abbot in his *Grammar of Shakespeare* to be "now only found in slang phrases." That may be so in England; in the United States nothing is more common than this addition, and General Grant's phrase, "I propose to fight *it* out on this line," has rendered it historical.

Item, though generally used in the sense of an article or separate particular in an account, has in America the meaning of a point of information for the press. "Local" reporters are forever in search of an *item* for their paper, and the New York *Times* quotes one of them as saying, "The moment you get the *item* you want, give it to me and I'll run to the office to have it printed."

J.

Jab, to, to handle harshly, or even to strike and stab, is a Western term. "The Missouri stoker pulls and *jabs* his plutonic monster as an irate driver would *regulate* his mule." (On the Plains. *Putnam's Magazine*, September, 1868.)

Jacket is in America almost exclusively used for "roundabout."

Jag, an old English word, long obsolete at home, survives in lower New Jersey especially, which was settled by Puritan immigrants from New England and Long Island, with a few English quakers, and hence has preserved many words no longer known in England. "He had brought a *jag* of hay to town."

Jaw, to, quoted by Todd and Halliwell in the sense of to scold, is much used in the New England States.

"But, neighbor, ef they prove their claim at law,
The best way is to settle, an' not to *jaw*."
(J. R. Lowell. *Biglow Papers*, II., p. 61.)

It is, however, also used as a common slang term for talking simply, as in the lines—

"The neighbors round the corners drawed,
And ca'mly drinked and *jawed*."
(John Hay. *The Mystery of Gilgal.*)

Jeames is the universal pronunciation of James in Virginia, since the time when English settlers brought it first with them from home. Hence "the noble *Jeames*" is the facetious name of James River, and the Thorn-apple is never called anything but *Jimson* weed. The same tendency has led to the change of Jane into

Jean (from Genoa, French *Gènes*), a twilled cotton-cloth; the term is commonly used in the plural in America.

Jew, to, colloquially known in England as meaning to cheat, is here often used in the sense of haggling, bargaining. "Don't you think the old hunks wanted to *jew* me down to three thousand dollars?" (California *Flush Times.*)

Jest and *jist* are favorite forms for "just."

Jine is in like manner substituted for "join," especially in New England, and has the fact in its favor that Dryden and Pope both rhyme *join* and *shine* more than once, and that this pronunciation of *oi* as *i* was once orthodox in England.

Job, originally a cant word, has made good its place, first in political language, and then in our speech generally. Nor has

England been able to prevent its introduction. "The House was very temperate, to-day, in the way of legislation, and with an evident determination to pass no *jobs*, adjourned early." (New York *Tribune*, March 23, 1871.) Grose quotes the word as meaning, in Norfolk, a piece of labor, undertaken at a stated price, and this meaning it still preserves. In political phraseology, however, it denotes almost always a good thing obtained by secret influence or unfair means. "Two centuries ago a *job* was declared to mean an arranged robbery. What does it mean now?" (*Slang Dictionary.*)

Jole is the common way of writing—according to the sound—the word *jowl*, and when applied to the cheek of a pig, served up with "turnip-greens," forms the favorite dish of the Virginian.

Jumper, the characteristic name of a rude kind of sleigh, made of two elastic poles on which a box is fastened, and much used in the North and Northwest. "Here two voyageurs were waiting for us with their *jumpers*, and, uninviting as the frail structures looked at first sight, we soon found that they were quite comfortable, and admirably adapted to the mode of travelling in this howling wilderness." (*A Winter in Canada*, p. 137.)

Junk is in New England constantly substituted for *chunk*, and means "a fragment of any solid substance." (J. R. Lowell, *Glossary to Biglow Papers.*)

K.

Keener, a noun made from the adjective, is a Western term for a sharp man. "I tell you he is a *keener*, you can't get on his blind side."

Keep, to, in the sense of to live, to have a place of business, is common here, while in England it is only provincial and local, as *e. g.* in Cambridge, where "to keep" means to lodge. *Keeping-room* instead of drawing-room, almost universal in New England, is in like manner found in Norfolk and Suffolk (England), proving once more how many of the early settlers must have come from the eastern counties of England.

Kellick or *Killock* is the peculiar name of a small anchor, mentioned by Forby, and still heard in some small seaports of England, but quite common here in the Eastern States. "The boatmen occasionally dropped the *kellick* in the river-channel, and plied the oyster-tongs." (*Connecticut Georgics.*)

Kilter, quoted by Grose and by Brockett, and derived from the Danish *Kilter*, continues to be used in Pennsylvania as well as in the New England States; the former preferring the form of *Kelter*. It means order and good condition, and what is not in such a state is said to be "out of *Kelter*."

> "But it's all out of *Kilter* ('twas tu good to last.")
> (J. R. Lowell. *Biglow Papers*, II., p. 144.)

It is probable that this is the origin of the term helter-*skelter*, which Grose humorously explains as consisting of *helter* to hang, and *kelter*, order, so that it literally means, hang order!

Key for Quay or Kay, is not an Americanism, although many localities in the United States are so called, as the *South Keys* in Nansemond County, Virginia. (The Florida *Keys* are Spanish *Cayos*.) Pepys writes, November 7, 1665, when the plague was raging in London: "Lord! to see how he (Carteret) wondered to see the river so empty of boats, nobody working at the Custom-House *Keys*."

Killing-Time denotes, in the South, the season of the year when, the first frosts having set in, hogs can be slaughtered—a time of overflowing abundance and great rejoicing in former days.

Kinkle is the more common form here for *kink*, in the sense of notion, idea, although *kinky* remains unchanged, and means eccentric, fanciful.

> "I love, I say, to start upon a tramp
> To shake the *kinkles* out o' back an' legs."
> (J. R. Lowell. *Biglow Papers*, II., p. 52.)

"It is said—and we are not prepared to deny it—that all the members of the Randolph family have been more or less *kinky*." (Richmond *Enquirer*, June 17, 1847.)

Kiver for cover, common in New England and southward as far as Pennsylvania, is merely old English preserved, being frequently met with in the earlier dramatists. "I am a mere shell-fish—an oyster with the *kivers* off." (J. C. Neal, *Charcoal Sketches*.) "Gill charges the Eastern counties of England with *kiver* for cover." (J. R. Lowell.) The word *kivered*, on the other hand, is frequently heard in the South also, precisely as the early English settlers pronounced it and as the Cockney to this day sings: "I have *kivered* my head with green baize."

Knife, to, a newly-made verb, which has already found its way back to England. It means, to cut as with a knife, to stab.

> "the blast
> That *knifes* your vitals in hurrying past."
> (Sleigh-Riding. Troy *Whig*, December, 1848.)

L.

Lamper-eel seems to be a favorite corruption of lamprey in America as well as at home. "Mr. Van Buren hung on like a *lamper-eel* to the tail of General Jackson's horse." (Major J. Downing's *Letters*, p. 23.) The term shows once more how eagerly the uneducated seize upon every opportunity to shape an unknown word into a more familiar form. The Middle Latin *lampreta*, from *lambe petram* (because the fish with its sucking mouth adhered to stones), conveyed, of course, no meaning to them; hence already in Anglo-Saxon the fish was called a *mere-naedre*, sea-adder, the same name as that given to the eel—and hence the corruption.

Lane is in the South the common name given to all roads which are enclosed on both sides by fences.

Lather, to, is used here as in some parts of England, in the sense of to beat. It was originally to *leather*, a term derived from the leather belt worn by soldiers and policemen, which was often used as a weapon in street-rows, when firearms were forbidden. (*Slang Dictionary*, p. 90.) "I'll *leather* you heartily." (Grose.) "You'll get a mighty fine *leathering*, if you don't make haste and clear out." (*Harper's Monthly*, January, 1851.)

Lawyer is in America the uniform name of the person who in England is called a solicitor, if attending to our legal business, and a barrister, if appearing for us at court—the distinction not being observed in this country.

Lay, to, instead of lie, although undoubtedly incorrect, if judged by the usage established by the best writers of our day, may still be excused on the plea that the older writers seem to have employed it unhesitatingly. Chaucer says in his well-known lines—

> "Befell that in that season, on a day
> At Southwark at the Tabart I did *lay*."

"I used to *lay* on the sofa in the stately hall, during the sultry part of the day, and read a MS. work with wonderful gusto." (*Letters from the South*, I., p. 81.)

Laylock for lilac has the same authority for its use.

> " The cat-bird in the *laylock* bush is loud."
> (J. R. Lowell. *Biglow Papers*, II., p. 157.)

Laze, to, instead of to idle and waste time, is used in this sense by South, who says: "He lay *lazing* and looking upon his couch."

Lean-to, in New England generally pronounced *linter*, is not unknown in England, but much more common in the Eastern States of the Union. It designates a small addition to a house, the roof of which leans to or against the main wall. "For a kitchen I have nothing but a small *lean-to* with a shingle-roof, through which the rain kindly furnishes me all the water I need for cooking." (Mrs. Cleveland, *A Summer in the West*, p. 148.)

Leave, to, used as a neuter verb, without an object, is as common as it is incorrect. R. G. White says indignantly: "To wind up a story with, then he *left*, is as bad as to say, then he sloped—worse, for sloped is recognized slang." (*Words and their Uses*, p. 134.)

Lick, as a noun, means in the South and West a place where rock-salt and salt-springs attract great numbers of buffalo and deer. It is often called a *Salt-Lick*, and has, in return, given a name to many localities. The *Big Bone Lick* in Kentucky is a place, which having once been a favorite resort of deer, buffalo, and wild cattle, presents now an incredible number of bones and whole skeletons; among the latter are some of the wild bisons of former days, and of mastodons. *Lick* has, moreover, from the verb, the meaning of a piece or a part, as in the following sentence: "The father hunted 'possums, cultivated a little patch of corn, and did an occasional *lick* of work for some well-to-do neighbor, taking his pay in corn." *Big Licks* mean, hence, vigorous efforts. As a verb, *to lick* retains in full force its ancient meaning of to thrash, which it had already under its quaint form of to *lycke*, in Thomas Harman's *Canting Dictionary*, published under Queen Elizabeth, and the first ever written. "'Tain't no use to talk about honor with them, Cap.; they hain't got no such thing in 'em, and they won't show fair fight, anyway you can fix it. Don't they kill and sculp a white man whenar they get the better on him? The mean varmints, they'll never behave themselves until you give um a clean out-and-out *licking*. They can't understand white folks' ways, and they won't learn 'um, and ef you treat 'um decently, they think you are afeard. You may depen' on it, Cap., the only way to treat Injuns is to thrash them well at first, and then the balance will sorter take to you and behave themselves." (Colonel Marcy's *Expedition in the West*.)

Lief, *liever*, and *lieves* are all used here as in England colloquially.

Lieutenant is almost universally pronounced *leftenant* in the United States, and the distinction between army and navy lieutenants treated with republican indifference.

Lift takes here the place of the more usual *liftgate* in England.

Light-bread designates wheat-bread, in contradistinction from corn-bread, which really is much heavier, while

Light-wood is so called from yielding a bright light, much used where candles and oil are too expensive, and from kindling readily. It consists generally of small chips of resinous pine wood, technically called *kindlings*. "I have heard a piece of pine forest called, The *lightwood* knot woods, *i. e.*, the woods where they get the pine-knots for kindlings." (S. S. Haldeman.)

Like instead of *as*, used mainly in the South, but not unknown elsewhere, is almost exclusively an Americanism, being but rarely heard in England. "I did not feel *like* saying another word, after he had treated me so badly." "Why can't you come this evening after meeting, *like* you always do?" (E. Phelps, *The Gates Ajar*.)

Lily-pads is the curious name given to places where a number of the leaves of the water-lily form, as it were, floating islands on the surface of a pond. "I have seen boys secure pickerel taking their unwary siesta beneath the *lily-pads* too nigh the surface, with a gun and small shot." (J. R. Lowell, *Biglow Papers*, I., p. 30.)

Limb, instead of *leg*, one of the ludicrous evidences of the false prudishness prevailing in certain classes of American society. R. G. White, in his sharp, incisive way, says of people who use *limb* for *leg*: "Perhaps these persons think that it is indelicate for women to have legs, and that therefore they are concealed by garments and should be concealed in speech. If so, heaven help them!" (*Words and their Uses*.) This mock-modesty is carried so far that we even find: "One of her *larger limbs* was fractured in the attempt to rescue her from the prison-walls." (*Upham Witchcraft*, II., p. 248.) The statements that Southern ladies at table ask for a chicken *limb*, and that the principal of a fashionable boarding-school for girls in Baltimore had the *limbs* of her pianos clad in muslin-trousers, are, we trust, what the French call *un peu plus beau que la vérité.*

Limbo, much used in America, as in England, is not slang, as often stated. The Catholic Prayer-Book says: "Christ descended into *Limbo*."

Lime-kill, for *lime-kiln*, very common in New England, has Gayton's authority in its favor, who so writes it in his "*Festivous Notes on Don Quixote*." (J. R. Lowell.)

Lives, another form under which, in the West especially, *lief* and *lieves* appear. "Just as *lives* as not," is a phrase occurring in the Eastern States also—"Well, captain, I'll go with you, too, I guess, if you jest as *lives*." (*Overland Monthly*, October, 1870, p. 343.)

Lit, the old preterite of *light*, much censured as an Americanism, is used by Addison, who says: "I *lit* my pipe with paper," and actually occurs in a leader of the London *Times*, June 17, 1861.

Live, in the sense of quick, green, active, is rarely heard in England, where *quick* takes its place mainly, but very common in America. *Live* oaks and *live* men, *live* hedges and *live* words, are constantly quoted. A new application of the term has been recently made: "This is the first instance in which, within the territory of the United States (Alaska, of course, excepted), *live* glaciers have been found, though in the East as well as in the West there are so many indications of glacial action. The glaciers on Mount Shasta, now detected, have hitherto escaped notice." (King, *Explorations in the Rocky Mountains*, p. 157.)

Lopsided is, in Pennsylvania, the usual form of *lab* or *lap*sided, written as it was used in England in old times. (*Slang Dictionary*, p. 173.) "He illustrates the *lopsided* consequences of giving one leg more to do than another." (J. C. Neal, *Charcoal Sketches*.)

Log, to, as a verb, is used only in America, and means to get out logs. From this verb are derived *logging* and the noun *logger*. "These men were on their way to the upper portage, where the *logging* was to commence." "The poet must from time to time travel the *logger's* path and the Indian trail, to drink at some new and more bracing fountain of the muses, far in the recesses of the mountains." (*American Monthly*, August, 1858.) The *logging camp* is a close-built, snug log-hut, erected by lumbermen for their residence during their winter work, and the place where the timber is felled and cut is called the *logging*-swamp, however dry it may happen to be, because generally the finest logs are cut in swamps.

Long, as an adverb, instead of "it is long," is used in some parts of America, especially in the Cumberland Valley, merging into the meaning of the kindred word "to *long*." "Don't you think *long* to be at home?" "A relic doubtless of English in the Middle Ages, for to *think long* is still common in the Cumbrian districts of England, supplying the missing link between the adjective *long* and the verb *long*. We *long* for a thing, when we think it is *long* before we attain it." (Henry Reeves.)

Lope, the old participle of to leap, in the sense of a leap, a long step, is "often heard in the streets of London." (*Slang Dictionary*, p. 173.)

> "Up he *lope* and the window broke,
> And he had thirty feet to fall."
> (*Percy's Relics.*)

As a verb, *to lope* is very generally used in the West, and in this sense generally looked upon as an abbreviation of to *gallop*. It is far more likely, however, to be a remnant of the Dutch verb *lopen*, which was once much used in England, and is referred to in Beaumont and Fletcher's line, "It goes like a Dutch *lopeman*." The former derivation was evidently in F. B. Harte's mind when he wrote, "Horses are always ready saddled in Spanish ranchos, and in half an hour from the time of our arrival, we were again *loping* in the staring sunlight." (*Luck of Roaring Camp*, p. 214.) The noun *loper*, used like *loafer*, would hardly admit such an etymology: "Nature never intended such a climate for lazy *lopers*; she never gin six months' sunshine to be slept and smoked away." (*Ibidem*, p. 201.)

Lumber, in England only known as meaning useless and cumbrous things, literally and figuratively, denotes in America also timber cut and sawed for use. As the business of getting out *lumber* is a very extensive one, the term is used as a verb as well as a noun, and has furnished the additional words, *lumberer* and *lumberman*, for persons engaged in this business.

> "In unploughed Maine, he sought the *lumberers'* gang
> Where from a hundred lakes young rivers sprang."
> (R. W. Emerson. *Wood Notes.*)

A *lumber*-wagon, consisting of a plain, square box on wheels, is used by farmers everywhere to carry produce to market.

Lummox, the odd provincial word of old England, is quite common with us. "The Roman cart-horse," says A. A. Bartlett in a recent number of *Old and New*, "will seldom weigh over a thousand or eleven hundred pounds, but I would trust him to keep on pulling long after your mere *lummoxes* had fallen in their shafts." (June, 1871.)

M.

Mad, in the sense of angry, and as a substitute for the English *wild*, was denounced as a vile Americanism when W. Irving first used it in one of his earlier works. Like many such terms, it is excellent old English. Middleton has: "They are *mad;* she graced me with one private minute above their fortunes." (*Your Five Gallants.*) "I was *mad* at him." (*Old Plays*, 2d ed., I., p. 65.) "And being exceedingly *mad* against them, I persecuted them even unto strange cities." (*Acts* xxvi. 11.) "This made him *halfe madde* to be the owner of such strange jewells." (Captain John Smith, *Virginia*, I., p. 168.) Even the familiar phrase, *like mad*, has old and high authority in its favor. Pepys, in his *Diary*, writes, June 13, 1663: "Thence by coach with a mad coachman, that drove *like mad*, and down bye-ways through Bucklesbury home." "Said I: 'Sister, while I was preaching, did you get *mad?*' She answered: 'Yes, very *mad;* I could have cut your throat. But I am not *mad* now, and I love you, and God has blessed me.'" (Rev. P. Cartwright, *Autobiography*, p. 222.) The word is even used as a noun, meaning anger: "The Squire's *mad* riz." (*New Era*, April, 1871.)

Madstone is the name of a round stone of the size of an egg, of dark color, preserved in some families in the South, to which the power is ascribed of curing persons bitten by mad dogs or venomous serpents. It is placed upon the wound, from which it draws much matter, and this process being repeated frequently, extracts the venom—by faith.

Madam is the title given in many parts of the country, where old English customs are still held in remembrance, in New England and in Virginia for instance, to married ladies who have married daughters of their own name. Besides, as the first President's wife was universally known as Lady Washington, ladies of old age and high social position are often honored with the title of *Madam*. *Marm* is the familiar corruption of the word, peculiar to New England.

Magnetic, denounced by the *Athenæum*, with its usual tenderness for the United States, as a "useless and objectionable Americanism," is not only used by Donne—

> "She that had all *magnetic* force alone"—

but has, since this was done, established itself in England also, as a useful and legitimate part of the language.

Mail, to, applied to letters and newspapers, has in America entirely usurped the place of the English, to post. In like manner, the post-boy of England is here a *mail-rider*, while the mail-coach there re-appears here as a *mail*-stage.

Manor denotes in America a tract of land occupied by tenants, and held by the owner in virtue of a grant from the former sovereigns, who governed this country as colonies.

Mantle-place is the curious form which the English *mantle-piece* has assumed in some parts of the South. As the term originally meant a piece of mantle or cloak, hung over the chimney to hide it by a kind of drapery (lambrequin), and only subsequently was applied to the whole framework itself, it conveyed no very distinct idea to persons unfamiliar with such luxuries, and hence the *piece* very naturally changed into a *place*. "You have a very singular ornament for your *mantle-place*." (W. G. Simms, *The Last Wager*.)

Marvel has, in like manner, usurped, first in pronunciation and afterward even in writing, the place of *marble*, especially in the play with "marbles," so popular in the South, that men now living can recollect having seen grave judges and renowned senators engage in it with much zest and pleasure. Even the great Chief-Justice Marshall, of Virginia, is said to have enjoyed it up to a good old age. A Kentucky divine is reported to have once preached against this "frivolous and childish sport" from the text, "*Marvel* not, brethren!" (1 *John* iii. 13.)

Mash, a corruption of *marsh,* is common in the South, where the letter *r* is grievously ill-treated, being dropped where it ought to be heard and tacked on to words that require no such help. The *Mash*-market in Baltimore thus derives its name from the fact that it was built upon low, marshy ground, where a very humble class of people formerly resided.

Matter, in the sense of amount, extent, etc., is frequently heard in the South and West. "I suppose the lad had been with us a *matter* of six weeks, getting better, but so slowly that he had not, at the end of that time, been able to leave the picket." (W. G. Simms, *The Two Camps.*)

Maying, a celebration of the return of spring, is little known in America; the term survives, however, in Pennsylvania, in the sense of having a picnic or a strolling after flowers. (S. S. Haldeman.)

Maypole. "There was formerly in the centre square of the village of Maytown, Lancaster County, Pennsylvania, a pole like a very tall mast, permanently erected, and called the *maypole.* It had a vane on the top." (S. S. Haldeman.) Probably the only instance of the existence of *maypoles* in the United States.

Meeching, more rarely *miching,* still survives here in the sense in which it was used by Shakespeare (skulking), while in England it has become obsolete.

> "But I ain't of the *meechin'* kind, that sets and thinks for weeks,
> The bottom's out o' th' Universe, 'coz their own gillpot leaks."
> (J. R. Lowell. *Biglow Papers,* II., p. 13.)

Middling, in the sense of tolerably well, is used from New England southward as far as Pennsylvania. "How are your folks? Only *middling,* thank you." It is, of course, good old English, mentioned in Bailey, and thus used by Dryden: "Longinus preferred the sublime genius that sometimes errs to the *middling* or indifferent one, which makes few faults but seldom rises to any excellence." The Scotch-Irish in the valley of the Alleghanies have improved upon it, and speak of a man as *middling smart.* "Mister Sawin, sir, you're *middlin'* well now, be ye?" (J. R.

Lowell, *Biglow Papers*, I., p. 27.) The plural, *middlings*, is used in the South and West to denote the parts of the hogs between the shoulders and the hams, which are cured separately, and quoted, as pork in the market, under this name.

Million, a common corruption for *melon*, used in the South by the whole black race and not a few whites, is not new. Pepys in his *Diary* says, August 5, 1666, "We landed and walked to Barne-elmes and bought a *millon*."

Minced-pies represent in America the English Christmas-pies. They continue to be popular in the South; in the North they, as well as plum porridge, fell under the interdict of the Puritans at Christmas times, though they allowed that they might be lawfully and piously eaten in any month but December. Hence the quaint complaint—

" All plums the prophets' sons deny,
And spice broths are too hot;
Treason's in a Deo pye,
And death within the pot.

Christmas, farewell! Thy days, I fear,
And merry days, are gone,
So they may keep feast all the year,
Our Saviour shall have none."
(Needham. *History of the Rebellion.*)

Mind, to, is used in America very much as in Scotland, to denote remembering. "I *minded* me of my sins." Wherever the Scotch-Irish have settled in large numbers, the word is so used. "A month's *mind*," is a series of ecclesiastical services, especially relating to one subject, and also a stated prayer for the dead. In the same manner to *mind* is used in the sense of to take care. "Never *mind* now; you ought to have *minded* the child better." In popular language the fuller form, to have a *mind*, is preferred. "You can call me when you have a *mind* to." (*Lippincott's Magazine*, March 27, 1871, p. 282.)

Misery, in the South, means simply pain. "I was suffering with such a *misery* in my head, and nothing would do me any good." (Longstreet, *Flush Times.*) The word is a special favorite with the negroes, to whose mind it represents any feeling which they cannot definitely describe. As they are never perfectly well, but only "jest tullable," so they are ever ready to have "a *misery* in the leg, the chest, or the throat."

Mistress is in the South very frequently yet heard pronounced fully, without the usual contraction into "Missess."

Mizzle, to, a term borrowed from English slang, is well known in America. The term is a frequentative of *mist*, and originally meant, in the forms of to *mistle* and then to *misle* (Bailey), to rain in small drops. As the *mizzle* is apt to come after a rain, the disappearance is transferred to persons who are said in like manner to *mizzle*, and hence the play upon those words in Thomas Hood's lines:

> "How monarchs die is easily explained,
> And thus it might upon their tombs be chiselled:
> As long as George IV. could reign, he reigned,
> And then he *mizzled*."
>
> (*On a Royal Demise.*)

"They say the treasurer has *mizzled*, and as there is a small sum of a hundred thousand dollars missing, the presumption is not a very violent one." (New York *Herald*, June 17, 1857.)

Mobee or *Mobby*, declared by Bailey to be "a potable liquor made of potato roots, used in America," and afterward a kind of wine made in the West Indies, is frequently applied in the South to what in England would be simply called a "punch."

Molasses, universally substituted for syrup and treacle—the latter being almost unknown in America—is in the West often misapprehended and treated as a plural. "Where did you get *these molasses*? at the store?"

Monkey-spoon, is the name of a spoon, bearing the figure of an ape or monkey, carved in solid silver on the extremity of the handle, and given at the funerals of great people in the State of New York to the pall-bearers. At the death of Philip Livingston in February, 1719, we are told "a pipe of wine was spiced for the occasion, and to each of the eight bearers, with a pair of gloves, a mourning ring, scarf, and handkerchief, and a *Monkey-spoon* was given." (Old paper.)

Monstrous, for anything great or striking, was precisely so used in Horace Walpole's time, and is now revived again.

Most, instead of almost, is inexcusable, but so generally in use that it has crept into the newspapers, and appears unblushingly even in otherwise well-written articles. "We have seen *most* every kind of trickery and deception at election time, but in this, Tammany has surpassed all precedent." (New York *Tribune*, March 30, 1870.)

Mought, the old preterite of *may*, obsolete in England, is frequently heard in the South, where the negroes especially use it almost exclusively. Derived from the ancient verb *mowe*, the ancestor of *may*, and corresponding to the German *mochte*, it was once correct, and hence Fairfax says—

"Yet mould with death, then chastise, tho' he *mought*."

In North Carolina "*it mout be*" is a standing phrase for perhaps.

Mud-lumps, is the technical name of the earliest appearance of soft, spongy land at the mouth of the Mississippi, the evil genii of the Passes, as they have been called, and the dread of the navigators. They are at first conical, not unlike miniature volcanoes, and have little craters at the top, from which flows muddy water, much salter and heavier than that of the Gulf. They have been known to rise to the height of twenty feet, and to become several hundred feet in circumference.

Mulling means, in the United States, bustling, stirring, with the additional idea, at times, of its being done in an underhand way. The metaphor is evidently derived from the *mulling* of wine, which takes place "when wine is burnt and sweetened." (Hanmer.) "What a *mullin'* there was among the lasses when he came home from college, and appeared at church in all his city splendor." (*Life in a Village*, p. 117.)

Mum, a probable corruption of ma'am, is the common pronunciation of the latter word in many parts of the Union, and often written, as in the case of the famous *Mum Bet*. This was the popular name of Elizabeth Freeman, a colored woman, born in slavery in 1742, who heard, while waiting at table, the Bill of Rights and the new Constitution of Massachusetts (1772) discussed. She thought she understood, from what she heard, that all but "dumb beasts" had a right, under these laws, to claim their personal liberty. She consulted an eminent lawyer, Judge Sedgwick, who took her case up seriously and obtained her freedom, with wages for her services since she came of age. This led, as a matter of convenience, to the abolition of slavery in Massachusetts, and made *Mum* Bet a historical personage.

Musical, in certain localities in New England, has the meaning of humorous; and a damsel will say to her lover: "Git away, you are so *musical,*" when she thinks he is becoming too pressing.

Muss, perhaps a corruption of *mess,* and meaning a difficulty, a state of disorder, is very popular in all parts of the United States, and has Shakespeare's authority in its favor, who uses it in *Anthony and Cleopatra:*

> "Of late, when I said: Ho!
> Like boys into a *muss,* kings would strut forth
> And cry: Your will!"

"We have all been in such a *muss,* ever since you left us, that I heartily wish we had gone too." (J. P. Kennedy.) The verb is, in New England, often corrupted into, to *mux.* "Don't *mux* up my dress so, it's all mashed already." The same form occurs in New Jersey, and has led to the question whether the word may not come from the German "Musz," a hashed mixture of fruit, like apple-butter. In the west of England *mux* means dirt, and this meaning also is not unknown here.

N.

Naked possessor, is the odd title by which, in Texas and the Southwestern States, the occupant of a farm is known, who can show no title to his land.

Nasty, in England frequently meaning ill-tempered or cross-grained (*Slang Dictionary,* p. 186), and in this sense admitted into good society, denotes in America something disgusting in point of smell, taste, or even moral character, and is not considered a proper word to be used in the presence of ladies.

Natural is used in two peculiar meanings in America. One is derived from the association of what is natural with what is savage, belonging to man's lower nature, as suggested in the words, "The *natural* man receiveth not the things of the spirit of God." (1 *Corinthians* ii. 14.) Hence it means, fierce, savage. "Ned Hazard is a pretty hard horse to ride, too; only look at his eye, how *natural* it is!" (J. P. Kennedy, *Swallow Barn.*) The other use of *natural* is the result of ignorance, when it is employed instead of *native.* But this also has old English usage to excuse it, for an old book, printed in 1536, has this title: "The Complaynt of Roderyck More, somtyme a gray fryre, unto the parliament howse of Ingland, his *natural* country."

Neat, used formerly in England in the sense of free from admixture, as in Chapman's "Our old wine *neat,*" is in America often employed as an adverb, with the same meaning: "I knew the mixture to be good for the cholera, for I had tried it, though I had never ventured to take it *neat.*" (*Lippincott's Magazine,* March, 1871, p. 245.)

Neither added to a negation, as is the frequent custom in the South, has the authority of many old English writers for its use, and has been preserved in its former meaning. "The Indians, who have no pleasure in exercise and won't be at the pains to fish and hunt, and, indeed, not so well as they *neither.*" (R. B. Beverley, *History of Virginia,* p. 18.)

Nightfall, used by Swift in the sense of at the close of the day, and *After Night,* are both continued unchanged in Virginia and the Southern States generally. The New England States, instead, use *nights* for "of *nights,*" an adverb made after the model of the German *Nachts:* "So thievish, they hev to take in their stone-walls *nights.*" (J. R. Lowell.)

Nice and nicely, used with great freedom, both North and South, has full authority for this in Grose's statement: "*Nice,* clever, agreeable, fine, applied to anything." "Squire, how's your wife?" Thank ye, she's doing *nicely.*" (Alice Cary.)

Nip, as derived from the German *nippen* or *nipfen,* to sip, is a frequent word in America to denote a small drink. "One of our Western villages passed an ordinance forbidding taverns to sell liquor on the Sabbath to any persons except travellers. The next Sunday every man in town, who wanted a *nip,* was seen walking around with a valise in one hand and two carpet-bags in the other." (Editor's Drawer. *Harper's Magazine,* May, 1855.)

Nohow, an American expletive, used even in careful writing. "Well, I reckon a man never gets anything worth having without a tussle for it, and as to secrets, I don't believe in them *nohow.*" This is but one of the many evidences our speech bears of loving double negatives, in the same manner in which they were popular with the English in the days of Shakespeare. *Nohow* is frequently strengthened, in familiar language, by two additions: "*Nohow* by a long way," and "*Nohow* you can fix it."

Nor, is in New England frequently substituted for the proper word *than*. "Better *nor* a thousand o' 'em were killed;" "Better *nor* fifty bushels of them potatoes was spoiled by the rain."

Notch, a narrow passage through the mountains, as the famous White Mountain *Notch*, is in the Catskill mountains represented by *Cove*, and in the Southern States by *Gap*.

Notify, to, a verb in England only applied to things, the object of information, is in the United States connected with persons, as its direct object. Where the English, therefore, notify an order to a person, the Americans notify the person of the order. "Upon receipt of these papers, you will *notify* the agent of the decision of the Department." (Hon. Hamilton Fish to Mr. Motley, 1869.)

Notion, in the sense of inclination, is an Americanism, and by no means any longer confined to colloquial language. "I have a *notion* to an egg" (*Southern Literary Messenger*, August, 1849), is of course incorrect, but such expressions are often heard in the South. "She had a *notion* I would propose as soon as she gave me an opening, but there she was mistaken." (Miss Evans, *Beulah*.) The plural has acquired in New England a special popularity, denoting every variety of small wares, which have come to be regarded so exclusively the specialty of those States that they are advertised in shops and newspapers as "Yankee *Notions*." Even a "dealer in *notions*" has become a regular mercantile term. The word is not new, in either sense, for Fr. Bentley already says: "He may coin new *notions* of his own." (*On Freethinking*, 1703.) "Finally he swore that he would have nothing more to do with such a squatting, bundling, questioning, swapping, pumpkin-eating, molasses-daubing, shingle-splitting, cider-watering, horse-jockeying, *notion*-peddling crew." (W. Irving, *Knickerbocker History of New York*.)

O.

Obleeged, as Pope said:

> "Dreading e'en fools, by flatterers besieged,
> And so obliging, that he ne'er *obliged*,"

and as Earl Russell has never ceased to say, is in like manner still used by many a gentleman of the old school, especially in the South, where quiet rural life and greater seclusion seem to have secured an asylum to old words and old sounds, that have long since disappeared everywhere else. The phrase, *obliged to be*, as applied to things, is however, of modern date and unpardonably faulty. "When he heard of Anthon's ruin and our doubts about it, he only said he knew it was *obliged* to be so, since no man ever went on at a greater rate than Anthon had done." (*The Southern Bride*, p. 271.) The North has, on the other hand, the old term *obligement*, which is still heard occasionally in New England.

Of, as inserted between verbs and their direct object, is very frequent in all parts of the Union, and arose originally, no doubt, from an instinctive perception of the verb as a noun. "The feeling *of it* is quite soft." "He expects to be well paid for the letting *of it*."

Offal, in the English sense nothing but absolutely worthless refuse, resumes in America, constantly and legitimately, its ancient meaning, of those parts of a butchered animal which are small in size, and not worth salting. Thus, in pork-packing, the liver and the lights, the head, etc., are called *offal*. In New Jersey the word is quite frequently pronounced *off-fall*, and a plural *off-falls* is used, which may possibly point out the true origin of the word.

Old Country, generally used with reference to England, not unfrequently finds a wider application to all Europe, and naturalized citizens are thus represented as having returned to the *Old Country*, whenever they visit their native land. "When the tandem was brought to the Mayor's office, an ordinance was read from an *Old-Country*-looking, yellow book, made when New York was not New York City." (New York *Tribune*, February 15, 1871.)

Old Driver and *Old Splitfoot* are probably also reminiscences of those early days, and continue to be courteous substitutes for the name of the Evil One.

> "An' make *Ole Splitfoot* winch an' squirm for all he's used to singeing."
> (J. R. Lowell. *Biglow Papers*, II., p. 33.)

Omnibus retains in America very generally its full form, the English *'bus* being but rarely heard.

On seems to be a favorite preposition with Americans; at least it is constantly found where other prepositions would seem to be more correct and appropriate. F. G. Halleck already condemned this abuse, a result of the prevailing carelessness in the use of words, and quoted the phrases: "Going to Europe *on* a steamboat; writing a letter *on* Chambers-street, and delivering it *on*

Fifth avenue; being mentioned *on* the *Times* newspaper; and actually speaking of: Our Father which art *on* heaven." Persons are constantly heard to speak of friends whom they saw *on* the street, and having come *on* the cars, while in the South members are elected to sit *on* the Legislature. Hence the common phrase of being *on* time, instead of in time; "The engine-driver had been running extra risks, in order, as the Americans phrase it, to *make time,* so as to be *on time.*" (W. F. Rae, *Westward by Rail.*) The New England phrase: "I hearn him tell *on* it," instead of concerning it, has its precedent in the Hallamshire Glossary; but "She never thought *on it*" (E. S. Phelps, *A Woman's Pulpit*), can hardly be excused. *To be on it,* is a recent slang term, meaning to be ready for a fight.

> "At that he pranced around as if a bee were in his bonnet,
> And, with hostile demonstrations, inquired if *I was on it.*"
> (*Words and their Uses,* Galveston *News,* May 4, 1871.)

Once, at, is used in the United States, North and South, instead of the English immediately. "I will send it back *at once.*" Unfortunately, it is rarely heard pronounced correctly, even educated persons having a tendency to raise it to a superlative, and pronounce it *onst.* Hence its peculiar spelling, resembling English provincialisms. "Warn ye *wunst,* warn ye twyst, warn ye three times." (J. C. Neal, *Charcoal Sketches.*) The *Chester Plays* already have *at onst,* and J. R. Lowell quotes it with this commentary: "I am now inclined to consider it no corruption at all, but only an erratic and obsolete superlative, *at onest.*" This is proved by the *twyst,* quoted above, and the development of among into amongst, amid into amidst, and between into betwixt.

Onhitch, to, is a quaint rural substitute for to fire, much used in the New England States. It refers to the act of pulling the trigger.

> "So he *onhitched*—Jerusalem! the middle of next year
> Was right next door compared to where he kicked the crittur to."
> (J. R. Lowell. *Biglow Papers,* II., p. 28.)

Onto, in England condemned as obsolete and incorrect, is much affected by certain writers of the class of Mrs. Stowe. A reverend Doctor of Divinity, in a learned essay on Christian Baptism, says: "Pouring water *onto* the fists is the proper translation of a phrase in the Greek usually translated, Pouring water upon the hands." (*Christian Observer*, June, 1849.)

Osculate, to, as a substitute for to kiss, an utterly unwarrantable vulgarism.

Ouch, an interjection quoted in ancient glossaries, still survives in the Middle and some of the Southern States, as a cry uttered by persons who are suddenly hurt. "*Ouch*—my eye. How it hurts! Don't hit me again." (J. C. Neal, *Charcoal Sketches*.)

Outcry is occasionally used in remote districts, instead of a similar old term, at public *cry*, meaning at auction. "Tuesday, May 1st, will be sold at public *outcry*." The word is old Saxon, and found in almost all the North Country glossaries.

Outen, a vulgarism known to America as well as to England. "Oh, Simon! My son Simon! To be overcome this way. A Suggs to be humbugged! His own Jack to be taken *outen* his hand and turned on him. Oh, that I should have lived to see the day!" (*Simon Suggs*.)

Outside is, in conversation and in journalism, very often used for beside, or except. "*Outside* of the Secretary of War, no one knew anything of the transaction." (Philadelphia *Ledger*, December, 1870.)

Overly, a redundant term, meaning excessively. "He is awful conceited, and not *overly* polite." (*Lippincott's Magazine*, March, 1871, p. 284.)

P.

Paddy, the East Indian word, is in the South also used to designate unhusked rice.

Paint, in the South and Southwest, is used for a spotted horse, or wild animal. "He said it was a *paint*, but we found no spots on the animal," (G. W. Kendall. *Santa Fê Expedition*.)

Pair, as applied to stairs, in the sense of a flight of stairs, is not peculiar to America. The expression is found in Hakluyt, and still in use in Yorkshire.

Palatial, a favorite term with grandiloquent speakers and journalists, who love to dwell on "*palatial* residences," and even "stores of *palatial* proportions."

Pandowdy, a dish consisting of stewed apples, into which the crust covering them has been stirred, and "bearing," it has been said, "to apple-pie the relation of the vulgar to the well-bred," is, no doubt, the descendant of Halliwell's *pandoudle*. The word, like the dish, is known only in New England.

Pants have almost entirely superseded *pantaloons* in American conversation, as the latter have taken the place of the English "trousers." The word is still objected to by critics. "Certainly it is an astonishment to find the tailor's English, rolling up his *pants*, p. 401—in an imposing octavo volume by a University professor." (Criticism on Hartt's *Brazil*, New York *Tribune*, October 11, 1870.) Thus it is, that the historic associations connected with our words are gradually fading out of sight. How long shall we be able to recognize in the poor remnant the peculiar garb of the ancient pantaloon, who wore breeches and stockings of the same stuff, and joined together as one garment, when he became in Italian comedy the representative of the "Magnificent Venetian," after having been for centuries the patron-saint of Venice, under the name of St. Pantaleone? What a gulf between the haughty πάντα λεών and the *pants* of our day!

Paring-shears, in the tailor's language, are so called in contradistinction to cutting-shears, which were formerly used for "cutting out" garments. A literary tailor—not unknown to the scientific world as a good entomologist—tells us that the term "*Paring-shears* originated in the fact that, forty years ago, nearly everything that would bear it at all was made 'raw-edged,' and required the edges to be pared, as the finishing touch to the garment." (S. S. Rathvon, Lancaster *Intelligencer*, April 24, 1871.)

Parlor is in America uniformly used for the English "drawing-room."

Parquet, the term which in Paris and on the Continent is called the *parterre*, in Italian *platea*, and in Spanish *patio*, is probably in the United States alone used for that part of the theatre which was formerly known as the "pit." The term comes, of course, from the French *parquet*, an inlaid floor, and has thus been applied to the "floor" of the theatre. It is stated that the word "*parquet* was first introduced at the opening of the Academy of Music in the city of New York."

Partake, to, is a verb much abused by journalists, who are not content to limit it to its legitimate sense of sharing with others, but use it vaguely for eating or enjoying. "The man who was to be hanged about noon, *partook* of his solitary meal!"

Pavement denotes in the United States more frequently the sidewalk than the paved street. This arises from the fact that, in the countless new towns springing up every year in all the new States, the sidewalks are generally first made, long before the roads are macadamised or the streets paved, and hence they are first spoken of as the *pavement.*

Peke, to, or to *peak,* is the old English word, used by many of the poets for to see. "He's going about all day *peaking* into every hole, and never doing anything worth speaking of." (W. G. Simms, *Sketches.*) Shakespeare's use of the word in the sense of looking ill, has probably led to the employment of *peaked* or *peakish* for the same purpose. The origin of the term must be sought in *peak,* and growing into a peak or peaks suggests naturally the idea of growing thin from illness. *Peckish,* on the contrary, derived from the Gypsy word *peck* (meat), and quoted by Grose and all cant dictionaries as meaning hungry, is the old English word surviving in America; we have both the adjective, "I feel rather *peckish* this morning" (*Slang Dictionary,* p. 173), and the noun, "keep your *pecker* up" (*Adventures of Verdant Green*), in the same sense.

Peert—frequently written *peart,* and in all probability a corruption of *pert*—is common in all parts of the Union. It is one of the good old words, used once upon a time by English writers, but now obsolete in England, while surviving vigorously in America. "You shall know them by their very gate; they walk so *peartly* about." (Burroughs, *On Hosea,* p. 115 : 1652.) "Fust rate, never felt *pearter* in my life. Tell ye what, that was a busting medicine." (*Lippincott's Magazine,* March, 1871, p. 246.) "He observed that the master was looking *peartish,* and hoped he had gotten over the neuralgia and the rheumatism; he himself had been troubled with a dumb ager since last conference, but he had learnt to rastle (wrestle) and pray." (F. B. Harte, *Luck of Roaring Camp,* p. 166.) *Perk,* pronounced *peerk,* is probably but another corruption of the same root.

Periodicals, in the plural, is a frequent but unwarranted use of the term, since the latter is an adjective and not a noun. Thus here, also, the language loses in correctness what it may gain in brevity.

Permanent boarders, as persons are called who live for any length of time in a boarding-house or hotel, are opposed to *transient* guests, travellers who spend only a night or a few days there, and both terms are thus used exclusively in America. The same applies to

Permit, when it is used instead of leave to enter, or ticket of admission to any place of public amusement.

Peruse, to, a term much affected by unrefined persons, who invariably prefer a strange but high-sounding word to the more familiar expression. Hence they *peruse* a book, where others modestly "read" it, and do not "scan" but *peruse* a stranger's features. Still, there is good authority for this use of the word also, since English writers of the seventeenth century employ it continually in this manner. "Monsieur Soubise having *perused* the fleet, returned to the King and told him that nothing was ready." (MS. in Harleian Collection in British Museum, written before 1650.) "My children, have you so *perused* each other's countenances that when you meet you may recognize each other? said Magdalen Graeme to Catharine Seaton and Roland Graeme." (Sir W. Scott.) Hence we need not wonder if a Virginia overseer sent to examine some wood which his master wished to buy, returned, saying he had "*perused* the wood carefully." (Hugh Blair Grigsby, 1870.)

Pesky and *peskily* are intensative expressions, implying annoyance, and probably corruptions of "pestilent." (*Slang Dictionary*, p. 199.) "Bill was up in his room playing Seven-Up, or Four-in-Hand, or some of those *pesky* games." (*Wild Bill.*)

Petroleum takes in America the place of "rock-oil" in Canada and England, but, when used for domestic purposes, appears almost universally as "kerosene."

Philology is often heard with a broad *i*, as in psyche, and yet no one says "physic," with a long *y*; so unsettled is as yet the pronunciation of foreign words among the masses.

Picra, an electuary in England, is in America the officinal powder of aloes with canella, a cathartic, and often used to denote anything mean and objectionable. "Fips was tangled with some old debts, as poor as *picra*, as they say in the country, and totally without hitch or hold upon any actual capital, influence, or means of any kind." (*Putnam's Magazine*, August, 1868.)

Pie takes here entirely the place of the English "tart," in dishes not made of meat, and is, especially in New England, so great a favorite, that it appears almost on every table at breakfast, dinner, and supper alike.

Piece, in the sense of a while, a small distance, is provincial in the north of England, and, with us, in Pennsylvania. "Go *a piece* with me," and, "Won't you go along a *piece* farther?" are common expressions. The verb to *piece* means, in the same district, to take an irregular snack between meals. A child, not showing any appetite at dinner, is said to "have been *a-piecing* on it all the morning." (S. S. Haldeman.)

Pierce, to, is very often, and the proper name *Pierce* always, pronounced as if it were written Perse. This, however, is not incorrect; at least it was the orthodox sound of the word in the days of Spenser, who rhymes thus:

> "He red and measur'd many a sad verse,
> That horrour gave the virgin's hart to *perse,*
> Hearing him those same bloody lines reherse."
> (*Faëry Queen,* Bk. III., Canto XII., v. 36.)

Pike is quite common for "turnpike," following the example of English "van" and "bus," and assumes, not unfrequently, a figurative meaning. "Another champion walkist, Weston, the democratic Governor of New Hampshire, on a radical *Pike.*" (Philadelphia *Age,* March 17, 1871.)

Pillow-Slip and *pillow-bier* take in New England the place of the English pillow-case.

Pint, instead of point, and even *disappint,* are quite common in New England and in some of the Southern States, where the old English pronunciation has been preserved.

Pip, to, originally the same as to peep, denotes the first chirping or piping of young chickens, and hence is used to denote all very small beginnings. "I suppose radicalism had just *pipped.*" (Rev. P. Cartwright, *Autobiography,* p. 158.)

Pitcher, used for *jug,* is frequently adduced by Englishmen as a test-word by which Americans are recognized abroad. "This word is the best test, if indeed it is not the only test, of the nationality of a cultivated man of English blood. . . . If a man asks for the milk-jug, be sure that he is British bred; if for the milk-*pitcher*, be equally sure that he is an American." (R. G. White, *Words and their Uses*, p. 84.)

Plain, instead of plainly, clearly, is very much used by Americans. "These fellows are not smart; they cannot talk *plain*."

Plankroad, a roadway formed of sawed deals or boards of considerable thickness, laid even and close, crosswise, with much yield in them, is a common contrivance in regions where timber is abundant, and roads have to be made promptly and cheaply. They require, however, constant repair, and are very injurious to horses, whose knees they "knock up" in a very short time.

Play-actor, a pleonasm used in some parts of the United States by persons over-anxious to distinguish the common agent in any great event from the actor on the stage. "Mrs. Cora Ritchie is the first author who has led us behind the scenes, and allowed us to judge of the true life of the *play-actor*, whom most of us only know as he appears on the stage." (*Literary World*, March 27, 1868.)

Pled, instead of pleaded, is stated by English authority to be "sometimes used in Scotland, but never by good writers, who remember that verbs derived from Latin or any foreign language cannot have the strong inflection of Saxon verbs." (*Blackwood*, October, 1867.) The principle is true, no doubt, but language acts frequently upon analogy and not upon principle. Hence *pled*, used much in the United States, and laughed at by domestic and foreign critics, has, nevertheless, good authority to adduce in its behalf. If we turn to Lord Brougham's dedication of the *Edinburgh Cyclopedia*, edited by Sir D. Brewster in 1830, we find in the last paragraph but one: "The inalienable right of humanity has been *pled*," and the same form is used by the fastidious W. S. Landor, as it was by Spenser in his Faëry Queen,

"Many grave persons that against her *pled*."

"What would be said by his old friends in Virginia, when it reached their ears, that he had *plead* want of notice to get clear of a debt, when everybody knew it was the same thing as if he had got notice?" (*Flush Times of Alabama*, p. 217.)

Plow, the form under which *plough* constantly appears in American school-books even, to the intense disgust of English critics, is yet by no means an innovation, since it is rhymed with "inow" by Chaucer and all the writers of the fourteenth century. Robert of Gloucester, Wiclife, and all the earlier writers wrote *plow* more frequently than any other form, and Chaucer rhymes it thus:

> "I have a wyfe, parde! as wel as *thou*,
> Yet wolde I, for the oxen in my *plow*,
> Taken upon me more than *ynow*."
> (*Miller's Prologue*, v. 3518.)

Pluck, for courage, did not make its way into American speech at least till *Tom Brown's School-Days* made the term familiar here. The American people seem to have been reluctant to accept so vile a word, denoting the most worthless part of an animal's entrails, as the representative of what their fathers had called courage or heartiness, from the *cor*, the *heart* of man.

Plug is used in the United States for two purposes unknown in England. Dentists thus denote the foil or other matter with which they fill up hollow teeth, and lovers of tobacco call thus a flat-pressed cake of chewing-tobacco.

Plum, in the New England States, serves as a generic name for all berries, and thus is used for the brilliant berries of the *Diacæna borealis*, an elegant forest-plant bearing a few acid blueberries, the partridge-berries, the mountain-cranberries, and some other species.

Plunder, the word which obtained a certain celebrity in England by S. Coleridge's great outburst of wrath against it, has since been proved to have been used by English writers precisely in the same sense in which Americans employ it. Mr. Coleridge said: "An American, by his boasting of the superiority of Americans generally, but especially in their language, provoked me to tell him, that, on that head, the least said the better, as the Americans present the extraordinary anomaly of a people without a language; that they had mistaken the English word for baggage (which is called *plunder* in America), and had stolen it." (*Recollections and Conversations.*) The elder D'Israeli, on the contrary, says, in his *Curiosities of Literature*, that *plunder*, in the sense of "baggage," is an old word, long known and used in England, and Fuller states that it was introduced at the same time with the term Malignants. The fact is, that the term is a Dutch or Flemish word, meaning, as Mr. Douce quotes, property of any kind, and connected with the German "Plunder." The English troops which fought under the banner of the great Swedish king, Gustavus Adolphus, brought this word home with them, as they brought "lifeguard" and "gauntlet," and from that time it has been in constant use in England. "We had heard the steamboat-gun the night before, or something like it, and that, you know, is the signal to tell us when to look after our *plunder*." (W. G. Simms, *The Last Wager*.) "It is very rare here to see gentlemen-travellers carry their *plunder*, except in a small portmanteau fixed to the saddle, as it is not customary to dress fine at the springs or elsewhere." (*Letters from the South*, I., p. 39.)

Poke, the oldest form of the French word *poche*, is still used by the side of the modern "pocket." "To buy a pig in a *poke*," is often heard in England and in the United States, and shows how old, obsolete words survive in proverbial sentences. "Put the feathers in a *poke*," is a familiar phrase to Southerners. That *poke* should be used in the New England States for an ingenious instrument of torture, put upon animals to keep them from jumping fences, is natural enough, as the long pole pointing forward suggests the meaning of the verb, to *poke*, but it is not quite so clear, why a stupid person, a bore, should also be called a *poke*, unless it be on the plea that "a slow *poke*" annoys us continually, as if we were *poked* at by a thorn in the side. It is from the latter meaning of the word that Americans have derived the peculiar phrase of "*poking* fun," either for one's own delectation or at another person's expense. "Don't you be *poking fun* at me now, Judge; this is too serious a matter." (J. C. Neal, *Charcoal Sketches*, III., p. 24.) "It was often said of Mr. Lincoln that he liked nothing so much as to *poke fun* at his advisers in the Cabinet, but those who could appreciate him knew very well, what a depth of wisdom and earnest will lay under the slight drapery of jest." (*Life of A. Lincoln*, p. 137.) A *poke*-bonnet, also, is familiar to American eyes, worn generally by Quakers and Methodists, and so called because its long, straight sides *poke*, as it were, into everybody's face.

Poker, the old Danish name for the devil (pokker), retains its use in America, though it is here employed in the sense of a hobgoblin or any frightful object; hence also *pokerish*, a familiar word applied to what is likely to excite fear.

Polliwig, the name of a tadpole, as used by Forby, and frequently quoted, appears in America very generally as *pollywog*, removing it thus farther from the presumed original, periwig, of which Forby thought it was a corruption. It seems, however, to be merely a word imitative of the wriggling motions of the tadpole.

Polt, a blow, and *polter*, are still quite often heard in the South, and lead us back to the days of the first English settlers in Virginia, who brought the words from their distant home, and bequeathed them to their descendants. In England both words are obsolete. "He gave the stallion a tremendous *polt* on the head, and thus forced him to let go his hold." (Pennsylvania paper, 1867.) George Coleman already used *polter* in his day:

> "Oh, whack! Cupid's a mannikin,
> Smack on my heart he hit me a *polter*."
> (*The Review*, Act II., Scene 1.)

Pond, a sheet of water in the interior, smaller than a lake, but frequently of considerable size, has taken the place of the English "mere," which is almost unknown in the United States. "Here and there was a little lake—a *pond*—under the shadow of the woods, yielding water-lilies in summer and ice for exportation in winter." (*The Country near Salem, Massachusetts.*) The English use *pond* only for a sheet of water confined by artificial banks.

Poor, in the sense of lean, occurs already in Middleton's Plays, and remains to this day a favorite term in the South, where *poorly* also continues to be used in its early meaning of indifferently. "How is your father, to-day? Thank you, but *poorly*; he had a bad night."

Popular has, in the New England States, the curious meaning of conceited, and J. R. Lowell quotes, therefore, the Yankee phrase: "*Popular* as a hen with one chicken."

Potwalloper, a man, in England, who occupies a house, no matter how small, and boils a pot in it, thus qualifying himself for voting, is in the United States, where voting depends on no such trifling qualifications as property or intelligence, a scullion or a slovenly person. The figure is apparently taken from the manner in which such an unfortunate being would be apt to knock the kitchen-pots about. The English term has its origin in *wall*, from A. S. wealan (German *wallen*) and *up*, in the sense of making water, etc., "boil up," as appears in the old English proverb, quoted by Grose: "To scold like a wych *waller*," that is, like a salt-boiler. The American meaning is connected with the use of *wallop* in the sense of beating, striking. In Pennsylvania, *pot-wrestler* is occasionally used for the same purpose.

Pounds are in America exclusively used in estimating the weight of a person, etc., instead of the English "stone," which is unknown here. "He weighs at least two hundred *pounds*."

Power and *powerful*, once peculiar to Irish phrases, have now become not only English, but American also. "If you will follow my advice, it will do you a *power* of good, and you may be sure you will never repent it." (*Life of J. J. Astor*, p. 59.) *Powerful*, however, for "powerfully," is probably an American abuse of the word. "I hated *powerful* bad to part with him." (W. G. Simms, *The Lost Wager*.)

Preach, as a noun, belongs to the same category; the extreme desire to express much by the least possible exertion has led to this shortening of the proper word—preaching. "He told us, if we wanted to hear a regular *preach*, to stand fast." (J. P. Kennedy, *Swallow Barn*.)

Predicate, to, in the sense of basing an argument on certain facts, is very common in conversation, and perhaps even more so in fine writing. "You *predicate* an editorial on a wrong report of my speech in Brooklyn." (Letter of a Member of Congress to New York *Tribune*, February 1, 1871.) "I do not see how the member from Illinois can *predicate* any such conclusion on what I have said." (Speech of B. F. Butler, reported April 24, 1871.) This is one of the words put under the ban in W. C. Bryant's *Codex Expurgatorius*.

Present is, in the United States, placed on the back of letters addressed to persons living in the same place with the writer. "You can direct your letters 'at home,' but '*present*' is the universally adopted term for the purpose in this country." (*Harper's Bazar*, April, 1871.)

Preserves, instead of the English term, sweets, for fruits preserved in sugar, is one of the words that strike foreigners most forcibly when they first enter American households. "Here, too, is honey fresh taken from the *gum*, and here are various kinds of *preserves*." (P. H. Gosse, *Letters from Alabama*, p. 47.)

Progress, to, with the accent on the last syllable, is nothing but an old form, fallen into disuse in the mother-country, and retained in America. It was always thus used in Devonshire, from which county came a great number of the early settlers of the colonies; and hence Mr. Gifford, in his edition of *Ford*, acknowledges it "as one of the words lost to England, but which, having crossed the Atlantic, have been retained by the English race in America." The word was at one time represented in England as a daring Americanism; hence J. R. Lowell, after having quoted Ben Jonson in the *Alchemist*, saying,

"Progress so from extreme unto extreme,"

adds facetiously: "Surely we may sleep in peace now, and our English cousins will forgive us, since we have cleared ourselves from any suspicion of being original in the matter."

Proper and *properly*, in the sense of "very" or "very much," are colloquial in England as well as in America, although nothing can be said in excuse for the tautology. *Proper* meant formerly handsome, nice, and hence perhaps the familiar use of the word. "That sugar is *proper* good, but it might be whiter." "I tell you it smarts *properly*, when you ain't used to it." (*Pickings from the Picayune*, p. 119.)

Prox, meaning a list of candidates to be voted for on the day of election, and *proxy*, the day itself, are provincialisms confined to the two States of Connecticut and Rhode Island. For some time, however, they have failed to make their appearance in the newspapers, and are, probably, becoming obsolete.

Proven, instead of proved, originally a Scotticism, is used by the best American writers. "The trials of the witches awaken, by turns, pity, indignation, disgust, and dread—dread at the thought of what the human mind can be brought to believe not only probable, but *proven*." (J. R. Lowell, *Among my Books*, p. 136.)

Pub. Func., for Public Functionary, has long been a favorite term in political slang. "The radical manipulators have acted in good faith, but resident stevedores and professional office-holders, *pub. funcs.*, and political changelings, have lost their reward." (Tallahassee *Floridian*, March 21, 1871.)

Pucker, in the sense of, a state of apprehension, of anxiety, is familiarly used here as in England. "I was in such a *pucker*, I did not know what to do, for here were the guests, and nothing had been prepared." (W. Irving, *Sketch Book*.)

Pumpkin must have been a favorite dish with Americans, for the first recorded verse written in this country, bearing the date 1630, a doggerel list of "New England Annoyances," has already the following allusions to this preference:

"If fresh meat be wanting to fill up our dish,
We have carrots and *pumpkins* and turnips and fish;
We have *pumpkins* at morning and *pumpkins* at noon,
If it was not for *pumpkins* we should be undone."

Still worse is the explanation given in the *Classical Dictionary*: "*Pompkin*, a man or woman of Boston, America, from the number of *pompkins* raised and eaten by the people of that country. *Pompkins-hive*, for Boston and its dependencies." The old word *pompion* has entirely disappeared here, although it was used by the first settlers of Virginia: "In May also, amongst their corn, they plant *pumpeons*" (Captain John Smith, *Virginia*, I., p. 127), thus foreshadowing a custom which has never been abandoned to the present day. The *Hubbites*, as Bostonians are apt to be called now, from the fact that jealous rivals accuse them of cherishing the belief that Boston is the Hub of the Universe, are said to have derived, from their attachment to this vegetable, and the esteem in which it is universally held among them, the phrase *some pumpkins*, expressive of high appreciation. "Franklin was a poor printer-boy and Washington a land-surveyor, yet they growed to be *some pumpkins*." (*Sam Slick*.) "Your honor, although it is I who say, who oughtn't to say it, but I swow, my son Fred is a fine fellow; you may axe every rouster on the levee, and I'll be hanged if they don't tell you he is *some pumpkins* to hum." (*Pickings from the Picayune*, p. 237.) It is stated, however, by one high in authority among New Englanders, that this explanation of the term is not the true one, although the latter cannot well be stated, because it would offend ears polite. (J. H. Trumbull.) *Pumpkin-shell* was in olden times a term designating the peculiar form of the vegetable, and is still quite frequently so used in the New England States. "'And shall not the youth's hair be cut?' asked Peter Palfrey, looking with abhorrence at the love-lock and long glossy curls of the young man. 'Crop it forthwith, and that in the true *pumpkin-shell* style,' answered the Captain." (N. Hawthorne, *The May-Pole of Merry Mount.*) By assimilation the word is frequently corrupted into *pungkin* or *pungk'n*, the common Yankee pronunciation, thus written by J. R. Lowell:

> "Lazy as the bream,
> Whose only business is to head up-stream,
> We call 'em *punkin*-seed"—
> (*Biglow Papers,* II., p. 38.)

while in Pennsylvania, and in the South even, they have a nursery-rhyme, saying:

> "Peter, Peter, *Punkin*-eater,
> Had a wife and couldn't keep her;
> He put her in a *punkin*-shell,
> And then he kept her very well."
> (S. S. Haldeman.)

Punk, a species of fungus or rotten wood, easily set on fire, is rarely heard in England, but quite common here. "Fire-making is a simple process with mountaineers. Their bullet-pouches always contain a flint and steel, and sundry pieces of *punk* or tinder, and pulling a handful of dry grass, which they screw into a nest, they place the lighted *punk* in this, and closing the grass over it, wave it in the air, when it soon ignites and readily kindles, the dry sticks forming the foundation of the fire." (*Life in the Far West.*)

Punt, in England a flat-bottomed boat, used for a variety of purposes, means in America, especially in the South, a small boat made of a hollow tree.

Purchase, ordinarily used only to denote a mechanical hold or advantage, applied in raising or moving heavy bodies, is in America made to denote *any* good hold. Even the splitting of a pump was, in the Virginia papers, once ascribed to the "sun's having had such a *purchase* upon it." (1859.)

Purgery is the name of the room in which the sugar-cane juice is placed in hogsheads, and allowed to drain of its molasses.

Q.

Qualify, to, is but rarely found in English writers in the sense of to qualify one's self, by taking an oath, furnishing security, or complying with other conditions required before assuming an office. In the United States this is the common form. Official announcements of nominations made by the President run thus: "John Doe, Internal Revenue Collector, in place of Richard Roe, having failed to *qualify*." "On yesterday (*sic*) Mr. John Smith assumed his new duties, having duly *qualified* the day before, and his sureties being accepted." (Washington *Chronicle*, March 17, 1865.)

Quarter-Dollar is in Pennsylvania the common appellation of the coin elsewhere called a quarter of a dollar. (S. S. Haldeman.)

Quarters, in the South, used to be the name of the buildings on a farm inhabited by the negroes. "We found the *quarters* to consist of long rows of stone-cabins, each holding two families, with small but sufficient gardens attached to each of them." (*Letters from the South.*)

Quates is a common name of the game of *quoits* in Pennsylvania.

Queer or *quier*, in old English a common prefix, meaning bad or wicked, has now lost entirely its former signification, and denotes what is odd, curious, or strange. It is a very popular word in America, and generally coupled with odd terms, e. g., *queer stick*, *queer fish*, etc. Thus it has always more or less of the comic and ludicrous in it, while it never serves to express—as it does in English—the sensation of sudden illness or serious injury. A distinguished English practitioner, having been invited by Mr. Jefferson to fill a chair in the University of Virginia, met soon after his arrival a countryman, who accosted him, inquiring his name and profession, and then added: "Look here, Doctor, you haven't by chance any salts about you? I feel sorter *queer*." The word had its origin in the German *queer*, which means crooked, and thus came to be used at first as a cant word for a crooked mind; it has, however, "become respectable since 1500." (*Slang Dictionary.*)

Quilting-frolic, also called *quilting*-bee, a meeting of ladies for the purpose of making bed-quilts, generally from a charitable motive, is one of the few rural amusements still found in New England, but unfortunately confined to one sex.

Quit, to, in the sense of to leave off, is a favorite American term, though not unknown to Ben Jonson and Henry More, who both use it in precisely the same manner: "The old church considered actors, stage-players, choristers, and other gamesters and frequenters of the theatre worthy of excommunication, unless they *quit*." (*Southern Churchman*, January 5, 1871.) In the South the word is constantly heard as an order: "*Quit* that, do you hear?" "*Quit* teasing me, or I'll whip you."

Quitch-grass presents, probably, a not unfrequent corruption of "quick" and hence Tennyson even speaks of the "vicious *quitch*," but the further corruption into *witch*-grass, with a sly allusion to its apparently bewitched vitality, which defies all efforts at eradication, is purely American.

Quite used to mean in England nothing but wholly. In the United States it soon lost its special meaning, and became a general term for, very: "It is *quite* cold this morning." This vague meaning, the misapplication of a good word, we are told, "has lately become very common in England, an eminent member of Parliament declaring that an event had happened *quite* recently, and another that *quite* a number of people assembled in Trafalgar-square. Such phrases as *quite* warm, *quite* extraordinary, are heard every day, and are sometimes inadvertently employed by writers of otherwise irreproachable English." (*Blackwood*, October, 1867.) The lament is instructive, since these expressions appear to the American ear quite correct and "irreproachable," showing how little we are generally aware of the broad difference between home English and our English.

R.

Rag, in the sense of a piece of linen, has already been mentioned as an evidence of the carelessness with which Americans use words for a purpose for which they were never intended. A Southern lady will gravely say, "Tie it up nicely in a clean *rag* and carry it with my compliments to Mrs. A," precisely as she will speak of her boy's having thrown a *rock* at a little bird, or order her servant to fill her jardinière with "nice *dirt*." The slang use of *rags* for bank-notes and paper-money prevails here as well as in England.

Raise, to, is, in the West especially, often used in the sense of to procure, to obtain. "Meat has to be *raised* anyhow, or we'll starve before the week is out." (*Life in the Far West*, p. 221.) To *raise* a house is the term applied to the erection of the frame of a wooden building, and has furnished the noun, a *raising*, often called a *raising-bee*, when it is done by the help of friends and neighbors. *Raise*, too, has in America almost superseded the two words employed in England, to *grow* crops on a farm, and to *rear* children in a family. No one here says that he was "reared," but that he was *raised* in Pennsylvania, and a severe critic alludes sneeringly to the attempts recently made to *raise* an American literature. "You know I was *raised*, as they say in Virginia, among the mountains of the North." (*Letters from the South*, I., p. 85.) But this use of the word is not an Americanism; it is legitimate English of the 17th century, at which time it was brought over to Virginia. Mr. William Wirt used it in his sketches of Patrick Henry, and was laughed at in the North and abroad. But if we turn to Lord Herbert of Chertbury's *Memoirs*, written about 1645, we find this sentence: "My grandfather's power in the county was so great, that divers ancestors of the better families in Montgomeryshire were his servants, and *raised* by him." J. R. Bartlett says of the word: "To *raise* is applied in the Southern States to the breeding of negroes. It is also sometimes heard at the North among the illiterate, as, I was *raised* in Connecticut." The sting of the sneer in the first part of the sentence is happily removed by the Emancipation Act; the "illiterate" will be pleased to count in their number a man like Horace Binney, who said, in his eloquent remarks on John Sergeant before the Philadelphia bar (November, 1852): "It was the good fortune of Mr. Sergeant and myself to have been *raised* under the eye of such a man (Jared Ingersoll)."

Raising, for yeast, a favorite term in New England, is endorsed by J. R. Lowell, because it was thus used by Gayton in his *Festivous Notes on Don Quixote*, and because it is a literal translation of the French *levain*, our *leaven*.

Rake, to, is almost always accompanied by *up*, and then acquires in America a meaning directly opposite to that which it has in England. There, to *rake up* the fire, means to cover it with ashes; here we use to *rake up* in the sense of discovering, bringing to light. "You ought not to *rake up* old stories, it only makes bad blood." (Daniel Webster in Faneuil Hall.)

Rare, in the sense of underdone, is not considered in good taste now in England, though Dryden speaks of new-laid eggs

"Turned by a gentle fire and roasted *rare*,"

but universal in America. "How do you like it? well done or *rare?*" The word is not derived, as commonly stated, from the same root as "raw" (Icelandic hrar), but from the old English *rear*, of which already Grose says: "*Rear* (corruptly pronounced *rare*), early, soon. Meat under-roasted, boiled, or broiled, is said to be *rear* or *rare*, from being taken too *soon* from the fire. Kent." Pegge makes precisely the same statement with regard to the word, and quotes Middleton:

"and thy *rear* flesh
Tost all into poached eggs."
(*The World Lost at Tennis.*)

this derivation is all the more probable, when we bear in mind that in the South the verb to *rear*, used of horses, is pronounced *rare*, and hence *rare* may well be called *rear* in New England.

Reckon, to, a term looked upon as the favorite of the South, as "to calculate" is that of the North, in the endeavor to express a conjecture or a conclusion. A Virginian, asked if he means to go North in the summer, will promptly answer: "I *reckon* I shall." These are the very words quoted by Grose (p. 46) as used in the North of England, and prove that the use of the term is not new, but only revived after a long slumber. Still, it occurs also in English authors of more recent date, e. g., "He was *reckoned* for a madman." (Godwin, *Caleb Williams*, II., p. 54.) It has the same meaning in Holy Writ: "Likewise *reckon* ye also yourselves to be dead unto sin." (*Romans* vi. 11), and "For I *reckon* that the sufferings of this present time are not worthy," etc. (*Romans* viii. 18), a use of the word by the apostle which once led a pious but simple-minded preacher to tell his hearers that "St. Paul was a great mathematician, because he *reckoned* so much." The *reck'ning* of New England is the score at a public house, or a private account run up with a dealer.

Ready, to, in the sense of setting to rights, is an old English term surviving in our speech. Grose quotes: "*Ready*, to *ready* the hair, to comb it," and speaks of a "*Readying* comb, a wide-toothed comb." The word is often heard in America, but more generally assumes the equally old form, to *redd*, of which Grose says: "*Redd*, to untangle or separate. South." "To *redd* up a room" is a marked provincialism in Pennsylvania, from whence it has passed into Ohio. It originated with the Scotch immigrants, who settled those districts, and brought the word with them from the borders, where the old proverb is current:

> "A seamstress that sews and would make her work *redde*,
> Must use a long needle and a short thread."

In "Margaret Maitland," we find "a well *redd*-up house" mentioned, and in Jane Eyre the words, "you are *redd* up and made decent."

Redemptioner used to be the name of a person, who engaged to pay for his passage from Europe to this country by his services here for a given time. "From these German paupers," Bishop Kip tells us, "many of the wealthy farming families, now living in the Hudson River Counties, are descended; in an early day they purchased the lands, which enriched their children. They had often but one name, and took the name of the original proprietor. Hans took the name of Morris, etc., and gave it to his children; hence there are in the State of New York many families bearing the names of the old landed proprietaries, which are descended from *redemptioners*, thus named after early settlers."

Reliable, instead of trustworthy, is a malappropriation of a good word, now as common in England as in the United States.

Rench, for rinse, is so old a mispronunciation, that we find already in Lovelace *renched* for rinsed, and the same mistake is constantly made abroad and with us. "*Wrench* your mouth out," said a fashionable dentist one day to a lady. (*Slang Dictionary*, p. 213.) The use of this form is so frequent, that an effort has actually been made to trace *rinse* back to a Danish word, *renser*, which was to have furnished the modern *rench*. The derivation is improbable.

Rent is used in America for the English *rental*, which is almost unknown here.

Reprint is said to be an Americanism as far as it denotes the republication, here, of a work printed in a foreign country. It certainly used to be a charming euphemism in olden days, when the works of British authors were issued here without their sanction, and without giving them a fair compensation—a régime happily unknown in our day.

Resentment has in New England preserved the ancient meaning given it by Barrow, Cudworth, Bull, and other writers of that time. "A farmer in an interior town of New England, who had recently lost his wife, called upon a lawyer in the place for advice under his bereavement, remarking that he wished to make a proper *resentment* on the occasion." (*North American Review*, 1849.)

Retire, to, in the sense of going to bed, is a vulgar, but unfortunately very common, euphemism.

Revamp, to, a verb derived from to *vamp*, which meant to put new upper leather to shoes; this was lengthened into *revamp*, under a vague sense of something being done over again, and finally the new term was applied to other modes of repairing and refitting generally. Hence Edgar Poe said of Bulwer, "His Athens would have received an Etonian prize, and has all the happy air of an Etonian prize-essay *revamped*."

Ride, to, now limited in England to *riding* on horseback, has in the United States retained the more general meaning as applied to any mode of conveyance. As the Bible says: "He made him to *ride* in the chariot" (*Genesis* xlii. 43), we say of a person, that "he *rides* in his carriage," and we even "*ride* in the cars." "Out of *ride*," is said, in the South, of a river that is past fording on horseback, and most streams there have a so-called *riding rock* at or near a fording-place, which indicates to those familiar with its appearance, whether the water is too high for crossing or not.

Riffles, for *ripples*, is an odd corruption, applied in Pennsylvania to the rocky obstructions of the Susquehanna, with this effect, that the more grievous obstructions are *riffles*, the slighter ones *ripples*. (S. S. Haldeman.)

Rifle, retains in some parts of the Union the meaning it has in old English, viz., a whetstone for sharpening scythes, consisting either of the stone itself or of a strip of wood covered with emery. Its use is almost limited to the New England States and a few of the Eastern counties of Virginia. "The best man goes foremost, and the strong-backed scythemen, each with his *rifle* in his red, right hand, girded low and tight, stepping wide and bending forward, seem to gesture the falling grass into long, straight swathes." (*Connecticut Georgics.*)

Right, in the sense of *very,* is frequently charged upon the South as an unpardonable provincialism. Its use is as old as the English language. In Halliwell's edition of the "*Voiage and Travaile of Sir John Maundeville,*" page 96, we find—"And there *righte* nighe is the tomb," and so in, perhaps, fifty places in the same book. The Psalms have: "I gat me to my Lord *right* humbly;" "I myself will awake *right* early;" and Bailey already calls this use of the word "obsolete" in his day. Even the phrase *right here,* a favorite with American authors and editors, "turns up *passim* in the Chester and Coventry Plays." (J. R. Lowell.) *Right away,* another form for "straightway," it may be recollected, excited the wrath of Dickens on his first visit to Boston. A waiter at the Tremont House asked him if he wanted dinner *right away,* and the illustrious writer fancied it meant, in some particular place, instead of, directly. Now the phrase is quite common all over the United States, having long since ceased to be a Boston provincialism, if it ever was one, and has recently made its way to England also.

To-rights, with the adverbial *s,* which in England means excellent, very well, used to be employed in the United States instead of directly, soon, as in Major Jack Downing's *Letters:* "So *to-rights,* the express got back and brought a letter." (p. 129.) This use of the word has, however, become obsolete here as well as in England, and the phrase is now used only in the sense of "putting to-rights," setting things in order, though the verb is often omitted. "Being thus completely settled, and, to use his own word, *to-rights,* one would imagine that he would begin to enjoy the comforts of his situation, to read newspapers, talk politics, neglect his own business and attend to the affairs of the nation, like a useful and patriotic citizen." (W. Irving, *Knickerbocker History of New York.*) "Jenny had gone over the mountain, before she had time to put things *to-rights,* and she herself had enough to do besides." (*Letters from the South,* II., p. 7.) *Right-off,* not unknown to some of the best English writers, is a favorite expression in the West, conveying promptness and energy happily combined. A striking illustration of its use appears in the following announcement: "Mr. Forbes undertook to deliver a temperance lecture in Cheyenne, but the people justly took it as a personal insult, and shot him *right-off*." (April 17, 1871.)

Rile, to, is almost universally used for to *roil* or *royl*, which originally meant to render a liquid turbid, and then, as a figure of speech, came to denote a stirring up of anger. "There are dregs enough within to *royle* and distemper the spirit." (Gurnall, *Christian in Armor*, III., p. 296.) *Riled*, in the sense of made angry, is used by Roger North, but written *roiled*.

> "Here Brown come frowningly in, but smiled,
> When he found his wife seemed nothing *riled*,
> And begged his guest to be seated."
> (E. K. Yates. *Mirth and Meter*, 1855.)

The word, which has often been connected with the French verb *railler*, to make fun of, has long been obsolete in England; but being found useful, it is gradually making its way back again from this country, where it has never ceased to be used. The adjective *rily* is purely American; an ill-tempered, cross-grained person is apt to be called "a *rily* fellow."

Rising, in the sense of exceeding, is an Americanism derived from the general meaning of the word, but still considered "low." "How much wheat did you raise this year? A little *rising* of five thousand bushels." (*Letters from the South*, II., p. 93.)

Ris, an intense vulgarism for the preterite, and, as *riz* for the participle, a pronunciation peculiar to New England, must be traced back to forms like *risse* and *roze*, used by Middleton and Dryden. "I wish I had my big lamp here; it is a perfect prairie on fire. I set it out once, the darkest night that ever came over, and all creation *ris*, thinking it was daylight." (*Pickings from the Picayune*.) *Riz-cake*, for risen cake, is common to all the New England States. The humorist Mark Twain, having duly admired the Venus of Milo, in the Louvre, naturally inquired, according to American custom, what the statue cost, and exclaimed, when he heard the enormous sum, "Wal, stone gals must have *riz* lately."

Risibilities, in the plural form, are only heard in America. "I had hard work to keep down my *risibilities*." (Rev. P. Cartwright, *Autobiography*, p. 142.)

Risky, an adjective, made from risk, and denoting what is hazardous, is unexceptionable in meaning, whatever purists may think of the form of the hybrid.

River is placed by Americans more generally after the name than before, as in England. Thus they speak of Charles *River* in Massachusetts, and of James *River* in Virginia.

Roach, to, denotes the trimming of a horse's mane, which the English commonly call "hogged." "Look at the *roached* head of that boy!" The figure is probably taken from the peculiar curve or arch cut in some square sails, which, in nautical language, is called a *roach*.

Rock, used in the South and certain parts of New England for stone, has, at least, ancient authority for it. Halliwell quotes—

> "The false fox came into our yard,
> And there he made the geese afeard;
> The good wife came out in her smock,
> And at the fox she threw her *rock*."
> (*Reliquiae Antiquae*.)

From this use of the noun an odd verb is derived, to *rock*, meaning to throw stones at an object. "The boys cast *rocks* at the poor little bird, till it was stone-dead." "In the evening the house was *rocked*, and he himself threatened with instant death, if he did not leave the State within eight days." (Evidence before Committee of Members of Congress, April, 1871.)

Rolling has in the West the peculiar meaning of undulating, and hence *rolling-lands* are those which present to the eye a succession of elevations and depressions. Hence also the term *Rolling Prairies*. "The country was what was termed *rolling*, from some fancied resemblance to the ocean, when it is just undulating with a long ground-swell." (J. F. Cooper, *Oak Openings*.)

Rookery has obtained in California a new meaning, upon being applied to the seals that congregate on its shores. "A man's social standing here depends, in a great measure, upon his knowledge and judgment in selecting the seals to be killed from the immense *rookeries*, killing and skinning them, and salting the skins." (*Overland Monthly*, October, 1870, p. 298.)

Room, to, is a verb not unknown to England, though more generally used in America. In colleges, especially, the uniform expression is, that "such and such a student *rooms* in No. 10."

Rosum is a common corruption of *rosin*, which is almost universally pronounced *ros'm* by the mass of the people. "In this kind of weather you must tune yourself up and get *rosumed*—tuned up to concert-pitch." (J. C. Neal, *Charcoal Sketches.*)

Rough, denoting a rowdy, hardly known in England outside of London and the small boroughs at election time, is a familiar term in the large cities of the Union, and especially in Baltimore, which formerly suffered under an unenviable notoriety on account of its frequent and bloody rows. Mr. Forly in his notice of the word slily insinuates that "it may have been transported to the Western World many years ago with some East-Anglian thief." From the same word is derived the familiar phrase, *to rough it*, by no means a slang word. "Woman, too, must *rough it*, but she does not like to *rough it*, and she is hurt and demoralized, if the *roughing* is too rough or too long continued." (Mrs. Kirkland, *A New Home.*) "To *learn to rough it* is an educational phrase, in the dialect of the new countries, which would be of great service, adopted as a rule of government for the young in all." (W. G. Simms, *Oakatibbe.*) *Roughness* in South Carolina denotes shucks or cornhusks, on account, probably, of the roughness of the serrated blades.

Roundabout is in America almost exclusively used for the short "jacket" of the English, as worn by boys, sailors, and others. "Marion wore a close *roundabout*-jacket of coarse crimson cloth, and upon his head was the same cap and silver crescent which marked him as the recruiting officer in that region five years before." (B. F. Lossing, *Francis Marion.*)

Rubbers, for India-rubber overshoes, followed naturally after India-rubber itself had been shortened into *Rubber*.

Rugged, in the sense of vigorous and robust, is probably an Americanism. In other meanings it not unfrequently resumes the old English form of *ruggy*, as in Chaucer's line:

> "With flotery berd and *ruggy* ashy heres."

"It's a mighty *ruggy* trail, Mister, up the Shasta Mountain, and I wouldn't much mind staying behind, if so be you'll let me." (*Scenes in the Far West*, p. 119.)

Run, used in the South generally for a brook or small stream, as in *Bull Run*, the scene of the first fight in the late Civil War, has good and old authority to sustain it. "I remember on the road between Naples and Rome a *run* from a sulphurous spring." (Boswell, *Corsica*, p. 36, 1768.) The same use is made of the word in *Waymouth's Voyage* (1605), as quoted by J. R. Lowell. "The towns, rivers, crossroads, and *runs* of Virginia became names that thrilled the hearts of millions with triumph or agony." (H. T. Tuckerman.) The word is, of course, akin to the verb, to run, and corresponds, in this sense, to the Scottish runnock, a drain or small stream. This verb has acquired, of late, a peculiar and forcible application to any kind of business, from a first-class hotel to a petty grocery, which is said to be *run*, instead of managed or kept.

Runt, rarely used in England except among farmers, butchers, and like people, is in America very generally applied to cattle and to men inferior in size. "Every family has its *runt*," is a proverbial saying, arising from the fact that in every litter of pigs there is, almost invariably, one very diminutive in comparison with the rest. It is said that during the war of 1812, a young man, a member of a Kentucky family renowned for magnificent proportions, and not unknown to fame, was sent with a cartel on board a British man-of-war. The officers crowded around him, admiring his great height and magnificent form, but were not a little surprised at hearing him reply to their question, whether all the members of his family were as gigantic as he, that he "had the misfortune of being the *runt* of the family."

Rusties, in Pennsylvania and Ohio, the name given to the restive movements of an unquiet horse, probably represents in a slightly modified form the *rusty*, which Halliwell states to mean, restive and filthy. "It won't do for us to cut up *rusties* here at this time o' night." (J. C. Neal, *Charcoal Sketches*.)

S.

Sabbath is almost universally used in the United States for Sunday, certainly in the New England States, where the latter is rarely heard. The religious sentiment may account for the misuse of the word, for a misuse it is, since Sunday is the name of a day, while *Sabbath* is the name of an institution, and yet people will speak of the fine weather they had "last *Sabbath day*." The same peculiarity marks the Scotchman in England, he, like the

New Englander, having inherited the word from Puritan ancestors. The term *Sabbaday*, occasionally heard in rural districts of New England, is, of course, a corruption of *Sabbath day*, as incorrect in form as in meaning. "We're goin' sure enough, comin' *Sabbaday*, and no mistake, Deacon." (J. T. Trowbridge in *Our Young Folks.*)

Safe, a box or cupboard in which provisions are kept, has entirely superseded the English "larder," which is rarely used otherwise than figuratively.

Sag, to, frequently used in the figurative sense, is not, as Webster states, "rare," for Fuller has in his "Worthies," "That it may not *sag* from the intention of the founders," and Shakespeare, "The heart I bear shall never *sag* with fear." From the lost preterite of this verb, *I sog*, is derived the adjective *soggy*, much used in America to signify a wet, marshy soil, that yields to the foot. "We marched ten miles over a *soggy* wilderness." (New York *Tribune.*)

Sarcophagus almost universally serves in America to designate the metallic burying-cases, which are largely used to transport bodies from distant places to their last home, and presents a striking instance of the preference given here to high-sounding terms, however unmeaning or inappropriate they may be. The restless American, who must needs be moving even after death, orders his body to be enclosed in a *sarcophagus*, which once meant a stone eating up the body, and now represents a metal preserving the body!

Saw-buck takes in New Jersey the place of the "saw-horse" of other States, while farther South it is called a "wood-horse."

Scaly, in the sense of shabby or mean, is quoted already by Halliwell, and much used in the South. "We had a pretty *scaly* time after the war." (*Reminiscences of the Confederacy*, p. 224.) "The *scaliest* trick they ever played wuz bringin' on me hither." (J. R. Lowell, *Biglow Papers*, I., p. 99.) The term is said to have been originally connected with the scales of the serpent in Paradise, though the derivation from *scall* (scab) is probably correct.

Scart, a not uncommon form of *scared*, has been inherited from old English writers, though generally it is used by them with a long *a*. "Oh! Don't be *scart* at me! Come up to my house and see me. I will give you some peaches and make you happy." (Elder

Kimball at Nauvoo, as quoted by W. H. Dixon.) The verb itself is generally pronounced *skeer*, and often so written, and the noun, a *scare*, is an Americanism. "Nothing can exceed the grandeur of the scene, when a large cavallada or drove of horses takes a *scare*." (G. W. Kendall, *Santa Fé Expedition*, I., p. 97.)

Scoot, to,—written *skoot* by J. R. Lowell in his *Glossary to the Biglow Papers*, and *skute* by other writers—is evidently connected with skate and skeet, and hence means, to move or run swiftly. "An Iowa man, instead of going to the expense of a divorce, gave his wife a dollar, and told her to *scoot*." (Philadelphia *Age*, February, 1871.) "Notwithstanding his convulsive efforts to clutch the icy bricks, he *skuted* into the gutter." (J. C. Neal, *Charcoal Sketches*.) To *skeete* is used in the same manner and thus interpreted: "You must go, be off. *Skeet* represents exactly the classic abiit, excessit, evasit." (S. S. Haldeman.) In the South the boys and all the negroes say *skeating* instead of *skating*, which has evidently led to the formation of these two derivatives, *skeete* and *skute*. They have the authority of Pepys for their pronunciation, since in his *Diary*, December 1, 1662, he writes: "To my Lord Sandwich's to Mr. Moore, and then over the Parke, where I first in my life, it being a great frost, did see people sliding on their *skeates*." (Charles II., having, during his exile, learned to skate in Holland, had, at the Restoration, introduced the amusement in England.)

Score, to, is occasionally used in America in the peculiar sense of scoring by criticism. "I would praise Mr. Cooper's new work as readily as any other man, but no fear of so irate a man would deter me from *scoring* him when he merits such an application." (E. A. Poe, *Criticism*.)

Scranny—the *scrannel* of Milton—is much used to denote what is lean and thin, but is almost exclusively confined to women, whose delicate frame, in this country, unfortunately encourages the use of the word.

Scrawl, in New England only, means brushwood or broken branches of a tree. It is evidently connected with "scroll."

Screw, to, in the sense of being exactious, as quoted by Grose with reference to a bargain, is in College-cant applied to professors who examine students with unusual rigor.

"Who would let a tutor knave
Screw him like a Guinea slave!"
(Hall. *College Words.*)

Scrimp, to, occasionally heard in England to denote that a dress, etc., is made too short or tight, has furnished Americans with an adjective and a noun. "That the amount at his disposal might be as large as possible, he *scrimped* his children and his servants, in the minutest acts of expenditure." (G. M. Beard, M. D., *Putnam's Magazine,* November, 1868.) "Your dress is too *scrimp;* I wouldn't wear it again." "Every lovely lady who drives over from Lennox and returns, probably laughs at the *scrimpiness* of the Shaker's skirt just in the degree of the fullness of her own. The larger the hoop the louder the laugh." (*Atlantic Monthly,* 1870.)

Scringe, to, probably merely a corruption of *cringe,* is provincial in England, and quite common in the New England States.

"For the silver-spoon born in Democracy's mouth
Is a kind of a *scringe* thet they hev to the South."
(J. R. Lowell. *Biglow Papers,* I., p. 51.)

Season is, in the South, often misused for "weather." "This is a good *season* for planting," does not mean, this is the proper time, but, this is favorable weather for planting tobacco. As the latter is understood to be a shower, *season* often means a rain, or "spell" of wet weather.

Seem, to, is one of the words which, as J. R. Lowell says, the Yankee puts to an odd use: "I can't *seem* to be suited," or "I couldn't *seem* to know him."

Seep, to, means in New England to run through fine pores or any very small openings; it is evidently but an altered form of *sipe,* as quoted by Grose with the same meaning.

Segar, a very general form of *cigar,* is not as correct as the latter, which comes from the French *cigarre* or the Spanish *cigarro,* both of which terms come originally from the name of a certain variety of tobacco grown in Cuba.

Settle, designates in New England the almost unfailing long wooden seat which adorns the chimney-corner in country houses. It is generally very high in the back and very narrow in the seat, as far removed as possible from an easy lounge, and long enough to hold six to eight persons.

Shackly for shaky, is quite common in the United States, though only known as slang in England. "That's rather a *shackly* house, isn't it?"

Shakes are commonly fever and ague, from the manner in which that disease is apt to *shake* the sufferer. "Have you had the *shakes* again?—No, this is not my day."

Shanty, derived from the French *chantier*, and brought to the United States by Canadian immigrants, who had heard it used by voyageurs, is here almost exclusively used for the wooden sheds inhabited by laborers on railways, and similar classes of men. "My house is a mere *shanty*, but a bower of roses." (H. D. Thoreau.)

Shay, a corruption of chaise, does not mean a post-chaise, since these are unknown in the United States, but a two-wheeled vehicle drawn by one horse. O. W. Holmes has made the "One-Horse *Shay*" famous by his popular poems, and the term is now applied to anything small and insignificant.

Shet, the almost universal Yankee pronunciation of *shut*, is warmly defended by J. R. Lowell, who quotes in its behalf Golden's *Ovid*, and states that "Brampton Gurdon writes *shet* in a letter to Winthrop," showing that "our ancestors brought their pronunciation with them from the Old Country, and have not wantonly debased their mother-tongue. I need only cite the words *scriptur*, *Israll*, *athists* and *cherfulness* from Governor Bradford's *History*. So the good men wrote them, and so the good descendants of his fellow-exiles still pronounce them." (*Preface to Biglow Papers*, II., 32.) Precisely the same reasoning applies with equal force to the peculiar words of the South, fiercely denounced as Southern vulgarisms, while they were carried there from the Old Country by men as worthy as the Puritans, and preserved—not wantonly debased—by their descendants, who revere their memory.

Shine, to, designates in the South and West a mode of still-hunting by means of a pan with fire, which *shines* in the eyes of the deer and holds it spell-bound. "It is related that Daniel Boone, while fire-hunting, *shined* a pair of mild blue eyes which struck him as not belonging to the game he was seeking. He lowered his rifle and made further examination, when, to his surprise, he discovered a young girl who, with himself, was equally astonished at the adventure. Boone expressed the most eloquent gratitude that he had not fired his weapon, and waited upōn the woodland nymph to her home; in time the damsel became the wife of the most famous of backwoodsmen." (T. B. Thorpe.)

Shingle, in America a wooden tile, and also familiarly used for a modest signboard, placed over an office, since, in the West especially, a real shingle has often to answer the purpose. J. R. Lowell speaks of a "wooden *shingle*, painted so like marble that it sank in the water." In Pennsylvania the word is often pronounced *shindle*, partly, no doubt, under the influence of the numerous Germans in that State, whose vernacular says *Schindel* for shingle, but partly also because the word was often so written by old English authors. In Holland's *Plinio* we find: "Cornelius Nepos writeth that the housen in Rome were no otherwise covered over head but with *shindles*, untill the warre with King Pyrrhus." (Book xvi. ch. 10.)

Shinney, sounded and written as it appears in Halliwell's *Dictionary*, still serves to denote the game of that name, and the peculiar, crooked stick with which it is played.

Shoat is the common form given to the word in New England and Virginia, while elsewhere it is apt to appear as *shoot* and *shote*—according to Webster, from the fact that the young pig begins "shooting" up. It is the name of the pig between a sucker and a porker, but also applied, in a rather contemptuous manner, to young persons of pretentious manners. "Long 's you elect for Congressmen poor *shotes* that want to go." (J. R. Lowell.)

Shoo! the common exclamation to drive fowls from gardens, and hence generally coupled with *fly*, is more generally used in America, where fences are of little avail, than in England. The word is a simple, natural sound, and not derived from the German "scheuchen," which, on the contrary, is probably derived from the common root of both words. "Saying *shoo*, the farmer would be surprised to hear that he was talking German, and so would the fowls." (A. L. Elwyn, M.D., *Americanisms.*) "*Shoo! shoo!* Get out! 'Long there with you!" (*Atlantic Magazine*, March, 1870.)

Shorts, "the first remove above bran," as Halliwell defines it, is in constant use in the South, where it designates the bran and coarsest part of cornmeal, a favorite article of food for cattle. "By and by a west-country wagoner chanced to come jingling his bells that way, and, stopping his wagon, unhooked his horses, gave them some *shorts*, sat himself down on the top of the bank, and began to whistle: The batteaux-man robbed the old woman's henroost." (*Letters from the South*, I., p. 72.)

Shotgun is used for a smooth-bored fowling-piece, to distinguish it from a rifle.

Shut for shutter, and meaning also a small door, is an old English term preserved in some parts of New England.

Sick, in England used only for sickness of the stomach, is in America applied to indisposition of any kind, in the manner in which, as Sir C. Lyell already noticed, it was used by Shakespeare and the authors of the Liturgy of the Established Church. It is said that a Virginia lady in Europe, happening to be ill, sent for an English physician, who, hearing from her servant that she was *sick*, soon made his appearance with a stomach-pump and other instruments of the kind. Evelyn writes, November 16, 1652: "Visited Dean Stewart, who had been *sick* about two days." Pepys also employs *sick* in the same general sense (*Diary*, Vol. III., p. 264). It is curious to notice how *sickness* of the stomach changed in England first into *nausea*, which soon became vulgar and gave way to *throwing up*; this also fell in disfavor, and *vomit* was substituted, as it is used in the Bible; in its turn this gave way to *puking*, when the great king, with knee-buckles, silk-stockings, and gold-headed canes, also gave *pukes* to high-bred matrons and fastidious belles, some fifty years ago. This also was soon banished; but as people might get rid of the word but could not free themselves of the thing, they turned once more to their first love, and *sickness* was restored to favor.

Sight, in the sense of a number, a great many, is provincial in England, and in America serves the Northerner as *heap* serves the Southerner. "What a *sight* of people there was!" The verb to *sight* means simply to choose one's direction by the eye, and watching carefully the landmarks. "Having thus ventured into the depths of the forest as far as we dared, observing our due line of march by *sighting* at such trees as were in range of our course, we stopped short in our track." (*Putnam's Magazine*, September, 1854.)

Sizzle, to, an old English word, quoted by Forby, but almost forgotten in England, retains its vitality in some parts of the United States, meaning to shrivel up with a hissing sound. "Some pieces lay in the fire, half buried, and *sizzling* in the ashes." (*Atlantic Monthly,* August, 1858.)

Skin, to, in the sense of to extort, is probably an Americanism, although the idea of ill-treating and pressing a man "to his *skin,*" which has given rise to the meaning, is not unknown in English, as is shown by the word "*skin*flint."

> "Old miser Dyser, *skin* a fly, Sir,
> Sell the skin, and turn the money in,

as the boys used to rhyme about my old uncle Dyser." (*Putnam's Magazine,* January, 1868.)

Slab-sided and *slab-bridged,* both terms applied to persons of unreliable character, are taken from the *slabs,* outside pieces of timber which occasionally serve to make country bridges, of peculiarly unstable and unsafe character.

Slapjacks, in the North a kind of pancake, representing the English "flapjacks," but in the West all kinds of griddle-cakes. "Well, I'd just as lief live on *slapjacks* a spell." (*Atlantic Monthly,* March, 1870.)

Slashes are low grounds in the South and West, though openings in the woods are also called by that name. As Henry Clay was born in the *slashes* of Hanover, in Virginia, and in his youth was often sent to carry mealbags to and from the mill, he was popularly known in after-life as the "Millboy of the *Slashes:*" "I have seen great numbers of quail, plover, and snipe, within a couple or three hundred yards of the President's mansion, and they do say that deer abound in the *slashes,* as they are called, about half a mile from the building." (*Letters from the South,* II., p. 211.)

Slat, used in America as a noun, for a narrow piece of board used to fasten together larger pieces, and as a verb in the sense of doing anything with special violence, is probably a corruption of the word *sloat,* and intimately connected with *slatter.* "If you don't come into the house this minute, I'll *slat* your head off." The word was originally confined to the language of fishermen on the Eastern coast, who disengaged mackerel and other delicategilled fish by *slatting* them off the hook, but has long since rendered service as a term expressive of anger.

Slazy, a modification of *sleazy*, and denoting the flimsy, unsubstantial character of certain materials, is the common pronunciation of the word with us, though much less frequently heard in England.

Sleigh for sledge, denoting a vehicle on runners to carry passengers or goods on snow and ice, is universal in America. In England it is but just beginning to supersede *sledge*, which was heretofore almost exclusively used. "We have had hardly any *sleighing* at all this winter, though snow fell in abundance, but it never lay long enough to become firm." (Boston *Transcript*, March 7, 1867.) Hence also the word *sleigh-ride* for excursions made in *sleighs*.

Slick, the popular form, shortened and modified in sound, of *sleek*, has become almost exclusively popular, not in America only, but also in England, where "Sam Slick" first made it known. It is, however, by no means a new thing, but was already so used in the West of England long ago (though not in Mr. Jenning's *Glossaries*), and is mentioned in Pegge's *Supplement to Grose* as prevalent in Kent. The presumption, moreover, is that *sleek* was always pronounced *slick*, if we may judge from the older poets. Chaucer has—

> "Her flesh as tender as is a chicke,
> With bent browes, smooth and *slike*."
>
> (*Romaunt of the Rose.*)

"*Slick't* all with sweet oil" is found in Chapman's *Odyssey*, and Beaumont and Fletcher say, "Who will our palfrey *slick* with wisps of straw" (*Knight of the Baring Pestle*, II., sc. 1), and so does Ben Jonson show the early use of this form, both as an adjective and as a verb. Americans, however, make a difference between *sleek*, as meaning smooth and glossy, and *slick* in the sense of easily, readily; in the latter sense the word seems to be a genuine Americanism. Thus we say that "a man has a *sleek* and glossy appearance," and that "he goes *slick* about his business." The Yankee carries this meaning to an extreme, when he says that "Down East an animal's ear can be taken off so *slick*, that he does not know he is one ear short till he puts up his forefoot to scratch it."

Slim is in New England very frequently used in the sense of ordinary or even worthless—a meaning which it also has in some of the Northern counties of England. "He is but a *slim* fellow, I guess." (Mrs. Stowe, *Old Town Folks.*)

Slip has acquired in America two peculiar meanings, which are unknown in England. It means an opening between two wharves or in a dock, and hence many localities in New York bear that name, as Peck *Slip*, Coenties *Slip*, Burling *Slip*, etc. It is also used, in New England only, to denote a narrow pew in a church, somewhat resembling the *slip* in the wharves on a small scale. If the *slip* have a door it becomes a *pew*. As *slip* means also a long narrow piece of paper, it is frequently used for a cutting from a newspaper. "Send me the *slip* from the *Herald* and I will return it promptly."

Sliver is used as a verb and as a noun, meaning to cut or rend lengthwise, and the small pieces thus obtained. The English generally pronounce it with a long *i*, while Americans always give it a short *i*, but the latter has the authority of Chaucer, who rhymes *sliver* with "deliver," and Shakespeare, who says—

> "She that herself will *sliver*."

Slops, with the early settlers of Virginia and the West, meant tea and coffee, and in many parts of the country it retains this signification to the present day. "*Slops*," says Wills De Hass, "were tea and coffee, which, in the adage of the day, do not stick to the ribs. A genuine backwoodsman would have considered himself disgraced by showing a fondness for such *slops*. Indeed, many of them have, to this day, very little respect for them." (*History of Early Settlements*, etc., p. 73.)

Smack, to, divides its two principal meanings curiously between two different portions of the country. In New England to "*smack* a child" means to cover it with kisses and caresses; in Pennsylvania the same phrase means to punish the child by slapping it with the hand. In the latter sense the verb is used throughout the South. "If you don't behave yourself I'll *smack* you." The sharp, quick noise which the word suggests by an effort to imitate it, has probably led, in America, to its use as an adverb also, in the sense of suddenly. "He came *smack* against me, as I turned the corner."

Smart has as many meanings in America as in England, resembling, in this respect, *clever*, the English sense of which it represents here. The *smart* man is quick and intelligent, but apt to be suspected of taking advantage of his neighbors by these qualities. The "*smart* business man" may be irreproachable in all respects, but his *smartness* will always be looked upon with more or less apprehension. The extreme of the quality conveyed by the word is represented in the West by "a parcel of *smart* thieves, who stole a felled walnut-tree in the night-time, by drawing the log right slick out of the bark, and leaving the five watchmen, who had engaged to protect it, sitting fast asleep astride on the bark." In the South and West *smart* is, besides, used in the sense of great or considerable. "He has a *smart* chance of getting himself into trouble if he keeps on talking that way." (Richmond *Examiner*, July 15, 1864.) "We had a *smart* shower this morning, but it was not enough to lay the dust." The phrase "*smart* sprinkle" is used in Western slang to express a considerable quantity.

Smouch, to, obsolete in England, still survives in Pennsylvania, where it means to salute, kiss. It is probably connected with *smack* in the same sense, and imitative of the noise produced.

Smudge, which is used in England for an overwhelming smoke, is in America specially applied to the smoke produced by combustibles partly ignited, to drive away mosquitoes and flies, and to the heap of combustibles themselves. In Canada and the Northern States travellers, hunters, and lumberers make large *smudges* to protect themselves against the clouds of insects that abound there, and in the South, near country houses, similar *smudges* are set on fire to protect the inmates against mosquitoes. "I was sitting under the lee of a cedar-bark *smudge*, enjoying the fragrant smoke that drove away the mosquitoes." (*Putnam's Magazine*, July, 1870.)

Smut-mill or *smut-machine*, designates in the farmer's language a part of a flouring-mill which breaks and separates grains of wheat infected with smut (Uredo segetum). The name has subsequently been transferred to an abusive newspaper.

Snack, in the sense of share, and hence forming the phrase to go *snacks*, is as common in America now as it was in England in the days of Pope and Dryden, both of whom use it repeatedly.

The Rev. P. Cartwright speaks of a woman at a camp-meeting, who, "in a state of semi-frenzy implored the Almighty not to let her Sally *go snacks* with the devil."

Snarl, in England used only for an entanglement of thread and similar material, is in America applied to difficulties among men also, and even an angry person is said "to be in a *snarl*." "Again we hear reports from Washington that the members of the Cabinet have gotten into a *snarl* with each other or with the President. These rumors arise periodically and amount to nothing." (St. Louis *Democrat,* February 19, 1871.)

Snew, the old preterite of to snow, and its companion *snown,* the participle, are both still quite frequently heard in the United States; sometimes affectedly, as in Major Jack Downing's *Letters:* "First it blew, and then it *snew,* and finally it frizzed horrid;" but by the negroes in the South precisely as it was used by the first English settlers. "Yes, mas' Bob, it *snew* sure all night long, dat's so."

Snob has very curiously, in Massachusetts and Pennsylvania, retained its old meaning, quoted by Halliwell, but long forgotten everywhere else, of journeyman shoemaker. An acquaintance will sometimes jeer one of the trade with the salutation: "Wh't, *snob!*" whistling the first part of the address in imitation of the waxing process.

Snooze, as verb and as noun, rarely heard in England, is quite common with us: "Lead him off to the lock-up and let him *snooze* till he is quiet." (J. R. Lowell, *Biglow Papers,* I., p. 57.) *Snoozy* is hence frequently used for slightly drunk.

So is very often carelessly employed for *as,* and this abuse, formerly rare, threatens to become more general of late. "When we got on a new suit thus manufactured, and sallied out into the country, we thought ourselves *so* big as anybody." (Rev. P. Cartwright, *Autobiography,* p. 26.)

Soak, to, in the sense of drain, which is obsolete in England, is still used in America, especially as applied to bread, which is said "to be well soaked," if it is dry and thoroughly well baked.

Sobby, an adjective made from the verb to *sob,* after the analogy of *soggy,* and perhaps only an erroneous form of the latter, represents the English *sobbed,* and denotes land that is wet or marshy, and hence unfit for cultivation. "Cranberries will grow in *sobby* ground, where nothing else can be raised." (Norfolk *Journal*, June 27, 1859.) Occasionally the term is applied to other articles; thus certain United States Records, concerning the history of Georgia, saved from the wreck of a vessel bound to Liverpool, were said to have been "sent in their wet and *sobby* condition to New York." (North American *Review*, January, 1847.) *Sad* also is frequently used for *sodden*; for instance, when speaking of the bottom of a pie not properly baked.

Soft, rarely used in England for *fool*, is quite frequent in that sense in America, representing the Scottish *saft*.

Some, as an adverb, and meaning much, or of some account, is a modern perversion of the original meaning of the word, no longer limited to the United States. "She is *some* now, that's a fact, and the biggest kind of a punkin' at that." (*Blackwood*, July, 1848.) "I always thought he was *some*, but I am surprised to see him where he is now." (*Southern Quarterly*, 1853.)

Soon, instead of early, is used continually throughout the South. "I shall be there *soon* in the morning, if you will promise to be ready."

Sot, instead of set, probably nothing more than a broader sound of *sat*, and following in this the analogy of the modern *got* for the ancient *gat*, which J. R. Lowell tells us the Yankee further degrades into *gut*, is used universally North and South by the illiterate. The analogy is still stronger in Virginia, where the verb to *sit* is almost as unknown as among cockneys, and where, hence, the transition to *sot* must have been all the easier. "Who *sot* you up, Master Frank, to tell me how to fodder that 'are creatur, when I as good as nursed you on my knees?" (J. P. Kennedy, *Swallow Barn*.)

"We wanted one that felt all Chief
From roots o' hair to sole o' stockin',
Square-*sot* with thousan'-ton belief
In him and us, ef earth went rockin'."
(*J. R. Lowell.*)

Sots is the name of common yeast in Pennsylvania.

Souse, a mere modification of *sauce*, and often written *sowce* in New England and Virginia, means in Pennsylvania more generally pigs' feet.

Sparsely, for the obsolete sparsedly, is frequently said and written, especially with reference to "*sparsely* populated districts." "The country between Richmond and Danville is but *sparsely* settled, and only here and there a house is seen lording it over a cluster of cabins, formerly the slaves' quarters." (New York *Tribune*, April 26, 1871.)

Spell, a favorite expression in the United States for a little time or a short turn. Thus the "kink of laughter" is a "*spell* of laughter" in America. "We have had a wet *spell* of weather and the roads are almost unfathomable." (Hoffman, *Winter in the West*.)

"He stood a *spell* on one foot fust,
Then stood a *spell* on t'other,
An' on which one he felt the wust
He couldn't ha' told yer nuther."
(J. R. Lowell. *The Courtin'*.)

Spike-team is the American name for the English "Unicorn:" two horses preceded by a third.

Splendid, as applied to things not commonly associated in our mind with "splendor," as in speaking of "a *splendid* piece of mutton," is often objected to as an evidence of American grandiloquence. It sinks into utter insignificance by the side of *splendidious*, used by Drayton, the poet, in Queen Elizabeth's time. It was probably the Latin word *splendidus* he meant to employ, but there it is in print, and *splendiferous*, frequently met with in humorous English writings, is hardly worse.

Splurge, as noun and as verb, expressive of any violent, noisy demonstration, and much used in the South and West, is probably only a modification of *splairge*, quoted by Halliwell in his *Archaic Dictionary*, as a Northumbrian word with the same meaning. It referred originally to the floundering about of a great fish in the water, and the noise and splash it produced, and thence came to mean making a great swagger of wealth and importance. "Our would-be fashionables and shoddy aristocrats are off to Newport or Saratoga, to make a great *splurge*." (New York *Herald*, July, 1869.) The word is apparently connected with the old English *splorage*, from Scottish *splore*, which means a merry, riotous meeting.

Spree, a word traced back to a connection with French *esprit*, and thus closely related to *spry*, cannot have come to us from Louisiana, as is often stated, since it is already quoted by Halliwell as a provincialism. It was, on the contrary, brought here from England, as Dr. Elwyn says, "with Tom and Jerry, and is continued by the patrons of the firm."

Spunk, in the sense of mettle, is so far from being an Americanism that it is, on the contrary, admitted into good company in the north of England, and has been colloquially used from the oldest times in Scotland. Burns speaks, therefore, of "Erskine, a *spunkie* Norland billie" (*Cry and Prayer*), as Sir A. Wylie already said: "I did na think your Lordship was sic a *spunkie*." The adjective is used in America in precisely the same manner: "If you were not a minister, I should say you was *spunky*." (*A Woman's Pulpit.*)

Spurt, a perversion of *spirit*, and meaning a sudden, vigorous effort, is even more frequently used here than in England, where it is generally limited to accounts of various kinds of sport. It is one of the oldest words of the language, and has ever since 1619, when it first appears in print, retained the same meaning. "A short *spurt* does not tire me; the length and hardness of the way will at last tell me what leg I halt on." (A. Tuckney, *Sermon on Balm of Gilead*, p. 65.)

Squelch, to, expressive of the action of crushing anything soft, inanimate or animate, is good old English, and, although obsolete in the mother-country, in daily use in America. It had generally a humorous meaning, as in the well-known lines—

"He was the cream of Brecknock,
And flower of all the Welsh;
But Saint George he did the dragon fell
And gave him a plaguey *squelch*."
(*St. George and the Dragon.*)

Squiggle, to, for to *squirm*, to move about as eels and worms do, is an Americanism, the uncouth word having in England a different signification. It stands colloquially for the good old English verb, to

Squirm, which is now little heard in England. "The gentleman is suddenly seized with the retrenchment gripes, and *squirms* about like a long red worm on a pinhook." (Speech of Mr. Pitt in the Legislature of Missouri, 1867.) Grose already cites the word as meaning to wriggle and twist about actively, but as obsolete. It is well known that the same word is frequently substituted, in England as well as in the United States, for the verb to *swarm*, when applied to sailors hastening up to man the yards, or boys climbing up a tree without branches.

Staddle, the old English name of "the bottom of a corn-mow or haystack," as Grose says, is in America often applied to a young tree or sapling, till it has reached a certain size—a meaning well known to Bacon, but apparently obsolete in England. In the vast salt-marshes on the Eastern coast, stout stakes are driven in, on which the hayricks are set to raise them out of the reach of high tides, and these stakes are called *staddles*.

> "Lonesome ez *staddles* on a mash without no hayricks on."
> (J. R. Lowell. *Biglow Papers*, I., p. 130.)

Stamp, to, commonly pronounced *stomp*, has, in the South especially, the meaning of being very angry, derived no doubt from the violent *stamping* with the foot which so often accompanies ebullitions of wrath. "The General jumps up and he *stomps* about a spell, I tell you; he smashed down his pipe and it flew into more than forty pieces." (Major Jack Downing, *Letters*, p. 124.)

Stand, to, is used in Pennsylvania and some of the Western States for the more usual to *stand in*, meaning to cost. "This horse *stands* me two hundred dollars at least." (S. S. Haldeman.)

Start, to, is a verb very much used in the United States, and this popularity is explained thus by J. K. Paulding: "When folks set out to go anywhere in this country, it is called *starting*. Thus they *start* to the Westward; for our people are the most active in the world, and do everything by a *start*. Other people set out, as they term it, and will pause and ponder, ponder and pause, half a life over a journey of twenty miles, while an American decides at once upon going from the province of Maine to the banks of the Missouri. We are young quails, and run from the nest with the eggshells on our back." (*Letters from the South*, I., p. 108.)

Starvation was at one time denounced as an Americanism, but has been found to be an English word of considerable age, made incorrectly with a Latin termination to a Saxon word, after the analogy of "flirtation." Its first use is attributed to Mr. Dundas, afterward Lord Melville, in 1775, who, as Horace Walpole tells us, received from his daring innovation the nickname of "*Starvation* Dundas." To *starve* (German, sterben) was originally, and is now in England, applied only to dying of hunger, in the sense in which the trades-unions employ the grim word to *clem*; but in America *starvation* is used to denote death from exposure and cold also.

Steale, pronounced *stale*, the stock or handle of a tool, is provincial in England, but in daily use among the farmers of New England. The term is evidently the German *Stiel*.

Steep is not only used in its literal sense, but, by a kind of bold hyperbole, applied to things generally. Men speak of "a *steep* price for a farm," and complain of "a *steep* tax to be paid." J. R. Lowell gives a happy example of the extravagance with which such terms are used by country folks, even in their literal meaning: "I once asked a stage-driver if the other side of a hill was as steep as the one we were climbing? *Steep!* Chain-lightnin' couldn't go down it without puttin' the shoe on."

Stent, more commonly pronounced and written *stint*, almost forgotten in England, is still in daily use in the United States in the same manner in which Shakespeare spoke of his "*stint* of woe." The idea connected with the meaning of the term is evidently not merely that of a task, but of that amount of work which, when accomplished, will allow the worker to *stint* his efforts, that is, to cease working. Swift, however, uses the word *stint* as an allowance or portion: "How much wine do you drink in a day? My *stint* in company is a pint at noon." Theodore Parker spoke of "Little boys in the country working against time, with *stents* to do." (*Oration on the Death of Daniel Webster.*)

Stocking-feet, an expression long considered an Americanism by English critics, who made much of the "Yankee walking in his *stocking-feet* so as not to be heard." But either the word was long in use in Scotland also, or Mr. Thackeray had taken a fancy to it, in spite of its pretended foreign origin, for he says in his Newcomes: "Binnie found the Colonel in his sitting-room arranged in what are called in Scotland his *stocking-feet*." (I., ch. 8.)

Stone is occasionally used in America as an adverb to qualify an adjective, after the manner of the German *Stein* in *steinreich*, etc., probably an effect of the German, spoken so largely in the interior of Pennsylvania, where this usage most prevails. "I have heard the following story in the country: A young lady, who was so refined that she avoided saying *stone*, spoke thus: I took up a ground-seed (stone) and threw it at a he-biddy (cock) sitting on a turn-about (grinding-stone) and killed him *stone*-dead." (S. S. Haldeman.) *Stone*-dead is, however, quoted by Britton.

Stop, to, is very generally used here for to *stay*, and, we are told, now heard in England also, not only from illiterate people, but from many also who would be very angry if they were considered so. "The diplomats, who on this occasion are wont to greet our republican President in the splendor of their own court costumes, *stopped* quietly at home, and the day wore on without an incident." (Richmond *Dispatch*, January 4, 1871.) "Personal.—General George W. Deitzler, of Lawrence, is *stopping* at the Southern. Dr. Ernest Alexovitch, of Venice, Austria, is *stopping* with Captain Frederick Fuchs." (St. Louis *Democrat*, March 24, 1871.)

Stories of a house are counted differently in America from the English way: the story on the ground-floor is called the first, and the next above it, the first in England, is here called the second, and so on.

Stringy, in the sense of filamentous, consisting of long, thin strings, has recently obtained a new meaning in the United States, which is thus explained: "The excessive use of iron has given us an architecture which is technically known as *stringy*, like a man with a very large body on very thin legs." (New York *Tribune*, January 19, 1871.)

Stripper is not only the person who strips, but in Pennsylvania also a cow which is nearly dry, and has to be stripped of the little milk she gives.

Stub, to, instead of to *stump*, is often heard when persons strike their toes against a stone or a tree. The term is related to the German *stubben*, which has the same signification. *Stubby*, however, is used in the familiar sense of short and thick-set, mainly of persons.

Stud, in the very peculiar sense of stubbornness, was originally used only of horses who refuse to go on, and is connected with the verb to stand. Afterward it was applied to persons also, who were determined or obstinate:

> "Here lies Thomas Dudley, the trusty old *stud;*
> A bargain's a bargain and must be made good."
> (Governor Belcher's *Epitaph* on Governor Dudley. 17th century.)

Stumpy, very generally used like *stubby,* for a short and stout person. "*Stumpy* chaps, such as you, ain't got no troubles in this world.—That's all you know about it; *stumpies* have troubles." (J. C. Neal, *Charcoal Sketches.*)

Suant or *suent,* by some traced back to the fuller form of *pursuant,* by others believed to come from the old French *suiant,* following, means even or uniform, and is much used by the farmers of New England. It was carried there by their ancestors, and Jennings tells us that they say *suent* in the West of England, while Grose quotes in the Somersetshire dialect the phrase: "Zow the zeed *zuant.*"

Suicide is not unfrequently used as a verb. "John Pflug, of Pekin, Illinois, *suicided* from disgust at his name." (St. Louis *Democrat,* January, 1871.)

Suit, as applied to hair, is probably an Americanism. In the South a lady is said to "possess a wonderfully fine *suit* of hair." "You ought to have seen Cora, when she first appeared on the stage. Pale as death, and evidently very nervous, her beautiful fine features, radiant with intelligence and enthusiasm, almost shone in their brightness, relieved as they were by a back-ground formed of the most magnificent *suit* of hair ever seen flowing down woman's fair shoulders." (Richmond *Enquirer,* November 19, 1858.)

Summons, to, the old verb used by Swift, but long since regarded as obsolete in England, continues in use in the New England States. "It can't be that he really had you *summonsed* before the squire, Zek; what did he mean?" (Judd's *Margaret,* ed. 1871.)

Sundown, found in early English writers, and *sunup,* formed analogously, but probably a genuine Americanism, are both in constant use in New England and the Far West. "At *sundown* a drove of mustangs paid us a flying visit." (G. W. Kendall, *Santa Fé Expedition,* I., p. 88.) "I had walked fourteen miles since *sunup*, and felt ready for the fried chicken and hominy which are the regular breakfast of South Carolina planters." (Letter in New York *Tribune*, March 14, 1870.) "Mam's going to Brown's store at *sunup*, and I spose I've got to pack her and baby again." (F. B. Harte, *Luck of Roaring Camp*, p. 202.)

Supper is almost universally used for *tea* in the United States. "The meal which we are accustomed to call tea," says an English traveller, "is by Americans universally, I believe, called *supper*, and it is the final meal, there being only three in the day." (P. H. Gosse, *Letters from Alabama*, p. 68.)

Suspenders is the American substitute for the English "braces," and sometimes viewed as a delicate way to avoid the objectionable term "gallowses."

Suspicion, to, instead of to suspect, used by South, but long since obsolete in England, is still a favorite in Southern States, especially among the negroes, to whom the curtailed *'spect* is not expressive enough for their strong feelings. "Then the sergeant *suspicioned* me, for he turned on me and growled out, By God, I believe ye are a Yank!" (*Wild Bill.*)

Swad, an old English word for a lump or mass of earth, etc., survives in New England, as in the mother-country, as a colloquial or cant word only. "Such a *swad* of people as came to see the show! I never seen in all my life the like on it!" (*Our Young Folks*, December, 1869.)

Swale, in the sense of a tract of low, generally swampy, land, is, in like manner, an old word preserved in the remoter districts of New England and some parts of the Far West. "Branching from the Colorado, near the mouth, it glides easily down across the desert, through a *swale* a quarter of a mile wide." (T. F. Meagher, *Colorado*, etc.)

Swash, in the Southern and especially the Gulf States, designates a narrow channel of water between sandbanks, or near the shore. "It is said they took refuge in the *swash* behind the house, and thus escaped into the bayou, although others maintain that they only hid in the loft, while the officers were searching the lower story." (New Orleans *Bee*, May 17, 1869.)

Swinger is, in the West, the name given to the middle horses in a team of six. "Each wagon is usually drawn by three span of mules, of which the lighter and forward are leaders, the next pair *swingers*, and the rear, or heaviest pair, wheelers." (*A Trip to the West*, p. 137.)

Swingeing, often written *swindging*, is one of the good old English words which tenaciously cling to the soil, and sound like echoes from a far-off age. In Virginia and most parts of the South, white and black boys have for more than two centuries called a large snake or other formidable creature a *swindger*, or "a *swinging* big snake." The word, rarely if ever heard in the North, is duly laid down by Bailey, and applied by Milton in precisely the same sense to a dragon, who,

> "wroth to see his kingdom fail,
> *Swindges* the scaly horrour of his folded tail."
> (*Christmas Hymn*, St. VIII.)

"There will be a *swingeing* supper by-and-by." (*Putnam's Magazine*, January, 1868.)

Swingle-tree is rarely heard in the United States; an erroneous connection with the "double-tree," used in some cases, having led to the altered form of *single-tree*, which is nearly universal.

T.

Tackey, in the Southern States a common designation of an unkempt and uncouth-looking horse, is transferred to men also of neglected and forlorn appearance. "I rode along on my poor *tackey*, deep in thought, when I was suddenly recalled to the realities of life by a loud voice calling out to me: Halloa! stranger, what may you be after in my potato-patch?" (Lucian Minor, *New England Revisited*.)

Take, to, a newspaper, says the American, where the Englishman would say, to *take in* a paper.

Talented, a form perhaps first used in America, was strongly criticised and opposed by Coleridge, with many other apparent or genuine Americanisms. The term is, however, not objectionable in its mode of formation, eminently useful in designating persons who are endowed with talents, as "spirited and gifted" are made to serve for similar purposes, and has made its way so successfully in England, that it may be found now in her best and most fastidious writers. The "vile and barbarous vocable," as Coleridge called it, has thus established its claims and justified its authors.

Tall, like steep, is in America very frequently used in the sense of considerable, exceedingly, Western speech delighting in deriving such expressions from the prominent features of the landscape in the West. "My friend, said the agent to the Indian, when he had finished his harangue, that is pretty *tall* talk, but you had better take what the Great Father in Washington sends you, and be content." (*Official Report to Chief of Indian Bureau*, 1868.) The facility with which such words spread to regions where they are not indigenous, and hence often most ludicrously misapplied, may be seen in the phrase, "This is what I call *tall* fishing, anyhow." (*Newfoundland Fisheries*, 1870.)

Tarrify, to, has been for many generations a common expression in the South, for any undue pressure exercised by the powers that be. The word is generally referred back to a vulgar corruption of *torrified*, from the Latin *torrēre*, to roast, and this presumption is strengthened by the fact that the word is so used and written in an anonymous "Tour through North and South Carolina," published some years before the Revolution. A recent writer humorously alludes to the enormous tax on cotton and tobacco, which "tarrifies," if it does not "roast" the unfortunate planters of the South, and suggests that, if the word was not so old, it might very well be the result of being *tariff*-ied, since the Tariff has become a synonym of misery.

Tavern takes here almost universally the place of the English inn. In England the "tavern" furnishes entertainment and liquor, but provides no lodgings.

Tease, to, has taken in America the place of the English verb, to *chaff*, and its derivatives, which are rarely heard in this country, although so elegant and pure a writer as W. S. Landor uses them more than once.

Techy, instead of touchy, is neither a new form nor limited to the New England States. Shakespeare already has *tetchy* twice, and Ray mentions *techy* as a "North Country word."

Teeter, to, an American form of the English verb, to tilter, with its literal meaning, to seesaw, to move up and down on opposite ends of a plank, as children do; and, to be in a more or less painful state of suspense. "Because we want to watch the money-market, so many are *teetering* on the beam of speculation. Now gold goes up and they go down. Now stock goes down and they go up. Thus they *teeter* day after day, and when they tumble headlong in the crowd, they cannot see where the joke comes in." (*The Comic Side of Life.*)

Telegram, a much-discussed word, is an undoubted Americanism, used first by the editor of the Albany *Journal,* April 6, 1852, and formed after the analogy of "epigram," and "monogram," to distinguish the result of the process of telegraphing from the instrument. The term commended itself so strongly by its brevity that it soon supplanted its predecessor, "telegraphic dispatch," and a year or so later appeared in English journals also, which claimed it as an invention of their own. (*Notes and Queries,* November 21, 1852.) For some reason or other, however, the word has never become popular, and is still more or less confined to cases where brevity is of importance. Even the verb, to telegraph, is frequently forced to give way to the shorter, to *wire,* as a late telegram by Atlantic Cable from the British Premier to the Commissioner of Internal Revenue of the United States said: "*Cable* how match-tax works."

Temper is used by Americans in the majority of cases to denote passion, while in England it expresses, on the contrary, the control of passion. "Hook was nearly engaged in a duel," says his English biographer, "in which transaction, from first to last, he showed equal *temper* and spirit." This is also the meaning attached to its derivatives, *temperate* and *temperance,* in this country, but *temper* itself is rarely used thus: "It was the only time when I saw Mr. Lincoln really show *temper;* he seemed to have been literally worn out by insatiate petitioners and troublesome counsellors, and when the old lady declined leaving the room he spoke with serious anger." (*A Visit to Washington,* 1864.)

Tenement-houses are large buildings, erected generally in a very imperfect manner, for the purpose of being rented out in single rooms to poor families, thus producing very high rent and enriching the owner at the expense of the ill-lodged tenants.

Threap, to, meaning to argue, to contend, is quoted by Halliwell and by Ray among North Country words, but rarely heard in England, while it is still in daily use in Central Pennsylvania. "It's not for a man with a woman to *threapan.*" (*Percy's Rel-*

iques.) "I said to him, Come, let us *threap* and argue, but he, without saying another word, struck me over the head and knocked me down." (Harrisburgh *Journal*, January 17, 1851.)

Timber means in America not only the wood and the trees, but the whole forest—wooded land in contrast to open land. It is a remarkable feature of American landscape, that large parts of the country which were once covered with forests are now utterly bare; and in a late official report it was stated, that "Maine, in 1870, was bereft of almost her entire growth of old trees, New York was an extensive importer of *timber* from Canada and the West, and, as for the whole Union, it was believed that at the present rate of consumption the *timber* now growing will be all cut and marketed within fifteen or twenty years."

Tin, instead of tin-cup, is by no means American slang. Halliwell quotes it and English writers continually use it, Dickens speaking even of "a dinner-*tin*."

To, instead of *at*, is one of the most distinctive features of the Yankee lingo, as J. R. Lowell calls the dialect. "Now, I say, ef you don't bring the fashion-book, when you come home at Thanksgivin', you'll see what you'll git. You know we have sech lots of company *tu* our house, and I've got to be dressed, said a coarse, red-haired girl, who rejoiced in the mellifluous appellation of Serepty Hepzibah Smoot." (*Putnam's Magazine*, January, 1870.) It is thus written *tu*, because an additional peculiarity of the Yankee dialect requires that it and *too* should alike be pronounced *tŏ*, as in *touch*, when not emphatic, while both sound like *tu* in *tumult*, when emphatic. "There is such a thing as bein' *tu*," says the New Englander, with special satisfaction at never being found guilty of the crime. This confusion between *to* and too appears not so blameable, when it is borne in mind that formerly both words were written simply *to*. *To hum*, instead of, at home, is never heard outside of New England, but in daily use there. Even educated people are apt to say *to home*, as in the line praising a Governor, because

> "He stays *to* his home an' looks after his folks."
> (J. R. Lowell. *Biglow Papers*, I., p. 34.)

Equally remarkable is the American use of *to* as a kind of expletive, the infinitive of the verb that might follow it being universally omitted. "I meant to ask him *to*," means, to ask him to do what we are discussing. "Would you like *to?*" "I told him I did not want *to*," are phrases continually meeting the eye in reading works written by Northern authors. Even Mrs. H. B. Stowe, in her great work *Uncle Tom*, and in other writings, uses this phrase incessantly, and although perhaps not exactly a model of composition, her authority is of some weight, as she puts it into the mouth of educated as well as of illiterate people.

Tole, to, also written *toll*, and probably identical with the latter verb, is used in America to express the alluring of animals. "His son was found *toling* and coaxing the hogs to a gap." "We went down the bay, and saw plenty of ducks, but as we had no skiff and no means to *tole* them on, we did not get a shot." (Baltimore *American*, 1867.)

Tongue, instead of *pole* of wagon, is probably an Americanism, derived from an instinctive comparison with the *tongue* of a buckle, or a *tongue* of land stretching out, long and narrow, into the water.

Top, to, in the sense of *snuffing* a candle, is limited to Pennsylvania, where it is found in daily use.

Town is in New England very generally used for *township*, which, Miss Leslie tells us, explains Jonathan's difficulty, who

> "Said he could not see the *town*,
> There were so many houses."

It sounds odd, at first, to hear New Englanders speak of farms they own in Newton *Town*, or of the fine crops made in the whole *Town*.

Training and *training-day* are two old-fashioned terms, referring to the former usage of "*training* the militia" at certain seasons of the year, when they met on *training-days* to be reviewed. A militia-man, called out to do active service, is apt to be called a *trainer*—all these terms being derived from the process of *training* soldiers, as the modern "drill" used to be called.

Transpire, to, instead of, to happen, is unfortunately no longer slang, but has become a word in daily use with persons who ought not to be guilty of such bad usage. The original meaning of the word seems to have entirely disappeared, and whatever "happens" is now-a-days, in American newspapers especially, represented as having *transpired.* "After 12 o'clock last night it *transpired* that the Massachusetts delegation had voted unanimously in caucus to present the name of General Butler for Vice-President." (New York *Times,* 1869.) John Randolph, of Virginia, had a very tender ear for good English, and when one day a Member of Congress used the word *transpire* repeatedly, and always in the sense of occurring or taking place, he bore it for a time, but finally lost all patience: "'May I interrupt the gentleman a moment?' he asked. 'Certainly,' said the speaker. 'Well,' said Randolph, 'if you use the word *transpire* once more, I shall *expire.*'" In spite of such warning, and although whatever happens openly, in honest daylight, ought not to be slandered by being said to have *transpired,* the term is applied to every act and occurrence. "Our readers will recall the details of a horrible and unprovoked murder which *transpired* near Brighton, in the square before the railroad depot, and in presence of several hundred persons." (Alton *Telegraph,* January 30, 1871.)

Trash, in its vagueness and comprehensiveness of meaning, is a popular word with Americans, who apply it to persons and things alike, to express their worthlessness. It is also used, as an expressive term, of the leaves, sticks, and compact foam which accumulate by the side of a stream. In Louisiana, when the cane has been cut for the mill and stripped of its abundant leaves, the unripe joints are cut off, and with the leaves and canetons spread out upon the ground, so as to cover the roots with a thick mat of slowly-decaying vegetation. This *trash,* as it is called, is in spring, when no more frost is to be apprehended, removed and ploughed in by careful planters, while less prudent men simply burn it.

Trig, in the sense of trim, neat, but rarely heard in England, survives with many similar terms in Virginia, and the States that owe their existence to the Old Dominion. It is related to *trick,* in the sense of "tricked out," decorated. "This was a negro-boy equipped for service on horseback. He was rather more *trig* in appearance than I was accustomed to see the servants." (J. P. Kennedy, *Swallow Barn.*)

Turnpike, instead of turnpike-road, is universally used in the United States. In New England the word is pronounced *tunpike,* hence the play upon the word in the lines—

"Ef your soul
Don't sneak through *shunpikes* so's to save the toll."
(J. R. Lowell. *Biglow Papers*, I., p. 52.)

U.

Ugly, originally applied to want of beauty, has been almost entirely superseded by the word *plain*, as *comely* is nearly unknown in America, and its place supplied by pretty, handsome, or good-looking. *Ugly*, in the Northern States, means almost exclusively, ill-tempered, and is so constantly applied to disposition, that it is a common phrase to hear a girl represented as "being quite good-looking, but *ugly*." This use of the word is not new, but has come to be considered colloquial only, if not real cant, in England. "Governor Andros was inclined to be *ugly*, but they understood him, and, pretending indifference, secured a passport from him to visit the upper waters of the Hudson." (*Early Voyages to New Netherlands*.) H. Reeves states that "a British traveller, walking one day in the suburbs of Boston, saw a woman out on a doorstep whipping a screaming child. Good woman, said he, why do you whip the boy so severely? She answered, Because he is so *ugly!* The Englishman walked on and then put down in his journal: Mem. American mothers are so cruel as to whip their children because they are not handsome." The same term is applied to animals: "Squire Stebbin owned a bull that came from the same stock, and he turned out so dreadful *ugly* that he had to be killed for beef." (*Putnam's Magazine*, March, 1855.)

Uncle was, in the South, the universal term by which a colored man was addressed.

Underhew, as applied to timber, in Pennsylvania, denotes a piece of timber which should be square to come up to measure, but which has been hewn in such a manner that, while it looks full size, it really does not hold the requisite number of cubic feet. (S. S. Haldeman.)

Up, to, as a verb, is a familiar but quite common expression in the South. "And then he *ups* and tells me all." (J. C. Neal, *Charcoal Sketches*.)

Use, to, is in like manner an elliptic expression, common in the Southern States. "The sheep *used* in that field," means "used to graze" there. "A boy generally found no difficulty, before he was twelve years old, to learn to discover where deer *used*, and to notice the signs." (Wills De Hass, *History of Early Settlements*, p. 227.)

V.

Varmin, as all wild animals are called in hunter's phrase, whether they are hunted for sport, for profit, or for extermination, is considered a corrupt pronunciation of *Vermin*. This can apply, however, only to the strengthening *t* which is commonly added, since the *a* in the first syllable is simply a remnant of its former sound, when *er* was in England almost uniformly pronounced *ar*, and as it still is in Derby, clerk, and sergeant. "Would you have me suffer myself to be bullied all day by a *varmint?*" (W. Irving, *Astoria*, I., p. 260.) "You're not going to get 'possum from top of tree at one jump, I know. He come down-stairs presently. Terrible *varmint* for grabbing—his tail as good as his hand." (J. P. Kennedy, *Swallow Barn.*) "Oh, Land of Goshen, what are you prying and peeping into the *varmint's* hole; it is nothing but a bumble-bee, and the fish are come down to the sea and every man and boy in the place is after them." (*A Visit to Manasquam.*) P. H. Gosse gives a ludicrous account of the nice distinction which Americans, with all their apparent looseness of language, know how to apply, when it seems necessary: "I inadvertently spoke of it (a 'possum) as 'a singular creature,' but *creature* or rather *critter* is much too honorable a term for such an animal, being appropriated to cattle. A 'possum, sir, is not a critter but a *varmint*." (*Letters from Alabama*, p. 234.)

Ventilate, to, as applied to persons, is a most objectionable abuse of the picturesque word, which has forced its way irresistibly from the French into German and English. "In another article our correspondent promises to *ventilate* the President and his policy, and we promise our readers a rich treat." (New York *Herald*, July 27, 1868.)

Vest is in America almost universally used for the English *waistcoat*, while the latter is very appropriately applied to a garment worn immediately on the body, as a flannel-*waistcoat*. Sir C. Lyell, during his first visit to the United States, wrote home that "the American citizen deigns not to appear in public unless dressed in full evening costume of costly black broadcloth, with what he calls a *vest* of black satin."

Vige, a most violent and unwarrantable corruption of *voyage,* in constant use in New England, has been shown by J. R. Lowell to be of great antiquity. He quotes from Peel's *Sir Clymon and Sir Clamydes:* "And afterwards having met our *vige,*" while Chaucer writes at least *viage,* as it is written in Spanish.

Voyageur, a French word, perfectly naturalized in the United States, and used to designate Canadian boatmen and travelling fur-traders, on the upper Mississippi and in the great Northwest, was first used by Mr. Irving in his *Astoria* (I., p. 20) in 1847.

W.

Waggon, to, or, as it is almost universally written in the United States, to *wagon,* is constantly used instead of to carry or to transport. "The goods will have to be *wagoned* a long way, sir."

Wain, the old and obsolete form of wagon, is still in daily use in some parts of the United States, e. g., in the peninsula east of the Chesapeake, one of the first parts of Virginia and of North America that were colonized, the earliest settlements made there dating back to a few years after the foundation of Jamestown.

Wallop, to, or *Wallup,* in the sense of beating violently; an English pronunciation of old date, is frequently heard in familiar style in America also. The word seems to be intimately connected with *wallup,* in the literal sense of "walling (boiling) up," as used in *potwalloper,* and in Joel Barlow's lines on *Hasty Pudding:* "Then puffs and *wallops,* rises to the brim." The process of boiling up may have been transferred to the hot, hasty character of persons, as we also say that an irate man "boiled over." "All I know was *walloped* into me. I took larnin' through the skin." (J. C. Neal, *Charcoal Sketches.*)

Warn, to, in the sense of to notify, has occasionally been considered an Americanism, but the *warning* given by English servants would seem to show that it is used thus in England also. It is, besides, employed in the same meaning by Pecock (J. R. Lowell) and other old English writers, and repeatedly by Dickens.

Weddiner, a term derived from *wedding,* as the English "meetiner" is derived from "meeting," designates in Virginia the persons in attendance on the bridegroom. It is, of course, not a new word, having been handed down to the present generation from the time of the first settlers, and occurs, among others, in a poem in the Cumberland dialect, by John Stagg:

"The priest was ready within,
The *weddiners* just took gluts apiece,
While he his brick was lattin'."

Well is used by Americans with peculiar fondness to begin almost every sentence, but especially an answer to a question. This custom seems to have originated in New England, where it is still most generally prevailing, in order to gain time before replying, as the Yankee is commonly accused of answering only by a new question. He, therefore, dwells upon the *well*, perhaps even repeats it, and, as J. R. Lowell quaintly remarks, gives it "a variety of shades of meaning, conveyed by the difference of intonation, and by prolonging or abbreviating, which I should vainly attempt to describe. A friend of mine told me that once he heard five different *wells*, like pioneers, precede the answer to an inquiry about the price of land."

Whip, to, in the sense of beating, surpassing others, is an Americanism, and the slang phrase, "That *whips* all creation," commonly credited to Kentuckians, is characteristic of this use of the word. "He *whipped* me at leaping, but I reckon I can *whip* him at running." (S. S. Haldeman.)

Whitpotting, a term used in Nantucket and a few other places on the Eastern coast for visiting among relations and friends, is derived from the old English festival of Mothering-Sunday in Mid-Lent, when the servants and young people in England were allowed to go home, and when—especially in West England—the *white-pot*, a dish resembling hasty pudding, formed a staple dish.

Whittle, to, designating what is, abroad, considered the favorite and life-long occupation of the American, is probably derived from the Scottish *whittle*, a claspknife, as used by Burns:

"Gudeman, quoth he, put up your *whittle*,
I'm no designed to try its mettle."
(*Death and Dr. Hornbook.*)

Dryden also speaks of "a butcher's *whittle*," meaning his little knife, the term being a diminutive, and the root *whet*. That the word is by no means American in its meaning—whatever may be said of the practice of *whittling* sticks, tables, and furniture generally—may be seen from the fact that Horace Walpole wrote to Horace Mann, after the battle of Rocoux, October 14, 1746: "Then we have *whittled* down our loss extremely."

Whop, to, instead of *whip*, is universal in the South among the blacks and many whites. "Dis yere my boy, Miss, I wants him ter come ter school, an ef he don't 'have hisself, hopes you'll *whop* him. You hears dat 'are now? Ef yer don't mind de teacher, I'se gwine *whop* yer, 'sides de *whopping* she'll gib yer." (Sketches in Color, *Putnam's Magazine*, January, 1870.) The word is an old English cant term, a corruption of *whip*, and was often written *whap*; hence comes the term *whopper*, mentioned by Pegge as a "thumper, anything uncommonly large. North," and representing in our day mainly a big lie (*Slang Dictionary*, p. 270). "If Colfax had not told such a *whopper* in his definition, it would have been the champion joke of the season." (Macon *Telegraph*, April 1, 1871.)

Wicket is, in Maine and the timber regions of the Northwest, the name of a shed or "camp" made of boughs, to shelter the lumbermen at night and in bad weather.

Wilt, to, is applied in America to flowers and plants which begin to lose their freshness, and to become flaccid when exposed to the heat on a dry day.

> "Tediously pass the hours,
> And vegetation *wilts* with blistered roots."
> (*W. D. Gallagher.*)

J. R. Lowell commends the word as useful to fill the gap between drooping and withering, the previous and the succeeding stage, and thinks the "imaginative phrase, he *wilted* right down, like, he caved right in, a true Americanism." Artemus Ward punned upon the word atrociously. "I said to her, *Wilt* thou? and she *wilted*." Its better use is beautifully illustrated in the lines—

> "We never thought to see her droop her fair and noble head,
> Till she lay stretched before our eyes, *wilted* and cold and dead."
> (J. R. Lowell. *The Morning Glory.*)

Witness, to, frequently substituted for the simpler to see, is another evidence of the American tendency to grandiloquence. "I never *witnessed* a more splendid sight in all my life." (Baltimore *Sun*, April 17, 1871.)

Wolfish, in the sense of very hungry, is a strong and picturesque Western term. "When we reached camp my half-breed said he was *wolfish* hungry, but as we had nothing whatever to eat, and even the parfleche failed to give us any comfort, he buckled his belt tighter and lay down to sleep." (T. Winthrop, *The Canoe and the Saddle*, 1863.)

Workhouse, generally associated in our mind with paupers, has recently obtained a new and nobler meaning in Boston, where a *workhouse* has been established for weak girls, which is in reality a horticultural school or hospital. Weak girls attend here to learn ostensibly how to cultivate flowers, but in reality to accustom them gradually to such hard work as will restore them to health. When new-comers first attempt work, they can with difficulty endure it two hours a day. After a short time they are able to spend eight hours in work, their health, appetite, and strength increasing in corresponding proportions. All the flowers that can be raised are quickly bought up, and, although this was not the primary object of the institution, it is "making money."

Worryment, made after the manner of "wonderment," and similar factitious words, can hardly be said to be in use, as it does not occur outside of certain works, the humor of which has to be sought for largely in bad spelling and unusual words.

Wrathy, a familiar substitute for *wroth*, is not unfrequently heard in the West. "The general was as *wrathy* as thunder, and when he gets his dander up it's no joke." (Major Jack Downing's *Letters*, p. 34.)

Y.

Yallo is the almost uniform pronunciation of *yellow* as far South as Virginia, and to the West. In New England it appears as *yellers*, and then often denotes a peculiar disease of peach-trees which makes their leaves turn yellow.

Yammer, used to express a whine or a whimper in Pennsylvania, owes its origin evidently to the influence of German in that State, as it reproduces, almost unchanged, the German word *Jammer* in one of its meanings.

You is curiously enough in the South almost invariably accompanied by the word all, and a person meeting a bachelor friend, will not hesitate to ask him, "How are *you all?*" *Yourn*, instead of *yours*, retaining the old adjective termination which is concealed in mine and thine (my-en, thy-en), is frequently enlarged in the South into *you-uns*, and followed up with the same addition in other pronouns.

"I have heern the tale a thousand ways,
But never could git through the maze,
That hangs around that queer day's doin's :
But I'll tell the yarn to *you-uns*."
(John Hay. *The Mystery of Gilgal.*)

A story is told of a soldier in the late Civil War, who had been captured by Sheridan in his charge through Rockfish Gap, on the raid down to the White House, and who, sent back to Winchester, reported thus: "We didn't know *you-uns* was around us all, and *we-uns* reckoned we was all safe, till *you-uns* came ridin' down like mad through the gap and scooped up *we-uns* jest like so many herrin'." These terms, and *you-ens* and *us-ens*, are but extensions of the English vulgarism, which says *yourn, hisn, hern*, in Berkshire not only, where it seems to be most prevalent, but in other parts of England also. A Berkshire ditty runs thus:

"But tother young maiden looked sly at me,
And from her seat she ris'n—
Let's you and I go our own way
And we'll let she go *shis'n*."

This is more than a precedent for J. R. Lowell's—

"She thought no voice had such a swing
Ez *hiz'n* in the choir;
My! when he made Ole Hundred ring
She know'd the Lord was nigher."
(*The Courtin'*.)

Even a reverend minister of the Hardshell Baptists, we are told, may use the words: "He had laid sixpence on the desk, and, after the manner of those people, bet us that no one in the congregation could tell him where his text was found. Brother, said an old man present, it's a small bet, but I never let them pass; and then referred to the passage correctly and sat down. The money's *yourn,* said the preacher, and then began his sermon." (*Putnam's Magazine,* February, 1855.

XI.

Cant and Slang.

CANT AND SLANG.

" No expression can become a vulgarism which has not a broad foundation. The language of the vulgar hath its source in physics, in known, comprehended, and operative things."

(*Walter Savage Landor.*)

THE number of really new American words is but very small, and many of these even will, no doubt, upon more careful investigation, be found to be mere imitations of well-known terms. After all, human nature differs very little wherever society is well organized, and what may appear original for a time, in the efforts at reform, or in startling innovations, is speedily discovered to be but a repetition of former experiments. New habits and new occupations do not always call for new terms, since they bear generally sufficient resemblance to others of well-known character, to allow of old names receiving a new application. It is only where special importance is attached to a custom, as in the case of "Forefathers' Day;" where a casual word happens to strike the fancy of the people with such force as to make a word popular, like "boost;" or where the usefulness and power of a modified form makes itself felt at once, as in "mailable," that really new words establish their claim to be considered essential parts of the language. Some of these even disappear again after a short period of usefulness; such are especially the names of political parties and fractions of parties, which are manufactured at nearly every election, certainly whenever a change in politics takes place, and are forgotten again when a new emergency produces new names. Their number is legion; their interest often merely local, and always only ephemeral; so that it has been deemed better to omit them here altogether. They have been quite as numerous in Europe, and quite as fleeting. But for the help afforded by the charming *Memoirs of the Duke of Guise,* few but the most ardent students of history would, for instance, know of the existence of "Beggars," as the revolters of Flanders were called in his time, while those of Guienne took the name of "Eaters," those of Normandy that of "Bare Feet," and those of Beausse and Boulogne that of "Woollen Pattens." These names convey to us no more meaning than will after a few years those of *Barnburners* and *Old Hunkers, Copperheads* and *Butternuts, Scallawags* and *Carpetbaggers,* which in their time stirred up the passions of a great nation, and were in everybody's mouth and on every page of the public journals.

It has, also, been thought unnecessary to repeat here those colloquial or genuine cant and slang terms, which either owe their origin to a foreign tongue or belong to a special department of social life, such as religious or political institutions, railways or counting-rooms, or hunting or fishing pursuits. These have already been mentioned in their proper connection.

Attention has, on the other hand, been bestowed upon the cant and slang terms which are not simply importations from England; the latter being introduced only when they have been modified in some essential point as to form or meaning. American cant and slang have some peculiarities unknown to the Old World. The women even contribute to it largely, availing themselves of the national gallantry extended to their sex on all occasions, for the purpose of indulging to the utmost in unbridled license of expression, both in public and in private. There is as much truth as wit in the conundrum: Wherein do the women of the day resemble St. Paul? In that they speak after the manner of men.

Then the Great West contributes its characteristic features, demanding from its popular speakers free manners and bold words, and, conscious of its political importance and exhaustless resources, caring as little for the canons of verbal criticism as for the dictates of European lawgivers. Its speech is impregnated with the racy flavor of the backwoods and the prairie, and reflects in form and intonation the primitive life in the settler's log cabin. Its vast extent, the boundless plains and gigantic rivers, and all the matchless features of Nature on the largest scale ever beheld by man, impress upon language also a certain freedom from restraint and a certain tendency to employ vast terms and large-sounding phrases, which give an air of unconscious grandiloquence and genuine slang even to ordinary conversation.

The most fertile source of cant and slang, however, is, beyond doubt, the low-toned newspaper, written for the masses, which, instead of being a monitor and an instrument of improvement in the hands of great men, has become a flatterer of the populace, and a panderer to their lowest vices. The common tendency to slang which characterizes the American people, the colloquial inelegancies that mark our conversation, and the downright vulgarities which deface so much of our literature, are all, more or less, due to the pernicious influence of the low-toned party newspaper of the day. Thanks to this influence, any sudden excitement, political event, or popular literary production, originates and sets a-going a number of slang words, vulgar at first, and rejected by the few who are careful of the people's English, but soon adopted as semi-respectable by the force of habit and the innate indolence of the American in such matters. How truly was it said by Grose, as far back as 1785, that "those burlesque phrases, quaint allusions, and nicknames for persons, things, and places, which from long, uninterrupted usage, are made classical by prescription," form an essential part of the English language. Englishmen have always been distinguished by their fondness for vulgar equivalents, and their descendants on this continent have not forgotten the customs of their fathers. They constantly coin new words, and give new force to half-obsolete terms; and as Mr. Buckle often used to say, "many of these words are but serving their apprenticeship, and will eventually become the active strength of our language." America has sent a fair supply of cant terms to the home-country, and they have been welcomed and readily adopted by English politicians and English merchants especially, while at home they spread with a rapidity heretofore unknown in the history of language—thanks to the fact that there is no country where reading is so universal and newspapers are so numerous. The gradual growth of such terms has been well described. "These vulgarisms and corruptions of language do not come at once into general use; they creep in stealthily; they often spring from ignorance or caprice; then they do some service in an humble way, in the market or the courts, ministering to the wants of the poor and the ignorant; then they attract the favor of the press in its least authoritative form, and finally, partly by assumption and partly from necessity, they come to be acknowledged as good citizens and freeholders of the realm."]

Among the fertile sources of slang, sound must not be forgotten, which contributes a large number of words, although etymology is but too apt to overlook its productive powers. Nothing pleases ignorant persons so much as high-sounding terms, "full of fury," and hence they delight in words melodious to their ear, like "rumbumptious, slantindicular, splendiferous, rumbustious, and ferricadouzer." (*Slang Dictionary.*) Thus Americans have invented "catawampiously, karnuption and conniption-fits," and love to devise new terms like "skeet, skoot, and skit," to represent, by the mere sound, brisk action and energetic movement. It is this same love of sound which leads to the marked preference of Western people for high-flown, intense, or grandiloquent expressions. "The Western man," says a recent writer on the subject, "touches the high keys of conversation when he speaks of condiments, instead of sugar and cream, in his coffee, and uses propelling for walking. He says his neighbor speaks *judgmatically;* he talks of going out as *prospecting;* when he wishes to know what he has to pay, he asks, What's the *damage?* or, not so charitably, What's the *swindle?* He talks of your *plunder,* and his *betterments* on his farm. He speaks soberly of *building* a pair of shoes, and says of an old goose, We biled it, and biled it, but it was tougher than the wrath of God." (Henry Reeves.) [Nothing is more amusing than to listen to a group of hunters or Western backwoodsmen, as they lie around the fire, smoking their short pipes and talking quietly in a tone and a style which, to the person unaccustomed to their speech, sounds like the height of extravagance and absurdity. Thus a literary tailor relates of his wandering associates, that "One would declare that for thirty days, in the city of London, he had not seen a 'patch' of blue sky big enough to 'seat a pair of breeches of the Jack of Clubs.' Another would aver that he knew a restaurant in some town, where he could get coffee strong enough to 'bear an iron wedge.' A third, in discussing the social qualities of his landlady, would allege that she could 'talk off the ears of a cast-iron dog,' whilst still another declared he knew an Irishman who lay six weeks speechless in the month of August, overcome by heat, and 'all his cry was water.'"

A.

About, in newspaper-slang and the pages of careless writers, is used in the sense of "here and there." "In last night's row, Mr. —— was badly beaten *about* the head and face;" and with an intensifying addition, "It is fair to infer that, distributing his attentions, he had been, as usual, *about in spots*."

About right, are called those things and acts which are judged to be very nearly right. "Well, that'll be *about right*, I reckon, but I think you might have done better, Pete." (J. P. Kennedy, *Horseshoe Robinson*.)

Above one's bend means, above one's power of bending all his strength to a certain purpose. "It would be *above my bend* to attempt telling you all we saw among the Redskins." (J. F. Cooper, *The Oak Openings*.) J. R. Lowell calls attention to Hamlet's expression, "To the top of my *bent*." In the South the phrase is apt to expand into "above my *huckleberry*."

Absquatulate, to, to run away, with the more or less forcible idea of running away in disgrace—a fictitious word, considered in England an Americanism, and perhaps made from the Latin *ab* and the American *squat*, which was first used by "Nimrod Wildfire," a Kentucky character, in a play called "The Kentuckian," by Bernard, and acted by Mr. Hackett, in 1833.

Africanize, to, in the sense of placing under the control of Africans, is a cant term which has of late acquired very general and very melancholy currency, since several of the Southern States have been literally *Africanized*.

Afterclap represents in Pennsylvania and the Western States an additional and generally unjust demand beyond the agreement or bargain originally made. "None of your *afterclaps!*" In Scotch the same word means "evil consequences."

Agur-forty, a curious corruption, showing the almost irrepressible tendency of the uneducated to give some intelligible and suggestive form to terms which they do not comprehend. It is the *aqua fortis* of medicine. "Your Honor needn't say another word; I knock under; this man's whiskey ain't Red Eye, it ain't Chain Lightnin' either, it's regular *Agur-forty*, and there isn't a man living can stand a glass and keep his senses." (New Orleans *Picayune*. *Police Reports*, December 25, 1867.)

Airly, for early, is New England slang, though not unknown in Pennsylvania, and derived from its orthodox sound in the 17th century. It is well represented in J. R. Lowell's line: "A man must get up *airly*, if he wants to take in God."

All any more, or simply *all*, is a Pennsylvania vulgarism, the latter form probably derived from the German *alle*, which is familiarly used in the sense of "gone." "Die Suppe ist *alle*," means, "the soup is (all) gone." Thus the waiter at a hotel will say, "The pies are *all any more*, Sir," meaning that there are no more.

All-fired, meaning excessively, in the highest degree, is suspected by J. R. Bartlett to be a corruption of *hell-fired*, which is very likely. "That's an *all-fired* lie, cried the Kentucky man, drawing his bowie-knife from behind him, and you'll have to swallow every word of it, or your soul will see daylight pretty quick." (*Western Scenes*, 1839, p. 147.)

All sorts of suggests the idea of persons or things which are nothing particularly, but of that indifferent nature which may be anything and everything. The phrase is confined to the South and West, where it is very popular. "He was *all sorts of* a man to most people, but if you knew him better, you could not help liking him." (Eulogy in House of Delegates of Virginia, January 17, 1849.)

Along, to get, is the American substitute for the English phrase to get on. Mrs. Trollope already noticed it as a peculiarity of our speech. "'Well, Sir, how are you *getting along*? were Mr. Webster's words, as the little fellow ran up to him, hugging his knees and looking up into his face." (*A Visit to Marshfield*, 1851.)

Alpaca, a well-known material, is extensively corrupted by traders, who call it *Alla Packa* and *Alley Packa*, confounding it apparently with "Ali Pacha," as pronounced by them.

Among the missing, to be, or to be found, is a common slang phrase to denote simply to be absent. "I tell you what, Jake, if this goes on, I'll be *among the missing* before sundown; it ain't human nature to stand bein' fired at by them varmin, and not to have a crack at 'em in return." (*Across the Great Desert*, 1869.)

Animules is, in California and the Southwestern Territories, a favorite substitute for *animals*, with a sly pun upon *mules*.

Anti, the professional term for a bet placed *anti*, or in opposition to the dealer's bet, in playing the Southern game of cards called Poker, has been transferred to other transactions also, and to *anti* means to bet or risk generally. "What will you *anti* he won't be re-elected?"

Antony Over, a game of ball played by two parties of boys, on opposite sides of a schoolhouse, over which the ball is thrown. Used in Pennsylvania. *Antony* is merely a proper name, pressed into the service here, as Reynard, Robin, and others are for the same purpose, and *Over* requires no explanation. (S. S. Haldeman.)

Anything else is often added with *not,* to any assertion which in the speaker's mind requires strengthening, and if the latter be strongly negative, is changed into *nothing else.* "He's a brick, I swear, and *nothing else.*" (*Pickings from the Picayune,* p. 156.) The same result is obtained by adding

Anyhow or *anyhow you can fix it.* "I am going to try, *anyhow.*" "I don't see how you can convince me of that, *anyhow you can fix it.*"

Ary, for *ever a,* is common in New England, as in England. (*Slang Dictionary,* p. 68.) "Take *ary* one on 'em you like." The older form was *airy,* and in Tom Jones it is even written *arrow:* "And yet I warrants me, there is *narrow* a one of all these officer-fellows but looks upon himself as good as *arrow* a squire of five hundred pounds a year."

As I can, following generally a phrase like I don't know, is frequently heard in the rural districts of New England, where it represents the cautious hesitation by which the Yankee thinks it prudent to qualify every promise or assertion. The particle *as* is substituted for *but,* and already N. S. Dodge has remarked the resemblance of this class of phrases to the Spanish "Quien-sabe?" "A traveller," he adds, "passing a few weeks at Mount Desert, Maine, asked the innkeeper if he could change a hundred-dollar note? Putting his hand in his pocket and taking out his wallet, the latter replied: I don't know I can and I don't know *as I can.*"

Asininity, an *asinine* stupidity. "The editor is not asked to restrain his loquacity, but to let it be truthful . . . even if he should have to avoid *asininities* like his *Oxycocus verburnum.*" (S. S. Haldeman, *Notes on Willson's Readers,* 1864, § 126.)

Assentatious, ready and willing to assent to all that is said—made from *assentation.* "One who listens well, a respectable, *assentatious* stranger." (J. P. Kennedy, *Swallow Barn.*)

Assign, to, is in the South used by illiterate persons and by an astounding number of men who ought to know better, instead of *sign*. "I will *assign* the paper, sir, as soon as you bring it to me, and then you can have it recorded in Court." (*Southern Literary Messenger*, September, 1849.) The word is a striking illustration of the force with which analogy fashions words that are not understood by the speaker. Ignorant persons derive from the frequent use of words like assent, assert, approve, ascribe, etc., a vague conception of a peculiar force adhering to the initial *a*, and thus add it where it is superfluous and incongruous.

Ater, for after, is a corruption which the New Englander has inherited from his Puritan ancestors, while the Virginian, with his apparent inability to pronounce the *r* where it ought to be heard, and to omit it where it is not in place, says more frequently *arter* or even *arfter*. While the latter, even in the pulpit, is occasionally heard to speak of "us *poo motals*," and orders the servant to "shet the *doo*," he calls his uncle's wife *Arnt Mariar*, and asks her "when she goes back to *Starnton*."

Avalanche, a corruption of ambulance, was already before the late Civil War much used in Texas and the outlying territories, but is said to have caused no small merriment in the Confederate Camp, when Prince Polignac was sent to hold an obscure command in the Southwest, and once showed very great excitement upon being informed by a sergeant that the "*avalanche* was just coming down the hill as fast as fury."

B.

Back, to, down, or to *back out*, are both Western phrases, quite picturesque in form and suggestive in meaning. The metaphor may have been taken from the stable—as is maintained by English writers—but corresponds so evidently to the opposite phrase of *going ahead*, that the sea appears far more likely to have been the birthplace of the phrase. "It is not expected now that the Democrats will *back out* from their position, as the Radicals can no longer command the two-thirds which enabled them last session to enforce the previous question." (New York *Herald*, December 10, 1870.) "He was one of those men who never *back down*, even when they know they are clearly in the wrong: their pride is sure to be too strong for their judgment." (*New Eclectic*, March, 1870.)

Bald-face, one of the many slang terms under which bad whiskey passes in the West.

Bald-headed, to go it, is a very peculiar but not unfrequent phrase in New England, suggestive of the eagerness with which men rush to do a thing without taking time to cover their head. "Whenever he had made up his mind to do a thing he went at it *bald-headed*." (*Our Young Folks*, 1869.) To *snatch bald-headed*, on the other hand means to defeat a person in a street-fight:

> "The crowd then gave a specimen of calumny broke loose,
> And said I'd *snatched him bald-headed*, and likewise cooked his goose."
> (*Words and their Uses.* Galveston *News*, May 4, 1871.)

Bamsquabbled, first used in the "Legend of the American War," and expressing discomfiture, is an evidently manufactured word, and but rarely heard except in humorous writings.

Bango, an onomatopoetic term, imitative of the sound which calls forth the exclamation. Confined to the negroes in all the States.

Bar represents in the West almost uniformly the *bear*, and reappears in *bar-meat*. Another *bar* is the verb made from the noun, a *bar*, in the sense of drinking-shop, used in the West. "He *bars* too much, and won't stand it long." (*Western Scenes*, 1839, p. 771.)

Barberize, to, is a word fortunately confined to barbers, whose occupation it is intended to express.

Beast is in Virginia and some of the Southern States used for a horse, as it was the custom with Englishmen at the time when the Old Dominion was settled, and when the translators of the Bible wrote, "A certain Samaritan set him on his own *beast*." (Luke x. 34.) "Entertainment for man and *beast*," is a common inscription over the doors of village taverns.

Bellmare, a horse chosen to lead a "caravan" or drove of mules in the Southwest. "Why the gray mare should be the better horse in the estimation of mules I cannot say, but such is certainly the fact. Though very cautious animals, when relying solely upon their own judgment, they would appear to have a consciousness of their inferiority, which induces them to entertain a great regard for the sagacity of the horse, and especially for that of a white mare. The wily Californians, taking advantage of this amiable weakness, employ a steady, old, white mare of known gentleness and good character, to act as a kind of mother and guide to each drove of unruly mules." (*A Ride with Kit Carson.*) This is the familiar *bellmare*, who in her turn gives, in slang language, her name to the leader of political parties. "Mr. Eastman will probably be the *bellmare* of the scalawags in the approaching session." (Houston *Telegraph*, 1869.)

Begin is frequently used, accompanied by *not*, to express a very emphatic negation. A caterpillar being about to be consigned to a small box, not wide enough to receive the body, nor even the smallest part, a servant exclaimed indignantly, "Law, sir! he wouldn't *begin* to go in." (Gosse, *Letters from Alabama*, p. 293.)

Bender, in the sense of a spree, a course of drinking, is the facetious name given to the arm, which becomes a *bender* from being so frequently bent or "crooked" to lift the glass to the mouth. The word originated with the Scotch, among whom it designated the hard drinker as well as the drinking. "Most of the owners of these names had been tempted by the festivities of the day to go on a regular *bender*, and had to pay the penalty for their New Year's frolic by appearing this morning in the police-court." (Richmond *Dispatch*, January 3, 1864.) Allan Ramsay already sang—

"Now lend your lugs, ye *benders* fine
Wha ken the benefit of wine."

Bet, you—a new asseveration, which has arisen in the Southwest, but shows a decided tendency to make its way upward. It means, You may bet on what I say. "We will be all right if Lower Georgia will do her duty as we do up here. We're all going to turn out in the upper country. Did you see all them that passed through the cars just now? Well, there's eighteen of them negroes, and we're going to take them all down to vote the Democratic ticket, and they'll vote it too, *you bet*." (Correspondence New York *Tribune*, December, 1870.)

Bettermost, a cumulative superlative after the model of many a similar form in Shakespeare, but not found in English writers. Common in New England. "I stopped the *bettermost* part of the time with my cousin, the deacon." (Mrs. Stowe.)

Betweenity, the state of being undecided, of halting between two opinions, a favorite slang term with so-called humorous writers. "Like the fabled coffin of Mohammed, he is always in a state of *betweenity*." (J. C. Neal, *Charcoal Sketches*, I., p. 217.) "*Betweenity* is still in daily use in Pennsylvania." (S. S. Haldeman.)

B'hoys, the name of young men in the city of New York who fill the streets with their noise, are prominent at the polls and at fires, and drive fast on Sundays on favorite roads leading out of town, often with their *g'hals* by their side. "The *b'hoy* is fast disappearing from among us, and the day is not far off, we apprehend, when the Bowery will know him no more." (New York *Home Journal*, June 17, 1868.)

Big Dog of the Tanyard is the name often given to an overbearing person who will allow no one else to speak or to differ from his views. The bold figure of speech is derived from the fact that tanyards are generally guarded by fierce bulldogs.

Big Figure, to do, or to go the big figure, denotes in the South mainly the venturing upon a great undertaking, the metaphor being taken from the game of poker, where players are said to *go* a certain figure. Hence also the phrase, "to go the *whole figure*." "When I saw that, I thought I might as well *go the big figure*, you see, and so I grabbed the bag; but mischief would have it, that just then the policeman grabbed me and took me to the caboose." (*Pickings from the Picayune*, p. 226.)

Biling (instead of *boiling*), the whole kit and biling, an expressive phrase, heard in the West, to designate the totality of persons or things. "At one time there was good reason to fear that *the whole kit and biling*, as our men invariably called our traps, would be swept away, but by a great effort they kept the boat upright, and, although thoroughly drenched, we saved everything." (*A Trip to the Rocky Mountains*, 1869.)

Bimeby, the popular contraction of by-and-by in New England, inherited, in all probability, from early settlers, who brought the word over from Somersetshire, where Halliwell quotes it as prevalent.

"When Ma *bimeby* upon 'em slips;
Huldy sot pale ez ashes."
(J. R. Lowell. *Courtin'*.)

Bit, a, in the sense of a little while. "If you'll wait *a bit*, I'll go with you."

Blazes, generally preceded by "like," is a euphemistic form for the lower regions. The term is as familiar to English ears as to ours, except, perhaps, in its occasional meaning of the Evil One.

"He looked, upon my word, like *Old Blazes* himself, with his clothing all on fire, and rage and despair in his face." (*Southern Literary Messenger*, June, 1849.)

Bloomer, the name of a lady, Mrs. Bloomer, who proposed to the ladies a costume which she herself wore, consisting of a very short dress with long and wide trousers, and a broad-brimmed hat. The costume, as well as the wearer of the costume, is called a *Bloomer*.

Blow, to, in the sense of boasting, is probably an Americanism. "You need not *blow* so, my friend, I don't believe a word of what you say." Hence also the noun *blower*, a braggart, with special reference to his success in imitating Baron Munchausen.

Blowth. Mr. Wright, in his *Dictionary of Obsolete and Provincial English*, explains it as meaning a blossom. With us a single blossom is a *blow*, while *blowth* means the blossoming in general. A farmer would say that there was a good *blowth* on the fruit-trees. The word retreats farther inland, and away from the railroads, year by year. (J. R. Lowell.) A *blow-out* is here, as in England, a great demonstration; a *blow-up*, a severe scolding. "He has a prompt alacrity at a *blow-out*, and has been skyed in a *blow-up*, two varieties of *blow* which frequently follow each other so closely as to be taken for cause and effect." (J. C. Neal, *Charcoal Sketches*.) The term *blow-up* is stated to be, in England, "now a recognized, respectable phrase." (*Slang Dictionary*, p. 77.) The American, fond of doing everything with unusual energy, likes to *blow-up sky-high*, an addition which makes it more probable that the phrase is originally a nautical one, and really borrowed from the *blowing-up* of a vessel, much as the meaning of the words must have evaporated before it reached the present stage.

Boat, in New England frequently pronounced *bŏat*, is one of a whole class of words with *oa* or *o*, which, in many parts of the Union, are pronounced with utter recklessness, now with an open and now with a close *o*. The Yankee is apt to make *oa* always short; the Southerner does the same with *oo*, and speaks of a *roŏt* and a *boŏt*. The extreme license in this matter is faithfully portrayed in O. W. Holmes' humorous lines:

> "Learning condemns beyond the reach of hope,
> The careless lips that speak of *soăp* for *soāp*;
> The edict exiles from her fair abode
> The clownish voice that utter *roăd* for *rōād*,

Less stern to him who calls his *cōăt* a *coăt*,
And steers his *bōăt*, believing it to be a *boăt*.
She pardoned one, our classic city's boast,
Who said at Cambridge *mŏst* instead of *mōst*,
But knit her brows and stamped her angry foot,
To hear a teacher call a *rōōt* a *roŏt*.
(*Urania*, 1846.)

Boatable, capable of being navigated by boats, originated in America, but proved so useful that it has found its way into English dictionaries. "The river is not *boatable* for several months in the summer." (E. A. Pollard, *Virginia*, 1870.)

Bob, to, around, to make frequent calls upon a number of friends, is probably as much English slang as American. "*Bobbing around*" is, however, a favorite expression in the United States.

Body, in the sense of person, often cited as American slang, may be slang, but has a good warrant in old English authors. Shakespeare says: "Unworthy *body* that I am;" and Hooker has, "A wise *body's* part it were to put out this fire." After that there seems to be no particular vulgarism in saying, "What can a *body* do under such circumstances but lie still and wait?"

Boggle, to, meaning to embarrass, is often used in the State of New York: "His affairs were found to be woefully *boggled*, and his creditors have little chance to recover anything." (Rochester *Democrat*, 1870.)

Bolt, to, for to rush, to escape, has made its way upward again, after having for generations served as a mere slang word, and is now nearly as respectable as when Dryden wrote: "I have reflected on those who, from time to time, have shot into the world, some *bolting* out on the stage with vast applause, and others hissed off." "Several of our contemporaries have announced it as a well-established fact, that Carl Schurz has *bolted* from the Republican party. We have the very best authority for denying the report." (St. Louis *Democrat*, April 3, 1871.)

Bones, one of the instruments used with great effect by so-called negro-minstrels, resembling castanets, but made of real bones. "To make no *bones*" of a man or a thing is old English slang, occurring already in Cotgrave; it originated with people living on the coast, who, eating fish in haste, say that they "*make no bones*."

Boohoo, to, a verb made from the noise which it represents, and coined by the witty Judge Haliburton, who, though not an American, is the father of a number of Americanisms. It is meant to express blubbering aloud, and answers the purpose. "When he heard that he was to be left behind, what do you think he did? He *boohooed* aloud, till we could bear it no longer." (*Sketches*, p. 132.)

Boost, to, in the sense of pushing or lifting one up a tree or a fence. J. R. Lowell uses it thus:

> "Whereas ole Abram 'd sink afore he'd let a darkie *boost* him."
> (*Biglow Papers*, II., 106.)

A negro-preacher in South Carolina made the following application of the word: "For, my bredderen, little Zaccheus was bound to see the Lord for once, dough he had to climb up de tree to do it. And how did he get up der tree? Ah, how did he get up der tree, my bredderen? Did he wait for some lazy nigger to bring him a ladder? Ah, no, my bredderen. Did he wait to be *boosted?* Ah, no, my bredderen. Not a *boost!* He climbed right straight up der tree hisself, like de possum, by his own hands and feet and de grace of God!" (T. A. Richards, *Rice-Fields of the South.*)

Both alike, a pleonasm arising from ignorance, but quite frequent in all the States.

Break-Bone Fever is the very expressive though vulgar name of a disease which, in the West Indies, is known as the *Dengue*, from a misapprehension of the English cant-term "Dandy Fever," which the Spaniards corrupted into Dengue. The rheumatism which causes the affection produces intense pain in all the bones of the body, and utterly exhausts the patient's strength, so that he literally feels as if "all his bones were broken," and hence the name.

Brickley, in the sense of *brittle*, is neither slang nor to be condemned as a corruption. From the German *brechlich* and the Scottish *brickle* the word could be legitimately derived, and T. Moore's "*brickle* earthen pots" are but a step behind the "*brickly* ware," which is met with in Southern writers. *Brittle* itself is curiously enough in Pennsylvania used when speaking of the weather, as a substitute for "fickle." "We have had *brickle* weather of late." (S. S. Haldeman.)

Britches is the almost universal pronunciation of *breeches* among the mass of the people.

Brown, to, is occasionally met with in the sense of to understand, and as such quoted as "American Slang" in the *Slang Dictionary* (p. 86). Its use is very rare, but the meaning is evidently connected with the familiar slang phrase, to *do a thing brown*, the figure being taken from the process of roasting, which is well done when the meat is well "browned."

Buck-party, like stag-party, denotes a company without ladies.

Bulger, from to *bulge* (French *bouger*), to swell out, is hence literally a *swell*, but in the United States generally designates anything very large. "That's a *bulger* of a story."

Bung-town, an imaginary town in New England, so called from the slang term to *bung*, meaning to lie. Hence, *Bung-town Copper* is a favorite name of the spurious English half-penny, which has no currency in the country. "These flowers wouldn't fetch a *bung-town* copper." (Judd, *Margaret*, p. 19.) It is said that such a coin was really once made—a counterfeit, of course—in a town then bearing the name of Bung-town, but since known as Rehoboth, in Massachusetts.

Bunk, connected with the Swedish word Bunke, and denoting a tub or a wooden case in taverns, which serves as a seat by day and as a bed at night, is thus derived in the same manner as the Scottish *bunker*, but in its shortened form peculiar to the United States. With their usual license, Americans use the term as a verb also, and sailors, especially, speak of *bunking*, when they go to their *bunks* to sleep. "I was too tired to work any more, and went to my *bunk* to sleep, but found it full of water." (J. H. Mayo, *Kaloolah*.)

Burglarize, to, a term creeping into journalism. "The Yankeeisms donated, collided, and *burglarized*, have been badly used up by an English magazine-writer." (*Southern Magazine*, April, 1871.) The word has a dangerous rival in the shorter *burgle*.

Bursted, a false participle from *burst*, is often used in the South to give emphasis to the word. "What has become of Dick Farish? He has *bursted* all to pieces." The more familiar slang phrase is to *bust*, and hence *buster*, in the sense of a reckless spree or frolic.

Buzzard is the half-facetious half-contemptuous term applied in several mechanical professions to a badly-spoiled piece of work. "Said the venerable Mr. G. to one of his jours: Sir, I pronounce that job an unmitigated *buzzard;* and, sir, promptly responded the jour, I pronounce it cut a *buzzard,* and, therefore, nothing else could be made of it." (Lancaster *Intelligencer,* May 6, 1871.)

By and again, instead of now and then, is peculiar to the South.

C.

Cabbage-head, a slang term for a fool, is used here as in England, where it is commonly explained as meaning "a soft-headed person."

> "For take my word for 't, when all's come an' past,
> The *cabbage-heads* 'll cair the day at last;
> Th' aint been a meetin' since the world begun,
> But they made (raw or bil'd ones) ten to one."
> (J. R. Lowell. *Biglow Papers,* II., p. 228.)

Cabbage designates in America as well as in Europe not only the well-known vegetable, but also the pieces of cloth purloined by dishonest tailors. They claim a noble ancestry for the usage, and state that it originated with no less a person than Sir Anthony Ashley. It is true that the latter was the first to introduce the cultivation of the close-hearted cabbage into England, and thus rendered his native country independent of Holland, from which heretofore the supply had been imported. It appears, however, that this "planter of cabbages" was also accused of having secured much loot during a command he held at Cadiz (also called Cales), in Spain, and especially by appropriating the jewels which a great lady had entrusted to his honor. Hence the well-known pun, that "Sir Anthony Ashley got more by Cales than by kale." On his monument at Wimborne, St. Giles, in Dorsetshire, England, a head of cabbage is sculptured, and the craft of tailors look back upon him as the author of the popular term. A somewhat ludicrous companion to the tailor's *cabbage* in America, is his *cold-slaw,* as he terms the smaller pieces of material which his skilful *crooking* enables him to save for his own use. The term is chosen in allusion to the fact that *cold-slaw* consists of finely-cut cabbage, thus representing the small remnants, which in other countries are known as "carpet-rags."

Caboodle, probably an enlargement of the word *boodle,* means, like the latter, crowd. "The whole *caboodle* came out and fell upon me, till I was as soft as a squash, and then they took me up for fighting." (New Orleans *Picayune*, February 23, 1858.)

Calibogus, quoted already by Grose as an "American beverage," is a mixture of rum and spruce-beer; the term is evidently made from *bogus*, a drink made of rum and ale. It is not unlikely that the French word *bagasse*, the refuse of sugar-cane, may be the common ancestor of this word as well as of the *bogus*, that is generally traced back to a Mr. Borghese; while the first part is the same used in *Calithump*, *Galli*nipper, and similar words. The latter term, often written

Callithump, seems, in like manner, to be of American origin. It represents the French *charivari*, the German *Katzenmusik*, and cannot be better described than in Butler's words:

> "One might distinguish different noise
> Of horns and pans, and dogs and boys,
> And kettle-drums, whose sullen dub
> Sounds like the hooping of a tub."
> (*Hudibras*, II., c. 2, v. 587.)

Camfire is the vulgar pronunciation of *camphor*, and not unfrequently found written as it is sounded.

Canacks, *Canucks*, and even *K'nucks*, are slang terms by which the Canadians are known in the United States and among themselves.

Can't come it, expressive of inability to do a thing, with a certain air of defiance inherent in the phrase. It may be noticed here that *cannot* (in one word) is universal in the Union, while in England *can not* (in two words) are used exclusively.

Cantankerous, in the sense of malicious and contentious, is used in America as in England, where even Mr. Thackeray speaks of "a *cantankerous* humor." The word was at one time regarded as an American corruption of *contentious*, but more careful investigations have traced it back to an Anglo-Norman word *contek*, cited by Bailey as "*conteke*, contentious, Spenserian," by the side of "old English *contekors*, quarrelsome persons." Halliwell has "*contankerous*, quarrelsome, West of England."

Carlicues, frequently written *curlicues*, and evidently derived from *curl* and *curly*, designates fantastic ornaments worn on a person or used in architecture. The second part of the word has been explained as *queue, cue,* so that it would literally mean *curly queues,* as vignette means little vine; but *cues* may be a mere fanciful termination, such as is often added to words of this class. "Architects have a wonderful predilection for all manner of *curly-cues* and breaks in your roof." (*Home Journal,* July 24, 1858.)

Carry on, to, to riot or frolic, is perhaps a phrase borrowed from a nautical term to *carry on sail.* The verb, as well as the noun made from it, *carryings-on,* is found in old English authors, and Butler has even the modern Yankee pronunciation already in his line—

"To which these *carr'ings-on* did tend."

"Such *carryings-on,* as the old Christmas-frolicking is called in Virginia, might be a heresy in Puritan eyes, but were entered into with such heartiness and simplicity by old and young, that I felt twenty years younger as I found myself playing blindman's-buff with half a dozen rosy children." (J. P. Kennedy.)

Case, a, designating persons objectionable for some reason or other, has its origin probably in the newspaper reports, where they are mentioned as "a case" of drunkenness, etc. "He is *a case,* I tell you, and no mistake."

Cashunk, with a very slight and indistinct sound of the first syllable, is an exclamation, imitative of a sudden noise, like *thump,* largely used in New England and the South and West. A purely onomatopoetic word, without original meaning, it has hence but a very uncertain form, and reappears, a very Proteus, in an almost endless variety of sounds and spellings. New England has *keshonk* and *keshwosh,* the West, *kerchug, kewosh,* and *cashwash. Keswollop* and *kewhollux,* known in England, are rare in America.

Catawampous, or *catawamptious,* a word enlarged in the West from *catamount.* This animal had already furnished the hunter with the expressive phrase, "he dropped on him like a *catamount* on a coon," and hence, no doubt, the further development of the word. "He was *catawamptiously* chawed up," was said of a political character, who had been fiercely attacked by a host of adversaries in the Legislature of Missouri; and even orators of greater pretension, addressing a body of national representatives, have not disdained to use the phrase. To *chaw up,* for demolish, is also used without such energetic qualification, and occasionally applied to one's own words, for the common term to *eat.* "I'll make you *chaw up* them words as quick as lightning, an' you don't stop instanly." (Longstreet, *Georgia Scenes.*)

Choke off, to, has of late become a favorite slang phrase of politicians to denote the forcible ending of a debate. The phrase is said to be worthily derived from the process of *choking* a bull-dog, who can by no other means be induced to let go his hold; and as the opposition is apt to try and make up by pertinacity what it lacks in power, the same means are sometimes used to enforce silence. "As usual, the call for the previous question was heard on the other side, and the members who had hoped to be heard on the momentous question were *choked off* by Republican courtesy." (Baltimore *Sun,* March 9, 1870.)

Cider appears frequently in political slang, and especially in the popular phrase, *All talk and no cider*, which is but another version of *Vox et praeterea nihil.* It is stated to have originated at a party in Bucks County, Pennsylvania, which had assembled to drink a barrel of superior cider; but politics being introduced, speeches were made, and discussion ensued, till some malcontents withdrew on the plea that it was a trap into which they had been lured, politics and not pleasure being the purpose of the meeting, or, as they called it, *All talk and no cider!*

Clean, in the phrase the *clean thing*, means the right, proper course to pursue. Bailey already quotes *clean* in such combination as meaning, "pure, free from moral impurity, guiltless," and this it still represents. "It would have been the *clean thing* to say at once that no debate would be allowed, instead of professing a readiness to go into debate, and then to refuse discussion." (Washington *Patriot,* April 3, 1871.)

Clear, to clear out, a phrase probably derived from Western usage, in speaking of the trees which have to be *cleared out* in order to afford room for a settlement, is now generally used for to disappear, go away. "You'll have to *clear out*, and that pretty quick, or I'll be after you with a sharp stick." (*Harper's Monthly*, August, 1861.)

Cocked hat, to knock into, a favorite phrase, denoting more or less complete destruction, from the habit which reckless rowdies have to knock the hats of unoffending persons into a shapeless mass, which is sneeringly called a "cocked hat," a process not unfrequently seen even in the Gold-Room of New York. "Although it took little more *to knock* Fort Sumter *into a cocked hat*, yet as the walls fell, and the bricks got pounded into dust, they covered the lower casemates with such a mass of débris as materially increased their strength." (E. A. Pollard, *The Lost Cause.*)

Come, to, serves for a number of slang phrases, most of which are, however, of English origin, and present no peculiarity of meaning connecting them with this country. To *come off* and to *come to time*, are both derived from the slang of the ring and the cockpit. To *come down*, in commercial parlance, means to reduce prices, and such an abatement is soberly announced in the newspapers as a "Tremendous *Coming Down*." To *come over* or *come it over* a person, means to get the better of a person by superiority of argument, while to *come around* him, means to persuade him by coaxing or wheedling. Colonel Ethan Allen, when a prisoner in England, asked for leave to send a letter to the "Illustrious Continental Congress," and was told that it had been sent to Lord North instead. "This," says Allen, "gave me inward satisfaction, though I carefully concealed it with a pretended resentment, for I found I had *come Yankee over him*, and that the letter had gone to the identical person I had designed it for."

Come-outers, is not only the name of a religious sect, numerous in New England, but a cant term for all who are said to have *come out* from some organized society. Thus it was recently said that "Brigham Young keeps up his 'religion,' with its many revolting and ridiculous absurdities, by sheer force of personal will. Up to the present time, the Mormon perverts had nowhere to go, nobody to sympathize with them, and no social status. With plenty of 'Gentiles' to keep them in countenance, trade with them, pray with them, protect them, the *come-outers* will increase rapidly." (New York *Tribune*, May 2, 1871.)

Concerned, in New England always pronounced *consarned*, is a popular euphemism for "damned." "That's a *concerned* ugly fix, and how we'll ever get out of it is more than I know." (*Southern Literary Messenger*, March, 1851.)

Condeript is of the same manufacture, limited to Kentucky, and meaning, thrown into fits.

Contraptions, a purely fictitious word, denoting new and peculiar things. "For my part, I can't say as how I see what's to be the end of all them new-fangled *contraptions*." (J. C. Neal, *Charcoal Sketches*.)

Cord, in the West, designates any large quantity, and not only a cord of wood. "There is a whole *cord* of fixings in the kitchen."

Cowlick, a peculiar arrangement of the hair, which to fanciful men suggests the smooth and glossy appearance of a place licked by a cow. "If it becomes distinctly apparent that the interests of the government will be subserved by our ministers combing their hair behind their ears, tousling it in picturesque dishevelment about the temples, or indulging the vain ostentation of a *cowlick*, we shall then ponder the matter with deliberation." (New York *Tribune*, February 15, 1871.)

Crack up, to, is old English, though now vulgar slang. It is generally used in the phrase, such and such a thing is not what it was *cracked up* to be, meaning, what it was boastfully represented to be.

Crook, to, viz., the elbow, is one of the many slang terms for drinking. *Crook* is, however, a far more important word in the noble art of tailoring. There, we are told by a master of the craft, "*crook* occupies the same position that a *boss* does to any other mechanical calling. But the term of *crook* has, more directly, reference to a garment *cutter*, than to an employer, or a mere conductor of the tailoring business. There is a unity, an individuality, and a dignity about the name of *crook*, which the tailor claims as peculiarly his own, and with this term is associated a distinctive meaning." (S. S. Rathvon, Lancaster *Intelligencer*, May 6, 1871.)

Crooked as a Virginia fence, denotes matters or persons which it is difficult to keep straight. The Virginia fence, also known as "snake fence," forms a zigzag of rails, which follow the inequalities of the soil, and hence is apt to be exceedingly crooked in every aspect.

Crowd is a common term used to denote a company, of whatever size it may happen to be, frequently heard in the South and West. "Was there any one in the *crowd* last night, I knew?" "When I entered the church, there were very few people there yet, and not one Methodist in the *crowd* as far as I could judge." (Rev. P. Cartwright, *Autobiography*, p. 321.)

Cut, to, enters, like *go* and *come*, into a number of slang phrases, the majority of which are, however, well-known English. Only a few have an American flavor about them, though often quite unsavory. To *cut dirt*, for running away in haste, is evidently taken from the fondness of Americans for fast driving. "Now you *cut dirt*, and don't let me see you here again for a coon's age, you hear!" (*Western Scenes.*) To *cut a swathe*, in the sense of cutting a dash, is evidently Western, and taken from the ambition of powerful, well-trained mowers to cut the widest swathe. To *cut one's stick*, used in England instead of to leave, has been enlarged in its meaning by American vigor of speech, and here often means to die. "I'm blowed if he *cut stick*." (N. Hawthorne.)

D.

Daddyism, a recent word made to represent the respect paid to good family and honorable descent. "An Eastern man commending the services of a young Philadelphian to a Chicago tradesman, said: 'He comes of a very good family; his grandfather was a distinguished man.' 'Was he?' replied the man of Chicago. 'That's of no account with us. There's less *daddyism* here than in any part of the United States. What's he himself?'" (Kate Field, *Harper's Bazar*, August, 1871.)

Darky, a former name of the freedman, in picturesque allusion to his color, and quite as familiar to Englishmen as to Americans. His recent fate has been such as to show one of the most remarkable fulfillments of men's wishes ever known to history. Not twenty years ago, a favorite negro-minstrel's song ran thus:

"I wish de legislatur' would set dis *darkie* free,
Oh! what a happy place den de *darkie* land would be;
We'd have a *darkie* parliament
An' *darkie* codes of law,
An' *darkie* judges on the bench,
Darkie barristers and *aw*,"

and to-day the *darkie's* wishes are fulfilled to the letter.

Darn and *darnation*, said to be American inventions, and with their superfluous *r* betraying Southern manufacture, belong to that painfully numerous class of half-veiled blasphemies which abound in all parts of the United States and in all classes of society. The honest *damn* is rarely heard, it is true, but, "fearful of committing an open profanity, yet nibbling slyly at the sin," men indulge in countless hypocritical evasions. *Darn, durn,* and *dang,* all but thinly disguised *damns,* appear far more vulgar than the open oath. It has been well said, that such slang terms are but a "whipping the devil round the stump," by persons who desire to enjoy the sweets of wickedness and yet to escape the penalty. The devil is in like manner concealed behind the *deuce* (stated by Junius and others to be from *deus*), and the *dickens,* Old *Nick,* Old *Harry,* Old *Scratch,* and Old *Splitfoot.* The Yankee is peculiarly fertile in variations on the name of God, and gives a striking proof of his ingenuity in inventing new forms for the forbidden *I swear.* He has his by *Gorram,* by *Goldam,* and by *Goshdang,* by the side of the English oath by *Golly,* which occurs as early as 1743. "The first person consulted a gentleman-farmer, and declared that he never read anything so good in his life. "'*By Golly,*' says he, 'he 'as mauled the parsons.'" (*Five Arguments against Tythes.* London, W. Warren.) It is popular also among the negroes in the South, like the mysterious by *Gum.* "In the United States," says a recent writer in England, "small boys are permitted by their guardians to say *Goldam* to anything, but they are on no account allowed the profanity of G—d—g anything. An effective ejaculation and moral waste-pipe for interior passion or wrath is seen in the exclamation, *By the Ever-Living Jumping Moses*—a harmless phrase, that for its length expends a considerable quantity of fiery anger." (*Slang Dictionary,* p. 92.) He has, in like manner, his *I swan, I swad, I swow, I swamp,* and *I vum,* for I swear, and I vow, and a number of other slang make-shifts for oaths, and sham exclamations for passion and temper. The old Puritan laws of New England, which made swearing not only a sin, but a crime against the commonwealth, have evidently left their marks on the expletives of the present generation even. Men seem still to remember the day when "Joseph Shorthose, for profane swearing, was sentenced to have his tongue fixed in a cleft stick, and so to continue for the space of half an hour." (Hutchinson, *History of Massachusetts,* p. 436.) It is a grave question whether this impression, surviving after so many generations, has a beneficial effect, in driving the descendants of the virtuous old settlers to such shifts to find substitutes for the objectionable words. In form, they are a disgrace to our speech; in sentiment, hardly an evidence of greater freedom from national profanity.

Darsent, a vile corruption of *dare not* (dares not) in all persons of the verb. The term has evidently originated in the South, perhaps with the negroes, who are fond of saying, "I dares not."

Dead, added to other adverbs in the sense of *utterly*, is so very common in England, from *dead beat* to *dead alive*, that it cannot be looked upon as an Americanism, except in its universal popularity. Even H. W. Longfellow, in his translation of Dante, where the poet describes his weariness of climbing, and says that but for the shortness of one ascent he had well-nigh overcome, "*io sarei ben vinto*," renders it thus: "I would be *dead beat*." Among new combinations for which the United States may, perhaps, be credited, is the phrase *dead broke*, for utterly ruined.

Dear me, also, is a purely English phrase, recently traced back to enthusiastic travellers who tried to imitate the Italian *Dio mio!* and thus produced the peculiar ejaculation. (?)

Death is dragged in by slang to denote the last extremity in everything. *To be death on anything* means to be completely master of it, or at least a capital hand at it, like the quack who advertises in the daily papers that his "Ready Relief is *death* on all pulmonary diseases," as it very likely is. It may, however, also mean to love passionately, in which sense it is used in Sam Slick: "Your friend Silas *is death on* sherry and gin-slings, and Sally on lace, and old Aunt Thankful goes the whole figure for furs." To *dress to death* suggests clothes cut in the very extreme of splendor or fashion, perhaps because they are intended to be *killing*. "The next day I met Davis and Nye, my two chums on board the Little Rhody, *dressed to death* and trunk empty, as they said of themselves." (*Newfoundland Fisheries*, 1869.) To *dress up drunk*, and to *dress to kill*, appear, after that, but attenuated versions.

Dicker, to, in the sense of bartering or chaffering, is a genuine Americanism, though the word itself may be easily traced back to the French *dix*, ten, and the old English noun *dicker*, derived from it, and also representing the number of *ten*.

"When selfish thrift and party held the scales,
For peddling *dicker*, not for honest sales,
Whom shall we strike?"
(J. G. Whittier. *The Panorama.*)

Dig, in college slang, represents a hard-working student, who is supposed to *dig* deep into his books, as opposed to the superficial reader.

Dike, denoting a man in full dress, or merely the dress, is a peculiar American cant term, as yet unexplained. To be *out on a dike* is said of persons, mainly young men, who are dressed more carefully than usual, in order to pay visits or to attend a party. It is not unlikely that the term is merely a corruption of the obsolete *dight*, which meant *decked out*, and is in this sense used by many old English writers.

Ding and *dinged* belong both to the class of faintly-disguised oaths, and are peculiar to the South.

Docious and *docity*, pronounced *dossity*, are substitutes for docile and docility, in daily use in the South; the latter generally qualified by a negative, as, he has no *docity*, in which sense it is not unknown in England also.

Dod, for God, common especially in New England and the South, and generally used in connection with some equally vulgar form, as, *Dod*rot or *Dod*fetched.

Dog plays a very prominent part in American slang, from the verb to *dog*, in the sense of following a person like a bloodhound, to *doggery*, a grogshop; but almost all the phrases in which the word appears have been imported from England. *Sick as a dog* is not as common here as abroad, the phrase being replaced by *sick as a cat*, while to "vomit as a cat" is said to have as little reference to the animal as *dog-cheap* has (Latham, *English Language*), but to mean throwing up like a *cat*aract, which, if true, would be quite American in its proportions. *Doggone* or *doggoned* is also, in all probability, original with us, and mainly used in the South. "I'll be *doggone* if you ever pick a pound of cotton." (*Putnam's Magazine*, July, 1868.) In California it is gracefully embellished by an addition, being expanded into *doggon'd cuss*.

Doin', instead of *doing*, is universal in most of the New England States to denote the state of the roads. How are the roads? is the question in Virginia and the Southern States generally; while in New York it is, How is travelling? in Massachusetts and Connecticut, How is the going? In the West the word *doing* is generally used in the plural, and qualified by an adjective, as in the case of *great doings*, which denotes high feasting or solemn ceremonies. "*Hard doings* when it comes to that—seeing a horse's tail eaten up by the mules, in the days of strait." (*Life in the Far West.*)

Done, instead of *did*, is one of the most common vulgarisms of the United States. "Who now *done* that?" But the main peculiarity of the word is its constant addition to every other verb used in the past tense, not only by the negroes of the South universally, but also by all but the best-educated whites. "I *done* do all you said I must do." "He *done* gone long ago." "When I awoke in the morning, refreshed and re-invigorated, I asked for my friend. 'He *done* come down early,' was the laughing reply of Jupiter, who had burnished my boots till they shone as bright as his ebony face." (*Letters from the South.*) To be *done* means, here as in England, to be cheated; but *done* is, in this sense also, used instead of *did* in both countries. "I *done* him," meaning I cheated him, or I paid him out. (*Slang Dictionary*, p. 121.)

Do tell, a cant phrase of New England, which occupies there the ground held in the South by, You don't say so, and expressive of surprise and wonder. An account of anything remarkable that has happened is received by the astonished Yankee with an emphatic *Do tell!* and if this should tempt the inexperienced narrator to repeat the story, he will be instantly rewarded by a second *do tell*. *Do*, as a noun, flourishes in America as well as in England, and even enjoys a far more extended usefulness here. "There is a *do* for you," means, there is noise and confusion enough for you. "Well, I must make a *do* of potatoes for supper, with a bit of pie and a mouthful of cake." (*Atlantic Magazine*, March, 1870.) Nor is the familiar phrase to *do* brown unknown in the Union, where meat is but rarely roasted on the spit, but generally cooked, and then simply *browned* before the fire.

"And some of the greenhorns
Resolved upon flight,
And vamosed the ranch
In a desperate plight;

While those who succeeded
In reaching the town,
Confessed they were *done*
Most exceedingly *brown*."
(*Harper's Monthly*, January, 1854.)

Thus the old phrase has safely passed down through a hundred generations, from Piers the Plowman, who is the first writer known to have used it, to the miners in California.

Donock or *don nock*, used to denote a stone, by J. R. Bartlett cited as almost peculiar to Arkansas, occurs throughout the Southwest, and is probably nothing more than a corruption of *doughnut*, humorously applied to a "rock."

"Then shape me out two little *donocks*,
Place one at my head and my toe,
And do not forget to scratch on it
The name of Old Rosin the Bow."
(*Song of Old Rosin the Bow* (alias Beau).)

It is not altogether out of question, however, that the word may have come down to us from the Gaelic doirneag, Irish doirneog, a stone of convenient size for throwing.

Don't, quite admissible, it seems, into good society, since the best of our writers employ it unhesitatingly, is still objectionable slang when connected with the third person, thus changing *does* into do. "He *don't* tell the truth." As the New Englander invariably says *doos* for *does*, he is not so likely to commit this blunder.

Doted is, in the South and West, not limited to persons who are in their dotage, but applied also to lifeless things. Thus, *doted* wood is rotten wood, and *doted* things are spoiled.

Drab-colored gentlemen are Quakers, in vulgar parlance, here as in England.

Drat, a corruption—if such it can be called—of *Dodrot*, takes, in the United States, the place of the English *Drabbit*, which is but rarely heard here. The latter is cited by Grose as "a vulgar exclamation, an abbreviation of *God rabbit it*, a foolish evasion of an oath." From *drat* Americans have derived the epithet *dratted*. "This is a *dratted* piece of business, and I wish we were safely out of it." (Judge Longstreet, *Georgia Scenes*.)

Draw a straight furrow, to, a figure evidently taken from rural pursuits, means to walk in paths of rectitude and live uprightly.

> "Governor B. is a sensible man,
> He stays to his home and looks arter his folks,
> He *draws his furrows as straight* as he can."
> (J. R. Lowell. *Biglow Papers.*)

Drink, in Western slang, is often used to designate a river or a pond, and the Mississippi thus appears quite frequently as the Big *Drink*. It is curious to notice the similar use made of the word by Shakespeare, when he says of Ophelia—

> "Till that her garments, heavy with her *drinke*,
> Pul'd the poor wretch . . . .
> To muddy death."

Drudge, another name for raw whiskey, originating in the Eastern States. "I doubt whether the word *drudge* is thirty years old." (S. S. Haldeman.)

Drunk, used as a noun, takes in the West frequently the place of spree or debauch. "It seems that Gamble went on a *drunk* last Monday evening and was arrested." (Philadelphia *Inquirer*, July 6, 1871.

Dubersome has been made in America from the English corruption *duberous*, used instead of *dubious*. It expresses, however, not the doubtful fact, but only the uncertain state of mind. "He was a *dubersome* man, who always meant well, but always hesitated between two opinions." (Mrs. H. B. Stowe.)

Dumfoundered, the Scottish form, is, in America, generally preferred to the English form *dumfounded*.

Dunnow'z, (do not know as) *I know*, says J. R. Lowell, "is the nearest your true Yankee ever comes to acknowledging ignorance."

E.

E'en a'most, for *even almost*, but meaning nothing more than *almost*, is a cant word peculiar to New England. "I thought I'd *e'en a'most* drop down dead on the spot, when Martha come in." (*Putnam's Magazine*, June, 1869.)

Elephant, to see the, a slang term taken from wandering menageries, in which the elephant generally closes the exhibition, as the most attractive feature of the show. Hence the phrase means to have seen all and to know everything, and is now as current in England as in America.

Everlasting, instead of very, exceeding. "What an *everlasting* great city this is!" (Mark Twain.)

Expect, to, is ludicrously used with the past tense, and yet countless well-educated people, who employ it so, appear utterly unconscious of the incompatibility, and say, "I *expect* it *was* really so."

Eye, all *in your*—a phrase expressive of utter unbelief in an account related by another. "That's all *in your eye*, I don't believe there's an Indian within a hundred miles of camp." (*Western Scenes.*)

F.

Face the music, to, a slang phrase, derived, according to J. F. Cooper, from the stage, and used by actors in the green-room, when they are nervously preparing to go on the boards and literally *face the music*. Another explanation traces it back to militia musters, where every man is expected to appear fully equipped and armed, when in rank and file, *facing the music*. The meaning of the phrase is, generally, to show one's hand, though it is often used as a summons to pay the bill. "Rabelais' unpleasant 'quarter' is by our more picturesque people called *facing the music*." (J. F. Cooper.)

Fair shake, a local vulgarism in some parts of New England for a fair trade.

Fair off, to, is said in the South when *fair* weather sets in and the sky is clearing. "I think it'll *fair off* before morning."

Farziner, a violent corruption of as *far as I know*, throughout New England and in parts of New York, but confined to the most ignorant classes, and rapidly disappearing.

Fellow-countrymen, a word often heard in public addresses, is only an apparent pleonasm, since in England, for instance, the term *countryman* indicates merely the common native land, but by no means social fellowship, while the republican equality which prevails in the United States, creates a new bond between all citizens, and makes them literally *fellow-countrymen*.

Few, a, in slang means *a little*. "Were you alarmed? No, but I was astonished *a few*." It is in this case synonymous with *rather*, which is used more frequently in the South. J. R. Lowell, in his enthusiastic attempts to vindicate Yankeeisms, traces *a few* back to the French *un peu*. (*Preface to Biglow Papers*, xxiv.)

Found, instead of *fined*, is an unpardonable blunder, and not mere slang.

First-rate, like *first-class*, is borrowed from mercantile pursuits, where goods and ships are *rated* and valued accordingly. In the United States *first-rate* alone is used by the mass of the people, and with unbounded license, even where no rating is possible. A man, asked how he feels, is quite ready to reply, "Oh, *first-rate!*" The Rev. P. Cartwright wrote: "The man had a *first-rate* wife and several interesting daughters, and, I will not forget to say, had some three hundred dollars hoarded up." (*Autobiography*, p. 251.) J. R. Lowell informs us that the Yankee increases the efficacy of the phrase by saying, "*first-rate* and a half." In the West a new form has been given to the phrase, by substituting *swathe* for rate. "She was a *first-swathe* gal, if ever there was one in our village, and the way she made the money fly, when she came to town to shop!" (*Western Scenes.*)

Fits, by their suddenness and painful violence, seem to have been regarded as a welcome slang term to form several expressions. *By fits and starts* means, of course, only by short and sudden intervals, as a *fit* is often used to express simply a short space of time. But *to give one fits*, or, as emphatic Yankees say, to give one *very particular fits*, suggests such severe punishment as will produce fits. "The man ran after the thievish Indian, and the corporal cried out to him to *give him fits* if he caught him; they seemed to be bent upon making an end, once for all, to the petty thefts by which we had been annoyed in camp." (G. W. Kendall, *Santa Fé Expedition.*)

Flambustious, a fictitious word made from *flam*, a lie, denotes something great and showy. "We will have a *flambustious* time." (*Putnam's Magazine*, January, 1868.)

Flat, to, in the West, means to jilt, and is probably derived from another slang phrase, to feel *flat*, denoting the depression which is apt to follow such a disappointment. "Not to hurt a gentleman's feelings and to make him *feel flat* afore the country." (J. C. Neal, *Charcoal Sketches.*) The same word enters into the phrase *flat broke*, meaning the same as "dead broke," from the idea of being so broken as to lie flat on the ground; while *to flat out* means simply to fail, or in other words not to stand.

Flummux, to, a slang term used in England in the sense of to hinder, to perplex, denotes in America the giving up of a purpose, and even to die. "We regularly *flummuxed,* and after that dared not say a word to our Mexican guards." (*Life of General Houston.*) In Arkansas the term is supplied by one of still more extraordinary form: a person who is "played out," as is said elsewhere, is there reported to be *flipfloppussed.* (Chicago *Evening Post,* February 27, 1871.) This quaint word is probably derived from the (English) slang term to *flop* down, which means, to fall suddenly, to collapse, both in the literal and the figurative sense of the phrase.

Flunky, in college parlance, means the man who backs out from recitation or examination for fear of failure; while in the slang of Wall-street it denotes the unlucky outsider who ventures to speculate in stocks without the necessary knowledge of monetary matters.

Fly, instead of *flee,* is so common as hardly to be observed in conversation, and even in the pulpit the warning is frequently heard: "*Fly* from temptation." To *fly around* is a familiar expression for making haste and being quick at some pressing work.

For short, a cant phrase, meaning "for brevity's sake," often very curiously misapplied, as in the lines, "My little gal's name is Helen, but we call her Heelen *for short.*" (Washington, *Watchman,* 1870.)

Fouty is used in Pennsylvania for trifling—the term being probably derived from the obsolete English word *fouter,* a despicable fellow, so quoted by Brockett.

Frills denotes, in California and the West generally, any assumption of style: "I can't bear his talk, it's all *frills.*" (Sacramento paper, 1870.)

Funk, to, and to *funkify,* the former of which means in England to be in great fear, are both in America used to express backing out from great fear, very much in the same way as to *flunk.* The metaphor is taken from the meaning of "smoking out," which is given to *funking* in the North of England—*funk* being a provincial name for a small, smoking fire, etymologically connected with the German *Funke.*

Furr is the Yankee's pronunciation of *far.*

G.

Galoot, a Southwestern expression of unknown parentage:

> "I'll hold her nozzle agin the bank,
> Till the last *galoot's* ashore."
> (John Hay. *Jim Bludsoe of the Prairie Belle.*)

Gambolling, a common corruption of *gambling*, as *gamboller* is of *gambler*. "No honest people wear beard onto their upper lip; I would not be surprised if he wasn't a *gamboller*." (*Lippincott's Magazine*, March, 1871, p. 286.)

Gauley, by, a Yankee oath.

Gawnicus, a fictitious word, manufactured in New England, and denoting a dolt—possibly an enlargement of *gawk*.

Gimbal-jawed, often corrupted into *gimber-jawed*, is used to denote a person whose lower jaw is apparently out of joint, projecting beyond the upper, and moving with unusual freedom. The phrase is taken from *gimbal*, a mechanical contrivance to secure free motion in suspension, such as supports a chronometer on board ship.

Git, and *git out*, is the uniform pronunciation of *get* among the people of the West. In California, near the town of Henroost Camp, is another settlement called *Git up and Git*.

Go, to, furnishes almost as many slang phrases as *to do*, but few of these also can claim an American origin. Among the latter is *to go by*, which utterly puzzles foreigners at first. In travelling through Virginia and most of the Southern States, nothing is more common than to be asked by the hospitable planters to *go by* and dine, or spend the night with them. Abroad the invitation would be taken literally to mean, not to stop, but to go by or on. In the South it means to leave the public road, go into the plantation, and take the road *by* the owner's house. Neighbors, therefore, coming from church together, will stop at their gates and invite each other to "*go by* and stop for dinner." Of all phrases formed by the aid of this verb none is perhaps more universally known than the American's watchword: *Go ahead!* Its origin is stated thus: David Crockett, a man of great originality and vigor of mind, was sent in 1830 from the young State of Kentucky to Washington as a member of Congress. Among his eccentric sayings, for which he had already then become famous, was that of, "Be sure you're right and then *go ahead*," which, with the aid of, "I leave this motto when I'm dead," was converted into a distich, of which he was probably not the author. This caused, however, the phrase *go ahead* to become extremely popular, and it soon spread abroad, becoming at once the representative of American nationality and of every kind of bold progress. Thus a Parisian candidate for the National Assembly, in the month of April, 1871, said in a card addressed to the voters, "Citoyens, je suis le représentant du *go ahead*." It soon became, moreover, the basis of new words, and thus were manufactured *goaheaditiveness*, first used August 4, 1860, and *goaheadifying*, used February 16, 1861, both made by N. P. Willis, and *goaheadness*, first printed in a Liverpool paper in 1862. One of the most recent slang phrases made by the aid of *go* has become surprisingly popular, and made its way into the pages of careful writers even. This is *going back* on somebody, which means to abandon him, to disappoint his just expectations. At a public dinner in New York, it is stated, "General Howard, being called on for a toast, took a glass of water in his hand and said: Gentlemen, I am from the State of Maine. I don't *go back* on my State. I give you, gentlemen, the Maine Law, the true beverage of the soldier." (August, 1865.)

> "Of all sharp cuts the sharpest,
> Of all mean turns the meanest,
> Vilest of all vile jobs,
> Worse than the Cowboy pillagers
> Are these Dobbs' Ferry villagers,
> A *going back* on Dobbs!
> 't wouldn't be more anom'lous,
> If Rome *went back* on Rom'lus!"
>
> (Dobbs His Ferry. *Putnam's Magazine*, January, 1868.)

To go and to *go it* is common gamblers' slang, as much English as American; to *go it strong* is probably strong American. But *to go through* a man is new; it means to overhaul him, and either to strip him literally of all his valuables, or to expose his political treachery, or any other weakness of which he may be guilty. "He was garroted, and the two robbers *went through* him before the police could reach the spot." (Baltimore *Sun*, November

13, 1869.) "It was a grand sight to see Farnsworth *go through* him; he did not leave him a single leg to stand upon." (*Ibidem*, April, 1871.) To *go the whole hog* is a slang phrase, well known in England and exceedingly popular in the West, which has sorely puzzled antiquarians. Some seek its source in the fact that in vernacular English *hog* was for many centuries the name of a piece of money; first of a shilling or six pence, as Halliwell states, and now of a five shilling-piece in England, but only of a shilling in Ireland. It is but fair to presume that one gambler would *go*, as their slang suggests, a shilling, another half a crown, and a third would say, "I'll *go the whole hog*," the whole piece of five shillings. Another explanation is suggested by the fact that the collections of coin-dealers contain numbers of large silver coins, on which the figure of a *hog* was stamped. These coins were frequently crossed deeply on the reverse for the convenience of breaking them into two or four pieces (fourth thing=farthing) should the bargain require it, and the parties have no small change. Persons who were willing to spend the whole coin would very naturally say, "I'll *go the whole hog.*" Either of these derivations is more probable than the suggestion made recently that *hog* might be, not the name of the animal, but an abbreviation of the Jewish word *hoger*, a ducat. "I told him that if he wanted to try politics, he might just as well go *the whole hog* and run for Congress, instead of peddling small-wares, and trying to be sent to the Legislature." (New York *Ledger*, July, 1870.) To go the whole *animal* is a frequent substitute in the West, while in the West Indies the phrase is changed into *going the whole dog*. *Go*, as a noun, has the meaning of strength or capacity, as in England. "I don't believe you have *go* enough in you to make much of a tyrant." (*Putnam's Magazine*, September, 1870.) *Goner* is the slang term for a ruined person, a politician, a merchant, or even "an official who is *gone*, done for, finished." "Those who acted with us in 1869, and who have since gone off, will not return at the call of a convention, be it called Conservative, Democrat, or Republican. The few who have departed are *goners*. The clover was not luxuriant on our side of the fence, whilst it stood rank and inviting, in the way of Federal offices, on the other." (Fredericksburg *Herald*, December 29, 1870.) In the West, where the picturesque element always prevails over classic simplicity, *goner* is deemed too tame, and improved into *gone goose*, *gone gander*, or *gone coon*. Western mountaineers say of an invalid hunter, who can no longer "hunt for meat," that he is a *gone beaver*.

Gonoff, a corruption of the old English *gnoff* (by Dickens revived as *gonoph*), denotes a bungler at cheating. The idea is probably that he is *gone off* the right way, and thus has failed to accomplish his end. The term itself is as old as Chaucer, and in the reign of Edward VI. some insurgents had a song—

> "The country *gnoffes*, Hob, Dick, and Hick,
> With clubbes and clouted shoon,
> Shall fill up Dussin Dale
> With slaughtered bodies soone."
>
> (*Slang Dictionary*, p. 145.)

Gosh, by, a euphemistic oath.

Gotham and *Gothamites* are cant terms applied to the city of New York and its inhabitants, with a sly satirical acknowledgment of their superior wisdom. English readers know the renown of the town of *Gotham* in Northamptonshire, England, whose wise men attempted to hedge in the cuckoo. At Court Hill, in the parish of Gotham, a bush still bears the name of Cuckoo Bush, and more than one pleasant volume has been written on the blunders of the good people of the borough. Hence a *Gothamite*, in England, means a simple fellow. In America, W. Irving first applied the epithet to the Empire City, which has never been able to shake it off.

Gownd, a common corruption of *gown*, from a false analogy with ground, pound, sound, etc. In like manner the verb to *foal*, has, in Virginia and the South generally, a preterite, *foalded*, whence a gentleman who had remarked to a friend that his mare had *foalded* that morning, was told that it would have been more correct to say, she had *unfolded*.

Grandacious and *grandiferous*, mere fictitious words, which have no real existence in the language.

Gum, by, and *Gummy*, are again euphemistic oaths, mainly heard in the New England States.

Gwine, instead of *going*, is the uniform pronunciation of the negroes in the South. "I ain't a *gwine* do no such thing!"

H.

Hadn't ought, an utterly inexcusable combination of the two verbs, standing for "ought not to have," is, nevertheless, common in all parts of the Union among the uneducated. "You *hadn't ought* say a word about it, mister, and it wouldn't have been no difference to me after all." (*The Land We Love,* January, 1870.) Frequently the term is embellished by an addition, and appears in full vulgarity as *hadn't oughter,* the appendix being a faint echo of the *to* which is apt to follow the ill-treated verb.

Haines, my name is, a slang phrase used to express, I must be off, I am going at once—originated in an incident in the life of President Jefferson, and is still in use.

Hain't, instead of *have not,* common throughout New England.

Hard row to hoe, a very expressive figure of speech, taken from the cultivation of Indian corn, in which every row of plants has to be hoed or worked more than once. "You'll find courting Sallie a pretty *hard row to hoe,* and when you have got her, it's likely you'll wish you had never taken the job." (*The Hunter and the Squatter,* p. 217.) To *hoe one's own row* is an admonition, equal to minding one's own business. "Now that I have *hoed my own row* and rumor gives me a false condition, they deluge me with congratulations." (Prentice Mulford, San Francisco *Chronicle,* 1871.)

Hard-up, a nautical term expressive of distress, has found its way through English sailors to this country, and fairly divides popular favor with *hard-run* and *hard-pushed,* which have very nearly the same meaning of trouble and poverty. "This anxiety of the pedigreeless, traditionless, Mushroom, Abolition, Yankee, Shoddy party, shows conclusively that they are *hard-up* for political capital." (New York *Herald,* 1865.)

Hems is frequently said and written for *hames,* in Pennsylvania. (S. S. Haldeman.)

Here is in the South pronounced like *hyar,* like many words of similar formation, and those with *a* in the first syllable, which obtain an additional *y* (yerb, year, cyard, cyare, etc.)

High Dutchers, a cant term for skates, the blade of which is curled up high in front; while skates without such ornamental projections are known as *dumps.*

Hitch, originally meaning a substantial obstacle and its effects upon the gait of persons, is in America constantly applied to difficulties in business matters. "He has got a *hitch* in his gait." "I am afraid the silence of the officer in command shows that there is a *hitch* in the matter, and that the expedition has not been as successful as was hoped." (Official Report, 1869.) *Hitching* horses has suggested many a slang phrase, of which some have already been mentioned in connection with the word *hoss*. The process itself is commonly called *hitching to*. "Over we went, safe and sound, geared up, *hitched to*, and started on through the mud." (Rev. P. Cartwright, *Autobiography*, p. 337.) "I was much amused at the lordly air with which the fat driver ordered his assistants to *hitch up* quickly." (*Letters from the South*, II., 117.)

Hog-tight and *horse-tight* fences are such as will not let hogs pass nor horses trespass. Used throughout the South.

Hold on, in the sense of stop! is the result of German influence, *Halt an!* being the corresponding phrase used in Pennsylvania and some of the Western States by the numerous German settlers there. It is quite probable that the same term may also have been familiar in the great seaport towns, where the nautical phrase to *hold on* was apt to be heard from sailors.

Holloo or *hollow*, to, before one is out of the woods, meaning to boast of an escape before the danger is over, is much used in America. A curious paraphrase of the slang phrase occurs in the Preface to Morris' *Earthly Paradise*—

> "Yet, fellows, must I warn you not to shout,
> Ere we have left the troublous wood behind."

To *beat all hollow*, an old English phrase, may be derived from the idea of beating so as to leave the victim literally *hollow*, without strength, as Webster suggests; but there is at least as strong probability that it may have been originally *wholly*, which was afterward corrupted into *hollow*. Some old writers spell the word regularly *hole* or *holly*. "Yes, boys, and I beat black David Copeland *all hollow*—beat him blacker than he is—killed two birds to his one." (John Randolph of Virginia.)

"In physic we have Francis and McNeven,
  Famed for long heads, short lectures, and long bills,
And Quackenboss and others, who from heaven
  Were rained upon us in a shower of pills.
They *beat* the deathless Æsculapius *hollow*
And make a starveling druggist of Apollo."
(Halleck. *Fancy.*)

Hopping mad, a slang phrase suggestive of the effect violent anger produces on weak-minded persons.

Hot, a vicious preterite of *hit,* is very frequently heard both in New England and some of the Southern States. "He *hot* me a big lick." "He *hot* out right and left."

House is, when coupled with another word, very generally contracted into *'us,* as is done in some parts of England, from whence the custom, no doubt, was imported into the Old Colony. Our house becomes thus *our 'us,* and meeting-house, *meetin'us.*

How is the imperious way of the New Englander to ask for a repetition of what he has failed to understand—or more likely of what he wishes to hear once more before he is called upon to give an answer. *How come,* pronounced short, like *hucum,* is, on the other hand, a purely Southern phrase, meaning, How came that about? It is almost entirely confined to the negroes and the so-called Mean Whites, but was, in all probability, brought over as a provincialism by the first English settlers.

Humbly, derived from the characteristic Yankee phrase *to hum,* for *at home,* is used in New England instead of "homely," the *b* being inorganic, and produced by the meeting of *m* and *l,* as in *chimbley* and similar words. Whole is in the same manner pronounced *hull,* and produces the adverb *hully.*

Hungry as a graven image is a phrase peculiar to New England, and very graphic.

Hurry up the cakes, to, a slang phrase, originating in the great partiality Americans have for hot cakes at breakfast, which, in order to be satisfactory, must be brought to the table as soon as they are baked. Hence the phrase means, Be quick about it—be alive! In the West, on the contrary, they have a phrase, *Don't hurry, Hopkins!* meaning the same, but used ironically in speaking to persons who are very slow in their work, or in meeting an obligation. "It originated from the case of one Hopkins, who, having given one of his creditors a promissory note in regular form, added to it this extraordinary memorandum: It is expressly agreed, that the said Hopkins is not to be hurried in paying the above note." (Uneda, *Notes and Queries*, March 13, 1858.) The term *hurryment*, often used in the South, has no real existence in the language.

Hush up takes in America the place of simple Hush! whenever the vulgar but energetic *Shut up!* is not preferred.

I.

Idea, in the phrase *I have no idea*, means simply knowledge. It is unfortunately a favorite reply in the South, where, unlike the Yankee's strong reluctance to admit any ignorance on his part, a candid avowal of utter absence of knowledge is promptly made, to save trouble.

Ingens or *Ingins*, a frequent vulgarism for Indian, quite common throughout the country. "They are mighty rough on strangers, and they worship an *Ingin* baby." (F. B. Harte, *Luck of Roaring Camp*, p. 16.)

Inheaven, to, a badly-made and unmeaning word, manufactured by "Boston Transcendentalists," and unfortunately often used by careless writers in the sense of to lift us up to heaven. "Such music is well calculated to *inheaven* us; there is a spiritual power in it which well-tuned hearts cannot resist." (Boston *Transcript*, August 4, 1859.)

J.

Jam up, from the verb to *jam*, denotes a high degree of perfection.

Jamboree, a row, a disturbance, may possibly come from the same root; it is genuine American slang. "When all are assembled, we shall have a regular *jamboree*." (*Putnam's Magazine*. January, 18—.)

Jerusalem! a favorite New England exclamation, more correct than the corresponding old English term *Jerry-usalem!* In the West it is, as usual, improved to suit the louder taste of the people, and becomes *Jewhillikin*. "Now they are coming to the rich licks! *Jewhillikin!* There goes a drove of them! All stool-pigeons, every one of them!" (*The Country Merchant*, p. 221.)

Jenooary is the way the New Englander loves to pronounce January. Hence the startling simile of J. R. Lowell: "Cold as the north side of a *Jenooary* gravestone by starlight."

Jessie, to give, in the sense of giving a man a thrashing, is, perhaps, derived from the English slang phrase, unknown here, to give a man *gas*, through the (slang) adjective *gassy*. In the United States the popular phrase is made stronger by giving *particular Jessie*, or even *d—— particular Jessie*, according to the greater or lesser violence of the speaker's feelings. "The old general turned round and said: Well, gentlemen, I think we have given them very *particular Jessie* on this field." (*Campaign with General Price*, p. 27, 1867.)

Jingo, by, a favorite oath imported from England, where, Halliwell says, it was derived from Saint Gingoulph. Americans, in their desire to civilize and, perhaps, to annex Japan, have recently discovered that the Japanese *Gingko*, the name of a tree planted near almost all the temples in Japan and China, and hence a synonym of Deity, is the true ancestor of the odd-sounding phrase!

Jumping furnishes a number of slang phrases. To *jump at* a thing, means to seize it with eagerness. "When I offered him that, his whole face brightened wonderfully, and he *jumped at* the offer with a delight which proved to me how much I had been wanting in caution." (Judge Longstreet, *Georgia Scenes*.) To *jump with* means to accord, to agree with others. "On the whole, it *jumped with* his desires, and the matter was clinched." (J. C. Neal, *Charcoal Sketches*.) *From the jump* is constantly used as a more energetic expression than the prosy, from the first. "I knew how it would come *from the jump*, for in the man's face was written rascal, as clear as I have ever seen the letters." (*Wild Bill*.)

K.

Ketchup, a common mode of writing *catsup*, in imitation of the sound.

Killing is used less frequently in America as a slang term—whatever statisticians may say of the frequency of the act—than to *kill*. "When he came down after breakfast, to go over to the Judge's and to press his suit, he was *dressed to kill*." (*The Country Merchant*.) To *kill* is, moreover, frequently used to convey the idea of defeat. A political measure, being unsuccessful, is said to have been *killed* in Congress, and to *kill* a bill means to prevent its being taken into consideration.

Kind and *kinder* (instead of *kind of*) are both English slang as well as American, but the combination of *kinder sorter* may safely be claimed as a native phrase. "When I saw the red devil, I had *kinder sorter* a presentiment that we were in a bad box, but I didn't want to kick up a row before the persimmons were ripe." (*Sketches of Indian Warfare*, p. 118.)

Kiss-curl, a name for the little curls on ladies' temples, also known as "beau-catchers."

Knock about, to, is a favorite phrase applied to persons who have no regular business, and are said contemptuously "to be *knocking about* in spots," or "promiscuously." "I have been *knocking about* all day," may, however, also be said complacently, in the sense of having been busy stirring about all day long.

L.

La, for Lord! is generally pronounced *law*, and often so written. Even *laws* and *lawks* are heard in these contemptible efforts to avoid the charge of profanity, and yet to yield to the temptation. It avails little to say that *La!* may as justly be derived from the old English word that meant *look*, as Americans are apt to say, "Look a-here!" or "Look a-there!" Few who cry *La!* would think or are likely to know much of etymology.

Lap-tea is the quaint name given in New England to tea-parties where the guests sit in each other's laps for want of room.

Law, to, and to go to *lawing*, Western expressions for the more ceremonious expression, to go to *law*. "If I can't make anything out of him by *lawing*, I'll have to try what virtue there is in a Derringer." (Trial of Mrs. Fair, April, 1871.)

Let on, to, a phrase not unknown to English Slang Dictionaries, but far more common in America, means to betray a knowledge of something, without reference to enjoined secrecy. "I saw Mr. —— at the meeting, but I never *let on* that I knew he was present." (*Dean Ramsay's Reminiscenses.*) Burns forms his own preterite:

> "I never *loot* on that I ken'd it or car'd,
> But thought I might hae waur offers."

"Although the visitors, the gentlemanly keeper, and the prison-chaplain, all tried in every conceivable way to induce him to make a confession, he would never *let on* how the murder was committed, and all agree that Ruloff is the greatest mystery of the age." (Binghamton *Journal*, April, 1871.) *Let out*, to, in the sense of giving an account of an event, or making an explanation, is Western slang. "You bile the pot, and when I have had a smoke I'll *let out*, but not afore." (*Western Scenes.*) To *let up*, on the other hand, is a phrase borrowed from the ring, and denotes a relief, as when the money-market is reported to have experienced a *let-up*, or when the poor stokers on board a river-steamer complain of being kept at work near the fires "for fourteen hours in a stretch, without more *let-up* than to have a drink." To *let her rip*, a phrase borrowed from Western steamboats, which, when racing down the river, are very apt to be allowed to *rip* themselves open upon snags and sawyers rather than to disappoint the ambitious pilot, has entered into common life as an expression of indifference or despair. "Cuthbert Bede" suggested the humorous explanation that *Rip* was the American way of reading the letters R. I. P. (*Requiescat In Pace*) on a tombstone, taking them to be one word, and commenting upon it thus: "*Rip!* well, he was an old *Rip*, and no mistake!" "As to the Constitution, I would *let her rip* any time rather than that one citizen of these United States should not feel safe in my State, because of his color or his political convictions." (*Congressional Globe*, January 17, 1871.) A recent substitute for the phrase is *Let her slide*, an expression so old in English speech that it has been traced back to the earliest times. Shakespeare, in *Taming the Shrew*, has the energetic words, "*Let* the world *slide*;" Lord Walter, in Chaucer's *Clerke's Tale*, was so fond of hawking, that he "well-nigh *let* all other cures *slide*;" and Dorigen, in the *Franklin's Tale*, gives a mourner the good advice—

"But natheless she must a time abide;
And with good hope must *let* her sorrow *slide*;"

and yet the phrase was hailed as a new invention of marvellous force, when General Banks of Massachusetts, in his exuberant eloquence, said at the beginning of the late Civil War, "*Let* the

Union *slide!*" The phrase was soon after repeated in the United States Senate, when the orator said, "If California is going to cost the Union so much, it would be better to *let* California *slide*."

Level, a term probably borrowed from the diggings for precious metals, has of late entered into a number of slang expressions. When two persons are bargaining with each other, the seller is apt to say that he "will make an offer on a *broad level*," to imply that he proposes to offer his property at the lowest price possible. A Western man, making fair promises, says earnestly, "Mister, I'll do my *level* best;" and if he wishes to bestow great praise on a friend, he says of him that "his head is *level*," meaning that he is a man of eminent good, practical sense; "well-balanced," as it would be called from a different standpoint. The origin of the phrase is seen in the words of a dying miner: "Now, pardner, I feel that I can't drift no further on this *level*, and I guess I've got to go down lower." (*Overland Monthly,* March, 1871.)

Lift, on the, represents in the United States the English phrase, on the twig, not in the sense of dying, but of being ready to move to some other place. "I can conceive but of one extenuation; Bolus was *on the lift* for Texas, and the desire was natural to qualify himself for citizenship." (*Flush Times of Alabama.*)

Linkhorn is the corruption of Lincoln, and, e. g., regularly applied to *Linkhorn* County in Pennsylvania, which had been named after the unfortunate President.

Linkister is the common pronunciation of a New England cant term, *linguister,* which the Yankees employ to designate talkative persons and all who possess the "gift of the gab" in a special degree.

Lockrums, a slang term apparently made after the analogy of "tantrums," means, odd notions, eccentric or unpopular views. "I'd say to the members, Don't come down here to Halifax with your *lockrums* about politics!" (Sam Slick, *The Clockmaker,* p. 204.)

'Long on, a slang phrase much in use in the New England States, meaning "occasioned by," is traced back by J. R. Lowell to Middleton, but seems to have disappeared from English everywhere else. "Who's this *'long on?*" means, Who did this?

"The darkest, strangest mystery,
I ever read, or heern, or see,
Is *'long* of a drink at Taggart's Hall,
Tom Taggart's at Gilgal."
(John Hay. *The Mystery of Gilgal.*)

Looseness, a favorite Western term, to express, in a faint manner, the ideal freedom from all restraint. "He went at it with a perfect *looseness*, and didn't he make the chips fly!" (*Western Scenes.*) The energetic term has found its way, long since, to the Eastern cities. "The perfect *looseness* with which books not on the invoice were sold, was illustrated by the sale of a volume of Anthon's series." (New York *Express*, September, 1855.)

Lord'a mussy or *Luddy Mussy*, for Lord have mercy! are ejaculations heard with almost equal frequency in New England and in the South, where they are much affected by the negroes. "*Lud a mussy*, Mas Bob, is dat you? whar on arth is you gwine to?"

Lowbelia, a corruption of Lobelia (Lobelia inflata), much used by so-called herb-doctors, obtained that name from these ignorant quacks, and their still more ignorant dupes, while another plant of the same family (Lobelia cardinalis), of much greater size, became accordingly known as "Highbelia."

M.

Ma'am, in the combination of *school-ma'am*, and denoting a female teacher, used to be exclusively heard in New England; but since that estimable class of instructors has been so largely represented in the Southern States by enthusiasts who devote themselves to the teaching of the children of the freedmen, the term is as familiar in the South as in its native land. With those who do not appreciate her self-sacrificing zeal, the *school-ma'am* is apt to be rather the *Yankee ma'am* or *marm*.

Mammoxed means, in Southern and Western slang, to be seriously injured. The origin of the term is not very clear—if it ever had a legitimate pedigree outside of Shakespeare's *mummocked*. "He was right smartly *mammoxed*, and at first we thought he was done for, but the damage wasn't very great, after all." (*With the Comanches*, 1867.)

Maul and wedges, the woodchopper's tools, are often used to denote the whole of a man's possessions, his movables. "He went across-lots, *maul and wedges*, and we never seen nor hearn of him sence." (*Western Scenes.*) The *maul* is the large "mallet," also used for driving in stakes.

Mean Whites were, in the days of slavery, the white citizens of the South who had no slaves to work for them, and yet deemed themselves too good to work themselves. Ignorant and intemperate as a class, and imbued with that pride which is the greatest hindrance to culture, they were a cancer in the body politic of many of the Southern States, and are now (1871) a serious obstacle to their regeneration. A more contemptuous term is *poor white folks*, or even *poor white trash.*

Marblehead turkeys, in the slang of Massachusetts denoting codfish.

Mercy's sake alive, a most emphatic ejaculation, descended from the imperative summons in great danger: For Mercy's sake, be alive! *Mercy* is, especially with the negroes, always pronounced *mussy.*

Missing, to be found, denotes, in Western parlance, to be absent, or to run away. "I tell you this was a poser; the young lawyer was struck dumb, and presently was *found missing.*" (Rev. P. Cartwright, *Autobiography*, p. 194.)

Miscellaneous imbecility, a political slang phrase, is said to have originated with a Western general, dining at the Tremont House in Chicago, in 1863. He was criticising other Federal generals who were politicians, and, in order to express his utter disregard for their capacity in the army as well as in civil life, he denounced them as "men of *miscellaneous imbecility.*"

Mistake, and no, one of the most popular phrases in all parts of the United States, to clinch a matter. "That's so, *and no mistake.*" "I'll pay you Monday, *and no mistake.*"

Moke, possibly a remnant of the obsolete *moky*, which is related to "murky," is used in New York to designate an old fogy or any old person, disrespectfully spoken to. A hackdriver is thus represented to reply to a stranger who had upbraided him for his violent language, "See here, my lively *moke*, said he, you sling on too much style." (Galveston *News*, May 4, 1871.) In the Northwest the term is generally applied to negroes, with whom the original "murky" may be associated in some minds. "The young *mokes*, who had often denounced Mr. Ham for having incurred the displeasure of his aged sire, in consequence of which their heads were covered with tufts of hair." (Dubuque *Herald*, 1871.)

Momicks, is, in Pennsylvania, the curious slang term for a bad carver. It arose, in all probability, from a suggestion that such a person was apt to *mommox* the joints placed before him.

Much, to be, means, to be valuable in some capacity. "He *is not much* of a lawyer," he is not a very good lawyer. "That *was not much* of a speech." "*Is he much* of a speaker?" *Much of a muchness* is used here, as in England, instead of, nearly the same thing.

Muckrakes, a slang term in politics for persons who "fish in troubled waters," from the idea of their raking up the muck to see what valuable waifs and strays they may find in it. The term is generally used in the form of *muckrakes and placemongers*.

Musicianer, long considered pure slang, has recently been raised in public estimation by J. R. Lowell's statement that it occurs in an extract made by Collier as early as 1642, while the great English scholar, Mr. Wright, cites it as a Norfolk word. Henceforth New Englanders may with impunity enjoy their *musicianers* at their militia musters.

Mudsill, originally denoting the timber laid down to form a foundation for a railway-track, was subsequently applied to the lowest class of society, and has since become a favorite term with speakers who prefer energy to elegance. "I say that labor is not the *mudsill* of society, and I thank God that the old colonial aristocracy of Virginia, which despised mechanical and manual labor, is nearly run out." (H. A. Wise, Richmond *Enquirer*, May, 1858.)

Music is in many parts of the Union used as a synonym for fun or frolic, and hence, perhaps, *musical* means, in New England at least, humorous, funny. "Jake is not without his vein of fun, *music* they call it down here, and his eye sparkles with delight at the humor of others as well as at his own wit." (*Letters from the South*.) "I can't say it's *musical*." (O. W. Holmes.)

Mung, the old preterite of the old English verb to *ming* (from which our modern mingle), seems to have been brought to this country, with many kindred forms, by the earliest settlers, and has been preserved here in its purity and power. *Mung* news means confused news; statements which seem contradictory are, in like-manner, called *mung*. The original meaning of mingling is retained in the Scottish noun *mung*, which means a porridge of two kinds of meal.

N.

Nary, the contracted form of "ne'er a one," dating back to the days when *e* and *a* were used in speaking and writing as synonyms, in the same way as words like clerk, sergeant, and Derby, are still almost universally pronounced clark, sargeant, and Darby. (To the last day of their lives, great Americans even, like Chief-Justice Marshall, pronounced Berkeley, Barkeley—as it was written in early colonial records—and Perkins, Parkins.) The next step was probably the form *narra one* or *narra* simply (*Slang Dictionary*, p. 186), as used by Sir W. Scott, whose (English) landlord of the town of Darlington says of the Highlanders, "They are all gentlemen, though they ha' *narra* shirt to their back." (*Rob Roy*, I., c. 7.) The modern tendency is to couple *nary* with every noun in the language, as in the familiar phrase, "*nary* red cent," meaning, not a single red cent, and "*nary* president appeared at the meeting." The word is, however, still in the slang state.

Nation, possibly a euphemistic and modest abbreviation of *damnation*, is quite well known in provincial dialects in England, but probably less so in this country. Its meaning is simply, extremely, an emphatic "very." In Yankee Doodle it is used thus:

> "And every time they shoot it off
> It takes a horn of powder,
> And makes a noise like father's gun,
> Only a *nation* louder."
> (*Yankee Doodle.*)

Needcessity, a corruption of *necessity*, is continually heard in the South and often so written, from a desire to give the familiar meaning of *need* to the foreign word. "But it was a *needcessity* to keep in till the sounds died off pretty much, so as not to give them any scare this side, till they had dashed pretty far ahead on the other." (W. G. Simms, *Wigwam and Cabin.*)

Nigh unto and *nigh upon* are both used for the simpler nearly, from no other reason apparently than to be more grandiloquent. "I was *nigh unto* givin' out."

Nimshi, is the Connecticut term for nincompoop.

Nip and tuck expresses the closeness of a race, or of competition in any enterprise. "It was *nip and tuck* all along, who was to win her." (*Putnam's Magazine*, January, 1869.)

Nose to the grindstone, a very expressive phrase, denoting the ill-treatment received at the hands of a successful adversary who takes full advantage of his triumph. "At all events he had his *nose to the grindstone*, an operation which should make men keen." (J. C. Neal, *Charcoal Sketches.*)

Nothing else and *nothing to nobody* are both Southern phrases, the first a mere expletive, added to any statement or assertion which it is desired to render emphatic; the latter expressing defiant indifference to the opinion of others. "If he chooses to make a fool of hisself and marry the widow, why, that's *nothing to nobody*, and he oughtn't to be pestered." (*Flush Times of Alabama.*)

Nowhere, to be, denotes utter failure or complete ignorance. "Where was Flora? Flora! why, she was *nowhere*—came in last but one." (*Spirit of the Times*, 1859.) "When he began to ask me questions about surgery, I was just *nowhere*, and I can't tell, to save my life, what I said to him." (*De Bow's Magazine*, July, 1868.)

'Nuity, a word believed by some writers to be derived from *annuity*, and by others to be an absurd form of *knew*, is thus explained: "Tom had what the Capemen call *'nuity*, which means what the rest of Americans call go-aheaditiveness — a barbarous word, which no nation could coin, that did not find it easier to coin money than words." (Charles Nordhoff.)

Nurly, a vulgar corruption of *gnarly*, and thus applied to persons, who are said to be *nurly* when they are ill-tempered and cross-grained.

Nutmegs, when made of wood, as were those immortalized by Sam Slick, have become so familiar to the public mind, that they have passed into a slang term for any cunning deception. Not only is Connecticut called the *Nutmeg* State—although a factious native says the true reason is "because you will have to look for a *grater*,"—but in the press and in Congress *wooden nutmegs* have to answer for forged telegrams, political tricks, and falsified election-returns. "I leave the honorable gentleman from Massachusetts to his *wooden nutmegs* and silver spoons; he will receive his deserts before the people are done with him." (*Congressional Globe*, March, 1871.)

O.

Obscute and *obscutely*, fictitious words, manufactured in New England to express indirectness, and characteristic of the makers of wooden oats and nutmegs.

Obtusity, an unnecessary substitute for *obtuseness*, is peculiar to the New England States.

Odd, when applied to persons, has apparently a tendency to unite with odd epithets, such as *odd-fish* or *odd-stick*. "What an *odd-fish* the old man is, sure enough, but mighty good, and as pious a soul as ever lived." (*Southern Quarterly Review*, October, 1848.)

Offish, an adjective made from *off*, and quite suggestive of its meaning as reserved, shy, is mainly used in the North. When the reserve is attributed to pride, the epithet is changed into *uppish*. "I don't like him; to me he looks rather *uppish*."

Oldermost, made after the model of *furthermost* and *hindermost*, is quite common in the West, where it takes the place of *oldest*. "Where is your *oldermost* child, said the man to the unfortunate father?" (Rev. P. Cartwright, *Autobiography*.)

Once and again frequently takes, in the South, the place of once in a while. Generally, however, it is correctly used, meaning again and again. "I have told you, *once and again*, not to do that." "I have seen that man, *once and again*, riding by the gate, but I don't know who he is." (H. C. Pate, *Vademecum*.)

On end, or, as Yankees prefer to sound it, *on eend*, denotes such a state of excitement from wonder or from anger that the hairs stand at an end, and this is transferred to the person himself. "I wuz all *on eend* at seein' her thar." (*Our Young Folks*, 1868.)

Onplush, a corruption of *nonplus*, and of late a favorite term with Southern legislators, who, fresh from rural pursuits, bring the language of the stable and the cornfield to the Halls of Assembly.

Ornery, is not only a corruption but a higher degree of *ordinary*, for which it is largely used in the West and the South. It conveys generally an idea of contempt. "That ar Black Bess is the *ornarest* animule I ever see." (*Overland Monthly*, January,

1870.) "Coparisoned to me, I know few people that arn't *ornery* as to brains." (J. C. Neal, *Charcoal Sketches.*)

Opinuated, for *opinionated,* is frequently heard in the South, especially as used by the negroes. "That mule is mighty *opinuated.*"

Outquash, to, a more energetic than elegant term, used in the South to denote the peculiar process of law called *quashing* an indictment, in its full force. "Those were quashing times, and they were the *outquashingest* set of fellows ever known. In one court, forthcoming bonds to the amount of some hundred thousand dollars, were quashed, because the execution was written State of Mississippi, instead of The State of Mississippi—the constitution requiring the style of process to be, The State of Mississippi—an *outquashing* process, which vindicated the constitution at the expense of foreign creditors." (*Flush Times of Alabama.*)

Owdacious, for audacious, is often written as it is pronounced by illiterate people. "That's an *owdacious* and willful lie."

P.

Palmateer, to, frequently called and written *parmateer,* owes its origin evidently to *parliamentary,* a word unknown in its precise meaning to the illiterate, and hence easily corrupted in form and in application. It was formerly often heard in the State of Rhode Island for "electioneering," but has almost disappeared.

Pardner, is the popular form under which *partner* appears in colloquial intercourse. It has made its way to California, and is at the mines considered so correct that to say *partner* excites unpleasant attention.

Patent-outside, in newspaper cant, is the name of an outside of a newspaper printed and purchased from a firm, which furnishes it with the paper required for the whole edition. The firm not only makes its own selections, but has the right to publish therein a certain amount of advertising, which is also selected without consulting the country journalist. A Republican editor may thus be surprised by finding his first or fourth page taken up with elaborate and extended eulogies on his Democratic rival. "The editor who surrenders control of one-half of his paper to some manufacturer of *patent-outsides,* may make a slight reduction in his current expenses, but in the end he will lose both money and influence." (Lancaster *Intelligencer*, April 3, 1871.)

Peatime, the season of pease, is of sufficient importance in the New England States to give a number of phrases to their speech. The *last of peatime*, represents the era in a man's life when he is in great trouble, perhaps at his wit's ends; and *peatime is over*, when no chance remains. "People that can't see that *peatime is past*." (J. R. Lowell, *Biglow Papers*, II., p. 11.)

Passenger, to wake up the wrong,—a phrase derived from the frequent mistakes made in waking up passengers who were to start early in the morning,—means to be mistaken in a man, to "catch a Tartar." "When General Farnsworth had gotten so far, General Butler's face began to show evident signs of distress; he had clearly found out that in making the attack he had *waked up the wrong passenger*." (Chicago *Evening Post*, April 21, 1871.)

Peg, to rise a, or to take one down a *peg*, is old English, revived in America as a slang phrase. It originated in the days of St. Dunstan, who, having found that quarrels often arose in taverns from disputes among the topers as to their share of liquor, served in a common measure, advised King Edward to order gold or silver *pegs* to be fastened to the pot, so that every man should exactly know how "deep he might drink." (Hook, *Lives of the Archbishops of Canterbury*.) Now the *peg* of the alepot is the rung in the ladder of social rank.

> "To rise a *peg* an' jine the crowd that went for reconstruction."
> (J. R. Lowell, *Biglow Papers*, II., p. 99.)

Persuasion has recently been sadly perverted from its legitimate purpose of denoting private persuasion in arguing or religious belief, publicly avowed. It is one of the most recent slang terms introduced into the language, and forced to take the place of almost every other designation of class, rank, or occupation. The New York *Herald* speaks thus of "passengers being mainly of the *female persuasion*," and another paper in Washington said: "Mr. Harper (a speaker at a public meeting) complained of the absence of public reporters, when a gentleman of that *persuasion* was actually taking notes of what he said." The Southern papers especially are fond of designating the freedmen on every occasion as "gentlemen of the Fifteenth Amendment *persuasion,*" and a lady proposing to lecture in New Orleans on Women's Rights, was announced as "Mrs. Oates, of the Advanced Female *persuasion.*"

Philadelphia Lawyer, as smart as a, is a common phrase abroad as well as at home, to express supreme acuteness in legal matters and others. It is said that early in the history of the Republic, British sailors learnt to appreciate the shrewdness of members of the Philadelphia bar in helping them out of their difficulties, and that through their reports the reputation of these gentlemen spread far and wide. "You would beat a *Philadelphia lawyer,* wife, with your smartness and your gab." (*Every-Day Tales,* I., p. 54.)

Pinch, in a, represents, in Western parlance, to be in straits for money, or embarrassed in any way. *On a pinch* means in an emergency. "I could lend you a hundred dollars *on a pinch,* but farther than that I could not possibly go." (*Southern Literary Messenger,* July, 1860.) "He said he did not know what he might be able to do *upon a pinch,* but for the present he was unable to help you."

Pineblank is the popular pronunciation of *pointblank.* "His temper was sharp and high, but steady; as it never fell into feebleness, so it never rose into rage; the *percisely* and *pineblank* tone of feeling, ever present, kept him too well balanced for that." (General Ogle, *A Character.*)

Pitch it strong, to, a Western phrase, descriptive of an energetic effort, perhaps beyond the strict limits of truth in telling a story. "It seems to me, stranger, you *pitch* it rayther *strong,* but I donow, thar mout be a God after all." (Sacramento paper, July, 1870.) "*Pitching it strong* is the most obvious characteristic of American humor." (*North British Review,* November, 1860.) To *pitch in,* a term constantly used in the Western settlements, when they speak of going to work with a special effort, is, like the former phrase, graphically descriptive of American superabundant energy, which *starts* an enterprise, *pitches into it* with a will, and *rushes it through* in *less than no time.* "Grace Greenwood, supposed to be buried somewhere in the West, recently gave signs of remaining vitality by *pitching into* a younger pseudonyme, the sparkling and saucy Gail Hamilton." (*Lippincott's Magazine,* July, 1869.)

Pizarro, a quaint corruption of *piazza,* peculiar to New England.

Played out, a slang term taken from the gambler's language, has of late become very popular, and is applied to anything which has come to a more or less disastrous end. "General Butler is about *played out,* said a Western man to me after the disgraceful scene between Butler and Farnsworth." (Correspondence New York *Herald,* April, 1871.) "The Crimea got *played out,* and we turned it into Fort Sumter." (*Genial Showman.*)

Politicate, to, denotes the profession of but too large a number of Americans who, without the slightest qualification, and for the sole purpose of avoiding work, make politics their trade.

Prehaps, for perhaps, is not merely the result of carelessness, but has acquired a mysterious power of being more emphatic than the correct form—a peculiarity which it shares with *percisely,* which is also considered stronger than *precisely.* "*Prehaps,* young man, you did not understand me, but I rather guess you did, and if you didn't I'll make you aware of my meaning in mighty quick time." (*Western Scenes.*)

Pretty, as a noun, is in slang made to represent anything that is to be considered pretty. "The girls wouldn't let the boys go up with them in the gallery, while they were having their *pretties* taken." (Western newspaper, 1870.)

Puke, as a noun, and in the sense of a low, contemptible fellow, is unenviable American slang.

Pull foot, to, means, in Western slang, to make great haste. "I look'd up; it was another shower, by gosh. I *pulls foot* for dear life." (*Sam Slick in England.*) To *pull* up, a metaphor derived from the pull on the reins in making horses stop, means to stop. "Driver, when will you *pull up?* I don't *pull up* at no tavern till I gets home." (*A Trip through Virginia,* 1868.) To *pull wool over the eyes,* as is done to make sheep go into the water or into the pen where they are to be shorn, means proverbially to try and blind a person's judgment. "He tried hard to *pull the wool over my eyes,* but I was on my guard, for, you know, Forewarned, forearmed." (*Southern Literary Messenger,* June, 1851.)

Put, to, seems to be a favorite term with the New Englander, if we may judge from the frequency with which he uses it, and the variety of meanings which it is made to assume. One of the most frequent purposes for which it is used by him, is to express going away. The Yankee says, "Now, *put!*" for, Now, begone! and with him the word has wandered to the West, where it is now universally heard instead of Go! Whatever he finds will not remain as he has "fixed" it, he says will "not stay *put*," and if he sends a messenger, he recommends to him to be quick, by saying: "Now, be sure and *put out!*" "I knew there was no time to lose, if his life was to be saved; so I *put out* as fast as I could, and luckily met the doctor about halfway to his house." (*Our Young Folks*, 1868.) To *put in*, means to *put in* a word, and thus to interrupt, but the addition is not considered necessary. "By this time Stanton *put in* and stopped whatever more Robert had to say." (W. G. Simms, *The Snake of the Cabin.*) *To put a head* on somebody, is a slang term of recent origin, and used by combative persons, who convey by it their purpose of annihilating their adversary.

> "But all his jargon was surpassed, in wild absurdity,
> By threats, profanely emphasized, to *put a head* on me!
> No son of Belial, said I, that miracle can do!
> Whereat he fell upon me with blows and curses, too;
> But failed to work that miracle—if such was his design—
> Instead of *putting on a head*, he strove to smite off mine."
> (*Words and Their Uses.* Galveston *News*, May 4, 1871.)

To put through, means: To carry out successfully. "That bill can never be *put through*, unless it is modified in every section." (*Congressional Globe*, April, 1871.) In such cases the figure is, of course, taken from the process of carrying a bill through the necessary readings to its final adoption.

R.

R, the pronunciation of *r*, defective in all Americans, is especially charged upon Southerners as a mark of imperfect enunciation and neglected education. It cannot be denied, that if the true, rolling sound of the *r*, as affected by Englishmen, is rarely heard in the United States, from the national habit of speaking leisurely and even lazily, the South is guilty of frequently dropping the troublesome letter entirely from the roll of sounds. Even clergymen and public speakers are apt to forget the duty they owe this ill-treated letter. One reverend reader has been accused of pronouncing doorposts as if it was *dawposts*, while the firstborn always appeared in the disguise of *fustborn*. Another had the habit of pronouncing hearts as *haats*, and the Lord appeared always as the *Lawd*. But it ought to be borne in mind that similar differences exist in England. In Dorsetshire the sportsman hears of nothing but parrteridges and, in the shop, of shirrts, while the gamekeepers of Suffolk are only acquainted with pattridges, the parish-clerks speak of chutch-potches, and the laundresses get up shutts. (Dr. Donaldson.) The sins of the present generation ought, therefore, to be laid, in part at least, upon the shoulders of the guilty forefathers, the first English settlers, many of whom came from Suffolk and the districts belonging to the East-Anglians, and, no doubt, brought over with them this disregard for the letter *r*.

Raise, to, in Western slang, means to obtain something, without distinction as to the manner by which this is accomplished. The backwoodsman *raises meat* by shooting game, the frontiersman *raises hair* by killing Indians, and the drunkard *raises a racket* by making a disturbance at the grogshop. The most violent kind of row is called *raising Cain*, a fearfully suggestive word. "Thinks I, may be, old fellow, your gun has bust or you've pawned it for rum and can't *raise* skins enough to redeem it, and you want mine, and perhaps you'll get it." (W. S. Mayo, *Kaloolah.*) "I made a *raise* of a horse and a saw, after being a wood-piler's apprentice for a while." (J. C. Neal, *Charcoal Sketches.*) "They had an almighty row in the Legislature that day, and some outsiders having come in, armed to the teeth, there was a smart chance of a big fight; but Mike, who generally is ready enough to *raise Cain* whenever he is in liquor, happened to be sober, for a wonder, and General Hollins at last succeeded in restoring order." (Leavenworth paper, August, 1867.)

Rale, is the common sound of *real* with the illiterate throughout the country, as *rare* is for *rear*. "Beat you the *rale* gum and hickory." (J. C. Neal, *Charcoal Sketches.*)

Rantankerous, probably derived from the old English *rantan*, a row, a drunken frolic, means given to quarrelling. "On the *rantan*," drunk. (*Household Words*, No. 183.) "He was a regular *rantankerous* fellow, with whom nobody could get on. I say: Peace be to his ashes! as there certainly will be peace, now that he is dead." (Judge Longstreet, *Sketches.*)

Red, a, does not mean a Red Republican, as in England, but "a *red* cent," the smallest coin of the United States. "He isn't worth a *red.*"

Retiracy, in the sense of retirement, as well as, still worse, in the sense of a competency on which a man may retire, is irredeemable slang, although used by many American writers. "Yes, Mr. Speaker, I'd a powerful sight sooner go into *retiracy* among the wild, red aborigines of our wooden country, nor consent to this bill." (Carlton, *New Purchase.*) "When Mr. Watson found he had a sufficient *retiracy,* he gave up his lucrative business, and devoted himself to horticultural pursuits." (New Haven *Palladium,* 1860.)

Ride and tie, to, is the curious phrase by which, in Maryland and in the South, the arrangement is designated, according to which two travellers, having but one horse between them, will alternately ride and walk.

Right off, is more of an American slang term than *right away,* which was once considered a provincialism, belonging exclusively to Massachusetts and Virginia. It means, immediately. A Federal colonel, Fisk, during the late Civil War, tried to stop the habit of swearing in his regiment, and induced the men, by his influence, to covenant, that he should be made to do all the swearing, and they would abstain hereafter. The thousand men rose like one, and pledged themselves. The colonel became a brigadier-general, and one fine day heard a mule-driver swear fearfully at his animals; recognizing in him one of his own men, he asked him if he did not remember the covenant entered into at Benton Barracks, St. Louis, that he should do all the swearing for his old regiment? "To be sure I do, general," was the answer, "but then you were not there to do it, and it had to be done *right off.*"

Rip out, to, an energetic slang phrase, rarely ever used except with the addition of an *oath.* "With that, he *ripped out* a most fearful oath, and, running up to the second mate, knocked him down and stabbed him twice with the marlin-spike in his hand." (W. S. Mayo.)

Robustious, instead of *robust,* used by persons who love to be emphatic, even at the cost of vulgarity. "A pair of spanking bays flanked the pole, and a strapping, *robustious*, fellow with immense whiskers rode on the box." (*Putnam's Magazine*, September, 1853.)

Rope in, to, in the sense of gathering in, enlisting, is a bold metaphor derived from the common practice of gathering the cut hay of a meadow by means of a long rope, drawn by a horse, which *ropes in* the whole of a so-called windrow. Passing into slang, the term has subsequently acquired the unpleasant meaning of catching or cheating, probably from the idea that the rope was not seen by the dupes. "I'll lay bank, if you must have a game, but I'll make one condition: no *roping in!* I won't have it." (*Georgia Scenes*, ed. 1849.)

Rubbishy, an adjective made from *rubbish*, unknown to the Dictionaries. "Foot by foot the historic but useless old fortifications of Quebec are steadily disappearing. It was the reconstruction of St. John's Gate a few years ago, and now it is St. Louis, all the *rubbishy* old walls encumbering the approaches to which are now to be swept away in pursuance of an order from England." (*New Era*, April, 1871.)

Ruinatious, an enlarged and intensified form of *ruinous*, frequently used in the West and South.

Run into the ground, to, means, in Western parlance, literally to force beavers, and all burrowing animals, to seek refuge in their holes underground; but the phrase has long since been adopted, in all parts of the Union, as a metaphor, expressive of constant and close persecution, ending in destruction. "The temperance question is likely to be *run into the ground*, sooner or later, but only to be replaced by some other question of the same kind, which will be taken up, in its turn, to answer the purposes of politicians." (Springfield *Republican*, July, 1861.)

Rushers, in California and all the gold-bearing districts of the West, is the comprehensive name of persons going to the mines.

S.

Sanctimoniouslyfied, a horrible barbarism, is nevertheless reported by J. R. Bartlett as an American slang term, and its use proved by David Crockett, who wrote that he recollected "a *sanctimoniouslyfied* fellow, who made his negroes whistle while they were picking cherries for fear they should eat some." (*Tour Down East.*)

Savagerous, like ruinatious, used in the South to give still greater force to *savage.* "The most *savagerous* painter you ever saw in your life." (W. G. Simms.)

Save one's bacon, to, a slang phrase very frequently heard in spite of its objectionable character—for *bacon* does not mean smoked meat in this case—suggests a lucky escape from danger. "But virtue, if nothing more and no sooner, is its own reward, and in time to *save its bacon.*" (N. P. Willis, *Dashes at Life,* III., p. 90.)

Saw, as a noun and verb, is much used in the United States to designate a joke, and the process of playing a so-called practical joke upon others. In New Orleans this is called "running a *saw,*" and if the joke is very serious and perhaps even dangerous, it becomes a *vertical saw.*

Scott, Great! a curious euphemistic oath, in which the name of a well-known general is substituted for the original word, probably merely because of its monosyllabic form. "*Great Scott!* I'd rather give my name to a horticultural triumph like that there, than be Senator." (*Lippincott's Magazine,* March, 1871, p. 289.)

Seat, to, means in tailors' cant, to give employment to "jours," as the wandering members of that craft are called, who work by the day. When an employer has sufficient work for half a dozen or more laborers in his occupation, he says he "can *seat* half a dozen jours." The phrase probably originated in the fact that a generation ago all, or nearly all, master-tailors kept a "back-shop" of their own, and literally did *seat* their jours. It is altogether different now, as the trade is almost wholly supplied by what was then called "piece-masters," that is, operatives who take their work home and make it in their own houses.

Seed and *seen,* are both used for *saw* among the illiterate—a vulgarism which is probably as common to England as to America.

Semi-occasionally, for occasionally simply, which apparently did not express the meaning with sufficient clearness for emphatic speakers. "We see such really well-dressed men *semi-occasionally* in good society, but they are rare, our men on the whole preferring a more flashy style, and paying less attention to what is appropriate than to what is fashionable." (New York *Mirror*, January, 1854.)

Sense, to, instead of to comprehend, is a very brief term, popular in New England. "I can't say as I *sense* that."

Settle one's hash, to, a picturesque phrase expressive of such manner of acting as will finally silence an opponent and make an end to his hostility. "If you don't vamos this instant, I'll *settle your hash* with this here toothpick in a minit." (*Life in Mississippi*, p. 114.)

Shad-eaters, is the slang term very generally applied to members of the Legislature of the State of Connecticut—from an imaginary fondness for the excellent shad caught in those rivers.

Shake, a fair, is a good bargain, from the very simple process by which a measure, "well *shaken* down," suggests the fairness of the bargain. To be *no great shakes*, is a favorite phrase with Americans, borrowed from their English cousins, among whom it has risen high enough to be admitted even into Lord Byron's letters. *To shake a stick at*, denotes, for some mysterious reason, the utmost ability to count or to comprehend numbers. "I've been licked fifty times, and got more black eyes and bloody noses than you could *shake a stick at*." (J. C. Neal, *Charcoal Sketches*.)

Sharpshin, a slang term, denoting the smallest quantity. "This inconsiderable claim—for it is not the value of a *sharpshin*." (J. P. Kennedy, *Swallow Barn*.) The *sharp stick* plays, in Western slang, a prominent part, and is especially used in the phrase: "to be after a man with *a sharp stick*." "If you stay much longer, the old man will be after you with *a sharp stick*, and I don't know what you'll do to keep him from killing you." (*Western Scenes*.) "We are pleased to see that the New York *Tribune* is still after Senators Carpenter, Conkling, and others, with a *very sharp stick*, for their ridiculous course in the arrest and imprisonment of the *Tribune* correspondents, for daring to be true to themselves and to the profession of which they are honorable members and martyrs." (Trenton *State Sentinel*, May 26, 1871.)

Shenannigan, probably a purely fictitious word (though a Dutch origin has been claimed for it), frequently heard in the South and West, and denoting groundless bragging for the purpose of getting the better of another. "*Shenannigan* means any kind of chaff, foolery, nonsense, advanced to cover some little scheme or game."

Hence Miss Vinnie Ream, the artist, whose skill was said to have been largely measured by her personal charms, was recently admonished by a writer in the Chicago *Evening Post* to "go to work and try better next time, instead of fooling members of Congress by a pair of black eyes and a mass of beautiful curls. No *shenannigan*, Vinnie!" (January, 1871.)

Shin, to, applied to efforts to ascend a tree, means that the person who does it, tries to climb up by the aid of feet and hands only, which is apt to endanger the safety of his shins. In financial slang, Americans use the verb *to shin* simply, where the English use *to break shins*, to denote a desperate effort to procure money in an emergency by running about to friends and acquaintances.

Shine, to take a, means the same as to take a fancy to a person. "My gracious! it's a scorpion thet's *took a shine* to play with 't." (J. R. Lowell, *Biglow Papers*, I., p. 23.). To *take the shine off*, a metaphor taken from the meaning of *shine* as synonymous to gloss or beauty, means to excel or surpass another, not only in appearance but in any point. "If that does not *take the shine off* her altogether, I don't know her wits as well as I thought I did." (J. C. Neal, *Charcoal Sketches*.) *Shine* has also become, in the large cities, the slang term used by bootblacks, when they offer to "black your boots, sir?" pledging themselves, laconically, to make them *shine*. Hence the Quaker's lament upon his first visit to New York—

"As I left the cars, an imp with smutty face,
Said : *Shine?*—Nay, I'll not shine, I said, except with inward grace.
Is inward grace a liquid or a paste? asked this young Turk,
Hi, Daddy! What is inward grace? How does the old thing work?"
Words and Their Uses. Galveston *News*, May 4, 1871.)

Shoemake, the vulgar but very common pronunciation of the name of the *sumach*-tree, which every now and then even creeps into print.

Short metre has, in the New England States, where everybody is presumed to be familiar with psalm-singing, the peculiar meaning of quickly, in great haste.

"This goin' where glory waits ye, hain't one agreeable feature,
And if it warn't for wakin' snakes, I'd be home again *short metre*."
(J. R. Lowell. *Biglow Papers*, I.)

Shot in the neck, one of the numerous expressions for being drunk, which abound in the Union. "Your Honor, I found this man dead drunk in the gutter on the Place d'Armes, and when I tried to help him up he offered to fight me, saying that he was not drunk, but only *shot in the neck*." (New Orleans *Picayune*, March 17, 1870.)

Shut to, to, instead of *to shut*, furnishes another evidence of the influence which a large German population is apt to exercise, in limited localities, on the speech of the majority. The phrase is evidently derived from the German *zumachen*, to close, and quite common in some parts of Pennsylvania, where people do not say, "Close the door," but "*Shut* the door *to*." To *shut up* means, as has already been stated, to hush up, to be silent. To *get shut* of anybody, in the sense of to get rid of him, is not an Americanism, but an old phrase familiar to the North Briton, and preserved in some parts of the United States, which were mainly settled by immigrants of that race. Thus Chester County in Pennsylvania was settled mainly by Quakers from the North of England, and nothing is more common there than to hear men speak of "*getting shut* of a farm or a house," when they have disposed of the one or the other. A widow, importuned by a man whom she did not much care for, though her worldly substance was too considerable to be neglected, married him, as she said, "to *get shut* of the man." (Dr. A. L. Elwyn.) The word *shut* is, in its applications to slang, almost uniformly pronounced *shet*, a sound which it receives in the South, and especially from the negroes, under all circumstances.

Skary, or *skeary*, is a corruption of the new adjective *scary*, made from the verb to scare, and meaning easily intimidated. The transition is seen in the following phrase:—"Instead of *skeering* them away, my style of doing it would almost coax them to come and be took up." (J. C. Neal, *Charcoal Sketches*.) "You don't say you're *skeery*? Well, I declare, that beats all creation!" (*The Honeymoon*, p. 137.)

Skesicks, *skeezicks*, and a number of similar slang terms, apparently made at random as a mere expression of contempt, but, in reality, variations upon the Dutch word for vagabond, an idle, unprofitable person, is used very frequently to denote a good-for-nothing. "Thar ain't nobody but him within ten miles of the shanty, and that 'ar d—d old *skeezicks* knows it." (F. B. Harte, *Luck of Roaring Camp*, p. 43.)

Skunner, a strange corruption of *scorner*, frequent in Pennsylvania, and generally used not for the person who scorns, but for the dislike which he feels.

Slang whanger, derived from *slang* and to *whang*, to beat, is said to be not unknown as a provincial word in England, and was actually used more than once by T. Hood, though it attracted much attention abroad, when W. Irving first used it in his early writings to designate a noisy politician. "He is nothing but a miserable *slang whanger*, to whom nobody listens, when he addresses the house." (New York *Evening Mail*, May 17, 1870.) "To use the favorite word of *slang whangers*." (J. C. Neal, *Charcoal Sketches*, 1865.) Odder still is

Slantendicular, a word evidently made up from the verb to *slant* and the latter part of the word *perpendicular*, and now well known in English High Life below Stairs. "No, stop, I'll get at him as it were *slantendicularly* round a corner." (Sam Slick.)

Slink, occurs but rarely, and means a sneaking fellow; it is evidently a derivative of *sly*.

Slope, to, in the sense of disappearing from sight as if gliding down a slope, and apparently connected in the mind of Americans with the idea underlying expressions like, "going *down* South," is probably an Americanism. The same general idea, however, is felt in Tennyson's famous lines—

> "Many a night, from yonder ivied casement, as I went to rest,
> Did I look on great Orion, *sloping* slowly to the West."
> (*Locksley Hall.*)

The term came first into use here, when the new State of Texas offered a ready asylum to unfortunate speculators, dishonest creditors, and even escaped criminals, so that the words Gone To Texas (G. T. T.) meant to be gone to the American Alsatia, and the act of going so far "down South," became known as *sloping*. It implied, virtually, that the *sloper* had cheated his creditors, plundered a bank, or robbed his employers. The precise meaning of the word has been elucidated in the statement that "a mean fellow does not *slope*, he sneaks or slinks away; but the scoundrel, bold and unabashed, when defeated, *slopes* to parts unknown." It is not unlikely, moreover, that the signification of the popular word is instinctively connected with the idea of *eloping*.

Slosh around, to, a Western slang phrase, taking its force from the colloquial term *slosh* or *slush* (*sludge* in old English), denoting the unpleasant and unhealthy state of the roads, when deep snow is beginning to yield to a thaw. To *slosh around* means to go about, frequenting grogshops, in a half-muddled state. "Tim isn't good for much now; all the good he ever had in him is fast oozing out; since he's taken to *sloshing about*, he hasn't done a lick, and isn't worth a red cent." (*Flush Times of Alabama.*)

Snacked, for drunk, used in the South—probably the same as the more familiar *snapped.*

Sniptious and *resniptious*, two Western terms for smart and finical. *Snippy* has very nearly the same meaning, and has, no doubt, furnished the two enlarged forms.

Snore, I, belongs to the numerous class of thinly-veiled oaths, peculiar to New England.

Sockdolager, said to be a corruption of *doxology*, and to have thence derived the meaning of a final argument or a conclusive evidence, which closes a debate as decisively as the singing of the doxology ends religious service, has gradually enlarged its usefulness far beyond the original limits. It now denotes anything conclusive, from a word that closes a debate to a blow that finishes a fight. "The Radicals evidently consider the Kuklux Bill a *sockdolager*, after which the South will have nothing more to say, but to knock under and obey." (Memphis *Avalanche*, April 24, 1871.) *Sockdolager* means also a double hook, the two parts of which close with a spring as soon as the fish bites, as if in grim expression of the unavoidable result.

Soft sawder, a corruption of *solder*, which is generally pronounced *sodder*, the Scots especially always absorbing the *l*, and *soft corn*, are the two American terms for that kind of flattery which in English slang appears as *soft-soap*. In this country all three terms are, moreover, freely used as verbs. "Nor can't be hired to fool ye an' *soft-soap* ye at the caucus." (J. R. Lowell, *Biglow Papers*, II., p. 118.) "I don't like to be left alone with a gal; it's plaguy apt to set me a *soft sawderin'* and a courtin'." (*Sam Slick in England*, p. 19.) Mr. Johnston, in his notes on America, says happily, "*Soft sawder*, we presume, is the proper

American equivalent for the stinging *sobriquet* with which Persius stigmatized some Chatfield—some supple Attorney-General of his day: *Palpo, quem ducit hiantem cretata ambitio.*"

Solemncoly, a half-humorous half-ignorant corruption of melancholy, is a slang term still much used even by persons who are fully aware of the absurdity of thus coupling *solemn* and *choly* for the sake of making a new word. "The *solemncoly* man, Mem., the man that stays so long and is always so hard to go." (J. C. Neal, *Charcoal Sketches.*)

Sossle, to, or *to sozzle,* is an American verb made from the obsolete English verb *to soss,* used by Swift in the sense of sitting in a lazy, careless manner. To *sozzle* means to lounge about, but is used also of water which is splashed or spilt for want of attention.

Spill, to, used of persons instead of things, is American slang now, though it was thus used by Chaucer—

> "To chese whether she would have him save or *spill.*"
> (*Wife of Bathe's Tale.*)

"The member from Austin was badly *spilled* in the debate, and won't be apt to be heard again this session." (Texas paper, June, 1868.)

Spruce, as referring to neatness of apparel, with an insinuation that it is smarter than usual, is, in like manner, often censured as slang, while it has the authority of Evelyn in its favor, who writes, January 18, 1645: "Those of Amboise on the Loire in France are something of this invention, but nothing so *spruce.*"

Spots, in, one of the suggestive and graphic phrases which the West originates every now and then for a shortlived popularity, means occasionally, or here and there. The phrase, "He is clever in *spots,*" gives a man credit for fragmentary ability, and when a poor hunter comes to a town or a digging, where lodgings are scarce and high, he is quite ready to "sleep in *spots,*" *i. e.,* wherever he can find a sheltered place.

Spread, to, meaning to enlarge one's self and one's power or territory, is American. "England was not to be allowed to take Cuba or hold Oregon, because we, the people of the United States, had *spread,* were *spread,* and intended to *spread,* and should *spread*, and go on to *spread*." (Speech of Hon. Mr. Baker, of Illinois, in Congress, 1845.)

Spunk, made from *punk*, a word considered extremely vulgar slang in England, and denounced as such in Todd, is, in the United States, also considered a slang word, but looked upon with far more indulgence. *Spunk* means "touchwood" in English, and hence its figurative meaning, sanctioned by no less an authority than Sir Walter Scott: "He showed muckle more *spunk* too, than I thought had been in him; I thought he wad hae sent iron through the vagabond." (*Antiquary*.) "That boy of yours is a *spunky* chap, but you'll have to put a bit into his mouth or he'll give you a heap of trouble." (J. P. Kennedy.)

Square, either as an adjective qualifying a noun, as "a *square* trade," or as a phrase, *on the square*, refers to the open, fair character of a transaction. In either case the metaphor is borrowed from the Masonic emblem, the square being the symbol of evenness and rectitude. Thus *all squares* is used in the *Pickwick Papers*, p. 434. "It ain't no *square* game. They've jest put up the keerds on the chap from the start." (F. B. Harte, *Preface to Luck of Roaring Camp*, p. 1.) "Can you give us a *square* meal?" "This is all a fair, *square*, bona fide (fide to be pronounced as a monosyllable) business enterprise, is it?" (*Putnam's Magazine*, August, 1868.)

Sqush, to, is genuine, unmeaning slang, the word being made simply to imitate the sound produced by crushing a soft substance, like *squelch*. "The next time I meet the critter, I'll take my stick and kill it. I'll *sqush* it with my foot." (J. C. Neal, *Charcoal Sketches*.)

Steboy or *seboy*, often written *St, boy!* a favorite term to set dogs at other animals, the origin of which is shown in the last form.

Stevedore, to, shortened into *steve* occasionally, is constantly heard on wharves and in warehouses. "Sugar . . . not *stevedored*." (U. S. Congress, 1862.) "All hands were called aboard to *steeve*." (R. H. Dana, 1840.) "Each morning we brought off as many hides as we could *steeve* in the course of the day." (Ibidem.)

Streaked or *streaky*, well known to English low life, are favorite words with Western men, to whom "to feel *streaked*," conveys the utmost apprehension of which they are capable. New

Englanders, also, have inherited the word and the idea from the early settlers; hence—

> "But when it comes to bein' killed, I tell ye I felt *streaked*
> The first time ever I found out wy baggonets were peaked."
> (J. R. Lowell, *Biglow Papers*, I., p. 17.)

"Stranger, yon needn't look amused; it's no joke, I tell ye, to have a dozen red devils arter you in a hurry to raise your hair, and a man needn't be ashamed to feel *streaky*, when his mule's about giving out and the Ingins begin to yell like a pack of coyotes." (*Wild Western Scenes.*) From this meaning of fear the verb to *streak* obtains probably its meaning of running to escape from some danger. Americans prefer generally the fuller phrase, to make *streaks*, which means the same as to make *tracks*, while English slang is content with the simple term, to *streak*. "I *streaked* it for Washington, and it was well-nigh upon midnight, when I reached the White House." (Major Downing's *Letters*, p. 91.)

Stuck, to be, means, in slang phraseology, to be taken in by false pretences. "Did he buy the horse? Yes, and he was dreadfully *stuck*: the horse wasn't worth twenty dollars." (New Orleans *Picayune*, January 28, 1870.)

Stucked, a most emphatic participle of to *stick*, is heard with surprising frequency in the West, furnishing a double-dyed slang term, as *stuck* already has the slang meaning of being taken in or cheated. The literal meaning will be seen in this phrase: "He lived just long enough to send his respects to his wife, and tell his son to be a good boy, and then he died just like a *stucked* hog" (*Putnam's Magazine*, December, 1869), while the metaphor is used thus: "When Thomas came down the river, he looked demoralized, and to all our questions about his luck, he had only one answer: I am *stucked*, awfully *stucked*, and what's to become of the store is more than I can tell." (*The Country Merchant*, p. 258.) *Stuck up*, also, is used in slang as a substitute for proud or conceited: "He had, as a new-comer, perhaps fairly earned the reputation of being *stuck up*." (F. B. Harte, *Luck of Roaring Camp*, p. 74.)

Subside, to, as applied to persons, is a modern slang term, expressive of their giving up, or at least, becoming silent. "Thereupon the doughty General *subsided*, but it would be a great mistake to suppose that he will remain silent. He will *bottle up* his wrath, having had some experience in the line of *bottling up* during the war, and pour out his vials upon General Farnsworth's head, whenever the occasion offers." (Cincinnati *Commercial*, April, 1871.)

Suck in, as a noun and as a verb, is a graphic Western phrase to express deception of a more or less violent character. The figure is taken from the quicksands found on the banks of some of the Southwestern rivers especially, which literally *suck in* men and cattle. "Speculating in land is all very well, and great fortunes can be made and have been made in that line. But, Colonel, mind my word, there's a heap of *sucking-in* going on there, and my opinion is, you had better not venture too far at first." (*Western Scenes.*)

Sure, as a mere affirmative expletive, serves many purposes in American conversation. Constantly used instead of the adverb *surely*, it is often strengthened by strange additions. "Do you mean so, *sure?*" "I met him and he payed me all he owed. You don't say so? *Sure enough.*" (J. C. Neal, *Charcoal Sketches.*) "If you do so, I'll never say another word to you, and you'll be sorry for it, as *sure* as you are born." (*Putnam's Magazine*, June, 1852.) This latter phrase takes the place of the English "as *sure* as a gun," which is rarely heard in this country.

Suzz, a corruption of *sirs*, peculiar to New England, and as J. R. Bartlett states, frequently embellished by an additional *law*. "*Law, suzz*, what do you mean?"

Swan or *swon*, and *swow* or *swown*, euphemistic oaths of the New Englander, are substitutes for "swear;" "I *swan to man*" being considered particularly strong. *I swow* is used by J. R. Lowell.

T.

T, to suit to a, is an American phrase as well as English—arising probably from the *T* square of the carpenters, by which the accuracy of their work is tested.

> "An John P.
> Robinson, he
> Sez this is his view o' the thing to a *T*."
> (J. R. Lowell, *Biglow Papers*, I., p. 35.)

Tack, to, is the familiar abbreviation of *attack* in the South.

Take, to, furnishes a number of slang and colloquial expressions, most of which have been mentioned in connection with the noun which is added to *take*. To *take it*, is a very frequent substitute for I surmise: "You are all aware, I *take it*, that this is a most important question, and one that cannot be shirked any longer." (Speech of Colonel Forney in Washington, April, 1871.) To *take on*, in the sense of grieving, or fretting at a misfortune, is common throughout the United States, but of ancient use in England, and by no means an American phrase. "Alas, good soul, she cries and *takes on*." (Beaumont and Fletcher, *Scornful Lady*.) To *take up*, besides being applied to land, which is *taken up*, when it is brought under cultivation, also refers to horses and cattle, when they are taken from pasture to be made useful for riding, milking, etc. "Horses ought not to be *taken up* before their third year, and then only to be gentled." (*Rural Register*.) *To take to do*, in New England only, means to take to task, to reprove. "When she returned she was seriously *taken to do* for staying out so long." (*Our Young Folks*. 1869.)

Talk turkey, to, means to talk in a silly, foolish way, from the extremely ludicrous way in which the wild turkey during pairing-time gobbles while strutting about on a branch, with eyes closed, and feathers spread out wide. "When you tell me that you ain't afraid of a Redskin, and that you had just as lieves meet one of them bloody Ingins on the perairy as a perairy wolf, and knock him down, I calls that *talking turkey*, and no mistake." (W. G. Simms.)

Tanglefoot, one of the many popular names given in the West to bad liquor, which picturesquely describes the effect it has on the walk of the consumer.

'Tarnal and *'tarnation*, corruptions of *eternal* and *damnation*, both heard occasionally in England, used jocularly, while *tarnal* is nearly confined to the New England States, are favorite phrases with those who wish to be energetic without becoming profane. The antiquity of *tarnation* is proved by the lines—

"Poor honest John! 'tis plain he knowes
But liddle of live's range,
Or he'd aknow'd, gals oft, at fust
Have ways *tarnation* strange."
(*John Noakes' and Mary Styles*.)

Teetotal and its various derivatives, though of English manufacture, have acquired new and superior force in America with the growth of the agitation in favor of Total Abstinence. The word, formed by a duplication of the initial *t* of *total* for the sake of greater emphasis and force, had been in existence in Preston, England, and in many other localities, for several generations. When a proposal was made to change the Temperance movement into a new agitation in favor of excluding all intoxicating liquors, a working-man in Preston, of the name of Richard Turner, applied to the plan the familiar term *teetotal*. As he had a habit of stammering, and thus found difficulty in uttering the word, the attention of the public was specially directed toward the curious word, and thus it became, in course of time, the watchword of millions of men, and, as *Teetotalism*, the name of one of the greatest moral movements of the age. In the United States it is, however, far more frequently used in the sense of altogether or thoroughly, than with reference to the Temperance question. "There you are out, Sir, *teetotally* out, wofully out, Sir." (*Western Scenes.*) "Things were'nt going on right, so I pretty nearly gave myself up *teetotally* to the good of the republic." (J. C. Neal, *Charcoal Sketches.*) In the West an effort is sometimes made to increase the force of the strange word, by enlarging it into *teetotaciously.*

Tell, I can't, meaning I am unable to inform you, is universal in America, but not peculiar to this country. J. R. Lowell already calls attention to the fact that the phrase is explained by Dyce in a note to Middleton by the gloss, I could not say. To *tell* is, moreover, in the South, continually substituted for to say. "*Tell* the gentleman good-bye now."

Tend, to, in the sense of attending, as in Shakespeare's "He *tends* upon my father," is rarely if ever heard now in England, while in the New England States it is almost universal; and in certain combinations, as "*tending* bar" and "*tending* store," quite common in all parts of the Union. "Will you *tend* baby while I run down and open the door to father?" (*Atlantic Monthly*, December, 1869.) "He wanted to write up books, to *tend* store, or do anything to make an honest living." (*The Young Merchant*, p. 271.)

There, or rather *thar*, as it is more generally pronounced, means, in Western parlance, either the consent given to a proposition, or the familiarity with the subject in question. "Want me to liquor, stranger? I am *thar!*" (F. B. Harte, *Luck of Roaring Camp.*) "If you talk about hunting for meat, I am *there;* if you want me to follow a trail, I am *there,* and, by Jingo, if you want me to snuff you out as you are, I am *there* too." (*Wild Bill.*)

Thousand of brick, a, is a very forcible expression, conveying the most cordial approbation of a person who in England would have to be contented with being called "a brick." "When it came to the breakdown, Your Honor, he kicked up a row like a drove of contrary mules, and when we wanted to turn him out, he fell upon us like a *thousand of bricks,* and threatened to make minced meat of the police and every one of us." (Police Report. New Orleans *Picayune,* April 27, 1860.)

Thundering, an English slang term for very great, excessive, is very common especially in New England, where J. R. Lowell says, it is "a euphemism for the profane English *devilish,* perhaps derived from the belief common formerly, that thunder was caused by the prince of the air, for some of whose accomplishments, see Cotton Mather." (*Glossary to Biglow Papers.*)

Tickler has, in America, two special meanings: it denotes a small flask for holding liquor, and also a book in which merchants enter the names of those debtors whose memory has to be "tickled" in order to make them pay their dues. In one of the side-streets of New York the following advertisement used to hang over the door of a large and imposing building: "Pocket-pistols charged, and *ticklers* supplied, on Saturday night up to 12 o'clock, for use next day." In the South the phrase, to "take a *tickler,*" is often used as an invitation to "join in a drink."

Tie to, to, has in the West the figurative meaning of to rely, and hence a reliable man is qualified as a man it will do to *tie to.* To *tie up,* on the other hand, is used with reference to boats, which are secured at the landing. Flatboats and steamboats alike, are said, on the Mississippi, to *tie up.* "The Crevasse was so threatening, and the current of the river changing so continually, that the larger steamers even did not venture below, but *tied up* above Helena, till there was not room for another boat." (New Orleans *Bee,* June 30, 1861.)

Tiger, the slang term for a peculiar howl or yell, which is given after the usual cheers, and by an excited fancy has been compared to the howl of a tiger. It is of purely American origin, and common on occasions of great excitement and wild enthusiasm. "Gentlemen, I call for nine cheers and a *tiger* in honor of our guests." (New York *Herald*, November 17, 1870.)

Time, to have a good, is also a thorough Americanism, a great favorite, especially with young ladies, and hence abounding in the works of Mrs. Stowe, the Misses Wetherell, and their professional sisters. There is, however, good authority for this phrase also, though perhaps in a slightly modified sense, in old English authors: Swift has in his Journal to Stella: "I hope Mrs. Wells has *had a good time*." (February 14, 1710–11.) "What kind of a time did you have at your uncle's? Oh! we *had a delightful time*." (*The Wide Wide World*, II.)

Tom Dog, made after the manner of *Tom* Cat, belongs to the West exclusively.

Tomfoolery, for foolish trifling, is quite common throughout the country. It is, of course, derived from the English term Tom Fool, as in

> "Red and Yellow
> *Tom Fool's* colors."
> (*Proverb.*)

"None of your *tomfoolery*, Bob; you keep quiet and we'll settle it all."

Tormented, another New England euphemism for the stronger term denoting eternal torment. "Not a *tormented* cent." (J. R. Lowell.)

Tote, to, a verb which of all colloquial Americanisms has probably excited the most general interest and led to innumerable disquisitions, remains still unexplained as far as its first origin is concerned. It is universally used in the South to denote the carrying something weighty by personal effort and unaided by any convenience. The strangest of all explanations is probably that given by the learned Noah Webster in his admirable Dictionary. He says of the word, "said to be of African origin." This suggestion has nothing in its favor except the simple fact, that the negroes never use any other word for carrying. It is almost as improbable, that the word should have been derived from the old English word to *tote*, which was used to express the process of summing up the *total* amount, and which is still in use in

Lincolnshire, where people say, "Come, *tote* it up and tell me what is the whole amount." (*Notes and Queries*, 1853.) Chaucer also uses the word in this sense. It seems far more probable, that the word should owe its present use to the fact, that when Virginia was settled, and the term, to *tote*, was brought to this country, the English emigrants were familiar with it from two entirely different sources. One was the Anglo-Saxon verb, *totian*, to lift up, to elevate. ("*Totodun* ut tha heafdu: eminebant capita, Past. 16, 5. Bosworth, *Anglo-Saxon Dictionary*, and *English Dictionary*, p. 226.) This old Saxon word, used in its primitive sense, still survived in the provinces, and was carried by persons, accustomed to its sound and use, to America, where it has never ceased to be used. At the same time, Englishmen were all more or less familiar with the word *tolt*, the name of a writ, by which the proceedings on a writ of right are removed (carried) from the Court Baron into the County Court, the precept of the sheriff being, "quia *tollit* atque eximit causam e curia baronum" (3 C., Blackstone, *Commentaries*, p. 34.) Blount's *Law Dictionary* (1691), states that the familiar term *tolt*, was derived from the Latin verb *tolle*, to lift or remove. In the colonies this word and the Anglo-Saxon *tote* combined to express the process of removing corporeal things as well as incorporeal, and being short and easy of pronunciation, the negroes especially readily seized upon it, to denote the lifting a thing with a view of carrying it from one place to another. That the word is by no means unknown in England may be seen from the fact that already Piers Plowman says in his Crede: "Then *toted* I into a taverne and there I espyede two frere Carmes" (Ed. 1553, B. III.); and that the handle of a carpenter's plane is to this day called a *tote* in England, evidently from the Anglo-Saxon verb mentioned above.

Touch of the liver, a euphemism for more serious affections. "The Sulphur Springs, where I am now (White Sulphur), are much resorted to by persons who have a *touch of the liver*, as it is called, or who are afflicted with bilious complaints of any kind." (*Letters from the South*, I., p. 155.)

Tracks, to follow in one's, means to follow him so immediately and closely as to step into his footmarks. The phrase, of Western origin, is quite common in New England, and compared by J. R. Lowell, with his touching tenderness for all his native expressions, to the Latin *e vestigio* and the Norman-French *chezlespas*, both of which have the same meaning, although in no way connected with the modern form. "She is an excellent woman, and if you *follow close in her tracks*, you may be sure to do what is right." (*Our Young Folks*, 1870.)

Trampoose, to, an enlargement of the English "to tramp," is a genuine Americanism, and means, to wander about listlessly. "I felt as lonely as a catamount, and as dull as a bachelor beaver, so I *trampousses* off to the stable." (*Sam Slick in England.*) "The sergeant has successfully *trampoosed* this, the whole South, with the Stars and Stripes fluttering in the breeze, but, beyond the mere bravado of having done so, it is hard to tell what good he or his friends can imagine to have been accomplished by the exploit." (Cincinnati *Commercial*, September, 1866.)

Trash a trail, to, means, in Western parlance, to conceal the traces of your march. The phrase has its literal meaning, when it denotes the taking to the water, or covering up footmarks in some cunning way, to mislead pursuers; but it is almost as frequently employed in a figurative meaning, when speaking of the efforts made to conceal acts that could hereafter be used as evidence against a man's political integrity or financial prudence. "What we admire most in Carl Schurz's movement, is, that he comes out boldly and takes no pains to *trash his trail.* We admire plain dealings." (St. Louis *Republican*, April, 1871.)

Try it on, to, instead of the simple *to try*, is of course taken from tailors' slang, and hence frequently coupled with the personal pronoun. "You needn't *try it on* me, I have heard all that before." "You must find somebody else to *try it on*, I have cut my wisdom teeth long ago." (New Orleans *Bee*, July 31, 1870.)

Tuk is a common corruption of *took*.

Turkey, as poor as Job's, a phrase, not a genuine Americanism, but intensified, in American fashion, by some energetic addition; for instance, "As poor as Job's turkey, that had but one feather in its tail," or, "As poor as Job's turkey, that had to lean against a fence to gobble." (*Once a Week*, May, 1871.)

Twistical, denotes in slang that which has a moral *twist*, and is hence unfair, and not straightforward. "I wouldn't go deep into that matter, Sam is raythe *twistical*, and it's pretty hard, I hearn tell, to get along with him smoothly." (*New Englander*, June, 1870.)

U.

Uncultivatable, but for its inconvenient length, has nothing objectionable in form or meaning. "The land around the Light is a perfect desert of loose sand, and perfectly *uncultivatable,* except in one or two of the hollows." (*Putnam's Magazine,* September, 1870.) Equally unsupported is

Universanimous, apparently an effort to make *unanimous* more comprehensive, is perhaps nothing more than a facetious fabrication of J. R. Lowell, who says, "They are *universanimous,* both as to its rusticity and its capacity of rising to the level of more elevated sentiments." (*Biglow Papers,* II., p. 36.)

Upper Crust, Upper Ten Thousand, and *Uppertendom,* with a host of similar crudities, owe their origin to the unfortunate taste of a writer of great ability and well-earned popularity, N. P. Willis. A brother poet criticises him thus—

"Gad, what a polish *uppertendom* gives
This polisher of adjectives;
This man who chokes the English worse than Thuggists,
And turns the trade to trunkmakers or druggists."
(Duganne. *Parnassus in Pillory.*)

"What the *Upper Ten Thousand* will do until Paris is once more at peace and able to resume the sceptre of fashion, is a question which deeply agitates the most profound minds of our society." (New York *Herald,* March 14, 1871.)

Usable, one of the latest manufactures, but already making its way into the daily journals. "Government lands at one dollar per acre. Land scrip *usable* by pre-emptors. For sale by G. F. Lewis, Cleveland, Ohio." (New York *Tribune,* May 1, 1871.)

Used to be, and even *used to could,* are frequently heard in the United States, as they occur, though rarely, in provincial dialects in England. The former is even used as an adverb, instead of formerly.

"But maugre all the croaking
Of the Raven, and the joking
Of the verdant little fellow of the *used to be* review,
The people, in derision
Of their impudent decision,
Have declared, without division, that the mystery will do."
(Hartford *Columbian,* 1849.)

V.

V is pronounced *w* in words like vinegar, veil, veal, etc., in the neighborhood of Burlington in New Jersey and Marblehead in Massachusetts, precisely as it is done by the cockneys of London.

Virginia Fence, to make a, means to walk like a drunken man, in humorous allusion to the zigzag shape of a snake-fence. *Virginia Reel*, on the contrary, is the name given to the old English country dance, throughout the United States, as for some time in Virginia alone of all the Colonies the national dance was permitted, and from thence made its way to other parts of the country. "The dancing wound up, as usual, with a genuine *Virginia Reel*, which lasted far into the small hours, and enlisted the energies of old and young alike." (*America by Rail and River.*)

Vum, I, instead of *I vow*, a favorite oath in disguise, in New England.

W.

Walking-papers is a cant term denoting letters of dismissal, as if in derisive allusion to the liberty granted to an official to walk out of office and whithersoever he likes. "It was said, yesterday, that a number of town officials, as well as many of the officers of the former District, had already received their *walking-papers*, but the announcement is premature." (Washington *Patriot*, April 21, 1871.)

Wan't, like *hain't*, is, in New England especially, used indifferently for *was not* and *were not*.

Ways is used constantly, and throughout the United States, for the singular, to denote a short distance. "Won't you go *a little ways* further?" "We had only proceeded a *little ways* down the road, when we noticed a large crowd of men running all in one direction." (J. P. Kennedy.) *There is no two ways about it*, an energetic assertion of being certain beyond doubt. "I tell you, general, we'll have to fight our way out, and that at once, there is *no two ways* about it; for if we don't do it pretty quickly, we shall be surrounded on all sides, and have to go up, sure enough." (*Campaign with General Price*, p. 119.)

Whapper or *whopper*, a slang term not unknown to England in the sense of a big lie, is much used in the West to designate anything unusually large or remarkable. At times it is exchanged for the adjective *whapping*, which has the same signification. "Once, however, my spear entered the back of a *whapper*, and my determination to keep hold was nearly the cause of my being drowned. It must have been a thrilling, yet a ridiculous sight to see me astraddle of the sturgeon, and passing down the river like lightning." (C. Lanman, *A Summer in the Wilderness.*)

Whipping the cat, an old English phrase used only by tailors and carpenters, has maintained its existence in New England, Pennsylvania, and a few other States, where it denotes the annual visit of a tailor to repair the clothes of a household. It is said to have originated in a very rough practical joke, which bears the same name in Hampshire, England, and of which, it is surmised, the tailor may have been the victim. (J. R. Lowell.) The simple tailors of former days liked thus to go from house to house in the rural districts, providing the families with clothing. The chief romance for the happy "Schneider" was in the abundant and wholesome cheer of the farmer who employed him, and as his annual visits fell in the pudding and sausage season, he was usually crammed with that kind of "vegetables," as he facetiously called them, to his heart's content. The only objection made to *catwhipping*, was that it afforded no opportunity to "cabbage," and in former days this was a serious grievance. The introduction of large manufacturing establishments, low-priced ready-made clothing, and the advent of the sewing-machine, have now nearly made an end to this itinerant occupation. The terms *catwhipper* and *catwhipping* were often facetiously, and sometimes very irreverently, applied to other itinerant professions: even "schoolmasters"—there were no "teachers," much less "educators," in those benighted days—were called *catwhippers*, when they boarded, as was quite usual, in turns with the parents of their scholars. Itinerating preachers also were, by the initiated, included in this category.

Whipstitch, every, a phrase of the Far West, expressive of what is done continually. "The laborers are off *every whipstitch*." (*Overland Magazine*, March, 1869.)

White frost, a common expression for hoar frost, in the South and West.

Whole-footed, whole-hearted, and *whole-souled*, are popular cant terms, used with a profusion and want of discrimination which has utterly destroyed their original meaning. Any devising man, who invites a crowd to "drinks all around" is instantly praised as a "*whole-footed* man," and the calculating speculator, who gives a piece of land for a church with a view to the enhanced value of the adjoining lots, which he retains, appears in the newspapers as "a noble, *whole-souled* gentleman, whose liberality will earn him the thanks of his countrymen and the gratitude of coming generations." (Philadelphia *Age*, January 14, 1851.)

Winter-kill, to, a verb made for the sake of brevity and convenience, means, to be killed by the frosts of winter. "Our clover was completely *winter-killed*." "Who would go to the Northwest, with its terrible frosts and short summers, when in Virginia all kind of stock can stay out during the whole year without shelter, and such a thing as *winter-killed* crops are utterly unknown?" (Richmond *Whig*, August 11, 1863.)

Wonst, a slang term for *once* (compare German *einst*).

Wrath, like all, a strong but suggestive phrase, frequently heard in the South and the West, and expressive of great emphasis. "When we went down to the beach, the waves came tumbling up *like all wrath*, and the sight of our little bay, usually so quiet and peaceful, was grand beyond description." (*A Summer in Florida*, p. 47.)

Y.

Yank, used as a noun and a verb, denotes the action of violently jerking or twitching a person or a thing, and in figurative meaning, a great effort of mind. An attempt has been made to find in the slang term an allusion to the energy and ingenuity with which the *Yank*, as the Yankee is often called by the vulgar, overcomes all difficulties. "He *yanked* and *yanked*, but the sapling wouldn't come, and thar he was caught in his own trap." (*A Visit to Nantucket*, 1867.) *Yankee* used to be also the name of a New England drink, made of whiskey and molasses, but the term has nearly fallen into disuse.

> "You fine Miss Boston Lady gay,
> For this your speech I thank ye,
> Call on me, when you come this way,
> And take a dram of *Yankee*."
>
> (Fessenden, *Yankee Doodle*, B.)

Young America, a cant term, when used to denote the supposed characteristics of the generation of Americans now growing up, as when the popular writer, J. G. Holland, says: "What we call *Young America* is made up of about equal parts of irreverence, conceit, and that moral quality familiarly known as brass."

Z.

Zit, to, a verb evidently made in imitation of the sound which it describes—the peculiar hissing of bullets when striking water—is frequently heard in the West. "It was the hottest bath I ever took. For about two minutes the bullets *zitted* and skipped on the water; I thought I was hit again and again, but the rebel sharpshooters were bothered by the splash we made." (*Wild Bill.*)

XII.

New Forms and Nicknames.

NEW FORMS AND NICKNAMES.

Severe critics are apt to place among the slang terms of America the large number of new forms, which have been made here from well-known words, and are gradually gaining ground, as they become popular with journalists, and thus familiar to a large class of intelligent persons. Grammatically, they are abominations, and æsthetically, not one of them, perhaps, can be justified. The pure well of English undefiled ought not to be contaminated by such misshapen forms, and their influence is disastrous in the extreme, by removing all landmarks in language, and accustoming the ear to the utmost license in the use of words. With all this, they are apparently suited to supply a want; at least they are largely employed, easily understood, and have, almost invariably, the one great merit of brevity. This is the feature which has led to their creation in the first place: they are, to a large extent, the offspring of the telegraph-wire and the cable. The heavy expense incurred by private correspondents, and still more by great companies, such as the leading daily papers of London or New York, and especially the "Associated Press" of the United States, engendered promptly a tendency to shorten messages, and developed great ingenuity in accomplishing this purpose. The last-named company, for instance, at once adopted certain well-known abbreviations: this evening and this morning, became *sevening* and *smorning; fob,* meant free on board, and *swells,* as well as; New York and New Orleans appeared simply as *York* and *Orleans;* Rio de Janeiro as *Rio;* Buenos Ayres as *Bayres,* and San Francisco as *Frisco.* Then came less pardonable forms, such as sleeting, conflagrating, incendiaried, and interviewed, and finally a whole class of violent contractions, derived from well-known and well-formed words, like *burgled, injuncted,* and *excurted.* It is this class of words which contains the most objectionable and most dangerous terms, attractive as they have proved by their novelty and their brevity. They led to the use of other terms for which no such excuse could be made, and as their number daily increases, they threaten to corrupt American English to a mournful extent. The absence of sound criticism, and the little respect paid to the authority of good writers and sound teachers, favor the contamination, and, unless the good sense of the people, and the conscience of editors and writers for the press, come to the rescue, serious danger may be apprehended.

Among these new-fangled terms we find *complected*, in the sense of having a certain complexion. "The woman had evidently had chills recently; she was feeble and emaciated, and *complected* as I have never seen any one out of malarious regions." (Cincinnati *Commercial*, June 9, 1868.) The noun *eruption* has, in like manner, suffered violent curtailment in order to furnish a new verb, to *erupt*. "This person had, at the peak and tip of a gigantic volcano of infuriated scolding against everything whatever, *erupted* in a final blaze of fury." (*Putnam's Magazine*, September, 1870.) Old English writers, however, have *erupt* quite frequently. *Excursion* has been forced to produce to *excurt*. "President Grant has once more *excurted* from Washington; he has gone on a visit to Mr. Cameron's home, but will be back in time for the Cabinet-meeting on Monday." (Washington *Chronicle*, April 17, 1870.) An amusing evidence of the utter insecurity which such license creates in the use of the most familiar words, has been furnished by the fate of the word *resurrection*. A verb was apparently required, and forthwith two were manufactured to meet the demand, which now compete with each other for the supremacy; but, whichever may prove victorious, the language will be seriously damaged by its admission. "The invention described in yesterday's *Times*, and displayed on Saturday in Newark, by which a person who may happen to be buried alive, is enabled to *resurrect* himself from the grave, may lead some people to fancy there is actual danger of their being buried alive." (New York *Times*, quoted by R. G. White, *Words and their Uses*, p. 229.) "Mr. Butler said, he had long since learned the wisdom of the maxim, *de mortuis nil nisi bonum*, and if Admiral Porter only lay still in his grave, if his friends did not *resurrect* him to offend the nostrils of the House, he (Mr. Butler) would not have said a word about him." (New York *Tribune*, February 7, 1871.) Then there arose a formidable rival to this "amazing formation," as R. G. White justly calls it, and being a little more imposing and grandiloquent, now threatens to supersede the shorter term. "Body-snatching continues to be a business in Cincinnati. The leading gentleman of the *resurrectionizing* profession is one Cunningham, who, with two assistants, dug up the subjects and carried them to the medical schools in an express-wagon." (Cincinnati *Commercial*, February 6, 1871.) In like manner the burglar's occupation has been designated as *burglarizing;* when caught he is *custodized*, and the news of his capture is promptly *itemized* by the penny-a-liner.

The frequency with which *resolutions* are spoken of in newspapers and public reports, has led, in the same way, to the formation of a new verb to take the place of *resolve*. "I tell you, gentlemen, you may keep this up as long as you choose, but when you have done *resoluting*, you will only have lost your time, because we of the majority won't stand it." (Savannah *Republican*, March 13, 1860.)

"You may *resoloot* till the cows come home,
But ef one of you teches the boy
He'll rastle his bones to-night in hell."
(John Hay, *Banty Tim.*)

Another class of such words is the offspring of the agitation of so-called Women's Rights, and pretends to furnish terms for the many new professions to which women claim admission. A couple of ladies having established their "Exchange Office" in that quiet and respectable neighborhood so eminently suited for persons of their sex, called Wall-street, they were at once spoken of in the New York papers as *bankeresses* or *brokeresses*. Fortunately, the word seemed to please the public as little as the new occupation, and neither term has been adopted. *Doctoresses*, however, abound in the land, to the utmost disgust of Miss Mary Walker, the most notorious of the class, who, like all her learned "sisters," claims the right to be called *Doctor*. "Miss A——, the young and attractive *doctoress*, who yesterday appeared in Court to testify in the great will-case, made a most pleasing impression upon the bar and the jury, by her clear, intelligent answer, and her simple, modest behavior while in the witness-stand." (Philadelphia *Inquirer*, 1868.) Since Miss Hosmer began her brilliant career, the word *Sculptoress* has become familiar to American ears. "We all remember the time when the old doctor's charming daughter uncoupled the cars as the train ran over the mill-dam, and imperilled the lives of nearly a hundred passengers, who were left on the track at the mercy of the approaching mail-train. The young *sculptoress* was hardly aware of the frightful responsibility she incurred by her thoughtless prank." (Boston *Bee*, March 23, 1855.) Even the grave and mysterious masons have seen their sacred precincts invaded by the enemy. "We are now informed of the great secret of Miss Vinnie Ream's grand success as a *sculptoress*. It appears that she is a mason, or a *masoness*, as you please. She belongs to a Female Lodge, which has some sort of connection with Male Lodges—a very mysterious and recondite connection, no doubt, only we don't know what it is. The statutes of the old, original order forbid the initiation of women most emphatically, but there used to be a sort of branch kind, called the Daughters of Jerusalem. However, Miss V. Ream has taken eight degrees in something or other, and is very high in the mysteries. This accounts for the elegance, beauty, and generally fine mason-work of the Lincoln statue." (New York *Tribune*, February 2, 1871.) A different formation is attempted in the following notice: "Mrs. E. Tupper Wilkes, the Minnesota *clergywoman*, has a salary of $2000 a year, and is to get more." (Chicago *Tribune*, February 17, 1871.) An effort was made to vindicate the honor of the sex by having *Chairwomen* to preside over Women's Rights meetings, but Irish sympathizers would appeal to the *chairwoman* so persistently, that the association became offensive, and the new title was abandoned.

Perhaps the worst of all these malformations, and perhaps, for that very reason, the most numerous and most popular of all, is the class of new nouns made promiscuously from French and Latin, German and Saxon words, by the simple addition of the termination *ist*. This produces naturally most shocking hybrids, but the gain of time and exertion seems to be deemed ample compensation for the barbarous character of the process. Thus we find the following advertisement: "A nurseryman wanted, who is a thorough master of his business; one who understands taking care of a greenhouse and plants preferred; must be complete master in propagating evergreens and deciduous trees and shrubs; also a good *fruitist*." (New York *Tribune*, February 16, 1871.) An excellent and generally very carefully-written journal, *Appleton's Weekly Journal*, speaks nevertheless of the great painter, A. B. Durand, as a distinguished *landscapist* (May 7, 1870), thus proving the extreme danger with which license in speech is fraught. Absurd grandiloquence is quaintly illustrated in a notice, under the startling title "Thanatopsis," and beginning with the sentence: "It is very seldom that the *obituarist* is called upon to speak with honest truthfulness of departed humbleness." (Mrs. Van Lew, Postmaster of Richmond, Virginia, in Richmond *Dispatch*, April 27, 1871.) Another distinguished speaker at public meetings, held to advocate the rights of the downtrodden sex, Mrs. Isabella Beecher Hooker, is thus described: "Every one admires her and her course; she never oversteps the line of strict propriety: whether on the platform or off it, she is modest and sensible, and she has done more to commend the new doctrines of the female *suffragists* than a dozen of her associates. The only wonder is, that she can associate with the Woodhulls and Claflins." (New York *Tribune*, March 20, 1871.) A term which has become very popular with the steadily-increasing interest in the culture of vines throughout the United States is one of the worst manufactures of this kind; it is used thus: "This year a French winemaker and *vineyardist* came from Kentucky to cultivate the Great Mustang grape of Texas." (*American Wines*, p. 613.) There is but one newly-made term of this class that falls perhaps even more painfully upon the ear, and yet it also is found daily more frequently: "A Wisconsin *walkist* has done one hundred miles within twenty-four hours, and his name is Simmons." (St. Louis *Democrat*, January 4, 1871.) It is not to be wondered at, that as soon as the door is once opened to such abominations, by those who ought to be the guardians of the purity of the language, a whole host of similar terms should rush in and try to make a lodgment, for nothing thrives like weeds, in language as well as in nature. Hence, no sooner had men's ears become somewhat accustomed to hear a pedestrian called a *walkist*, than the man whose rifle brought down the largest amount of game became known as a famous *shootist*, the Nilsson was praised in numerous journals as one of the greatest *singists* that had ever come to America, and the man of violence, who had heretofore been denounced as a murderer, now appeared before the charitable jury as a modest *stabbist*, or, at worst, called a formidable *strikist.*

Among the familiar terms peculiar to our American speech, we must, finally, not forget the names which are given to several of the States of the Union, and of the principal cities, from some striking peculiarity in their appearance, or from remarkable incidents connected with their history. The following are the most common:

Arkansas is called the *Bear State,* although within its limits and throughout the West the name is pronounced *Bar* State. The epithet was bestowed in days when bears abounded in that part of the Union.

California enjoys the same title, but in this instance it is a grizzly bear which gives the name, and reappears in the coat of arms of the State, where the huge and formidable animal is seen standing on a railway track, thus graphically symbolizing the marvellous growth of a State which, thirty years ago, was a wilderness, and now is behind no other part of the Union in wealth and culture.

Connecticut enjoys quite a number of *sobriquets* by which it is popularly known. Sometimes it is called the *Blue Law State,* from the unenviable fame acquired by the first regulations of the government of New Haven Plantation, known as the Blue Laws. The valuable quarries of freestone, to which the State is largely indebted for its revenue, have procured for it the name of the *Freestone State,* while at other times it appears as the *Nutmeg State,* from the famous speculation in wooden spices, immortalized by Sam Slick, or, as a factious native prefers to explain it, "because you will have to look for a *grater!*"

Delaware is known as the *Blue Hen,* from the unenviable notoriety which one of her sons, Captain Caldwell, acquired in the War of the Revolution for his fondness of cockfighting. Fortunately he was, at the same time, renowned for his spirit and undaunted gallantry, as well as for admirable skill in drilling his men, so that the latter became known in the army as his "gamecocks." He held the peculiar notion that no cock could be true game that did not come from a blue hen, and this led to the substitution of Blue Hen Chickens for the former term of Gamecocks. As the whole regiment in which he served became famous through him, all the men from Delaware were surnamed thus, and finally the epithet was transferred to the State from which they came.

Florida is the *Gulf State,* although Arkansas, Louisiana, Mississippi, and Texas share with it the common name of Gulf States.

Georgia, one of the most thriving States of the Union, and beyond comparison the most enterprising and energetic Southern State, little deserves the name of *Cracker State,* by which it is occasionally designated, from the Crackers, the lowest and most ignorant of its citizens before the abolition of slavery.

Illinois is known as the *Sucker State,* because its inhabitants are known throughout the Union as suckers. The origin of the odd term is said to be this: "The Western prairies are, in many places, full of holes made by the crawfish, which descends to the water beneath. In early times, when travellers wended their way over these immense plains, they very prudently provided themselves with a long hollow reed, and when thirsty, thrust it into these natural Artesian wells, and thus easily supplied their longings. The crawfish-well generally contains pure water, and the manner in which the traveller drew forth the refreshing element gave him the name of Sucker." (Providence *Journal.*) A more pleasing and more appropriate name, under which Illinois is equally well known, is that of the *Prairie State.*

Indiana is the *Hoosier State.* "The citizens of this State, known as Hoosiers, who gave the State its name, are proverbially inquisitive. They are said to have got their nickname, because they could not pass a house without pulling the latchstring and crying out, Who's here?" (W. Ferguson, *America by River and by Rail,* p. 338.) Another version derives the name from the word *husher,* denoting a man of superior strength and skill, who could *hush* or overcome every adversary, and hence an equivalent for the modern "bully."

Iowa has adopted the name of a famous Indian chief, who was long the terror of all settlers within her boundary lines, and hence is known as the *Hawkeye State.*

Kansas is often called the *Garden State,* from the beautiful appearance of rolling prairies and vast cultivated fields which abound in that fertile region. It appears occasionally as *Squatter State,* from the pertinacity with which squatter-sovereignty was discussed there, and settlers poured in by the two contending parties.

Kentucky shares with Arkansas the name of the Bear State, and for the same reason; but it is also known as the *Corn-Cracker*, that being a common epithet given to the inhabitants.

Louisiana is known as the *Pelican State*, the bird being frequent on its shores, and hence chosen as its emblem in its coat of arms. It also appears as the *Creole State*, on account of the large number of its inhabitants who are descendants of the original French and Spanish settlers.

Massachusetts, known as the Colony of Massachusetts Bay before the formation of the present Union, still continues to be called the *Bay State*.

Maine obtains its name as the *Pine-Tree State* from the extensive pine-forests which cover its central and northern parts, while the occupation they afford to a large number of inhabitants, engaged in felling and rafting the trees, and in converting them into shingles, boards, and the like, has made it also known as the *Lumber State*.

Maryland bears the proud title of *Old-Line State* from the *Old-Line* regiments which she contributed to the Continental Army in the War of the Revolution—the only State that had regular troops of "the line."

Michigan appears as *Wolverine State*, from the number of wolverines (literally, little wolves) which used to abound in the peninsula, and gave the inhabitants their name of Wolverines, by which they are still generally known. Michigan, surrounded by the four magnificent lakes (Superior, Michigan, Huron, and Erie), derives from this position also the name of *Lake State*.

Minnesota is known as the *New England of the West*, on account of the number of New England people to be found there.

Mississippi is occasionally spoken of humorously as the *Mud-cat State*, the inhabitants being quite generally known as Mud-cats, a name given to the large catfish abounding in the swamps and the mud of the rivers.

Missouri owes its name of *Bullion State* to one of her most distinguished sons, Col. Thomas H. Benton, who, as a statesman, was a staunch advocate of gold and silver currency, and became himself known in Congress and among the people as Old Bullion.

New Hampshire, originally so called by the early settlers, who wished to perpetuate the memory of the county from which many had emigrated, is now known as the *Granite State,* its mountains being largely composed of that material.

New York, once known as New Amsterdam, under Dutch rule, then assuming its present name as an English colony, assumes in the Union the proud title of *Empire State,* as surpassing all others in wealth and population, and thus forming an Empire of its own. The motto, "Excelsior," upon its coat of arms has made it also known as the *Excelsior State.*

North Carolina, producing from her immense pine-forests large quantities of valuable products, derives from one of them the name of the *Turpentine State.*

Ohio owes to the *Buck-Eye,* one of the most beautiful trees of America, and poetically so called from the resemblance its chestnut-like fruit bears to a deer's eye, the name of *Buckeye State,* as its inhabitants also are familiarly known as Buckeyes.

Pennsylvania is proud of the name of the *Keystone State,* derived from the fact of its being the central State at the time when the Union was formed. The names of the States, arranged in the form of an arch, according to their geographical position, leave Pennsylvania in the centre, where the keystone would be placed. The great importance of the State, due to its extent, wealth, and immense manufacturing interests, make the name quite appropriate also in a higher sense of the word, and Pennsylvania is not loth to claim the full meaning.

Rhode Island, the smallest State in the Union, is therefore affectionately called *Little Rhody.*

South Carolina is indebted for her name as *Palmetto State* to the valuable tree growing abundantly on its shores, and hence furnishing the emblem in her coat of arms. A palmetto is carefully kept growing in the streets of Charleston, and the Palmetto Flag earned a sad distinction in the late Civil War by its ill-fated connection with Fort Sumter.

Texas, once a province of Mexico, then an independent republic, bore a single star in its coat of arms, and being for a time left to struggle unaided against the whole power of her formidable enemy, became then honorably known as the *Lone Star State*—a name which she has ever since retained.

Vermont is generally, by simple translation of the original name given by the French settlers, called the *Green Mountain State*, the principal ridge of mountains within its boundaries being known by that name.

Virginia retains to this day her name of the *Old Dominion*, honorably earned in times of great peril by her loyalty to her legitimate sovereign, Charles II.

Wisconsin, abounding during early days in badgers, has ever since retained the name of *Badger State*.

Among the names given to the prominent cities of the United States, the following are most familiar:

Baltimore, in Maryland, appears as the *Monumental City*, having had, for a long time, alone monuments in her squares before other towns had followed the example, and boasting still of the oldest and largest monument erected in honor of Washington. (Richmond, in Virginia, has, however, recently finished the finest monument found in this country, an equestrian statue of General Washington, surrounded by a number of colossal statues.)

Boston, in Massachusetts, rejoices in a number of nicknames. Now she is called the *Classic City*, in appreciation of the high culture of her inhabitants, whose proverbial modesty, however, has claimed for their native town the name of the *Athens* of America. The sarcastic Virginia statesman, John Randolph, hearing Daniel Webster use this term, remarked: "Boston may be the Athens of America, but it has never been my good fortune to meet with any of the Athenians." Less appreciative outsiders indulge in calling it the *City of Notions*, the latter furnishing the staple of the native trade in mercantile goods as well as in matters of mind and thought; while one of her own most gifted sons, the poet Holmes, nicknamed her, good-naturedly, the *Hub of the Universe*, a term which has become by far the most popular of all her names. An older designation, *Trimountain City*, has been almost entirely lost, although the three mountains upon which the city is built, and which gave rise to the epithet, still survive in Tremont-street and Tremont House.

Brooklyn, in New York, a city of marvellous growth, and

promising soon to have half a million inhabitants, enjoys the enviable name of *City of Churches*, which it well deserves, on account of the unusual number and superior beauty of its churches.

Buffalo, in New York, derives, from its vast commerce on the great lakes, the name of *Queen City of the Lakes.*

Chicago, in Illinois, famous for the number and beauty of its gardens, is hence known everywhere as the *Garden City*, while

Cincinnati, in Ohio, unparalleled in rapidity of growth and extent of wealth, is called the *Queen City.*

Cleveland, in Ohio, is known as the *Forest City*, her streets being bordered by beautiful forest-trees—in the same manner in which *Portland*, in Maine, also has earned this name by her stately elms and numerous shade-trees.

Detroit, in Michigan, translates the French name given by the early settlers, into *City of the Straits*, in allusion to the Strait connecting Lake St. Clair with Lake Erie, on which the city is situated.

Duluth, one of the youngest cities of the Union, claims, according to Bayard Taylor's experiences, the remarkable name of *Zenith City of the Unsalted Seas!*

Galena, in Illinois, owing its first name to the galena, a species of lead ore found in abundance in the neighborhood, is indebted to its remarkably quick growth for the familiar name of *Crescent City* of the Northwest.

Hannibal, in Missouri, is known as the *Bluff City*, being built on high bluffs overhanging the river.

Hartford, in Connecticut, derives the name of *Charter Oak City*, from a large oak-tree, now no longer in existence, in the cavity of which the Charter of the Colony of Connecticut was concealed by the Legislature when King James II., in 1686, sent over Sir Edmund Andros to resume the charters granted to the colonies.

Indianapolis, in Indiana, has the perfectly modern title of *Rail-Road City*, being the central point from which radiate an unusual number of railways.

Keokuk, in Iowa, situated at the foot of the Lower Rapids of the Mississippi River, is hence poetically called *Gate City*, since here opens to navigation the largest river of the Union.

Louisville, in Kentucky, is in like manner called *Falls City*, because it lies at the head of the Louisville Falls of the Ohio River.

Lowell, in Massachusetts, famous for its immense cotton factories, which it owes to the carefully-improved water-power of the Pawtucket Falls in the Merrimac River, is hence known as *Spindle City.*

Montpelier, in Vermont, derives its name of *Green Mountain City,* from the name of the State, of which it is the capital.

Nashville, in Tennessee, situated on an elevation of 460 feet above the sea, deserves its descriptive name, *City of Rocks.*

New Haven, in Connecticut, is known throughout the United States as *Elm City,* from the number and magnificent size of the elm-trees that adorn the public squares and most of the principal streets.

New Orleans, situated on a bend of the Mississippi River, which assumes the form of a crescent, is hence called *Crescent City,* a name now no longer appropriate, as the buildings have long since extended far beyond the original half-moon.

New York, the largest city in the Union, is not inaptly called *Empire City,* in appreciation of its size, wealth, and political influence. W. Irving, in his *Salmagundi,* is said to have been the first to apply to the true metropolis of the United States the derogatory name of *Gotham,* in allusion to the town of Gotham, in Northamptonshire, England, as famous there as Abdera was once in Greece, and noted for the lack of wisdom manifested by its citizens on many occasions.

Philadelphia, in Pennsylvania, owes to the meaning of its Greek name, the epithet, *City of Brotherly Love,* while the religious associations of its founder, W. Penn, and the number of Quakers still residing there, have procured for it the additional name, *Quaker City.*

Pittsburg, in Pennsylvania, derives, from its enormous iron manufactories, the name of *Iron City,* by which it is universally known.

Rochester, in New York, rejoices in the double name of *Flour City* and *Flower City,* being as famous for her love of flowers and unrivalled nursery-trade, as for the peculiarly fine flour made in her numerous mills, for which the rich valley of the Genesee furnishes the grain, while the falls of the river supply the water-power.

Savannah, in Georgia, is the third city claiming the name of *Garden City*, in virtue of the numerous and beautiful parks with which it is adorned.

Springfield, in Illinois, in like manner derives from the countless gardens, in which most of the houses are embowered, and from the beauty of its surroundings, the name of *Flower City*.

Saint Louis, in Missouri, is known as *Mound City*, being built upon numerous mounds, believed to have been burial-places of the former owners of the soil, the Indians.

San Francisco, in California, the youngest among American cities of that size, finds compensation for the curt way in which it is treated by Western men, who call it simply Frisco, in the high-sounding name, *Golden City*, under which it is elsewhere known.

Washington, the capital of the Union, still deserves the hollow-sounding title, *City of Magnificent Distances*, as the superb public buildings and stately private residences in which the city abounds, are still separated from each other by wide, waste tracts, or clusters of wretched hovels. Washington is also known as *Federal City*, from its metropolitan character in the Union.

We append a list of the *noms de plume*, under which some of the principal American writers are even better known than by their own, while in the case of some others, not included here, the real name is more frequently mentioned.

Carl Benson,	Mr. Charles Astor Bristed.
Josh Billings,	Mr. Henry G. Shaw.
Hans Breitmann,	Mr. Charles G. Leland.
Ned Buntline,	Mr. E. Z. C. Judson.
Philander Q. K. Doesticks,	Mr. Mortimer Thompson, Fanny Fern's son-in-law.
Major Jack Downing,	Mr. Seba Smith.
Fanny Fern,	Mrs. Sarah P. Parton.
Fanny Forrester,	Mrs. Adoniram Judson (*née* Emily Chudbuck, 1817–1854).
Frank Forrester,	Mr. Henry William Herbert.
Grace Greenwood,	Mrs. Sarah Jane Lippincott (*née* Clarke).

Gail Hamilton,	Miss Mary Abigail Dodge (of Hamilton, Massachusetts).
Marion Harland,	Mrs. Virginia Terhune.
Irenæus,	Rev. S. I. Prime.
Orpheus C. Kerr, (pronounced Office Seeker,)	Mr. R. H. Newalls.
Ike Marvel,	Mr. Donald G. Mitchell.
Petroleum V. Nasby,	Mr. D. R. Locke.
Oliver Optic,	Mr. W. T. Adams.
U. Donough Outis, (pronounced You don' know who't is,)	Mr. Richard Grant White.
Peter Parley,	Mr. Samuel G. Goodrich. (1793–1860.)
Mrs. Partington,	Mr. B. P. Shillaber.
K. N. Pepper, (pronounced Cayenne Pepper)	Mr. James M. Morris.
Kate Putnam,	Miss Kate Putnam Osgood.
Sparrowgrass,	Mr. F. S. Cozzens.
Talvj,	Mrs. (*T*heresa *A*lbertine *L*ouisa *v*on *J*acob) Robinson.
Dick Tinto,	Mr. Frank B. Goodrich.
Timothy Titcombe,	Dr. J. G. Holland.
Artemus Ward,	Mr. Charles F. Brown.
Christian Reid,	Miss Fanny Fischer.
Mark Twain	Mr. Samuel Clemens.

INDEX.

Y.

Z.

www.ingramcontent.com/pod-product-compliance
Lightning Source LLC
LaVergne TN
LVHW021047110826
845150LV00001B/3

9781425568610